THE OXFORD

Essential
Quotations
Dictionary

AMERICAN EDITION

Also available

THE OXFORD DESK DICTIONARY AND THESAURUS

THE OXFORD ESSENTIAL DICTIONARY

THE OXFORD ESSENTIAL SPELLING DICTIONARY

THE OXFORD ESSENTIAL THESAURUS

THE OXFORD FRENCH DICTIONARY

THE OXFORD GERMAN DICTIONARY

THE OXFORD ITALIAN DICTIONARY

THE OXFORD PORTUGUESE DICTIONARY

THE OXFORD RUSSIAN DICTIONARY

THE OXFORD SPANISH DICTIONARY

THE OXFORD

Essential
Quotations
Dictionary

AMERICAN EDITION

B

BERKLEY BOOKS, NEW YORK

Executive Editor: Elizabeth Knowles
Project Editors: Patricia G. Baldwin, Sue Ellen Thompson
Assistant Editors: Deborah Argosy, Andrea R. Nagy,
Laurie H. Ongley, Christine A. Lindberg
Proofreader: Julie Marsh
Data Entry: Kimberly Roberts

Editor-in-chief: Frank R. Abate
Managing Editor: Elizabeth J. Jewell

THE OXFORD ESSENTIAL QUOTATIONS DICTIONARY

A Berkley Book / published in mass market paperback
by arrangement with Oxford University Press, Inc.

PRINTING HISTORY
Berkley edition / August 1998

The Penguin Putnam Inc. World Wide Web site address is
http://www.penguinputnam.com

ISBN: 0-425-16387-3

BERKLEY®
Berkley Books are published by The Berkley Publishing Group,
a member of Penguin Putnam Inc.,
200 Madison Avenue, New York, New York 10016.
BERKLEY and the "B" design
are trademarks belonging to Berkley Publishing Corporation.

PRINTED IN THE UNITED STATES OF AMERICA

10 9 8 7 6 5 4 3 2 1

Contents

Introduction

The *Oxford Essential Quotations Dictionary: American Edition* offers a view of the central stock of our figurative language, bringing together over 7,000 quotations in a structure that at once allows access to individual items and expresses the essential relationship between them.

This dictionary arranges quotations by thematic category. From **Absence** and **Achievement** through **Broadcasting, Chance and Luck, Festivals and Celebrations, Government, Human Nature, Science, The Seasons**, and **Towns and Cities**, to **Warfare** and **Youth**, the category titles have been chosen to reflect as wide a range of subjects as possible, while accurately representing the actual evidence. Classification of quotations is by category or subject rather than keyword. Thus Montaigne's "When I play with my cat, who knows whether she isn't amusing herself with me more than I am with her" (*Essais*, 1580) is found at **Cats**, but Mark Twain's quip "One of the most striking differences between a cat and a lie is that a cat has only nine lives" (*Pudd'nhead Wilson*, 1894) illustrates **Lies and Lying**, and Shakespeare's "What though care killed a cat, thou hast mettle enough in thee to kill care" (*Much Ado About Nothing*, 1598) illustrates **Worry**.

Categories bring together disparate aspects of a single topic, and the chronological arrangement of quotations within each category allows us to hear the different voices speak over the centuries. For example, **Winning and Losing** offers a variety of views of competition. "One more such victory and we are lost," said Pyrrhus of his costly defeat of the Romans at Asculum in 279 B.C., a comment which led to the phrase *Pyrrhic victory*. On the other hand, Winston Churchill asserted in 1940, "What is our aim? . . . victory, victory at all costs . . . for without victory there is no survival." Then again, Ralph Waldo Emerson proposes a philosophical middle ground:

"For everything you have missed, you have gained something else; and for everything you gain, you lose something." In the category **Bribery and Corruption**, we find more unanimity. Sallust evaluated first-century B.C. Rome as "A venal city ripe to perish, if a buyer can be found," and over 1600 years later, Robert Walpole agrees: "All these men have their price," he said of English parliamentarians in the eighteenth century.

Allusions are part of our linguistic stock-in-trade, and this dictionary allows the reader to find examples of both source and modification. " 'The question is,' said Humpty-Dumpty, "which is to be master—that's all.' " This passage from Lewis Carroll's *Through the Looking-Glass* (1872) was quoted by the British Labour politician Hartley Shawcross in a speech in the House of Commons in 1946, often summarized in the statement, "We are the masters now." The category **Power** finds room for both these items and gives the reader explicit links between them.

"Quotation" is a broad term, and inevitably editorial selection is needed for a book of this scope. We have employed as our criteria for selection a combination of values each important for elevating any comment into a "quotable quote." Most of the quotations in this dictionary are *pithy*, that is, they capture the essence of an idea, or express a core human value or interest in a dramatic, charming, or humorous way. Others are simply *famous*—whether because delivered by a famous individual, or perhaps said of or at a critical juncture in history. We hope that the quotations we have included will allow the reader to share our pleasure and interest in noting the variety, vitality, and veracity of things well said down through the centuries.

How to Use the Dictionary

Entries are arranged in thematic categories alphabetically from **Absence** and **Achievement** to **Writing** and **Youth**. Category titles have been chosen to reflect as wide a range of subjects as possible, and related topics may be covered by a single category, for example **Actors and Acting** and **Ways and Means**. Opposites may also be grouped in a single topic, such as **Beginnings and Endings, Heaven and Hell, Trust and Treachery**, and **Winning and Losing**. A cross-reference from the second element of the pair, for example, "**Losing** *see Winning and Losing*," appears in its appropriate place in the alphabetic sequence both in the main text and in the **List of Thematic Categories**.

Where categories are closely related, "see also" references are given immediately following the title. The heading **Belief and Unbelief** is thus followed by the direction "see also **Certainty and Doubt, Faith**," and **Danger** by "see also **Caution, Courage**."

Within each category quotations are listed in chronological order. Where possible, quotations are precisely dated, either by the composition date of a letter or diary or the publication of a book published in the author's lifetime, or by external circumstances, such as a contemporary comment on a specific event. When the date is uncertain or unknown and the quotation cannot be related to a particular event, the author's date of death has been used to date the quotation.

Contextual information regarded as essential to a full appreciation of the quotation precedes the quotation itself in an italicized note; information seen as providing useful amplification follows the quotation in an italicized note.

Each quotation is accompanied by the name of the author or source to whom it is attributed; dates of birth and death (where known) are also given. In general, the authors' names are given in the form by which they are best known, so that we have "Mark Twain" rather than "Samuel Clemens." Bibliographical information follows the author's name; titles and dates of publication are also given. Where a quotation cannot be traced to a citable source, "attributed" is used to indicate that the attribution is generally accepted, but that a specific reference has not been traced.

Quotations are numbered in a single sequence within each category. Cross-references are made between items in the same category and to and from specific items in other categories. Cross-references between items in the same category are expressed in the form "see **12** above" or "cf. **34** below." The use of "see" indicates that following up the cross-reference will supply essential information; "cf." is used to indicate information that amplifies what is already given. Cross-references to items in other categories use a similar style but identify the target category: "see **Excess 6**" or "cf. **Marriage 38**."

Index

The index allows you to find individual quotations by author. References show the category name, sometimes in a shortened form (**Festivals** for **Festivals and Celebrations**; **Seasons** for **The Seasons**) followed by the number of the item within the category: **Science 7** therefore means the seventh item under the category **Science**.

List of Thematic Categories

Absence

see also **Meeting and Parting**

1 The Lord watch between me and
thee, when we are absent one
from another.
Bible: Genesis

2 Hang yourself, brave Crillon; we
fought at Arques and you were
not there.
*traditional form given by Voltaire to
the actual words, "My good man,
Crillon, hang yourself for not having
been at my side last Monday at the
greatest event that's ever been seen
and perhaps ever will be seen"*
Henri IV (Henri of Navarre) 1553–
1610: letter to Crillon, 20 September
1597

3 Absence diminishes commonplace
passions and increases great ones,
as the wind extinguishes candles
and kindles fire.
Duc de la Rochefoucauld 1613–80:
Maximes (1678)

4 I wish you could invent some
means to make me at all happy
without you. Every hour I am
more and more concentrated in
you; every thing else tastes like
chaff in my mouth.
John Keats 1795–1821: letter to
Fanny Brawne, August 1820

5 *Partir c'est mourir un peu,*
C'est mourir à ce qu'on aime:
On laisse un peu de soi-même
En toute heure et dans tout lieu.
To go away is to die a little, it is
to die to that which one loves:
everywhere and always, one
leaves behind a part of oneself.
Edmond Haraucourt 1856–1941:
"Rondel de l'Adieu" (1891)

6 The more he looked inside the
more Piglet wasn't there.
A. A. Milne 1882–1956: *The House at
Pooh Corner* (1928)

7 The heart may think it knows
better: the senses know that
absence blots people out. We
have really no absent friends.
Elizabeth Bowen 1899–1973: *Death
of the Heart* (1938)

8 When I came back to Dublin, I
was courtmartialled in my
absence and sentenced to death
in my absence, so I said they
could shoot me in my absence.
Brendan Behan 1923–64: *Hostage*
(1958)

9 A day away from Tallulah is like
a month in the country.
Howard Dietz 1896–1983: *Dancing in
the Dark* (1974)

Achievement and Endeavor

see also **Ambition, Problems and
Solutions, Success and Failure,
Thoroughness**

1 The desire accomplished is sweet
to the soul.
Bible: Proverbs

2 *Parturient montes, nascetur*
   ridiculus mus.
Mountains will go into labor, and
a silly little mouse will be born.
Horace 65–8 BC: *Ars Poetica*

3 *Non omnia possumus omnes.*
We can't all do everything.
Virgil 70–19 BC: *Eclogues*

4 I have fought a good fight, I have
finished my course, I have kept
the faith.
Bible: II Timothy

5 *Considerate la vostra semenza:*
Fatti non foste a viver come bruti,
Ma per seguir virtute e conoscenza.
Consider your origins: you were
not made to live as brutes, but to
follow virtue and knowledge.
Dante Alighieri 1265–1321: *Divina
Commedia* "Inferno"

6 Also say to them, that they suffre
hym this day to wynne his
spurres, for if god be pleased, I
woll this journey be his, and the
honoure therof.
*speaking of the Black Prince at the
battle of Crécy, 1346; commonly
quoted as "Let the boy win his
spurs"*
Edward III 1312–77: *The Chronicle of
Froissart* (translated by John
Bourchier 1523–5)

7 Things won are done; joy's soul
lies in the doing.
William Shakespeare 1564–1616:
Troilus and Cressida (1602)

8 None climbs so high as he who
knows not whither he is going.
Oliver Cromwell 1599–1658:
attributed

9 I had done all that I could; and
no man is well pleased to have
his all neglected, be it ever so
little.
Samuel Johnson 1709–84: letter to
Lord Chesterfield, 7 February 1755

10 But the fruit that can fall without
shaking,
Indeed is too mellow for me.
Lady Mary Wortley Montagu 1689–
1762: "Answered, for Lord William
Hamilton" (1758)

11 The General [Wolfe] . . . repeated
nearly the whole of Gray's Elegy
. . . adding, as he concluded, that
he would prefer being the author
of that poem to the glory of
beating the French tomorrow.
James Wolfe 1727–59: J. Playfair
Biographical Account of J. Robinson
(1815)

12 The distance is nothing; it is only
the first step that is difficult.
*commenting on the legend that St.
Denis, carrying his head in his
hands, walked two leagues*
Mme. Du Deffand 1697–1780: letter

to Jean Le Rond d'Alembert, 7 July
1763

13 He has, indeed, done it very well;
but it is a foolish thing well done.
*on Goldsmith's apology in the
London Chronicle for physically
assaulting Thomas Evans, who had
published a letter mocking
Goldsmith*
Samuel Johnson 1709–84: James
Boswell *Life of Johnson* (1791) 3
April 1773

14 Twenty-two acknowledged
concubines, and a library of sixty-
two thousand volumes, attested
the variety of his inclinations, and
from the productions which he
left behind him, it appears that
the former as well as the latter
were designed for use rather than
ostentation. [Footnote] By each of
his concubines the younger
Gordian left three or four
children. His literary productions
were by no means contemptible.
of the Emperor Gordian
Edward Gibbon 1737–94: *The
Decline and Fall of the Roman
Empire* (1776–88)

15 Now, gentlemen, let us do
something today which the world
may talk of hereafter.
*before the Battle of Trafalgar, 21
October 1805*
Admiral Collingwood 1748–1810: G.
L. Newnham Collingwood (ed.) *A
Selection from the Correspondence
of Lord Collingwood* (1828)

16 *J'ai vécu.*
I survived.
*when asked what he had done
during the French Revolution*
Emmanuel Joseph Sieyès 1748–1836:
F. A. M. Mignet *Notice historique sur
la vie et les travaux de M. le Comte
de Sieyès* (1836)

17 The shades of night were falling
fast,
As through an Alpine village
passed

A youth, who bore, 'mid snow
    and ice,
A banner with the strange device,
Excelsior!
Henry Wadsworth Longfellow 1807–
82: "Excelsior" (1841)

18 The reward of a thing well done
is to have done it.
Ralph Waldo Emerson 1803–82:
*Essays: Second Series, New England
Reformers* (1844)

19 It is a folly to expect men to do
all that they may reasonably be
expected to do.
Richard Whately 1787–1863:
Apophthegms (1854)

20 Say not the struggle naught
    availeth,
The labour and the wounds are
    vain,
The enemy faints not, nor faileth,
And as things have been, things
    remain.
Arthur Hugh Clough 1819–61: "Say
not the struggle naught availeth"
(1855)

21 That low man seeks a little thing
    to do,
Sees it and does it:
This high man, with a great
    thing to pursue,
Dies ere he knows it.
That low man goes on adding
    one to one,
His hundred's soon hit:
This high man, aiming at a
    million,
Misses an unit.
Robert Browning 1812–89: "A
Grammarian's Funeral" (1855)

22 Now, *here*, you see, it takes all
the running *you* can do, to keep
in the same place. If you want to
get somewhere else, you must
run at least twice as fast as that!
Lewis Carroll 1832–98: *Through the
Looking-Glass* (1872)

23 It is not the going out of port,
but the coming in, that
determines the success of the
voyage.
Henry Ward Beecher 1813–87:
Proverbs from Plymouth Pulpit
(1887)

24 If a man write a better book,
preach a better sermon, or make
a better mouse-trap than his
neighbor, tho' he build his house
in the woods, the world will
make a beaten path to his door.
Ralph Waldo Emerson 1803–82:
attributed to Emerson in Sarah S. B.
Yule *Borrowings* (1889); Mrs. Yule
states in *The Docket* February 1912
that she copied this in her
handbook from a lecture delivered
by Emerson; the quotation was the
occasion of a long controversy
owing to Elbert Hubbard's claim to
its authorship

25 There are two tragedies in life.
One is not to get your heart's
desire. The other is to get it.
George Bernard Shaw 1856–1950:
Man and Superman (1903)

26 We combat obstacles in order to
get repose, and, when got, the
repose is insupportable.
Henry Brooks Adams 1838–1918: *The
Education of Henry Adams* (1907)

27 Because it's there.
*on being asked why he wanted to
climb Mount Everest*
George Leigh Mallory 1886–1924: in
New York Times 18 March 1923

28 Those who believe that they are
exclusively in the right are
generally those who achieve
something.
Aldous Huxley 1894–1963: *Proper
Studies* (1927) "Note on Dogma"

29 The world is divided into people
who do things and people who
get the credit. Try, if you can, to

belong to the first class. There's far less competition.
Dwight Morrow 1873–1931: letter to his son; Harold Nicolson *Dwight Morrow* (1935)

30 Here is the answer which I will give to President Roosevelt . . . Give us the tools and we will finish the job.
Winston Churchill 1874–1965: radio broadcast, 9 February 1941

31 The world is an oyster, but you don't crack it open on a mattress.
Arthur Miller 1915– : *Death of a Salesman* (1949)

32 Well, we knocked the bastard off!
on conquering Mount Everest, 1953
Edmund Hillary 1919– : *Nothing Venture, Nothing Win* (1975)

33 I could have had class. I could have been a contender.
Budd Schulberg 1914– : *On the Waterfront* (1954 film); spoken by Marlon Brando

34 These are the voyages of the starship *Enterprise*. Its five-year mission . . . to boldly go where no man has gone before.
Gene Roddenberry 1921–91: *Star Trek* (television series, from 1966)

35 That's one small step for man, one giant leap for mankind.
Neil Armstrong 1930– : in *New York Times* 21 July 1969; interference in the transmission obliterated "a" between "for" and "man"

36 It is sobering to consider that when Mozart was my age he had already been dead for a year.
Tom Lehrer 1928– : N. Shapiro (ed.) *An Encyclopedia of Quotations about Music* (1978)

37 Just as Oliver Cromwell aimed to bring about the kingdom of God on earth and founded the British Empire, so Bunyan wanted the

millennium and got the novel.
Christopher Hill 1912– : *A Turbulent, Seditious, and Factious People: John Bunyan and his Church, 1628-1688* (1988)

38 Big things are expected of us, and nothing big ever came of being small.
Bill Clinton 1946– : second Inaugural Address, 20 January 1997

Acting
see **Actors and Acting**

Action and Inaction
see also **Idleness, Words and Deeds**

1 One man by delaying put the state to rights for us.
referring to the Roman general Fabius Cunctator ("The Delayer")
Ennius 239–169 BC: *Annals*

2 Nowher so bisy a man as he ther nas,
And yet he semed bisier than he was.
Geoffrey Chaucer c. 1343–1400: *The Canterbury Tales* "The General Prologue"

3 Iron rusts from disuse; stagnant water loses its purity and in cold weather becomes frozen; even so does inaction sap the vigour of the mind.
Leonardo da Vinci 1452–1519: Edward McCurdy (ed. and trans.) *Leonardo da Vinci's Notebooks* (1906)

4 But men must know, that in this theatre of man's life it is reserved only for God and angels to be lookers on.
Francis Bacon 1561–1626: *The Advancement of Learning* (1605)

5 If it were done when 'tis done, then 'twere well
It were done quickly.

William Shakespeare 1564–1616:
Macbeth (1606)

6 A first impulse was never a crime.
Pierre Corneille 1606–84: *Horace*
(1640)

7 You have sat too long here for
any good you have been doing.
Depart, I say, and let us have
done with you. In the name of
God, go!
*addressing the Rump Parliament, 20
April 1653; quoted by Leo Amery to
Neville Chamberlain in the House of
Commons, 7 May 1940*
Oliver Cromwell 1599–1658: oral
tradition

8 We have left undone those things
which we ought to have done;
And we have done those things
which we ought not to have done;
And there is no health in us.
The Book of Common Prayer 1662:
Morning Prayer General Confession

9 They also serve who only stand
and wait.
John Milton 1608–74: "When I
consider how my light is spent"
(1673)

10 He who desires but acts not,
breeds pestilence.
William Blake 1757–1827: *The
Marriage of Heaven and Hell* (1790–
3) "Proverbs of Hell"

11 Think nothing done while aught
remains to do.
Samuel Rogers 1763–1855: "Human
Life" (1819)

12 *Étourdir de grelots l'esprit qui veut
penser.*
To daze with little bells the spirit
that would think.
Victor Hugo 1802–85: *Le Roi
s'amuse* (1833)

13 I find the great thing in this
world is not so much where we
stand, as in what direction we are
moving: To reach the port of

heaven, we must sail sometimes
with the wind and sometimes
against it, —but we must sail,
and not drift, nor lie at anchor.
Oliver Wendell Holmes, Sr. 1841–
1935: *The Autocrat of the Breakfast
Table* (1891)

14 Action is consolatory. It is the
enemy of thought and the friend
of flattering illusions.
Joseph Conrad 1857–1924: *Nostromo*
(1904)

15 Henry has always led what could
be called a sedentary life, if only
he'd ever got as far as actually
sitting up.
Henry Reed 1914–86: *Not a Drum
was Heard* (unpublished radio play,
1959)

16 Under conditions of tyranny it is
far easier to act than to think.
Hannah Arendt 1906–75: W. H.
Auden *A Certain World* (1970)

17 The world can only be grasped by
action, not by contemplation . . .
The hand is the cutting edge of
the mind.
Jacob Bronowski 1908–74: *The
Ascent of Man* (1973)

18 I grew up in the Thirties with our
unemployed father. He did not
riot, he got on his bike and
looked for work.
Norman Tebbit 1931– : speech at
Conservative Party Conference, 15
October 1981

19 I do nothing, granted. But I see
the hours pass—which is better
than trying to fill them.
E. M. Cioran 1911–95: in *Guardian* 11
May 1993

Actors and Acting
see also **The Movies and Hollywood,
Shakespeare, The Theater**

1 Be not too tame neither, but let
your own discretion be your tutor:

suit the action to the word, the word to the action; with this special observance, that you o'erstep not the modesty of nature; for anything so overdone is from the purpose of playing, whose end, both at the first and now, was and is, to hold, as 'twere, the mirror up to nature.
William Shakespeare 1564–1616: *Hamlet* (1601)

2 *on attempting to paint two actors, David Garrick and Samuel Foote:*
Rot them for a couple of rogues, they have everybody's faces but their own.
Thomas Gainsborough 1727–88: Allan Cunningham *The Lives of the Most Eminent Painters, Sculptors and Architects* (1829)

3 To see him act, is like reading Shakespeare by flashes of lightning.
on Edmund Kean
Samuel Taylor Coleridge 1772–1834: *Table Talk* (1835) 27 April 1823

4 He played the King as though under momentary apprehension that someone else was about to play the ace.
of Creston Clarke as King Lear
Eugene Field 1850–95: review attributed to Field, in the *Denver Tribune c.* 1880

5 How different, how very different from the home life of our own dear Queen!
comment overheard at a performance of Cleopatra by Sarah Bernhardt
Anonymous: Irvin S. Cobb *A Laugh a Day* (1924); probably apocryphal

6 Ladies, just a little more virginity, if you don't mind.
to a motley collection of women, assembled to play ladies-in-waiting to a queen
Herbert Beerbohm Tree 1852–1917: Alexander Woollcott *Shouts and Murmurs* (1923)

7 She ran the whole gamut of the emotions from A to B.
of Katharine Hepburn at a Broadway first night, 1933
Dorothy Parker 1893–1967: attributed

8 Don't put your daughter on the stage, Mrs. Worthington,
Don't put your daughter on the stage.
Noël Coward 1899–1973: "Mrs. Worthington" (1935 song)

9 Actors are cattle.
Alfred Hitchcock 1899–1980: in *Saturday Evening Post* 22 May 1943

10 Acting is merely the art of keeping a large group of people from coughing.
Ralph Richardson 1902–83: in *New York Herald Tribune* 19 May 1946

11 Wet, she was a star—dry she ain't.
of the swimmer Esther Williams and her 1940s film career
Joe Pasternak 1901–91: attributed

12 For an actress to be a success, she must have the face of a Venus, the brains of a Minerva, the grace of Terpsichore, the memory of a Macaulay, the figure of Juno, and the hide of a rhinoceros.
Ethel Barrymore 1879–1959: George Jean Nathan *The Theatre in the Fifties* (1953)

13 "Playing our parts." Yes, we all have to do that and from childhood on, I have found that my own character has been much harder to play worthily and far harder at times to comprehend than any of the roles I have portrayed.
Bette Davis 1908–89: *New York Herald Tribune* (22 July 1956)

14 An actor is a kind of a guy who if you ain't talking about him ain't listening.

George Glass 1910–84: Bob Thomas
Brando (1973); often quoted by
Marlon Brando, 1956 onward

15 Garbo's visage had a kind of
emptiness into which anything
could be projected—nothing can
be read into Bardot's face.
Simone de Beauvoir 1908–86:
*Brigitte Bardot and the Lolita
Syndrome* (1959)

16 Stage nudity is disgusting,
shameful and damaging to all
things American. But if I were 22
with a great body, it would be
artistic, tasteful, patriotic and a
progressive religious experience.
Shelley Winters 1922– : *News
summaries* (13 September 1965)

17 Just say the lines and don't trip
over the furniture.
advice on acting
Noël Coward 1899–1973: D. Richards
The Wit of Noël Coward (1968)

18 There is something about seeing
real people on a stage that makes
a bad play more intimately, more
personally offensive than any
other art form.
Anatole Broyard 1920–90: *New York
Times* (6 February 1976)

19 Acting is a masochistic form of
exhibitionism. It is not quite the
occupation of an adult.
Laurence Olivier 1907–89: in *Time* 3
July 1978

20 I've made so many movies
playing a hooker that they don't
pay me in the regular way
anymore. They leave it on the
dresser.
Shirley MacLaine 1934– : *Out on a
Limb* (1983)

21 There are times when Richard
Gere has the warm effect of a
wind tunnel at dawn, waiting for
work, all sheen, inner curve, and
posed emptiness.

David Thomson 1941– : *A
Biographical Dictionary of Film*
(1994)

22 I have pale blue eyes and I was
receding in my late twenties. And
if you look like this and you're
twenty-eight, you play rapists.
Patrick Malahide: in *Daily Telegraph*
20 July 1996

Administration and Bureaucracy

1 For forms of government let fools
contest;
Whate'er is best administered is
best.
Alexander Pope 1688–1744: *An Essay
on Man* Epistle 3 (1733)

2 I have in general no very exalted
opinion of the virtue of paper
government.
Edmund Burke 1729–97: *On
Conciliation with America* (1775)

3 If any man will draw up his case,
and put his name at the foot of
the first page, I will give him an
immediate reply. Where he
compels me to turn over the
sheet, he must wait my leisure.
*on appeals made by officers to the
Navy Board*
Lord Sandwich 1718–92: N. W.
Wraxall *Memoirs* (1884) vol. 1

4 Whatever was required to be
done, the Circumlocution Office
was beforehand with all the
public departments in the art of
perceiving—HOW NOT TO DO IT.
Charles Dickens 1812–70: *Little
Dorrit* (1857)

5 A place for everything and
everything in its place.
Mrs. Beeton 1836–65: *The Book of
Household Management* (1861);
often attributed to Samuel Smiles

6 It is an inevitable defect, that bureaucrats will care more for routine than for results.
Walter Bagehot 1826–77: *The English Constitution* (1867) "On Changes of Ministry"

7 No academic person is ever voted into the chair until he has reached an age at which he has forgotten the meaning of the word "irrelevant."
Francis M. Cornford 1874–1943: *Microcosmographia Academica* (1908)

8 Sack the lot!
on overmanning and overspending within government departments
John Arbuthnot Fisher 1841–1920: letter to *The Times* (UK), 2 September 1919

9 The concept of the "official secret" is its [bureaucracy's] specific invention.
Max Weber 1864–1920: "Politik als Beruf" (1919)

10 This high official, all allow, Is grossly overpaid; There wasn't any Board, and now There isn't any Trade.
A. P. Herbert 1890–1971: "The President of the Board of Trade" (1922)

11 Where there is officialism every human relationship suffers.
E. M. Forster 1879–1970: *A Passage to India* (1924)

12 Let's find out what everyone is doing, And then stop everyone from doing it.
A. P. Herbert 1890–1971: "Let's Stop Somebody from Doing Something!" (1930)

13 Official dignity tends to increase in inverse ratio to the importance of the country in which the office is held.
Aldous Huxley 1894–1963: *Beyond the Mexique Bay* (1934)

14 In the case of nutrition and health, just as in the case of education, the gentleman in Whitehall really does know better what is good for people than the people know themselves.
Douglas Jay 1907–96: *The Socialist Case* (1939)

15 This island is made mainly of coal and surrounded by fish. Only an organizing genius could produce a shortage of coal and fish at the same time.
Aneurin Bevan 1897–1960: speech at Blackpool 24 May 1945

16 Are you laboring under the impression that I read these memoranda of yours? I can't even lift them.
to Leon Henderson
Franklin D. Roosevelt 1882–1945: J. K. Galbraith *Ambassador's Journal* (1969)

17 What is official Is incontestable. It undercuts The problematical world and sells us life At a discount.
Christopher Fry 1907– : *The Lady's not for Burning* (1949)

18 By the time the civil service has finished drafting a document to give effect to a principle, there may be little of the principle left.
Lord Reith 1889–1971: *Into the Wind* (1949)

19 Committee—a group of men who individually can do nothing but as a group decide that nothing can be done.
Fred Allen 1894–1956: attributed

20 Time spent on any item of the agenda will be in inverse proportion to the sum involved.
C. Northcote Parkinson 1909–93: *Parkinson's Law* (1958)

21 Here lies a civil servant. He was
civil
To everyone, and servant to the
devil.
C. H. Sisson 1914– : in *The London
Zoo* (1961)

22 The Civil Service is profoundly
deferential — "Yes, Minister! No,
Minister! If you wish it, Minister!"
Richard Crossman 1907–74: diary,
22 October 1964

23 The length of a meeting rises
with the square of the number of
people present.
Eileen Shanahan: in *New York Times
Magazine* 17 March 1968

24 In a hierarchy every employee
tends to rise to his level of
incompetence.
Laurence J. Peter 1919– : *The Peter
Principle* (1969)

25 Guidelines for bureaucrats:
(1) When in charge, ponder.
(2) When in trouble, delegate.
(3) When in doubt, mumble.
James H. Boren 1925– : in *New
York Times* 8 November 1970

26 A memorandum is written not to
inform the reader but to protect
the writer.
Dean Acheson 1893–1971: in *Wall
Street Journal* 8 September 1977

27 *when his secretary suggested
throwing away out-of-date files:*
A good idea, only be sure to
make a copy of everything before
getting rid of it.
Sam Goldwyn 1882–1974: Michael
Freedland *The Goldwyn Touch*
(1986)

28 Back in the East you can't do
much without the right papers,
but *with* the right papers you can
do *anything*. They *believe* in
papers. Papers are power.
Tom Stoppard 1937– : *Neutral
Ground* (1983)

29 Give a civil servant a good case
and he'll wreck it with clichés,
bad punctuation, double
negatives and convoluted
apology.
Alan Clark 1928– : diary 22 July
1983

30 I think it will be a clash between
the political will and the
administrative won't.
Jonathan Lynn 1943– and **Antony Jay**
1930– : *Yes Prime Minister* (1987)
vol. 2

31 A camel is a horse designed by a
committee.
Alec Issigonis 1906–88: attributed;
in *Guardian* 14 January 1991 "Notes
and Queries"

32 We make a house call on every
home and every business six days
a week . . . for 29 cents. Plumbers
charge 58 bucks.
on delivering the mail
**U.S. Postmaster General Anthony
Frank** 1931– : *Time* (4 March 1991)

33 Thank heavens we do not get all
of the government that we are
made to pay for.
Milton Friedman 1912– : quoted in
the House of Lords, 24 November
1994

Adversity
see also **Misfortunes, Suffering**

1 No stranger to trouble myself I
am learning to care for the
unhappy.
Virgil 70–19 BC: *Aeneid*

2 Sweet are the uses of adversity,
Which like the toad, ugly and
venomous,
Wears yet a precious jewel in his
head.
William Shakespeare 1564–1616: *As
You Like It* (1599)

3 Prosperity doth best discover vice,
but adversity doth best discover
virtue.
Francis Bacon 1561–1626: *Essays*
(1625) "Of Adversity"

4 Adversity is sometimes hard upon
a man; but for one man who can
stand prosperity, there are a
hundred that will stand adversity.
Thomas Carlyle 1795–1881: *On
Heroes, Hero-Worship, and the
Heroic* (1841)

5 But there, everything has its
drawbacks, as the man said when
his mother-in-law died, and they
came down upon him for the
funeral expenses.
Jerome K. Jerome 1859–1927: *Three
Men in a Boat* (1889)

6 By trying we can easily learn to
endure adversity. Another man's,
I mean.
Mark Twain 1835–1910: *Following
the Equator* (1897)

7 Adversity, if a man is set down to
it by degrees, is more supportable
with equanimity by most people
than any great prosperity arrived
at in a single lifetime.
Samuel Butler 1835–1902: *Way of All
Flesh* (1903)

8 The heart *prefers* to move against
the grain of circumstance;
perversity is the soul's very life.
John Updike 1932– : *Assorted
Prose* (1965) "More Love in the
Western World"

9 A woman is like a teabag—only
in hot water do you realize how
strong she is.
Nancy Reagan 1923– : in *Observer*
29 March 1981

Advertising

1 Promise, large promise, is the soul
of an advertisement.

Samuel Johnson 1709–84: in *The
Idler* 20 January 1759

2 You can tell the ideals of a nation
by its advertisements.
Norman Douglas 1868–1952: *South
Wind* (1917)

3 It is far easier to write ten
passably effective sonnets, good
enough to take in the not too
enquiring critic, than one effective
advertisement that will take in a
few thousand of the uncritical
buying public.
Aldous Huxley 1894–1963: *On the
Margin* (1923) "Advertisement"

4 Advertising may be described as
the science of arresting human
intelligence long enough to get
money from it.
Stephen Leacock 1869–1944: *Garden
of Folly* (1924) "The Perfect
Salesman"

5 Half the money I spend on
advertising is wasted, and the
trouble is I don't know which
half.
Lord Leverhulme 1851–1925: David
Ogilvy *Confessions of an Advertising
Man* (1963)

6 We are living in an age of
publicity. It used to be only
saloons and circuses that wanted
their name in the paper, but now
it's corporations, churches,
preachers, scientists, colleges, and
cemeteries.
Will Rogers 1879–1935: *Daily
Telegrams* (23 June 1931)

7 Those who prefer their English
sloppy have only themselves to
thank if the advertisement writer
uses his mastery of vocabulary
and syntax to mislead their weak
minds . . . The moral of all this . . .
is that we have the kind of
advertising we deserve.
Dorothy L. Sayers 1893–1957: in
Spectator (UK) 9 November 1937

8 Advertising is the rattling of a stick inside a swill bucket.
George Orwell 1903–50: attributed

9 It is not necessary to advertise food to hungry people, fuel to cold people, or houses to the homeless.
John Kenneth Galbraith 1908– : *American Capitalism* (1952)

10 The hidden persuaders.
Vance Packard 1914– : title of a study of the advertising industry (1957)

11 The consumer isn't a moron; she is your wife.
David Ogilvy 1911– : *Confessions of an Advertising Man* (1963)

12 As advertising blather becomes the nation's normal idiom, language becomes printed noise.
George F. Will 1941– : *The Pursuit of Happiness and Other Sobering Thoughts* (1976)

13 The cheap contractions and revised spellings of the advertising world which have made the beauty of the written word almost unrecognizable—surely any society that permits the substitution of "kwik" for "quick" and "e.z." for "easy" does not deserve Shakespeare, Eliot or Michener.
Russell Baker 1925– : column in *New York Times*; Ned Sherrin *Cutting Edge* (1984)

14 Society drives people crazy with lust and calls it advertising.
John Lahr 1941– : in *Guardian* (UK) 2 August 1989

Advice

1 A word spoken in due season, how good is it!
Bible: Proverbs

2 Who is this that darkeneth counsel by words without knowledge?
Bible: Job

3 Books will speak plain when counsellors blanch.
Francis Bacon 1561–1626: *Essays* (1625) "Of Counsel"

4 Early to bed and early to rise, makes a man healthy, wealthy, and wise.
Benjamin Franklin 1706–90: *Poor Richard's Almanack* (1735)

5 Advice is seldom welcome; and those who want it the most always like it the least.
Lord Chesterfield 1694–1773: *Letters to his Son* (1774) 29 January 1748

6 In matters of religion and matrimony I never give any advice; because I will not have anybody's torments in this world or the next laid to my charge.
Lord Chesterfield 1694–1773: letter to Arthur Charles Stanhope, 12 October 1765

7 It was, perhaps, one of those cases in which advice is good or bad only as the event decides.
Jane Austen 1775–1817: *Persuasion* (1818)

8 Of all the horrid, hideous notes of woe,
Sadder than owl-songs or the midnight blast,
Is that portentous phrase, "I told you so."
Lord Byron 1788–1824: *Don Juan* (1819–24)

9 Get the advice of everybody whose advice is worth having— they are very few—and then do what you think best yourself.
Charles Stewart Parnell 1846–91: Conor Cruise O'Brien *Parnell* (1957)

10 I always pass on good advice. It is
the only thing to do with it. It is
never of any use to oneself.
Oscar Wilde 1854–1900: *An Ideal
Husband* (1895)

11 It's the worst thing that can ever
happen to you in all your life,
and you've got to mind it . . .
They'll come saying, "Bear up—
trust to time." No, no; they're
wrong. Mind it.
E. M. Forster 1879–1970: *The
Longest Journey* (1907)

12 The Miss Lonelyhearts are the
priests of twentieth-century
America.
Nathaniel West 1903–40: *Miss
Lonelyhearts* (1933)

13 My advice to you is not to inquire
why or whither, but just to enjoy
your ice cream while it's on your
plate—that's my philosophy.
Thornton Wilder 1897–1975: *The
Skin of Our Teeth* (1942)

14 Ben—I want to say one word to
you—just one word—plastics.
Calder Willingham 1922– : *The
Graduate* (screenplay) (1967)

15 Don't panic.
Douglas Adams 1952– :
Hitchhiker's Guide to the Galaxy
(1979)

Alcohol
see also **Drunkenness**

1 Wine is a mocker, strong drink is
raging.
Bible: Proverbs

2 No verse can give pleasure for
long, nor last, that is written by
drinkers of water.
Horace 65–8 BC: *Epistles*

3 If all be true that I do think,
There are five reasons we should
drink;

Good wine—a friend—or being
dry—
Or lest we should be by and by—
Or any other reason why.
Henry Aldrich 1647–1710: "Reasons
for Drinking" (1689)

4 It would be port if it could.
his judgment on claret
Richard Bentley 1662–1742: R. C.
Jebb *Bentley* (1902)

5 Let schoolmasters puzzle their
brain,
With grammar, and nonsense,
and learning,
Good liquor, I stoutly maintain,
Gives genius a better discerning.
Oliver Goldsmith 1730–74: *She
Stoops to Conquer* (1773)

6 Claret is the liquor for boys; port,
for men; but he who aspires to be
a hero (smiling) must drink
brandy.
Samuel Johnson 1709–84: James
Boswell *Life of Johnson* (1791) 7
April 1779

7 Freedom and Whisky gang
thegither!
Robert Burns 1759–96: "The
Author's Earnest Cry and Prayer"
(1786)

8 O, for a draught of vintage! that
hath been
Cooled a long age in the deep-
delvèd earth,
Tasting of Flora and the country
green,
Dance, and Provençal song, and
sunburnt mirth!
O for a beaker full of the warm
South,
Full of the true, the blushful
Hippocrene,
With beaded bubbles winking at
the brim,
And purple-stainèd mouth.
John Keats 1795–1821: "Ode to a
Nightingale" (1820)

9 If ever I marry a wife,
I'll marry a landlord's daughter,

For then I may sit in the bar,
And drink cold brandy and water.
Charles Lamb 1775–1834: "Written in
a copy of *Coelebs in Search of a
Wife*"

10 Therefore I *do* require it, which I
makes confession, to be brought
reg'lar and draw'd mild.
*Mrs. Gamp on her "half a pint of
porter"*
Charles Dickens 1812–70: *Martin
Chuzzlewit* (1844)

11 Man wants but little drink below,
But wants that little strong.
Oliver Wendell Holmes 1809–94: "A
Song of other Days" (1848); see **Life
17**

12 Your lips, on my own, when they
printed "Farewell,"
Had never been soiled by the
"beverage of hell"
But they come to me now with
the bacchanal sign,
And the lips that touch liquor
must never touch mine.
George W. Young 1846–1919: "The
Lips That Touch Liquor Must Never
Touch Mine" (*c.* 1870); also
attributed, in a different form, to
Harriet A. Glazebrook, 1874

13 Fifteen men on the dead man's
chest
Yo-ho-ho, and a bottle of rum!
Drink and the devil had done for
the rest—
Yo-ho-ho, and a bottle of rum!
Robert Louis Stevenson 1850–94:
Treasure Island (1883)

14 We drink one another's healths,
and spoil our own.
Jerome K. Jerome 1859–1927: *Idle
Thoughts of an Idle Fellow* (1886)

15 A torchlight procession marching
down your throat.
describing whisky
John L. O'Sullivan 1813–95: G. W. E.
Russell *Collections and Recollections*
(1898)

16 And malt does more than Milton
can
To justify God's ways to man.
Ale, man, ale's the stuff to drink
For fellows whom it hurts to
think.
A. E. Housman 1859–1936: *A
Shropshire Lad* (1896); see **Writing
11**

17 I'm only a beer teetotaller, not a
champagne teetotaller.
George Bernard Shaw 1856–1950:
Candida (1898)

18 And Noah he often said to his
wife when he sat down to dine,
"I don't care where the water
goes if it doesn't get into the
wine."
G. K. Chesterton 1874–1936: "Wine
and Water" (1914)

19 A drink that tasted, she thought,
like weak vinegar mixed with a
packet of pins.
of champagne
H. G. Wells 1866–1946: *Joan and
Peter* (1918)

20 Let's get out of these wet clothes
and into a dry Martini.
*line coined in the 1920s by Robert
Benchley's press agent and adopted
by Mae West in* Every Day's a
Holiday *(1937 film)*
Anonymous: Howard Teichmann
Smart Alec (1976)

21 Our country has deliberately
undertaken a great social and
economic experiment, noble in
motive and far-reaching in
purpose.
*on the Eighteenth Amendment
enacting Prohibition*
Herbert Hoover 1874–1964: letter to
Senator W. H. Borah, 23 February
1928

22 Prohibition makes you want to
cry into your beer and denies you
the beer to cry into.

Don Marquis 1878–1937: *Sun Dial Time* (1936)

23 It's a naïve domestic Burgundy without any breeding, but I think you'll be amused by its presumption.
James Thurber 1894–1961: cartoon caption in *New Yorker* 27 March 1937

24 Some weasel took the cork out of my lunch.
W. C. Fields 1880–1946: *You Can't Cheat an Honest Man* (1939 film)

25 I've made it a rule never to drink by daylight and never to refuse a drink after dark.
H. L. Mencken 1880–1956: in *New York Post* 18 September 1945

26 The proper union of gin and vermouth is a great and sudden glory; it is one of the happiest marriages on earth, and one of the shortest lived.
Bernard De Voto 1897–1955: in *Harper's Magazine* December 1949

27 A good general rule is to state that the bouquet is better than the taste, and vice versa.
on wine-tasting
Stephen Potter 1900–69: *One-Upmanship* (1952)

28 A medium Vodka dry Martini—with a slice of lemon peel. Shaken and not stirred.
Ian Fleming 1908–64: *Dr. No* (1958)

29 One reason why I don't drink is because I wish to know when I am having a good time.
Nancy Astor 1879–1964: in *Christian Herald* June 1960

30 A man shouldn't fool with booze until he's fifty; then he's a damn fool if he doesn't.
William Faulkner 1897–1962: James M. Webb and A. Wigfall Green *William Faulkner of Oxford* (1965)

31 I have taken more out of alcohol than alcohol has taken out of me.
Winston Churchill 1874–1965: Quentin Reynolds *By Quentin Reynolds* (1964)

32 What you need for breakfast, they say in East Tennessee, is a jug of good corn liquor, a thick beefsteak, and a hound dog. Then you feed the beefsteak to the hound dog.
Charles Kuralt 1934–97: *Dateline America* (1979)

Ambition
see also **Achievement and Endeavor, Success and Failure**

1 [I] had rather be first in a village than second at Rome.
Julius Caesar 100–44 BC: Francis Bacon *The Advancement of Learning*; based on Plutarch *Parallel Lives*

2 *Aut Caesar, aut nihil.*
Caesar or nothing.
motto inscribed on his sword
Cesare Borgia 1476–1507: John Leslie Garner *Caesar Borgia* (1912)

3 Who shoots at the mid-day sun, though he be sure he shall never hit the mark; yet as sure he is he shall shoot higher than who aims but at a bush.
Philip Sidney 1554–86: *Arcadia* ("New Arcadia," 1590)

4 When that the poor have cried, Caesar hath wept;
Ambition should be made of sterner stuff.
William Shakespeare 1564–1616: *Julius Caesar* (1599)

5 Fain would I climb, yet fear I to fall.
line written on a window-pane
Walter Ralegh c. 1552–1618: Thomas Fuller *Worthies of England* (1662)

6 If thy heart fails thee, climb not
at all.
*line after Sir Walter Ralegh, written
on a window-pane*
Elizabeth I 1533–1603: Thomas Fuller
Worthies of England (1662)

7 Cromwell, I charge thee, fling
away ambition:
By that sin fell the angels.
William Shakespeare 1564–1616:
Henry VIII (1613)

8 Ambition, in a private man a
vice,
Is in a prince the virtue.
Philip Massinger 1583–1640: *The
Bashful Lover* (1636)

9 Better to reign in hell, than serve
in heaven.
John Milton 1608–74: *Paradise Lost*
(1667)

10 In friendship false, implacable in
hate:
Resolved to ruin or to rule the
state.
John Dryden 1631–1700: *Absalom
and Achitophel* (1681)

11 My father was an eminent button
maker ... but I had a soul above
buttons ... I panted for a liberal
profession.
George Colman, the Younger 1762–
1836: *New Hay at the Old Market*
(1795)

12 Well is it known that ambition
can creep as well as soar.
Edmund Burke 1729–97: *Third Letter
... on the Proposals for Peace with
the Regicide Directory* (1797)

13 Before this time to-morrow I shall
have gained a peerage, or
Westminster Abbey.
before the battle of the Nile, 1798
Horatio, Lord Nelson 1758–1805:
Robert Southey *Life of Nelson* (1813)

14 Whenever a man has cast a
longing eye on them [official
positions], a rottenness begins in
his conduct.
Thomas Jefferson 1743–1826: letter
to Tench Coxe, 21 May 1799

15 Remember that there is not one
of you who does not carry in his
cartridge-pouch the marshal's
baton of the duke of Reggio; it is
up to you to bring it forth.
Louis XVIII 1755–1824: speech to
Saint-Cyr cadets, 9 August 1819

16 I had rather be right than be
President.
*to Senator Preston of South
Carolina, 1839*
Henry Clay 1777–1852: S. W. McCall
Life of Thomas Brackett Reed (1914)

17 Ah, but a man's reach should
exceed his grasp,
Or what's a heaven for?
Robert Browning 1812–89: "Andrea
del Sarto" (1855)

18 All ambitions are lawful except
those which climb upwards on
the miseries or credulities of
mankind.
Joseph Conrad 1857–1924: *Some
Reminiscences* (1912)

19 There are two things to aim at in
life: first, to get what you want;
and, after that, to enjoy it. Only
the wisest of mankind achieve the
second.
Logan Pearsall Smith 1865–1946:
Afterthoughts (1931)

20 He is loyal to his own career but
only incidentally to anything or
anyone else.
of Richard Crossman
Hugh Dalton 1887–1962: diary, 17
September 1941

21 Do you sincerely want to be rich?
stock question to salespeople
Bernard Cornfeld 1927– : Charles
Raw et al. *Do You Sincerely Want to
be Rich?* (1971)

America and Americans
see also **Countries and Peoples, Towns and Cities**

1 We must consider that we shall be a city upon a hill, the eyes of all people are on us; so that if we shall deal falsely with our God in this work we have undertaken, and so cause Him to withdraw His present help from us, we shall be made a story and a byword through the world.
John Winthrop 1588–1649: *Christian Charity, A Model Hereof* (sermon, 1630)

2 Westward the course of empire takes its way;
The first four acts already past,
A fifth shall close the drama with the day:
Time's noblest offspring is the last.
George Berkeley 1685–1753: "On the Prospect of Planting Arts and Learning in America" (1752)

3 I always consider the settlement of America with reverence and wonder, as the opening of a grand scene and design in providence for the illumination of the ignorant and the emancipation of the slavish part of mankind all over the earth.
John Adams 1735–1826: *Notes for "A Dissertation on the Canon and Feudal Law"* (1765)

4 Then join hand in hand, brave Americans all,—
By uniting we stand, by dividing we fall.
John Dickinson 1732–1808: "The Liberty Song" (1768)

5 The preservation of the sacred fire of liberty and the destiny of the republican model of government, are justly considered as deeply, perhaps as finally staked, on the experiment entrusted to the hands of the American people.
George Washington 1732–99: Address to the Continental Army before the battle of Long Island (27 August 1776)

6 O say does that star-spangled banner yet wave
O'er the land of the free, and the home of the brave!
Francis Scott Key 1779–1843: "The Star-Spangled Banner" (1814)

7 I called the New World into existence, to redress the balance of the Old.
George Canning 1770–1827: speech on the affairs of Portugal, House of Commons, 12 December 1826

8 If California ever becomes a prosperous country, this bay [San Francisco] will be the center of its prosperity.
Richard Henry Dana 1815–82: *Two Years Before the Mast* (1840)

9 I have heard something said about allegiance to the South. I know no South, no North, no East, no West, to which I owe any allegiance . . . The Union, sir, is my country.
Henry Clay 1777–1852: speech in the US Senate, 1848

10 I was born an American; I will live an American; I shall die an American.
Daniel Webster 1782–1852: speech in the Senate on "The Compromise Bill," 17 July 1850

11 Go West, young man, and grow up with the country.
Horace Greeley 1811–72: *Hints toward Reforms* (1850)

12 The United States themselves are essentially the greatest poem.
Walt Whitman 1819–92: *Leaves of Grass* (1855)

13 A house divided against itself cannot stand. I believe this

government cannot endure
permanently half slave and half
free.
Abraham Lincoln 1809–65:
Republican State Convention (16
June 1858)

14 A Star for every State, and a
State for every Star.
Robert Charles Winthrop 1809–94:
speech on Boston Common, 27
August 1862

15 A man may stand there [Cape
Cod] and put all America behind
him.
Henry David Thoreau 1817–62: *Cape
Cod* (1865)

16 The Constitution, in all its
provisions, looks to an
indestructible Union composed of
indestructible States.
Salmon Portland Chase 1808–73:
decision in Texas v. White, 1868

17 Give me your tired, your poor,
Your huddled masses yearning to
breathe free.
*inscription on the Statue of Liberty,
New York*
Emma Lazarus 1849–87: "The New
Colossus" (1883)

18 Isn't this a billion dollar country?
*responding to a Democratic gibe
about a "million dollar Congress"*
Charles Foster 1828–1904: at the
51st Congress, in *North American
Review* March 1892; also attributed
to Thomas B. Reed

19 America! America!
God shed His grace on thee
And crown thy good with
brotherhood
From sea to shining sea!
Katherine Lee Bates 1859–1929:
"America the Beautiful" (1893)

20 It is by the goodness of God that
in our country we have those
three unspeakably precious things:

freedom of speech, freedom of
conscience, and the prudence
never to practice either of them.
Mark Twain 1835–1910: *Following
the Equator* (1897)

21 I'm a Yankee Doodle Dandy,
A Yankee Doodle, do or die;
A real live nephew of my Uncle
Sam's,
Born on the fourth of July.
George M. Cohan 1878–1942:
"Yankee Doodle Boy" (1904 song)

22 America is God's Crucible, the
great Melting-Pot where all the
races of Europe are melting and
re-forming!
Israel Zangwill 1864–1926: *The
Melting Pot* (1908)

23 There is no room in this country
for hyphenated Americanism . . .
The one absolutely certain way of
bringing this nation to ruin, of
preventing all possibility of its
continuing to be a nation at all,
would be to permit it to become a
tangle of squabbling nationalities.
Theodore Roosevelt 1858–1919:
speech in New York, 12 October
1915

24 The chief business of the
American people is business.
Calvin Coolidge 1872–1933: speech
in Washington, 17 January 1925

25 The American system of rugged
individualism.
Herbert Hoover 1874–1964: speech
in New York City, 22 October 1928

26 I pledge you, I pledge myself, to a
new deal for the American
people.
Franklin D. Roosevelt 1882–1945:
speech to the Democratic
Convention in Chicago, 2 July 1932,
accepting the presidential
nomination

27 In the United States there is more
space where nobody is than

where anybody is. That is what
makes America what it is.
Gertrude Stein 1874–1946: *The
Geographical History of America*
(1936)

28 Every American woman has two
souls to call her own, the other
being her husband's.
James Agate 1877–1947: diary 15
May 1937

29 California is a fine place to live—
if you happen to be an orange.
Fred Allen 1894–1956: *American
Magazine* December 1945

30 I live in New Hampshire so I can
get a better view of Vermont.
Maxfield Parrish 1870–1966:
Vermont Life (1952)

31 The thing that impresses me most
about America is the way parents
obey their children.
Edward VIII 1894–1972: in *Look* 5
March 1957

32 America is a nation created by all
the hopeful wanderers of Europe,
not out of geography and
genetics, but out of purpose.
Theodore White 1915–86: *Making of
the President* (1960)

33 The immense popularity of
American movies abroad
demonstrates that Europe is the
unfinished negative of which
America is the proof.
Mary McCarthy 1912–89: *On the
Contrary* (1961)

34 America was discovered
accidentally by a great seaman
who was looking for something
else; when discovered it was not
wanted; and most of the
exploration for the next fifty years
was done in the hope of getting
through or around it. America
was named after a man who
discovered no part of the New

World. History is like that, very
chancy.
Samuel Eliot Morison 1887–1976:
*The Oxford History of the American
People* (1965)

35 Don't forget the Western is not
only the history of this country, it
is what the Saga of the
Nibelungen is for the European.
Fritz Lang 1890–1976: Peter
Bogdanovich *Fritz Lang in America*
(1967)

36 The land of the dull and the
home of the literal.
Gore Vidal 1925– : *Reflections
upon a Sinking Ship* (1969)

37 High school is closer to the core
of American experience than
anything else.
Kurt Vonnegut, Jr. 1922– : *Our
Time Is Now* (1970)

38 The weakness of American
civilization, and perhaps the chief
reason why it creates so much
discontent, is that it is so
curiously abstract. It is a
bloodless extrapolation of a
satisfying life . . . You dine off the
advertisers "sizzling" and not the
meat of the steak.
J. B. Priestley 1894–1984: in *New
Statesman* (UK) 10 December 1971

39 America is a vast conspiracy to
make you happy.
John Updike 1932– : *Problems*
(1980) "How to love America and
Leave it at the Same Time"

40 The microwave, the waste
disposal, the orgasmic elasticity of
the carpets, this soft resort-style
civilization irresistibly evokes the
end of the world.
Jean Baudrillard 1929– : *America*
(1986)

41 We are a nation of communities
. . . a brilliant diversity spread like

stars, like a thousand points of
light in a broad and peaceful sky.
George Bush 1924– : Republican
National Convention (18 August
1988)

42 I had forgotten just how flat and
empty it [middle America] is.
Stand on two phone books almost
anywhere in Iowa and you get a
view.
Bill Bryson 1951–   : *The Lost
Continent* (1989)

Anger

1 A soft answer turneth away
wrath.
Bible: Proverbs

2 *Ira furor brevis est.*
Anger is a short madness.
Horace 65–8 BC: *Epistles*

3 Be ye angry and sin not: let not
the sun go down upon your
wrath.
Bible: Ephesians

4 Anger makes dull men witty, but
it keeps them poor.
Francis Bacon 1561–1626:
"Baconiana" (1859); often attributed
to Queen Elizabeth I from a
misreading of the text

5 Anger is one of the sinews of the
soul.
Thomas Fuller 1608–61: *The Holy
State and the Profane State* (1642)

6 Anger is never without an
argument, but seldom with a
good one.
Lord Halifax 1633–95: *Political,
Moral, and Miscellaneous Thoughts
and Reflections* (1750)

7 The tygers of wrath are wiser
than the horses of instruction.
William Blake 1757–1827: *The
Marriage of Heaven and Hell* (1790–
3) "Proverbs of Hell"

8 We boil at different degrees.
Ralph Waldo Emerson 1803–82:
Society and Solitude (1870)

9 When angry, count four; when
very angry, swear.
Mark Twain 1835–1910: *Pudd'nhead
Wilson* (1894)

10 Speak when you are angry, and
you will make the best speech
you will ever regret.
Ambrose Bierce 1842–1913?: *The
Devil's Dictionary* (1906)

11 I'll thcream and thcream and
thcream till I'm thick.
Violet Elizabeth's threat
Richmal Crompton 1890–1969: *Still—
William* (1925)

12 It's my rule never to lose me
temper till it would be
dethrimental to keep it.
Sean O'Casey 1880–1964: *The
Plough and the Stars* (1926)

Animals
see also **Birds, Cats, Dogs**

1 There went in two and two unto
Noah into the Ark, the male and
the female.
Bible: Genesis

2 A righteous man regardeth the
life of his beast: but the tender
mercies of the wicked are cruel.
Bible: Proverbs

3 Nature's great masterpiece, an
elephant,
The only harmless great thing.
John Donne 1572–1631: "The
Progress of the Soul" (1601)

4 The serpent subtlest beast of all
the field.
John Milton 1608–74: *Paradise Lost*
(1667)

5 Of all Insects no one is more
wonderful than the spider
especially with Respect to their

sagacity and admirable way of working . . . I . . . once saw a very large spider to my surprise swimming in the air . . . and others have assured me that they often have seen spiders fly, the appearance is truly very pretty and pleasing.
Jonathan Edwards 1703–58: *The Flying Spider—Observations by Jonathan Edwards when a boy* "Of Insects"

6 Tyger Tyger, burning bright,
In the forests of the night;
What immortal hand or eye,
Could frame thy fearful
symmetry?
William Blake 1757–1827: *Songs of Experience* (1794) "The Tiger"

7 Animals, whom we have made our slaves, we do not like to consider our equal.
Charles Darwin 1809–82: Notebook B (1837–8)

8 I think I could turn and live with animals, they are so placid and self-contained,
I stand and look at them long and long.
They do not sweat and whine about their condition,
They do not lie awake in the dark and weep for their sins,
They do not make me sick discussing their duty to God,
Not one is dissatisfied, not one is demented with the mania of owning things.
Walt Whitman 1819–92: "Song of Myself" (written 1855)

9 Cats is "dogs" and rabbits is "dogs" and so's Parrats, but this 'ere "Tortis" is a insect, and there ain't no charge for it.
Punch: (UK) 1869

10 But I freely admit that the best of my fun
I owe it to horse and hound.
George John Whyte-Melville 1821–78: "The Good Grey Mare" (1933)

11 When people call this beast to mind,
They marvel more and more
At such a little tail behind,
So large a trunk before.
Hilaire Belloc 1870–1953: *A Bad Child's Book of Beasts* (1896) "The Elephant"

12 The Llama is a woolly sort of fleecy hairy goat,
With an indolent expression and an undulating throat
Like an unsuccessful literary man.
Hilaire Belloc 1870–1953: *More Beasts for Worse Children* (1897) "The Llama"

13 With monstrous head and sickening cry
And ears like errant wings,
The devil's walking parody
On all four-footed things.
G. K. Chesterton 1874–1936: "The Donkey" (1900)

14 All animals, except man, know that the principal business of life is to enjoy it—and they do enjoy it as much as man and other circumstances will allow.
Samuel Butler 1835–1902: *The Way of All Flesh* (1903)

15 'Twould ring the bells of Heaven
The wildest peal for years,
If Parson lost his senses
And people came to theirs,
And he and they together
Knelt down with angry prayers
For tamed and shabby tigers
And dancing dogs and bears,
And wretched, blind, pit ponies,
And little hunted hares.
Ralph Hodgson 1871–1962: "Bells of Heaven" (1917)

16 The rabbit has a charming face:
Its private life is a disgrace.
I really dare not name to you
The awful things that rabbits do.
Anonymous: "The Rabbit" (1925)

17 The giraffe, in their queer, inimitable, vegetative gracefulness . . . a family of rare, long-stemmed, speckled gigantic flowers slowly advancing.
Isak Dinesen 1885–1962: *Out of Africa* (1937)

18 I am fond of pigs. Dogs look up to us. Cats look down on us. Pigs treat us as equals.
Winston Churchill 1874–1965: attributed; M. Gilbert *Never Despair* (1988)

19 To my mind, the only possible pet is a cow. Cows love you . . . They will listen to your problems and never ask a thing in return. They will be your friends for ever. And when you get tired of them, you can kill and eat them. Perfect.
Bill Bryson 1951– : *Neither Here Nor There* (1991)

20 I'm not over-fond of animals. I am merely astounded by them.
David Attenborough 1926– : in *Independent* (UK) 14 January 1995

Apology and Excuses

1 Never make a defence or apology before you be accused.
Charles I 1600–49: letter to Lord Wentworth, 3 September 1636

2 A man should never be ashamed to own he has been in the wrong, which is but saying, in other words, that he is wiser to-day than he was yesterday.
Alexander Pope 1688–1744: *Miscellanies* (1727) vol. 2 "Thoughts on Various Subjects"

3 Never complain and never explain.
Benjamin Disraeli 1804–81: J. Morley *Life of William Ewart Gladstone* (1903)

4 Never explain—your friends do not need it and your enemies will not believe you anyway.
Elbert Hubbard 1859–1915: *The Motto Book* (1907)

5 As I waited I thought that there's nothing like a confession to make one look mad; and that of all confessions a written one is the most detrimental all round. Never confess! Never, never!
Joseph Conrad 1857–1924: *Chance* (1913)

6 It is a good rule in life never to apologize. The right sort of people do not want apologies, and the wrong sort take a mean advantage of them.
P. G. Wodehouse 1881–1975: *The Man Upstairs* (1914)

7 Very sorry can't come. Lie follows by post.
telegraphed message to the Prince of Wales, on being summoned to dine at the eleventh hour
Lord Charles Beresford 1846–1919: Ralph Nevill *The World of Fashion 1837–1922* (1923)

8 Several excuses are always less convincing than one.
Aldous Huxley 1894–1963: *Point Counter Point* (1928)

Appearance
see also **The Body**

1 A merry heart maketh a cheerful countenance.
Bible: Proverbs

2 He was as fressh as is the month of May.
Geoffrey Chaucer c. 1343–1400: *The Canterbury Tales* "The General Prologue"

3 There's no art
To find the mind's construction in the face;
William Shakespeare 1564–1616: *Macbeth* (1606)

4 He was one of a lean body and visage, as if his eager soul, biting for anger at the clog of his body, desired to fret a passage through it.
Thomas Fuller 1608–61: *The Holy State and the Profane State* (1642) "Life of the Duke of Alva"

5 Has he not a rogue's face? . . . a hanging-look to me . . . has a damned Tyburn-face, without the benefit o' the Clergy.
William Congreve 1670–1729: *Love for Love* (1695)

6 An unforgiving eye, and a damned disinheriting countenance!
Richard Brinsley Sheridan 1751–1816: *The School for Scandal* (1777)

7 Fat, fair and forty were all the toasts of the young men.
John O'Keeffe 1747–1833: *The Irish Mimic* (1795)

8 Like the silver plate on a coffin.
describing Robert Peel's smile
John Philpot Curran 1750–1817: quoted by Daniel O'Connell, House of Commons, 26 February 1835

9 She was a gordian shape of dazzling hue,
Vermilion-spotted, golden, green, and blue;
Striped like a zebra, freckled like a pard,
Eyed like a peacock, and all crimson barred.
John Keats 1795–1821: "Lamia" (1820)

10 Beware of all enterprises that require new clothes.
Henry David Thoreau 1817–62: *Walden* (1854)

11 The Lord prefers common-looking people. That is why he makes so many of them.
Abraham Lincoln 1809–65: attributed; James Morgan *Our Presidents* (1928)

12 It's as large as life, and twice as natural!
Lewis Carroll 1832–98: *Through the Looking-Glass* (1872)

13 She may very well pass for forty-three
In the dusk with a light behind her!
W. S. Gilbert 1836–1911: *Trial by Jury* (1875)

14 Most women are not so young as they are painted.
Max Beerbohm 1872–1956: *The Yellow Book* (1894)

15 Your two stout lovers frowning at one another across the hearth rug, while your small, but perfectly formed one kept the party in a roar.
Duff Cooper 1890–1954: letter to Lady Diana Manners, later his wife, October 1914

16 You look rather rash my dear your colors dont quite match your face.
Daisy Ashford 1881–1972: *The Young Visiters* (1919)

17 Have you ever noticed, Harry, that many jewels make women either incredibly fat or incredibly thin?
J. M. Barrie 1860–1937: *The Twelve-Pound Look and Other Plays* (1921)

18 The photograph is not quite true to my own notion of my gentleness and sweetness of nature, but neither perhaps is my external appearance.
A. E. Housman 1859–1936: letter 12 June 1922

19 Though I yield to no one in my admiration for Mr. Coolidge, I do wish he did not look as if he had been weaned on a pickle.
Anonymous: Alice Roosevelt Longworth *Crowded Hours* (1933)

20 At 50, everyone has the face he deserves.
George Orwell 1903–50: last words in his notebook, 17 April 1949

21 My face looks like a wedding-cake left out in the rain.
W. H. Auden 1907–73: Humphrey Carpenter *W. H. Auden* (1981)

22 No power on earth, however, can abolish the merciless class distinction between those who are physically desirable and the lonely, pallid, spotted, silent, unfancied majority.
John Mortimer 1923– : *Clinging to the Wreckage* (1982)

23 You can never be too rich or too thin.
Duchess of Windsor 1896–1986: attributed

Architecture

1 Well building hath three conditions. Commodity, firmness, and delight.
Henry Wotton 1568–1639: *Elements of Architecture* (1624)

2 Houses are built to live in and not to look on; therefore let use be preferred before uniformity, except where both may be had.
Francis Bacon 1561–1626: *Essays* (1625) "Of Building"

3 Light (God's eldest daughter) is a principal beauty in building.
Thomas Fuller 1608–61: *The Holy State and the Profane State* (1642)

4 Architecture in general is frozen music.
Friedrich von Schelling 1775–1854: *Philosophie der Kunst* (1809)

5 As if St. Paul's had come down and littered.
on Brighton Pavilion
Sydney Smith 1771–1845: Peter Virgin *Sydney Smith* (1994)

6 He builded better than he knew;— The conscious stone to beauty grew.
Ralph Waldo Emerson 1803–82: "The Problem" (1847)

7 When we build, let us think that we build for ever.
John Ruskin 1819–1900: *Seven Lamps of Architecture* (1849)

8 Form follows function.
Louis Henri Sullivan 1856–1924: *The Tall Office Building Artistically Considered* (1896)

9 A house is a machine for living in.
Le Corbusier 1887–1965: *Vers une architecture* (1923)

10 Architecture, of all the arts, is the one which acts the most slowly, but the most surely, on the soul.
Ernest Dimnet: *What We Live By* (1932)

11 The existence of St. Sophia is atmospheric; that of St. Peter's, overpoweringly, imminently substantial. One is a church to God: the other a salon for his agents. One is consecrated to reality, the other, to illusion. St. Sophia in fact is large, and St. Peter's is vilely, tragically small.
Robert Byron 1905–41: *The Road to Oxiana* (1937)

12 Fan-vaulting . . . from an aesthetic standpoint frequently belongs to the "Last-supper-carved-on-a-peach-stone" class of masterpiece.
Osbert Lancaster 1908–86: *Pillar to Post* (1938)

13 Less is more.
Mies van der Rohe 1886–1969: P. Johnson *Mies van der Rohe* (1947)

14 The physician can bury his mistakes, but the architect can

only advise his client to plant vines—so they should go as far as possible from home to build their first buildings.
Frank Lloyd Wright 1867–1959: in *New York Times* 4 October 1953

15 Architecture is the art of how to waste space.
Philip Johnson 1906– : in *New York Times* 27 December 1964

16 God is in the details.
Mies van der Rohe 1886–1969: in *New York Times* 19 August 1969

17 In my experience, if you have to keep the lavatory door shut by extending your left leg, it's modern architecture.
Nancy Banks-Smith: in *Guardian* (UK) 20 February 1979

18 A monstrous carbuncle on the face of a much-loved and elegant friend.
on the proposed extension to the National Gallery, London
Prince Charles 1948– : speech to the Royal Institute of British Architects, 30 May 1984

19 It looks like a portable typewriter full of oyster shells, and to the contention that it echoes the sails of yachts on the harbour I can only point out that the yachts on the harbour don't waste any time echoing opera houses.
of the Sydney Opera House
Clive James 1939– : *Flying Visits* (1984)

Argument and Conflict
see also **Opinion**

1 It is better to dwell in a corner of the housetop, than with a brawling woman in a wide house.
Bible: Proverbs

2 You cannot argue with someone who denies the first principles.

Auctoritates Aristotelis: a compilation of medieval propositions

3 Give you a reason on compulsion! if reasons were as plentiful as blackberries I would give no man a reason upon compulsion, I.
William Shakespeare 1564–1616: *Henry IV, Part 1* (1597)

4 Our disputants put me in mind of the skuttle fish, that when he is unable to extricate himself, blackens all the water about him, till he becomes invisible.
Joseph Addison 1672–1719: in *The Spectator* 5 September 1712

5 My uncle Toby would never offer to answer this by any other kind of argument, than that of whistling half a dozen bars of Lillabullero.
Laurence Sterne 1713–68: *Tristram Shandy* (1759–67)

6 There is no arguing with Johnson; for when his pistol misses fire, he knocks you down with the butt end of it.
Oliver Goldsmith 1730–74: James Boswell *Life of Johnson* (1791) 26 October 1769

7 I hate a fellow whom pride, or cowardice, or laziness drives into a corner, and who does nothing when he is there but sit and *growl*; let him come out as I do, and *bark*.
Samuel Johnson 1709–84: James Boswell *Life of Johnson* 10 October 1782

8 Who can refute a sneer?
William Paley 1743–1805: *Principles of Moral and Political Philosophy* (1785)

9 Persuasion is the resource of the feeble; and the feeble can seldom persuade.
Edward Gibbon 1737–94: *The Decline and Fall of the Roman Empire* (1776–88)

10 He never wants anything but what's right and fair; only when you come to settle what's right and fair, it's everything that he wants and nothing that you want. And that's his idea of a compromise. Give me the Brown compromise when I'm on his side.
Thomas Hughes 1822–96: *Tom Brown's Schooldays* (1857)

11 I maintain that two and two would continue to make four, in spite of the whine of the amateur for three, or the cry of the critic for five.
James McNeill Whistler 1834–1903: *Whistler v. Ruskin. Art and Art Critics* (1878)

12 There is no good in arguing with the inevitable. The only argument available with an east wind is to put on your overcoat.
James Russell Lowell 1819–91: *Democracy and other Addresses* (1887)

13 I am not arguing with you—I am telling you.
James McNeill Whistler 1834–1903: *The Gentle Art of Making Enemies* (1890)

14 It takes in reality only one to make a quarrel. It is useless for the sheep to pass resolutions in favour of vegetarianism, while the wolf remains of a different opinion.
William Ralph Inge 1860–1954: *Outspoken Essays: First Series* (1919) "Patriotism"

15 Any stigma, as the old saying is, will serve to beat a dogma.
Philip Guedalla 1889–1944: *Masters and Men* (1923)

16 The argument of the broken window pane is the most valuable argument in modern politics.
Emmeline Pankhurst 1858–1928: George Dangerfield *The Strange Death of Liberal England* (1936)

17 Making noise is an effective means of opposition.
Joseph Goebbels 1897–1945: Ernest K. Bramsted *Goebbels and National Socialist Propaganda 1925–45* (1965)

18 The Catholic and the Communist are alike in assuming that an opponent cannot be both honest and intelligent.
George Orwell 1903–50: in *Polemic* January 1946

19 "Yes, but not in the South," with slight adjustments, will do for any argument about any place, if not about any person.
Stephen Potter 1900–69: *Lifemanship* (1950)

20 I've never won an argument with her; and the only times I thought I had I found out the argument wasn't over yet.
referring to his wife
Jimmy Carter 1924– : *Reader's Digest* (March 1979)

21 That happy sense of purpose people have when they are standing up for a principle they haven't really been knocked down for yet.
P. J. O'Rourke 1947– : *Give War a Chance* (1992)

The Armed Forces
see also **Warfare, Wars, World War I, World War II**

1 For a city consists in men, and not in walls nor in ships empty of men.
speech to the defeated Athenian army at Syracuse, 413 BC
Nicias c. 470–413 BC: Thucydides *History of the Peloponnesian Wars*

2 Then a soldier,
Full of strange oaths, and bearded like the pard,
Jealous in honor, sudden and quick in quarrel,

Seeking the bubble reputation
Even in the cannon's mouth.
William Shakespeare 1564–1616: *As
You Like It* (1599)

3 I would rather have a plain russet-
coated captain that knows what
he fights for, and loves what he
knows, than that which you call
"a gentleman" and is nothing
else.
Oliver Cromwell 1599–1658: letter to
Sir William Spring, September 1643

4 It is upon the navy under the
good Providence of God that the
safety, honor, and welfare of this
realm do chiefly depend.
Charles II 1630–85: "Articles of War"
preamble; Sir Geoffrey Callender *The
Naval Side of British History* (1952);
probably a modern paraphrase

5 Cowards in scarlet pass for men
of war.
George Granville, Baron Lansdowne
1666–1735: *The She Gallants* (1696)

6 Rascals, would you live for ever?
*to hesitant Guards at Kolin, 18 June
1757*
Frederick the Great 1712–86:
attributed

7 Heart of oak are our ships,
Heart of oak are our men:
We always are ready;
Steady, boys, steady;
We'll fight and we'll conquer
again and again.
David Garrick 1717–79: "Heart of
Oak" (1759 song)

8 Every man thinks meanly of
himself for not having been a
soldier, or not having been at sea.
Samuel Johnson 1709–84: James
Boswell *Life of Samuel Johnson*
(1791) 10 April 1778

9 Without a decisive naval force we
can do nothing definitive. And

with it, everything honorable and
glorious.
George Washington 1732–99: to
Lafayette, 15 November 1781

10 Some talk of Alexander, and some
of Hercules;
Of Hector and Lysander, and such
great names as these;
But of all the world's brave
heroes, there's none that can
compare
With a tow, row, row, row, row,
row, for the British Grenadier.
Anonymous: "The British Grenadiers"
(traditional song)

11 A willing foe and sea room.
Anonymous: naval toast in the time
of Nelson; W. N. T. Beckett *A Few
Naval Customs, Expressions,
Traditions, and Superstitions* (1931)

12 As Lord Chesterfield said of the
generals of his day, "I only hope
that when the enemy reads the
list of their names, he trembles as
I do."
*usually quoted as "I don't know
what effect these men will have
upon the enemy, but, by God, they
frighten me"*
Duke of Wellington 1769–1852:
letter, 29 August 1810

13 *La Garde meurt, mais ne se rend
pas.*
The Guards die but do not
surrender.
*when called upon to surrender at
Waterloo, 1815*
Pierre, Baron de Cambronne 1770–
1842: attributed to Cambronne, but
later denied by him; H. Houssaye *La
Garde meurt et ne se rend pas*
(1907)

14 The Assyrian came down like the
wolf on the fold,
And his cohorts were gleaming in
purple and gold;

And the sheen of their spears was
like stars on the sea,
When the blue wave rolls nightly
on deep Galilee.
Lord Byron 1788–1824: "The
Destruction of Sennacherib" (1815)

15 An army marches on its stomach.
Napoleon I 1769–1821: attributed,
but probably condensed from a long
passage in E. A. de Las Cases
Mémorial de Ste-Hélène (1823) vol.
4, 14 November 1816; also attributed
to Frederick the Great

16 Ours [our army] is composed of
the scum of the earth—the mere
scum of the earth.
Duke of Wellington 1769–1852:
Philip Henry Stanhope *Notes of
Conversations with the Duke of
Wellington* (1888) 4 November 1831

17 A good uniform must work its
way with the women, sooner or
later.
Charles Dickens 1812–70: *Pickwick
Papers* (1837)

18 *C'est magnifique, mais ce n'est pas
la guerre.*
It is magnificent, but it is not
war.
*on the charge of the Light Brigade at
Balaclava, 25 October 1854*
Pierre Bosquet 1810–61: Cecil
Woodham-Smith *The Reason Why*
(1953)

19 Theirs not to make reply,
Theirs not to reason why,
Theirs but to do and die:
Into the valley of Death
Rode the six hundred.
Alfred, Lord Tennyson 1809–92: "The
Charge of the Light Brigade" (1854);
cf. **20** below

20 As far as it engendered
excitement the finest run in
Leicestershire could hardly bear
comparison.

*the second-in-command's view of
the charge of the Light Brigade*
Lord George Paget 1818–80: *The
Light Cavalry Brigade in the Crimea*
(1881); cf. **19** above

21 I have considered the pension list
of the republic a roll of honor.
Grover Cleveland 1837–1908: veto of
Dependent Pension Bill, 5 July 1888

22 For it's Tommy this, an' Tommy
that, an' "Chuck him out, the
brute!"
But it's "Saviour of 'is country"
when the guns begin to shoot.
Rudyard Kipling 1865–1936:
"Tommy" (1892)

23 The 'eathen in 'is blindness must
end where 'e began.
But the backbone of the Army is
the non-commissioned man!
Rudyard Kipling 1865–1936: "The
'Eathen" (1896); cf. **Religion 22**

24 You can always tell an old soldier
by the inside of his holsters and
cartridge boxes. The young ones
carry pistols and cartridges; the
old ones, grub.
George Bernard Shaw 1856–1950:
Arms and the Man (1898)

25 Your friend the British soldier can
stand up to anything except the
British War Office.
George Bernard Shaw 1856–1950:
The Devil's Disciple (1901)

26 We're foot—slog—slog—slog—
sloggin' over Africa!—
Foot—foot—foot—foot—sloggin'
over Africa—
(Boots—boots—boots—boots—
movin' up and down again!)
There's no discharge in the war!
Rudyard Kipling 1865–1936: "Boots"
(1903); the final line is from
Ecclesiastes

27 If these gentlemen had their way,
they would soon be asking me to

defend the moon against a possible attack from Mars.
of his senior military advisers, and their tendency to see threats which did not exist
Lord Salisbury 1830–1903: Robert Taylor *Lord Salisbury* (1975)

28 What passing-bells for these who die as cattle?
Only the monstrous anger of the guns.
Only the stuttering rifles' rapid rattle
Can patter out their hasty orisons.
Wilfred Owen 1893–1918: "Anthem for Doomed Youth" (1917)

29 If I were fierce, and bald, and short of breath,
I'd live with scarlet Majors at the Base,
And speed glum heroes up the line to death.
Siegfried Sassoon 1886–1967: "Base Details" (1918)

30 LUDENDORFF: The English soldiers fight like lions.
HOFFMAN: True. But don't we know that they are lions led by donkeys.
during World War I
Max Hoffman 1869–1927: attributed; Alan Clark *The Donkeys* (1961)

31 O Death, where is thy sting-a-ling-a-ling,
O grave, thy victory?
The bells of Hell go ting-a-ling-a-ling
For you but not for me.
Anonymous: "For You But Not For Me" (World War I song); see **Death** 7

32 Nor law, nor duty bade me fight,
Nor public man, nor angry crowds,
A lonely impulse of delight
Drove to this tumult in the clouds;
I balanced all, brought all to mind,

The years to come seemed waste of breath,
A waste of breath the years behind
In balance with this life, this death.
W. B. Yeats 1865–1939: "An Irish Airman Foresees his Death" (1919)

33 Old soldiers never die,
They simply fade away.
J. Foley 1906–70: "Old Soldiers Never Die" (1920 song); possibly a "folk-song" from World War I

34 Their shoulders held the sky suspended;
They stood, and earth's foundations stay;
What God abandoned, these defended,
And saved the sum of things for pay.
A. E. Housman 1859–1936: "Epitaph on an Army of Mercenaries" (1922)

35 My only great qualification for being put at the head of the Navy is that I am very much at sea.
Edward Carson 1854–1935: Ian Colvin *Life of Lord Carson* (1936)

36 Naval tradition? Monstrous. Nothing but rum, sodomy, prayers, and the lash.
often quoted as, "rum, sodomy, and the lash," as in Peter Gretton Former Naval Person *(1968)*
Winston Churchill 1874–1965: Harold Nicolson diary 17 August 1950

37 The world has turned over many times since I took the oath on the plain at West Point . . . but I still remember the refrain of one of the most popular barracks ballads of that day which proclaimed most proudly that old soldiers never die; they just fade away.
Douglas MacArthur 1880–1964: Address to Congress (19 April 1951)

38 If there is one basic element in our Constitution, it is civilian control of the military.
Harry S. Truman 1884–1972: *Memoirs: Years of Trial and Hope* (1956)

39 The best service a retired general can perform is to turn in his tongue along with his suit and to mothball his opinions.
Omar N. Bradley 1893–1981: *News summaries* (17 May 1959)

40 Only when our arms are sufficient beyond doubt can we be certain beyond doubt that they will never be employed.
John F. Kennedy 1917–63: Inaugural (20 January 1961)

41 I don't object to it being called "McNamara's war" . . . It is a very important war and I am pleased to be identified with it and do whatever I can to win it.
Robert S. McNamara 1916– : *New York Times* (25 April 1964)

42 Some nervous Nellies . . . will turn on their own leaders and their own country, and on our own fighting men.
Lyndon B. Johnson 1908–73: statement (17 May 1966)

43 I didn't fire him because he was a dumb son of a bitch, although he was, but that's not against the law for generals. If it was, half to three-quarters of them would be in jail.
of General MacArthur
Harry S. Truman 1884–1972: Merle Miller *Plain Speaking* (1974)

44 The sergeant is the Army.
Dwight D. Eisenhower 1890–1969: *New York Times* (24 December 1972)

45 I've spent my life fighting the Germans and the politicians. It is much easier to fight the Germans.
Bernard Law Montgomery 1887–1976: (24 March 1976)

46 Most people are relieved to find a superior on whose judgement they can rest. That, indeed, is the difference between most people and Generals.
Barbara W. Tuchman 1912–89: *Practicing History* (1981)

47 Once you're committed to war, then be ferocious enough to do whatever is necessary to get it over with as quickly as possible in victory.
H. Norman Schwarzkopf III 1934– : *New York Times* (28 January 1991)

48 I don't consider myself dovish and I certainly don't consider myself hawkish. Maybe I would describe myself as owlish—that is, wise enough to understand that you want to do everything possible to avoid war.
H. Norman Schwarzkopf III 1934– : *New York Times* (28 January 1991)

49 We are required to pledge our sacred honor to a document that looks at the military . . . as a necessary, but undesirable, institution useful in times of crisis and to be watched carefully at all other times.
Colin L. Powell 1937– : *U.S News & World Report* (4 February 1991)

50 Any soldier worth his salt should be antiwar.
H. Norman Schwarzkopf III 1934– : *U.S. News & World Report* (11 February 1991)

51 I have fewer disciplinary problems commanding a third of a million troops now than I did in 1973 commanding 1,000 men.
John J. Yeosock 1937– : *Time* (18 March 1991)

52 We of the Kennedy and Johnson administrations who participated in the decisions on Vietnam acted according to what we thought were the principles and traditions

of this nation. We made our
decisions in light of those values.
Yet we were wrong, terribly
wrong.
Robert S. McNamara 1916– : *In
Retrospect: The Tragedy and
Lessons of Vietnam* (1995)

The Arts
see also **Arts and Sciences, The
Movies and Hollywood, Music,
Painting and the Visual Arts, The
Theater, Writing**

1 Painting is silent poetry, poetry is
eloquent painting.
Simonides c. 556–468 BC: Plutarch
Moralia

2 The poet ranks far below the
painter in the representation of
visible things, and far below the
musician in that of invisible
things.
Leonardo da Vinci 1452–1519: Irma
A. Richter (ed.) *Selections from the
Notebooks of Leonardo da Vinci*
(1952)

3 In art the best is good enough.
Johann Wolfgang von Goethe 1749–
1832: *Italienische Reise* (1816–17) 3
March 1787

4 *L'art pour l'art, sans but, car tout
but dénature l'art. Mais l'art atteint
au but qu'il n'a pas.*
Art for art's sake, with no
purpose, for any purpose perverts
art. But art achieves a purpose
which is not its own.
*describing a conversation with Crabb
Robinson about the latter's work on
Kant's aesthetics*
Benjamin Constant 1767–1834: diary
11 February 1804

5 The arts babblative and
scribblative.
Robert Southey 1774–1843:
*Colloquies on the Progress and
Prospects of Society* (1829)

6 Politics in the middle of things
that concern the imagination are
like a pistol-shot in the middle of
a concert.
Stendhal 1783–1842: *Scarlet and
Black* (1830)

7 God help the Minister that
meddles with art!
Lord Melbourne 1779–1848: Lord
David Cecil *Lord M* (1954)

8 I believe the right question to ask,
respecting all ornament, is simply
this: Was it done with enjoyment—
was the carver happy while he
was about it?
John Ruskin 1819–1900: *Seven
Lamps of Architecture* (1849)

9 The artist must be in his work as
God is in creation, invisible and
all-powerful; one must sense him
everywhere but never see him.
Gustave Flaubert 1821–80: letter to
Mademoiselle Leroyer de Chantepie,
18 March 1857

10 Art is a jealous mistress.
Ralph Waldo Emerson 1803–82: *The
Conduct of Life* (1860)

11 Human life is a sad show,
undoubtedly: ugly, heavy and
complex. Art has no other end,
for people of feeling, than to
conjure away the burden and
bitterness.
Gustave Flaubert 1821–80: letter to
Amelie Bosquet, July 1864

12 Then a sentimental passion of a
    vegetable fashion must excite
    your languid spleen,
An attachment à la Plato for a
    bashful young potato, or a not
    too French French bean!
Though the Philistines may jostle,
    you will rank as an apostle in
    the high aesthetic band,
If you walk down Piccadilly with
    a poppy or a lily in your
    medieval hand.
W. S. Gilbert 1836–1911: *Patience*
(1881)

13 Listen! There never was an
artistic period. There never was
an Art-loving nation.
James McNeill Whistler 1834–1903:
Mr. Whistler's "Ten O'Clock" (1885)

14 All that I desire to point out is
the general principle that Life
imitates Art far more than Art
imitates Life.
Oscar Wilde 1854–1900: *Intentions*
(1891)

15 The nineteenth century dislike of
Realism is the rage of Caliban
seeing his own face in the glass.
Oscar Wilde 1854–1900: *The Picture
of Dorian Gray* (1891)

16 We know that the tail must wag
      the dog, for the horse is drawn
      by the cart;
But the Devil whoops, as he
      whooped of old: "It's clever, but
      is it Art?"
Rudyard Kipling 1865–1936: "The
Conundrum of the Workshops"
(1892)

17 We work in the dark—we do
what we can—we give what we
have. Our doubt is our passion
and our passion is our task. The
rest is the madness of art.
Henry James 1843–1916: "The Middle
Years" (short story, 1893)

18 I always said God was against art
and I still believe it.
Edward Elgar 1857–1934: letter to
A. J. Jaeger, 9 October 1900

19 The history of art is the history of
revivals.
Samuel Butler 1835–1902:
Notebooks (1912)

20 The true artist will let his wife
starve, his children go barefoot,
his mother drudge for his living
at seventy, sooner than work at
anything but his art.
George Bernard Shaw 1856–1950:
Man and Superman (1903)

21 Life being all inclusion and
confusion, and art being all
discrimination and selection.
Henry James 1843–1916: *The Spoils
of Poynton* (1909 ed.)

22 The artist, like the God of the
creation, remains within or
behind or beyond or above his
handiwork, invisible, refined out
of existence, indifferent, paring
his fingernails.
James Joyce 1882–1941: *A Portrait of
the Artist as a Young Man* (1916)

23 Art is vice. You don't marry it
legitimately, you rape it.
Edgar Degas 1834–1917: Paul Lafond
Degas (1918)

24 Another unsettling element in
modern art is that common
symptom of immaturity, the
dread of doing what has been
done before.
Edith Wharton 1862–1937: *The
Writing of Fiction* (1925)

25 The artist is not a special kind of
man, but every man is a special
kind of artist.
Ananda Coomaraswamy 1877–1947:
Transformation of Nature in Art
(1934)

26 The proletarian state must bring
up thousands of excellent
"mechanics of culture,"
"engineers of the soul."
Maxim Gorky 1868–1936: speech at
the Writers' Congress 1934; cf. **34**
below

27 Art is significant deformity.
Roger Fry 1866–1934: Virginia Woolf
Roger Fry (1940)

28 I suppose art is the only thing
that can go on mattering once it
has stopped hurting.
Elizabeth Bowen 1899–1973: *Heat of
the Day* (1949)

29 It is closing time in the gardens of the West and from now on an artist will be judged only by the resonance of his solitude or the quality of his despair.
Cyril Connolly 1903–74: in *Horizon* December 1949–January 1950

30 *L'art est un anti-destin.*
Art is a revolt against fate.
André Malraux 1901–76: *Les Voix du silence* (1951)

31 Art is born of humiliation.
W. H. Auden 1907–73: Stephen Spender *World Within World* (1951)

32 Artists are the antennae of the race, but the bullet-headed many will never learn to trust their great artists.
Ezra Pound 1885–1972: *Literary Essays* (1954)

33 Art is . . . pattern informed by sensibility.
Herbert Read 1893–1968: *The Meaning of Art* (1955)

34 In free society art is not a weapon . . . Artists are not engineers of the soul.
John F. Kennedy 1917–63: speech at Amherst College, Mass., 26 October 1963; see **26** above

35 Art is the objectification of feeling, and the subjectification of nature.
Susanne Langer 1895–1985: in *Mind* (1967)

36 We all know that Art is not truth. Art is a lie that makes us realize truth.
Pablo Picasso 1881–1973: Dore Ashton *Picasso on Art* (1972)

37 An artist is someone who produces things that people don't need to have but that he — for *some reason* — thinks it would be a good idea to give them.

Andy Warhol 1927–87: *Philosophy of Andy Warhol (From A to B and Back Again)* (1975)

38 Do not imagine that Art is something which is designed to give gentle uplift and self-confidence. Art is not a *brassière*. At least, not in the English sense. But do not forget that *brassière* is the French for life-jacket.
Julian Barnes 1946– : *Flaubert's Parrot* (1984)

39 You've got to have two out of death, sex and jewels.
the ingredients for a successful exhibition
Roy Strong 1935– : in *Sunday Times* 23 January 1994

Arts and Sciences

1 Histories make men wise; poets, witty; the mathematics, subtile; natural philosophy, deep; moral, grave; logic and rhetoric, able to contend.
Francis Bacon 1561–1626: *Essays* (1625) "Of Studies"

2 In science, read, by preference, the newest works; in literature, the oldest.
Edward George Bulwer-Lytton 1803–73: *Caxtoniana* (1863) "Hints on Mental Culture"

3 A contemporary poet has characterized this sense of the personality of art and of the impersonality of science in these words—"Art is myself; science is ourselves"
Claude Bernard 1813–78: *Introduction à l'étude de la médecin expérimentale* (1865)

4 Poets do not go mad; but chess-players do. Mathematicians go mad, and cashiers; but creative artists very seldom. I am not, as

will be seen, in any sense
attacking logic: I only say that
this danger does lie in logic, not
in imagination.
G. K. Chesterton 1874–1936:
Orthodoxy (1908)

5 Why is it that the scholar is the
only man of science of whom it is
ever demanded that he should
display taste and feeling?
A. E. Housman 1859–1936:
"Cambridge Inaugural Lecture" (1911)

6 We believe a scientist because he
can substantiate his remarks, not
because he is eloquent and
forcible in his enunciation. In
fact, we distrust him when he
seems to be influencing us by his
manner.
I. A. Richards 1893–1979: *Science
and Poetry* (1926)

7 Every good poem, in fact, is a
bridge built from the known,
familiar side of life over into the
unknown. Science too, is always
making expeditions into the
unknown. But this does not mean
that science can supersede poetry.
For poetry enlightens us in a
different way from science; it
speaks directly to our feelings or
imagination. The findings of
poetry are no more and no less
true than science.
C. Day-Lewis 1904–72: *Poetry for
You* (1944)

8 Art is meant to disturb, science
reassures.
Georges Braque 1882–1963: *Le Jour
et la nuit: Cahiers 1917–52*

9 Science must begin with myths,
and with the criticism of myths.
Karl Popper 1902–94: "The
Philosophy of Science" C. A. Mace
(ed.) *British Philosophy in the Mid-
Century* (1957)

10 The true men of action in our
time, those who transform the

world, are not the politicians and
statesmen, but the scientists.
Unfortunately poetry cannot
celebrate them, because their
deeds are concerned with things,
not persons, and are, therefore,
speechless. When I find myself in
the company of scientists, I feel
like a shabby curate who has
strayed by mistake into a drawing
room full of dukes.
W. H. Auden 1907–73: *The Dyer's
Hand* (1963) "The Poet and the City"

11 If a scientist were to cut his ear
off, no one would take it as
evidence of a heightened
sensibility.
Peter Medawar 1915–87: "J. B. S."
(1968)

12 Shakespeare would have grasped
wave functions, Donne would
have understood complementarity
and relative time. They would
have been excited. What richness!
They would have plundered this
new science for their imagery.
And they would have educated
their audiences too. But you
"arts" people, you're not only
ignorant of these magnificent
things, you're rather proud of
knowing nothing.
Ian McEwan 1948– : *The Child in
Time* (1987)

13 If Watson and Crick had not
discovered the nature of DNA,
one can be virtually certain that
other scientists would eventually
have determined it. With art—
whether painting, music or
literature — it is quite different. If
Shakespeare had not written
Hamlet, no other playwright
would have done so.
Lewis Wolpert 1929– : *The
Unnatural Nature of Science* (1993)

Australia and New Zealand

1 The loss of America what can
repay?

New colonies seek for at Botany
  Bay.
John Freeth c. 1731–1808: "Botany
Bay" (1786)

2 True patriots we; for be it
    understood,
  We left our country for our
    country's good.
  *prologue, written for, but not recited
  at, the opening of the Playhouse,
  Sydney, New South Wales, 16
  January 1796, when the actors were
  principally convicts*
  Henry Carter d. 1806: A. W. Jose and
  H. J. Carter (eds,) *The Australian
  Encyclopaedia* (1927); previously
  attributed to George Barrington (b.
  1755)

3 I have been disappointed in all
    my expectations of Australia,
    except as to its wickedness; for it
    is far more wicked than I have
    conceived it possible for any place
    to be, or than it is possible for me
    to describe to you in England.
  Henry Parkes 1815–95: letter, 1 May
  1840 *An Emigrant's Home Letters*
  (1896)

4 Earth is here so kind, that just
    tickle her with a hoe and she
    laughs with a harvest.
  Douglas Jerrold 1803–57: *The Wit
  and Opinions of Douglas Jerrold*
  (1859)

5 The crimson thread of kinship
    runs through us all.
  on Australian federation
  Henry Parkes 1815–95: speech at
  banquet in Melbourne 6 February
  1890; *The Federal Government of
  Australasia* (1890)

6 Once a jolly swagman camped by
    a billabong,
  Under the shade of a coolibah
    tree;
  And he sang as he watched and
    waited till his "Billy" boiled:
  "You'll come a-waltzing, Matilda,
    with me."

"Banjo" Paterson 1864–1941:
"Waltzing Matilda" (1903 song)

7 Australia has a marvellous sky
    and air and blue clarity, and a
    hoary sort of land beneath it, like
    a Sleeping Princess on whom the
    dust of ages has settled.
  D. H. Lawrence 1885–1930: letter to
  Jan Juta, 20 May 1922

8 Sing 'em muck! It's all they can
    understand!
  *advice to Dame Clara Butt, prior to
  her departure for Australia*
  Dame Nellie Melba 1861–1931: W. H.
  Ponder *Clara Butt* (1928)

9 And her five cities, like teeming
    sores,
  Each drains her: a vast parasite
    robber-state
  Where second-hand Europeans
    pullulate
  Timidly on the edge of alien
    shores.
  A. D. Hope 1907– : "Australia"
  (1939)

10 What Great Britain calls the Far
    East is to us the near north.
  Robert Gordon Menzies 1894–1978:
  in *Sydney Morning Herald* 27 April
  1939

11 Above our writers—and other
    artists—looms the intimidating
    mass of Anglo-Saxon culture.
    Such a situation almost inevitably
    produces the characteristic
    Australian Cultural Cringe—
    appearing either as the Cringe
    Direct, or as the Cringe Inverted,
    in the attitude of the Blatant
    Blatherskite, the God's-Own-
    Country and I'm-a-better-man-
    than-you-are Australian bore.
  Arthur Angell Phillips 1900–85:
  Meanjin (1950) "The Cultural Cringe"
  cf. **17** below

12 [The average Australian practises]
    that hateful religion of
    ordinariness.

Patrick White 1912–90: letter to Ben Huebsch, 20 January 1960

13 Australia is a lucky country run mainly by second-rate people who share its luck.
Donald Richmond Horne 1921– : *The Lucky Country: Australia in the Sixties* (1964)

14 In all directions stretched the great Australian Emptiness, in which the mind is the least of possessions.
Patrick White 1912–90: *The Vital Decade* (1968) "The Prodigal Son"

15 Australia is a huge rest home, where no unwelcome news is ever wafted on to the pages of the worst newspapers in the world.
Germaine Greer 1939– : in *Observer* 1 August 1982

16 Australia is the flattest, driest, ugliest place on earth. Only those who can be possessed by her can know what secret beauty she holds.
Eric Paul Willmot 1936– : *Australia The Last Experiment* (1987)

17 Even as it [Great Britain] walked out on you and joined the Common Market, you were still looking for your MBEs and your knighthoods, and all the rest of the regalia that comes with it. You would take Australia right back down the time tunnel to the cultural cringe where you have always come from.
addressing Australian Conservative supporters of Great Britain
Paul Keating 1944– : on 27 February 1992; cf. 11 above

18 A broad school of Australian writing has based itself on the assumption that Australia not only has a history worth bothering about, but that all the

history worth bothering about happened in Australia.
Clive James 1939– : *The Dreaming Swimmer* (1992)

Beauty
see also **The Body**

1 A beautiful face is a mute recommendation.
Publilius Syrus: *Sententiae*

2 Consider the lilies of the field, how they grow; they toil not, neither do they spin:
And yet I say unto you, That even Solomon in all his glory was not arrayed like one of these.
Bible: St. Matthew

3 And she was fayr as is the rose in May.
Geoffrey Chaucer c. 1343–1400: *The Legend of Good Women* "Cleopatra"

4 Was this the face that launched a thousand ships,
And burnt the topless towers of Ilium?
Sweet Helen, make me immortal with a kiss!
Christopher Marlowe 1564–93: *Doctor Faustus* (1604)

5 Love built on beauty, soon as beauty, dies.
John Donne 1572–1631: *Elegies* "The Anagram" (c. 1595)

6 O! she doth teach the torches to burn bright.
It seems she hangs upon the cheek of night
Like a rich jewel in an Ethiop's ear;
Beauty too rich for use, for earth too dear.
William Shakespeare 1564–1616: *Romeo and Juliet* (1595)

7 There is no excellent beauty that hath not some strangeness in the proportion.

Francis Bacon 1561–1626: *Essays* (1625) "Of Beauty"

8 Beauty is the lover's gift.
William Congreve 1670–1729: *The Way of the World* (1700)

9 No woman can be a beauty without a fortune.
George Farquhar 1678–1707: *The Beaux' Stratagem* (1707)

10 The flowers anew, returning seasons bring;
But beauty faded has no second spring.
Ambrose Philips c. 1675–1749: *The First Pastoral* (1708)

11 Beauty is no quality in things themselves. It exists merely in the mind which contemplates them.
David Hume 1711–76: *Essays, Moral, Political, and Literary* (ed. T. H. Green and T. H. Grose, 1875) "Of the Standard of Taste" (1757)

12 She walks in beauty, like the night
Of cloudless climes and starry skies;
And all that's best of dark and bright
Meet in her aspect and her eyes.
Lord Byron 1788–1824: "She Walks in Beauty" (1815)

13 A thing of beauty is a joy for ever:

Its loveliness increases; it will never
Pass into nothingness.
John Keats 1795–1821: *Endymion* (1818); cf. **Men 12**

14 "Beauty is truth, truth beauty,"—that is all
Ye know on earth, and all ye need to know.
John Keats 1795–1821: "Ode on a Grecian Urn" (1820); cf. **Truth 18**

15 There is nothing ugly; *I never saw an ugly thing in my life*: for let the

form of an object be what it may,—light, shade, and perspective will always make it beautiful.
John Constable 1776–1837: C. R. Leslie *Memoirs of the Life of John Constable* (1843)

16 Remember that the most beautiful things in the world are the most useless; peacocks and lilies for instance.
John Ruskin 1819–1900: *Stones of Venice* vol. 1 (1851)

17 If you get simple beauty and naught else,
You get about the best thing God invents.
Robert Browning 1812–89: "Fra Lippo Lippi" (1855)

18 All things counter, original, spare, strange;
Whatever is fickle, freckled (who knows how?)
With swift, slow; sweet, sour; adazzle, dim;
He fathers-forth whose beauty is past change:
Praise him.
Gerard Manley Hopkins 1844–89: "Pied Beauty" (written 1877)

19 The awful thing is that beauty is mysterious as well as terrible. God and devil are fighting there, and the battlefield is the heart of man.
Fyodor Dostoevsky 1821–81: *The Brothers Karamazov* (1879–80)

20 I have a left shoulder-blade that is a miracle of loveliness. People come miles to see it. My right elbow has a fascination that few can resist.
W. S. Gilbert 1836–1911: *The Mikado* (1885)

21 When a woman isn't beautiful, people always say, "You have lovely eyes, you have lovely hair."
Anton Chekhov 1860–1904: *Uncle Vanya* (1897)

22 A woman of so shining loveliness
That men threshed corn at
    midnight by a tress,
A little stolen tress.
W. B. Yeats 1865–1939: "The Secret
Rose" (1899)

23 Beauty is all very well at first
sight; but who ever looks at it
when it has been in the house
three days?
George Bernard Shaw 1856–1950:
Man and Superman (1903)

24 I always say beauty is only sin
deep.
Saki 1870–1916: *Reginald* (1904)

25 A pretty girl is like a melody
That haunts you night and day.
Irving Berlin 1888–1989: "A Pretty
Girl is like a Melody" (1919 song)

26 Beauty for some provides escape,
Who gain a happiness in eyeing
The gorgeous buttocks of the ape
Or Autumn sunsets exquisitely
    dying.
Aldous Huxley 1894–1963: "Ninth
Philosopher's Song" (1920)

27 He was afflicted by the thought
that where Beauty was, nothing
ever ran quite straight, which, no
doubt, was why so many people
looked on it as immoral.
John Galsworthy 1867–1933: *In
Chancery* (1920)

28 Oh no, it wasn't the aeroplanes.
It was Beauty killed the Beast.
James Creelman 1901–41 and **Ruth
Rose**: *King Kong* (1933 film) final
words

29 I'm tired of all this nonsense
about beauty being only skin-
deep. That's deep enough. What
do you want—an adorable
pancreas?
Jean Kerr 1923– : *The Snake has
all the Lines* (1958)

Beginnings and Endings
see also **Change**

1 In the beginning God created the
heaven and the earth. And the
earth was without form, and void;
and darkness was upon the face
of the deep. And the Spirit of God
moved upon the face of the
waters.
And God said, Let there be light:
and there was light.
Bible: Genesis

2 Better is the end of a thing than
the beginning thereof.
Bible: Ecclesiastes

3 *Dies irae, dies illa,*
Solvet saeclum in favilla,
Teste David cum Sibylla.
That day, the day of wrath, will
turn the universe to ashes, as
David foretells (and the Sibyl too).
The Missal: *Order of Mass for the
Dead* "Sequentia" (commonly known
as *Dies Irae*); attributed to Thomas
of Celano, *c.* 1190–1260

4 In my end is my beginning.
Mary, Queen of Scots 1542–87:
motto; letter from William
Drummond of Hawthornden to Ben
Jonson in 1619; cf. **15** below

5 The rest is silence.
William Shakespeare 1564–1616:
Hamlet (1601)

6 Finish, good lady; the bright day
    is done,
And we are for the dark.
William Shakespeare 1564–1616:
Antony and Cleopatra (1606–7)

7 What if this present were the
    world's last night?
John Donne 1572–1631: *Holy Sonnets*
(after 1609)

8 And so I betake myself to that
course, which is almost as much
as to see myself go into my grave—

for which, and all the discomforts
that will accompany my being
blind, the good God prepare me!
Samuel Pepys 1633–1703: diary 31
May 1669, closing words

9 Ere time and place were, time and
place were not;
Where primitive nothing
something straight begot;
Then all proceeded from the great
united what.
John Wilmot, Lord Rochester 1647–
80: "Upon Nothing" (1680)

10 This is the beginning of the end.
*on the announcement of Napoleon's
Pyrrhic victory at Borodino, 1812*
Charles-Maurice de Talleyrand 1754–
1838: attributed; Sainte-Beuve *M. de
Talleyrand* (1870); cf. **13** below

11 All tragedies are finished by a
death,
All comedies are ended by a
marriage;
The future states of both are left
to faith.
Lord Byron 1788–1824: *Don Juan*
(1819–24)

12 "Where shall I begin, please your
Majesty?" he asked. "Begin at the
beginning," the King said,
gravely, "and go on till you come
to the end: then stop."
Lewis Carroll 1832–98: *Alice's
Adventures in Wonderland* (1865)

13 Now this is not the end. It is not
even the beginning of the end.
But it is, perhaps, the end of the
beginning.
on the Battle of Egypt
Winston Churchill 1874–1965: speech
at the Mansion House, London, 10
November 1942; cf. **10** above

14 All this will not be finished in the
first 100 days. Nor will it be
finished in the first 1,000 days,
nor in the life of this
Administration, nor even perhaps

in our lifetime on this planet. But
let us begin.
John F. Kennedy 1917–63: inaugural
address, 20 January 1961

15 Eternity's a terrible thought. I
mean, where's it all going to end?
Tom Stoppard 1937– : *Rosencrantz
and Guildenstern are Dead* (1967)

16 It ain't over till it's over.
Yogi Berra 1925– : comment on
National League pennant race, 1973,
quoted in many versions

Behavior
see also **Manners, Words and Deeds**

1 *O tempora, O mores!*
Oh, the times! Oh, the manners!
Cicero 106–43 BC: *In Catilinam*

2 When I go to Rome, I fast on
Saturday, but here [Milan] I do
not. Do you also follow the
custom of whatever church you
attend, if you do not want to give
or receive scandal.
St. Ambrose c. 339–97: "Letter 54 to
Januarius" (AD c. 400)

3 This noble ensample to his sheep
he yaf,
That first he wroghte, and
afterward he taughte.
Geoffrey Chaucer c. 1343–1400: *The
Canterbury Tales* "The General
Prologue"

4 Never *in* the way, and never *out*
of the way.
*of Lord Godolphin, who had been
raised as page to the king*
Charles II 1630–85: in *Dictionary of
National Biography* (1917–)

5 Careless she is with artful care,
Affecting to seem unaffected.
William Congreve 1670–1729:
"Amoret"

6 Take the tone of the company
that you are in.

Lord Chesterfield 1694–1773: *Letters to his Son* (1774) 16 October 1747

7 They teach the morals of a whore, and the manners of a dancing master.
of the Letters *of Lord Chesterfield*
Samuel Johnson 1709–84: James Boswell *Life of Samuel Johnson* (1791) 1754

8 While he felt like a victim, he acted like a hero.
of Admiral Byng, on the day of his execution, 1757
Horace Walpole 1717–97: *Memoirs of the Reign of King George II* (ed. Lord Holland, 1846)

9 Always ding, dinging Dame Grundy into my ears—what will Mrs. Grundy zay? What will Mrs. Grundy think?
Thomas Morton c. 1764–1838: *Speed the Plough* (1798); cf. **Morality 4**

10 May I ask whether these pleasing attentions proceed from the impulse of the moment, or are the result of previous study?
Jane Austen 1775–1817: *Pride and Prejudice* (1813)

11 There was a little girl
Who had a little curl
Right in the middle of her forehead,
When she was good
She was very, very good,
But when she was bad she was horrid.
composed for, and sung to, his second daughter while a babe in arms, c. 1850
Henry Wadsworth Longfellow 1807–82: B. R. Tucker-Macchetta *The Home Life of Henry W. Longfellow* (1882)

12 It is almost a definition of a gentleman to say that he is one who never inflicts pain.
John Henry Newman 1801–90: *The Idea of a University* (1852)

13 He only does it to annoy,
Because he knows it teases.
Lewis Carroll 1832–98: *Alice's Adventures in Wonderland* (1865)

14 Go directly—see what she's doing, and tell her she mustn't.
Punch: (UK) 1872

15 Conduct is three-fourths of our life and its largest concern.
Matthew Arnold 1822–88: *Literature and Dogma* (1873)

16 He combines the manners of a Marquis with the morals of a Methodist.
W. S. Gilbert 1836–1911: *Ruddigore* (1887)

17 Be a good animal, true to your instincts.
D. H. Lawrence 1885–1930: *The White Peacock* (1911)

18 In the rotation of crops there was a recognized season for wild oats; but they were not sown more than once.
Edith Wharton 1862–1937: *The Age of Innocence* (1920)

19 Vulgarity has its uses. Vulgarity often cuts ice which refinement scrapes at vainly.
Max Beerbohm 1872–1956: letter 21 May 1921

20 Being tactful in audacity is knowing how far one can go too far.
Jean Cocteau 1889–1963: *Le Rappel à l'ordre* (1926)

21 Airing one's dirty linen never makes for a masterpiece.
Francois Truffaut 1932–84: *Bed and Board* (1972)

22 Whatever it is that makes a person charming, it needs to remain a mystery.
Rex Harrison 1908–90: *Los Angeles Herald Examiner* (24 June 1978)

23 Already at four years of age I had begun to apprehend that refinement was very often an extenuating virtue; one that excused and eclipsed almost every other unappetizing trait.
Barry Humphries 1934– : *More Please* (1992)

Belief and Unbelief
see also **Certainty and Doubt, Faith**

1 The fool hath said in his heart: There is no God.
Bible: Psalm 14

2 It is convenient that there be gods, and, as it is convenient, let us believe that there are.
Ovid 43 BC–AD c. 17: *Ars Amatoria*

3 Lord, I believe; help thou mine unbelief.
Bible: St. Mark

4 Except ye see signs and wonders, ye will not believe.
Bible: St. John

5 *Certum est quia impossibile est.*
It is certain because it is impossible.
often quoted as "Credo quia impossibile [I believe because it is impossible]"
Tertullian AD c. 160–c. 225: *De Carne Christi*

6 The confidence and faith of the heart alone make both God and an idol.
Martin Luther 1483–1546: *Large Catechism* (1529) "The First Commandment"

7 'Twas God the word that spake it, He took the bread and brake it; And what the word did make it; That I believe, and take it.
answer on being asked her opinion of Christ's presence in the Sacrament
Elizabeth I 1533–1603: S. Clarke *The Marrow of Ecclesiastical History* (1675)

8 For what a man would like to be true, that he more readily believes.
Francis Bacon 1561–1626: *Novum Organum* (1620)

9 A little philosophy inclineth man's mind to atheism, but depth in philosophy bringeth men's minds about to religion.
Francis Bacon 1561–1626: *Essays* (1625) "Of Atheism"

10 By night an atheist half believes a God.
Edward Young 1683–1765: *Night Thoughts* (1742–5) "Night 5"

11 Truth, Sir, is a cow, that will yield such people [sceptics] no more milk, and so they are gone to milk the bull.
Samuel Johnson 1709–84: James Boswell *Life of Samuel Johnson* (1791) 21 July 1763

12 Confidence is a plant of slow growth in an aged bosom: youth is the season of credulity.
William Pitt, Earl of Chatham 1708–78: speech, House of Commons, 14 January 1766

13 It is necessary to the happiness of man that he be mentally faithful to himself. Infidelity does not consist in believing, or in disbelieving, it consists in professing to believe what one does not believe.
Thomas Paine 1737–1809: *The Age of Reason* pt. 1 (1794)

14 Credulity is the man's weakness, but the child's strength.
Charles Lamb 1775–1834: *Essays of Elia* (1823) "Witches, and Other Night-Fears"

15 *We can believe what we choose.* We are answerable for what we choose to believe.

John Henry Newman 1801–90: letter to Mrs. William Froude, 27 June 1848

16 Just when we are safest, there's a
   sunset-touch,
A fancy from a flower-bell, some
   one's death,
A chorus-ending from Euripides,—

And that's enough for fifty hopes
   and fears
As old and new at once as
   nature's self . . .
The grand Perhaps!
Robert Browning 1812–89: "Bishop
Blougram's Apology" (1855)

17 And almost every one when age,
Disease, or sorrows strike him,
Inclines to think there is a God,
Or something very like Him.
Arthur Hugh Clough 1819–61:
Dipsychus (1865)

18 The Sea of Faith
Was once, too, at the full, and
   round earth's shore
Lay like the folds of a bright
   girdle furled.
But now I only hear
Its melancholy, long, withdrawing
   roar,
Retreating, to the breath
Of the night-wind, down the vast
   edges drear
And naked shingles of the world.
Matthew Arnold 1822–88: "Dover
Beach" (1867)

19 Why, sometimes I've believed as
many as six impossible things
before breakfast.
Lewis Carroll 1832–98: *Through the
Looking-Glass* (1872)

20 Be not afraid of life. Believe that
life is worth living, and your
belief will help create the fact.
William James 1842–1910: *The
Principles of Psychology* (1890)

21 I do not pretend to know where
many ignorant men are sure —
that is all that agnosticism means.

Clarence Darrow 1857–1938: speech
at the trial of John Thomas Scopes,
15 July 1925

22 Every time a child says "I don't
believe in fairies" there is a little
fairy somewhere that falls down
dead.
J. M. Barrie 1860–1937: *Peter Pan*
(1928)

23 Of course not, but I am told it
works even if you don't believe in
it.
*when asked whether he really
believed a horseshoe hanging over
his door would bring him luck, c.
1930*
Niels Bohr 1885–1962: A. Pais
Inward Bound (1986)

24 The dust of exploded beliefs may
make a fine sunset.
Geoffrey Madan 1895–1947: *Livre
sans nom: Twelve Reflections*
(privately printed 1934)

25 George [Gershwin] died on July
11, 1937, but I don't have to
believe that if I don't want to.
John O'Hara 1905–70: in *Newsweek*
15 July 1940

26 An atheist is a man who has no
invisible means of support.
John Buchan 1875–1940: H. E.
Fosdick *On Being a Real Person*
(1943)

27 Man is a credulous animal, and
must believe *something*; in the
absence of good grounds for
belief, he will be satisfied with
bad ones.
Bertrand Russell 1872–1970:
Unpopular Essays (1950) "Outline of
Intellectual Rubbish"

28 A young man who wishes to
remain a sound atheist cannot be
too careful of his reading.
C. S. Lewis 1898–1963: *Surprised by
Joy* (1955)

29 If it were an innocent, passive gullibility it would be excusable; but all too clearly, alas, it is an active willingness to be deceived.
Peter Medawar 1915–87: review of Teilhard de Chardin *The Phenomenon of Man* (1961)

30 I do not believe . . . I know.
Carl Gustav Jung 1875–1961: L. van der Post *Jung and the Story of our Time* (1976)

31 I confused things with their names: that is belief.
Jean-Paul Sartre 1905–80: *Les Mots* (1964)

32 Of course, Behaviourism "works." So does torture. Give me a no-nonsense, down-to-earth behaviourist, a few drugs, and simple electrical appliances, and in six months I will have him reciting the Athanasian Creed in public.
W. H. Auden 1907–73: *A Certain World* (1970)

33 There is a lot to be said in the Decade of Evangelism for believing more and more in less and less.
John Yates 1925– : in *Gloucester Diocesan Gazette* (UK) August 1991

The Bible

1 The devil can cite Scripture for his purpose.
William Shakespeare 1564–1616: *The Merchant of Venice* (1596–8)

2 The pencil of the Holy Ghost hath laboured more in describing the afflictions of Job than the felicities of Solomon.
Francis Bacon 1561–1626: *Essays* (1625) "Of Adversity"

3 *Scrutamini scripturas*
[Let us look at the scriptures]. These two words have undone the world.
John Selden 1584–1654: *Table Talk* (1689) "Bible Scripture"

4 We present you with this Book, the most valuable thing that this world affords. Here is wisdom; this is the royal Law; these are the lively Oracles of God.
Coronation Service 1689: The Presenting of the Holy Bible

5 The English Bible, a book which, if everything else in our language should perish, would alone suffice to show the whole extent of its beauty and power.
Lord Macaulay 1800–59: "John Dryden" (1828)

6 There's a great text in Galatians, Once you trip on it, entails Twenty-nine distinct damnations, One sure, if another fails.
Robert Browning 1812–89: "Soliloquy of the Spanish Cloister" (1842)

7 We have used the Bible as if it was a constable's handbook—an opium-dose for keeping beasts of burden patient while they are being overloaded.
Charles Kingsley 1819–75: *Letters to the Chartists*

8 LORD ILLINGWORTH: The Book of Life begins with a man and a woman in a garden.
MRS. ALLONBY: It ends with Revelations.
Oscar Wilde 1854–1900: *A Woman of No Importance* (1893)

9 An apology for the Devil: It must be remembered that we have only heard one side of the case. God has written all the books.
Samuel Butler 1835–1902: *Notebooks* (1912)

10 I know of no book which has been a source of brutality and sadistic conduct, both public and

private, that can compare with the Bible.
Reginald Paget 1908–90: in *Observer* (UK) 28 June 1964 "Sayings of the Week"

Biography

1 Nobody can write the life of a man, but those who have eat and drunk and lived in social intercourse with him.
Samuel Johnson 1709–84: James Boswell *Life of Samuel Johnson* (1791) 31 March 1772

2 Lives of great men all remind us
We can make our lives sublime,
And, departing, leave behind us
Footprints on the sands of time.
Henry Wadsworth Longfellow 1807–82: "A Psalm of Life" (1838)

3 A well-written Life is almost as rare as a well-spent one.
Thomas Carlyle 1795–1881: *Critical and Miscellaneous Essays* (1838) "Jean Paul Friedrich Richter"

4 There is no life of a man, faithfully recorded, but is a heroic poem of its sort, rhymed or unrhymed.
Thomas Carlyle 1795–1881: *Critical and Miscellaneous Essays* (1838) "Sir Walter Scott"

5 There is properly no history; only biography.
Ralph Waldo Emerson 1803–82: *Essays* (1841) "History"

6 Then there is my noble and biographical friend who has added a new terror to death.
on Lord Campbell's Lives of the Lord Chancellors *being written without the consent of heirs or executors*
Charles Wetherell 1770–1846: Lord St. Leonards *Misrepresentations in Campbell's Lives of Lyndhurst and Brougham* (1869); also attributed to Lord Lyndhurst (1772–1863)

7 No quailing, Mrs. Gaskell! no drawing back!
apropos her undertaking to write the life of Charlotte Brontë
Patrick Brontë 1777–1861: letter from Mrs. Gaskell to Ellen Nussey, 24 July 1855

8 *refusing an offer to write his memoirs:*
I should be trading on the blood of my men.
Robert E. Lee 1807–70: attributed, perhaps apocryphal

9 Every great man nowadays has his disciples, and it is always Judas who writes the biography.
Oscar Wilde 1854–1900: *Intentions* (1891) "The Critic as Artist"

10 It is not a Life at all. It is a Reticence, in three volumes.
on J. W. Cross's Life of George Eliot
W. E. Gladstone 1809–98: E. F. Benson *As We Were* (1930)

11 The Art of Biography
Is different from Geography.
Geography is about Maps,
But Biography is about Chaps.
Edmund Clerihew Bentley 1875–1956: *Biography for Beginners* (1905)

12 I write no memoirs. I'm a gentleman. I cannot bring myself to write nastily about persons whose hospitality I have enjoyed.
John Pentland Mahaffy 1839–1919: W. B. Stanford and R. B. McDowell *Mahaffy* (1971)

13 Discretion is not the better part of biography.
Lytton Strachey 1880–1932: Michael Holroyd *Lytton Strachey* vol. 1 (1967)

14 Reformers are always finally neglected, while the memoirs of the frivolous will always eagerly be read.
Henry "Chips" Channon 1897–1958: diary 7 July 1936

15 To write one's memoirs is to speak ill of everybody except oneself.
Henri Philippe Pétain 1856–1951: in *Observer* 26 May 1946

16 He made the books and he died.
his own "sum and history of my life"
William Faulkner 1897–1962: letter to Malcolm Cowley, 11 February 1949

17 Every autobiography . . . becomes an absorbing work of fiction, with something of the charm of a cryptogram.
H. L. Mencken 1880–1956: *Minority Report* (1956)

18 Only when one has lost all curiosity about the future has one reached the age to write an autobiography.
Evelyn Waugh 1903–66: *A Little Learning* (1964)

19 An autobiography is an obituary in serial form with the last instalment missing.
Quentin Crisp 1908– : *The Naked Civil Servant* (1968)

20 I used to think I was an interesting person, but I must tell you how sobering a thought it is to realize your life's story fills about thirty-five pages and you have, actually, not much to say.
Roseanne Arnold 1953– : *Roseanne* (1990)

21 It's an excellent life of somebody else. But I've really lived inside myself, and she can't get in there.
on a biography of himself
Robertson Davies 1913–95: interview in *The Times* (UK) 4 April 1995

Birds
see also **Animals**

1 And smale foweles maken melodye,
That slepen al the nyght with open ye
(So priketh hem nature in hir corages),
Thanne longen folk to goon on pilgrimages.
Geoffrey Chaucer c. 1343–1400: *The Canterbury Tales* "The General Prologue"

2 The silver swan, who, living had no note,
When death approached unlocked her silent throat.
Orlando Gibbons 1583–1625: "The Silver Swan" (1612 song)

3 While the cock with lively din
Scatters the rear of darkness thin,
And to the stack, or the barn door,
Stoutly struts his dames before.
John Milton 1608–74: "L'Allegro" (1645)

4 A robin red breast in a cage
Puts all Heaven in a rage.
William Blake 1757–1827: "Auguries of Innocence" (c. 1803)

5 O blithe new-comer! I have heard, I hear thee and rejoice:
O Cuckoo! Shall I call thee bird, Or but a wandering voice?
William Wordsworth 1770–1850: "To the Cuckoo" (1807)

6 Hail to thee, blithe Spirit!
Bird thou never wert,
That from Heaven, or near it,
Pourest thy full heart
In profuse strains of unpremeditated art.
Percy Bysshe Shelley 1792–1822: "To a Skylark" (1819)

7 The red-breast whistles from a garden-croft;
And gathering swallows twitter in the skies.
John Keats 1795–1821: "To Autumn" (1820)

8 Alone and warming his five wits,
   The white owl in the belfry sits.
   Alfred, Lord Tennyson 1809–92:
   "Song—The Owl" (1830)

9 That's the wise thrush; he sings
      each song twice over,
   Lest you should think he never
      could recapture
   The first fine careless rapture!
   Robert Browning 1812–89: "Home-
   Thoughts, from Abroad" (1845)

10 I once had a sparrow alight upon
   my shoulder for a moment while
   I was hoeing in a village garden,
   and I felt that I was more
   distinguished by that
   circumstance than I should have
   been by any epaulette I could
   have worn.
   Henry David Thoreau 1817–62:
   Walden (1854) "Winter Animals"

11 I caught this morning morning's
   minion, kingdom of daylight's
   dauphin, dapple-dawn-drawn
   Falcon.
   Gerard Manley Hopkins 1844–89:
   "The Windhover" (written 1877)

12 At once a voice outburst among
   The bleak twigs overhead
   In a full-hearted evensong
   Of joy illimited;
   An aged thrush, frail, gaunt, and
      small,
   In blast-beruffled plume,
   Had chosen thus to fling his soul
   Upon the growing gloom.
   Thomas Hardy 1840–1928: "The
   Darkling Thrush" (1902)

13 It was the Rainbow gave thee
      birth,
   And left thee all her lovely hues.
   W. H. Davies 1871–1940: "Kingfisher"
   (1910)

14 Oh, a wondrous bird is the
      pelican!
   His beak holds more than his
      belican.
   He takes in his beak
   Food enough for a week.

But I'll be darned if I know how
   the helican.
Dixon Lanier Merritt 1879–1972: in
Nashville Banner 22 April 1913

15 From troubles of the world
   I turn to ducks
   Beautiful comical things.
   F. W. Harvey b. 1888: "Ducks" (1919)

Birth
see **Pregnancy and Birth**

The Body
see also **Appearance, The Senses**

1 I will give thanks unto thee, for I
   am fearfully and wonderfully
   made.
   Bible: Psalm 139

2 Doth not even nature itself teach
   you, that if a man have long
   hair, it is a shame unto him?
   But if a woman have long hair, it
   is a glory to her.
   Bible: I Corinthians

3 He does smile his face into more
   lines than are in the new map
   with the augmentation of the
   Indies.
   William Shakespeare 1564–1616:
   Twelfth Night (1601)

4 Raised by that curious engine,
      your white hand.
   John Webster c. 1580–c. 1625: *The
   Duchess of Malfi* (1623)

5 Wise nature did never put her
   precious jewels into a garret four
   stories high: and therefore . . .
   exceeding tall men had ever very
   empty heads.
   Francis Bacon 1561–1626: J.
   Spedding (ed.) *The Works of Francis
   Bacon* vol. 7 (1859) "Additional
   Apophthegms"

6 Her feet beneath her petticoat,
   Like little mice, stole in and out,

As if they feared the light.
John Suckling 1609–42: "A Ballad upon a Wedding" (1646)

7 The hands are a sort of feet, which serve us in our passage towards Heaven, curiously distinguished into joints and fingers, and fit to be applied to any thing which reason can imagine or desire.
Thomas Traherne c. 1637–74: *Meditations on the Six Days of Creation* (1717)

8 Why has not man a microscopic eye?
For this plain reason, man is not a fly.
Alexander Pope 1688–1744: *An Essay on Man* Epistle 1 (1733)

9 And our carcases, which are to rise again, are they worth raising? I hope, if mine is, that I shall have a better pair of legs than I have moved on these two-and-twenty years, or I shall be sadly behind in the squeeze into Paradise.
Lord Byron 1788–1824: letter 13 September 1811

10 I sing the body electric.
Walt Whitman 1819–92: title of poem (1855)

11 Our body is a machine for living. It is organized for that, it is its nature. Let life go on in it unhindered and let it defend itself, it will do more than if you paralyse it by encumbering it with remedies.
Leo Tolstoy 1828–1910: *War and Peace* (1865–9)

12 Bah! the thing is not a nose at all, but a bit of primordial chaos clapped on to my face.
H. G. Wells 1866–1946: *Select Conversations with an Uncle* (1895) "The Man with a Nose"

13 A large nose is in fact the sign of an affable man, good, courteous, witty, liberal, courageous, such as I am.
Edmond Rostand 1868–1918: *Cyrano de Bergerac* (1897)

14 An impersonal and scientific knowledge of the structure of our bodies is the surest safeguard against prurient curiosity and lascivious gloating.
Marie Stopes 1880–1958: *Married Love* (1918)

15 She fitted into my biggest armchair as if it had been built round her by someone who knew they were wearing armchairs tight about the hips that season.
P. G. Wodehouse 1881–1975: *My Man Jeeves* (1919)

16 Anatomy is destiny.
Sigmund Freud 1856–1939: *Collected Writings* (1924)

17 There is more felicity on the far side of baldness than young men can possibly imagine.
Logan Pearsall Smith 1865–1946: *Afterthoughts* (1931)

18 Imprisoned in every fat man a thin one is wildly signalling to be let out.
Cyril Connolly 1903–74: *The Unquiet Grave* (1944); cf. **20** below

19 I came in here in all good faith to help my country. I don't mind giving a reasonable amount [of blood], but a pint . . . why that's very nearly an armful.
Ray Galton 1930– and **Alan Simpson** 1929– : *The Blood Donor* (1961 BBC television program) words spoken by Tony Hancock

20 Outside every fat man there was an even fatter man trying to close in.
Kingsley Amis 1922–95: *One Fat Englishman* (1963); cf. **23** above

21 When self-indulgence has reduced
a man to the shape of Lord
Hailsham, sexual continence
requires no more than a sense of
the ridiculous.
Reginald Paget 1908–90: speech in
the House of Commons during the
Profumo affair, 17 June 1963

22 The body of a young woman is
God's greatest achievement . . . Of
course, He could have built it to
last longer but you can't have
everything.
Neil Simon 1927– : *The
Gingerbread Lady* (1970)

23 My brain? It's my second favorite
organ.
Woody Allen 1935– : *Sleeper* (1973
film, with Marshall Brickman)

24 Fat is a feminist issue.
Susie Orbach 1946– : title of book
(1978)

Books
see also **Fiction and Storytelling,
Libraries, Reading, Writing**

1 Of making many books there is
no end; and much study is a
weariness of the flesh.
Bible: Ecclesiastes

2 Some books are to be tasted,
others to be swallowed, and some
few to be chewed and digested;
that is, some books are to be read
only in parts; others to be read
but not curiously; and some few
to be read wholly, and with
diligence and attention. Some
books also may be read by
deputy, and extracts made of
them by others.
Francis Bacon 1561–1626: *Essays*
(1625) "Of Studies"

3 A good book is the precious life-
blood of a master spirit,

embalmed and treasured up on
purpose to a life beyond life.
John Milton 1608–74: *Areopagitica*
(1644)

4 An empty book is like an infant's
soul, in which anything may be
written. It is capable of all things,
but containeth nothing.
Thomas Traherne c. 1637–74:
Centuries of Meditations

5 I hate books; they only teach us
to talk about things we know
nothing about.
Jean-Jacques Rousseau 1712–78:
Émile (1762)

6 ELPHINSTON: What, have you not
read it through?
JOHNSON: No, Sir, do *you* read
books *through*?
Samuel Johnson 1709–84: James
Boswell *Life of Samuel Johnson*
(1791) 19 April 1773

7 The reading or non-reading a
book—will never keep down a
single petticoat.
Lord Byron 1788–1824: letter to
Richard Hoppner, 29 October 1819

8 Your *borrowers of books*—those
mutilators of collections, spoilers
of the symmetry of shelves, and
creators of odd volumes.
Charles Lamb 1775–1834: *Essays of
Elia* (1823) "The Two Races of Men"

9 A good book is the best of friends,
the same to-day and for ever.
Martin Tupper 1810–89: *Proverbial
Philosophy* Series I (1838) "Of
Reading"

10 No furniture so charming as
books.
Sydney Smith 1771–1845: Lady
Holland *Memoir* (1855)

11 Books must be read as deliberately
and reservedly as they were
written.
Henry David Thoreau 1817–62:
Walden (1854)

12 Books are made not like children but like pyramids . . . and they're just as useless! and they stay in the desert! . . . Jackals piss at their foot and the bourgeois climb up on them.
Gustave Flaubert 1821–80: letter to Ernest Feydeau, November/December 1857

13 "What is the use of a book," thought Alice, "without pictures or conversations?"
Lewis Carroll 1832–98: *Alice's Adventures in Wonderland* (1865)

14 There is no such thing as a moral or an immoral book. Books are well written, or badly written.
Oscar Wilde 1854–1900: *The Picture of Dorian Gray* (1891)

15 "*Classic.*" A book which people praise and don't read.
Mark Twain 1835–1910: *Following the Equator* (1897)

16 All books are either dreams or swords,
You can cut, or you can drug, with words.
Amy Lowell 1874–1925: "Sword Blades and Poppy Seed" (1914)

17 A bad book is as much of a labour to write as a good one: it comes as sincerely from the author's soul.
Aldous Huxley 1894–1963: *Point Counter Point* (1928)

18 From the moment I picked up your book until I laid it down, I was convulsed with laughter. Some day I intend reading it.
blurb written for S. J. Perelman's book Dawn Ginsberg's Revenge *(1928)*
Groucho Marx 1895–1977: Hector Arce *Groucho* (1979)

19 A best-seller is the gilded tomb of a mediocre talent.
Logan Pearsall Smith 1865–1946: *Afterthoughts* (1931)

20 Books can not be killed by fire. People die, but books never die. No man and no force can abolish memory . . . In this war, we know, books are weapons. And it is a part of your dedication always to make them weapons for man's freedom.
Franklin D. Roosevelt 1882–1945: "Message to the Booksellers of America" 6 May 1942

21 The principle of procrastinated rape is said to be the ruling one in all the great best-sellers.
V. S. Pritchett 1900– : *The Living Novel* (1946) "Clarissa"

22 Some books are undeservedly forgotten; none are undeservedly remembered.
W. H. Auden 1907–73: *The Dyer's Hand* (1963) "Reading"

23 The possession of a book becomes a substitute for reading it.
Anthony Burgess 1917–93: in *New York Times Book Review* 4 December 1966

24 This is not a novel to be tossed aside lightly. It should be thrown with great force.
Dorothy Parker 1893–1967: R. E. Drennan *Wit's End* (1973)

25 Long books, when read, are usually overpraised, because the reader wishes to convince others and himself that he has not wasted his time.
E. M. Forster 1879–1970: note from commonplace book; O. Stallybrass (ed.) *Aspects of the Novel and Related Writings* (1974)

26 Book—what they make a movie out of for television.
Leonard Louis Levinson: Laurence J. Peter (ed.) *Quotations for our Time* (1977)

27 Books say: she did this because.
Life says: she did this. Books are
where things are explained to
you; life is where things aren't . . .
Books make sense of life. The
only problem is that the lives
they make sense of are other
people's lives, never your own.
Julian Barnes 1946–　: *Flaubert's
Parrot* (1984)

28 What literature can and should
do is change the people who
teach the people who don't read
the books.
A. S. Byatt 1936–　: interview in
Newsweek 5 June 1995

Bores and Boredom

1 After three days men grow weary,
of a wench, a guest, and weather
rainy.
Benjamin Franklin 1706–90: *Poor
Richard's Almanack* (1733)

2 The secret of being a bore . . . is
to tell everything.
Voltaire 1694–1778: *Discours en vers
sur l'homme* (1737)

3 He is not only dull in himself, but
the cause of dullness in others.
on a dull law lord
Samuel Foote 1720–77: James
Boswell *Life of Samuel Johnson*
(1791) 1783

4 Society is now one polished
horde,
Formed of two mighty tribes, the
Bores and *Bored*.
Lord Byron 1788–1824: *Don Juan*
(1819–24)

5 I am like a man yawning at a
ball; the only reason he does not
go home to bed is that his
carriage has not arrived yet.
Mikhail Lermontov 1814–41: *A Hero
of our Time* (1840)

6 A desire for desires—boredom.
Leo Tolstoy 1828–1910: *Anna
Karenina* (1873–6)

7 Some people can stay longer in
an hour than others can in a
week.
William Dean Howells 1837–1920:
attributed

8 He is an old bore. Even the grave
yawns for him.
of Israel Zangwill
Herbert Beerbohm Tree 1852–1917:
Max Beerbohm *Herbert Beerbohm
Tree* (1920)

9 Boredom is . . . a vital problem for
the moralist, since half the sins of
mankind are caused by the fear of
it.
Bertrand Russell 1872–1970: *The
Conquest of Happiness* (1930)

10 Someone has somewhere
commented on the fact that
millions long for immortality who
don't know what to do with
themselves on a rainy Sunday
afternoon.
Susan Ertz 1894–1985: *Anger in the
Sky* (1943)

11 Nothing happens, nobody comes,
nobody goes, it's awful!
Samuel Beckett 1906–89: *Waiting for
Godot* (1955)

12 A healthy male adult bore
consumes *each year* one and a
half times his own weight in
other people's patience.
John Updike 1932–　: *Assorted
Prose* (1965) "Confessions of a Wild
Bore"

13 He was not only a bore; he bored
for England.
of Anthony Eden
Malcolm Muggeridge 1903–90: *Tread
Softly* (1966)

14 What's wrong with being a
boring kind of guy?

*during the campaign for the
Republican nomination*
George Bush 1924– : in *Daily
Telegraph* (UK) 28 April 1988

Borrowing
see **Debt and Borrowing**

Bribery and Corruption

1 A venal city ripe to perish, if a
buyer can be found.
of Rome
Sallust 86–35 BC: *Jugurtha*

2 . . . *Omnia Romae
Cum pretio.*
Everything in Rome—at a price.
Juvenal AD c. 60–c. 130: *Satires*

3 If gold ruste, what shall iren do?
Geoffrey Chaucer c. 1343–1400: *The
Canterbury Tales* "The General
Prologue"

4 Let me tell you, Cassius, you
yourself
Are much condemned to have an
itching palm.
William Shakespeare 1564–1616:
Julius Caesar (1599)

5 Nothing to be done without a
bribe I find, in love as well as
law.
Susannah Centlivre c. 1669–1723:
The Perjured Husband (1700)

6 I am not worth purchasing, but
such as I am, the King of Great
Britain is not rich enough to do
it.
*replying to an offer from Governor
George Johnstone of £10,000, and
any office in the Colonies in the
King's gift, if he were able
successfully to promote a Union
between Britain and America*
Joseph Reed 1741–85: W. B. Read
*Life and Correspondence of Joseph
Reed* (1847)

7 All those men have their price.
of fellow parliamentarians
Robert Walpole 1676–1745: W. Coxe
Memoirs of Sir Robert Walpole
(1798)

8 But the jingling of the guinea
helps the hurt that Honour
feels.
Alfred, Lord Tennyson 1809–92:
"Locksley Hall" (1842)

9 It is always a temptation to a rich
and lazy nation,
To puff and look important and
to say:-
"Though we know we should
defeat you, we have not the
time to meet you,
We will therefore pay you cash to
go away."
And that is called paying the
Dane-geld;
But we've proved it again and
again,
That if once you have paid him
the Dane-geld
You never get rid of the Dane.
Rudyard Kipling 1865–1936: "What
Dane-geld means" (1911)

10 Men are more often bribed by
their loyalties and ambitions than
money.
Robert H. Jackson 1892–1954:
dissenting opinion in *United States
v. Wunderlich* 1951

11 I stuffed their mouths with gold.
*on his handling of the consultants
during the establishment of the
National Health Service*
Aneurin Bevan 1897–1960: Brian Abel-
Smith *The Hospitals 1800–1948*
(1964)

Britain
see also **England and the English**

1 Rule, Britannia, rule the waves;
Britons never will be slaves.
James Thomson 1700–48: *Alfred: a
Masque* (1740)

2 It must be owned, that the Graces
do not seem to be natives of
Great Britain; and I doubt, the
best of us here have more of
rough than polished diamond.
Lord Chesterfield 1694–1773: *Letters
to his Son* (1774) 18 November 1748

3 Born and educated in this
country, I glory in the name of
Briton.
George III 1738–1820: *The King's
Speech on Opening the Session* 18
November 1760

4 He [the Briton] is a barbarian,
and thinks that the customs of
his tribe and island are the laws
of nature.
George Bernard Shaw 1856–1950:
Caesar and Cleopatra (1901)

5 Other nations use "force" we
Britons alone use "Might."
Evelyn Waugh 1903–66: *Scoop*
(1938)

6 The British nation is unique in
this respect. They are the only
people who like to be told how
bad things are, who like to be
told the worst.
Winston Churchill 1874–1965: speech
in the House of Commons, 10 June
1941

7 Britain will be honoured by
historians more for the way she
disposed of an empire than for the
way in which she acquired it.
Lord Harlech 1918–85: in *New York
Times* 28 October 1962

8 Great Britain has lost an empire
and has not yet found a role.
Dean Acheson 1893–1971: speech at
the Military Academy, West Point, 5
December 1962

9 A soggy little island huffing and
puffing to keep up with Western
Europe.
John Updike 1932– : "London Life"
(written 1969)

10 We did have a form of Afro-Asian
studies which consisted of
colouring bits of the map red to
show the British Empire.
Michael Green 1927– : *The Boy
Who Shot Down an Airship* (1988)

11 [The Commonwealth] is a largely
meaningless relic of Empire—like
the smile on the face of the
Cheshire Cat which remains when
the cat has disappeared.
Nigel Lawson 1932– : attributed,
1993

12 Fifty years on from now, Britain
will still be the country of long
shadows on county [cricket]
grounds, warm beer, invincible
green suburbs, dog lovers, and—
as George Orwell said—old maids
bicycling to Holy Communion
through the morning mist.
John Major 1943– : speech to the
Conservative Group for Europe, 22
April 1993

Broadcasting

1 Nation shall speak peace unto
nation.
Montague John Rendall 1862–1950:
motto of the BBC; after *Isaiah*: see
Peace 2

2 *Television?* The word is half Greek,
half Latin. No good can come of
it.
C. P. Scott 1846–1932: Asa Briggs
The BBC: the First Fifty Years (1985)

3 TV—a clever contraction derived
from the words Terrible
Vaudeville . . . we call it a
medium because nothing's well
done.
Goodman Ace 1899–1982: letter to
Groucho Marx, *c.* 1953

4 So much chewing gum for the
eyes.
*small boy's definition of certain
television programs*
Anonymous: James Beasley Simpson
Best Quotes of '50, '55, '56 (1957)

5 When the politicians complain
that TV turns their proceedings
into a circus, it should be made
plain that the circus was already
there, and that TV has merely
demonstrated that not all the
performers are well trained.
Ed Murrow 1908–65: attributed, 1959

6 Radio and television . . . have
succeeded in lifting the
manufacture of banality out of
the sphere of handicraft and
placed it in that of a major
industry.
Nathalie Sarraute 1902– : in *Times
Literary Supplement* (UK) 10 June
1960

7 The charm of television
entertainment is its ability to
bridge the chasm between dinner
and bedtime without mental
distraction.
Russell Baker 1925– : *All Things
Considered* (1962)

8 It [television] is a medium of
entertainment which permits
millions of people to listen to the
same joke at the same time, and
yet remain lonesome.
T. S. Eliot 1888–1965: *New York Post*
(22 September 1963)

9 Like having your own licence to
print money.
*on the profitability of commercial
television in Britain*
Roy Thomson 1894–1976: R.
Braddon *Roy Thomson* (1965)

10 It used to be that we in films
were the lowest form of art. Now
we have something to look down
on.
of television
Billy Wilder 1906– : A. Madsen
Billy Wilder (1968)

11 Americans have never quite
digested television. The mystique
which should fade grows stronger.
We make celebrities not only of

the men who cause events but of
the men who read reports of them
aloud.
Joe McGinniss 1942– : *The Selling
of the President 1968* (1969)

12 Television brought the brutality of
war into the comfort of the living
room. Vietnam was lost in the
living rooms of America—not the
battlefields of Vietnam.
Marshall McLuhan 1911–80: in
Montreal Gazette 16 May 1975

13 Let's face it, there are no plain
women on television.
Anna Ford 1943– : in *Observer* (UK)
23 September 1979

14 Television is simultaneously
blamed, often by the same people,
for worsening the world and for
being powerless to change it.
Clive James 1939– : *Glued to the
Box* (1981)

15 If we may say that the Age of
Andrew Jackson took political life
out of the hands of aristocrats
and turned it over to the masses,
then we may say, with equal
justification, that the Age of
Television has taken politics away
from the adult mind altogether.
Neil Postman 1931– : *The
Disappearance of Childhood* (1982)

16 For all its flexibility, television is
more a mirror of taste than a
shaper of it.
Russell Lynes 1910– : *The
Phenomenon of Change* (1984)

17 Television contracts the
imagination and radio expands it.
Terry Wogan 1938– : attributed,
1984

18 Television . . . thrives on
unreason, and unreason thrives
on television . . . [It] strikes at the
emotions rather than the intellect.
Robin Day 1923– : *Grand Inquisitor*
(1989)

19 They [men] are happier with women who make their coffee than make their programmes.
Denise O'Donoghue: G. Kinnock and F. Miller (eds.) *By Faith and Daring* (1993)

20 In 1957, when I was in second grade, black children integrated Central High School in Little Rock, Arkansas. We watched it on TV. All of us watched it. I don't mean Mama and Daddy and Rocky. I mean all the colored people in America watched it, together, with one set of eyes.
Henry Louis Gates, Jr. 1950– : *Colored People* (1994)

21 It is stupidvision—where most of the presenters look like they have to pretend to be stupid because they think their audience is . . . It patronises. It talks to the vacuum cleaner and the washing machine without much contact with the human brain.
of daytime television
Polly Toynbee 1946– : in *Daily Telegraph* (UK) 7 May 1996

Bureaucracy
see **Administration and Bureaucracy**

Business and Commerce

1 A merchant shall hardly keep himself from doing wrong.
Bible: Ecclesiasticus

2 They [corporations] cannot commit treason, nor be outlawed, nor excommunicate, for they have no souls.
Edward Coke 1552–1634: *The Reports of Sir Edward Coke* (1658) "The case of Sutton's Hospital" cf. **9** below

3 A Company for carrying on an undertaking of Great Advantage, but no one to know what it is.
Anonymous: Company Prospectus at the time of the South Sea Bubble (1711)

4 There is nothing more requisite in business than dispatch.
Joseph Addison 1672–1719: *The Drummer* (1716)

5 I have heard of a man who had a mind to sell his house, and therefore carried a piece of brick in his pocket, which he showed as a pattern to encourage purchasers.
Jonathan Swift 1667–1745: *The Drapier's Letters* (1724)

6 It is the nature of all greatness not to be exact; and great trade will always be attended with considerable abuses.
Edmund Burke 1729–97: *On American Taxation* (1775)

7 People of the same trade seldom meet together, even for merriment and diversion, but the conversation ends in a conspiracy against the public, or in some contrivance to raise prices.
Adam Smith 1723–90: *Wealth of Nations* (1776)

8 To found a great empire for the sole purpose of raising up a people of customers, may at first sight appear a project fit only for a nation of shopkeepers. It is, however, a project altogether unfit for a nation of shopkeepers; but extremely fit for a nation whose government is influenced by shopkeepers.
Adam Smith 1723–90: *Wealth of Nations* (1776); cf. **England 14**

9 Corporations have neither bodies to be punished, nor souls to be condemned, they therefore do as they like.
often quoted as "Did you ever expect a corporation to have a

conscience, when it has no soul to be damned, and no body to be kicked?"
Lord Thurlow 1731–1806: John Poynder *Literary Extracts* (1844); cf. **2** above

10 Here's the rule for bargains: "Do other men, for they would do you." That's the true business precept.
Charles Dickens 1812–70: *Martin Chuzzlewit* (1844)

11 Perpetual devotion to what a man calls his business, is only to be sustained by perpetual neglect of many other things.
Robert Louis Stevenson 1850–94: *Virginibus Puerisque* (1881)

12 The public be damned! I'm working for my stockholders.
William H. Vanderbilt 1821–85: *Comment to a news reporter* (2 October 1882)

13 The growth of a large business is merely a survival of the fittest . . . The American beauty rose can be produced in the splendor and fragrance which bring cheer to its beholder only by sacrificing the early buds which grow up around it.
John D. Rockefeller 1839–1937: W. J. Ghent *Our Benevolent Feudalism* (1902)

14 *Le client n'a jamais tort.*
The customer is never wrong.
César Ritz 1850–1918: R. Nevill and C. E. Jerningham *Piccadilly to Pall Mall* (1908)

15 The best of all monopoly profits is a quiet life.
J. R. Hicks 1904– : *Econometrica* (1935)

16 NINOTCHKA: Why should you carry other people's bags?

PORTER: Well, that's my business, Madame.
NINOTCHKA: That's no business. That's social injustice.
PORTER: That depends on the tip.
Charles Brackett 1892–1969 and **Billy Wilder** 1906– : *Ninotchka* (1939 film, with Walter Reisch)

17 For a salesman, there is no rock bottom to the life . . . A salesman is got to dream, boy. It comes with the territory.
Arthur Miller 1915– : *Death of a Salesman* (1949)

18 Let Wall Street have a nightmare and the whole country has to help get them back in bed again.
Will Rogers 1879–1935: *The Autobiography of Will Rogers* (1949)

19 How to succeed in business without really trying.
Shepherd Mead 1914– : title of book (1952)

20 For years I thought what was good for our country was good for General Motors and vice versa.
Charles E. Wilson 1890–1961: testimony to the Senate Armed Services Committee on his proposed nomination for Secretary of Defense, 15 January 1953

21 Accountants are the witch-doctors of the modern world and willing to turn their hands to any kind of magic.
Lord Justice Harman 1894–1970: speech, February 1964; A. Sampson *The New Anatomy of Britain* (1971)

22 Could Henry Ford produce the Book of Kells? Certainly not. He would quarrel initially with the advisability of such a project and then prove it was impossible.
Flann O'Brien 1911–66: *Myles Away from Dublin* (1990)

23 The car, the furniture, the wife, the children—everything has to be disposable. Because you see the main thing today is—shopping.
Arthur Miller 1915– : *The Price* (1968)

24 In a consumer society there are inevitably two kinds of slaves: the prisoners of addiction and the prisoners of envy.
Ivan Illich 1926– : *Tools for Conviviality* (1973)

25 In the factory we make cosmetics; in the store we sell hope.
Charles Revson 1906–75: A. Tobias *Fire and Ice* (1976)

26 Nothing is illegal if one hundred well-placed business men decide to do it.
Andrew Young 1932– : Morris K. Udall *Too Funny to be President* (1988)

27 We even sell a pair of earrings for under £1, which is cheaper than a prawn sandwich from Marks & Spencers. But I have to say the earrings probably won't last as long.
Gerald Ratner 1949– : speech to the Institute of Directors, Albert Hall, 23 April 1991

28 The green shoots of economic spring are appearing once again.
often quoted as "the green shoots of recovery"
Norman Lamont 1942– : speech at Conservative Party Conference, 9 October 1991

29 We used to build civilizations. Now we build shopping malls.
Bill Bryson 1951– : *Neither Here Nor There* (1991)

30 Only the paranoid survive.
dictum on which he has long run his company, the Intel Corporation

Andrew Grove 1936– : in *New York Times* 18 December 1994

Canada

1 *J'estime mieux que autrement, que c'est la terre que Dieu donne à Caïn.*
I am rather inclined to believe that this is the land God gave to Cain.
on discovering the northern shore of the Gulf of St. Lawrence (now Labrador and Quebec) in 1534; after the murder of Abel, Cain was exiled to the desolate land of Nod
Jacques Cartier 1491–1557: *La Première Relation*

2 These two nations have been at war over a few acres of snow near Canada, and . . . they are spending on this fine struggle more than Canada itself is worth.
of the struggle between the French and the British for the control of colonial north Canada
Voltaire 1694–1778: *Candide* (1759)

3 The twentieth century belongs to Canada.
encapsulation of a view expressed in a speech to the Canadian Club of Ottawa, 18 January 1904, "The nineteenth century was the century of the United States. I think we can claim that it is Canada that shall fill the twentieth century"
Wilfrid Laurier 1841–1919: popularly attributed in this form

4 If some countries have too much history, we have too much geography.
William Lyon Mackenzie King 1874–1950: speech on Canada as an international power, 18 June 1936

5 Canada could have enjoyed:
English government,
French culture,
and American know how.

Instead it ended up with:
English know-how,
French government,
and American culture.
*a similar (prose) summary has been
attributed to Lester Pearson (1897–
1972), "Canada was supposed to get
British government, French culture,
and American know-how. Instead it
got French government, American
culture, and British know-how"*
John Robert Colombo 1936– : "O
Canada" (1965)

6 Canada has, for practical
purposes, no Atlantic seaboard.
The traveller from Europe edges
into it like a tiny Jonah entering
an inconceivably large whale,
slipping past the Straits of Belle
Isle into the Gulf of St. Lawrence,
where five Canadian provinces
surround him, for the most part
invisible . . . To enter the United
States is a matter of crossing an
ocean; to enter Canada is a
matter of being silently swallowed
by an alien continent.
Northrop Frye 1912–91: "Conclusion
to a *Literary History of Canada*"
(1965)

7 *Vive Le Québec Libre.*
Long Live Free Quebec.
Charles de Gaulle 1890–1970:
speech in Montreal, 24 July 1967

8 Canadians do not like heroes, and
so they do not have them.
George Woodcock 1912–95: *Canada
and the Canadians* (1970)

9 A Canadian is somebody who
knows how to make love in a
canoe.
Pierre Berton 1920– : in *The
Canadian* 22 December 1973

10 I have to spend so much time
explaining to Americans that I
am not English and to
Englishmen that I am not
American that I have little time
left to be Canadian . . . (On second
thought, I am a true
cosmopolitan—unhappy
anywhere.)
Laurence J. Peter 1919–90:
Quotations for our Time (1977)

11 Ours is a sovereign nation
Bows to no foreign will
But whenever they cough in
  Washington
They spit on Parliament Hill.
Joe Wallace: attributed

12 Canadians are Americans with no
Disneyland.
Margaret Mahy 1936– : *The
Changeover* (1984)

13 I see Canada as a country torn
between a very northern, rather
extraordinary, mystical spirit
which it fears and its desire to
present itself to the world as a
Scotch banker.
Robertson Davies 1913–95: *The
Enthusiasms of Robertson Davies*
(1990)

Capitalism and Communism
see also **Class, Political Parties**

1 The Riches and Goods of
Christians are not common, as
touching the right, title, and
possession of the same, as certain
Anabaptists do falsely boast.
The Book of Common Prayer 1662:
Articles of Religion (1562)

2 In the first stone which he [the
savage] flings at the wild animals
he pursues, in the first stick that
he seizes to strike down the fruit
which hangs above his reach, we
see the appropriation of one
article for the purpose of aiding in
the acquisition of another, and
thus discover the origin of capital.
Robert Torrens 1780–1864: *An Essay
on the Production of Wealth* (1821)

3 A spectre is haunting Europe—
the spectre of Communism.

Karl Marx 1818–83 and **Friedrich
Engels** 1820–95: *The Communist
Manifesto* (1848)

4 What is a communist? One who
hath yearnings
For equal division of unequal
earnings.
Ebenezer Elliott 1781–1849:
"Epigram" (1850)

5 Communism is a Russian
autocracy turned upside down.
Alexander Ivanovich Herzen 1812–70:
*The Development of Revolutionary
Ideas in Russia* (1851)

6 All I know is that I am not a
Marxist.
Karl Marx 1818–83: attributed in a
letter from Friedrich Engels to
Conrad Schmidt, 5 August 1890

7 The worker is the slave of
capitalist society, the female
worker is the slave of that slave.
James Connolly 1868–1916: *The Re-
conquest of Ireland* (1915)

8 Imperialism is the monopoly stage
of capitalism.
V. I. Lenin 1870–1924: *Imperialism
as the Last Stage of Capitalism*
(1916) "Briefest possible definition of
imperialism"

9 I have seen the future; and it
works.
*following a visit to the Soviet Union
in 1919*
Lincoln Steffens 1866–1936: *Letters*
(1938)

10 Communism is Soviet power plus
the electrification of the whole
country.
V. I. Lenin 1870–1924: Report to 8th
Congress, 1920

11 The State is an instrument in the
hands of the ruling class, used to
break the resistance of the
adversaries of that class.
Joseph Stalin 1879–1953:
Foundations of Leninism (1924)

12 Nature has no cure for this sort
of madness [Bolshevism], though I
have known a legacy from a rich
relative work wonders.
F. E. Smith 1872–1930: *Law, Life and
Letters* (1927)

13 Communism is like prohibition,
it's a good idea but it won't work.
Will Rogers 1879–1935: in 1927;
Weekly Articles (1981)

14 From Stettin in the Baltic to
Trieste in the Adriatic an iron
curtain has descended across the
Continent.
*the expression "iron curtain"
previously had been applied by
others to the Soviet Union or her
sphere of influence*
Winston Churchill 1874–1965: speech
at Westminster College, Fulton,
Missouri, 5 March 1946

15 There is a good deal of solemn
cant about the common interests
of capital and labour. As matters
stand, their only common interest
is that of cutting each other's
throat.
Brooks Atkinson 1894–1984: *Once
Around the Sun* (1951)

16 Whether you like it or not,
history is on our side. We will
bury you.
Nikita Khrushchev 1894–1971:
speech to Western diplomats in
Moscow, 18 November 1956

17 Capitalism, it is said, is a system
wherein man exploits man. And
communism—is vice versa.
quoting "a Polish intellectual"
Daniel Bell 1919–   : *The End of
Ideology* (1960)

18 Normally speaking, it may be said
that the forces of a capitalist
society, if left unchecked, tend to
make the rich richer and the poor
poorer and thus increase the gap
between them.

Jawaharlal Nehru 1889–1964: "Basic Approach" in Vincent Shean *Nehru* . . . (1960)

19 He enjoys prophesying the imminent fall of the capitalist system and is prepared to play a part, any part, in its burial, except that of mute.
of Aneurin Bevan
Harold Macmillan 1894–1986: Michael Foot *Aneurin Bevan* (1962)

20 Capitalism is using its money; we socialists throw it away.
Fidel Castro 1927– : in *Observer* 8 November 1964

21 In the service of the people we followed such a policy that socialism would not lose its human face.
Alexander Dubček 1921–92: in *Rudé Právo* 19 July 1968

22 It is as wholly wrong to blame Marx for what was done in his name, as it is to blame Jesus for what was done in his.
Tony Benn 1925– : Alan Freeman *The Benn Heresy* (1982)

23 A theater where no one is allowed to walk out and everyone is forced to applause.
on Eastern Europe
Arthur Miller 1915– : on *Omnibus* (BBC TV) 30 October 1987

24 The clock of communism has stopped striking. But its concrete building has not yet come crashing down. For that reason, instead of freeing ourselves, we must try to save ourselves being crushed by the rubble.
Alexander Solzhenitsyn 1918– : in *Komsomolskaya Pravda* 18 September 1990

25 Communism died this year . . . [and] the Cold War didn't "end," it was won.

George Bush 1924– : *State of the Union* (28 January 1992)

26 The Iron Curtain did not reach the ground and under it flowed liquid manure from the West.
Alexander Solzhenitsyn 1918– : speaking at Far Eastern Technical University, Vladivostok, 30 May 1994

Cats
see also **Animals**

1 When I play with my cat, who knows whether she isn't amusing herself with me more than I am with her?
Montaigne 1533–92: *Essais* (1580)

2 For I will consider my Cat Jeoffrey. . . .
For he counteracts the powers of darkness by his electrical skin and glaring eyes.
For he counteracts the Devil, who is death, by brisking about the life.
Christopher Smart 1722–71: *Jubilate Agno* (c. 1758–63)

3 When I observed he was a fine cat, saying, "Why yes, Sir, but I have had cats whom I liked better than this" and then as if perceiving Hodge to be out of countenance, adding, "but he is a very fine cat, a very fine cat indeed."
Samuel Johnson 1709–84: James Boswell *Life of Samuel Johnson* (1791) 1783

4 Cruel, but composed and bland, Dumb, inscrutable and grand, So Tiberius might have sat, Had Tiberius been a cat.
Matthew Arnold 1822–88: "Poor Matthias" (1885)

5 He walked by himself, and all places were alike to him.
Rudyard Kipling 1865–1936: *Just So*

Stories (1902) "The Cat that Walked by Himself"

6 Cats seem to go on the principle that it never does any harm to ask for what you want.
Joseph Wood Krutch 1893–1970: *Twelve Seasons* (1949)

Causes and Consequences

1 He that diggeth a pit shall fall into it.
Bible: Ecclesiastes

2 They have sown the wind, and they shall reap the whirlwind.
Bible: Hosea

3 Whatsoever a man soweth, that shall he also reap.
Bible: Galatians

4 Who buys a minute's mirth to wail a week?
Or sells eternity to get a toy?
For one sweet grape who will the vine destroy?
William Shakespeare 1564–1616: *The Rape of Lucrece* (1594)

5 One leak will sink a ship, and one sin will destroy a sinner.
John Bunyan 1628–88: *The Pilgrim's Progress* (1684)

6 A little neglect may breed great mischief . . . for want of a nail the shoe was lost; for want of a shoe the horse was lost; and for want of a horse the rider was lost.
Benjamin Franklin 1706–90: *Poor Richard's Almanack, Preface: Courteous Reader* (1758)

7 Whoever wills the end, wills also (so far as reason decides his conduct) the means in his power which are indispensably necessary thereto.
Immanuel Kant 1724–1804: *Fundamental Principles of the Metaphysics of Ethics* (1785)

8 Sow an act, and you reap a habit. Sow a habit and you reap a character. Sow a character, and you reap a destiny.
Charles Reade 1814–84: attributed; in *Notes and Queries* 17 October 1903

9 The present contains nothing more than the past, and what is found in the effect was already in the cause.
Henri Bergson 1859–1941: *L'Évolution créatrice* (1907)

10 The captain is in his bunk, drinking bottled ditch-water; and the crew is gambling in the forecastle. She will strike and sink and split. Do you think the laws of God will be suspended in favour of England because you were born in it?
George Bernard Shaw 1856–1950: *Heartbreak House* (1919)

11 As it will be in the future, it was at the birth of Man —
There are only four things certain since Social Progress began:
That the Dog returns to his Vomit and the Sow returns to her Mire,
And the burnt Fool's bandaged finger goes wobbling back to the Fire;
And that after this is accomplished, and the brave new world begins
When all men are paid for existing and no man must pay for his sins,
As surely as Water will wet us, as surely as Fire will burn,
The Gods of the Copybook Headings with terror and slaughter return!
Rudyard Kipling 1865–1936: "The Gods of the Copybook Headings" (1919)

12 The English . . . are paralysed by fear. That is what thwarts and distorts the Anglo-Saxon existence

. . . Nothing could be more lovely and fearless than Chaucer. But already Shakespeare is morbid with fear, fear of consequences. That is the strange phenomenon of the English Renaissance: this mystic terror of the consequences, the consequences of action.
D. H. Lawrence 1885–1930: *Phoenix* (1936)

13 The structure of a play is always the story of how the birds came home to roost.
Arthur Miller 1915– : in *Harper's Magazine* August 1958

14 Every positive value has its price in negative terms . . . The genius of Einstein leads to Hiroshima.
Pablo Picasso 1881–1973: F. Gilot and C. Lake *Life With Picasso* (1964)

Caution
see also **Danger**

1 Happy is that city which in time of peace thinks of war.
inscription found in the armory of Venice
Anonymous: Robert Burton *The Anatomy of Melancholy* (1621–51)

2 Beware of desperate steps. The darkest day
(Live till tomorrow) will have passed away.
William Cowper 1731–1800: "The Needless Alarm" (written *c.* 1790)

3 Prudence is a rich, ugly, old maid courted by Incapacity.
William Blake 1757–1827: *The Marriage of Heaven and Hell* (1790–3) "Proverbs of Hell"

4 Have no truck with first impulses for they are always generous ones.
Casimir, Comte de Montrond 1768–1843: attributed; Comte J. d'Estourmel *Derniers Souvenirs*

(1860), where the alternative attribution to Talleyrand is denied

5 Tar-baby ain't sayin' nuthin', en Brer Fox, he lay low.
Joel Chandler Harris 1848–1908: *Uncle Remus and His Legends of the Old Plantation* (1881)

6 Put all your eggs in the one basket, and—WATCH THAT BASKET.
Mark Twain 1835–1910: *Pudd'nhead Wilson* (1894)

7 Five and twenty ponies,
Trotting through the dark—
Brandy for the Parson,
'Baccy for the Clerk;
Laces for a lady, letters for a spy,
Watch the wall, my darling,
while the Gentlemen go by!
Rudyard Kipling 1865–1936: "A Smuggler's Song" (1906)

8 Of all forms of caution, caution in love is perhaps the most fatal to true happiness.
Bertrand Russell 1872–1970: *The Conquest of Happiness* (1930)

9 All the same, sir, I would put some of the colonies in your wife's name.
Joseph Herman Hertz 1872–1946: the Chief Rabbi to George VI, summer 1940; Chips Channon diary 3 June 1943

10 All the security around the American president is just to make sure the man who shoots him gets caught.
Norman Mailer 1923– : in *Sunday Telegraph* (UK) 4 March 1990

Celebrations
see **Festivals and Celebrations**

Censorship

1 If these writings of the Greeks agree with the book of God, they

are useless and need not be preserved; if they disagree, they are pernicious and ought to be destroyed.
on burning the library of Alexandria, AD c. 641
Caliph Omar d. 644: Edward Gibbon *The Decline and Fall of the Roman Empire* (1776–88)

2 As good almost kill a man as kill a good book: who kills a man kills a reasonable creature, God's image; but he who destroys a good book, kills reason itself, kills the image of God, as it were in the eye.
John Milton 1608–74: *Areopagitica* (1644)

3 I disapprove of what you say, but I will defend to the death your right to say it.
his attitude toward Helvétius following the burning of the latter's De l'esprit in 1759
Voltaire 1694–1778: attributed to Voltaire, the words are in fact S. G. Tallentyre's summary; *The Friends of Voltaire* (1907)

4 Wherever books will be burned, men also, in the end, are burned.
Heinrich Heine 1797–1856: *Almansor* (1823)

5 You have not converted a man, because you have silenced him.
Lord Morley 1838–1923: *On Compromise* (1874)

6 Assassination is the extreme form of censorship.
George Bernard Shaw 1856–1950: *The Showing-Up of Blanco Posnet* (1911)

7 We have long passed the Victorian Era when asterisks were followed after a certain interval by a baby.
W. Somerset Maugham 1874–1965: *The Constant Wife* (1926)

8 Everybody favors free speech in the slack moments when no axes are being ground.
Heywood Broun 1888–1939: in *New York World* 23 October 1926

9 God forbid that any book should be banned. The practice is as indefensible as infanticide.
Rebecca West 1892–1983: *The Strange Necessity* (1928)

10 So cryptic as to be almost meaningless. If there is a meaning, it is doubtless objectionable.
banning Jean Cocteau's film The Seashell and the Clergyman (1929)
British Board of Film Censors: J. C. Robertson *Hidden Cinema* (1989)

11 Don't you see that the whole aim of Newspeak is to narrow the range of thought? In the end we shall make thoughtcrime literally impossible, because there will be no words in which to express it.
George Orwell 1903–50: *Nineteen Eighty-Four* (1949)

12 Those who want the Government to regulate matters of the mind and spirit are like men who are so afraid of being murdered that they commit suicide to avoid assassination.
Harry S. Truman 1884–1972: address at the National Archives, Washington, D.C., 15 December 1952

13 We are paid to have dirty minds.
on British Film Censors
John Trevelyan: in *Observer* 15 November 1959

14 Is it a book you would even wish your wife or your servants to read?
of D. H. Lawrence's Lady Chatterley's Lover
Mervyn Griffith-Jones 1909–79: speech for the prosecution at the Central Criminal Court, Old Bailey, 20 October 1960

15 One has to multiply thoughts to the point where there aren't enough policemen to control them.
Stanislaw Lec 1909–66: *Unkempt Thoughts* (1962)

16 If decade after decade the truth cannot be told, each person's mind begins to roam irretrievably. One's fellow countrymen become harder to understand than Martians.
Alexander Solzhenitsyn 1918– : *Cancer Ward* (1968)

17 The Khomeini cry for the execution of Rushdie is an infantile cry. From the beginning of time we have seen that. To murder the thinker does not murder the thought.
Arnold Wesker 1932– : in *Weekend Guardian* (UK) 3 June 1989

18 What is freedom of expression? Without the freedom to offend, it ceases to exist.
Salman Rushdie 1947– : in *Weekend Guardian* 10 February 1990

Certainty and Doubt
see also **Belief and Unbelief, Faith, Indecision**

1 How long halt ye between two opinions?
Bible: I Kings

2 O thou of little faith, wherefore didst thou doubt?
Bible: St. Matthew

3 If a man will begin with certainties, he shall end in doubts; but if he will be content to begin with doubts, he shall end in certainties.
Francis Bacon 1561–1626: *The Advancement of Learning* (1605)

4 I beseech you, in the bowels of Christ, think it possible you may be mistaken.

Oliver Cromwell 1599–1658: letter to the General Assembly of the Kirk of Scotland, 3 August 1650

5 Negative Capability, that is when man is capable of being in uncertainties, mysteries, doubts, without any irritable reaching after fact and reason.
John Keats 1795–1821: letter to George and Thomas Keats, 21 December 1817

6 I wish I was as cocksure of anything as Tom Macaulay is of everything.
Lord Melbourne 1779–1848: Lord Cowper's preface to *Lord Melbourne's Papers* (1889)

7 There lives more faith in honest doubt,
Believe me, than in half the creeds.
Alfred, Lord Tennyson 1809–92: *In Memoriam A. H. H.* (1850)

8 Ah, what a dusty answer gets the soul
When hot for certainties in this our life!
George Meredith 1828–1909: *Modern Love* (1862)

9 Ten thousand difficulties do not make one doubt.
John Henry Newman 1801–90: *Apologia pro Vita Sua* (1864)

10 What, never?
No, never!
What, *never*?
Hardly ever!
W. S. Gilbert 1836–1911: *HMS Pinafore* (1878)

11 I am too much of a sceptic to deny the possibility of anything.
T. H. Huxley 1825–95: letter to Herbert Spencer, 22 March 1886

12 Oh! let us never, never doubt What nobody is sure about!
Hilaire Belloc 1870–1953: "The Microbe" (1897)

13 Poor Tom Arnold has lost his
faith *again*.
of a frequent convert
Eliza Conybeare 1820–1903: Rose
Macaulay letter to Father Johnson, 8
April 1951

14 Life is doubt,
And faith without doubt is
nothing but death.
Miguel de Unamuno 1864–1937:
"Salmo II" (1907)

15 Certitude is not the test of
certainty.
Oliver Wendell Holmes, Jr. 1841–1935:
Natural Law (1918)

16 I respect faith but doubt is what
gets you an education.
Wilson Mizner 1876–1933: H. L.
Mencken *A New Dictionary of
Quotations* (1942)

17 My mind is not a bed to be made
and re-made.
James Agate 1877–1947: *Ego 6*
(1944) 9 June 1943

18 Human beings are perhaps never
more frightening than when they
are convinced beyond doubt that
they are right.
Laurens van der Post 1906–96: *The
Lost World of the Kalahari* (1958)

19 The trouble with the world is that
the stupid are cocksure and the
intelligent are full of doubt.
Bertrand Russell 1872–1970:
attributed

Chance and Luck

1 Cast thy bread upon the waters:
for thou shalt find it after many
days.
Bible: Ecclesiastes

2 Fortune's a right whore:
If she give aught, she deals it in
small parcels,

That she may take away all at
one swoop.
John Webster *c.* 1580–*c.* 1625: *The
White Devil* (1612)

3 What a world is this, and how
does fortune banter us!
Henry St. John, Lord Bolingbroke
1678–1751: letter to Jonathan Swift,
3 August 1714

4 Care and diligence bring luck.
Thomas Fuller 1654–1734:
Gnomologia (1732)

5 The chapter of knowledge is a
very short, but the chapter of
accidents is a very long one.
Lord Chesterfield 1694–1773: letter
to Solomon Dayrolles, 16 February
1753

6 O! many a shaft, at random sent,
Finds mark the archer little
meant!
And many a word, at random
spoken,
May soothe or wound a heart
that's broken.
Sir Walter Scott 1771–1832: *The Lord
of the Isles* (1813)

7 All you know about it [luck] for
certain is that it's bound to
change.
Bret Harte 1836–1902: *The Outcasts
of Poker Flat* (1871)

8 The ball no question makes of
Ayes and Noes,
But here or there as strikes the
player goes.
Edward Fitzgerald 1809–83: *The
Rubáiyát of Omar Khayyám* (4th ed.,
1879)

9 A throw of the dice will never
eliminate chance.
Stéphane Mallarmé 1842–98: title of
poem (1897)

10 There is much good luck in the
world, but it is luck. We are none

of us safe. We are children,
playing or quarrelling on the line.
E. M. Forster 1879–1970: *The Longest Journey* (1907)

11 A million million spermatozoa,
All of them alive:
Out of their cataclysm but one
poor Noah
Dare hope to survive.
And among that billion minus
one
Might have chanced to be
Shakespeare, another Newton, a
new Donne—
But the One was Me.
Aldous Huxley 1894–1963: "Fifth Philosopher's Song" (1920)

12 At any rate, I am convinced that
He [God] does not play dice.
often quoted as "God does not play dice"
Albert Einstein 1879–1955: letter to Max Born, 4 December 1926

13 I come from a vertiginous
country where the lottery forms a
principal part of reality.
Jorge Luis Borges 1899–1986:
Fictions (1956) "The Babylon Lottery"

14 Predictability: Does the flap of a
butterfly's wings in Brazil set off a
tornado in Texas?
Edward N. Lorenz: title of paper given to the American Association for the Advancement of Science, Washington, 29 December 1979

Change
see also **Beginnings and Endings, Progress**

1 Can the Ethiopian change his
skin, or the leopard his spots?
Bible: Jeremiah

2 Everything flows and nothing
stays . . . You can't step twice into
the same river.

Heraclitus *c.* 540–*c.* 480 BC: Plato *Cratylus*

3 Times go by turns, and chances
change by course,
From foul to fair, from better hap
to worse.
Robert Southwell *c.* 1561–95: "Times go by Turns" (1595)

4 Bless thee, Bottom! bless thee!
thou art translated.
William Shakespeare 1564–1616: *A Midsummer Night's Dream* (1595–6)

5 He that will not apply new
remedies must expect new evils;
for time is the greatest innovator.
Francis Bacon 1561–1626: *Essays* (1625) "Of Innovations"

6 At last he rose, and twitched his
mantle blue:
Tomorrow to fresh woods, and
pastures new.
John Milton 1608–74: "Lycidas"(1638)

7 When it is not necessary to
change, it is necessary not to
change.
Lucius Cary, Lord Falkland 1610–43: "A Speech concerning Episcopacy" delivered in 1641

8 The world's a scene of changes,
and to be
Constant, in Nature were
inconstancy.
Abraham Cowley 1618–67: "Inconstancy" (1647)

9 Who will change old lamps for
new ones? . . . new lamps for old
ones?
Arabian Nights: "The History of Aladdin"

10 Change is not made without
inconvenience, even from worse
to better.
Samuel Johnson 1709–84: *A Dictionary of the English Language* (1755)

11 If we do not find anything
pleasant, at least we shall find
something new.
Voltaire 1694–1778: *Candide* (1759)

12 *Sint ut sunt aut non sint.*
Let them be as they are or not be
at all.
*replying to a request for changes in
the constitutions of the Society of
Jesus*
Pope Clement XIII 1693–1769: J. A.
M. Crétineau-Joly *Clément XIV et les
Jésuites* (1847)

13 Variety's the very spice of life,
That gives it all its flavour.
William Cowper 1731–1800: *The Task*
(1785) bk. 2 "The Timepiece"

14 There is nothing stable in the
world—uproar's your only music.
John Keats 1795–1821: letter to
George and Thomas Keats, 13
January 1818

15 There is a certain relief in change,
even though it be from bad to
worse . . . it is often a comfort to
shift one's position and be bruised
in a new place.
Washington Irving 1783–1859: *Tales
of a Traveller* (1824)

16 A foolish consistency is the
hobgoblin of little minds, adored
by little statesmen and
philosophers and divines. With
consistency a great soul has
simply nothing to do.
Ralph Waldo Emerson 1803–82:
Essays (1841) "Self-Reliance"

17 Forward, forward let us range,
Let the great world spin for ever
down the ringing grooves of
change.
Alfred, Lord Tennyson 1809–92:
"Locksley Hall" (1842)

18 Change and decay in all around I
see;
O Thou, who changest not, abide
with me.

Henry Francis Lyte 1793–1847:
"Abide with Me" (probably written in
1847)

19 *Plus ça change, plus c'est la même
chose.*
The more things change, the
more they are the same.
Alphonse Karr 1808–90: *Les Guêpes*
January 1849

20 It is not best to swap horses
while crossing the river.
Abraham Lincoln 1809–65: *comment
to delegate from National Union
League* (9 June 1864)

21 Change is inevitable in a
progressive country. Change is
constant.
Benjamin Disraeli 1804–81: speech at
Edinburgh, 29 October 1867

22 There is in all change something
at once sordid and agreeable,
which smacks of infidelity and
household removals. This is
sufficient to explain the French
Revolution.
Charles Baudelaire 1821–67:
Journaux intimes (1887) "Mon coeur
mis à nu"

23 The old order changeth, yielding
place to new,
And God fulfils himself in many
ways,
Lest one good custom should
corrupt the world.
Alfred, Lord Tennyson 1809–92:
Idylls of the King "The Passing of
Arthur" (1869)

24 All conservatism is based upon
the idea that if you leave things
alone you leave them as they are.
But you do not. If you leave a
thing alone you leave it to a
torrent of change.
G. K. Chesterton 1874–1936:
Orthodoxy (1908)

25 Most of the change we think we
see in life
Is due to truths being in and out
of favor.

Robert Frost 1874–1963: "The Black Cottage" (1914)

26 I write it out in a verse—
MacDonagh and MacBride
And Connolly and Pearse
Now and in time to be,
Wherever green is worn,
Are changed, changed utterly:
A terrible beauty is born.
W. B. Yeats 1865–1939: "Easter, 1916" (1921)

27 Consistency is contrary to nature, contrary to life. The only completely consistent people are the dead.
Aldous Huxley 1894–1963: *Do What You Will* (1929)

28 God, give us the serenity to accept what cannot be changed;
Give us the courage to change what should be changed;
Give us the wisdom to distinguish one from the other.
Reinhold Niebuhr 1892–1971: prayer said to have been first published in 1951; Richard Wightman Fox *Reinhold Niebuhr* (1985); adapted and used by Alcoholics Anonymous

29 If we want things to stay as they are, things will have to change.
Giuseppe di Lampedusa 1896–1957: *The Leopard* (1957)

30 The wind of change is blowing through this continent.
Harold Macmillan 1894–1986: speech at Cape Town, 3 February 1960

Chaos
see **Order and Chaos**

Character
see also **Human Nature**

1 A man's character is his fate.
Heraclitus c. 540–c. 480 BC: *On the Universe*

2 He was a verray, parfit gentil knyght.
Geoffrey Chaucer c. 1343–1400: *The Canterbury Tales* "The General Prologue"

3 He was a man, take him for all in all,
I shall not look upon his like again.
William Shakespeare 1564–1616: *Hamlet* (1601)

4 Nature is often hidden, sometimes overcome, seldom extinguished.
Francis Bacon 1561–1626: *Essays* (1625) "Of Nature in Men"

5 Youth, what man's age is like to be doth show;
We may our ends by our beginnings know.
John Denham 1615–69: "Of Prudence" (1668)

6 I've tried him drunk and I've tried him sober but there's nothing in him.
of his niece Anne's husband George of Denmark
Charles II 1630–85: Gila Curtis *The Life and Times of Queen Anne* (1972)

7 I am fit for nothing but to carry candles and set chairs all my life.
Lord Hervey 1696–1743: letter to Sir Robert Walpole, 1737

8 Thy body is all vice, and thy mind all virtue.
to Beauclerk
Samuel Johnson 1709–84: James Boswell *Life of Samuel Johnson* (1791) March 1752

9 Then he does not wear them out in practice.
on hearing that a certain person was "a man of good principles"
Topham Beauclerk 1739–80: James Boswell *Life of Samuel Johnson* (1791) 14 April 1778

10 It is not in the still calm of life, or the repose of a pacific station, that great characters are formed ... Great necessities call out great virtues.
Abigail Adams 1744–1818: letter to John Quincy Adams, 19 January 1780

11 Talent develops in quiet places, character in the full current of human life.
Johann Wolfgang von Goethe 1749–1832: *Torquato Tasso* (1790)

12 Qualities too elevated often unfit a man for society. We don't take ingots with us to market; we take silver or small change.
Nicolas-Sébastien Chamfort 1741–94: *Maximes et Pensées* (1796)

13 I am not at all the sort of person you and I took me for.
Jane Carlyle 1801–66: letter to Thomas Carlyle, 7 May 1822

14 Character is higher than intellect.
Ralph Waldo Emerson 1803–82: *The American Scholar* (1837)

15 Affection beaming in one eye, and calculation shining out of the other.
Charles Dickens 1812–70: *Martin Chuzzlewit* (1844)

16 I desire so to conduct the affairs of this administration that if at the end, when I come to lay down the reins of power, I have lost every other friend on earth, I shall at least have one friend left, and that friend shall be down inside me.
Abraham Lincoln 1809–65: *Reply to the Missouri Committee of Seventy* (1864)

17 The great qualities, the imperious will, the rapid energy, the eager nature fit for a great crisis are not required—are impediments—in common times.
Walter Bagehot 1826–77: *The English Constitution* (1867)

18 Though I've belted you and flayed you,
By the livin' Gawd that made you,
You're a better man than I am, Gunga Din!
Rudyard Kipling 1865–1936: "Gunga Din" (1892)

19 A man of great common sense and good taste, meaning thereby a man without originality or moral courage.
George Bernard Shaw 1856–1950: *Notes to Caesar and Cleopatra* (1901) "Julius Caesar"

20 If you can trust yourself when all men doubt you,
But make allowance for their doubting too;
If you can wait and not be tired by waiting,
Or being lied about, don't deal in lies,
Or being hated, don't give way to hating,
And yet don't look too good, nor talk too wise.
Rudyard Kipling 1865–1936: "If—" (1910)

21 She did her work with the thoroughness of a mind which reveres details and never quite understands them.
Sinclair Lewis 1885–1951: *Babbitt* (1922)

22 Slice him where you like, a hellhound is always a hellhound.
P. G. Wodehouse 1881–1975: *The Code of the Woosters* (1938)

23 It is the nature, and the advantage, of strong people that they can bring out the crucial questions and form a clear opinion about them. The weak

always have to decide between alternatives that are not their own.
Dietrich Bonhoeffer 1906–45: *Widerstand und Ergebung* (Resistance and Submission, 1951)

24 There exists a great chasm between those, on one side, who relate everything to a single central vision . . . and, on the other side, those who pursue many ends, often unrelated and even contradictory . . . The first kind of intellectual and artistic personality belongs to the hedgehogs, the second to the foxes.
Isaiah Berlin 1909–97: *The Hedgehog and the Fox* (1953); cf. **Knowledge 1**

25 A thick skin is a gift from God.
Konrad Adenauer 1876–1967: in *New York Times* 30 December 1959

26 Underneath this flabby exterior is an enormous lack of character.
Oscar Levant 1906–72: *Memoirs of an Amnesiac* (1965)

27 We are all worms. But I do believe that I am a glow-worm.
Winston Churchill 1874–1965: Violet Bonham-Carter *Winston Churchill as I Knew Him* (1965)

28 Those who stand for nothing fall for anything.
Alex Hamilton 1936– : "Born Old" (radio broadcast), in *Listener* (UK) 9 November 1978

29 You can tell a lot about a fellow's character by his way of eating jellybeans.
Ronald Reagan 1911– : in *New York Times* 15 January 1981

30 Claudia's the sort of person who goes through life holding on to the sides.
Alice Thomas Ellis 1932– : *The Other Side of the Fire* (1983)

31 Nice guys, when we turn nasty, can make a terrible mess of it, usually because we've had so little practice, and have bottled it up for too long.
Matthew Parris 1949– : in *The Spectator* (UK) 27 February 1993

32 If you have bright plumage, people will take pot shots at you.
Alan Clark 1928– : in *Independent* (UK) 25 June 1994

Charity
see also **Gifts and Giving**

1 When thou doest alms, let not thy left hand know what thy right hand doeth.
Bible: St. Matthew

2 Friends, I have lost a day.
on reflecting that he had done nothing to help anybody all day
Titus AD 39–81: Suetonius *Lives of the Caesars* "Titus"

3 Thy necessity is yet greater than mine.
on giving his water-bottle to a dying soldier on the battlefield of Zutphen, 1586; commonly quoted "thy need is greater than mine"
Philip Sidney 1554–86: Fulke Greville *Life of Sir Philip Sidney* (1652)

4 'Tis not enough to help the feeble up,
But to support him after.
William Shakespeare 1564–1616: *Timon of Athens* (c. 1607)

5 Defer not charities till death; for certainly, if a man weigh it rightly, he that doth so is rather liberal of another man's than of his own.
Francis Bacon 1561–1626: *Essays* (1625) "Of Riches"

6 For Charity is cold in the multitude of possessions, and the

rich are covetous of their crumbs.
Christopher Smart 1722–71: *Jubilate Agno* (c. 1758–63)

7 He has enough of misanthropy to be a philanthropist.
of Lord Brougham
Walter Bagehot 1826–77: in *National Review* (UK) July 1857 "Lord Brougham"

8 The living need charity more than the dead.
George Arnold 1834–65: "The Jolly Old Pedagogue" (1866)

9 Much benevolence of the passive order may be traced to a disinclination to inflict pain upon oneself.
George Meredith 1828–1909: *Vittoria* (1866)

10 The Christian usually tries to give away his own money, whilst the philosopher usually tries to give away the money of someone else.
Lord Salisbury 1830–1903: C. S. Kenny *Property for Charitable Uses* (1880)

11 People often feed the hungry so that nothing may disturb their own enjoyment of a good meal.
W. Somerset Maugham 1874–1965: *A Writer's Notebook* (1949) written in 1896

12 I have always depended on the kindness of strangers.
Tennessee Williams 1911–83: *A Streetcar Named Desire* (1947)

13 No one would remember the Good Samaritan if he'd only had good intentions. He had money as well.
Margaret Thatcher 1925– : television interview, 6 January 1980

14 There is no greater joy in life than giving to worthy causes.
announcing his decision to donate $1 billion to the United Nations

Ted Turner 1938– : in *New York Times* 26 December 1997

Children
see also **The Family, Parents, Youth**

1 Like as the arrows in the hand of the giant: even so are the young children.
Happy is the man that hath his quiver full of them: they shall not be ashamed when they speak with their enemies in the gate.
Bible: Psalm 127

2 Train up a child in the way he should go: and when he is old, he will not depart from it.
Bible: Proverbs

3 Suffer the little children to come unto me, and forbid them not: for of such is the kingdom of God.
Bible: St. Mark

4 A child is owed the greatest respect; if you ever have something disgraceful in mind, don't ignore your son's tender years.
Juvenal AD c. 60–c. 130: *Satires*

5 A child is not a vase to be filled, but a fire to be lit.
François Rabelais c. 1494–c. 1553: attributed

6 It should be noted that children at play are not playing about; their games should be seen as their most serious-minded activity.
Montaigne 1533–92: *Essais* (1580)

7 My son—and what's a son? A thing begot
Within a pair of minutes, thereabout,
A lump bred up in darkness.
Thomas Kyd 1558–94: *The Spanish Tragedy* (1592) The Third Addition (1602 ed.)

8 At first the infant,
Mewling and puking in the
nurse's arms.
And then the whining schoolboy,
with his satchel,
And shining morning face,
creeping like snail
Unwillingly to school.
William Shakespeare 1564–1616: *As
You Like It* (1599)

9 Children sweeten labours, but
they make misfortunes more
bitter.
Francis Bacon 1561–1626: *Essays*
(1625) "Of Parents and Children"

10 Men are generally more careful of
the breed of their horses and dogs
than of their children.
William Penn 1644–1718: *Some
Fruits of Solitude* (1693)

11 Behold the child, by Nature's
kindly law
Pleased with a rattle, tickled with
a straw.
Alexander Pope 1688–1744: *An Essay
on Man* Epistle 2 (1733)

12 Alas, regardless of their doom,
The little victims play!
No sense have they of ills to
come,
Nor care beyond to-day.
Thomas Gray 1716–71: *Ode on a
Distant Prospect of Eton College*
(1747)

13 The Child is father of the Man;
And I could wish my days to be
Bound each to each by natural
piety.
William Wordsworth 1770–1850: "My
heart leaps up when I behold"
(1807)

14 A child's a plaything for an hour.
Charles Lamb 1775–1834: "Parental
Recollections" (1809); often
attributed to Lamb's sister Mary

15 The place is very well and quiet
and the children only scream in a
low voice.

Lord Byron 1788–1824: letter to Lady
Melbourne, 21 September 1813

16 There was never a child so lovely
but his mother was glad to get
asleep.
Ralph Waldo Emerson 1803–82:
Journal (1836)

17 You are a human boy, my young
friend. A human boy. O glorious
to be a human boy! . . . O running
stream of sparkling joy
To be a soaring human boy!
Charles Dickens 1812–70: *Bleak
House* (1853)

18 A torn jacket is soon mended; but
hard words bruise the heart of a
child.
Henry Wadsworth Longfellow 1807–
82: *Driftwood* (1857)

19 Go practise if you please
With men and women: leave a
child alone
For Christ's particular love's sake!
Robert Browning 1812–89: *The Ring
and the Book* (1868–9)

20 You will find as the children
grow up that as a rule children
are a bitter disappointment—their
greatest object being to do
precisely what their parents do
not wish and have anxiously
tried to prevent.
Queen Victoria 1819–1901: letter to
the Crown Princess of Prussia, 5
January 1876

21 Oh, for an hour of Herod!
*at the first night of J. M. Barrie's
Peter Pan in 1904*
Anthony Hope 1863–1933: Denis
Mackail *The Story of JMB* (1941)

22 Children are given us to
discourage our better emotions.
Saki 1870–1916: *Reginald* (1904)

23 If there is anything that we wish
to change in the child, we should

first examine it and see whether it is not something that could better be changed in ourselves.
Carl Gustav Jung 1875–1961: "Vom Werden der Persönlichkeit" (1932)

24 There is no end to the violations committed by children on children, quietly talking alone.
Elizabeth Bowen 1899–1973: *The House in Paris* (1935)

25 There is always one moment in childhood when the door opens and lets the future in.
Graham Greene 1904–91: *The Power and the Glory* (1940)

26 There is no finer investment for any community than putting milk into babies.
Winston Churchill 1874–1965: radio broadcast, 21 March 1943

27 What do we ever get nowadays from reading to equal the excitement and the revelation in those first fourteen years?
Graham Greene 1904–91: *The Lost Childhood and Other Essays* (1951) title essay

28 [Toys] can summon up in an instant, in colors stronger than life, the whole of childhood at its happiest.
Anonymous: *Sports Illustrated* (26 December 1960)

29 Children have never been very good at listening to their elders, but they have never failed to imitate them.
James Baldwin 1924–87: *Nobody Knows My Name* (1961)

30 Literature is mostly about having sex and not much about having children. Life is the other way round.
David Lodge 1935– : *The British Museum is Falling Down* (1965)

31 A child becomes an adult when he realizes that he has a right not only to be right but also to be wrong.
Thomas Szasz 1920– : *The Second Sin* (1973)

32 Childhood is Last Chance Gulch for happiness. After that, you know too much.
Tom Stoppard 1937– : *Where Are They Now?* (1973)

33 Nothing has a stronger influence on their children than the unlived lives of their parents.
Dr. Carl Jung 1875–1961: *Boston Magazine* (June 1978)

34 Children are the living messages we send to a time we will not see.
John W. Whitehead 1946– : *The Stealing of America* (1983)

35 Our schools are improving. It's childhoods that are not.
Keith Geiger 1941– : *New York Times* (5 July 1991)

36 With the birth of each child, you lose two novels.
Candia McWilliam 1955– : in *Guardian* (UK) 5 May 1993

37 Allowing children to be free of child-rearing did not, after all, produce a generation of happy, carefree, uncomplicated, altruistic and creative people. The experiment seems to suggest that a great deal of what we think of as "human nature" in the best sense—compassion, fairness, conscience—is, in fact, taught. We had always assumed that guilt and remorse were a natural consequence of doing wrong, but judges are now encountering legions of young criminals who have no such feelings.
Judith Martin 1938– : *Miss Manners Rescues Civilization* (1996)

Choice

see also **Indecision**

1 For many are called, but few are
  chosen.
  Bible: St. Matthew

2 To be, or not to be: that is the
  question:
  Whether 'tis nobler in the mind
  to suffer
  The slings and arrows of
  outrageous fortune,
  Or to take arms against a sea of
  troubles,
  And by opposing end them?
  William Shakespeare 1564–1616:
  Hamlet (1601)

3 How happy could I be with
  either,
  Were t'other dear charmer away!
  John Gay 1685–1732: *The Beggar's
  Opera* (1728)

4 From this day you must be a
  stranger to one of your parents.—
  Your mother will never see you
  again if you do *not* marry Mr.
  Collins, and I will never see you
  again if you *do*.
  Jane Austen 1775–1817: *Pride and
  Prejudice* (1813)

5 What man wants is simply
  independent choice, whatever that
  independence may cost and
  wherever it may lead.
  Fyodor Dostoevsky 1821–81: *Notes
  from Underground* (1864)

6 A woman can hardly ever choose
  . . . she is dependent on what
  happens to her. She must take
  meaner things, because only
  meaner things are within her
  reach.
  George Eliot 1819–80: *Felix Holt*
  (1866)

7 White shall not neutralize the
  black, nor good

Compensate bad in man, absolve
  him so:
  Life's business being just the
  terrible choice.
  Robert Browning 1812–89: *The Ring
  and the Book* (1868–9)

8 Any customer can have a car
  painted any color that he wants
  so long as it is black.
  on the Model T Ford, 1909
  Henry Ford 1863–1947: *My Life and
  Work* (with Samuel Crowther, 1922)

9 Two roads diverged in a wood,
  and I—
  I took the one less traveled by,
  And that has made all the
  difference.
  Robert Frost 1874–1963: "The Road
  Not Taken" (1916)

10 If it has to choose who is to be
  crucified, the crowd will always
  save Barabbas.
  Jean Cocteau 1889–1963: *Le Rappel
  à l'ordre* (1926)

11 Many men would take the death-
  sentence without a whimper to
  escape the life-sentence which fate
  carries in her other hand.
  T. E. Lawrence 1888–1935: *The Mint*
  (1955)

12 Between two evils, I always pick
  the one I never tried before.
  Mae West 1892–1980: *Klondike
  Annie* (1936 film)

13 Whose finger do you want on the
  trigger?
  *headline alluding to the atom bomb,
  apropos the failure of both the
  Labour and Conservative parties to
  purge their leaders of proven failures*
  Anonymous: in *Daily Mirror* (UK) 21
  September 1951

14 If one cannot catch the bird of
  paradise, better take a wet hen.
  Nikita Khrushchev 1894–1971: in
  Time 6 January 1958

15 Chips with everything.
Arnold Wesker 1932– : title of play
(1962)

16 Was there ever in anyone's life
span a point free in time, devoid
of memory, a night when choice
was any more than the sum of all
the choices gone before?
Joan Didion 1934– : *Run River*
(1963)

17 I'll make him an offer he can't
refuse.
Mario Puzo 1920– : *The Godfather*
(1969)

18 A compromise in the sense that
being bitten in half by a shark is
a compromise with being
swallowed whole.
P. J. O'Rourke 1947– : *Parliament
of Whores* (1991)

The Christian Church
see also **Clergy, God, Religion**

1 Thou art Peter, and upon this
rock I will build my church; and
the gates of hell shall not prevail
against it.
Bible: St. Matthew

2 As often as we are mown down
by you, the more we grow in
numbers; the blood of Christians
is the seed.
Tertullian AD *c.* 160–*c.* 225:
Apologeticus

3 He cannot have God for his father
who has not the church for his
mother.
St. Cyprian *c.* AD 200–258: *De
Ecclesiae Catholicae Unitate*

4 *In hoc signo vinces.*
In this sign shalt thou conquer.
*traditional form of Constantine's
vision of the cross* (AD 312)
Constantine the Great AD *c.* 288–337:
reported in Greek "By this, conquer";
Eusebius *Life of Constantine*

5 Rome has spoken; the case is
concluded.
St. Augustine of Hippo AD 354–430:
traditional summary of words found
in *Sermons* (Antwerp, 1702) no. 131

6 Take heed of thinking, *The farther
you go from the church of Rome,
the nearer you are to God.*
Henry Wotton 1568–1639: Izaak
Walton *Reliquiae Wottonianae* (1651)

7 The papacy is not other than the
ghost of the deceased Roman
Empire, sitting crowned upon the
grave thereof.
Thomas Hobbes 1588–1679:
Leviathan (1651)

8 As some to church repair,
Not for the doctrine, but the
music there.
Alexander Pope 1688–1744: *An
Essay on Criticism* (1711)

9 The Gospel of Christ knows of no
religion but social; no holiness
but social holiness.
John Wesley 1703–91: *Hymns and
Sacred Poems* (1739) preface

10 The Christian religion not only
was at first attended with
miracles, but even at this day
cannot be believed by any
reasonable person without one.
David Hume 1711–76: *An Enquiry
Concerning Human Understanding*
(1748)

11 We have a Calvinistic creed, a
Popish liturgy, and an Arminian
clergy.
of the Church of England
William Pitt, Earl of Chatham 1708–
78: speech in the House of Lords, 19
May 1772

12 A mere gossiping entertainment:
a few child's squalls, a few
mumbled amens, and a few
mumbled cakes, and a few smirks
accompanied by a few fees.
on the christening of his godson

Leigh Hunt 1784–1859: letter to
Marianne Kent, February 1806

13 Christians have burnt each other,
quite persuaded
That all the Apostles would have
done as they did.
Lord Byron 1788–1824: *Don Juan*
(1819–24)

14 He who begins by loving
Christianity better than Truth will
proceed by loving his own sect or
church better than Christianity,
and end by loving himself better
than all.
Samuel Taylor Coleridge 1772–1834:
Aids to Reflection (1825)

15 He may be one of its [the
Church's] buttresses, but certainly
not one of its pillars, for he is
never found within it.
*of John Scott, Lord Eldon (1751–
1838)*
Anonymous: H. Twiss *Public and
Private Life of Eldon* (1844); later
attributed to Lord Melbourne

16 She [the Roman Catholic Church]
may still exist in undiminished
vigour when some traveller from
New Zealand shall, in the midst of
a vast solitude, take his stand on
a broken arch of London Bridge
to sketch the ruins of St. Paul's.
Lord Macaulay 1800–59: *Essays
Contributed to the Edinburgh Review*
(1843) "Von Ranke"

17 The Church's one foundation
Is Jesus Christ, her Lord;
She is his new creation
By water and the word.
Samuel John Stone 1839–1900: "The
Church's one foundation" (1866
hymn)

18 If the Church of England were to
fail, it would be found in my
parish.
John Keble 1792–1866: D. Newsome
The Parting of Friends (1966)

19 His Christianity was muscular.
Benjamin Disraeli 1804–81:
Endymion (1880)

20 Scratch the Christian and you
find the pagan—spoiled.
Israel Zangwill 1864–1926: *Children
of the Ghetto* (1892)

21 People may say what they like
about the decay of Christianity;
the religious system that produced
green Chartreuse can never really
die.
Saki 1870–1916: *Reginald* (1904)

22 It was a divine sermon. For it
was like the peace of God—which
passeth all understanding. And
like his mercy, it seemed to
endure for ever.
Henry Hawkins 1817–1907: Gordon
Lang *Mr. Justice Avory* (1935); cf.
Peace 3

23 The Christian ideal has not been
tried and found wanting. It has
been found difficult; and left
untried.
G. K. Chesterton 1874–1936: *What's
Wrong with the World* (1910)

24 SAINT, *n.* A dead sinner revised
and edited.
Ambrose Bierce 1842–*c.* 1914: *The
Devil's Dictionary* (1911)

25 The sinner is at the heart of
Christianity . . . No one is as
competent as the sinner in
matters of Christianity. No one,
except a saint.
Charles Péguy 1873–1914: *Basic
Verities* (1943) "Un Nouveau
théologien . . . " (1911)

26 The Church should go forward
along the path of progress and be
no longer satisfied only to
represent the Conservative Party
at prayer.
Maude Royden 1876–1956: address
at Queen's Hall, London, 16 July
1917

27 Christianity is the most materialistic of all great religions.
William Temple 1881–1944: *Readings in St. John's Gospel* vol. 1 (1939)

28 The two dangers which beset the Church of England are good music and bad preaching.
Lord Hugh Cecil 1869–1956: K. Rose *The Later Cecils* (1975)

29 The chief contribution of Protestantism to human thought is its massive proof that God is a bore.
H. L. Mencken 1880–1956: *Minority Report* (1956)

30 Anybody can be pope; the proof of this is that I have become one.
Pope John XXIII 1881–1963: Henri Fesquet *Wit and Wisdom of Good Pope John* (1964)

31 You have no idea how much nastier I would be if I was not a Catholic. Without supernatural aid I would hardly be a human being.
Evelyn Waugh 1903–66: Noel Annan *Our Age* (1990)

32 I see it as an elderly lady, who mutters away to herself in a corner, ignored most of the time.
on the Church of England
George Carey 1935– : in *Readers Digest* (British ed.) March 1991

33 The crisis of the Church of England is that too many of its bishops, and some would say of its archbishops, don't quite realise that they are atheists, but have begun to suspect it.
Clive James 1939– : *The Dreaming Swimmer* (1992)

34 We must recall that the Church is always "one generation away from extinction."
George Carey 1935– : Working Party Report *Youth A Part: Young People and the Church* (1996) foreword

Christmas

1 For unto us a child is born, unto us a son is given: and the government shall be upon his shoulder: and his name shall be called Wonderful, Counselor, The mighty God, The everlasting Father, The Prince of Peace.
Bible: Isaiah

2 She brought forth her firstborn son, and wrapped him in swaddling clothes, and laid him in a manger; because there was no room for them in the inn.
Bible: St. Luke

3 Welcome, all wonders in one sight!
Eternity shut in a span.
Richard Crashaw c. 1612–49: "Hymn of the Nativity" (1652)

4 I have often thought, says Sir Roger, it happens very well that Christmas should fall out in the Middle of Winter.
Joseph Addison 1672–1719: *The Spectator* (UK) 8 January 1712

5 'Twas the night before Christmas, when all through the house
Not a creature was stirring, not even a mouse;
The stockings were hung by the chimney with care,
In hopes that St. Nicholas soon would be there.
Clement C. Moore 1779–1863: "A Visit from St. Nicholas" (December 1823)

6 "Bah," said Scrooge. "Humbug!"
Charles Dickens 1812–70: *A Christmas Carol* (1843)

7 It is Christmas Day in the Workhouse.
George R. Sims 1847–1922: "In the Workhouse—Christmas Day" (1879)

8 Yes, Virginia, there is a Santa
Claus.
*replying to a letter from eight-year-
old Virginia O'Hanlon*
Francis Pharcellus Church 1839–1906:
editorial in New York *Sun*, 21
September 1897

9 The darkness drops again but
now I know
That twenty centuries of stony
sleep
Were vexed to nightmare by a
rocking cradle,
And what rough beast, its hour
come round at last,
Slouches towards Bethlehem to be
born?
W. B. Yeats 1865–1939: "The Second
Coming" (1921)

10 Still xmas is a good time with all
those presents and good food and
i hope it will never die out or at
any rate not until i am grown up
and hav to pay for it all.
Geoffrey Willans 1911–58 and **Ronald
Searle** 1920–   : *How To Be Topp*
(1954)

Circumstance and Situation

1 Every honourable action has its
proper time and season, or rather
it is this propriety or observance
which distinguishes an
honourable action from its
opposite.
Agesilaus 444–400 BC: Plutarch *Lives*
"Agesilaus"

2 But for the grace of God there
goes John Bradford.
*on seeing a group of criminals being
led to their execution; usually
quoted as, "There but for the grace
of God go I"*
John Bradford c. 1510–55: in
Dictionary of National Biography
(1917–)

3 The time is out of joint; O cursèd
spite,

That ever I was born to set it
right!
William Shakespeare 1564–1616:
Hamlet (1601); cf. **Opportunity 13**

4 My nature is subdued
To what it works in, like the
dyer's hand.
William Shakespeare 1564–1616:
sonnet 111

5 And, spite of Pride, in erring
Reason's spite,
One truth is clear, "Whatever IS,
is RIGHT."
Alexander Pope 1688–1744: *An
Essay on Man* Epistle 1 (1733)

6 *No se puede mirar.*
One cannot look at this.
Goya 1746–1828: *The Disasters of
War* (1863) title of etching

7 We shall generally find that the
triangular person has got into the
square hole, the oblong into the
triangular, and a square person
has squeezed himself into the
round hole. The officer and the
office, the doer and the thing
done, seldom fit so exactly that
we can say they were almost
made for each other.
Sydney Smith 1771–1845: *Sketches
of Moral Philosophy* (1849)

8 For of all sad words of tongue or
pen,
The saddest are these: "It might
have been!"
John Greenleaf Whittier 1807–92:
"Maud Muller" (1854); cf. **10** below

9 It was the best of times, it was
the worst of times, it was the age
of wisdom, it was the age of
foolishness, it was the epoch of
belief, it was the epoch of
incredulity, it was the season of
Light, it was the season of
Darkness, it was the spring of
hope, it was the winter of despair,
we had everything before us, we
had nothing before us, we were

all going direct to Heaven, we
were all going direct the other
way.
Charles Dickens 1812–70: *A Tale of
Two Cities* (1859)

10 If, of all words of tongue and pen,
The saddest are, "It might have
    been,"
More sad are these we daily see:
"It is, but hadn't ought to be!"
Bret Harte 1836–1902: "Mrs. Judge
Jenkins" (1867); see **8** above

11 We are so made, that we can
only derive intense enjoyment
from a contrast, and only very
little from a state of things.
Sigmund Freud 1856–1939:
Civilization and its Discontents
(1930)

12 Anyone who isn't confused
doesn't really understand the
situation.
on the Vietnam War
Ed Murrow 1908–65: Walter Bryan
The Improbable Irish (1969)

Cities
see **Towns and Cities**

Civilization
see **Culture and Civilization**

Class
see also **Capitalism and Communism,
Rank and Title**

1 When Adam dalfe and Eve spane
Go spire if thou may spede,
Where was than the pride of man
That now merres his mede?
Richard Rolle de Hampole c. 1290–
1349: G. G. Perry *Religious Pieces*
(1914)

2 I must have the gentleman to
haul and draw with the mariner,
and the mariner with the
gentleman . . . I would know him,

that would refuse to set his hand
to a rope, but I know there is not
any such here.
Francis Drake c. 1540–96: J. S.
Corbett *Drake and the Tudor Navy*
(1898)

3 Take but degree away, untune
    that string,
And, hark! what discord follows.
William Shakespeare 1564–1616:
Troilus and Cressida (1602)

4 That in the captain's but a
    choleric word,
Which in the soldier is flat
    blasphemy.
William Shakespeare 1564–1616:
Measure for Measure (1604)

5 The people have little intelligence,
the great no heart . . . if I had to
choose I should have no
hesitation: I would be of the
people.
Jean de la Bruyère 1645–96: *Les
Caractères ou les moeurs de ce
siècle* (1688)

6 He told me . . . that mine was the
middle state, or what might be
called the upper station of low
life, which he had found by long
experience was the best state in
the world, the most suited to
human happiness.
Daniel Defoe 1660–1731: *Robinson
Crusoe* (1719)

7 O let us love our occupations,
Bless the squire and his relations,
Live upon our daily rations,
And always know our proper
    stations.
Charles Dickens 1812–70: *The
Chimes* (1844) "The Second Quarter"

8 The proletarians have nothing to
lose but their chains. They have a
world to win. WORKING MEN OF
ALL COUNTRIES, UNITE!
*commonly rendered as "Workers of
the world, unite!"*
Karl Marx 1818–83 and **Friedrich**

Engels 1820–95: *The Communist Manifesto* (1848); cf. **22** below

9 The rich man in his castle,
The poor man at his gate,
God made them, high or lowly,
And ordered their estate.
Cecil Frances Alexander 1818–95:
"All Things Bright and Beautiful"
(1848)

10 *Il faut épater le bourgeois.*
One must astonish the bourgeois.
Charles Baudelaire 1821–67:
attributed; also attributed to Privat
d'Anglemont (c. 1820–59) in the
form "*Je les ai épatés, les bourgeois*
[I flabbergasted them, the
bourgeois]"

11 The so called immorality of the
lower classes is not to be named
on the same day with that of the
higher and highest. This is a
thing which makes my blood boil,
and they will pay for it.
Queen Victoria 1819–1901: letter to
the Crown Princess of Prussia, 26
June 1872

12 All the world over, I will back the
masses against the classes.
W. E. Gladstone 1809–98: speech in
Liverpool, 28 June 1886

13 The bourgeois are other people.
Jules Renard 1864–1910: diary, 28
January 1890

14 Bourgeois . . . is an epithet which
the riff-raff apply to what is
respectable, and the aristocracy to
what is decent.
Anthony Hope 1863–1933: *The Dolly
Dialogues* (1894)

15 You may tempt the upper classes
With your villainous demi-tasses,
But; Heaven will protect a
working-girl!
Edgar Smith 1857–1938: "Heaven
Will Protect the Working-Girl" (1909
song)

16 Dear me, I never knew that the
lower classes had such white
skins.
*supposedly said when watching
troops bathing during the First World
War*
Lord Curzon 1859–1925: K. Rose
Superior Person (1969)

17 The British Bourgeoise
Is not born,
And does not die,
But, if it is ill,
It has a frightened look in its
eyes.
Osbert Sitwell 1892–1969: *At the
House of Mrs. Kinfoot* (1921)

18 The bourgeois prefers comfort to
pleasure, convenience to liberty,
and a pleasant temperature to the
deathly inner consuming fire.
Hermann Hesse 1877–1962: *Der
Steppenwolf* (1927)

19 Any who have heard that sound
will shrink at the recollection of it;
it is the sound of English county
families baying for broken glass.
Evelyn Waugh 1903–66: *Decline and
Fall* (1928)

20 Civilization has made the
peasantry its pack animal. The
bourgeoisie in the long run only
changed the form of the pack.
Leon Trotsky 1879–1940: *History of
the Russian Revolution* (1933)

21 Destroy him as you will, the
bourgeois always bounces up—
execute him, expropriate him,
starve him out *en masse*, and he
reappears in your children.
Cyril Connolly 1903–74: in *Observer*
(UK) 7 March 1937

22 We of the sinking middle class . . .
may sink without further
struggles into the working class
where we belong, and probably
when we get there it will not be
so dreadful as we feared, for, after

all, we have nothing to lose but
our aitches.
George Orwell 1903–50: *The Road to
Wigan Pier* (1937); see **8** above

23 Ladies were ladies in those days;
they did not do things
themselves.
Gwen Raverat 1885–1957: *Period
Piece* (1952)

24 You can be in the Horseguards
and still be common, dear.
Terence Rattigan 1911–77: *Separate
Tables* (1954)

25 Impotence and sodomy are
socially O.K. but birth control is
flagrantly middle-class.
Evelyn Waugh 1903–66: "An Open
Letter" in Nancy Mitford (ed.)
Noblesse Oblige (1956)

26 I can't help feeling wary when I
hear anything said about the
masses. First you take their faces
from 'em by calling 'em the
masses and then you accuse 'em
of not having any faces.
J. B. Priestley 1894–1984: *Saturn
Over the Water* (1961)

27 Will the people in the cheaper
seats clap your hands? All the
rest of you, if you'll just rattle
your jewellery.
John Lennon 1940–80: at the Royal
Variety Performance, 4 November
1963

28 The real solvent of class
distinction is a proper measure of
self-esteem—a kind of
unselfconsciousness. Some people
are at ease with themselves, so
the world is at ease with them.
My parents thought this kind of
ease was produced by education
. . . they didn't see that what
disqualified them was
temperament—just as, though
educated up to the hilt, it
disqualifies me. What keeps us in
our place is embarrassment.
Alan Bennett 1934– : *Dinner at
Noon* (BBC television, 1988)

29 There are those who think that
Britain is a class-ridden society,
and those who think it doesn't
matter either way as long as you
know your place in the set-up.
Miles Kington 1941– : *Welcome to
Kington* (1989)

30 I am pretty middle class.
John Prescott 1938– : on BBC
Radio Four *Today* program; in
Observer (UK) 14 April 1996 "Sayings
of the Week"; cf. **31** below

31 I have little or no time for people
who aspire to be members of the
middle class.
*on John Prescott, at the launch of
the Socialist Labour Party*
Arthur Scargill 1938– : in *Observer*
(UK) 5 May "Sayings of the Week"
see **30** above

Clergy
see also **The Christian Church**

1 A bishop then must be blameless,
the husband of one wife, vigilant,
sober, of good behavior, given to
hospitality, apt to teach;
Not given to wine, no striker, not
greedy of filthy lucre; but patient,
not a brawler, not covetous.
Bible: I Timothy

2 In old time we had treen chalices
and golden priests, but now we
have treen priests and golden
chalices.
John Jewel 1522–71: *Certain Sermons
Preached Before the Queen's
Majesty* (1609)

3 A single life doth well with
churchmen, for charity will
hardly water the ground where it
must first fill a pool.
Francis Bacon 1561–1626: *Essays*
(1625) "Of Marriage and the Single
Life"

4 New *Presbyter* is but old *Priest*
   writ large.
   John Milton 1608–74: "On the New
   Forcers of Conscience under the
   Long Parliament" (1646)

5 And of all plagues with which
   mankind are curst,
   Ecclesiastic tyranny's the worst.
   Daniel Defoe 1660–1731: *The True-
   Born Englishman* (1701)

6 I look upon all the world as my
   parish.
   John Wesley 1703–91: *Journal* 11
   June 1739

7 In all ages of the world, priests
   have been enemies of liberty.
   David Hume 1711–76: *Essays, Moral,
   Political, and Literary* (1875) "Of the
   Parties of Great Britain" (1741–2)

8 They seem to know no medium
   between a mitre and a crown of
   martyrdom. If the clergy are not
   called to the latter, they never
   deviate from the pursuit of the
   former. One would think their
   motto was, *Canterbury or
   Smithfield.*
   Horace Walpole 1717–97: *Memoirs of
   the Reign of King George II* (1758)

9 I never saw, heard, nor read, that
   the clergy were beloved in any
   nation where Christianity was the
   religion of the country. Nothing
   can render them popular, but
   some degree of persecution.
   Jonathan Swift 1667–1745: *Thoughts
   on Religion* (1765)

10 Men may call me a knave or a
   fool, a rascal, a scoundrel, and I
   am content; but they shall never
   by my consent call me a Bishop!
   John Wesley 1703–91: Betty M.
   Jarboe *Wesley Quotations* (1990)

11 A Curate—there is something
   which excites compassion in the
   very name of a Curate!!!
   Sydney Smith 1771–1845:

"Persecuting Bishops" in *Edinburgh
Review* (1822)

12 *Merit*, indeed! . . . We are come to
   a pretty pass if they talk of *merit*
   for a bishopric.
   John Fane, Lord Westmorland 1759–
   1841: Lady Salisbury's diary, 9
   December 1835

13 Damn it! Another Bishop dead! I
   believe they die to vex me.
   as Prime Minister (1834, 1835–41)
   Lord Melbourne 1779–1848:
   attributed; Lord David Cecil *Lord M*
   (1954)

14 As the French say, there are three
   sexes—men, women, and
   clergymen.
   Sydney Smith 1771–1845: Lady
   Holland *Memoir* (1855)

15 How can a bishop marry? How
   can he flirt? The most he can say
   is, "I will see you in the vestry
   after service."
   Sydney Smith 1771–1845: Lady
   Holland *Memoir* (1855)

16 Pray remember, Mr. Dean, no
   dogma, no Dean.
   Benjamin Disraeli 1804–81: W.
   Monypenny and G. Buckle *Life of
   Benjamin Disraeli* vol. 4 (1916)

17 There is a species of person called
   a "Modern Churchman" who
   draws the full salary of a
   beneficed clergyman and need not
   commit himself to any religious
   belief.
   Evelyn Waugh 1903–66: *Decline and
   Fall* (1928)

18 Don't like bishops. Fishy lot.
   Blessed are the meek my foot!
   They're all on the climb. Ever
   heard of meekness stopping a
   bishop from becoming a bishop?
   Nor have I.
   Maurice Bowra 1898–1971: Arthur
   Marshall *Life's Rich Pageant* (1984)

Commerce
see **Business and Commerce**

Communism
see **Capitalism and Communism**

Conformity

1 While we were talking came by
several poor creatures carried by,
by constables, for being at a
conventicle . . . I would to God
they would either conform, or be
more wise, and not be catched!
Samuel Pepys 1633–1703: diary 7
August 1664

2 "It's always best on these
occasions to do what the mob
do." "But suppose there are two
mobs?" suggested Mr. Snodgrass.
"Shout with the largest," replied
Mr. Pickwick.
Charles Dickens 1812–70: *Pickwick
Papers* (1837)

3 Whoso would be a man must be
a nonconformist.
Ralph Waldo Emerson 1803–82:
Essays (1841) "Self-Reliance"

4 Teach him to think for himself?
Oh, my God, teach him rather to
think like other people!
on her son's education
Mary Shelley 1797–1851: Matthew
Arnold *Essays in Criticism* Second
Series (1888) "Shelley"

5 If a man does not keep pace with
his companions, perhaps it is
because he hears a different
drummer. Let him step to the
music which he hears, however
measured or far away.
Henry David Thoreau 1817–62:
Walden (1854)

6 You cannot make a man by
standing a sheep on its hind-legs.
But by standing a flock of sheep

in that position you can make a
crowd of men.
Max Beerbohm 1872–1956: *Zuleika
Dobson* (1911)

7 I've broken Anne of gathering
bouquets.
It's not fair to the child. It can't
be helped though:
Pressed into service means
pressed out of shape.
Robert Frost 1874–1963: "The Self-
Seeker" (1914)

8 Imitation lies at the root of most
human actions. A respectable
person is one who conforms to
custom. People are called good
when they do as others do.
Anatole France 1844–1924:
Crainquebille (1923)

9 I feel like a fugitive from th' law
of averages.
Bill Mauldin 1921– : cartoon
caption in *Up Front* (1945)

10 These are the days when men of
all social disciplines and all
political faiths seek the
comfortable and the accepted;
when the man of controversy is
looked upon as a disturbing
influence; when originality is
taken to be a mark of instability;
and when, in minor modification
of the scriptural parable, the
bland lead the bland.
John Kenneth Galbraith 1908– : *The
Affluent Society* (1958); see
Leadership 1

11 Never forget that only dead fish
swim with the stream.
Malcolm Muggeridge 1903–90:
quoting a supporter; in *Radio Times*
9 July 1964

12 Her exotic daydreams do not
prevent her from being small-
town bourgeois at heart, clinging
to conventional ideas or
committing this or that
conventional violation of the
conventional, adultery being a

most conventional way to rise
above the conventional.
Vladimir Nabokov 1899–1977:
Lectures on Literature (1980)
"Madame Bovary"

13 The Normal is the good smile in a
child's eyes—all right. It is also
the dead stare in a million adults.
It both sustains and kills—like a
God. It is the Ordinary made
beautiful; it is also the Average
made lethal.
Peter Shaffer 1926–   : *Equus* (1983
ed.)

Conscience
see also **Forgiveness and
Repentance, Sin**

1 Then I, however, showed again,
by action, not in word only, that
I did not care a whit for death . . .
but that I did care with all my
might not to do anything unjust
or unholy.
*on being ordered by the Thirty
Commissioners to take part in the
liquidation of Leon of Salamis*
Socrates 469–399 BC: Plato *Apology*

2 *O dignitosa coscienza e netta,
Come t'è picciol fallo amaro morso!*
O pure and noble conscience,
how bitter a sting to thee is a
little fault!
Dante 1265–1321: *Divina Commedia*
"Purgatorio"

3 Every subject's duty is the king's;
but every subject's soul is his
own.
William Shakespeare 1564–1616:
Henry V (1599)

4 Thus conscience doth make
cowards of us all.
William Shakespeare 1564–1616:
Hamlet (1601)

5 If I am obliged to bring religion
into after-dinner toasts (which
indeed does not seem quite the

thing) I shall drink—to the Pope,
if you please—still, to Conscience
first, and to the Pope afterwards.
John Henry Newman 1801–90: *A
Letter Addressed to the Duke of
Norfolk . . .* (1875)

6 Conscience is thoroughly well-
bred and soon leaves off talking
to those who do not wish to hear
it.
Samuel Butler 1835–1902: *Further
Extracts from Notebooks* (1934)

7 Conscience: the inner voice which
warns us that someone may be
looking.
H. L. Mencken 1880–1956: *A Little
Book in C major* (1916)

8 Most people sell their souls, and
live with a good conscience on
the proceeds.
Logan Pearsall Smith 1865–1946:
Afterthoughts (1931)

9 Sufficient conscience to bother
him, but not sufficient to keep
him straight.
of Ramsay MacDonald
David Lloyd George 1863–1945: A. J.
Sylvester *Life with Lloyd George*
(1975)

10 I cannot and will not cut my
conscience to fit this year's
fashions.
Lillian Hellman 1905–84: letter to
John S. Wood, 19 May 1952

Consequences

see **Causes and Consequences**

Consolation
see **Sympathy and Consolation**

Constancy and Inconstancy

1 My true love hath my heart and I
have his,
   By just exchange one for the
   other giv'n;

I hold his dear, and mine he
  cannot miss,
There never was a better bargain
  driv'n.
Philip Sidney 1554–86: *Arcadia*
(1581)

2 If I could pray to move, prayers
    would move me;
But I am constant as the
    northern star,
Of whose true-fixed and resting
    quality
There is no fellow in the
    firmament.
William Shakespeare 1564–1616:
Julius Caesar (1599)

3 Why, I hold fate
Clasped in my fist, and could
    command the course
Of time's eternal motion, hadst
    thou been
One thought more steady than an
    ebbing sea.
John Ford 1586–after 1639: *'Tis Pity
She's a Whore* (1633)

4 I loved thee once. I'll love no
    more,
Thine be the grief, as is the blame;

Thou art not what thou wast
    before,
What reason I should be the
    same?
Robert Aytoun 1570–1638: "To an
Inconstant Mistress"

5 A mistress should be like a little
country retreat near the town,
not to dwell in constantly, but
only for a night and away.
William Wycherley c. 1640–1716: *The
Country Wife* (1675)

6 Tell me no more of constancy,
  that frivolous pretence,
Of cold age, narrow jealousy,
  disease and want of sense.
John Wilmot, Lord Rochester 1647–
80: "Against Constancy" (1676)

7 An inconstant woman, tho' she
  has no chance to be very happy,
can never be very unhappy.
John Gay 1685–1732: "Polly" (1729)

8 No, the heart that has truly loved
    never forgets,
But as truly loves on to the close,
As the sun-flower turns on her
    god, when he sets,
The same look which she turned
    when he rose.
Thomas Moore 1779–1852: "Believe
me, if all those endearing young
charms" (1807)

9 Bright star, would I were
    steadfast as thou art—.
John Keats 1795–1821: "Bright star,
would I were steadfast as thou art"
(written 1819)

10 "Yes," I answered you last night;
  "No," this morning, sir, I say.
Colours seen by candle-light
Will not look the same by day.
Elizabeth Barrett Browning 1806–61:
"The Lady's Yes" (1844)

11 The shackles of an old love
    straitened him,
His honour rooted in dishonour
    stood,
And faith unfaithful kept him
    falsely true.
Alfred, Lord Tennyson 1809–92:
Idylls of the King "Lancelot and
Elaine" (1859)

12 But I was desolate and sick of an
    old passion,
Yea, all the time, because the
    dance was long:
I have been faithful to thee,
    Cynara! in my fashion.
Ernest Dowson 1867–1900: "Non
Sum Qualis Eram" (1896); also
known as "Cynara" cf. **Memory** 15

13 *of an unwelcome supporter:*
He pursues us with malignant
  fidelity.
Arthur James Balfour 1848–1930:
Winston Churchill *Great
Contemporaries* (1937)

14 Your idea of fidelity is not having
more than one man in bed at the
same time.
Frederic Raphael 1931– : *Darling*
(1965)

Conversation
see also **Gossip, Speech, Speeches**

1 I am not bound to please thee
with my answer.
William Shakespeare 1564–1616: *The
Merchant of Venice* (1596–8)

2 JOHNSON: Well, we had a good
talk.
BOSWELL: Yes, Sir; you tossed and
gored several persons.
James Boswell 1740–95: *Life of
Samuel Johnson* (1791) Summer 1768

3 Religion is by no means a proper
subject of conversation in a mixed
company.
Lord Chesterfield 1694–1773: *Letters
. . . to his Godson and Successor*
(1890) Letter 142

4 Questioning is not the mode of
conversation among gentlemen. It
is assuming a superiority.
Samuel Johnson 1709–84: James
Boswell *Life of Samuel Johnson*
(1791) 25 March 1776

5 John Wesley's conversation is
good, but he is never at leisure.
He is always obliged to go at a
certain hour. This is very
disagreeable to a man who loves
to fold his legs and have out his
talk, as I do.
Samuel Johnson 1709–84: James
Boswell *Life of Samuel Johnson*
(1791) 31 March 1778

6 On every formal visit a child
ought to be of the party, by way
of provision for discourse.
Jane Austen 1775–1817: *Sense and
Sensibility* (1811)

7 He talked on for ever; and you
wished him to talk on for ever.
of Coleridge
William Hazlitt 1778–1830: *Lectures
on the English Poets* (1818)

8 Two may talk and one may hear,
but three cannot take part in a
conversation of the most sincere
and searching sort.
Ralph Waldo Emerson 1803–82:
Essays: First Series, Friendship
(1841)

9 "Not to put too fine a point upon
it"—a favourite apology for plain-
speaking with Mr. Snagsby.
Charles Dickens 1812–70: *Bleak
House* (1853)

10 If you are ever at a loss to
support a flagging conversation,
introduce the subject of eating.
Leigh Hunt 1784–1859: A. Gere and
John Sparrow (eds.) *Geoffrey
Madan's Notebooks* (1981);
attributed

11 The fun of talk is to find what a
man really thinks, and then
contrast it with the enormous lies
he has been telling all dinner,
and, perhaps, all his life.
Benjamin Disraeli 1804–81: *Lothair*
(1870)

12 "The time has come," the Walrus
said,
"To talk of many things:
Of shoes—and ships—and sealing
wax—
Of cabbages—and kings—
And why the sea is boiling hot—
And whether pigs have wings."
Lewis Carroll 1832–98: *Through the
Looking-Glass* (1872)

13 It is the province of knowledge to
speak and it is the privilege of
wisdom to listen.
Oliver Wendell Holmes 1809–94: *The
Poet at the Breakfast-Table* (1872)

14 The tribute which intelligence
pays to humbug.
definition of tact
St. John Brodrick 1856–1942: Lady
Ribblesdale to Lord Curzon 3 April
1891; Kenneth Rose *Superior Person*
(1969)

15 He speaks to Me as if I was a
public meeting.
of Gladstone
Queen Victoria 1819–1901: G. W. E.
Russell *Collections and Recollections*
(1898)

16 Most English talk is a quadrille in
a sentry-box.
Henry James 1843–1916: *The
Awkward Age* (1899)

17 Although there exist many
thousand subjects for elegant
conversation, there are persons
who cannot meet a cripple
without talking about feet.
Ernest Bramah 1868–1942: *The
Wallet of Kai Lung* (1900)

18 She plunged into a sea of
platitudes, and with the powerful
breast stroke of a channel
swimmer made her confident way
towards the white cliffs of the
obvious.
W. Somerset Maugham 1874–1965:
A Writer's Notebook (1949) written
in 1919

19 How time flies when you's doin'
all the talking.
Harvey Fierstein 1954– : *Torch
Song Trilogy* (1979)

20 The opposite of talking isn't
listening. The opposite of talking
is waiting.
Fran Lebowitz 1946– : *Social
Studies* (1981)

Cooking and Eating
see also **Food and Drink, Greed**

1 You won't be surprised that
diseases are innumerable—count
the cooks.
Seneca ("the Younger") *c.* 4 BC–AD
65: *Epistles*

2 Now good digestion wait on
appetite,
And health on both!
William Shakespeare 1564–1616:
Macbeth (1606)

3 A good, honest, wholesome,
hungry breakfast.
Izaak Walton 1593–1683: *The
Compleat Angler* (1653)

4 Strange to see how a good dinner
and feasting reconciles everybody.
Samuel Pepys 1633–1703: diary 9
November 1665

5 I look upon it, that he who does
not mind his belly will hardly
mind anything else.
Samuel Johnson 1709–84: James
Boswell *Life of Samuel Johnson*
(1791) 5 August 1763

6 If ever I ate a good supper at
night,
I dreamed of the devil, and waked
in a fright.
Christopher Anstey 1724–1805: *The
New Bath Guide* (1766)

7 For my part now, I consider
supper as a turnpike through
which one must pass, in order to
get to bed.
Oliver Edwards 1711–91: James
Boswell *Life of Samuel Johnson*
(1791) 17 April 1778

8 Some have meat and cannot eat,
Some cannot eat that want it:
But we have meat and we can
eat,
Sae let the Lord be thankit.
Robert Burns 1759–96: "The

Kirkudbright Grace" (1790), also known as "The Selkirk Grace"

9 . . . That all-softening, overpowering knell,
The tocsin of the soul—the dinner bell.
Lord Byron 1788–1824: *Don Juan* (1819–24)

10 Tell me what you eat and I will tell you what you are.
Anthelme Brillat-Savarin 1755–1826: *Physiologie du Goût* (1825); cf. **25** below

11 Cooking is the most ancient of the arts, for Adam was born hungry.
Anthelme Brillat-Savarin 1755–1826: *Physiologie du Goût* (1825)

12 Anyone who tells a lie has not a pure heart, and cannot make a good soup.
Ludwig van Beethoven 1770–1827: Ludwig Nohl *Beethoven Depicted by his Contemporaries* (1880)

13 "It's very easy to talk," said Mrs. Mantalini. "Not so easy when one is eating a demnition egg," replied Mr. Mantalini; "for the yolk runs down the waistcoat, and yolk of egg does not match any waistcoat but a yellow waistcoat, demmit."
Charles Dickens 1812–70: *Nicholas Nickleby* (1839)

14 Home-made dishes that drive one from home.
Thomas Hood 1799–1845: *Miss Kilmansegg and her Precious Leg* (1841–3) "Her Misery"

15 I'll fill hup the chinks wi' cheese.
R. S. Surtees 1805–64: *Handley Cross* (1843)

16 Let onion atoms lurk within the bowl,
And, scarce-suspected, animate the whole.
Sydney Smith 1771–1845: Lady

Holland *Memoir* (1855) "Receipt for a Salad"

17 Kissing don't last: cookery do!
George Meredith 1828–1909: *The Ordeal of Richard Feverel* (1859)

18 They dined on mince, and slices of quince,
Which they ate with a runcible spoon.
Edward Lear 1812–88: "The Owl and the Pussy-Cat" (1871)

19 We each day dig our graves with our teeth.
Samuel Smiles 1812–1904: *Duty* (1880)

20 He sows hurry and reaps indigestion.
Robert Louis Stevenson 1850–94: *Virginibus Puerisque* (1881) "An Apology for Idlers"

21 The healthy stomach is nothing if not conservative. Few radicals have good digestions.
Samuel Butler 1835–1902: *Notebooks* (1912)

22 The cook was a good cook, as cooks go; and as good cooks go, she went.
Saki 1870–1916: *Reginald* (1904)

23 "Oh, my Friends, be warned by me,
That Breakfast, Dinner, Lunch, and Tea
Are all the Human Frame requires . . . "
With that, the Wretched Child expires.
Hilaire Belloc 1870–1953: *Cautionary Tales* (1907) "Henry King"

24 It is said that the effect of eating too much lettuce is "soporific."
Beatrix Potter 1866–1943: *The Tale of the Flopsy Bunnies* (1909)

25 It's a very odd thing—
As odd as can be—

That whatever Miss T eats
Turns into Miss T.
Walter de la Mare 1873–1956: "Miss
T" (1913); cf. **10** above

26 I discovered that dinners follow
the order of creation — fish first,
then entrées, then joints, lastly
the apple as dessert. The soup is
chaos.
Sylvia Townsend Warner 1893–1978:
diary 26 May 1929

27 Time for a little something.
A. A. Milne 1882–1956: *Winnie-the-
Pooh* (1926)

28 Be content to remember that
those who can make omelettes
properly can do nothing else.
Hilaire Belloc 1870–1953: *A
Conversation with a Cat* (1931)

29 The tragedy of English cooking is
that "plain" cooking cannot be
entrusted to "plain" cooks.
Countess Morphy fl. 1930–50:
English Recipes (1935)

30 Last night we went to a Chinese
dinner at six and a French dinner
at nine, and I can feel the sharks'
fins navigating unhappily in the
Burgundy.
Peter Fleming 1907–71: letter from
Yunnanfu, 20 March 1938

31 On the Continent people have
good food; in England people have
good table manners.
George Mikes 1912– : *How to be
an Alien* (1946)

32 Dinner at the Huntercombes'
possessed "only two dramatic
features—the wine was a farce
and the food a tragedy."
Anthony Powell 1905– : *The
Acceptance World* (1955)

33 Gluttony is an emotional escape,
a sign something is eating us.
Peter De Vries 1910– : *Comfort Me
With Apples* (1956)

34 I never see any home cooking.
All I get is fancy stuff.
Prince Philip, Duke of Edinburgh
1921– : in *Observer* (UK) 28
October 1962

Cooperation

1 The wolf also shall dwell with the
lamb, and the leopard shall lie
down with the kid; and the calf
and the young lion and the
fatling together; and a little child
shall lead them.
Bible: Isaiah; cf. **14** below

2 If a house be divided against
itself, that house cannot stand.
Bible: St. Mark

3 When bad men combine, the
good must associate; else they
will fall, one by one, an unpitied
sacrifice in a contemptible
struggle.
Edmund Burke 1729–97: *Thoughts
on the Cause of the Present
Discontents* (1770)

4 We must indeed all hang
together, or, most assuredly, we
shall all hang separately.
Benjamin Franklin 1706–90: at the
signing of the Declaration of
Independence, 4 July 1776; possibly
not original

5 Now who will stand on either
    hand,
And keep the bridge with me?
Lord Macaulay 1800–59: "Horatius"
(1842)

6 All for one, one for all.
motto of the Three Musketeers
Alexandre Dumas 1802–70: *Les Trois
Mousquetaires* (1844)

7 You may call it combination, you
may call it the accidental and
fortuitous concurrence of atoms.
*on a projected Palmerston–Disraeli
coalition*

Lord Palmerston 1784–1865: speech, House of Commons, 5 March 1857

8 Government and co-operation are in all things the laws of life; anarchy and competition the laws of death.
John Ruskin 1819–1900: *Unto this Last* (1862)

9 His blade struck the water a full second before any other: the lad had started well. Nor did he flag as the race wore on . . . as the boats began to near the winning-post, his oar was dipping into the water nearly twice as often as any other.
often quoted as "All rowed fast, but none so fast as stroke"
Desmond Coke 1879–1931: *Sandford of Merton* (1903)

10 My apple trees will never get across
And eat the cones under his pines, I tell him.
He only says, "Good fences make good neighbors."
Robert Frost 1874–1963: "Mending Wall" (1914)

11 To my daughter Leonora without whose never-failing sympathy and encouragement this book would have been finished in half the time.
P. G. Wodehouse 1881–1975: *The Heart of a Goof* (1926) dedication

12 Why don't you do something to *help* me?
Stan Laurel 1890–1965: *Drivers' Licence Sketch* (1947 film); words spoken by Oliver Hardy

13 We must learn to live together as brothers or perish together as fools.
Martin Luther King, Jr. 1929–68: speech at St. Louis, 22 March 1964

14 The lion and the calf shall lie down together but the calf won't get much sleep.

Woody Allen 1935– : in *New Republic* 31 August 1974; see **1** above

Corruption
see **Bribery and Corruption**

Countries and Peoples
see also **America, Australia and New Zealand, Canada, England, France, International Relations, Russia, Towns and Cities**

1 *Civis Romanus sum.*
I am a Roman citizen.
Cicero 106–43 BC: *In Verrem*

2 *Semper aliquid novi Africam adferre.*
Africa always brings [us] something new.
often quoted as "Ex Africa semper aliquid novi [Always something new out of Africa]"
Pliny the Elder AD 23–79: *Historia Naturalis*

3 The Netherlands have been for many years, as one may say, the very cockpit of Christendom.
James Howell *c.* 1594–1666: *Instructions for Foreign Travel* (1642)

4 England is a paradise for women, and hell for horses: Italy a paradise for horses, hell for women, as the diverb goes.
Robert Burton 1577–1640: *The Anatomy of Melancholy* (1621–51)

5 This agglomeration which was called and which still calls itself the Holy Roman Empire was neither holy, nor Roman, nor an empire.
Voltaire 1694–1778: *Essai sur l'histoire générale et sur les moeurs et l'esprit des nations* (1756)

6 We are . . . a nation of dancers, singers and poets.
of the Ibo people

Olaudah Equiano c. 1745–c. 1797:
*Narrative of the Life of Olaudah
Equiano* (1789)

7 She has made me in love with a
cold climate, and frost and snow,
with a northern moonlight.
*on Mary Wollstonecraft's letters from
Sweden and Norway*
Robert Southey 1774–1843: letter to
his brother Thomas, 28 April 1797

8 I look upon Switzerland as an
inferior sort of Scotland.
Sydney Smith 1771–1845: letter to
Lord Holland, 1815

9 The isles of Greece, the isles of
Greece!
Where burning Sappho loved and
sung,
Where grew the arts of war and
peace,
Where Delos rose, and Phoebus
sprung!
Eternal summer gilds them yet,
But all, except their sun, is set!
Lord Byron 1788–1824: *Don Juan*
(1819–24)

10 Holland . . . lies so low they're
only saved by being dammed.
Thomas Hood 1799–1845: *Up the
Rhine* (1840)

11 A quiet, pilfering, unprotected
race.
John Clare 1793–1864: "The Gipsy
Camp" (1841)

12 Some people . . . may be
Rooshans, and others may be
Prooshans; they are born so, and
will please themselves. Them
which is of other naturs thinks
different.
Charles Dickens 1812–70: *Martin
Chuzzlewit* (1844)

13 Lump the whole thing! say that
the Creator made Italy from
designs by Michael Angelo!
Mark Twain 1835–1910: *The
Innocents Abroad* (1869)

14 Except the blind forces of Nature,
nothing moves in this world
which is not Greek in its origin.
Henry Maine 1822–88: *Village
Communities* (3rd ed., 1876)

15 I'm Charley's aunt from Brazil—
where the nuts come from.
Brandon Thomas 1856–1914:
Charley's Aunt (1892)

16 The traveller who has gone to
Italy to study the tactile values of
Giotto, or the corruption of the
Papacy, may return remembering
nothing but the blue sky and the
men and women under it.
E. M. Forster 1879–1970: *Room with
a View* (1908)

17 The people of Crete unfortunately
make more history than they can
consume locally.
Saki 1870–1916: *Chronicles of Clovis*
(1911)

18 He is crazed with the spell of far
Arabia,
They have stolen his wits away.
Walter de la Mare 1873–1956:
"Arabia" (1912)

19 Poor Mexico, so far from God and
so close to the United States.
Porfirio Diaz 1830–1915: attributed

20 What cleanliness everywhere!
You dare not throw your
cigarette into the lake. No graffiti
in the urinals. Switzerland is
proud of this; but I believe this is
just what she lacks: manure.
André Gide 1869–1951: diary,
Lucerne, 10 August 1917

21 Nothing in India is identifiable,
the mere asking of a question
causes it to disappear or to merge
in something else.
E. M. Forster 1879–1970: *A Passage
to India* (1924)

22 I don't like Norwegians at all.
The sun never sets, the bar never

opens, and the whole country smells of kippers.
Evelyn Waugh 1903–66: letter to Lady Diana Cooper, 13 July 1934

23 A country is a piece of land surrounded on all sides by boundaries, usually unnatural.
Joseph Heller 1923– : *Catch-22* (1961)

24 There are very few Eskimos, but millions of Whites, just like mosquitoes. It is something very special and wonderful to be an Eskimo—they are like the snow geese. If an Eskimo forgets his language and Eskimo ways, he will be nothing but just another mosquito.
Abraham Okpik: attributed

25 America is a land whose center is nowhere; England one whose center is everywhere.
John Updike 1932– : *Picked Up Pieces* (1976) "London Life" (written 1969)

26 Whereas in England all is permitted that is not expressly prohibited, it has been said that in Germany all is prohibited unless expressly permitted and in France all is permitted that is expressly prohibited. In the European Common Market (as it then was) no-one knows what is permitted and it all costs more.
Robert Megarry 1910– : "Law and Lawyers in a Permissive Society" (5th Riddell Lecture delivered in Lincoln's Inn Hall 22 March 1972)

27 It's where they commit suicide and the king rides a bicycle, Sweden.
Alan Bennett 1934– : *Enjoy* (1980)

28 Westerners have aggressive problem-solving minds; Africans experience people.
Kenneth Kaunda 1924– : attributed, 1990

The Country and the Town

1 O farmers excessively fortunate if only they recognized their blessings!
Virgil 70–19 BC: *Georgics*

2 What is the city but the people?
William Shakespeare 1564–1616: *Coriolanus* (1608)

3 As one who long in populous city pent,
Where houses thick and sewers annoy the air,
Forth issuing on a summer's morn to breathe
Among the pleasant villages and farms
Adjoined, from each thing met conceives delight.
John Milton 1608–74: *Paradise Lost* (1667)

4 God the first garden made, and the first city Cain.
Abraham Cowley 1618–67: "The Garden" (1668); cf. 5 below

5 God made the country, and man made the town.
William Cowper 1731–1800: *The Task* (1785) bk. 1 "The Sofa" cf. 4 above

6 Nothing can be said in his vindication, but that his abolishing Religious Houses and leaving them to the ruinous depredations of time has been of infinite use to the landscape of England in general.
of Henry VIII
Jane Austen 1775–1817: *The History of England* (written 1791)

7 'Tis distance lends enchantment to the view,
And robes the mountain in its azure hue.
Thomas Campbell 1777–1844: *Pleasures of Hope* (1799)

8 We do not look in great cities for our best morality.

Jane Austen 1775–1817: *Mansfield Park* (1814)

9 There is nothing good to be had in the country, or if there is, they will not let you have it.
William Hazlitt 1778–1830: *The Round Table* (1817) "Observations on Mr. Wordsworth's Poem *The Excursion*"

10 If you would be known, and not know, vegetate in a village; if you would be known, and not be known, live in a city.
Charles Caleb Colton c. 1780–1832: *Lacon* (1820)

11 But a house is much more to my mind than a tree,
And for groves, O! a good grove of chimneys for me.
Charles Morris 1745–1838: "Country and Town" (1840)

12 I have no relish for the country; it is a kind of healthy grave.
Sydney Smith 1771–1845: letter to Miss G. Harcourt, 1838

13 We plough the fields, and scatter
The good seed on the land,
But it is fed and watered
By God's almighty hand.
Jane Montgomery Campbell 1817–78: "We plough the fields, and scatter" (1861 hymn)

14 Anybody can be good in the country.
Oscar Wilde 1854–1900: *The Picture of Dorian Gray* (1891)

15 It is my belief, Watson, founded upon my experience, that the lowest and vilest alleys in London do not present a more dreadful record of sin than does the smiling and beautiful countryside.
Arthur Conan Doyle 1859–1930: *The Adventures of Sherlock Holmes* (1892) "The Copper Beeches"

16 Sylvia . . . was accustomed to nothing much more sylvan than "leafy Kensington." She looked on the country as something excellent and wholesome in its way, which was apt to become troublesome if you encouraged it overmuch.
Saki 1870–1916: *The Chronicles of Clovis* (1911)

17 The Farmer will never be happy again;
He carries his heart in his boots;
For either the rain is destroying his grain
Or the drought is destroying his roots.
A. P. Herbert 1890–1971: "The Farmer" (1922)

18 So *that's* what hay looks like.
said at Badminton House, where she was evacuated during World War II
Queen Mary 1867–1953: James Pope-Hennessy *Life of Queen Mary* (1959)

19 Slums may well be breeding-grounds of crime, but middle-class suburbs are incubators of apathy and delirium.
Cyril Connolly 1903–74: *The Unquiet Grave* (1944)

20 A farm is an irregular patch of nettles bounded by short-term notes, containing a fool and his wife who didn't know enough to stay in the city.
S. J. Perelman 1904–79: *The Most of S. J. Perelman* (1959) "Acres and Pains"

21 The city is not a concrete jungle, it is a human zoo.
Desmond Morris 1928– : *The Human Zoo* (1969)

22 "You are a pretty urban sort of person though, wouldn't you say?"
"Only nor'nor'east," I said. "I know a fox from a fax-machine."
Stephen Fry 1957– : *The Hippopotamus* (1994); cf. **Madness 3**

Courage

see also **Fear**

1 The wicked flee when no man pursueth: but the righteous are bold as a lion.
Bible: Proverbs

2 Cowards die many times before their deaths;
The valiant never taste of death but once.
William Shakespeare 1564–1616: *Julius Caesar* (1599)

3 Boldness be my friend!
Arm me, audacity.
William Shakespeare 1564–1616: *Cymbeline* (1609–10)

4 He either fears his fate too much,
Or his deserts are small,
That puts it not unto the touch
To win or lose it all.
James Graham, Marquess of Montrose 1612–50: "My Dear and Only Love" (written *c.* 1642)

5 For all men would be cowards if they durst.
John Wilmot, Lord Rochester 1647–80: "A Satire against Mankind" (1679)

6 None but the brave deserves the fair.
John Dryden 1631–1700: *Alexander's Feast* (1697)

7 Tender-handed stroke a nettle,
And it stings you for your pains;
Grasp it like a man of mettle,
And it soft as silk remains.
Aaron Hill 1685–1750: "Verses Written on a Window in Scotland"
cf. **Danger 2**

8 Perhaps those, who, trembling most, maintain a dignity in their fate, are the bravest: resolution on reflection is real courage.
Horace Walpole 1717–97: *Memoirs of the Reign of King George II* (1757)

9 My valour is certainly going!—it is sneaking off!—I feel it oozing out as it were at the palms of my hands!
Richard Brinsley Sheridan 1751–1816: *The Rivals* (1775)

10 The fate of unborn millions will now depend, under God, on the courage and conduct of this army . . . We have, therefore, resolved to conquer or die.
George Washington 1732–99: *Address to the Continental Army before the battle of Long Island* (27 August 1776)

11 It is thus that mutual cowardice keeps us in peace. Were one half of mankind brave and one half cowards, the brave would be always beating the cowards. Were all brave, they would lead a very uneasy life; all would be continually fighting: but being all cowards, we go on very well.
Samuel Johnson 1709–84: James Boswell *Life of Samuel Johnson* (1791) 28 April 1778

12 Boldness, and again boldness, and always boldness!
Georges Jacques Danton 1759–94: speech to the Legislative Committee of General Defence, 2 September 1792

13 As to moral courage, I have very rarely met with two o'clock in the morning courage: I mean instantaneous courage.
Napoleon I 1769–1821: E. A. de Las Cases *Mémorial de Ste-Hélène* (1823) 4–5 December 1815

14 Was none who would be foremost
To lead such dire attack;
But those behind cried "Forward!"
And those before cried "Back!"
Lord Macaulay 1800–59: "Horatius" (1842)

15 No coward soul is mine,
No trembler in the world's storm-
    troubled sphere:
I see Heaven's glories shine,
And faith shines equal, arming
    me from fear.
Emily Brontë 1818–48: "No coward
soul is mine" (1846)

16 In the fell clutch of circumstance,
I have not winced nor cried aloud:

Under the bludgeonings of chance
My head is bloody, but unbowed.
W. E. Henley 1849–1903: "Invictus.
In Memoriam R.T.H.B." (1888)

17 At times he regarded the
wounded soldiers in an envious
way. He conceived persons with
torn bodies to be peculiarly
happy. He wished that he, too,
had a wound, a red badge of
courage.
Stephen Crane 1871–1900: *The Red
Badge of Courage* (1895)

18 As an old soldier I admit the
cowardice: it's as universal as sea
sickness, and matters just as little.
George Bernard Shaw 1856–1950:
Man and Superman (1903)

19 Had we lived, I should have had
a tale to tell of the hardihood,
endurance, and courage of my
companions which would have
stirred the heart of every
Englishman. These rough notes
and our dead bodies must tell the
tale.
Robert Falcon Scott 1868–1912:
"Message to the Public" in late
editions of *The Times* (UK) 11
February 1913

20 Courage is the thing. All goes if
courage goes!
J. M. Barrie 1860–1937: Rectorial
Address at St. Andrews, 3 May 1922

21 Grace under pressure.
*when asked what he meant by
"guts," in an interview with Dorothy
Parker*
Ernest Hemingway 1899–1961: in
New Yorker 30 November 1929

22 Cowardice, as distinguished from
panic, is almost always simply a
lack of ability to suspend the
functioning of the imagination.
Ernest Hemingway 1899–1961: *Men
at War* (1942)

23 Courage is not simply *one* of the
virtues but the form of every
virtue at the testing point.
C. S. Lewis 1898–1963: Cyril
Connolly *The Unquiet Grave* (1944)

Courtship
see also **Love**

1 She is a woman, therefore may be
wooed;
She is a woman, therefore may be
won.
William Shakespeare 1564–1616:
Titus Andronicus (1590)

2 Why so pale and wan, fond lover?
Prithee, why so pale?
Will, when looking well can't
move her,
Looking ill prevail?
Prithee, why so pale?
John Suckling 1609–42: *Aglaura*
(1637)

3 Had we but world enough, and
time,
This coyness, lady, were no
crime.
Andrew Marvell 1621–78: "To His
coy Mistress" (1681)

4 Courtship to marriage, as a very
witty prologue to a very dull play.
William Congreve 1670–1729: *The
Old Bachelor* (1693)

5 I court others in verse: but I love
thee in prose:

And they have my whimsies, but
thou hast my heart.
Matthew Prior 1664–1721: "A Better
Answer" (1718)

6 My only books
Were woman's looks,
And folly's all they've taught me.
Thomas Moore 1779–1852: "The
time I've lost in wooing" (1807)

7 For talk six times with the same
single lady,
And you may get the wedding
dresses ready.
Lord Byron 1788–1824: *Don Juan*
(1819–24)

8 She knew how to allure by
denying, and to make the gift
rich by delaying it.
Anthony Trollope 1815–82: *Phineas
Finn* (1869)

9 You think that you are Ann's
suitor; that you are the pursuer
and she the pursued . . . Fool: it is
you who are the pursued, the
marked down quarry, the
destined prey.
George Bernard Shaw 1856–1950:
Man and Superman (1903)

10 Wooing, so tiring.
Nancy Mitford 1904–73: *The Pursuit
of Love* (1945)

11 Woe betide the man who dares to
pay a woman a compliment today
. . . Forget the flowers, the
chocolates, the soft word—rather
woo her with a self-defence
manual in one hand and a family
planning leaflet in the other.
Alan Ayckbourn 1939– : *Round and
Round the Garden* (1975)

12 Dating is a social engagement
with the threat of sex at its
conclusion.
P. J. O'Rourke 1947– : *Modern
Manners* (1984)

Creativity

1 Nothing can be created out of
nothing.
Lucretius c. 94–55 BC: *De Rerum
Natura*

2 All things were made by him;
and without him was not any
thing made that was made.
Bible: St. John

3 For the sake of a few fine
imaginative or domestic passages,
are we to be bullied into a certain
philosophy engendered in the
whims of an egotist?
*on the overbearing influence of
Wordsworth upon his
contemporaries*
John Keats 1795–1821: letter to J. H.
Reynolds, 3 February 1818

4 The urge for destruction is also a
creative urge!
Michael Bakunin 1814–76: *Jahrbuch
für Wissenschaft und Kunst* (1842)
"Die Reaktion in Deutschland"
(under the pseudonym "Jules
Elysard")

5 Urge and urge and urge,
Always the procreant urge of the
world.
Walt Whitman 1819–92: "Song of
Myself" (written 1855)

6 Could Hamlet be written by a
committee, or the Mona Lisa
painted by a club? Could the New
Testament have been composed
as a conference report? Creative
ideas do not spring from groups.
They spring from individuals. The
divine spark leaps from the finger
of God to the finger of Adam,
whether it takes ultimate shape in
a law of physics or a law of the
land, a poem, or a policy, a
sonata or a mechanical computer.
A. Whitney Griswold 1906–63:
*Baccalaureate address, Yale
University* (9 June 1957)

7 If the devil doesn't exist, but man
has created him, he has created
him in his own image and
likeness.
Fyodor Dostoevsky 1821–81: *The
Brothers Karamazov* (1879–80)

8 Birds build—but not I build; no,
but strain,
Time's eunuch, and not breed one
work that wakes.
Mine, O thou lord of life, send my
roots rain.
Gerard Manley Hopkins 1844–89:
"Thou art indeed just, Lord" (written
1889)

9 Poems are made by fools like me,
But only God can make a tree.
Joyce Kilmer 1886–1918: "Trees"
(1914)

10 An artist has no need to express
his thought directly in his work
for the latter to reflect its quality;
it has even been said that the
highest praise of God consists in
the denial of Him by the atheist
who finds creation so perfect that
it can dispense with a creator.
Marcel Proust 1871–1922:
Guermantes Way (1921)

11 Like a piece of ice on a hot stove
the poem must ride on its own
melting. A poem may be worked
over once it is in being, but may
not be worried into being.
Robert Frost 1874–1963: *Collected
Poems* (1939) "The Figure a Poem
Makes"

12 Think before you speak is
criticism's motto; speak before
you think creation's.
E. M. Forster 1879–1970: *Two Cheers
for Democracy* (1951)

13 All men are creative but few are
artists.
Paul Goodman 1911–72: *Growing up
Absurd* (1961)

14 There is, perhaps, no more
dangerous man in the world than

the man with the sensibilities of
an artist but without creative
talent. With luck such men make
wonderful theatrical impresarios
and interior decorators, or else
they become mass murderers or
critics.
Barry Humphries 1934– : *More
Please* (1992)

Crime and Punishment
see also **Guilt and Innocence, Justice,
The Law and Lawyers, Murder**

1 I the Lord thy God am a jealous
God, visiting the iniquity of the
fathers upon the children unto
the third and fourth generation of
them that hate me.
*often alluded to in the form "the
sins of the fathers"*
Bible: Exodus

2 He that spareth his rod hateth his
son.
Bible: Proverbs

3 My father hath chastised you
with whips, but I will chastise
you with scorpions.
Bible: I Kings

4 This is the first of punishments,
that no guilty man is acquitted if
judged by himself.
Juvenal AD *c.* 60–*c.* 130: *Satires*

5 Opportunity makes a thief.
Francis Bacon 1561–1626: "A Letter
of Advice to the Earl of Essex . . . "
(1598)

6 'Tis a sharp remedy, but a sure
one for all ills.
*on feeling the edge of the axe prior
to his execution*
Walter Ralegh *c.* 1552–1618: D.
Hume *History of Great Britain* (1754)

7 Severity breedeth fear, but
roughness breedeth hate. Even

reproofs from authority ought to be grave, and not taunting.
Francis Bacon 1561–1626: *Essays* (1625) "Of Great Place"

8 I went out to Charing Cross, to see Major-general Harrison hanged, drawn, and quartered; which was done there, he looking as cheerful as any man could do in that condition.
Samuel Pepys 1633–1703: diary 13 October 1660

9 Hanging is too good for him, said Mr. Cruelty.
John Bunyan 1628–88: *The Pilgrim's Progress* (1678)

10 Men are not hanged for stealing horses, but that horses may not be stolen.
Lord Halifax 1633–95: *Political, Moral, and Miscellaneous Thoughts and Reflections* (1750) "Of Punishment"

11 He found it inconvenient to be poor.
of a burglar
William Cowper 1731–1800: "Charity" (1782)

12 All punishment is mischief: all punishment in itself is evil.
Jeremy Bentham 1748–1832: *Principles of Morals and Legislation* (1789)

13 Lay then the axe to the root, and teach governments humanity. It is their sanguinary punishments which corrupt mankind.
Thomas Paine 1737–1809: *The Rights of Man* (1791)

14 Whenever the offence inspires less horror than the punishment, the rigour of penal law is obliged to give way to the common feelings of mankind.
Edward Gibbon 1737–94: attributed

15 As for rioting, the old Roman way of dealing with that is always the right one; flog the rank and file, and fling the ringleaders from the Tarpeian rock.
Thomas Arnold 1795–1842: letter written before 1828, quoted by Matthew Arnold in *Cornhill Magazine* August 1868

16 Prisoner, God has given you good abilities, instead of which you go about the country stealing ducks.
William Arabin 1773–1841: Frederick Pollock *Essays in the Law* (1922); sometimes attributed to a Revd. Mr. Alderson

17 A clever theft was praiseworthy amongst the Spartans; and it is equally so amongst Christians, provided it be on a sufficiently large scale.
Herbert Spencer 1820–1903: *Social Statics* (1850)

18 The best of us being unfit to die, what an inexpressible absurdity to put the worst to death!
Nathaniel Hawthorne 1804–64: diary 13 October 1851

19 Better build schoolrooms for "the boy,"
Than cells and gibbets for "the man."
Eliza Cook 1818–89: "A Song for the Ragged Schools" (1853)

20 Thou shalt not steal; an empty feat,
When it's so lucrative to cheat.
Arthur Hugh Clough 1819–61: "The Latest Decalogue" (1862)

21 To crush, to annihilate a man utterly, to inflict on him the most terrible punishment so that the most ferocious murderer would shudder at it beforehand, one need only give him work of an

absolutely, completely useless and irrational character.
Fyodor Dostoevsky 1821–81: *House of the Dead* (1862)

22 My object all sublime
I shall achieve in time—
To let the punishment fit the crime—
The punishment fit the crime.
W. S. Gilbert 1836–1911: *The Mikado* (1885)

23 Between the possibility of being hanged in all innocence, and the certainty of a public and merited disgrace, no gentleman of spirit could long hesitate.
Robert Louis Stevenson 1850–94: *The Wrong Box* (with Lloyd Osbourne, 1889)

24 Singularity is almost invariably a clue. The more featureless and commonplace a crime is, the more difficult is it to bring it home.
Arthur Conan Doyle 1859–1930: *The Adventures of Sherlock Holmes* (1892) "The Boscombe Valley Mystery"

25 Ex-Professor Moriarty of mathematical celebrity . . . is the Napoleon of crime, Watson.
Arthur Conan Doyle 1859–1930: *The Memoirs of Sherlock Holmes* (1894) "The Final Problem"

26 Thieves respect property. They merely wish the property to become their property that they may more perfectly respect it.
G. K. Chesterton 1874–1936: *The Man who was Thursday* (1908)

27 For de little stealin' dey gits you in jail soon or late. For de big stealin' dey makes you Emperor and puts you in de Hall o' Fame when you croaks.
Eugene O'Neill 1888–1953: *The Emperor Jones* (1921)

28 Any one who has been to an English public school will always feel comparatively at home in prison. It is the people brought up in the gay intimacy of the slums, Paul learned, who find prison so soul-destroying.
Evelyn Waugh 1903–66: *Decline and Fall* (1928)

29 Once in the racket you're always in it.
Al Capone 1899–1947: in *Philadelphia Public Ledger* 18 May 1929

30 *reply to a prison visitor who asked if he were sewing:*
No, reaping.
Horatio Bottomley 1860–1933: S. T. Felstead *Horatio Bottomley* (1936)

31 Major Strasser has been shot. Round up the usual suspects.
Julius J. Epstein 1909– et al.: *Casablanca* (1942 film)

32 Crime isn't a disease, it's a symptom. Cops are like a doctor that gives you aspirin for a brain tumor.
Raymond Chandler 1888–1959: *The Long Good-Bye* (1953)

33 I hate victims who respect their executioners.
Jean-Paul Sartre 1905–80: *Les Séquestrés d'Altona* (1960)

34 The thoughts of a prisoner— they're not free either. They keep returning to the same things.
Alexander Solzhenitsyn 1918– : *One Day in the Life of Ivan Denisovich* (1962)

35 I'm all for bringing back the birch, but only between consenting adults.
Gore Vidal 1925– : in *Sunday Times Magazine* (UK) 16 September 1973

36 Even the most hardened criminal a few years ago would help an

old lady across the road and give
her a few quid if she was skint.
Charlie Kray c. 1930– : in *Observer*
28 December 1986

37 Society needs to condemn a little
more and understand a little less.
John Major 1943– : interview with
Mail on Sunday 21 February 1993

38 Labour is the party of law and
order in Britain today. Tough on
crime and tough on the causes of
crime.
as Shadow Home Secretary
Tony Blair 1953– : speech at the
Labour Party Conference, 30
September 1993

Crises

1 The die is cast.
*at the crossing of the Rubicon often
quoted in Latin "Iacta alea est" but
originally spoken in Greek*
Julius Caesar 100–44 BC: Suetonius
Lives of the Caesars "Divus Julius";
Plutarch *Parallel Lives* "Pompey"

2 For it is your business, when the
wall next door catches fire.
Horace 65–8 BC: *Epistles*

3 An event has happened, upon
which it is difficult to speak, and
impossible to be silent.
Edmund Burke 1729–97: speech at
the trial of Warren Hastings, 5 May
1789

4 The illustrious bishop of Cambrai
was of more worth than his
chambermaid, and there are few
of us that would hesitate to
pronounce, if his palace were in
flames, and the life of only one of
them could be preserved, which
of the two ought to be preferred.
William Godwin 1756–1836: *An
Enquiry concerning the Principles of
Political Justice* (1793)

5 Whatever might be the extent of
the individual calamity, I do not

consider it of a nature worthy to
interrupt the proceedings on so
great a national question.
*on hearing that his theater was on
fire, during a debate on the
campaign in Spain*
Richard Brinsley Sheridan 1751–1816:
speech, House of Commons 24
February 1809

6 We have the wolf by the ears;
and we can neither hold him, nor
safely let him go. Justice is in one
scale, and self-preservation in the
other.
on slavery
Thomas Jefferson 1743–1826: letter
to John Holmes, 22 April 1820

7 Swimming for his life, a man does
not see much of the country
through which the river winds.
W. E. Gladstone 1809–98: diary, 31
December 1868

8 If you can keep your head when
all about you
Are losing theirs and blaming it
on you . . .
Rudyard Kipling 1865–1936: "If—"
(1910); cf. **12** below

9 The British people have taken for
themselves this motto—"Business
carried on as usual during
alterations on the map of Europe."
Winston Churchill 1874–1965: speech
at Guildhall, 9 November 1914

10 I felt as if I was walking with
destiny, and that all my past life
had been but a preparation for
this hour and this trial.
on becoming Prime Minister
Winston Churchill 1874–1965: on 10
May 1940

11 Comin' in on a wing and a
pray'r.
*the contemporary comment of a war
pilot, speaking from a disabled
plane to ground control*
Harold Adamson 1906–80: title of
song (1943)

12 As someone pointed out recently,
if you can keep your head when
all about you are losing theirs, it's
just possible you haven't grasped
the situation.
Jean Kerr 1923– : *Please Don't Eat
the Daisies* (1957); see **8** above

13 I myself have always deprecated
. . . in crisis after crisis, appeals to
the Dunkirk spirit as an answer
to our problems.
Harold Wilson 1916–95: in the House
of Commons, 26 July 1961

14 We're eyeball to eyeball, and I
think the other fellow just
blinked.
on the Cuban missile crisis
Dean Rusk 1909– : comment, 24
October 1962

15 In bygone days, commanders
were taught that when in doubt,
they should march their troops
towards the sound of gunfire. I
intend to march my troops
towards the sound of gunfire.
Jo Grimond 1913– : speech at
Liberal Party Annual Assembly, 14
September 1963

16 There cannot be a crisis next
week. My schedule is already full.
Henry Kissinger 1923– : in *New
York Times Magazine* 1 June 1969

17 I'm at my best in a messy, middle-
of-the-road muddle.
Harold Wilson 1916–95: remark in
Cabinet, 21 January 1975; Philip
Ziegler *Wilson* (1993)

18 Crisis? What Crisis?
*headline summarizing James
Callaghan's remark of 10 January
1979: "I don't think other people in
the world would share the view
there is mounting chaos"*
Anonymous: in *Sun* (UK) 11 January
1979

19 We do not experience and thus
we have no measure of the
disasters we prevent.

John Kenneth Galbraith 1908– : *A
Life in our Times* (1981)

20 It is exciting to have a real crisis
on your hands, when you have
spent half your political life
dealing with humdrum issues like
the environment.
on the Falklands campaign, 1982
Margaret Thatcher 1925– : speech
to Scottish Conservative Party
conference, 14 May 1982; Hugo
Young *One of Us* (1990)

21 All I can do is look at where I
keep my suitcases and feel like
packing them and disappearing
from here very quickly.
*as the Israeli polls showed that the
right wing was likely to defeat
Yizhak Rabin's successor Shimon
Peres*
Leah Rabin : in a television
interview, 30 May 1996

Critics and Criticism
see also **Likes and Dislikes, Taste**

1 Critics are like brushers of
noblemen's clothes.
Henry Wotton 1568–1639: Francis
Bacon *Apophthegms New and Old*
(1625)

2 One should look long and
carefully at oneself before one
considers judging others.
Molière 1622–73: *Le Misanthrope*
(1666)

3 You who scribble, yet hate all
who write . . .
And with faint praises one
another damn.
of theater critics
William Wycherley c. 1640–1716: *The
Plain Dealer* (1677)

4 How science dwindles, and how
volumes swell,
How commentators each dark
passage shun,

And hold their farthing candle to
the sun.
Edward Young 1683–1765: *The Love
of Fame* (1725–8)

5 Yet malice never was his aim;
He lashed the vice, but spared the
name;
No individual could resent,
Where thousands equally were
meant.
Jonathan Swift 1667–1745: "Verses
on the Death of Dr. Swift" (1731)

6 You *may* abuse a tragedy, though
you cannot write one. You may
scold a carpenter who has made
you a bad table, though you
cannot make a table. It is not
your trade to make tables.
on literary criticism
Samuel Johnson 1709–84: James
Boswell *Life of Samuel Johnson*
(1791) 25 June 1763

7 I have always suspected that the
reading is right, which requires
many words to prove it wrong;
and the emendation wrong, that
cannot without so much labour
appear to be right.
Samuel Johnson 1709–84: *Plays of
William Shakespeare . . .* (1765)

8 Of all the cants which are canted
in this canting world,—though
the cant of hypocrites may be the
worst,—the cant of criticism is
the most tormenting!
Laurence Sterne 1713–68: *Tristram
Shandy* (1759–67)

9 If it is abuse,—why one is always
sure to hear of it from one
damned goodnatured friend or
another!
Richard Brinsley Sheridan 1751–1816:
The Critic (1779)

10 Oh! I could thresh his old jacket
till I made his pension jingle in
his pockets.

*on Johnson's inadequate treatment
of* Paradise Lost
William Cowper 1731–1800: letter to
the Revd. William Unwin, 31 October
1779

11 A man must serve his time to
every trade
Save censure—critics all are ready
made.
Lord Byron 1788–1824: *English Bards
and Scotch Reviewers* (1809)

12 This will never do.
on Wordsworth's The Excursion
(1814)
Francis, Lord Jeffrey 1773–1850: in
Edinburgh Review November 1814

13 'Tis strange the mind, that very
fiery particle,
Should let itself be snuffed out by
an article.
*on Keats "who was killed off by one
critique"*
Lord Byron 1788–1824: *Don Juan*
(1819–24)

14 He took the praise as a greedy
boy takes apple pie, and the
criticism as a good dutiful boy
takes senna-tea.
*of Bulwer-Lytton, whose novels he
had criticized*
Lord Macaulay 1800–59: letter 5
August 1831

15 He wreathed the rod of criticism
with roses.
of Pierre Bayle
Isaac D'Israeli 1766–1848: *Curiosities
of Literature* (9th ed., 1834)

16 I never read a book before
reviewing it; it prejudices a man
so.
Sydney Smith 1771–1845: H. Pearson
The Smith of Smiths (1934)

17 You know who the critics are?
The men who have failed in
literature and art.
Benjamin Disraeli 1804–81: *Lothair*
(1870)

18 The good critic is he who relates the adventures of his soul in the midst of masterpieces.
Anatole France 1844–1924: *La Vie littéraire* (1888)

19 We must grant the artist his subject, his idea, his *donnée*: our criticism is applied only to what he makes of it.
Henry James 1843–1916: *Partial Portraits* (1888) "Art of Fiction"

20 The lot of critics is to be remembered by what they failed to understand.
George Moore 1852–1933: *Impressions and Opinions* (1891) "Balzac"

21 I am sitting in the smallest room of my house. I have your review before me. In a moment it will be behind me.
responding to a savage review by Rudolph Louis in Münchener Neueste Nachrichten, *7 February 1906*
Max Reger 1873–1916: Nicolas Slonimsky *Lexicon of Musical Invective* (1953)

22 She was one of the people who say "I don't know anything about music really, but I know what I like."
Max Beerbohm 1872–1956: *Zuleika Dobson* (1911)

23 You don't expect me to know what to say about a play when I don't know who the author is, do you?
George Bernard Shaw 1856–1950: *Fanny's First Play* (1914)

24 People ask you for criticism, but they only want praise.
W. Somerset Maugham 1874–1965: *Of Human Bondage* (1915)

25 Never trust the artist. Trust the tale. The proper function of a critic is to save the tale from the artist who created it.
D. H. Lawrence 1885–1930: *Studies in Classic American Literature* (1923)

26 Parodies and caricatures are the most penetrating of criticisms.
Aldous Huxley 1894–1963: *Point Counter Point* (1928)

27 Literature is strewn with the wreckage of men who have minded beyond reason the opinions of others.
Virginia Woolf 1882–1941: *A Room of One's Own* (1929)

28 Remember, a statue has never been set up in honor of a critic!
Jean Sibelius 1865–1957: Bengt de Törne *Sibelius: A Close-Up* (1937)

29 Whom the gods wish to destroy they first call promising.
Cyril Connolly 1903–74: *Enemies of Promise* (1938)

30 When the reviews are bad I tell my staff that they can join me as I cry all the way to the bank.
Liberace 1919–87: *Autobiography* (1973); joke coined in the mid-1950s

31 As I grew older I realized that hurting people through criticism was a form of failure . . . One hurt them for things one hadn't done oneself.
Cyril Connolly 1903–74: interview on BBC radio, 9 November 1956; Clive Fisher *Cyril Connolly: a Nostalgic Life* (1995)

32 Long experience has taught me that to be criticized is not always to be wrong.
speech at Lord Mayor's Guildhall banquet during the Suez crisis
Anthony Eden 1897–1977: in *Daily Herald* 10 November 1956

33 A critic is a bundle of biases held loosely together by a sense of taste.
Whitney Balliett 1926– : *Dinosaurs in the Morning* (1962)

34 One cannot review a bad book
without showing off.
W. H. Auden 1907–73: *Dyer's Hand*
(1963) "Reading"

35 Interpretation is the revenge of
the intellect upon art.
Susan Sontag 1933–   : in *Evergreen
Review* December 1964

36 A critic is a man who knows the
way but can't drive the car.
Kenneth Tynan 1927–80: in *New
York Times Magazine* 9 January 1966

37 When I read something saying
I've not done anything as good as
Catch-22 I'm tempted to reply,
"Who has?"
Joseph Heller 1923–   : in *The Times*
(UK) 9 June 1993

38 [Roger Fry] gave us the term
"Post-Impressionist," without
realising that the late twentieth
century would soon be entirely
fenced in with posts.
Jeanette Winterson 1959–   : *Art
Objects* (1995)

Cruelty

1 Boys throw stones at frogs for
fun, but the frogs don't die for
"fun," but in sober earnest.
Bion *c.* 325–*c.* 255 BC: Plutarch
Moralia

2 Strike him so that he can feel
that he is dying.
Caligula AD 12–41: Suetonius *Lives of
the Caesars* "Gaius Caligula"

3 I must be cruel only to be kind.
William Shakespeare 1564–1616:
Hamlet (1601); cf. **10** below

4 Man's inhumanity to man
Makes countless thousands
mourn!
Robert Burns 1759–96: "Man was
Made to Mourn" (1786)

5 *There* were his young barbarians
all at play,
There was their Dacian mother—
he, their sire,
Butchered to make a Roman
holiday.
Lord Byron 1788–1824: *Childe
Harold's Pilgrimage* (1812–18)

6 Is not the pleasure of feeling and
exhibiting *power* over other
beings, a principal part of the
gratification of cruelty?
John Foster 1770–1843: *Journal* Item
772 in *Life and Correspondence*
(1846)

7 Cruelty, like every other vice,
requires no motive outside itself—
it only requires opportunity.
George Eliot 1819–1880: *Scenes from
a Clerical Life* (1858)

8 With many women I doubt
whether there be any more
effectual way of touching their
hearts than ill-using them and
then confessing it. If you wish to
get the sweetest fragrance from
the herb at your feet, tread on it
and bruise it.
Anthony Trollope 1815–82: *Miss
Mackenzie* (1865)

9 The infliction of cruelty with a
good conscience is a delight to
moralists. That is why they
invented Hell.
Bertrand Russell 1872–1970:
Sceptical Essays (1928) "On the
Value of Scepticism"

10 Being cruel to be kind is just
ordinary cruelty with an excuse
made for it ... And it is right that
it should be more resented, as it
is.
Ivy Compton-Burnett 1884–1969:
Daughters and Sons (1937); see **3**
above

11 The wish to hurt, the momentary
intoxication with pain, is the
loophole through which the

pervert climbs into the minds of ordinary men.
Jacob Bronowski 1908–74: *The Face of Violence* (1954)

12 Our language lacks words to express this offense, the demolition of a man.
of a year spent in Auschwitz
Primo Levi 1919–87: *If This is a Man* (1958)

Culture and Civilization

1 Our love of what is beautiful does not lead to extravagance; our love of the things of the mind does not make us soft.
funeral oration, Athens, 430 BC
Pericles c. 495–429 BC: Thucydides *History of the Peloponnesian War*

2 In the youth of a state arms do flourish; in the middle age of a state, learning; and then both of them together for a time; in the declining age of a state, mechanical arts and merchandise.
Francis Bacon 1561–1626: *Essays* (1625) "Of Vicissitude of Things"

3 I must study politics and war that my sons may have liberty to study mathematics and philosophy. My sons ought to study mathematics and philosophy, geography, natural history, naval architecture, navigation, commerce, and agriculture, in order to give their children a right to study painting, poetry, music, architecture, statuary, tapestry, and porcelain.
John Adams 1735–1826: *Letter to Abigail Adams* (12 May 1780)

4 If a nation expects to be ignorant and free, in a state of civilization, it expects what never was and never will be.
Thomas Jefferson 1743–1826: letter to Colonel Charles Yancey, 6 January 1816

5 The three great elements of modern civilization, Gunpowder, Printing, and the Protestant Religion.
Thomas Carlyle 1795–1881: *Critical and Miscellaneous Essays* (1838) "The State of German Literature" cf.
Inventions 4

6 Philistinism!—We have not the expression in English. Perhaps we have not the word because we have so much of the thing.
Matthew Arnold 1822–88: *Essays in Criticism* First Series (1865) "Heinrich Heine"

7 Civilized ages inherit the human nature which was victorious in barbarous ages, and that nature is, in many respects, not at all suited to civilized circumstances.
Walter Bagehot 1826–77: *Physics and Politics* (1872) "The Age of Discussion"

8 Jesus wept; Voltaire smiled. Of that divine tear and of that human smile the sweetness of present civilization is composed. (*Hearty applause.*)
Victor Hugo 1802–85: centenary oration on Voltaire, 30 May 1878

9 What are we waiting for, gathered in the market-place? The barbarians are to arrive today.
Constantine Cavafy 1863–1933: "Waiting for the Barbarians" (1904)

10 Civilization advances by extending the number of important operations which we can perform without thinking about them.
Alfred North Whitehead 1861–1947: *Introduction to Mathematics* (1911)

11 Mrs. Ballinger is one of the ladies who pursue Culture in bands, as though it were dangerous to meet it alone.
Edith Wharton 1862–1937: *Xingu and Other Stories* (1916)

12 All civilization has from time to
time become a thin crust over a
volcano of revolution.
Havelock Ellis 1859–1939: *Little
Essays of Love and Virtue* (1922)

13 The nations which have put
mankind and posterity most in
their debt have been small states—
Israel, Athens, Florence,
Elizabethan England.
William Ralph Inge 1860–1954:
Outspoken Essays: Second Series
(1922) "State, visible and invisible"

14 Cultured people are merely the
glittering scum which floats upon
the deep river of production.
*on hearing his son Randolph criticize
the lack of culture of the Calgary oil
magnates, probably c. 1929*
Winston Churchill 1874–1965: Martin
Gilbert *In Search of Churchill* (1994)

15 [A journalist] asked, "Mr. Gandhi,
what do you think of modern
civilization?" And Mr. Gandhi
said, "That would be a good
idea."
on arriving in England in 1930
Mahatma Gandhi 1869–1948: E. F.
Schumacher *Good Work* (1979)

16 Whenever I hear the word
culture . . . I release the safety-
catch of my Browning!
*often quoted: "Whenever I hear the
word culture, I reach for my pistol!"*
Hanns Johst 1890–1978: *Schlageter*
(1933); often attributed to Hermann
Goering; cf. **23**, **26** below

17 It is stupid of modern civilization
to have given up believing in the
devil, when he is the only
explanation of it.
Ronald Knox 1888–1957: *Let Dons
Delight* (1939)

18 Civilization is an active deposit
which is formed by the
combustion of the Present with
the Past.
Cyril Connolly 1903–74: *The Unquiet
Grave* (1944)

19 Culture may even be described
simply as that which makes life
worth living.
T. S. Eliot 1888–1965: *Notes Towards
a Definition of Culture* (1948)

20 In Italy for thirty years under the
Borgias they had warfare, terror,
murder, bloodshed —they
produced Michelangelo, Leonardo
da Vinci and the Renaissance. In
Switzerland they had brotherly
love, five hundred years of
democracy and peace and what
did that produce . . . ? The cuckoo
clock.
Orson Welles 1915–85: *The Third
Man* (1949 film); words added by
Welles to Graham Greene's script

21 Rousseau was the first militant
lowbrow.
Isaiah Berlin 1909–97: in *Observer*
(UK) 9 November 1952

22 The soul of any civilization on
earth has ever been and still is
Art and Religion, but neither has
ever been found in commerce, in
government or the police.
Frank Lloyd Wright 1867–1959: *A
Testament* (1957)

23 When politicians and civil
servants hear the word "culture"
they feel for their blue pencils.
Lord Esher 1913– : speech, House
of Lords, 2 March 1960; see **16**
above

24 "Sergeant Pepper"—a decisive
moment in the history of Western
Civilisation.
Kenneth Tynan 1927–80: in 1967;
Howard Elson *McCartney* (1986)

25 All my wife has ever taken from
the Mediterranean—from that
whole vast intuitive culture—are
four bottles of Chianti to make
into lamps.
Peter Shaffer 1926– : *Equus* (1973)

26 It is unlikely that the government reaches for a revolver when it hears the word culture. The more likely response is to search for a dictionary.
David Glencross 1936– : Royal Television Society conference on the future of television, 26-27 November 1988; see **16** above

Cursing and Swearing

1 Swear not at all: neither by heaven; for it is God's throne: Nor by the earth; for it is his footstool.
Bible: St. Matthew

2 You taught me language; and my profit on't
Is, I know how to curse: the red plague rid you,
For learning me your language!
William Shakespeare 1564–1616: *The Tempest* (1611)

3 "Our armies swore terribly in Flanders," cried my uncle Toby,— "but nothing to this."
Laurence Sterne 1713–68: *Tristram Shandy* (1759–67)

4 Though "Bother it" I may Occasionally say,
I never use a big, big D—
W. S. Gilbert 1836–1911: *HMS Pinafore* (1878)

5 A swear-word in a rustic slum A simple swear-word is to some, To Masefield something more.
Max Beerbohm 1872–1956: *Fifty Caricatures* (1912)

6 If ever I utter an oath again may my soul be blasted to eternal damnation!
George Bernard Shaw 1856–1950: *Saint Joan* (1924)

7 Orchestras only need to be sworn at, and a German is consequently at an advantage with them, as English profanity, except in America, has not gone beyond the limited terminology of perdition.
George Bernard Shaw 1856–1950: Harold Schonberg *The Great Conductors* (1967)

8 The man who first abused his fellows with swear-words instead of bashing their brains out with a club should be counted among those who laid the foundations of civilization.
John Cohen 1911– : in *Observer* (UK) 21 November 1965

9 Don't swear, boy. It shows a lack of vocabulary.
Alan Bennett 1934– : *Forty Years On* (1969)

10 Expletive deleted.
Anonymous: *Submission of Recorded Presidential Conversations to the Committee on the Judiciary of the House of Representatives by President Richard M. Nixon* 30 April 1974

Custom and Habit

1 *Consuetudo est altera natura.*
Habit is second nature.
Auctoritates Aristotelis: a compilation of medieval propositions

2 But to my mind,—though I am native here,
And to the manner born,—it is a custom
More honoured in the breach than the observance.
William Shakespeare 1564–1616: *Hamlet* (1601)

3 Custom that is before all law, Nature that is above all art.
Samuel Daniel 1563–1619: *A Defence of Rhyme* (1603)

4 Custom, that unwritten law,
By which the people keep even
kings in awe.
Charles D'Avenant 1656–1714: *Circe*
(1677)

5 Actions receive their tincture
from the times,
And as they change are virtues
made or crimes.
Daniel Defoe 1660–1731: *A Hymn to
the Pillory* (1703)

6 Custom reconciles us to
everything.
Edmund Burke 1729–97: *On the
Sublime and Beautiful* (1757)

7 The satirist may laugh, the
philosopher may preach, but
Reason herself will respect the
prejudices and habits which have
been consecrated by the
experience of mankind.
Edward Gibbon 1737–94: *Memoirs of
My Life* (1796)

8 Habit with him was all the test of
truth,
"It must be right: I've done it
from my youth."
George Crabbe 1754–1832: *The
Borough* (1810)

9 People wish to be settled: only as
far as they are unsettled is there
any hope for them.
Ralph Waldo Emerson 1803–82:
Essays (1841) "Circles"

10 The tradition of all the dead
generations weighs like a
nightmare on the brain of the
living.
Karl Marx 1818–83: *The Eighteenth
Brumaire of Louis Bonaparte* (1852)

11 Habit is stronger than reason.
George Santayana 1863–1952:
*Interpretations of Poetry and
Religion* (1900)

12 Tradition means giving votes to
the most obscure of all classes,

our ancestors. It is the democracy
of the dead.
G. K. Chesterton 1874–1936:
Orthodoxy (1908)

13 Every public action, which is not
customary, either is wrong, or, if
it is right, is a dangerous
precedent. It follows that nothing
should ever be done for the first
time.
Francis M. Cornford 1874–1943:
Microcosmographia Academica
(1908)

14 One can't carry one's father's
corpse about everywhere.
Guillaume Apollinaire 1880–1918: *Les
peintres cubistes* (1965) "Méditations
esthétiques: Sur la peinture"

15 Tradition is entirely different from
habit, even from an excellent
habit, since habit is by definition
an unconscious acquisition and
tends to become mechanical,
whereas tradition results from a
conscious and deliberate
acceptance . . . Tradition
presupposes the reality of what
endures.
Igor Stravinsky 1882–1971: *Poetics
of Music* (1947)

16 The air is full of our cries. (*He
listens*) But habit is a great
deadener.
Samuel Beckett 1906–89: *Waiting for
Godot* (1955)

Cynicism
see **Disillusion and Cynicism**

Dance

1 My men, like satyrs grazing on
the lawns,
Shall with their goat feet dance
an antic hay.
Christopher Marlowe 1564–93:
Edward II (1593)

2 This wondrous miracle did Love
    devise,
  For dancing is love's proper
    exercise.
  John Davies 1569–1626: "Orchestra,
  or a Poem of Dancing" (1596)

3 A dance is a measured pace, as a
  verse is a measured speech.
  Francis Bacon 1561–1626: *The
  Advancement of Learning* (1605)

4 Come, and trip it as ye go
  On the light fantastic toe.
  John Milton 1608–74: "L'Allegro"
  (1645)

5 On with the dance! let joy be
    unconfined:
  No sleep till morn, when Youth
    and Pleasure meet
  To chase the glowing Hours with
    flying feet.
  Lord Byron 1788–1824: *Childe
  Harold's Pilgrimage* (1812–18)

6 Will you, won't you, will you,
  won't you, will you join the
  dance?
  Lewis Carroll 1832–98: *Alice's
  Adventures in Wonderland* (1865)

7 I wish I could shimmy like my
    sister Kate,
  She shivers like the jelly on a
    plate.
  Armand J. Piron: *Shimmy like Kate*
  (1919 song)

8 Can't act. Slightly bald. Also
  dances.
  *studio official's comment on Fred
  Astaire*
  Anonymous: Bob Thomas *Astaire*
  (1985)

9 To learn to dance by practicing
  dancing or to live by practicing
  living, the principles are the same
  . . . One becomes, in some area,
  an athlete of God.
  Martha Graham 1894–1991: (15 May
  1945)

10 [Dancing is] a perpendicular
   expression of a horizontal desire.
   George Bernard Shaw 1856–1950: in
   New Statesman 23 March 1962

11 Dance is the hidden language of
   the soul.
   Martha Graham 1894–1991: *Blood
   Memory* (1991)

Danger
see also **Caution, Courage**

1 I am escaped with the skin of my
  teeth.
  Bible: Job

2 Out of this nettle, danger, we
  pluck this flower, safety.
  William Shakespeare 1564–1616:
  Henry IV, Part 1 (1597); cf. **Courage
  7**

3 It is the bright day that brings
    forth the adder;
  And that craves wary walking.
  William Shakespeare 1564–1616:
  Julius Caesar (1599)

4 Our God and soldiers we alike
    adore
  Ev'n at the brink of danger; not
    before:
  After deliverance, both alike
    requited,
  Our God's forgotten, and our
    soldiers slighted.
  Francis Quarles 1592–1644: "Of
  Common Devotion" (1632); cf.
  Human Nature 4

5 When there is no peril in the
  fight, there is no glory in the
  triumph.
  Pierre Corneille 1606–84: *Le Cid*
  (1637)

6 Dangers by being despised grow
  great.
  Edmund Burke 1729–97: speech on
  the Petition of the Unitarians, 11 May
  1792

7 In skating over thin ice, our safety is in our speed.
Ralph Waldo Emerson 1803–82: *Essays* (1841) "Prudence"

8 We took risks, we knew we took them; things have come out against us, and therefore we have no cause for complaint.
Robert Falcon Scott 1868–1912: "The Last Message" in *Scott's Last Expedition* (1913)

9 My inclination to go by Air Express is confirmed by the crash they had yesterday, which will make them careful in the immediate future.
A. E. Housman 1859–1936: letter 17 August 1920

10 Fasten your seat-belts, it's going to be a bumpy night.
Joseph L. Mankiewicz 1909– : *All About Eve* (1950 film); spoken by Bette Davis

11 Security is when everything is settled, when nothing can happen to you; security is the denial of life.
Germaine Greer 1939– : *The Female Eunuch* (1970)

12 It is no good putting up notices saying "Beware of the bull" because very rude things are sometimes written on them. I have found that one of the most effective notices is "Beware of the Agapanthus."
Lord Massereene and Ferrard 1914–93: speech on the Wildlife and Countryside Bill, House of Lords 16 December 1980

Day and Night

1 Night's candles are burnt out, and jocund day
Stands tiptoe on the misty mountain tops.
William Shakespeare 1564–1616: *Romeo and Juliet* (1595)

2 Night hath a thousand eyes.
John Lyly c. 1554–1606: *The Maydes Metamorphosis* (1600)

3 But, look, the morn, in russet mantle clad,
Walks o'er the dew of yon high eastern hill.
William Shakespeare 1564–1616: *Hamlet* (1601)

4 'Tis now the very witching time of night,
When churchyards yawn and hell itself breathes out
Contagion to this world.
William Shakespeare 1564–1616: *Hamlet* (1601)

5 Dear Night! this world's defeat;
The stop to busy fools; care's check and curb.
Henry Vaughan 1622–95: *Silex Scintillans* (1650–5) "The Night"

6 Lighten our darkness, we beseech thee, O Lord; and by thy great mercy defend us from all perils and dangers of this night.
The Book of Common Prayer 1662: *Evening Prayer*

7 Now came still evening on, and twilight grey
Had in her sober livery all things clad.
John Milton 1608–74: *Paradise Lost* (1667)

8 The curfew tolls the knell of parting day,
The lowing herd wind slowly o'er the lea,
The ploughman homeward plods his weary way,
And leaves the world to darkness and to me.
Thomas Gray 1716–71: *Elegy Written in a Country Churchyard* (1751)

9 The Sun's rim dips; the stars rush out;
At one stride comes the dark.
Samuel Taylor Coleridge 1772–1834:

"The Rime of the Ancient Mariner"
(1798)

10 It is a beauteous evening, calm
and free;
The holy time is quiet as a nun
Breathless with adoration.
William Wordsworth 1770–1850: "It
is a beauteous evening, calm and
free" (1807)

11 When I behold, upon the night's
starred face
Huge cloudy symbols of a high
romance.
John Keats 1795–1821: "When I have
fears that I may cease to be"
(written 1818)

12 The cares that infest the day
Shall fold their tents, like the
Arabs,
And as silently steal away.
Henry Wadsworth Longfellow 1807–
82: "The Day is Done" (1844)

13 And ghastly through the drizzling
rain
On the bald street breaks the
blank day.
Alfred, Lord Tennyson 1809–92: *In
Memoriam A. H. H.* (1850)

14 Only that day dawns to which we
are awake. There is more day to
dawn. The sun is but a morning
star.
Henry David Thoreau 1817–62:
Walden (1854)

15 Awake! for Morning in the bowl
of night
Has flung the stone that puts the
stars to flight:
And Lo! the Hunter of the East
has caught
The Sultan's turret in a noose of
light.
Edward Fitzgerald 1809–83: *The
Rubáiyát of Omar Khayyám* (1859)

16 There's a certain Slant of light,
Winter Afternoons—

That oppresses like the Heft
Of Cathedral Tunes—
Emily Dickinson 1830–86: "There's a
certain Slant of light" (c. 1861)

17 There midnight's all a glimmer,
and noon a purple glow,
And evening full of the linnet's
wings.
W. B. Yeats 1865–1939: "The Lake
Isle of Innisfree" (1892)

18 Let us go then, you and I,
When the evening is spread out
against the sky
Like a patient etherized upon a
table.
T. S. Eliot 1888–1965: "The Love
Song of J. Alfred Prufrock" (1917)

19 The winter evening settles down
With smell of steaks in
passageways.
Six o'clock.
The burnt-out ends of smoky
days.
T. S. Eliot 1888–1965: "Preludes"
(1917)

20 I have a horror of sunsets, they're
so romantic, so operatic.
Marcel Proust 1871–1922: *Cities of
the Plain* (1922)

Death
see also **Epitaphs, Last Words,
Mourning and Loss, Murder, Suicide**

1 I would rather be tied to the soil
as another man's serf, even a
poor man's, who hadn't much to
live on himself, than be King of
all these the dead and destroyed.
Homer: *The Odyssey*

2 For dust thou art, and unto dust
shalt thou return.
Bible: Genesis

3 Whatsoever thy hand findeth to
do, do it with thy might; for there

is no work, nor device, nor knowledge, nor wisdom, in the grave, whither thou goest.
Bible: Ecclesiastes

4 Death, therefore, the most awful of evils, is nothing to us, seeing that, when we are death is not come, and when death is come, we are not.
Epicurus 341–271 BC: Diogenes Laertius *Lives of Eminent Philosophers*

5 *Non omnis moriar.*
I shall not altogether die.
Horace 65–8 BC: *Odes*

6 Behold, I shew you a mystery: We shall not all sleep, but we shall all be changed.
In a moment, in the twinkling of an eye, at the last trump: for the trumpet shall sound, and the dead shall be raised incorruptible, and we shall be changed.
Bible: I Corinthians

7 O death, where is thy sting? O grave, where is thy victory?
Bible: I Corinthians; cf. **Armed Forces 31**

8 And I looked, and behold a pale horse: and his name that sat on him was Death.
Bible: Revelation

9 *Abiit ad plures.* He's gone to join the majority [the dead].
Petronius d. AD 65: *Satyricon*; cf. **Elections 6**

10 Anyone can stop a man's life, but no one his death; a thousand doors open on to it.
Seneca ("the Younger") c. 4 BC–AD 65: *Phoenissae*; cf. **24 below**

11 Finally he paid the debt of nature.
Robert Fabyan d. 1513: *The New Chronicles of England and France* (1516)

12 We are as near to heaven by sea as by land!
Humphrey Gilbert c. 1537–83: Richard Hakluyt *Third and Last Volume of the Voyages . . . of the English Nation* (1600)

13 I care not; a man can die but once: we owe God a death.
William Shakespeare 1564–1616: *Henry IV, Part 2* (1597)

14 Brightness falls from the air;
Queens have died young and fair;
Dust hath closed Helen's eye.
I am sick, I must die.
Lord have mercy on us.
Thomas Nashe 1567–1601: *Summer's Last Will and Testament* (1600)

15 This fell sergeant, death,
Is swift in his arrest.
William Shakespeare 1564–1616: *Hamlet* (1601)

16 To die: to sleep;
No more: and, by a sleep to say we end
The heart-ache and the thousand natural shocks
That flesh is heir to, 'tis a consummation
Devoutly to be wished. To die, to sleep;
To sleep: perchance to dream: ay, there's the rub;
For in that sleep of death what dreams may come
When we have shuffled off this mortal coil,
Must give us pause.
William Shakespeare 1564–1616: *Hamlet* (1601)

17 Nothing in his life
Became him like the leaving it.
William Shakespeare 1564–1616: *Macbeth* (1606)

18 Death be not proud, though some have called thee
Mighty and dreadful, for thou art not so.
John Donne 1572–1631: *Holy Sonnets* (1609)

19 One short sleep past, we wake
    eternally,
  And death shall be no more;
    Death thou shalt die.
  John Donne 1572–1631: *Holy Sonnets*
  (1609)

20 He that dies pays all debts.
  William Shakespeare 1564–1616: *The
  Tempest* (1611)

21 O eloquent, just, and mighty
  Death! . . . thou hast drawn
  together all the farstretched
  greatness, all the pride, cruelty,
  and ambition of man, and
  covered it all over with these two
  narrow words, *Hic jacet.*
  Walter Ralegh c. 1552–1618: *The
  History of the World* (1614),
  commenting on the Latin words
  meaning "here lies" that precede
  the name of the deceased on old
  gravestones

22 Only we die in earnest, that's no
  jest.
  Walter Ralegh c. 1552–1618: "On the
  Life of Man"

23 Cover her face; mine eyes dazzle:
    she died young.
  John Webster c. 1580–c. 1625: *The
  Duchess of Malfi* (1623)

24 I know death hath ten thousand
    several doors
  For men to take their exits.
  John Webster c. 1580–c. 1625: *The
  Duchess of Malfi* (1623); see **10**
  above

25 Any man's death diminishes me,
  because I am involved in
  Mankind; And therefore never
  send to know for whom the bell
  tolls; it tolls for thee.
  John Donne 1572–1631: *Devotions
  upon Emergent Occasions* (1624)

26 Revenge triumphs over death;
  love slights it; honour aspireth to
  it; grief flieth to it.
  Francis Bacon 1561–1626: *Essays*
  (1625) "Of Death"

27 How little room
  Do we take up in death, that,
    living know
  No bounds?
  James Shirley 1596–1666: *The
  Wedding* (1629)

28 One dies only once, and it's for
  such a long time!
  Molière 1622–73: *Le Dépit amoureux*
  (1662)

29 The long habit of living
  indisposeth us for dying.
  Thomas Browne 1605–82:
  Hydriotaphia (Urn Burial, 1658)

30 We shall die alone.
  Blaise Pascal 1623–62: *Pensées*
  (1670)

31 In the midst of life we are in
  death.
  The Book of Common Prayer 1662:
  The Burial of the Dead; cf. **Debt 10**

32 Forasmuch as it hath pleased
  Almighty God of his great mercy
  to take unto himself the soul of
  our dear brother here departed,
  we therefore commit his body to
  the ground; earth to earth, ashes
  to ashes, dust to dust; in sure and
  certain hope of the Resurrection
  to eternal life.
  The Book of Common Prayer 1662:
  The Burial of the Dead Interment

33 Death never takes the wise man
  by surprise; he is always ready to
  go.
  Jean de la Fontaine 1621–95: *Fables*
  (1678–9) "La Mort et le Mourant"

34 They that die by famine die by
  inches.
  Matthew Henry 1662–1714: *An
  Exposition on the Old and New
  Testament* (1710)

35 Can storied urn or animated bust
  Back to its mansion call the
    fleeting breath?
  Thomas Gray 1716–71: *Elegy Written
  in a Country Churchyard* (1751)

36 The boast of heraldry, the pomp
of pow'r,
And all that beauty, all that
wealth e'er gave,
Awaits alike th' inevitable hour,
The paths of glory lead but to the
grave.
Thomas Gray 1716–71: *Elegy Written
in a Country Churchyard* (1751)

37 The bodies of those that made
such a noise and tumult when
alive, when dead, lie as quietly
among the graves of their
neighbours as any others.
Jonathan Edwards 1703–58:
Miscellaneous Discourses sermon on
procrastination

38 "There is no terror, brother Toby,
in its [death's] looks, but what it
borrows from groans and
convulsions—and the blowing of
noses, and the wiping away of
tears with the bottoms of
curtains, in a dying man's room—
Strip it of these, what is it?"—
"'Tis better in battle than in bed,"
said my uncle Toby.
Laurence Sterne 1713–68: *Tristram
Shandy* (1759–67)

39 It matters not how a man dies,
but how he lives. The act of
dying is not of importance, it lasts
so short a time.
Samuel Johnson 1709–84: James
Boswell *Life of Samuel Johnson*
(1791) 26 October 1769

40 Depend upon it, Sir, when a man
knows he is to be hanged in a
fortnight, it concentrates his mind
wonderfully.
on the execution of Dr. Dodd
Samuel Johnson 1709–84: James
Boswell *Life of Samuel Johnson*
(1791) 19 September 1777

41 My name is Death: the last best
friend am I.
Robert Southey 1774–1843: "The Lay
of the Laureate" (1816)

42 Darkling I listen; and, for many a
time
I have been half in love with
easeful Death,
Called him soft names in many a
musèd rhyme,
To take into the air my quiet
breath;
Now more than ever seems it rich
to die,
To cease upon the midnight with
no pain.
John Keats 1795–1821: "Ode to a
Nightingale" (1820)

43 The cemetery is an open space
among the ruins, covered in
winter with violets and daisies. It
might make one in love with
death, to think that one should
be buried in so sweet a place.
Percy Bysshe Shelley 1792–1822:
Adonais (1821)

44 From the contagion of the world's
slow stain
He is secure, and now can never
mourn
A heart grown cold, a head
grown grey in vain.
Percy Bysshe Shelley 1792–1822:
Adonais (1821)

45 With the dead there is no rivalry.
In the dead there is no change.
Plato is never sullen. Cervantes is
never petulant. Demosthenes
never comes unseasonably. Dante
never stays too long. No
difference of political opinion can
alienate Cicero. No heresy can
excite the horror of Bossuet.
Lord Macaulay 1800–59: *Essays
Contributed to the Edinburgh Review*
(1843) "Lord Bacon"

46 He'd make a lovely corpse.
Charles Dickens 1812–70: *Martin
Chuzzlewit* (1844)

47 Death must be distinguished from
dying, with which it is often
confused.
Sydney Smith 1771–1845: H.
Pearson *The Smith of Smiths* (1934)

48 Even the death of friends will inspire us as much as their lives. . . . Their memories will be encrusted over with sublime and pleasing thoughts, as monuments of other men are overgrown with moss; for our friends have no place in the graveyard.
Henry David Thoreau 1817–62: *Civil Disobedience* (1849)

49 Just try and set death aside. It sets you aside, and that's the end of it!
Ivan Turgenev 1818–83: *Fathers and Sons* (1862)

50 Fear death?—to feel the fog in my throat,
The mist in my face.
Robert Browning 1812–89: "Prospice" (1864)

51 He could not die when the trees were green,
For he loved the time too well.
John Clare 1793–1864: "The Dying Child"

52 This quiet Dust was Gentlemen and Ladies
And Lads and Girls—
Was laughter and ability and Sighing
And Frocks and Curls.
Emily Dickinson 1830–86: "This quiet Dust was Gentlemen and Ladies" (c. 1864)

53 The Bustle in a House
The Morning after Death
Is solemnest of industries
Enacted upon Earth—
The Sweeping up the Heart
And putting Love away
We shall not want to use again
Until Eternity.
Emily Dickinson 1830–86: "The Bustle in a House" (c. 1866)

54 And all our calm is in that balm—
Not lost but gone before.
Caroline Norton 1808–77: "Not Lost but Gone Before"

55 The candle by which she had been reading the book filled with trouble and deceit, sorrow and evil, flared up with a brighter light, illuminating for her everything that before had been enshrouded in darkness, flickered, grew dim, and went out for ever.
Leo Tolstoy 1828–1910: *Anna Karenina* (1875–7)

56 No it is better not. She would only ask me to take a message to Albert.
on his death-bed, declining a proposed visit from Queen Victoria
Benjamin Disraeli 1804–81: Robert Blake *Disraeli* (1966)

57 "Well, poor soul; she's helpless to hinder that or anything now," answered Mother Cuxsom. "And all her shining keys will be took from her, and her cupboards opened; and things a' didn't wish seen, anybody will see; and her little wishes and ways will all be as nothing!"
Thomas Hardy 1840–1928: *Mayor of Casterbridge* (1886)

58 For though from out our bourne of time and place
The flood may bear me far,
I hope to see my pilot face to face
When I have crossed the bar.
Alfred, Lord Tennyson 1809–92: "Crossing the Bar" (1889)

59 "Justice" was done, and the President of the Immortals (in Aeschylean phrase) had ended his sport with Tess.
Thomas Hardy 1840–1928: *Tess of the D'Urbervilles* (1891)

60 Life levels all men: death reveals the eminent.
George Bernard Shaw 1856–1950: *Man and Superman* (1903) "Maxims: Fame"

61 In the arts of life man invents nothing; but in the arts of death he outdoes Nature herself, and produces by chemistry and machinery all the slaughter of plague, pestilence and famine.
George Bernard Shaw 1856–1950: *Man and Superman* (1903)

62 What I like about Clive
Is that he is no longer alive.
There is a great deal to be said
For being dead.
Edmund Clerihew Bentley 1875–1956: "Clive" (1905)

63 There are no dead.
Maurice Maeterlinck 1862–1949: *L'Oiseau bleu* (1909)

64 Death is nothing at all; it does not count. I have only slipped away into the next room.
Henry Scott Holland 1847–1918: sermon preached on Whitsunday 1910

65 Blow out, you bugles, over the rich Dead!
There's none of these so lonely and poor of old,
But, dying, has made us rarer gifts than gold.
Rupert Brooke 1887–1915: "The Dead" (1914)

66 Why fear death? It is the most beautiful adventure in life.
last words before drowning in the Lusitania, *7 May 1915*
Charles Frohman 1860–1915: I. F. Marcosson and D. Frohman *Charles Frohman* (1916); cf. **72** below

67 So here it is at last, the distinguished thing!
on experiencing his first stroke
Henry James 1843–1916: Edith Wharton *A Backward Glance* (1934)

68 The pallor of girls' brows shall be their pall;
Their flowers the tenderness of patient minds,

And each slow dusk a drawing-down of blinds.
Wilfred Owen 1893–1918: "Anthem for Doomed Youth" (written 1917)

69 Webster was much possessed by death
And saw the skull beneath the skin;
And breastless creatures underground
Leaned backward with a lipless grin.
T. S. Eliot 1888–1965: "Whispers of Immortality" (1919)

70 The dead don't die. They look on and help.
D. H. Lawrence 1885–1930: letter to J. Middleton Murry, 2 February 1923

71 A man's dying is more the survivors' affair than his own.
Thomas Mann 1875–1955: *The Magic Mountain* (1924)

72 To die will be an awfully big adventure.
J. M. Barrie 1860–1937: *Peter Pan* (1928); cf. **66** above

73 Ain't it grand to be blooming well dead?
Leslie Sarony 1897–1985: title of song (1932)

74 The King's life is moving peacefully towards its close.
bulletin, drafted on a menu card at Buckingham Palace on the eve of the king's death, 20 January 1936
Lord Dawson of Penn 1864–1945: Kenneth Rose *King George V* (1983)

75 One death is a tragedy, a million deaths a statistic.
Joseph Stalin 1879–1953: attributed

76 Life is a great surprise. I do not see why death should not be an even greater one.
Vladimir Nabokov 1899–1977: *Pale Fire* (1962)

77 If there wasn't death, I think you
couldn't go on.
Stevie Smith 1902–71: in *Observer*
(UK) 9 November 1969

78 This parrot is no more! It has
ceased to be! It's expired and
gone to meet its maker! This is a
late parrot! It's a stiff! Bereft of
life it rests in peace — if you
hadn't nailed it to the perch it
would be pushing up the daisies!
It's rung down the curtain and
joined the choir invisible! THIS IS
AN EX-PARROT!
Graham Chapman 1941–89, **John
Cleese** 1939–, et al.: *Monty Python's
Flying Circus* (BBC TV program,
1969)

79 Death is nothing if one can
approach it as such. I was just a
tiny night-light, suffocated in its
own wax, and on the point of
expiring.
E. M. Forster 1879–1970: Philip
Gardner (ed.) *E. M. Forster:
Commonplace Book* (1985)

80 It's not that I'm afraid to die. I
just don't want to be there when
it happens.
Woody Allen 1935–   : *Death* (1975)

81 Even death is unreliable: instead
of zero it may be some ghastly
hallucination, such as the square
root of minus one.
Samuel Beckett 1906–89: attributed

82 My specialty is death.
Dr. Jack Kevorkian 1928–: *Time* (31
May 1993)

83 The key to dying well is for you
to decide where, when, how and
whom to invite to the last party.
*during the last days of his final
illness, to a visitor*
Timothy Leary 1920–96: in *Daily
Telegraph* (UK) 3 May 1996; cf.
Epitaphs 31, Last Words 31

Debt and Borrowing
see also **Thrift and Extravagance**

1 Be not made a beggar by
banqueting upon borrowing.
Bible: Ecclesiasticus

2 Neither a borrower, nor a lender
be;
For loan oft loses both itself and
friend,
And borrowing dulls the edge of
husbandry.
William Shakespeare 1564–1616:
Hamlet (1601)

3 The human species, according to
the best theory I can form of it, is
composed of two distinct races,
the men who borrow, and *the men
who lend*.
Charles Lamb 1775–1834: *Essays of
Elia* (1823) "The Two Races of Men"

4 Dreading that climax of all
human ills,
The inflammation of his weekly
bills.
Lord Byron 1788–1824: *Don Juan*
(1819–24)

5 Three things I never lends—my
'oss, my wife, and my name.
R. S. Surtees 1805–64: *Hillingdon
Hall* (1845)

6 Annual income twenty pounds,
annual expenditure nineteen
nineteen six, result happiness.
Annual income twenty pounds,
annual expenditure twenty
pounds ought and six, result
misery.
Charles Dickens 1812–70: *David
Copperfield* (1850)

7 Let us all be happy, and live
within our means, even if we
have to borrer the money to do it
with.
Artemus Ward 1834–67: *Artemus
Ward in London* (1867)

8 Worm or beetle—drought or
tempest—on a farmer's land
may fall,
Each is loaded full o' ruin, but a
mortgage beats 'em all.
William McKendree Carleton 1845–
1912: "The Tramp's Story" (1881)

9 One must have some sort of
occupation nowadays. If I hadn't
my debts I shouldn't have
anything to think about.
Oscar Wilde 1854–1900: *A Woman of
No Importance* (1893)

10 In the midst of life we are in debt.
Ethel Watts Mumford 1878–1940 et
al.: *Altogether New Cynic's Calendar*
(1907); see **Death** 31

11 To take usury is contrary to
Scripture; it is contrary to
Aristotle; it is contrary to nature,
for it is to live without labour; it
is to sell time, which belongs to
God, for the advantage of wicked
men; it is to rob those who use
the money lent, and to whom,
since they make it profitable, the
profits should belong.
R. H. Tawney 1880–1962: *Religion
and the Rise of Capitalism* (1926)

12 The National Debt is a very Good
Thing and it would be dangerous
to pay it off, for fear of Political
Economy.
W. C. Sellar 1898–1951 and **R. J.
Yeatman** 1898–1968: *1066 and All
That* (1930)

13 They hired the money, didn't
they?
*on the subject of war debts incurred
by England and others*
Calvin Coolidge 1872–1933: John H.
McKee *Coolidge: Wit and Wisdom*
(1933)

14 Should we really let our people
starve so we can pay our debts?
Julius Nyerere 1922– : in *Guardian*
21 March 1985

Deception
see also **Hypocrisy, Lies and Lying**

1 Deceive boys with toys, but men
with oaths.
Lysander d. 395 BC: Plutarch *Parallel
Lives* "Lysander"

2 And if, to be sure, sometimes you
need to conceal a fact with
words, do it in such a way that it
does not become known, or, if it
does become known, that you
have a ready and quick defence.
Niccolò Machiavelli 1469–1527:
"Advice to Raffaello Girolami when
he went as Ambassador to the
Emperor" (October 1522)

3 A false report, if believed during
three days, may be of great
service to a government.
Catherine de' Medici 1518–89: Isaac
D'Israeli *Curiosities of Literature
Second Series* vol. 2 (1849)

4 Like strawberry wives, that laid
two or three great strawberries at
the mouth of their pot, and all
the rest were little ones.
*describing the tactics of the
Commission of Sales, in their
dealings with her*
Elizabeth I 1533–1603: Francis Bacon
Apophthegms New and Old (1625)

5 Doubtless the pleasure is as great
Of being cheated, as to cheat.
As lookers-on feel most delight,
That least perceive a juggler's
sleight.
Samuel Butler 1612–80: *Hudibras* pt.
2 (1664)

6 An open foe may prove a curse,
But a pretended friend is worse.
John Gay 1685–1732: *Fables* (1727)
"The Shepherd's Dog and the Wolf"

7 Wise fear, you know,
Forbids the robbing of a foe;
But what, to serve our private
ends,

Forbids the cheating of our
   friends?
Charles Churchill 1731–64: *The Ghost*
(1763)

8 O what a tangled web we weave,
   When first we practise to deceive!
   Sir Walter Scott 1771–1832: *Marmion*
   (1808)

9 You may fool all the people some
   of the time; you can even fool
   some of the people all the time;
   but you can't fool all of the
   people all the time.
   Abraham Lincoln 1809–65: Alexander
   K. McClure *Lincoln's Yarns and
   Stories* (1904); also attributed to
   Phineas Barnum; cf. **Politics 15**

10 If he paid for each day's comfort
   with the small change of his
   illusions, he grew daily to value
   the comfort more and set less
   store upon the coin.
   Edith Wharton 1862–1937: *The
   Descent of Man* (1904) "The Other
   Two"

11 It was beautiful and simple as all
   truly great swindles are.
   O. Henry 1862–1910: *Gentle Grafter*
   (1908)

12 That branch of the art of lying
   which consists in very nearly
   deceiving your friends without
   quite deceiving your enemies.
   on propaganda
   Francis M. Cornford 1874–1943:
   Microcosmographia Academica (1922
   ed.)

Deeds
see **Words and Deeds**

Defiance
see also **Determination and
Perseverance**

1 They are as venomous as the
   poison of a serpent: even like the
   deaf adder that stoppeth her ears;
   Which refuseth to hear the voice
   of the charmer: charm he never
   so wisely.
   Bible: Psalm 58

2 He will give him seven feet of
   English ground, or as much more
   as he may be taller than other
   men.
   *his offer to the invader Harald
   Hardrada, before the battle of
   Stamford Bridge*
   •**Harold II** *c.* 1019–66: Snorri
   Sturluson *Heimskringla* (*c.* 1260)
   "King Harald's Saga"

3 If I had heard that as many devils
   would set on me in Worms as
   there are tiles on the roofs, I
   should none the less have ridden
   there.
   Martin Luther 1483–1546: to the
   Princes of Saxony, 21 August 1524;
   Sämmtliche Schriften vol. 16 (1745)

4 I grow, I prosper;
   Now, gods, stand up for bastards!
   William Shakespeare 1564–1616:
   King Lear (1605–6)

5 . . . What though the field be lost?
   All is not lost; the unconquerable
      will,
   And study of revenge, immortal
      hate,
   And courage never to submit or
      yield:
   And what is else not to be
      overcome?
   John Milton 1608–74: *Paradise Lost*
   (1667)

6 "Do you not see your country is
   lost?" asked the Duke of
   Buckingham. "There is one way
   never to see it lost" replied
   William, "and that is to die in the
   last ditch."
   William III 1650–1702: Bishop Gilbert
   Burnet *History of My Own Time*
   (1838 ed.)

7 Should the whole frame of nature
round him break,
In ruin and confusion hurled,
He, unconcerned, would hear the
mighty crack,
And stand secure amidst a falling
world.
Joseph Addison 1672–1719:
translation of Horace *Odes*

8 I was ever a fighter, so—one fight
more,
The best and the last!
I would hate that death bandaged
my eyes, and forbore,
And bade me creep past.
No! let me taste the whole of it,
fare like my peers
The heroes of old,
Bear the brunt, in a minute pay
glad life's arrears
Of pain, darkness and cold.
Robert Browning 1812–89:
"Prospice" (1864)

9 *No pasarán.*
They shall not pass.
Dolores Ibarruri 1895–1989: radio
broadcast, Madrid, 19 July 1936; see
World War I 11

Delay
see **Haste and Delay**

Democracy
see also **Elections, Politics**

1 And those people should not be
listened to who keep saying the
voice of the people is the voice of
God, since the riotousness of the
crowd is always very close to
madness.
Alcuin c. 735–804: letter 164; *Works*
(1863)

2 Let no one oppose this belief of
mine with that well-worn proverb:
"He who builds on the people
builds on mud."
Niccolò Machiavelli 1469–1527: *The
Prince* (written 1513)

3 Nor is the people's judgement
always true:
The most may err as grossly as
the few.
John Dryden 1631–1700: *Absalom
and Achitophel* (1681)

4 I never could believe that
Providence had sent a few men
into the world, ready booted and
spurred to ride, and millions
ready saddled and bridled to be
ridden.
on the scaffold
Richard Rumbold c. 1622–85: T. B.
Macaulay *History of England* vol. 1
(1849)

5 If one must serve, I hold it better
to serve a well-bred lion, who is
naturally stronger than I am,
than two hundred rats of my
own breed.
Voltaire 1694–1778: letter to a friend;
Alexis de Tocqueville *The Ancien
Régime* (1856)

6 One man shall have one vote.
John Cartwright 1740–1824: *The
People's Barrier Against Undue
Influence* (1780)

7 All, too, will bear in mind this
sacred principle, that though the
will of the majority is in all cases
to prevail, that will to be rightful
must be reasonable; that the
minority possess their equal
rights, which equal law must
protect, and to violate would be
oppression.
Thomas Jefferson 1743–1826:
inaugural address, 4 March 1801

8 I know no safe depositor of the
ultimate powers of society but the
people themselves; and if we
think them not enlightened
enough to exercise their control
with a wholesome discretion, the
remedy is not to take it from
them, but to inform their
discretion.

Thomas Jefferson 1743–1826: *Letter to William Charles Jarvis* (28 September 1820)

9 It is impossible that the whisper of a faction should prevail against the voice of a nation.
Lord John Russell 1792–1878: reply to an Address from a meeting of 150,000 persons at Birmingham on the defeat of the second Reform Bill, October 1831

10 Minorities . . . are almost always in the right.
Sydney Smith 1771–1845: H. Pearson *The Smith of Smiths* (1934)

11 A majority is always the best repartee.
Benjamin Disraeli 1804–81: *Tancred* (1847)

12 Fourscore and seven years ago our fathers brought forth upon this continent a new nation, conceived in liberty, and dedicated to the proposition that all men are created equal . . . we here highly resolve that the dead shall not have died in vain, that this nation, under God, shall have a new birth of freedom; and that government of the people, by the people, and for the people, shall not perish from the earth.
the Lincoln Memorial inscription reads "by the people, for the people"
Abraham Lincoln 1809–65: address at the Dedication of the National Cemetery at Gettysburg, 19 November 1863, as reported the following day

13 The majority never has right on its side. Never I say! That is one of the social lies that a free, thinking man is bound to rebel against. Who make up the majority in any given country? Is it the wise men or the fools? I think we must agree that the fools are in a terrible

overwhelming majority, all the wide world over. But, damn it, it can surely never be right that the stupid should rule over the clever!
Henrik Ibsen 1828–1906: *An Enemy of the People* (1882)

14 Democracy substitutes election by the incompetent many for appointment by the corrupt few.
George Bernard Shaw 1856–1950: *Man and Superman* (1903) "Maxims: Democracy"

15 Democracy is the theory that the common people know what they want, and deserve to get it good and hard.
H. L. Mencken 1880–1956: *A Little Book in C Major* (1916)

16 The world must be made safe for democracy.
Woodrow Wilson 1856–1924: speech to Congress, 2 April 1917

17 No, Democracy is *not* identical with majority rule. Democracy is a *State* which recognizes the subjection of the minority to the majority, that is, an organization for the systematic use of *force* by one class against the other, by one part of the population against another.
V. I. Lenin 1870–1924: *State and Revolution* (1919)

18 Democracy is the recurrent suspicion that more than half of the people are right more than half of the time.
E. B. White 1899–1985: in *New Yorker* 3 July 1944

19 Man's capacity for justice makes democracy possible, but man's inclination to injustice makes democracy necessary.
Reinhold Niebuhr 1892–1971: *Children of Light and Children of Darkness* (1944)

20 No one pretends that democracy is perfect or all-wise. Indeed, it has been said that democracy is the worst form of Government except all those other forms that have been tried from time to time.
Winston Churchill 1874–1965: speech, House of Commons, 11 November 1947

21 After each war there is a little less democracy to save.
Brooks Atkinson 1894–1984: *Once Around the Sun* (1951)

22 So Two cheers for Democracy: one because it admits variety and two because it permits criticism. Two cheers are quite enough: there is no occasion to give three. Only Love the Beloved Republic deserves that.
E. M. Forster 1879–1970: *Two Cheers for Democracy* (1951)

23 Democracy means government by discussion, but it is only effective if you can stop people talking.
Clement Attlee 1883–1967: speech at Oxford, 14 June 1957

24 It's not the voting that's democracy, it's the counting.
Tom Stoppard 1937– : *Jumpers* (1972); cf. **Elections 11**

25 Every government is a parliament of whores. The trouble is, in a democracy the whores are us.
P. J. O'Rourke 1947– : *Parliament of Whores* (1991)

Despair

see also **Hope, Optimism and Pessimism, Sorrow**

1 My God, my God, look upon me; why hast thou forsaken me?
Bible: Psalm 22

2 Magnanimous Despair alone Could show me so divine a thing,

Where feeble Hope could ne'er have flown
But vainly flapped its tinsel wing.
Andrew Marvell 1621–78: "The Definition of Love" (1681)

3 The black dog I hope always to resist, and in time to drive, though I am deprived of almost all those that used to help me . . . When I rise my breakfast is solitary, the black dog waits to share it, from breakfast to dinner he continues barking, except that Dr. Brocklesby for a little keeps him at a distance . . . Night comes at last, and some hours of restlessness and confusion bring me again to a day of solitude. What shall exclude the black dog from a habitation like this?
on his attacks of melancholia; more recently associated with Winston Churchill, who used the phrase "black dog" when alluding to his own periodic bouts of depression
Samuel Johnson 1709–84: letter to Mrs. Thrale, 28 June 1783

4 The very knowledge that he lived in vain,
That all was over on this side the tomb,
Had made Despair a smilingness assume.
Lord Byron 1788–1824: *Childe Harold's Pilgrimage* (1812–18)

5 Everywhere I see bliss, from which I alone am irrevocably excluded.
Mary Shelley 1797–1851: *Frankenstein* (1818)

6 I am in that temper that if I were under water I would scarcely kick to come to the top.
John Keats 1795–1821: letter to Benjamin Bailey, 25 May 1818

7 I give the fight up: let there be an end,

A privacy, an obscure nook for
me.
I want to be forgotten even by
God.
Robert Browning 1812–89:
Paracelsus (1835)

8 Take thy beak from out my heart,
and take thy form from off my
door!
Quoth the Raven, "Nevermore."
Edgar Allan Poe 1809–49: "The
Raven" (1845)

9 There is no despair so absolute as
that which comes with the first
moments of our first great
sorrow, when we have not yet
known what it is to have suffered
and be healed, to have despaired
and have recovered hope.
George Eliot 1819–80: *Adam Bede*
(1859)

10 In despair there are the most
intense enjoyments, especially
when one is very acutely
conscious of the hopelessness of
one's position.
Fyodor Dostoevsky 1821–81: *Notes
from Underground* (1864)

11 Not, I'll not, carrion comfort,
Despair, not feast on thee;
Not untwist—slack they may be—
these last strands of man
In me or, most weary, cry *I can
no more*. I can;
Can something, hope, wish day
come, not choose not to be.
Gerard Manley Hopkins 1844–89:
"Carrion Comfort" (written 1885)

12 We have done with Hope and
Honour, we are lost to Love
and Truth,
We are dropping down the ladder
rung by rung,
And the measure of our torment
is the measure of our youth,
God help us, for we knew the
worst too young!

Rudyard Kipling 1865–1936:
"Gentleman-Rankers" (1892)

13 In a real dark night of the soul it
is always three o'clock in the
morning.
F. Scott Fitzgerald 1896–1940:
"Handle with Care" in *Esquire* March
1936

14 Human life begins on the far side
of despair.
Jean-Paul Sartre 1905–80: *Les
Mouches* (1943)

15 Despair is the price one pays for
setting oneself an impossible aim.
Graham Greene 1904–91: *Heart of
the Matter* (1948)

Determination and Perseverance
see also **Defiance**

1 Faint, yet pursuing.
Bible: Judges

2 No man, having put his hand to
the plough, and looking back, is
fit for the kingdom of God.
Bible: St. Luke

3 *Hoc volo, sic iubeo, sit pro ratione
voluntas.*
I will have this done, so I order it
done; let my will replace reasoned
judgement.
Juvenal AD *c.* 60–*c.* 130: *Satires*

4 Thought shall be the harder,
heart the keener, courage the
greater, as our might lessens.
Anonymous: *The Battle of Maldon*
(*c.* 1000)

5 Here stand I. I can do no other.
God help me. Amen.
Martin Luther 1483–1546: speech at
the Diet of Worms, 18 April 1521;
attributed

6 The drop of rain maketh a hole in
the stone, not by violence, but by
oft falling.

Hugh Latimer c. 1485–1555: *The Second Sermon preached before the King's Majesty*, 19 April 1549

7 Perseverance, dear my lord,
Keeps honour bright.
William Shakespeare 1564–1616: *Troilus and Cressida* (1602)

8 Obstinacy in a bad cause, is but constancy in a good.
Thomas Browne 1605–82: *Religio Medici* (1643)

9 Who would true valour see,
Let him come hither;
One here will constant be,
Come wind, come weather.
There's no discouragement
Shall make him once relent
His first avowed intent
To be a pilgrim.
John Bunyan 1628–88: *The Pilgrim's Progress* (1684)

10 She's as headstrong as an allegory on the banks of the Nile.
Richard Brinsley Sheridan 1751–1816: *The Rivals* (1775)

11 Obstinacy, Sir, is certainly a great vice . . . It happens, however, very unfortunately, that almost the whole line of the great and masculine virtues, constancy, gravity, magnanimity, fortitude, fidelity, and firmness are closely allied to this disagreeable quality.
Edmund Burke 1729–97: *On American Taxation* (1775)

12 I have not yet begun to fight.
as his ship was sinking, 23 September 1779, having been asked whether he had lowered his flag
John Paul Jones 1747–92: Mrs. Reginald De Koven *Life and Letters of John Paul Jones* (1914)

13 I have only one eye,—I have a right to be blind sometimes . . . I really do not see the signal!
at the battle of Copenhagen

Horatio, Lord Nelson 1758–1805: Robert Southey *Life of Nelson* (1813)

14 I am in earnest—I will not equivocate—I will not excuse—I will not retreat a single inch—and I will be heard!
William Lloyd Garrison 1805–79: in *The Liberator* 1 January 1831

15 That which we are, we are;
One equal temper of heroic hearts,
Made weak by time and fate, but strong in will
To strive, to seek, to find, and not to yield.
Alfred, Lord Tennyson 1809–92: "Ulysses" (1842)

16 I purpose to fight it out on this line, if it takes all summer.
Ulysses S. Grant 1822–85: dispatch to Washington, from headquarters in the field, 11 May 1864

17 "If seven maids with seven mops Swept it for half a year,
Do you suppose," the Walrus said,
"That they could get it clear?"
"I doubt it," said the Carpenter,
And shed a bitter tear.
Lewis Carroll 1832–98: *Through the Looking-Glass* (1872)

18 For twenty years he has held a season-ticket on the line of least resistance and has gone wherever the train of events has carried him, lucidly justifying his position at whatever point he has happened to find himself.
of Herbert Asquith
Leo Amery 1873–1955: in *Quarterly Review* July 1914

19 The best way out is always through.
Robert Frost 1874–1963: "A Servant to Servants" (1914)

20 It's a great life if you don't weaken.
John Buchan 1875–1940: *Mr. Standfast* (1919)

21 One man that has a mind and knows it can always beat ten men who haven't and don't.
George Bernard Shaw 1856–1950: *The Apple Cart* (1930)

22 If at first you don't succeed, try, try again. Then quit. No use being a damn fool about it.
W. C. Fields 1880–1946: attributed

23 What is the victory of a cat on a hot tin roof?—I wish I knew . . . Just staying on it, I guess, as long as she can.
Tennessee Williams 1911–83: *Cat on a Hot Tin Roof* (1955)

24 There comes a time in a man's life when to get where he has to go—if there are no doors or windows—he walks through a wall.
Bernard Malamud 1914–86: *Rembrandt's Hat* (1972)

25 We shall not be diverted from our course. To those waiting with bated breath for that favourite media catch-phrase, the U-turn, I have only this to say. "You turn if you want; the lady's not for turning."
final line from alteration of the title of Christopher Fry's 1949 play The Lady's Not For Burning
Margaret Thatcher 1925– : speech at Conservative Party Conference in Brighton, 10 October 1980

Diaries

1 A page of my Journal is like a cake of portable soup. A little may be diffused into a considerable portion.
James Boswell 1740–95: *Journal of a Tour to the Hebrides* (1785) 13 September 1773

2 I never travel without my diary. One should always have something sensational to read in the train.
Oscar Wilde 1854–1900: *The Importance of Being Earnest* (1895)

3 What sort of diary should I like mine to be? . . . I should like it to resemble some deep old desk, or capacious hold-all, in which one flings a mass of odds and ends without looking them through.
Virginia Woolf 1882–1941: diary 20 April 1919

4 One need not write in a diary what one is to remember for ever.
Sylvia Townsend Warner 1893–1978: diary 22 October 1930

5 What is more dull than a discreet diary? One might just as well have a discreet soul.
Henry ("Chips") Channon 1897–1958: diary (26 July) 1935

6 I always say, keep a diary and some day it'll keep you.
Mae West 1892–1980: *Every Day's a Holiday* (1937 film)

7 I want to go on living even after death!
Anne Frank 1929–45: diary 4 April 1944

8 Now that I am finishing the damned thing I realise that diary-writing isn't wholly good for one, that too much of it leads to living for one's diary instead of living for the fun of living as ordinary people do.
James Agate 1877–1947: letter 7 December 1946

9 To be a good diarist one must have a little snouty, sneaky mind.
Harold Nicolson 1886–1968: diary 9 November 1947

10 To write a diary every day is like returning to one's own vomit.
Enoch Powell 1912– : interview in *Sunday Times* (UK) 6 November 1977

11 I have decided to keep a full journal, in the hope that my life will perhaps seem more interesting when it is written down.
Sue Townsend 1946– : *Adrian Mole: The Wilderness Years* (1993)

Difference
see **Similarity and Difference**

Diplomacy
see also **International Relations**

1 An ambassador is an honest man sent to lie abroad for the good of his country.
Henry Wotton 1568–1639: written in the album of Christopher Fleckmore in 1604; Izaak Walton *Reliquiae Wottonianae* (1651)

2 We are prepared to go to the gates of Hell—but no further.
attempting to reach an agreement with Napoleon, c. 1800–1
Pope Pius VII 1742–1823: J. M. Robinson *Cardinal Consalvi* (1987)

3 The gentleman can not have forgotten his own sentiment, uttered even on the floor of this House, "peaceably if we can, forcibly if we must."
of Josiah Quincy
Henry Clay 1777–1852: speech in Congress, 8 January 1813

4 The Congress makes no progress; it dances.
on the Congress of Vienna
Charles-Joseph, Prince de Ligne 1735–1814: Auguste de la Garde-Chambonas *Souvenirs du Congrès de Vienne* (1820)

5 The compact which exists between the North and the South is "a covenant with death and an agreement with hell."
William Lloyd Garrison 1805–79: resolution adopted by the Massachusetts Anti-Slavery Society, 27 January 1843; in allusion to *Isaiah* "We have made a covenant with death, and with hell are we at agreement"

6 I do not regard the procuring of peace as a matter in which we should play the role of arbiter between different opinions . . . more that of an honest broker who really wants to press the business forward.
Otto von Bismarck 1815–98: speech to the Reichstag, 19 February 1878

7 The agonies of a man who has to finish a difficult negotiation, and at the same time to entertain four royalties at a country house can be better imagined than described.
Lord Salisbury 1830–1903: letter to Lord Lyons, 5 June 1878

8 There is a homely old adage which runs: "Speak softly and carry a big stick; you will go far." If the American nation will speak softly, and yet build and keep at a pitch of the highest training a thoroughly efficient navy, the Monroe Doctrine will go far.
Theodore Roosevelt 1858–1919: speech in Chicago, 3 April 1903

9 What do you expect when I'm between two men of whom one [Lloyd George] thinks he is Napoleon and the other [Woodrow Wilson] thinks he is Jesus Christ?
to André Tardieu, on being asked why he always gave in to Lloyd George at the Paris Peace Conference, 1918
Georges Clemenceau 1841–1929: letter from Harold Nicolson to his wife, 20 May 1919

10 I gather it has now been decided not to embrace the Russian bear, but to hold out a hand and accept its paw gingerly. No more. The worst of both worlds.

Henry ("Chips") Channon 1897–1958: diary 16 May 1939

11 Personally I feel happier now that we have no allies to be polite to and to pamper.
to Queen Mary, 27 June 1940
George VI 1895–1952: John Wheeler-Bennett *King George VI* (1958)

12 Negotiating with de Valera . . . is like trying to pick up mercury with a fork.
to which de Valera replied, "Why doesn't he use a spoon?"
David Lloyd George 1863–1945: M. J. MacManus *Eamon de Valera* (1944)

13 I do not see any other way of realizing our hopes about World Organization in five or six days. Even the Almighty took seven.
to Franklin Roosevelt on the likely duration of the Yalta conference with Stalin
Winston Churchill 1874–1965: *The Second World War* (1954)

14 To jaw-jaw is always better than to war-war.
Winston Churchill 1874–1965: speech at White House, 26 June 1954

15 A diplomat these days is nothing but a head-waiter who's allowed to sit down occasionally.
Peter Ustinov 1921– : *Romanoff and Juliet* (1956)

16 A diplomat . . . is a person who can tell you to go to hell in such a way that you actually look forward to the trip.
Caskie Stinnett 1911– : *Out of the Red* (1960)

17 Let us never negotiate out of fear. But let us never fear to negotiate.
John F. Kennedy 1917–63: inaugural address, 20 January 1961

Discontent
see **Satisfaction and Discontent**

Discoveries
see **Inventions and Discoveries**

Disillusion and Cynicism

1 To get practice in being refused.
on being asked why he was begging for alms from a statue
Diogenes 404–323 BC: Diogenes Laertius *Lives of the Philosophers*

2 Kill them all; God will recognize his own.
when asked how the true Catholics could be distinguished from the heretics at the massacre of Béziers, 1209
Arnald-Amaury, abbot of Citeaux : Jonathan Sumption *The Albigensian Crusade* (1978)

3 Tell zeal it wants devotion;
Tell love it is but lust;
Tell time it metes but motion;
Tell flesh it is but dust:
And wish them not reply,
For thou must give the lie.
Walter Ralegh *c.* 1552–1618: "The Lie" (1608)

4 Paris is well worth a mass.
Henri of Navarre, a Huguenot, on becoming King of France
Henri IV (Henri of Navarre) 1553–1610: attributed to Henri IV; alternatively to his minister Sully, in conversation with Henri

5 What makes all doctrines plain and clear?
About two hundred pounds a year.
And that which was proved true before,
Prove false again? Two hundred more.
Samuel Butler 1612–80: *Hudibras* pt. 3 (1680)

6 Everything has been said, and we are more than seven thousand years of human thought too late.
Jean de la Bruyère 1645–96: *Les Caractères ou les moeurs de ce siècle* (1688)

7 "Blessed is the man who expects nothing, for he shall never be disappointed" was the ninth beatitude.
Alexander Pope 1688–1744: letter to Fortescue, 23 September 1725

8 And finds, with keen discriminating sight,
Black's not so black;—nor white so very white.
George Canning 1770–1827: "New Morality" (1821)

9 Now my sere fancy "falls into the yellow
Leaf," and imagination droops her pinion,
And the sad truth which hovers o'er my desk
Turns what was once romantic to burlesque.
with allusion to Shakespeare
Macbeth *"My way of life is fall'n Into the sear, the yellow leaf"*
Lord Byron 1788–1824: *Don Juan* (1819–24)

10 I never nursed a dear Gazelle, to glad me with its soft black eye, but when it came to know me well, and love me, it was sure to marry a market-gardener.
Charles Dickens 1812–70: *The Old Curiosity Shop* (1841); see **Transience** 10

11 Never glad confident morning again!
Robert Browning 1812–89: "The Lost Leader" (1845)

12 Cynicism is intellectual dandyism without the coxcomb's feathers.
George Meredith 1828–1909: *The Egoist* (1879)

13 Take the life-lie away from the average man and straight away you take away his happiness.
Henrik Ibsen 1828–1906: *The Wild Duck* (1884)

14 The flesh, alas, is wearied; and I have read all the books there are.
Stéphane Mallarmé 1842–98: "Brise Marin" (1887)

15 A man who knows the price of everything and the value of nothing.
definition of a cynic
Oscar Wilde 1854–1900: *Lady Windermere's Fan* (1892)

16 No man in his heart is quite so cynical as a well-bred woman.
W. Somerset Maugham 1874–1965: *A Writer's Notebook* (1949) written in 1896

17 CYNIC, *n.* A blackguard whose faulty vision sees things as they are, not as they ought to be.
Ambrose Bierce 1842–?1914: *Cynic's Word Book* (1906)

18 And nothing to look backward to with pride,
And nothing to look forward to with hope.
Robert Frost 1874–1963: "The Death of the Hired Man" (1914)

19 Disillusionment in living is the finding out nobody agrees with you not those that are and were fighting with you. Disillusionment in living is the finding out nobody agrees with you not those that are fighting for you. Complete disillusionment is when you realize that no one can for they can't change.
Gertrude Stein 1874–1946: *Making of Americans* (1934)

20 Cynicism is an unpleasant way of saying the truth.
Lillian Hellman 1905–84: *The Little Foxes* (1939)

21 Reason and Progress, the old firm,
is selling out! Everyone get out
while the going's good. Those
forgotten shares you had in the
old traditions, the old beliefs are
going up—up and up and up.
John Osborne 1929–94: *Look Back in
Anger* (1956)

22 If someone tells you he is going
to make a "realistic decision,"
you immediately understand that
he has resolved to do something
bad.
Mary McCarthy 1912–89: *On the
Contrary* (1961) "American Realist
Playwrights"

23 Like all dreamers, I mistook
disenchantment for truth.
Jean-Paul Sartre 1905–80: *Les Mots*
(1964) "Écrire"

24 The children of these disillusioned
colored pioneers inherited the
total lot of their parents—the
disappointments, the anger. To
add to their misery, they had
little hope of deliverance. For
where does one run to when he's
already in the promised land?
Claude Brown 1937–   : *Manchild in
the Promised Land* (1965)

Dislikes
see **Likes and Dislikes**

Dogs
see also **Animals**

1 I am his Highness' dog at Kew;
Pray, tell me sir, whose dog are
you?
Alexander Pope 1688–1744:
"Epigram Engraved on the Collar of
a Dog which I gave to his Royal
Highness" (1738)

2 My dog! what remedy remains,
Since, teach you all I can,
I see you, after all my pains,
So much resemble man!
William Cowper 1731–1800: "On a
Spaniel called Beau, killing a young
bird" (written 1793)

3 Near this spot are deposited the
remains of one who possessed
beauty without vanity, strength
without insolence, courage
without ferocity, and all the
virtues of Man, without his vices.
Lord Byron 1788–1824: "Inscription
on the Monument of a
Newfoundland Dog" (1808)

4 The more one gets to know of
men, the more one values dogs.
*also attributed to Mme. Roland in
the form "The more I see of men,
the more I like dogs"*
A. Toussenel 1803–85: *L'Esprit des
bêtes* (1847)

5 We were regaled by a dogfight . . .
How odd that people of sense
should find any pleasure in being
accompanied by a beast who is
always spoiling conversation.
Lord Macaulay 1800–59: G. O.
Trevelyan *Life and Letters of
Macaulay* (1876)

6 They say a reasonable amount o'
fleas is good fer a dog—keeps him
from broodin' over bein' a dog,
mebbe.
Edward Noyes Westcott 1846–98:
David Harum (1898)

7 The great pleasure of a dog is
that you may make a fool of
yourself with him and not only
will he not scold you, but he will
make a fool of himself too.
Samuel Butler 1835–1902:
Notebooks (1912)

8 There is sorrow enough in the
natural way
From men and women to fill our
day;
But when we are certain of
sorrow in store,
Why do we always arrange for
more?

Brothers and Sisters, I bid you
beware
Of giving your heart to a dog to
tear.
Rudyard Kipling 1865–1936: "The
Power of the Dog" (1909)

9 I'm a lean dog, a keen dog, a
    wild dog, and lone;
I'm a rough dog, a tough dog,
    hunting on my own;
I'm a bad dog, a mad dog,
    teasing silly sheep;
I love to sit and bay at the moon,
    to keep fat souls from sleep.
Irene Rutherford McLeod 1891–1964:
"Lone Dog" (1915)

10 Any man who hates dogs and
    babies can't be all bad.
of W. C. Fields, and often attributed
to him
Leo Rosten 1908–97: speech at
Masquers' Club dinner, 16 February
1939

11 And our little girl, Tricia, the six-
    year-old, named it Checkers. And
    you know, the kids love the dog,
    and I just want to say this right
    now, that regardless of what they
    do about it, we're going to keep
    it.
Richard M. Nixon 1913–94:
"Checkers" speech (23 September
1952)

12 That indefatigable and unsavoury
    engine of pollution, the dog.
John Sparrow 1906–92: letter to *The
Times* (UK) 30 September 1975

Doubt
see **Certainty and Doubt**

Dreams
see also **Sleep**

1 O God! I could be bounded in a
    nut-shell, and count myself a king
    of infinite space, were it not that I
    have bad dreams.

William Shakespeare 1564–1616:
Hamlet (1601)

2 That children dream not in the
    first half year, that men dream
    not in some countries, are to me
    sick men's dreams, dreams out of
    the ivory gate, and visions before
    midnight.
Thomas Browne 1605–82: "On
Dreams"

3 The dream of reason produces
    monsters.
Goya 1746–1828: *Los Caprichos*
(1799)

4 Was it a vision, or a waking
    dream?
Fled is that music:—do I wake or
    sleep?
John Keats 1795–1821: "Ode to a
Nightingale" (1820)

5 The quick Dreams,
The passion-wingèd Ministers of
    thought.
Percy Bysshe Shelley 1792–1822:
Adonais (1821)

6 He cursed him in sleeping, that
    every night
He should dream of the devil, and
    wake in a fright.
R. H. Barham 1788–1845: "The
Jackdaw of Rheims" (1840)

7 I have spread my dreams under
    your feet;
Tread softly because you tread on
    my dreams.
W. B. Yeats 1865–1939: "He Wishes
for the Cloths of Heaven" (1899)

8 The interpretation of dreams is
    the royal road to a knowledge of
    the unconscious activities of the
    mind.
often quoted as, "Dreams are the
royal road to the unconscious"
Sigmund Freud 1856–1939: *The
Interpretation of Dreams* (2nd ed.,
1909)

9 How many of our daydreams
would darken into nightmares if
there seemed any danger of their
coming true!
Logan Pearsall Smith 1865–1946:
Afterthoughts (1931)

10 Have you noticed . . . there is
never any third act in a
nightmare? They bring you to a
climax of terror and then leave
you there. They are the work of
poor dramatists.
Max Beerbohm 1872–1956: S. N.
Behrman *Conversations with Max*
(1960)

11 All the things one has forgotten
scream for help in dreams.
Elias Canetti 1905–94: *Die Provinz
der Menschen* (1973)

Dress
see also **Fashion**

1 Costly thy habit as thy purse can
buy,
But not expressed in fancy; rich,
not gaudy;
For the apparel oft proclaims the
man.
William Shakespeare 1564–1616:
Hamlet (1601)

2 Robes loosely flowing, hair as free:
Such sweet neglect more taketh
me,
Than all the adulteries of art;
They strike mine eyes, but not
my heart.
Ben Jonson c. 1573–1637: *Epicene*
(1609)

3 Whenas in silks my Julia goes,
Then, then (methinks) how
sweetly flows
That liquefaction of her clothes.
Next, when I cast mine eyes and
see
That brave vibration each way
free;
O how that glittering taketh me!
Robert Herrick 1591–1674: "Upon
Julia's Clothes" (1648)

4 A lady, if undressed at Church,
looks silly,
One cannot be devout in
dishabilly.
George Farquhar 1678–1707: *The
Stage Coach* (1704)

5 She wears her clothes, as if they
were thrown on her with a
pitchfork.
Jonathan Swift 1667–1745: *Polite
Conversation* (1738)

6 Let it be observed, that
slovenliness is no part of religion;
that neither this, nor any text of
Scripture, condemns neatness of
apparel. Certainly this is a duty,
not a sin. "Cleanliness is, indeed,
next to godliness."
John Wesley 1703–91: *Sermons on
Several Occasions* (1788)

7 No perfumes, but very fine linen,
plenty of it, and country washing.
Beau Brummell 1778–1840: *Memoirs
of Harriette Wilson* (1825)

8 She just wore
Enough for modesty—no more.
Robert Buchanan 1841–1901: "White
Rose and Red" (1873)

9 The sense of being well-dressed
gives a feeling of inward
tranquillity which religion is
powerless to bestow.
Miss C. F. Forbes 1817–1911: R. W.
Emerson *Letters and Social Aims*
(1876)

10 You should never have your best
trousers on when you go out to
fight for freedom and truth.
Henrik Ibsen 1828–1906: *An Enemy
of the People* (1882)

11 Her frocks are built in Paris, but
she wears them with a strong
English accent.
Saki 1870–1916: *Reginald* (1904)

12 His socks compelled one's attention without losing one's respect.
Saki 1870–1916: *Chronicles of Clovis* (1911)

13 When you're all dressed up and have no place to go.
George Whiting: title of song (1912)

14 Satan himself can't save a woman who wears thirty-shilling corsets under a thirty-guinea costume.
Rudyard Kipling 1865–1936: *Debits and Credits* (1926)

15 From the cradle to the grave, underwear first, last and all the time.
Bertolt Brecht 1898–1956: *The Threepenny Opera* (1928)

16 The Right Hon. was a tubby little chap who looked as if he had been poured into his clothes and had forgotten to say "When!"
P. G. Wodehouse 1881–1975: *Very Good, Jeeves* (1930)

17 The trick of wearing mink is to look as though you were wearing a cloth coat. The trick of wearing a cloth coat is to look as though you are wearing mink.
Pierre Balmain 1914–82: in *Observer* (UK) 25 December 1955

18 *on being asked what she wore in bed*: Chanel No. 5.
Marilyn Monroe 1926–62: Pete Martin *Marilyn Monroe* (1956)

19 Haute Couture should be fun, foolish and almost unwearable.
Christian Lacroix 1951– : attributed, 1987

20 It is to impossible to be well dressed in cheap shoes.
Hardy Amies 1909– : *The Englishman's Suit* (1994)

21 Every time you open your wardrobe, you look at your clothes and you wonder what you are going to wear. What you are really saying is "Who am I going to be today?"
Fay Weldon 1931– : in *New Yorker* 26 June 1995

Drink
see **Food and Drink**

Drugs

1 Almighty God hath not bestowed on mankind a remedy of so universal an extent and so efficacious in curing divers maladies as opiates.
Thomas Sydenham 1624–89: *Observationes Medicae* (1676); MS version given in 1991 ed.

2 Thou hast the keys of Paradise, oh just, subtle, and mighty opium!
Thomas De Quincey 1785–1859: *Confessions of an English Opium Eater* (1822)

3 Have you ever seen the pictures of the wretched poet Coleridge? He smoked opium. Take a look at Coleridge, he was green about the gills and a stranger to the lavatory.
warning his son to avoid opium on account of its "terrible binding effect," c. 1937
Clifford Mortimer d. 1960: John Mortimer *Clinging to the Wreckage* (1982)

4 Cocaine habit-forming? Of course not. I ought to know. I've been using it for years.
Tallulah Bankhead 1903–68: *Tallulah* (1952)

5 In this country, don't forget, a habit is no damn private hell. There's no solitary confinement outside of jail. A habit is hell for those you love.

Billie Holiday 1915–59: *Lady Sings the Blues* (1956, with William F. Duffy)

6 Every form of addiction is bad, no matter whether the narcotic be alcohol or morphine or idealism.
Carl Gustav Jung 1875–1961: *Erinnerungen, Träume, Gedanken* (1962)

7 I'll die young, but it's like kissing God.
on his drug addiction
Lenny Bruce 1925–66: attributed

8 We can no more hope to end drug abuse by eliminating heroin and cocaine than we could alter the suicide rate by outlawing high buildings or the sale of rope.
Ben Whittaker 1934– : *The Global Fix* (1987)

9 Alcohol didn't cause the high crime rates of the '20s and '30s, Prohibition did. Drugs don't cause today's alarming crime rates, but drug prohibition does.
quoted by Judge James C. Paine, addressing the Federal Bar Association in Miami, 1991
David Boaz 1953– : "The Legalization of Drugs" 27 April 1988

10 I experimented with marijuana a time or two. And I didn't like it, and I didn't inhale.
Bill Clinton 1946– : in *Washington Post* 30 March 1992

11 Sure thing, man. I used to be a laboratory myself once.
on being asked to autograph a fan's school chemistry book
Keith Richards 1943– : in *Independent (UK) on Sunday* 7 August 1994

Drunkenness
see also **Alcohol**

1 Drink, sir, is a great provoker of three things . . . nose-painting, sleep, and urine. Lechery, sir, it provokes, and unprovokes; it provokes the desire, but it takes away the performance.
William Shakespeare 1564–1616: *Macbeth* (1606)

2 Lo! the poor toper whose untutored sense,
Sees bliss in ale, and can with wine dispense;
Whose head proud fancy never taught to steer,
Beyond the muddy ecstasies of beer.
George Crabbe 1754–1832: "Inebriety" (1775); cf. **Ignorance 3**

3 A man who exposes himself when he is intoxicated, has not the art of getting drunk.
Samuel Johnson 1709–84: James Boswell *Life of Samuel Johnson* (1791) 24 April 1779

4 Man, being reasonable, must get drunk;
The best of life is but intoxication.
Lord Byron 1788–1824: *Don Juan* (1819–24)

5 Better sleep with a sober cannibal than a drunken Christian.
Herman Melville 1819–91: *Moby Dick* (1851)

6 It would be better that England should be free than that England should be compulsorily sober.
William Connor Magee 1821–91: speech on the Intoxicating Liquor Bill, House of Lords, 2 May 1872

7 Licker talks mighty loud w'en it git loose fum de jug.
Joel Chandler Harris 1848–1908: *Uncle Remus: His Songs and His Sayings* (1880)

8 R-E-M-O-R-S-E!
Those dry Martinis did the work
   for me;
Last night at twelve I felt
   immense,
Today I feel like thirty cents.
My eyes are bleared, my coppers
   hot,
I'll try to eat, but I cannot.
It is no time for mirth and
   laughter,
The cold, grey dawn of the
   morning after.
George Ade 1866–1944: *The Sultan
of Sulu* (1903)

9 Love makes the world go round?
Not at all. Whisky makes it go
round twice as fast.
Compton Mackenzie 1883–1972:
Whisky Galore (1947)

10 A man you don't like who drinks
as much as you do.
definition of an alcoholic
Dylan Thomas 1914–53: Constantine
Fitzgibbon *Life of Dylan Thomas*
(1965)

11 The light did him harm, but not
as much as looking at things did;
he resolved, having done it once,
never to move his eyeballs again.
A dusty thudding in his head
made the scene before him beat
like a pulse. His mouth had been
used as a latrine by some small
creature of the night, and then as
its mausoleum.
Kingsley Amis 1922–95: *Lucky Jim*
(1953)

12 One more drink and I'd have
been under the host.
Dorothy Parker 1893–1967: Howard
Teichmann *George S. Kaufman*
(1972)

13 You're not drunk if you can lie
on the floor without holding on.
Dean Martin 1917–95: Paul Dickson
Official Rules (1978)

Duty and Responsibility

1 Had I but served God as diligently
as I have served the King, he
would not have given me over in
my grey hairs.
Thomas Wolsey *c.* 1475–1530:
George Cavendish *Negotiations of
Thomas Wolsey* (1641)

2 Do your duty, and leave the
outcome to the Gods.
Pierre Corneille 1606–84: *Horace*
(1640)

3 I could not love thee, Dear, so
much,
Loved I not honour more.
Richard Lovelace 1618–58: "To
Lucasta, Going to the Wars" (1649)

4 England expects that every man
will do his duty.
*at the battle of Trafalgar, 21 October
1805*
Horatio, Lord Nelson 1758–1805:
Robert Southey *Life of Nelson* (1813)

5 Stern daughter of the voice of
God!
O Duty!
William Wordsworth 1770–1850:
"Ode to Duty" (1807)

6 When a man assumes a public
trust, he should consider himself
as public property.
Thomas Jefferson 1743–1826: to
Baron von Humboldt, 1807; B. L.
Rayner *Life of Jefferson* (1834)

7 The brave man inattentive to his
duty, is worth little more to his
country, than the coward who
deserts her in the hour of danger.
*to troops who had abandoned their
lines during the battle of New
Orleans, 8 January 1815*
Andrew Jackson 1767–1845:
attributed

8 Do the work that's nearest,
Though it's dull at whiles,
Helping, when we meet them,

Lame dogs over stiles.
Charles Kingsley 1819–75: "The
Invitation. To Tom Hughes" (1856)

9 The words *God, Immortality, Duty*—
pronounced, with terrible
earnestness, how inconceivable
was the *first*, how unbelievable
the *second*, and yet how
peremptory and absolute the
third.
George Eliot 1819–80: F. W. H. Myers
"George Eliot," in *Century Magazine*
November 1881

10 On an occasion of this kind it
becomes more than a moral duty
to speak one's mind. It becomes a
pleasure.
Oscar Wilde 1854–1900: *The
Importance of Being Earnest* (1895)

11 Take up the White Man's burden—
Send forth the best ye breed—
Go, bind your sons to exile
To serve your captives' need.
Rudyard Kipling 1865–1936: "The
White Man's Burden" (1899)

12 When a stupid man is doing
something he is ashamed of, he
always declares that it is his duty.
George Bernard Shaw 1856–1950:
Caesar and Cleopatra (1901)

13 If we believe a thing to be bad,
and if we have a right to prevent
it, it is our duty to try to prevent
it and to damn the consequences.
Lord Milner 1854–1925: speech in
Glasgow, 26 November 1909

14 People will do things from a sense
of duty which they would never
attempt as a pleasure.
Saki 1870–1916: *The Chronicles of
Clovis* (1911)

15 The great peaks of honour we
had forgotten—Duty, Patriotism,
and—clad in glittering white—the
great pinnacle of Sacrifice,
pointing like a rugged finger to
Heaven.

David Lloyd George 1863–1945:
speech at Queen's Hall, London, 19
September 1914

16 A sense of duty is useful in work,
but offensive in personal relations.
People wish to be liked, not to be
endured with patient resignation.
Bertrand Russell 1872–1970: *The
Conquest of Happiness* (1930)

17 Power without responsibility: the
prerogative of the harlot
throughout the ages.
*summing up Lord Beaverbrook's
political standpoint as a newspaper
editor; Stanley Baldwin, Kipling's
cousin, subsequently obtained
permission to use the phrase in a
speech in London on 18 March 1931*
Rudyard Kipling 1865–1936: in
Kipling Journal December 1971

18 I know this—a man got to do
what he got to do.
John Steinbeck 1902–68: *Grapes of
Wrath* (1939)

19 The buck stops here.
Harry S. Truman 1884–1972:
unattributed motto on Truman's
desk

The Earth
see also **Nature, Pollution and the
Environment, The Universe**

1 The earth is the Lord's, and all
that therein is: the compass of the
world, and they that dwell
therein.
Bible: Psalm 24

2 Above the smoke and stir of this
dim spot,
Which men call earth.
John Milton 1608–74: *Comus* (1637)

3 As low as where this earth
Spins like a fretful midge.
Dante Gabriel Rossetti 1828–82:
"The Blessed Damozel" (1870)

4 The earth does not argue,
Is not pathetic, has no
    arrangements,
Does not scream, haste, persuade,
    threaten, promise,
Makes no discriminations, has no
    conceivable failures,
Closes nothing, refuses nothing,
    shuts none out.
Walt Whitman 1819–92: "A Song of
the Rolling Earth" (1881)

5 Let me enjoy the earth no less
Because the all-enacting Might
That fashioned forth its loveliness
Had other aims than my delight.
Thomas Hardy 1840–1928: "Let me
Enjoy" (1909)

6 The new electronic
interdependence recreates the
world in the image of a global
village.
Marshall McLuhan 1911–80: *The
Gutenberg Galaxy* (1962)

7 Now there is one outstandingly
important fact regarding
Spaceship Earth, and that is that
no instruction book came with it.
R. Buckminster Fuller 1895–1983:
*Operating Manual for Spaceship
Earth* (1969)

8 The Alps, the Rockies and all
other mountains are related to
the earth, the Himalayas to the
heavens.
John Kenneth Galbraith 1908– : *A
Life in our Times* (1981)

9 How inappropriate to call this
planet Earth when it is clearly
Ocean.
Arthur C. Clarke 1917– : in *Nature*
1990; attributed

Eating
see **Cooking and Eating**

Economics
see also **Debt and Borrowing, Money,
Thrift and Extravagance**

1 Finance is, as it were, the
stomach of the country, from
which all the other organs take
their tone.
W. E. Gladstone 1809–98: article on
finance, 1858; H. C. G. Matthew
Gladstone 1809–1874 (1986)

2 There can be no economy where
there is no efficiency.
Benjamin Disraeli 1804–81: address
to his constituents, 1 October 1868

3 Lenin was right. There is no
subtler, no surer means of
overturning the existing basis of
society than to debauch the
currency.
John Maynard Keynes 1883–1946:
*The Economic Consequences of the
Peace* (1919)

4 Costs merely register competing
attractions.
Frank H. Knight 1885–1973: *Risk,
Uncertainty and Profit* (1921)

5 The cold metal of economic
theory is in Marx's pages
immersed in such a wealth of
steaming phrases as to acquire a
temperature not naturally its
own.
Joseph Alois Schumpeter 1883–1950:
Capitalism, Socialism and Democracy
(1942)

6 Everyone is always in favour of
general economy and particular
expenditure.
Anthony Eden 1897–1977: in
Observer (UK) 17 June 1956

7 In a community where public
services have failed to keep

abreast of private consumption things are very different. Here, in an atmosphere of private opulence and public squalor, the private goods have full sway.
John Kenneth Galbraith 1908– : *The Affluent Society* (1958)

8 Expenditure rises to meet income.
C. Northcote Parkinson 1909–93: *The Law and the Profits* (1960)

9 What a country calls its vital economic interests are not the things which enable its citizens to live, but the things which enable it to make war.
Simone Weil 1909–43: W. II. Auden *A Certain World* (1971)

10 Small is beautiful. A study of economics as if people mattered.
E. F. Schumacher 1911–77: title of book (1973)

11 Call a thing immoral or ugly, soul-destroying or a degradation of man, a peril to the peace of the world or to the well-being of future generations: as long as you have not shown it to be "uneconomic" you have not really questioned its right to exist, grow, and prosper.
E. F. Schumacher 1911–77: *Small is Beautiful* (1973)

12 Inflation is the one form of taxation that can be imposed without legislation.
Milton Friedman 1912– : in *Observer* (UK) 22 September 1974

13 First of all the Georgian silver goes, and then all that nice furniture that used to be in the saloon. Then the Canalettos go.
on privatization; often quoted as "selling the family silver"
Harold Macmillan 1894–1986: speech to the Tory Reform Group, 8 November 1985

14 If the policy isn't hurting, it isn't working.
on controlling inflation
John Major 1943– : speech in Northampton, 27 October 1989

15 Balancing the budget is like going to heaven. Everybody wants to do it, but nobody wants to do what you have to do to get there.
Phil Gramm 1942– : in a television interview, 16 September 1990

16 Trickle-down theory—the less than elegant metaphor that if one feeds the horse enough oats, some will pass through to the road for the sparrows.
John Kenneth Galbraith 1908– : *The Culture of Contentment* (1992)

Education and Teaching
see also **Examinations, Universities**

1 Get learning with a great sum of money, and get much gold by her.
Bible: Ecclesiasticus

2 Whereas then a rattle is a suitable occupation for infant children, education serves as a rattle for young people when older.
Aristotle 384–322 BC: *Politics*

3 Even while they teach, men learn.
Seneca ("the Younger") c. 4 BC–AD 65: *Epistulae Morales*

4 And gladly wolde he lerne and gladly teche.
Geoffrey Chaucer c. 1343–1400: *The Canterbury Tales* "The General Prologue"

5 That lyf so short, the craft so long to lerne.
Geoffrey Chaucer c. 1343–1400: *The Parliament of Fowls*; cf. **Medicine 2**

6 There is no such whetstone, to sharpen a good wit and

encourage a will to learning, as is
praise.
Roger Ascham 1515–68: *The
Schoolmaster* (1570)

7 I would I had bestowed that time
in the tongues that I have in
fencing, dancing, and bear-
baiting. O! had I but followed the
arts!
William Shakespeare 1564–1616:
Twelfth Night (1601)

8 Whilst others have been at the
balloo, I have been at my book,
and am now past the craggy
paths of study, and come to the
flowery plains of honour and
reputation.
Ben Jonson c. 1573–1637: *Volpone*
(1606)

9 And let a scholar all Earth's
volumes carry,
He will be but a walking
dictionary.
George Chapman c. 1559–1634: *The
Tears of Peace* (1609)

10 Reading maketh a full man;
conference a ready man; and
writing an exact man.
Francis Bacon 1561–1626: *Essays*
(1625) "Of Studies"

11 Studies serve for delight, for
ornament, and for ability.
Francis Bacon 1561–1626: *Essays*
(1625) "Of Studies"

12 Men must be taught as if you
taught them not,
And things unknown proposed as
things forgot.
Alexander Pope 1688–1744: *An
Essay on Criticism* (1711)

13 Delightful task! to rear the tender
thought,
To teach the young idea how to
shoot.
James Thomson 1700–48: *The
Seasons* (1746) "Spring"

14 Wear your learning, like your
watch in a private pocket; and do
not merely pull it out and strike
it, merely to show that you have
one.
Lord Chesterfield 1694–1773: *Letters
to his Son* (1774) 22 February 1748

15 There mark what ills the scholar's
life assail,
Toil, envy, want, the patron, and
the jail.
Samuel Johnson 1709–84: *The Vanity
of Human Wishes* (1749)

16 It is no matter what you teach
them [children] first, any more
than what leg you shall put into
your breeches first.
Samuel Johnson 1709–84: James
Boswell *Life of Samuel Johnson*
(1791) 26 July 1763

17 Few have been taught to any
purpose who have not been their
own teachers.
Joshua Reynolds 1723–92:
Discourses on Art 11 December 1769

18 Gie me ae spark o' Nature's fire,
That's a' the learning I desire.
Robert Burns 1759–96: "Epistle to J.
L[aprai]k" (1786)

19 Example is the school of mankind,
and they will learn at no other.
Edmund Burke 1729–97: *Two Letters
on the Proposals for Peace with the
Regicide Directory* (9th ed., 1796)

20 C-l-e-a-n, clean, verb active, to
make bright, to scour. W-i-n,
win, d-e-r, der, winder, a
casement. When the boy knows
this out of the book, he goes and
does it.
Charles Dickens 1812–70: *Nicholas
Nickleby* (1839)

21 Be a governess! Better be a slave
at once!
Charlotte Brontë 1816–55: *Shirley*
(1849)

22 I believe it will be absolutely necessary that you should prevail on our future masters to learn their letters.
popularized as "We must educate our masters"
Robert Lowe 1811–92: speech on the passing of the Reform Bill, House of Commons, 15 July 1867

23 Education makes a people easy to lead, but difficult to drive; easy to govern, but impossible to enslave.
Lord Brougham 1778–1868: attributed

24 Soap and education are not as sudden as a massacre, but they are more deadly in the long run.
Mark Twain 1835–1910: *A Curious Dream* (1872) "Facts concerning the Recent Resignation"

25 Let the children of the rich and poor take their seats together and know of no distinction save that of industry, good conduct, and intellect.
Townsend Harris 1804–78:

26 He who can, does. He who cannot, teaches.
George Bernard Shaw 1856–1950: *Man and Superman* (1903)

27 A teacher affects eternity; he can never tell where his influence stops.
Henry Brooks Adams 1838–1918: *The Education of Henry Adams* (1907)

28 The aim of education is the knowledge not of facts but of values.
William Ralph Inge 1860–1954: "The Training of the Reason" in A. C. Benson (ed.) *Cambridge Essays on Education* (1917)

29 The dawn of legibility in his handwriting has revealed his utter inability to spell.
Ian Hay 1876–1952: attributed; perhaps used in a dramatization of *The Housemaster* (1938)

30 To live for a time close to great minds is the best kind of education.
John Buchan 1875–1940: *Memory Hold-the-Door* (1940)

31 It [education] has produced a vast population able to read but unable to distinguish what is worth reading, an easy prey to sensations and cheap appeals.
G. M. Trevelyan 1876–1962: *English Social History* (1942)

32 The empires of the future are the empires of the mind.
Winston Churchill 1874–1965: speech at Harvard, 6 September 1943

33 Separate education facilities are inherently unequal.
Earl Warren 1891–1974: *Brown v. Board of Education* (17 May 1954)

34 Education ent only books and music—it's asking questions, all the time. There are millions of us, all over the country, and no one, not one of us, is asking questions, we're all taking the easiest way out.
Arnold Wesker 1932– : *Roots* (1959)

35 Education is the ability to listen to almost anything without losing your temper or your self-confidence.
Robert Frost 1874–1963: *Reader's Digest* (April 1960)

36 A child miseducated is a child lost.
John F. Kennedy 1917–63: *State of the Union* (11 January 1962)

37 The law of a boys' school is the law of the jungle. When you're strong, we're behind you, but if you're weak, we throw you to the boys.
Louis Auchincloss 1917– : *The Rector of Justin* (1964)

38 Education is what survives when what has been learned has been forgotten.
B. F. Skinner 1904–90: in *New Scientist* 21 May 1964

39 I read Shakespeare and the Bible and I can shoot dice. That's what I call a liberal education.
Tallulah Bankhead 1903–68: attributed

40 A liberal education is at the heart of a civil society, and at the heart of a liberal education is the act of teaching.
A. Bartlett Giamatti 1938–89: *Harper's* (July 1980)

41 If you are truly serious about preparing your child for the future, don't teach him to subtract—teach him to deduct.
Fran Lebowitz 1946– : *Social Studies* (1981)

42 A Harvard education consists of what you learn at Harvard while you are not studying.
James B. Conant 1893–1978: *Time* (29 September 1986)

43 I could always drop people from a helicopter into Lake Pontchartrain and see how many drown. But what we do is start from the shore and teach them how to swim.
on teaching college preparatory courses
J. W. Carmichael : *New York Times* (28 March 1990)

Elections
see also **Democracy**

1 The right of election is the very essence of the constitution.
"Junius": *Public Advertiser* 24 April 1769

2 To give victory to the right, not bloody bullets, but peaceful ballots only, are necessary.
usually quoted "The ballot is stronger than the bullet"
Abraham Lincoln 1809–65: speech, 18 May 1858

3 An election is coming. Universal peace is declared, and the foxes have a sincere interest in prolonging the lives of the poultry.
George Eliot 1819–80: *Felix Holt* (1866)

4 As for our majority . . . one is enough.
now often associated with Churchill
Benjamin Disraeli 1804–81: *Endymion* (1880)

5 I will not accept if nominated, and will not serve if elected.
on being urged to stand as Republican candidate in the 1884 US presidential election
William Tecumseh Sherman 1820–91: telegram to General Henderson; *Memoirs* (4th ed., 1891)

6 He has joined what even he would admit to be the majority.
on the death of a supporter of proportional representation
John Sparrow 1906–92: J. A. Gere and John Sparrow (eds.) *Geoffrey Madan's Notebooks* (1981); see **Death 9**

7 If there had been any formidable body of cannibals in the country he would have promised to provide them with free missionaries fattened at the taxpayer's expense.
of Harry Truman's success in the 1948 presidential campaign
H. L. Mencken 1880–1956: in *Baltimore Sun* 7 November 1948

8 Hell, I never vote *for* anybody. I always vote *against*.
W. C. Fields 1880–1946: Robert Lewis Taylor *W. C. Fields* (1950)

9 Don't buy a single vote more
than necessary. I'll be damned if
I'm going to pay for a landslide.
*telegraphed message from his
father, read at a Gridiron dinner in
Washington, 15 March 1958, and
almost certainly JFK's invention*
John F. Kennedy 1917–63: J. F. Cutler
Honey Fitz (1962)

10 Vote for the man who promises
least; he'll be the least
disappointing.
Bernard Baruch 1870–1965: Meyer
Berger *New York* (1960)

11 You won the elections, but I won
the count.
*replying to an accusation of ballot-
rigging*
Anastasio Somoza 1925–80: in
Guardian 17 June 1977; cf.
Democracy 24

12 You campaign in poetry. You
govern in prose.
Mario Cuomo 1932–   : in *New
Republic*, Washington, DC, 8 April
1985

Emotions

1 But I will wear my heart upon
my sleeve
For daws to peck at: I am not
what I am.
William Shakespeare 1564–1616:
Othello (1602–4)

2 A man whose blood
Is very snow-broth; one who
never feels
The wanton stings and motions of
the sense.
William Shakespeare 1564–1616:
Measure for Measure (1604)

3 Our passions are most like to
floods and streams;
The shallow murmur, but the
deep are dumb.
Walter Ralegh c. 1552–1618: "Sir
Walter Ralegh to the Queen" (1655)

4 The heart has its reasons which
reason knows nothing of.
Blaise Pascal 1623–62: *Pensées*
(1670)

5 Calm of mind, all passion spent.
John Milton 1608–74: *Samson
Agonistes* (1671)

6 The ruling passion, be it what it
will,
The ruling passion conquers
reason still.
Alexander Pope 1688–1744: *Epistles
to Several Persons* "To Lord
Bathurst" (1733)

7 What they call "heart" lies much
lower than the fourth waistcoat
button.
Georg Christoph Lichtenberg 1742–
99: notebook (1776–79)

8 You should have a softer pillow
than my heart.
*to his wife, who had rested her head
on his breast, c. 1814*
Lord Byron 1788–1824: E. C. Mayne
(ed.) *The Life and Letters of Anne
Isabella, Lady Noel Byron* (1929)

9 For ever warm and still to be
enjoyed,
For ever panting, and for ever
young;
All breathing human passion far
above,
That leaves a heart high-
sorrowful and cloyed,
A burning forehead, and a
parching tongue.
John Keats 1795–1821: "Ode on a
Grecian Urn" (1820)

10 We shall never learn to feel and
respect our real calling and
destiny, unless we have taught
ourselves to consider every thing
as moonshine, compared with the
education of the heart.
Sir Walter Scott 1771–1832: to J. G.
Lockhart, August 1825

11 There are strings . . . in the
human heart that had better not
be wibrated.
Charles Dickens 1812–70: *Barnaby
Rudge* (1841)

12 As you pass from the tender years
of youth into harsh and
embittered manhood, make sure
you take with you on your
journey all the human emotions!
Don't leave them on the road, for
you will not pick them up
afterwards!
Nikolai Gogol 1809–52: *Dead Souls*
(1842)

13 *on being told there was no English
word equivalent to* sensibilité:
Yes we have. Humbug.
Lord Palmerston 1784–1865:
attributed

14 One must have a heart of stone
to read the death of Little Nell
without laughing.
Oscar Wilde 1854–1900: Ada
Leverson *Letters to the Sphinx*
(1930)

15 The world of the emotions that
are so lightly called physical.
Colette 1873–1954: *Le Blé en herbe*
(1923)

16 The trumpets came out brazenly
with the last post. We all
swallowed our spittle, chokingly,
while our eyes smarted against
our wills. A man hates to be
moved to folly by a noise.
T. E. Lawrence 1888–1935: *The Mint*
(1955)

17 One may not regard the world as
a sort of metaphysical brothel for
emotions.
Arthur Koestler 1905–83: *Darkness
at Noon* (1940)

18 They had been corrupted by
money, and he had been
corrupted by sentiment.
Sentiment was the more

dangerous, because you couldn't
name its price. A man open to
bribes was to be relied upon
below a certain figure, but
sentiment might uncoil in the
heart at a name, a photograph,
even a smell remembered.
Graham Greene 1904–91: *The Heart
of the Matter* (1948)

19 Oh heavens, how I long for a
little ordinary human enthusiasm.
Just enthusiasm—that's all. I
want to hear a warm, thrilling
voice cry out Hallelujah!
Hallelujah! I'm alive!
John Osborne 1929–94: *Look Back in
Anger* (1956)

20 A man who has not passed
through the inferno of his
passions has never overcome
them.
Carl Gustav Jung 1875–1961:
Erinnerungen, Träume, Gedanken
(1962)

21 Sentimentality is the emotional
promiscuity of those who have no
sentiment.
Norman Mailer 1923– : *Cannibals
and Christians* (1966)

22 Passion always goes, and
boredom stays.
Coco Chanel 1883–1971: Frances
Kennett *Coco: the Life and Loves of
Gabrielle Chanel* (1989)

23 Do you know what "le vice
Anglais"—the English vice—
really is? Not flagellation, not
pederasty—whatever the French
believe it to be. It's our refusal to
admit our emotions. We think
they demean us, I suppose.
Terence Rattigan 1911–77: *In Praise
of Love* (1973)

24 There is no such thing as inner
peace. There is only nervousness
or death.
Fran Lebowitz 1946– : *Metropolitan
Life* (1978)

Employment
see also **Work**

1 For promotion cometh neither
  from the east, nor from the west:
  nor yet from the south.
  Bible: Psalm 75

2 I hold every man a debtor to his
  profession.
  Francis Bacon 1561–1626: *The
  Elements of the Common Law* (1596)

3 Thou art not for the fashion of
  these times,
  Where none will sweat but for
  promotion.
  William Shakespeare 1564–1616: *As
  You Like It* (1599)

4 'Tis the curse of service,
  Preferment goes by letter and
  affection,
  Not by the old gradation, where
  each second
  Stood heir to the first.
  William Shakespeare 1564–1616:
  Othello (1602–4)

5 Every time I make an
  appointment, I create a hundred
  malcontents and one ingrate.
  Louis XIV 1638–1715: Voltaire *Siècle
  de Louis XIV* (1768 ed.)

6 It is wonderful, when a
  calculation is made, how little the
  mind is actually employed in the
  discharge of any profession.
  Samuel Johnson 1709–84: James
  Boswell *Life of Samuel Johnson*
  (1791) 6 April 1775

7 Dr. — well remembered that he
  had a salary to receive, and only
  forgot that he had a duty to
  perform.
  Edward Gibbon 1737–94: *Memoirs of
  My Life* (1796)

8 To do nothing and get something,
  formed a boy's ideal of a manly
  career.

9 For more than five years I
  maintained myself thus solely by
  the labor of my hands, and I
  found, that by working about six
  weeks in a year, I could meet all
  the expenses of living.
  Henry David Thoreau 1817–62:
  Walden (1854) "Economy"

10 I pass my whole life, miss, in
   turning an immense pecuniary
   Mangle.
   Charles Dickens 1812–70: *A Tale of
   Two Cities* (1859)

11 Which of us . . . is to do the hard
   and dirty work for the rest—and
   for what pay? Who is to do the
   pleasant and clean work, and for
   what pay?
   John Ruskin 1819–1900: *Sesame and
   Lilies* (1865)

12 Naturally, the workers are
   perfectly free: the manufacturer
   does not force them to take his
   materials and his cards, but he
   says to them . . . "If you don't like
   to be frizzled in my frying-pan,
   you can take a walk into the
   fire."
   Friedrich Engels 1820–95: *The
   Condition of the Working Class in
   England in 1844* (1892)

13 When domestic servants are
   treated as human beings it is not
   worth while to keep them.
   George Bernard Shaw 1856–1950:
   Man and Superman (1903)

14 A man who has no office to go to—
   I don't care who he is—is a trial
   of which you can have no
   conception.
   George Bernard Shaw 1856–1950:
   The Irrational Knot (1905)

15 Lord Finchley tried to mend the
   Electric Light

Benjamin Disraeli 1804–81: *Sybil*
(1845)

Himself. It struck him dead: And
serve him right!
It is the business of the wealthy
man
To give employment to the
artisan.
Hilaire Belloc 1870–1953: "Lord
Finchley" (1911)

16 All professions are conspiracies
against the laity.
George Bernard Shaw 1856–1950:
The Doctor's Dilemma (1911)

17 Not a penny off the pay, not a
second on the day.
*often quoted with "minute"
substituted for "second"*
A. J. Cook 1885–1931: speech at
York, England, 3 April 1926

18 The most conservative man in
this world is the British Trade
Unionist when you want to
change him.
Ernest Bevin 1881–1951: speech,
Trades Union Congress, 8 September
1927

19 Had the employers of past
generations all of them dealt
fairly with their men there would
have been no unions.
Stanley Baldwin 1867–1947: speech
in Birmingham, 14 January 1931

20 Work is of two kinds: first,
altering the position of matter at
or near the earth's surface
relatively to other such matter;
second, telling other people to do
so. The first kind is unpleasant
and ill paid; the second is
pleasant and highly paid.
Bertrand Russell 1872–1970: *In
Praise of Idleness and Other Essays*
(1986) title essay (1932)

21 A professional is a man who can
do his job when he doesn't feel
like it. An amateur is a man who
can't do his job when he does feel
like it.
James Agate 1877–1947: diary 19 July
1945

22 If I would be a young man again
and had to decide how to make
my living, I would not try to
become a scientist or scholar or
teacher. I would rather choose to
be a plumber or a peddler in the
hope to find that modest degree
of independence still available
under present circumstances.
Albert Einstein 1879–1955: in
Reporter 18 November 1954

23 It's a recession when your
neighbor loses his job; it's a
depression when you lose yours.
Harry S. Truman 1884–1972: in
Observer (UK) 13 April 1958

24 By working faithfully eight hours
a day, you may eventually get to
be a boss and work twelve hours
a day.
Robert Frost 1874–1963: attributed

25 An industrial worker would
sooner have a £5 note but a
countryman must have praise.
Ronald Blythe 1922– : *Akenfield*
(1969)

26 How to be an effective secretary
is to develop the kind of lonely
self-abnegating sacrificial instincts
usually possessed only by the
early saints on their way to
martyrdom.
Jill Tweedie 1936–93: *It's Only Me*
(1980)

27 We spend most of our lives
working. So why do so few
people have a good time doing it?
Virgin is the possibility of good
times.
Richard Branson 1950– : interview
in *New York Times* 28 February 1993

28 Management that wants to
change an institution must first
show it loves that institution.

John Tusa 1936– : in *Observer* (UK)
27 February 1994

29 If management are using a word
you don't understand, nine times
out of ten they are making you
redundant.
John Edwards: on BBC Radio Four
Today, 10 June 1996

Endeavor
see **Achievement and Endeavor**

Endings
see **Beginnings and Endings**

Enemies

1 If thine enemy be hungry, give
him bread to eat; and if he be
thirsty, give him water to drink.
For thou shalt heap coals of fire
upon his head, and the Lord shall
reward thee.
Bible: Proverbs

2 *Delenda est Carthago.*Carthage
must be destroyed.
*warning included in every speech
made by Cato, whatever the subject*
Cato the Elder 234–149 BC: Pliny the
Elder *Naturalis Historia*

3 He that is not with me is against
me.
Bible: St. Matthew

4 Love your enemies, do good to
them which hate you.
Bible: St. Luke; cf. **Forgiveness 4**

5 I wish my deadly foe, no worse
Than want of friends, and empty
purse.
Nicholas Breton c. 1545–1626: "A
Farewell to Town" (1577)

6 Heat not a furnace for your foe so
hot
That it do singe yourself.
William Shakespeare 1564–1616:
Henry VIII (1613)

7 People wish their enemies dead—
but I do not; I say give them the
gout, give them the stone!
Lady Mary Wortley Montagu 1689–
1762: letter from Horace Walpole to
George Harcourt, 17 September 1778

8 He that wrestles with us
strengthens our nerves, and
sharpens our skill. Our antagonist
is our helper.
Edmund Burke 1729–97: *Reflections
on the Revolution in France* (1790)

9 Respect was mingled with
surprise,
And the stern joy which warriors
feel
In foemen worthy of their steel.
Sir Walter Scott 1771–1832: *The Lady
of the Lake* (1810)

10 He makes no friend who never
made a foe.
Alfred, Lord Tennyson 1809–92:
Idylls of the King "Lancelot and
Elaine" (1859)

11 A man cannot be too careful in
the choice of his enemies.
Oscar Wilde 1854–1900: *The Picture
of Dorian Gray* (1891)

12 You shall judge of a man by his
foes as well as by his friends.
Joseph Conrad 1857–1924: *Lord Jim*
(1900)

13 I am the enemy you killed, my
friend.
I knew you in this dark: for you
so frowned
Yesterday through me as you
jabbed and killed . . .
Let us sleep now.
Wilfred Owen 1893–1918: "Strange
Meeting" (written 1918)

14 Not while I'm alive 'e ain't!
*reply to the observation that Nye
Bevan was sometimes his own worst
enemy*
Ernest Bevin 1881–1951: Roderick

Barclay *Ernest Bevin and the Foreign Office* (1975)

15 Better to have him inside the tent pissing out, than outside pissing in.
of J. Edgar Hoover
Lyndon Baines Johnson 1908–73: David Halberstam *The Best and the Brightest* (1972)

16 Fidel Castro is right. You do not quieten your enemy by talking with him like a priest, but by burning him.
at a Communist Party meeting 17 December 1989
Nicolae Ceauşescu 1918–89: in *Guardian* 11 January 1990

England and the English
see also **Towns and Cities**

1 *Non Angli sed Angeli.*
Not Angles but Angels.
summarizing Bede Historia Ecclesiastica *"They answered that they were called Angles. 'It is well,' he said, 'for they have the faces of angels, and such should be the co-heirs of the angels of heaven'"*
Gregory the Great AD *c.* 540–604: oral tradition

2 This royal throne of kings, this sceptered isle,
This earth of majesty, this seat of Mars,
This other Eden, demi-paradise,
This fortress built by Nature for herself
Against infection and the hand of war,
This happy breed of men, this little world,
This precious stone set in the silver sea . . .
This blessèd plot, this earth, this realm, this England.
William Shakespeare 1564–1616: *Richard II* (1595)

3 That shire which we the Heart of England well may call.
of Warwickshire
Michael Drayton 1563–1631: *Poly-Olbion* (1612–22)

4 I know an Englishman,
Being flattered, is a lamb;
threatened, a lion.
George Chapman *c.* 1559–1634: *Alphonsus, Emperor of Germany* (1654)

5 The English take their pleasures sadly after the fashion of their country.
Maximilien de Béthune, Duc de Sully 1559–1641: attributed

6 Let not England forget her precedence of teaching nations how to live.
John Milton 1608–74: *The Doctrine and Discipline of Divorce* (1643)

7 Your Roman-Saxon-Danish-Norman English.
Daniel Defoe 1660–1731: *The True-Born Englishman* (1701)

8 The English are busy; they don't have time to be polite.
Montesquieu 1689–1755: *Pensées et fragments inédits . . .* vol. 2 (1901)

9 The English plays are like their English puddings: nobody has any taste for them but themselves.
Voltaire 1694–1778: Joseph Spence *Anecdotes* (ed. J. M. Osborn, 1966)

10 In England there are sixty different religions, and only one sauce.
Francesco Caracciolo 1752–99: attributed

11 England has saved herself by her exertions, and will, as I trust, save Europe by her example.
replying to a toast in which he had been described as the savior of his country in the wars with France

William Pitt 1759–1806: R. Coupland
War Speeches of William Pitt (1915)

12 We must be free or die, who
    speak the tongue
That Shakespeare spake; the faith
    and morals hold
Which Milton held.
William Wordsworth 1770–1850: "It
is not to be thought of that the
Flood" (1807)

13 I will not cease from mental fight,
Nor shall my sword sleep in my
    hand,
Till we have built Jerusalem,
In England's green and pleasant
    land.
William Blake 1757–1827: *Milton*
(1804–10) "And did those feet in
ancient time"

14 England is a nation of
    shopkeepers.
*the phrase "nation of shopkeepers"
had been used earlier by Samuel
Adams and Adam Smith*
Napoleon I 1769–1821: Barry E.
O'Meara *Napoleon in Exile* (1822); cf.
Business 8

15 Kent, sir—everybody knows Kent—
apples, cherries, hops, and
women.
Charles Dickens 1812–70: *Pickwick
Papers* (1837)

16 For he might have been a
    Roosian,
A French, or Turk, or Proosian,
Or perhaps Ital-ian!
But in spite of all temptations
To belong to other nations,
He remains an Englishman!
W. S. Gilbert 1836–1911: *HMS
Pinafore* (1878)

17 Winds of the World, give answer!
    They are whimpering to and
    fro—
And what should they know of
    England who only England
    know?

Rudyard Kipling 1865–1936: "The
English Flag" (1892)

18 When Adam and Eve were
    dispossessed
Of the garden hard by Heaven,
They planted another one down
    in the west,
'Twas Devon, glorious Devon!
Harold Edwin Boulton 1859–1935:
"Glorious Devon" (1902)

19 Ask any man what nationality he
would prefer to be, and ninety-
nine out of a hundred will tell
you that they would prefer to be
Englishmen.
Cecil Rhodes 1853–1902: Gordon Le
Sueur *Cecil Rhodes* (1913)

20 Englishmen never will be slaves:
they are free to do whatever the
Government and public opinion
allow them to do.
George Bernard Shaw 1856–1950:
Man and Superman (1903)

21 Smile at us, pay us, pass us; but
    do not quite forget.
For we are the people of England,
    that never have spoken yet.
G. K. Chesterton 1874–1936: "The
Secret People" (1915)

22 God! I will pack, and take a train,
And get me to England once
    again!
For England's the one land, I
    know,
Where men with Splendid Hearts
    may go.
Rupert Brooke 1887–1915: "The Old
Vicarage, Grantchester" (1915)

23 How can what an Englishman
believes be heresy? It is a
contradiction in terms.
George Bernard Shaw 1856–1950:
Saint Joan (1924)

24 It is not that the Englishman
can't feel—it is that he is afraid
to feel. He has been taught at his
public school that feeling is bad

form. He must not express great joy or sorrow, or even open his mouth too wide when he talks—his pipe might fall out if he did.
E. M. Forster 1879–1970: *Abinger Harvest* (1936) "Notes on English Character"

25 Down here it was still the England I had known in my childhood: the railway cuttings smothered in wild flowers . . . the red buses, the blue policemen—all sleeping the deep, deep sleep of England, from which I sometimes fear that we shall never wake till we are jerked out of it by the roar of bombs.
George Orwell 1903–50: *Homage to Catalonia* (1938)

26 It is a family in which the young are generally thwarted and most of the power is in the hands of irresponsible uncles and bed-ridden aunts. Still, it is a family. It has its private language and its common memories, and at the approach of an enemy it closes its ranks. A family with the wrong members in control.
of England
George Orwell 1903–50: *The Lion and the Unicorn* (1941) "England Your England"

27 Old maids biking to Holy Communion through the mists of the autumn mornings . . . these are not only fragments, but *characteristic* fragments, of the English scene.
George Orwell 1903–50: *The Lion and the Unicorn* (1941) "England Your England" cf. **Britain 12**

28 An Englishman, even if he is alone, forms an orderly queue of one.
George Mikes 1912– : *How to be an Alien* (1946)

29 You never find an Englishman among the under-dogs—except in England, of course.
Evelyn Waugh 1903–66: *The Loved One* (1948)

30 This is a letter of hate. It is for you my countrymen, I mean those men of my country who have defiled it. The men with manic fingers leading the sightless, feeble, betrayed body of my country to its death . . . damn you England.
John Osborne 1929–94: in *Tribune* (UK) 18 August 1961

31 England's not a bad country . . . It's just a mean, cold, ugly, divided, tired, clapped-out, post-imperial, post-industrial slag-heap covered in polystyrene hamburger cartons.
Margaret Drabble 1939– : *A Natural Curiosity* (1989)

Entertaining and Hospitality

1 Bring hither the fatted calf, and kill it.
Bible: St. Luke

2 Be not forgetful to entertain strangers: for thereby some have entertained angels unawares.
Bible: Hebrews

3 Unbidden guests
Are often welcomest when they are gone.
William Shakespeare 1564–1616: *Henry VI, Part 1* (1592)

4 This day my wife made it appear to me that my late entertainment this week cost me above £12, an expense which I am almost ashamed of, though it is but once in a great while, and is the end for which, in the most part, we live, to have such a merry day once or twice in a man's life.
Samuel Pepys 1633–1703: diary 6 March 1669

5 He showed me his bill of fare to tempt me to dine with him; poh, said I, I value not your bill of fare, give me your bill of company.
Jonathan Swift 1667–1745: *Journal to Stella* 2 September 1711

6 For I, who hold sage Homer's rule the best,
Welcome the coming, speed the going guest.
Alexander Pope 1688–1744: *Imitations of Horace* (1734); "speed the parting guest" in Pope's translation of *The Odyssey* (1725–6)

7 Like other parties of the kind, it was first silent, then talky, then argumentative, then disputatious, then unintelligible, then altogethery, then inarticulate, and then drunk.
Lord Byron 1788–1824: letter to Thomas Moore, 31 October 1815

8 The sooner every party breaks up the better.
Jane Austen 1775–1817: *Emma* (1816)

9 Everyone knows that the real business of a ball is either to look out for a wife, to look after a wife, or to look after somebody else's wife.
R. S. Surtees 1805–64: *Mr. Facey Romford's Hounds* (1865)

10 If one plays good music, people don't listen and if one plays bad music people don't talk.
Oscar Wilde 1854–1900: *The Importance of Being Earnest* (1895)

11 At a dinner party one should eat wisely but not too well, and talk well but not too wisely.
W. Somerset Maugham 1874–1965: *Writer's Notebook* (1949); written in 1896

12 Guests can be, and often are, delightful, but they should never

be allowed to get the upper hand.
Elizabeth, Countess von Arnim 1866–1941: *All the Dogs in My Life* (1936)

13 Standing among savage scenery, the hotel offers stupendous revelations. There is a French widow in every bedroom, affording delightful prospects.
supposedly quoting a letter from a Tyrolean landlord
Gerard Hoffnung 1925–59: speech at the Oxford Union, 4 December 1958

14 I'm a man more dined against than dining.
Maurice Bowra 1898–1971: John Betjeman *Summoned by Bells* (1960); in allusion to Shakespeare *King Lear* "I am a man More sinned against than sinning."

15 An office party is not, as is sometimes supposed, the Managing Director's chance to kiss the tea-girl. It is the tea-girl's chance to kiss the Managing Director.
Katharine Whitehorn 1928– : *Roundabout* (1962) "The Office Party"

16 The best number for a dinner party is two—myself and a dam' good head waiter.
Nubar Gulbenkian 1896–1972: in *Daily Telegraph* (UK) 14 January 1965

The Environment
see **Pollution and the Environment**

Envy and Jealousy

1 Thou shalt not covet thy neighbour's house, thou shalt not covet thy neighbour's wife, nor his manservant, nor his maidservant, nor his ox, nor his ass, nor any thing that is thy neighbour's.
Bible: Exodus; cf. **9** below

2 Love is strong as death; jealousy
is cruel as the grave.
Bible: Song of Solomon

3 Oh! how bitter a thing it is to
look into happiness through
another man's eyes.
William Shakespeare 1564–1616: *As
You Like It* (1599)

4 O! beware, my lord, of jealousy;
It is the green-eyed monster
which doth mock
The meat it feeds on.
William Shakespeare 1564–1616:
Othello (1602–4)

5 A certain fox, it is said, wanted to
become a wolf. Ah! who can say
why no wolf has ever craved the
life of a sheep?
Jean de la Fontaine 1621–95: *Fables
Choisies* (1693 ed.)

6 Malice is of a low stature, but it
hath very long arms.
Lord Halifax 1633–95: *Political,
Moral, and Miscellaneous Thoughts
and Reflections* (1750) "Of Malice
and Envy"

7 Fools out of favour grudge at
knaves in place.
Daniel Defoe 1660–1731: *The True-
Born Englishman* (1701)

8 If something pleasant happens to
you, don't forget to tell it to your
friends, to make them feel bad.
Casimir, Comte de Montrond 1768–
1843: attributed; Comte J.
d'Estourmel *Derniers Souvenirs*
(1860)

9 Thou shalt not covet; but
tradition
Approves all forms of competition.
Arthur Hugh Clough 1819–61: "The
Latest Decalogue" (1862); see **1**
above

10 Jealousy is no more than feeling
alone against smiling enemies.
Elizabeth Bowen 1899–1973: *The
House in Paris* (1935)

11 To jealousy, nothing is more
frightful than laughter.
Françoise Sagan 1935– : *La
Chamade* (1965)

Epitaphs
see also **Death**

1 Go, tell the Spartans, thou who
passest by,
That here obedient to their laws
we lie.
*epitaph for the Spartans who died at
Thermopylae*
Simonides *c.* 556–468 BC: attributed;
Herodotus *Histories*

2 Saul and Jonathan were lovely
and pleasant in their lives, and in
their death they were not divided.
Bible: II Samuel

3 And some there be, which have
no memorial . . . and are become
as though they had never been
born . . .
But these were merciful men,
whose righteousness hath not
been forgotten . . .
Their seed shall remain for ever,
and their glory shall not be
blotted out.
Their bodies are buried in peace;
but their name liveth for
evermore.
Bible: Ecclesiasticus

4 What wee gave, wee have;
What wee spent, wee had;
What wee kept, wee lost.
Anonymous: epitaph on Edward
Courtenay, Earl of Devonshire (d.
1419) and his wife, at Tiverton

5 Here lies he who neither feared
nor flattered any flesh.
*said of John Knox, as he was buried,
26 November 1572*
James Douglas, Earl of Morton *c.*
1516–81: George R. Preedy *The Life
of John Knox* (1940)

6 The waters were his winding
    sheet, the sea was made his
    tomb;
  Yet for his fame the ocean sea,
    was not sufficient room.
on the death of John Hawkins
Richard Barnfield 1574–1627: *The
Encomion of Lady Pecunia* (1598)

7 My friend, judge not me,
  Thou seest I judge not thee.
  Betwixt the stirrup and the
    ground
  Mercy I asked, mercy I found.
*epitaph for a gentleman falling off
his horse*
William Camden 1551–1623: *Remains
Concerning Britain* (1605)

8 Rest in soft peace, and, asked, say
    here doth lie
  Ben Jonson his best piece of
    poetry.
Ben Jonson c. 1573–1637: "On My
First Son" (1616)

9 Good friend, for Jesu's sake
    forbear
  To dig the dust enclosed here.
  Blest be the man that spares
    these stones,
  And curst be he that moves my
    bones.
William Shakespeare 1564–1616:
epitaph on his tomb, probably
composed by himself

10 Here lies my wife; here let her lie!
  Now she's at peace and so am I.
John Dryden 1631–1700: epitaph;
attributed but not traced in his
works

11 Life is a jest; and all things show
    it.
  I thought so once; but now I
    know it.
John Gay 1685–1732: "My Own
Epitaph" (1720)

12 *Si monumentum requiris,
  circumspice.*
  If you seek a monument, gaze
    around.

Anonymous: inscription in St. Paul's
Cathedral, London, attributed to the
son of Sir Christopher Wren, its
architect

13 The body of
  Benjamin Franklin, printer,
  (Like the cover of an old book,
    Its contents worn out,
  And stripped of its lettering and
    gilding)
  Lies here, food for worms!
  Yet the work itself shall not be
    lost,
  For it will, as he believed, appear
    once more
  In a new
  And more beautiful edition,
  Corrected and amended
  By its Author!
Benjamin Franklin 1706–90: epitaph
for himself (1728)

14 Under this stone, Reader, survey
  Dead Sir John Vanbrugh's house
    of clay.
  Lie heavy on him, Earth! for he
  Laid many heavy loads on thee!
Abel Evans 1679–1737: "Epitaph on
Sir John Vanbrugh, Architect of
Blenheim Palace"

15 Where fierce indignation can no
  longer tear his heart.
Swift's epitaph
Jonathan Swift 1667–1745: S. Leslie
The Skull of Swift (1928)

16 We carved not a line, and we
    raised not a stone—
  But we left him alone with his
    glory.
Charles Wolfe 1791–1823: "The
Burial of Sir John Moore at Corunna"
(1817)

17 Here lies one whose name was
  writ in water.
epitaph for himself
John Keats 1795–1821: Richard
Monckton Milnes *Life, Letters and
Literary Remains of John Keats*
(1848)

18 *Emigravit* is the inscription on the
tombstone where he lies;
Dead he is not, but departed,—for
the artist never dies.
of Albrecht Dürer
Henry Wadsworth Longfellow 1807–
82: "Nuremberg" (1844)

19 Were there but a few hearts and
intellects like hers this earth
would already become the hoped-
for heaven.
*epitaph (1859) inscribed on the
tomb of his wife, Harriet*
John Stuart Mill 1806–73: M. St. J.
Packe *Life of John Stuart Mill* (1954)

20 Here lie I, Martin Elginbrodde:
Hae mercy o' my soul, Lord God;
As I wad do, were I Lord God,
And ye were Martin Elginbrodde.
George MacDonald 1824–1905:
David Elginbrod (1863)

21 Now he belongs to the ages.
*of Abraham Lincoln, following his
assassination, 15 April 1865*
Edwin McMasters Stanton 1814–69:
I. M. Tarbell *Life of Abraham Lincoln*
(1900)

22 This be the verse you grave for
me:
"Here he lies where he longed to
be;
Home is the sailor, home from
sea,
And the hunter home from the
hill."
Robert Louis Stevenson 1850–94:
"Requiem" (1887)

23 Hereabouts died a very gallant
gentleman, Captain L. E. G. Oates
of the Inniskilling Dragoons. In
March 1912, returning from the
Pole, he walked willingly to his
death in a blizzard to try and
save his comrades, beset by
hardships.
*epitaph on cairn erected in the
Antarctic, 15 November 1912*
E. L. Atkinson 1882–1929 and **Apsley
Cherry-Garrard** 1882–1959: Apsley

Cherry-Garrard *The Worst Journey in
the World* (1922); cf. **Last Words 24**

24 They shall grow not old, as we
that are left grow old.
Age shall not weary them, nor
the years condemn.
At the going down of the sun
and in the morning
We will remember them.
*particularly associated with
Remembrance Day services*
Laurence Binyon 1869–1943: "For
the Fallen" (1914)

25 His foe was folly and his weapon
wit.
Anthony Hope 1863–1933:
inscription on W. S. Gilbert's
memorial on the Victoria
Embankment, London, 1915

26 When you go home, tell them of
us and say,
"For your tomorrows these gave
their today."
*particularly associated with the dead
of the Burma campaign of World
War II, in the form "For your
tomorrow we gave our today."*
John Maxwell Edmonds 1875–1958:
*Inscriptions Suggested for War
Memorials* (1919)

27 Excuse My Dust.
suggested epitaph for herself (1925)
Dorothy Parker 1893–1967:
Alexander Woollcott *While Rome
Burns* (1934)

28 Here lies W. C. Fields. I would
rather be living in Philadelphia.
suggested epitaph for himself
W. C. Fields 1880–1946: *Vanity Fair*
June 1925

29 The only thing that really
saddens me over my demise is
that I shall not be here to read
the nonsense that will be written
about me . . . There will be lists of
apocryphal jokes I never made
and gleeful misquotations of

words I never said. *What a pity I
shan't be here to enjoy them!*
Noël Coward 1899–1973: diary 19
March 1955

30 Without you, Heaven would be
    too dull to bear,
    And Hell would not be Hell if you
    are there.
    epitaph for Maurice Bowra
    John Sparrow 1906–92: in *Times
    Literary Supplement* (UK) 30 May
    1975

31 Timothy has passed . . .
    *message on his Internet home page
    announcing the death of Timothy
    Leary, 31 May 1996*
    Anonymous: in *Guardian* (UK) 1 June
    1996; cf. **Death 83, Last Words 31**

Equality
see also **Human Rights**

1 He maketh his sun to rise on the
  evil and on the good, and sendeth
  rain on the just and on the
  unjust.
  Bible: St. Matthew; cf. **Weather 13**

2 Hath not a Jew eyes? hath not a
  Jew hands, organs, dimensions,
  senses, affections, passions? fed
  with the same food, hurt with the
  same weapons, subject to the
  same diseases, healed by the same
  means, warmed and cooled by
  the same winter and summer, as
  a Christian is? If you prick us, do
  we not bleed? if you tickle us, do
  we not laugh? if you poison us,
  do we not die? and if you wrong
  us, shall we not revenge?
  William Shakespeare 1564–1616: *The
  Merchant of Venice* (1596–8)

3 Night makes no difference 'twixt
  the Priest and Clerk;
  Joan as my Lady is as good i' th'
  dark.
  Robert Herrick 1591–1674: "No
  Difference i' th' Dark" (1648)

4 Sir, there is no settling the point
  of precedency between a louse
  and a flea.
  *on the relative merits of two minor
  poets*
  Samuel Johnson 1709–84: James
  Boswell *Life of Samuel Johnson*
  (1791) 1783

5 A man's a man for a' that.
  Robert Burns 1759–96: "For a' that
  and a' that" (1790)

6 No one can be perfectly free till
  all are free; no one can be
  perfectly moral till all are moral;
  no one can be perfectly happy till
  all are happy.
  Herbert Spencer 1820–1903: *Social
  Statics* (1850)

7 There is no method by which
  men can be both free and equal.
  Walter Bagehot 1826–77: in *The
  Economist* 5 September 1863
  "France or England"

8 Join the union, girls, and together
  say Equal Pay for Equal Work.
  Susan B. Anthony 1820–1906: *The
  Revolution* (women's suffrage
  newspaper) (18 March 1869)

9 Make all men equal today, and
  God has so created them that
  they shall all be unequal
  tomorrow.
  Anthony Trollope 1815–82:
  Autobiography (1883)

10 When every one is somebodee,
   Then no one's anybody.
   W. S. Gilbert 1836–1911: *The
   Gondoliers* (1889)

11 Oh, East is East, and West is
   West, and never the twain shall
   meet,
   Till Earth and Sky stand presently
   at God's great Judgement Seat;
   But there is neither East nor
   West, Border, nor Breed, nor
   Birth,

When two strong men stand face
to face, tho' they come from
the ends of earth!
Rudyard Kipling 1865–1936: "The
Ballad of East and West" (1892)

12 His lordship may compel us to be
equal upstairs, but there will
never be equality in the servants'
hall.
J. M. Barrie 1860–1937: *The
Admirable Crichton* (1914)

13 While there is a lower class, I am
in it; while there is a criminal
element, I am of it; while there is
a soul in prison, I am not free.
Eugene Victor Debs 1855–1926:
speech at his trial for sedition in
Cleveland, Ohio, 14 September 1918

14 Those who dread a dead-level of
income or wealth . . . do not
dread, it seems, a dead-level of
law and order, and of security for
life and property.
R. H. Tawney 1880–1962: *Equality*
(4th ed., 1931)

15 The constitution does not provide
for first and second class citizens.
Wendell Willkie 1892–1944: *An
American Programme* (1944)

16 All animals are equal but some
animals are more equal than
others.
George Orwell 1903–50: *Animal Farm*
(1945)

17 I have a dream that one day on
the red hills of Georgia the sons
of former slaves and the sons of
former slave owners will be able
to sit down together at the table
of brotherhood.
Martin Luther King, Jr. 1929–68:
speech at Civil Rights March in
Washington, 28 August 1963

18 And now she is like everyone
else.
*on the death of his daughter, who
had been born with Down's
Syndrome*

Charles de Gaulle 1890–1970:
attributed

Europe and Europeans
see also **Countries and Peoples,
International Relations**

1 Pray enter
You are learned Europeans and
we worse
Than ignorant Americans.
Philip Massinger 1583–1640: *The
City Madam* (1658)

2 The age of chivalry is gone.—
That of sophisters, economists,
and calculators, has succeeded;
and the glory of Europe is
extinguished for ever.
Edmund Burke 1729–97: *Reflections
on the Revolution in France* (1790)

3 Roll up that map; it will not be
wanted these ten years.
*of a map of Europe, on hearing of
Napoleon's victory at Austerlitz,
December 1805*
William Pitt 1759–1806: Earl
Stanhope *Life of the Rt. Hon.
William Pitt* vol. 4 (1862)

4 Better fifty years of Europe than a
cycle of Cathay.
Alfred, Lord Tennyson 1809–92:
"Locksley Hall" (1842)

5 Whoever speaks of Europe is
wrong, [it is] a geographical
concept.
Otto von Bismarck 1815–98: marginal
note on a letter from the Russian
Chancellor Gorchakov, November
1876

6 We are part of the community of
Europe and we must do our duty
as such.
Lord Salisbury 1830–1903: speech at
Caernarvon, 10 April 1888

7 The European view of a poet is
not of much importance unless
the poet writes in Esperanto.

A. E. Housman 1859–1936: in
Cambridge Review 1915

8 Purity of race does not exist.
Europe is a continent of energetic
mongrels.
H. A. L. Fisher 1856–1940: *A History
of Europe* (1935)

9 If you open that Pandora's Box,
you never know what Trojan
'orses will jump out.
on the Council of Europe
Ernest Bevin 1881–1951: Roderick
Barclay *Ernest Bevin and the Foreign
Office* (1975)

10 Yes, It is Europe, from the
Atlantic to the Urals, it is Europe,
it is the whole of Europe, that will
decide the fate of the world.
Charles de Gaulle 1890–1970: speech
to the people of Strasbourg, 23
November 1959

11 When an American heiress wants
to buy a man, she at once crosses
the Atlantic. The only really
materialistic people I have ever
met have been Europeans.
Mary McCarthy 1912–89: *On the
Contrary* (1961) "America the
Beautiful"

12 It means the end of a thousand
years of history.
on a European federation
Hugh Gaitskell 1906–63: speech at
Labour Party Conference, 3 October
1962

13 Without Britain Europe would
remain only a torso.
Ludwig Erhard 1897–1977: remark
on West German television, 27 May
1962

14 "We went in," he said, "to screw
the French by splitting them off
from the Germans. The French
went in to protect their inefficient
farmers from commercial
competition. The Germans went
in to cleanse themselves of

genocide and apply for
readmission to the human race."
on the European Community
Jonathan Lynn 1943– and **Antony Jay**
1930– : *Yes, Minister* (1982) vol. 2

15 The policy of European
integration is in reality a question
of war and peace in the 21st
century.
Helmut Kohl 1930– : speech at
Louvain University, 2 February 1996

Evil
see **Good and Evil**

Examinations

1 Examinations are formidable even
to the best prepared, for the
greatest fool may ask more than
the wisest man can answer.
Charles Caleb Colton c. 1780–1832:
Lacon (1820)

2 *in his viva voce at Oxford, Wilde,
who had acquitted himself well in
translating a passage from the Greek
version of the New Testament, was
stopped:*
Oh, do let me go on, I want to
see how it ends.
Oscar Wilde 1854–1900: James
Sutherland (ed.) *The Oxford Book of
Literary Anecdotes* (1975)

3 Had silicon been a gas, I would
have been a major-general by
now.
*having been found "deficient in
chemistry" in a West Point
examination*
James McNeill Whistler 1834–1903:
E. R. and J. Pennell *The Life of
James McNeill Whistler* (1908)

4 In examinations those who do
not wish to know ask questions of
those who cannot tell.
Walter Raleigh 1861–1922: *Laughter
from a Cloud* (1923) "Some
Thoughts on Examinations"

5 Do not on any account attempt to write on both sides of the paper at once.
W. C. Sellar 1898–1951 and **R. J. Yeatman** 1898–1968: *1066 and All That* (1930) "Test Paper 5"

6 I wrote my name at the top of the page. I wrote down the number of the question "1." After much reflection I put a bracket round it thus "(1)." But thereafter I could not think of anything connected with it that was either relevant or true. . . . It was from these slender indications of scholarship that Mr. Welldon drew the conclusion that I was worthy to pass into Harrow. It is very much to his credit.
Winston Churchill 1874–1965: *My Early Life* (1930)

7 I evidently knew more about economics than my examiners.
explaining why he performed badly in the Civil Service examinations
John Maynard Keynes 1883–1946: Roy Harrod *Life of John Maynard Keynes* (1951)

8 If we have to have an exam at 11, let us make it one for humour, sincerity, imagination, character—and where is the examiner who could test such qualities.
A. S. Neill 1883–1973: letter to *Daily Telegraph* (UK) 1957; in *Daily Telegraph* 25 September 1973

9 Four times, under our educational rules, the human pack is shuffled and cut—at eleven-plus, sixteen-plus, eighteen-plus and twenty-plus—and happy is he who comes top of the deck on each occasion, but especially the last. This is called Finals, the very name of which implies that nothing of importance can happen after it.
David Lodge 1935– : *Changing Places* (1975)

Excellence and Mediocrity
see also **Perfection**

1 Not gods, nor men, nor even booksellers have put up with poets being second-rate.
Horace 65–8 BC: *Ars Poetica*

2 Nature made him, and then broke the mold.
Ludovico Ariosto 1474–1533: *Orlando Furioso* (1532)

3 The danger chiefly lies in acting well;
No crime's so great as daring to excel.
Charles Churchill 1731–64: *An Epistle to William Hogarth* (1763)

4 The best is the enemy of the good.
Voltaire 1694–1778: *Contes* (1772) "La Begueule" derived from an Italian proverb

5 It is a wretched taste to be gratified with mediocrity when the excellent lies before us.
Isaac D'Israeli 1766–1848: *Curiosities of Literature. Second Series* (1823)

6 The pretension is nothing; the performance every thing. A good apple is better than an insipid peach.
Leigh Hunt 1784–1859: *The Story of Rimini* (1832 ed.)

7 The best is the best, though a hundred judges have declared it so.
Arthur Quiller-Couch 1863–1944: *Oxford Book of English Verse* (1900) preface

8 The dullard's envy of brilliant men is always assuaged by the suspicion that they will come to a bad end.
Max Beerbohm 1872–1956: *Zuleika Dobson* (1911)

9 The best lack all conviction, while
the worst
Are full of passionate intensity.
W. B. Yeats 1865–1939: "The Second
Coming" (1921)

10 There's only one real sin, and
that is to persuade oneself that
the second-best is anything but
the second-best.
Doris Lessing 1919– : *Golden
Notebook* (1962)

Excess and Moderation

1 Nothing in excess.
Anonymous: inscribed on the temple
of Apollo at Delphi, and variously
ascribed to the Seven Wise Men

2 You will go most safely by the
middle way.
Ovid 43 BC–AD c. 17: *Metamorphoses*

3 Because thou art lukewarm, and
neither cold nor hot, I will spew
thee out of my mouth.
Bible: Revelation

4 To many, total abstinence is
easier than perfect moderation.
St. Augustine of Hippo AD 354–430:
On the Good of Marriage (AD 401)

5 To gild refinèd gold, to paint the
lily,
To throw a perfume on the violet,
To smooth the ice, or add
another hue
Unto the rainbow, or with taper
light
To seek the beauteous eye of
heaven to garnish,
Is wasteful and ridiculous excess.
William Shakespeare 1564–1616:
King John (1591–8)

6 No term of moderation takes
place with the vulgar.
Francis Bacon 1561–1626: *De
Dignitate et Augmentis Scientiarum*
(1623)

7 Don't, Sir, accustom yourself to
use big words for little matters. It

would *not* be *terrible*, though I
were to be detained some time
here.
*when Boswell said it would be
"terrible" if Johnson should not be
able to return speedily from Harwich*
Samuel Johnson 1709–84: James
Boswell *Life of Samuel Johnson*
(1791) 6 August 1763

8 By God, Mr. Chairman, at this
moment I stand astonished at my
own moderation!
Lord Clive 1725–74: reply during
Parliamentary cross-examination,
1773; G. R. Gleig *The Life of Robert,
First Lord Clive* (1848)

9 I know many have been taught
to think that moderation, in a
case like this, is a sort of treason.
Edmund Burke 1729–97: *Letter to
the Sheriffs of Bristol* (1777)

10 The road of excess leads to the
palace of wisdom.
William Blake 1757–1827: *The
Marriage of Heaven and Hell* (1790–
3) "Proverbs of Hell"

11 Above all, gentlemen, not the
slightest zeal.
Charles-Maurice de Talleyrand 1754–
1838: P. Chasles *Voyages d'un
critique à travers la vie et les livres*
(1868)

12 Eat not to dullness; drink not to
elevation.
Benjamin Franklin 1706–90:
Autobiography (1868)

13 Moderation is a fatal thing, Lady
Hunstanton. Nothing succeeds
like excess.
Oscar Wilde 1854–1900: *A Woman of
No Importance* (1893)

14 Fanaticism consists in redoubling
your effort when you have
forgotten your aim.
George Santayana 1863–1952: *The
Life of Reason* (1905)

15 Up to a point, Lord Copper.
meaning no
Evelyn Waugh 1903–66: *Scoop*
(1938)

16 We know what happens to people
who stay in the middle of the
road. They get run down.
Aneurin Bevan 1897–1960: in
Observer (UK) 6 December 1953

17 I would remind you that
extremism in the defense of
liberty is no vice! And let me
remind you also that moderation
in the pursuit of justice is no
virtue!
Barry Goldwater 1909– : accepting
the presidential nomination, 16 July
1964

Excuses
see **Apology and Excuses**

Experience
see also **Maturity**

1 *Experto credite.*
Trust one who has gone through
it.
Virgil 70–19 BC: *Aeneid*

2 No man's knowledge here can go
beyond his experience.
John Locke 1632–1704: *An Essay
concerning Human Understanding*
(1690)

3 We live and learn, but not the
wiser grow.
John Pomfret 1667–1702: "Reason"
(1700)

4 Courts and camps are the only
places to learn the world in.
Lord Chesterfield 1694–1773: *Letters
to his Son* (1774) 2 October 1747

5 The courtiers who surround him
have forgotten nothing and learnt
nothing.
of Louis XVIII, at the time of the
Declaration of Verona, September
1795
**Charles François du Périer
Dumouriez** 1739–1823: *Examen
impartial d'un Écrit intitulé
Déclaration de Louis XVIII* (1795);
quoted by Napoleon in his
Declaration to the French on his
return from Elba; a similar saying is
attributed to Talleyrand

6 He went like one that hath been
stunned,
And is of sense forlorn:
A sadder and a wiser man,
He rose the morrow morn.
Samuel Taylor Coleridge 1772–1834:
"The Rime of the Ancient Mariner"
(1798)

7 Axioms in philosophy are not
axioms until they are proved
upon our pulses: We read fine
things, but never feel them to the
full until we have gone the same
steps as the author.
John Keats 1795–1821: letter to J. H.
Reynolds, 3 May 1818

8 If men could learn from history,
what lessons it might teach us!
But passion and party blind our
eyes, and the light which
experience gives is a lantern on
the stern, which shines only on
the waves behind us!
Samuel Taylor Coleridge 1772–1834:
Table Talk (1835) 18 December 1831

9 I am a part of all that I have met;
Yet all experience is an arch
wherethrough
Gleams that untravelled world,
whose margin fades
For ever and for ever when I
move.
Alfred, Lord Tennyson 1809–92:
"Ulysses" (1842)

10 The years teach much which the
days never know.
Ralph Waldo Emerson 1803–82:
Essays. Second Series (1844)
"Experience"

11 Grace is given of God, but
knowledge is bought in the
market.
Arthur Hugh Clough 1819–61: *The
Bothie of Tober-na-Vuolich* (1848)

12 No, I ask it for the knowledge of
a lifetime.
*in his case against Ruskin, replying
to the question: "For two days'
labor, you ask two hundred
guineas?"*
James McNeill Whistler 1834–1903:
D. C. Seitz *Whistler Stories* (1913)

13 If I should certainly say to a
novice, "Write from experience
and experience only," I should
feel that this was rather a
tantalizing monition if I were not
careful immediately to add, "Try
to be one of the people on whom
nothing is lost."
Henry James 1843–1916: *The Art of
Fiction* (1888)

14 Experience is the name every one
gives to their mistakes.
Oscar Wilde 1854–1900: *Lady
Windermere's Fan* (1892)

15 All experience is an arch to build
upon.
Henry Brooks Adams 1838–1918: *The
Education of Henry Adams* (1907)

16 Experience is not what happens to
a man; it is what a man does
with what happens to him.
Aldous Huxley 1894–1963: *Texts and
Pretexts* (1932)

17 I've been things and seen places.
Mae West 1892–1980: *I'm No Angel*
(1933 film)

18 It's a funny old world—a man's
lucky if he gets out of it alive.
Walter de Leon and **Paul M. Jones**:
You're Telling Me (1934 film);
spoken by W. C. Fields

19 Experience isn't interesting till it
begins to repeat itself—in fact, till

it does that, it hardly *is*
experience.
Elizabeth Bowen 1899–1973: *Death
of the Heart* (1938)

20 You should make a point of
trying every experience once,
excepting incest and folk-dancing.
Anonymous: Arnold Bax (1883–
1953), quoting "a sympathetic Scot"
Farewell My Youth (1943)

21 I learned . . . that one can never
go back, that one should not ever
try to go back—that the essence
of life is going forward. Life is
really a One Way Street.
Agatha Christie 1890–1976: *At
Bertram's Hotel* (1965)

22 Education is when you read the
fine print; experience is what you
get when you don't.
Pete Seeger 1919– : L. Botts *Loose
Talk* (1980)

23 Damaged people are dangerous.
They know they can survive.
Josephine Hart: *Damage* (1991)

24 *after George Bush had laid stress on
the value of experience in the 1992
presidential debates:*
I don't have any experience in
running up a $4 trillion debt.
H. Ross Perot 1930– : in *Newsweek*
19 October 1992

25 Experience gives us the tests first
and the lessons later.
Naomi Judd 1946– : *Weekend
Edition* (29 January 1994)

Exploration
see **Travel and Exploration**

Extravagance
see **Thrift and Extravagance**

Fact
see **Hypothesis and Fact**

Failure
see **Success and Failure**

Faith
see also **Belief and Unbelief**

1 I know that my redeemer liveth,
and that he shall stand at the
latter day upon the earth:
And though after my skin worms
destroy this body, yet in my flesh
shall I see God.
Bible: Job

2 If ye have faith as a grain of
mustard seed, ye shall say unto
this mountain, Remove hence to
yonder place; and it shall remove.
Bible: St. Matthew

3 For the Jews require a sign, and
the Greeks seek after wisdom.
Bible: 1 Corinthians

4 Faith without works is dead.
Bible: James

5 A man with God is always in the
majority.
John Knox c. 1505–72: inscription on
the Reformation Monument, Geneva

6 At last, by singing and repeating
enthusiastic amorous hymns, and
ignorantly applying particular
texts of scripture, I got my
imagination to the proper pitch,
and thus was I born again in an
instant.
James Lackington 1746–1815:
Memoirs (1792 ed.)

7 Mock on mock on Voltaire
    Rousseau
Mock on mock on tis all in vain
You throw the sand against the
    wind

And the wind blows it back
    again.
William Blake 1757–1827: *MS Note-Book*

8 The faith that stands on authority
is not faith.
Ralph Waldo Emerson 1803–82:
Essays (1841) "The Over-Soul"

9 Let us have faith that right makes
might, and in that faith, let us, to
the end, dare to do our duty as
we understand it.
Abraham Lincoln 1809–65: speech,
27 February 1860

10 *to an undergraduate trying to excuse
himself from attendance at early
morning chapel on the plea of loss of
faith:*
You will find God by tomorrow
morning, or leave this college.
Benjamin Jowett 1817–93: Kenneth
Rose *Superior Person* (1969)

11 The great act of faith is when a
man decides he is not God.
Oliver Wendell Holmes, Jr. 1841–1935:
letter to William James, 24 March
1907

12 And I said to the man who stood
at the gate of the year: "Give me
a light that I may tread safely
into the unknown."
    And he replied:
    "Go out into the darkness and
put your hand into the Hand of
God. That shall be to you better
than light and safer than a
known way."
*quoted by King George VI in his
Christmas broadcast, 25 December
1939*
Minnie Louise Haskins 1875–1957:
Desert (1908) "God Knows"

13 Booth died blind and still by faith
he trod,
Eyes still dazzled by the ways of
God.
Vachel Lindsay 1879–1931: "General
William Booth Enters into Heaven"
(1913)

14 Faith may be defined briefly as an illogical belief in the occurrence of the improbable.
H. L. Mencken 1880–1956: *Prejudices* (1922)

15 A miracle, my friend, is an event which creates faith. That is the purpose and nature of miracles.... Frauds deceive. An event which creates faith does not deceive: therefore it is not a fraud, but a miracle.
George Bernard Shaw 1856–1950: *Saint Joan* (1924)

16 You'll never walk alone.
Oscar Hammerstein II 1895–1960: title of song (1945)

17 A faith is something you die for; a doctrine is something you kill for: there is all the difference in the world.
Tony Benn 1925– : in *Observer* (UK) 16 April 1989

Fame
see also **Reputation**

1 Let us now praise famous men, and our fathers that begat us.
Bible: Ecclesiasticus

2 So long as men can breathe, or eyes can see,
So long lives this, and this gives life to thee.
William Shakespeare 1564–1616: Sonnet 18

3 Glories, like glow-worms, afar off shine bright,
But looked to near, have neither heat nor light.
John Webster c. 1580–c. 1625: *The Duchess of Malfi* (1623)

4 Fame is like a river, that beareth up things light and swollen, and drowns things weighty and solid.
Francis Bacon 1561–1626: *Essays* (1625) "Of Praise"

5 Fame is the spur that the clear spirit doth raise
(That last infirmity of noble mind)
To scorn delights, and live laborious days;
John Milton 1608–74: "Lycidas" (1638)

6 To be nameless in worthy deeds exceeds an infamous history.
Thomas Browne 1605–82: *Hydriotaphia* (Urn Burial, 1658)

7 Seven wealthy towns contend for HOMER dead
Through which the living HOMER begged his bread.
Anonymous: epilogue to *Aesop at Tunbridge; or, a Few Selected Fables in Verse* By No Person of Quality (1698)

8 If you would not be forgotten
As soon as you are dead and rotten,
Either write things worthy reading,
Or do things worth the writing.
Benjamin Franklin 1706–90: *Poor Richard's Almanack* (1738)

9 Far from the madding crowd's ignoble strife,
Their sober wishes never learned to stray;
Along the cool sequestered vale of life
They kept the noiseless tenor of their way.
Thomas Gray 1716–71: *Elegy Written in a Country Churchyard* (1751)

10 Full many a flower is born to blush unseen,
And waste its sweetness on the desert air.
Thomas Gray 1716–71: *Elegy Written in a Country Churchyard* (1751)

11 Every man has a lurking wish to appear considerable in his native place.

Samuel Johnson 1709–84: letter to Joshua Reynolds, 17 July 1771; cf. **Familiarity 1**

12 One crowded hour of glorious life
Is worth an age without a name.
Thomas Osbert Mordaunt 1730–1809: "A Poem, said to be written by Major Mordaunt during the last German War," in *The Bee, or Literary Weekly Intelligencer* 12 October 1791

13 I awoke one morning and found myself famous.
on the instantaneous success of Childe Harold
Lord Byron 1788–1824: Thomas Moore *Letters and Journals of Lord Byron* (1830)

14 The deed is all, the glory nothing.
Johann Wolfgang von Goethe 1749–1832: *Faust* pt. 2 (1832) "Hochgebirg"

15 Martyrdom . . . the only way in which a man can become famous without ability.
George Bernard Shaw 1856–1950: *The Devil's Disciple* (1901)

16 I don't care what you say about me, as long as you say *something* about me, and as long as you spell my name right.
said to a newspaperman in 1912
George M. Cohan 1878–1942: John McCabe *George M. Cohan* (1973)

17 What price glory?
Maxwell Anderson 1888–1959 and **Lawrence Stallings** 1894–1968: title of play (1924)

18 It's better to be looked over than overlooked.
Mae West 1892–1980: *Belle of the Nineties* (1934 film)

19 Now who is responsible for this work of development on which so much depends? To whom must the praise be given? To the boys in the back rooms. They do not

sit in the limelight. But they are the men who do the work.
Lord Beaverbrook 1879–1964: in *Listener* (UK) 27 March 1941

20 He's always backing into the limelight.
of T. E. Lawrence
Lord Berners 1883–1950: oral tradition

21 The celebrity is a person who is known for his well-knownness.
Daniel J. Boorstin 1914– : *The Image* (1961)

22 There's no such thing as bad publicity except your own obituary.
Brendan Behan 1923–64: Dominic Behan *My Brother Brendan* (1965)

23 We're more popular than Jesus now: I don't know which will go first—rock 'n' roll or Christianity.
of The Beatles
John Lennon 1940–80: interview in *Evening Standard* 4 March 1966

24 In the future everybody will be world famous for fifteen minutes.
Andy Warhol 1927–87: *Andy Warhol* (1968)

25 Oh, the self-importance of fading stars. Never mind, they will be black holes one day.
Jeffrey Bernard 1932–97: in *The Spectator* (UK) 18 July 1992

26 The best fame is a writer's fame: it's enough to get a table at a good restaurant, but not enough that you get interrupted when you eat.
Fran Lebowitz 1946– : in *Observer* (UK) 30 May 1993

Familiarity

1 A prophet is not without honor, save in his own country, and in his own house.
Bible: St. Matthew; cf. **Fame 11**

2 There is nothing that God hath
established in a constant course
of nature, and which therefore is
done every day, but would seem
a Miracle, and exercise our
admiration, if it were done but
once.
John Donne 1572–1631: *LXXX
Sermons* (1640) Easter Day, 25
March 1627

3 Old friends are best. King James
used to call for his old shoes; they
were easiest for his feet.
John Selden 1584–1654: *Table Talk*
(1689) "Friends"

4 Let him go abroad to a distant
country; let him go to some place
where he is *not* known. Don't let
him go to the devil where he is
known!
*Boswell having asked if someone
should commit suicide to avoid
certain disgrace*
Samuel Johnson 1709–84: James
Boswell *Journal of a Tour to the
Hebrides* (1785) 18 August 1773

5 We can scarcely hate any one
that we know.
William Hazlitt 1778–1830: *Table
Talk* (1822) "On Criticism"

6 Think you, if Laura had been
Petrarch's wife,
He would have written sonnets
all his life?
Lord Byron 1788–1824: *Don Juan*
(1819–24)

7 A maggot must be born i' the
rotten cheese to like it.
George Eliot 1819–80: *Adam Bede*
(1859)

8 We do not expect people to be
deeply moved by what is not
unusual. That element of tragedy
which lies in the very fact of
frequency, has not yet wrought
itself into the coarse emotion of
mankind.
George Eliot 1819–80: *Middlemarch*
(1871–2)

9 There are no conditions of life to
which a man cannot get
accustomed, especially if he sees
them accepted by everyone about
him.
Leo Tolstoy 1828–1910: *Anna
Karenina* (1875–7)

10 Familiarity breeds contempt—and
children.
Mark Twain 1835–1910: *Notebooks*
(1935)

The Family
see also **Children, Parents**

1 Thy wife shall be as the fruitful
vine: upon the walls of thine
house.
Thy children like the olive-
branches: round about thy table.
Bible: Psalm 128

2 A little more than kin, and less
than kind.
William Shakespeare 1564–1616:
Hamlet (1601)

3 He that hath wife and children
hath given hostages to fortune;
for they are impediments to great
enterprises, either of virtue or
mischief.
Francis Bacon 1561–1626: *Essays*
(1625) "Of Marriage and the Single
Life"

4 We begin our public affections in
our families. No cold relation is a
zealous citizen.
Edmund Burke 1729–97: *Reflections
on the Revolution in France* (1790)

5 If a man's character is to be
abused, say what you will, there's
nobody like a relation to do the
business.
William Makepeace Thackeray 1811–
63: *Vanity Fair* (1847–8)

6 The worst families are those in
which the members never really
speak their minds to one another;

they maintain an atmosphere of unreality, and everyone always lives in an atmosphere of suppressed ill-feeling.
Walter Bagehot 1826–77: *The English Constitution* (ed. 2, 1872) introduction

7 All happy families resemble one another, but each unhappy family is unhappy in its own way.
Leo Tolstoy 1828–1910: *Anna Karenina* (1875–7)

8 Family! . . . the home of all social evil, a charitable institution for comfortable women, an anchorage for house-fathers, and a hell for children.
August Strindberg 1849–1912: *The Son of a Servant* (1886)

9 Relations are simply a tedious pack of people, who haven't got the remotest knowledge of how to live, nor the smallest instinct about when to die.
Oscar Wilde 1854–1900: *The Importance of Being Earnest* (1899)

10 The awe and dread with which the untutored savage contemplates his mother-in-law are amongst the most familiar facts of anthropology.
James George Frazer 1854–1941: *The Golden Bough* (2nd ed., 1900)

11 It takes patience to appreciate domestic bliss; volatile spirits prefer unhappiness.
George Santayana 1863–1952: *The Life of Reason* (1905)

12 I am the family face;
Flesh perishes, I live on,
Projecting trait and trace
Through time to times anon,
And leaping from place to place
Over oblivion.
Thomas Hardy 1840–1928: "Heredity" (1917)

13 It is no use telling me that there are bad aunts and good aunts. At the core, they are all alike. Sooner or later, out pops the cloven hoof.
P. G. Wodehouse 1881–1975: *The Code of the Woosters* (1938)

14 The family—that dear octopus from whose tentacles we never quite escape.
Dodie Smith 1896–1990: *Dear Octopus* (1938)

15 The Princesses would never leave without me and I couldn't leave without the King, and the King will never leave.
on the suggestion that the royal family be evacuated during the Blitz
Queen Elizabeth, the Queen Mother 1900– : Penelope Mortimer *Queen Elizabeth* (1986)

16 The most important thing a father can do for his children is to love their mother.
Theodore M. Hesburgh 1917– : *Reader's Digest* (January 1963)

17 As we read the school reports on our children we realize a sense of relief that . . . nobody is reporting in this fashion on us!
J. B. Priestley 1894– : *Reader's Digest* (June 1964)

18 Far from being the basis of the good society, the family, with its narrow privacy and tawdry secrets, is the source of all our discontents.
Edmund Leach 1910– : BBC Reith Lectures, 1967

19 I have never understood this liking for war. It panders to instincts already catered for within the scope of any respectable domestic establishment.
Alan Bennett 1934– : *Forty Years On* (1969)

20 The first child is made of glass, the second porcelain, the rest of rubber, steel and granite.
Richard J. Needham 1939– :
Toronto Globe & Mail (25 January 1977)

21 We have many things in common, the greatest of which is that we are both afraid of the children.
referring to his wife
Bill Cosby 1937– : *Fatherhood* (1986)

22 Having one child makes you a parent; having two you are a referee.
David Frost 1939– : in *Independent* (UK) 16 September 1989

23 Dinner together is one of the absolute critical symbols in the cohesion of the family.
John R. Kelly 1939– : *New York Times* (5 December 1990)

Fashion
see also **Dress**

1 The women come to see the show, they come to make a show themselves.
Ovid 43 BC–AD c. 17: *Ars Amatoria*

2 It is charming to totter into vogue.
Horace Walpole 1717–97: letter to George Selwyn, 2 December 1765

3 O Lord, Sir—when a heroine goes mad she always goes into white satin.
Richard Brinsley Sheridan 1751–1816: *The Critic* (1779)

4 A little of what you call frippery is very necessary towards looking like the rest of the world.
Abigail Adams 1744–1818: *letter to John Adams* (1 May 1780)

5 Fashion, though Folly's child, and guide of fools,
Rules e'en the wisest, and in learning rules.
George Crabbe 1754–1832: "The Library" (1808)

6 Fashion is something barbarous, for it produces innovation without reason and imitation without benefit.
George Santayana 1863–1952: *The Life of Reason* (1905)

7 You cannot be both fashionable and first-rate.
Logan Pearsall Smith 1865–1946: *Afterthoughts* (1931) "In the World"

8 The same costume will be
Indecent . . . 10 years before its time
Shameless . . . 5 years before its time
Outré (daring) 1 year before its time
Smart
Dowdy . . . 1 year after its time
Hideous . . . 10 years after its time
Ridiculous . . . 20 years after its time
Amusing . . . 30 years after its time
Quaint . . . 50 years after its time
Charming . . . 70 years after its time
Romantic . . . 100 years after its time
Beautiful . . . 150 years after its time
James Laver 1899–1975: *Taste and Fashion* (1937)

9 I don't really like knees.
Yves St. Laurent 1936– : in *Observer* (UK) 3 August 1958

10 Hip is the sophistication of the wise primitive in a giant jungle.
Norman Mailer 1923– : *Voices of Dissent* (1959) "The White Negro"

11 Radical Chic . . . is only radical in
Style; in its heart it is part of
Society and its tradition—Politics,
like Rock, Pop, and Camp, has its
uses.
Tom Wolfe 1931– : in *New York* 8
June 1970

12 Fashion is more usually a gentle
progression of revisited ideas.
Bruce Oldfield 1950– : in
Independent (UK) 9 September 1989

13 I never cared for fashion much.
Amusing little seams and witty
little pleats. It was the girls I
liked.
David Bailey 1938– : in
Independent (UK) 5 November 1990

14 My closet looks like a convention
of multiple-personality cases.
Anna Quindlen 1953– :
Newsmakers (1993)

Fate

1 Canst thou bind the sweet
influences of Pleiades, or loose the
bands of Orion?
Bible: Job

2 Each man is the smith of his own
fortune.
Appius Claudius Caecus fl. 312–279
BC: Sallust *Ad Caesarem Senem de
Re Publica Oratio*

3 *Dis aliter visum.*
The gods thought otherwise.
Virgil 70–19 BC: *Aeneid*

4 The fault, dear Brutus, is not in
our stars,
But in ourselves, that we are
underlings.
William Shakespeare 1564–1616:
Julius Caesar (1599)

5 There's a divinity that shapes our
ends,
Rough-hew them how we will.
William Shakespeare 1564–1616:
Hamlet (1601)

6 We are merely the stars' tennis-
balls, struck and bandied
Which way please them.
John Webster *c.* 1580–*c.* 1625: *The
Duchess of Malfi* (1623)

7 Every bullet has its billet.
William III 1650–1702: John Wesley's
diary, 6 June 1765

8 I feel that I am reserved for some
end or other.
*when his pistol twice failed to fire,
while attempting to take his own life*
Lord Clive 1725–74: G. R. Gleig *The
Life of Robert, First Lord Clive* (1848)

9 Must it be? It must be.
Ludwig van Beethoven 1770–1827:
String Quartet in F Major, Opus 135,
epigraph

10 By heaven, man, we are turned
round and round in this world,
like yonder windlass, and Fate is
the handspike.
Herman Melville 1819–91: *Moby Dick*
(1851)

11 There once was an old man who
said, "Damn!
It is borne in upon me I am
An engine that moves
In determinate grooves,
I'm not even a bus, I'm a tram."
Maurice Evan Hare 1886–1967:
"Limerick" (1905)

12 I [Death] was astonished to see
him in Baghdad, for I had an
appointment with him tonight in
Samarra.
W. Somerset Maugham 1874–1965:
Sheppey (1933)

13 Fate is not an eagle, it creeps like
a rat.
Elizabeth Bowen 1899–1973: *The
House in Paris* (1935)

14 The spring is wound up tight. It
will uncoil of itself. That is what
is so convenient in tragedy. The

least little turn of the wrist will do the job. Anything will set it going.
Jean Anouilh 1910–87: *Antigone* (1944)

15 We may become the makers of our fate when we have ceased to pose as its prophets.
Karl Popper 1902–94: *The Open Society and its Enemies* (1945)

16 The bad end unhappily, the good unluckily. That is what tragedy means.
Tom Stoppard 1937–   : *Rosencrantz and Guildenstern are Dead* (1967); cf. **Fiction 10**

Fear

1 Thou shalt not be afraid for any terror by night: nor for the arrow that flieth by day;
For the pestilence that walketh in darkness: nor for the sickness that destroyeth in the noon-day.
Bible: Psalm 91

2 Letting "I dare not" wait upon "I would,"
Like the poor cat i' the adage?
William Shakespeare 1564–1616: *Macbeth* (1606)

3 Present fears
Are less than horrible imaginings.
William Shakespeare 1564–1616: *Macbeth* (1606)

4 Every drop of ink in my pen ran cold.
Horace Walpole 1717–97: letter to George Montagu, 30 July 1752

5 No passion so effectually robs the mind of all its powers of acting and reasoning as fear.
Edmund Burke 1729–97: *On the Sublime and Beautiful* (1757)

6 Wee, sleekit, cow'rin', tim'rous beastie,

O what a panic's in thy breastie!
Robert Burns 1759–96: "To a Mouse" (1786)

7 Better be killed than frightened to death.
R. S. Surtees 1805–64: *Mr. Facey Romford's Hounds* (1865)

8 The horror! The horror!
Joseph Conrad 1857–1924: *Heart of Darkness* (1902)

9 I will show you fear in a handful of dust.
T. S. Eliot 1888–1965: *The Waste Land* (1922)

10 To fear love is to fear life, and those who fear life are already three parts dead.
Bertrand Russell 1872–1970: *Marriage and Morals* (1929)

11 The only thing we have to fear is fear itself.
Franklin D. Roosevelt 1882–1945: inaugural address, 4 March 1933

12 Terror . . . often arises from a pervasive sense of disestablishment; that things are in the unmaking.
Stephen King 1947–   : *Danse Macabre* (1981)

Festivals and Celebrations
see also **Christmas, The Seasons**

1 Beware the ides of March.
William Shakespeare 1564–1616: *Julius Caesar* (1599)

2 St. Agnes' Eve—Ah, bitter chill it was!
The owl, for all his feathers, was a-cold;
The hare limped trembling through the frozen grass,
And silent was the flock in woolly fold.
John Keats 1795–1821: "The Eve of St. Agnes" (1820)

3 Tomorrow 'ill be the happiest
   time of all the glad New-year;
   Of all the glad New-year, mother,
   the maddest merriest day;
   For I'm to be Queen o' the May,
   mother, I'm to be Queen o' the
   May.
   Alfred, Lord Tennyson 1809–92:
   "The May Queen" (1832)

4 Gay are the Martian Calends:
   December's Nones are gay:
   But the proud Ides, when the
   squadron rides,
   Shall be Rome's whitest day!
   Lord Macaulay 1800–59: *Lays of
   Ancient Rome* (1842) "The Battle of
   the Lake Regillus"

5 Ring out the old, ring in the new,
   Ring, happy bells, across the
   snow:
   The year is going, let him go;
   Ring out the false, ring in the
   true.
   Alfred, Lord Tennyson 1809–92: *In
   Memoriam A. H. H.* (1850)

6 Seasons pursuing each other the
   indescribable
   crowd is gathered, it is the fourth
   of Seventh-
   month, (what salutes of cannon
   and small-arms!)
   Walt Whitman 1819–92: "Song of
   Myself" (written 1855)

7 The holiest of all holidays are
   those
   Kept by ourselves in silence and
   apart;
   The secret anniversaries of the
   heart.
   Henry Wadsworth Longfellow 1807–
   82: "Holidays" (1877)

8 Time has no divisions to mark its
   passage, there is never a
   thunderstorm or blare of trumpets
   to announce the beginning of a
   new month or year. Even when a
   new century begins it is only we
   mortals who ring bells and fire off
   pistols.

Thomas Mann 1875–1955: *The Magic
Mountain* (1924)

Fiction and Storytelling
see also **Writers, Writing**

1 Storys to rede ar delitabill,
   Suppos that thai be nocht bot
   fabill.
   John Barbour c. 1320–95: *The Bruce*
   (1375)

2 With a tale forsooth he [the poet]
   cometh unto you, with a tale
   which holdeth children from play,
   and old men from the chimney
   corner.
   Philip Sidney 1554–86: *The Defence
   of Poetry* (1595)

3 If this were played upon a stage
   now, I could condemn it as an
   improbable fiction.
   William Shakespeare 1564–1616:
   Twelfth Night (1601)

4 "Oh! it is only a novel! . . . only
   Cecilia, or Camilla, or Belinda:"
   or, in short, only some work in
   which the most thorough
   knowledge of human nature, the
   happiest delineation of its
   varieties, the liveliest effusions of
   wit and humour are conveyed to
   the world in the best chosen
   language.
   Jane Austen 1775–1817: *Northanger
   Abbey* (1818)

5 I hate things all *fiction* . . . there
   should always be some
   foundation of fact for the most
   airy fabric and pure invention is
   but the talent of a liar.
   Lord Byron 1788–1824: letter to John
   Murray, 2 April 1817

6 A novel is a mirror which passes
   over a highway. Sometimes it
   reflects to your eyes the blue of
   the skies, at others the churned-
   up mud of the road.

Stendhal 1783–1842: *Le Rouge et le noir* (1830)

7 When I want to read a novel, I write one.
Benjamin Disraeli 1804–81: W. Monypenny and G. Buckle *Life of Benjamin Disraeli* vol. 6 (1920)

8 Merely corroborative detail, intended to give artistic verisimilitude to an otherwise bald and unconvincing narrative.
W. S. Gilbert 1836–1911: *The Mikado* (1885)

9 What is character but the determination of incident? What is incident but the illustration of character?
Henry James 1843–1916: *Partial Portraits* (1888) "The Art of Fiction"

10 The good ended happily, and the bad unhappily. That is what fiction means.
Oscar Wilde 1854–1900: *The Importance of Being Earnest* (1895); cf. **Fate** 16

11 Literature is a luxury; fiction is a necessity.
G. K. Chesterton 1874–1936: *The Defendant* (1901) "A Defence of Penny Dreadfuls"

12 The Story is just the spoiled child of art.
Henry James 1843–1916: *The Ambassadors* (1909 ed.) preface

13 Yes—oh dear yes—the novel tells a story.
E. M. Forster 1879–1970: *Aspects of the Novel* (1927)

14 If you try to nail anything down in the novel, either it kills the novel, or the novel gets up and walks away with the nail.
D. H. Lawrence 1885–1930: *Phoenix* (1936) "Morality and the Novel"

15 As artists they're rot, but as providers they're oil wells; they gush.
on lady novelists
Dorothy Parker 1893–1967: Malcolm Cowley *Writers at Work* 1st Series (1958)

16 When in doubt have a man come through the door with a gun in his hand.
Raymond Chandler 1888–1959: attributed

17 A beginning, a muddle, and an end.
on the "classic formula" for a novel
Philip Larkin 1922–85: in *New Fiction* January 1978

18 The central function of imaginative literature is to make you realize that other people act on moral convictions different from your own.
William Empson 1906–84: *Milton's God* (1981)

Films
see **The Movies and Hollywood**

Flattery
see **Praise and Flattery**

Flowers

1 That wel by reson men it calle may
The "dayesye," or elles the "ye of day,"
The emperice and flour of floures alle.
Geoffrey Chaucer c. 1343–1400: *The Legend of Good Women* "The Prologue"

2 Bring hither the pink and purple columbine,
With gillyflowers:
Bring coronation, and sops in wine,
Worn of paramours.

Strew me the ground with
daffadowndillies,
And cowslips, and kingcups, and
loved lilies.
Edmund Spenser c. 1552–99: *The
Shepherd's Calendar* (1579) "April"

3 I know a bank whereon the wild
thyme blows,
Where oxlips and the nodding
violet grows
Quite over-canopied with luscious
woodbine,
With sweet musk-roses, and with
eglantine:
William Shakespeare 1564–1616: *A
Midsummer Night's Dream* (1595–6)

4 Daffodils,
That come before the swallow
dares, and take
The winds of March with beauty;
violets dim,
But sweeter than the lids of
Juno's eyes
Or Cytherea's breath; pale prime-
roses,
That die unmarried, ere they can
behold
Bright Phoebus in his strength,—
a malady
Most incident to maids.
William Shakespeare 1564–1616: *The
Winter's Tale* (1610–11)

5 Ah, Sun-flower! weary of time,
Who countest the steps of the
Sun;
Seeking after that sweet golden
clime
Where the traveller's journey is
done.
William Blake 1757–1827: *Songs of
Experience* (1794) "Ah, Sun-flower!"

6 I never saw daffodils so beautiful.
They grew among the mossy
stones about and about them;
some rested their heads upon
these stones as on a pillow for
weariness; and the rest tossed and
reeled and danced, and seemed as
if they verily laughed with the

wind that blew upon them over
the lake.
Dorothy Wordsworth 1771–1855:
"Grasmere Journal" 15 April 1802

7 I wandered lonely as a cloud
That floats on high o'er vales and
hills,
When all at once I saw a crowd,
A host, of golden daffodils;
Beside the lake, beneath the trees,
Fluttering and dancing in the
breeze.
William Wordsworth 1770–1850: "I
wandered lonely as a cloud" (1815
ed.)

8 Here are sweet peas, on tip-toe for
a flight.
John Keats 1795–1821: "I stood tip-
toe upon a little hill" (1817)

9 Daisies, those pearled Arcturi of
the earth,
The constellated flower that never
sets.
Percy Bysshe Shelley 1792–1822:
"The Question" (1822)

10 The Amen! of nature is always a
flower.
Oliver Wendell Holmes, Sr. 1809–94:
The Autocrat of the Breakfast-Table
(1858)

11 Summer set lip to earth's bosom
bare,
And left the flushed print in a
poppy there.
Francis Thompson 1859–1907: "The
Poppy" (1913)

12 Oh, no man knows
Through what wild centuries
Roves back the rose.
Walter de la Mare 1873–1956: "All
That's Past" (1912)

13 Unkempt about those hedges
blows
An English unofficial rose.
Rupert Brooke 1887–1915: "The Old
Vicarage, Grantchester" (1915)

14 As well as any bloom upon a
    flower
  I like the dust on the nettles,
    never lost
  Except to prove the sweetness of a
    shower.
Edward Thomas 1878–1917: "Tall
Nettles" (1917)

Food and Drink
see also **Alcohol, Cooking and Eating**

1 Methinks sometimes I have no
more wit than a Christian or an
ordinary man has; but I am a
great eater of beef, and I believe
that does harm to my wit.
William Shakespeare 1564–1616:
Twelfth Night (1601)

2 Doubtless God could have made a
better berry, but doubtless God
never did.
on the strawberry
William Butler 1535–1618: Izaak
Walton *The Compleat Angler* (3rd
ed., 1661)

3 Coffee, (which makes the
    politician wise,
And see thro' all things with his
    half-shut eyes).
Alexander Pope 1688–1744: *The
Rape of the Lock* (1714)

4 Of soup and love, the first is the
best.
Thomas Fuller 1654–1732:
Gnomologia (1732)

5 A cucumber should be well sliced,
and dressed with pepper and
vinegar, and then thrown out, as
good for nothing.
Samuel Johnson 1709–84: James
Boswell *Journal of a Tour to the
Hebrides* (1785) 5 October 1773

6 I never see an egg brought on my
table but I feel penetrated with
the wonderful change it would
have undergone but for my
gluttony; it might have been a

gentle useful hen, leading her
chickens with a care and
vigilance which speaks shame to
many women.
St. John de Crèvecoeur 1735–1813:
Letters from an American Farmer
(1782)

7 It is as bad as bad can be: it is ill-
fed, ill-killed, ill-kept, and ill-drest.
*on the roast mutton he had been
served at an inn*
Samuel Johnson 1709–84: James
Boswell *Life of Samuel Johnson*
(1791) 3 June 1784

8 And, while the bubbling and loud-
    hissing urn
Throws up a steamy column, and
    the cups,
That cheer but not inebriate, wait
    on each,
So let us welcome peaceful
    evening in.
William Cowper 1731–1800: *The Task*
(1785) "The Winter Evening"

9 Fair fa' your honest, sonsie face,
  Great chieftain o' the puddin'-
    race!
Robert Burns 1759–96: "To a
Haggis" (1787)

10 An egg boiled very soft is not
unwholesome.
Jane Austen 1775–1817: *Emma* (1816)

11 And still she slept an azure-lidded
    sleep,
In blanchèd linen, smooth, and
    lavendered,
While he from forth the closet
    brought a heap
Of candied apple, quince, and
    plum, and gourd;
With jellies soother than the
    creamy curd,
And lucent syrops, tinct with
    cinnamon;
Manna and dates, in argosy
    transferred
From Fez; and spiced dainties,
    every one,

From silken Samarcand to cedared
Lebanon.
John Keats 1795–1821: "The Eve of
St. Agnes" (1820)

12 If there is a pure and elevated
pleasure in this world it is a roast
pheasant with bread sauce. Barn
door fowls for dissenters but for
the real Churchman, the thirty-
nine times articled clerk—the
pheasant, the pheasant.
Sydney Smith 1771–1845: letter to R.
H. Barham, 15 November 1841

13 Many's the long night I've
dreamed of cheese—toasted,
mostly.
Robert Louis Stevenson 1850–94:
Treasure Island (1883)

14 *to a waiter:*
When I ask for a watercress
sandwich, I do not mean a loaf
with a field in the middle of it.
Oscar Wilde 1854–1900: Max
Beerbohm letter to Reggie Turner, 15
April 1893

15 Cauliflower is nothing but
cabbage with a college education.
Mark Twain 1835–1910: *Pudd'nhead
Wilson* (1894)

16 Look here, Steward, if this is
coffee, I want tea; but if this is
tea, then I wish for coffee.
Punch: 1902

17 Roast Beef, Medium, is not only a
food. It is a philosophy.
Edna Ferber 1887–1968: *Roast Beef,
Medium* (1911)

18 Tea, although an Oriental,
Is a gentleman at least;
Cocoa is a cad and coward,
Cocoa is a vulgar beast.
G. K. Chesterton 1874–1936: "Song
of Right and Wrong" (1914)

19 MOTHER: It's broccoli, dear.
CHILD: I say it's spinach, and I say
the hell with it.

E. B. White 1899–1985: *New Yorker*
8 December 1928 (cartoon caption)

20 "Turbot, Sir," said the waiter,
placing before me two fishbones,
two eyeballs, and a bit of black
mackintosh.
Thomas Earle Welby 1881–1933: *The
Dinner Knell* (1932)

21 And now with some pleasure I
find that it's seven; and must
cook dinner. Haddock and
sausage meat. I think it is true
that one gains a certain hold on
sausage and haddock by writing
them down.
Virginia Woolf 1882–1941: diary, 8
March 1941

22 Milk's leap toward immortality.
of cheese
Clifton Fadiman 1904– : *Any
Number Can Play* (1957)

23 Take away that pudding—it has
no theme.
Winston Churchill 1874–1965: Lord
Home *The Way the Wind Blows*
(1976)

24 Salad. I can't bear salad. It grows
while you're eating it, you know.
Have you noticed? You start one
side of your plate and by the time
you've got to the other, there's a
fresh crop of lettuce taken root
and sprouted up.
Alan Ayckbourn 1939– : *Living
Together* (1975)

Fools and Foolishness
see also **Intelligence**

1 Answer not a fool according to
his folly, lest thou also be like
unto him.
Answer a fool according to his
folly, lest he be wise in his own
conceit.
Bible: Proverbs

2 As the crackling of thorns under a pot, so is the laughter of a fool.
Bible: Ecclesiastes

3 *Misce stultitiam consiliis brevem: Dulce est desipere in loco.*
Mix a little foolishness with your prudence: it's good to be silly at the right moment.
Horace 65–8 BC: *Odes*

4 For ye suffer fools gladly, seeing ye yourselves are wise.
Bible: II Corinthians

5 The world is full of fools, and he who would not see it should live alone and smash his mirror.
Anonymous: adaptation from an original form attributed to Claude Le Petit (1640–65) *Discours satiriques* (1686)

6 A knowledgeable fool is a greater fool than an ignorant fool.
Molière 1622–73: *Les Femmes savantes* (1672)

7 A fool can always find a greater fool to admire him.
Nicolas Boileau 1636–1711: *L'Art poétique* (1674)

8 The rest to some faint meaning make pretence,
But Shadwell never deviates into sense.
Some beams of wit on other souls may fall,
Strike through and make a lucid interval;
But Shadwell's genuine night admits no ray,
His rising fogs prevail upon the day.
John Dryden 1631–1700: *MacFlecknoe* (1682)

9 For fools rush in where angels fear to tread.
Alexander Pope 1688–1744: *An Essay on Criticism* (1711)

10 Be wise with speed;
A fool at forty is a fool indeed.
Edward Young 1683–1765: *The Love of Fame* (1725–8)

11 Experience keeps a dear school, but fools will learn in no other.
Benjamin Franklin 1706–90: *Poor Richard's Almanack* (1758)

12 The picture, placed the busts between,
Adds to the thought much strength:
Wisdom and Wit are little seen,
But Folly's at full length.
Jane Brereton 1685–1740: "On Mr. Nash's Picture at Full Length, between the Busts of Sir Isaac Newton and Mr. Pope" (1744)

13 'Tis hard if all is false that I advance
A fool must now and then be right, by chance.
William Cowper 1731–1800: "Conversation" (1782)

14 How much a dunce that has been sent to roam
Excels a dunce that has been kept at home.
William Cowper 1731–1800: "The Progress of Error" (1782)

15 A fool sees not the same tree that a wise man sees.
William Blake 1757–1827: *The Marriage of Heaven and Hell* (1790–3) "Proverbs of Hell"

16 If the fool would persist in his folly he would become wise.
William Blake 1757–1827: *The Marriage of Heaven and Hell* (1790–3) "Proverbs of Hell"

17 With stupidity the gods themselves struggle in vain.
Friedrich von Schiller 1759–1805: *Die Jungfrau von Orleans* (1801)

18 The ae half of the warld thinks the tither daft.
Sir Walter Scott 1771–1832: *Redgauntlet* (1824)

19 Experience keeps a dear school,
but fools will learn in no other.
Benjamin Franklin 1706–90: *Poor
Richard's Almanack* (1743)

20 Hain't we got all the fools in
town on our side? and ain't that
a big enough majority in any
town?
Mark Twain 1835–1910: *The
Adventures of Huckleberry Finn*
(1885)

21 The ultimate result of shielding
men from the effects of folly, is to
fill the world with fools.
Herbert Spencer 1820–1903: *Essays*
(1891) vol. 3 "State Tamperings with
Money and Banks"

22 There's a sucker born every
minute.
Phineas T. Barnum 1810–91:
attributed

23 Better to keep your mouth shut
and appear stupid than to open it
and remove all doubt.
Mark Twain 1835–1910: James
Munson (ed.) *The Sayings of Mark
Twain* (1992); attributed, perhaps
apocryphal

24 The follies which a man regrets
most, in his life, are those which
he didn't commit when he had
the opportunity.
Helen Rowland 1875–1950: *A Guide
to Men* (1922)

25 Never give a sucker an even
break.
W. C. Fields 1880–1946: title of a W.
C. Fields film (1941); the catch-
phrase (Fields's own) is said to have
originated in the musical comedy
Poppy (1923)

26 So dumb he can't fart and chew
gum at the same time.
of Gerald Ford
Lyndon Baines Johnson 1908–73:
Richard Reeves *A Ford, not a Lincoln*
(1975)

Football
see also **Sports and Games**

1 Football, wherein is nothing but
beastly fury, and extreme
violence, whereof proceedeth hurt,
and consequently rancour and
malice do remain with them that
be wounded.
Thomas Elyot 1499–1546: *Book of
the Governor* (1531)

2 Outlined against a blue-grey
October sky, the Four Horsemen
rode again. In dramatic lore they
were known as Famine,
Pestilence, Destruction, and
Death. These are only aliases.
Their real names are Stuhldreher,
Miller, Crowley, and Layden.
They formed the crest of the
South Bend cyclone before which
another fighting Army football
team was swept over the
precipice.
*report of football game between US
Military Academy at West Point NY
and University of Notre Dame*
Grantland Rice 1880–1954: in *New
York Tribune* 19 October 1924

3 For when the One Great Scorer
comes to mark against your
name,
He writes—not that you won or
lost—but how you played the
Game.
Grantland Rice 1880–1954: "Alumnus
Football" (1941)

4 Being in politics is like being a
football coach. You have to be
smart enough to understand the
game, and dumb enough to think
it's important.
*while campaigning for the
presidency*
Eugene McCarthy 1916– : in an
interview, 1968

Foresight
see also **The Future**

1 For which of you, intending to
build a tower, sitteth not down
first, and counteth the cost,
whether he have sufficient to
finish it?
Bible: St. Luke

2 If you can look into the seeds of
time,
  And say which grain will grow
  and which will not,
Speak then to me, who neither
  beg nor fear
Your favours nor your hate.
William Shakespeare 1564–1616:
Macbeth (1606)

3 The best way to suppose what
may come, is to remember what
is past.
Lord Halifax 1633–95: *Political,
Moral, and Miscellaneous Thoughts
and Reflections* (1750)
"Miscellaneous: Experience"

4 Prognostics do not always prove
prophecies,—at least the wisest
prophets make sure of the event
first.
Horace Walpole 1717–97: letter to
Thomas Walpole, 19 February 1785

5 The best laid schemes o' mice an'
men
  Gang aft a-gley.
Robert Burns 1759–96: "To a
Mouse" (1786)

6 You can never plan the future by
the past.
Edmund Burke 1729–97: *Letter to a
Member of the National Assembly*
(1791)

7 What all the wise men promised
has not happened, and what all
the d—d fools said would happen
has come to pass.
*of the Catholic Emancipation Act
(1829)*

Lord Melbourne 1779–1848: H.
Dunckley *Lord Melbourne* (1890)

8 She felt that those who prepared
for all the emergencies of life
beforehand may equip themselves
at the expense of joy.
E. M. Forster 1879–1970: *Howards
End* (1910)

9 God damn you all: I told you so.
*suggestion for his own epitaph, in
conversation with Sir Ernest Barker,
1939*
H. G. Wells 1866–1946: Ernest
Barker *Age and Youth* (1953)

10 Some of the jam we thought was
for tomorrow, we've already
eaten.
Tony Benn 1925– : attributed, 1969;
see **The Present 9**

11 We should not be surprised that
the Founding Fathers didn't
foresee everything, when we see
that the current Fathers hardly
ever foresee anything.
Henry Steele Commager 1902– :
American Heritage (February 1970)

12 It was déjà vu all over again.
Yogi Berra 1925– : attributed

Forgiveness and Repentance

1 Though your sins be as scarlet,
they shall be as white as snow.
Bible: Isaiah

2 Lord, how oft shall my brother
sin against me, and I forgive him?
till seven times?
Jesus saith unto him I say not
unto thee, Until seven times: but
Until seventy times seven.
Bible: St. Matthew

3 Charity shall cover the multitude
of sins.
Bible: I Peter

4 We read that we ought to forgive
our enemies; but we do not read

that we ought to forgive our
friends.
*speaking of what Bacon refers to as
"perfidious friends"*
Cosimo de' Medici 1389–1464:
Francis Bacon *Apophthegms* (1625);
see **Enemies** 4

5 And forgive us our trespasses, As
we forgive them that trespass
against us.
The Book of Common Prayer 1662:
Morning Prayer The Lord's Prayer

6 Repentance is but want of power
to sin.
John Dryden 1631–1700: *Palamon
and Arcite* (1700)

7 To err is human; to forgive,
divine.
Alexander Pope 1688–1744: *An
Essay on Criticism* (1711); cf.
Technology 19

8 Remorse, the fatal egg by
pleasure laid.
William Cowper 1731–1800: "The
Progress of Error" (1782)

9 You ought certainly to forgive
them as a Christian, but never to
admit them in your sight, or
allow their names to be
mentioned in your hearing.
Jane Austen 1775–1817: *Pride and
Prejudice* (1813)

10 The spirit burning but unbent,
May writhe, rebel—the weak
alone repent!
Lord Byron 1788–1824: *The Corsair*
(1814)

11 But with the morning cool
repentance came.
Sir Walter Scott 1771–1832: *Rob Roy*
(1817)

12 And blessings on the falling out
That all the more endears,
When we fall out with those we
love
And kiss again with tears!

Alfred, Lord Tennyson 1809–92: *The
Princess* (1847), song (added 1850)

13 God will pardon me, it is His
trade.
on his deathbed
Heinrich Heine 1797–1856: Alfred
Meissner *Heinrich Heine.
Erinnerungen* (1856); cf. **Power 8**

14 After such knowledge, what
forgiveness?
T. S. Eliot 1888–1965: "Gerontion"
(1920)

15 I never forgive but I always
forget.
Arthur James Balfour 1848–1930: R.
Blake *Conservative Party* (1970)

16 The stupid neither forgive nor
forget; the naïve forgive and
forget; the wise forgive but do not
forget.
Thomas Szasz 1920– : *The Second
Sin* (1973)

17 God of forgiveness, do not forgive
those murderers of Jewish
children here.
*at an unofficial ceremony at
Auschwitz on 26 January 1995,
commemorating the 50th anniversary
of its liberation*
Elie Wiesel 1928– : in *The Times*
(UK) 27 January 1995

France and the French
see also **Countries and Peoples,
International Relations, Towns and
Cities**

1 France, mother of arts, of warfare,
and of laws.
Joachim Du Bellay 1522–60: *Les
Regrets* (1558)

2 That sweet enemy, France.
Philip Sidney 1554–86: *Astrophil and
Stella* (1591)

3 Tilling and grazing are the two
breasts by which France is fed.

Maximilien de Béthune, Duc de Sully
1559–1641: *Mémoires* (1638)

4 What is not clear is not French.
Antoine de Rivarol 1753–1801:
*Discours sur l'Universalité de la
Langue Française* (1784)

5 Yet, who can help loving the land
   that has taught us
Six hundred and eighty-five ways
   to dress eggs?
Thomas Moore 1779–1852: *The
Fudge Family in Paris* (1818)

6 France was long a despotism
tempered by epigrams.
Thomas Carlyle 1795–1881: *History
of the French Revolution* (1837)

7 France, famed in all great arts, in
   none supreme.
Matthew Arnold 1822–88: "To a
Republican Friend—Continued"
(1849)

8 French art, if not sanguinary, is
usually obscene.
Herbert Spencer 1820–1903: *Home
Life with Herbert Spencer* (1906)
(authorship unknown)

9 If the French noblesse had been
capable of playing cricket with
their peasants, their chateaux
would never have been burnt.
G. M. Trevelyan 1876–1962: *English
Social History* (1942)

10 *on speaking French fluently rather
than correctly:*
It's nerve and brass, *audace* and
disrespect, and leaping-before-you-
look and what-the-hellism, that
must be developed.
Diana Cooper 1892–1986: Philip
Ziegler *Diana Cooper* (1981)

11 How can you govern a country
which has 246 varieties of
cheese?
Charles de Gaulle 1890–1970: Ernest
Mignon *Les Mots du Général* (1962)

Friendship
see also **Relationships**

1 Intreat me not to leave thee, or to
return from following after thee:
for whither thou goest, I will go;
and where thou lodgest, I will
lodge: thy people shall be my
people, and thy God my God.
Bible: Ruth

2 There is a friend that sticketh
closer than a brother.
Bible: Proverbs

3 One soul inhabiting two bodies.
*reply when asked "What is a
friend?"*
Aristotle 384–322 BC: Diogenes
Laertius *Lives of Philosophers*

4 I count myself in nothing else so
   happy
As in a soul remembering my
   good friends.
William Shakespeare 1564–1616:
Richard II (1595)

5 A crowd is not company, and
faces are but a gallery of pictures,
and talk but a tinkling cymbal,
where there is no love.
Francis Bacon 1561–1626: *Essays*
(1625) "Of Friendship"

6 It redoubleth joys, and cutteth
griefs in halves.
Francis Bacon 1561–1626: *Essays*
(1625) "Of Friendship"

7 It is more shameful to doubt
one's friends than to be duped by
them.
Duc de la Rochefoucauld 1613–80:
Maximes (1678)

8 If a man does not make new
acquaintance as he advances
through life, he will soon find
himself left alone. A man, Sir,
should keep his friendship in
constant repair.
Samuel Johnson 1709–84: James

Boswell *Life of Samuel Johnson*
(1791) 1755

9 The man that hails you Tom or
Jack,
And proves by thumps upon your
back
How he esteems your merit,
Is such a friend, that one had
need
Be very much his friend indeed
To pardon or to bear it.
William Cowper 1731–1800:
"Friendship" (1782)

10 Sir, I look upon every day to be
lost, in which I do not make a
new acquaintance.
Samuel Johnson 1709–84: James
Boswell *Life of Samuel Johnson*
(1791) November 1784

11 Should auld acquaintance be
forgot
And never brought to mind?
Robert Burns 1759–96: "Auld Lang
Syne" (1796)

12 Friendship is Love without his
wings!
Lord Byron 1788–1824: "L'Amitié est
l'amour sans ailes" (written 1806)

13 Give me the avowed, erect and
manly foe;
Firm I can meet, perhaps return
the blow;
But of all plagues, good Heaven,
thy wrath can send,
Save me, oh, save me, from the
candid friend.
George Canning 1770–1827: "New
Morality" (1821)

14 Of two close friends, one is always
the slave of the other.
Mikhail Lermontov 1814–41: *A Hero
of our Time* (1840)

15 A friend is a person with whom I
may be sincere. Before him, I may
think aloud.
Ralph Waldo Emerson 1803–82:

Essays: First Series, Friendship
(1841)

16 The only reward of virtue is
virtue; the only way to have a
friend is to be one.
Ralph Waldo Emerson 1803–82:
Essays (1841) "Friendship"

17 Friendships begin with liking or
gratitude—roots that can be
pulled up.
George Eliot 1819–80: *Daniel
Deronda* (1876)

18 A woman can become a man's
friend only in the following stages—
first an acquaintance, next a
mistress, and only then a friend.
Anton Chekhov 1860–1904: *Uncle
Vanya* (1897)

19 One friend in a lifetime is much;
two are many; three are hardly
possible. Friendship needs a
certain parallelism of life, a
community of thought, a rivalry
of aim.
Henry Brooks Adams 1838–1918: *The
Education of Henry Adams* (1907)

20 I have lost friends, some by death
. . . others through sheer inability
to cross the street.
Virginia Woolf 1882–1941: *The
Waves* (1931)

21 To find a friend one must close
one eye. To keep him—two.
Norman Douglas 1868–1952:
Almanac (1941)

22 My life is spent in a perpetual
alternation between two rhythms,
the rhythm of attracting people for
fear I may be lonely, and the
rhythm of trying to get rid of them
because I know that I am bored.
C. E. M. Joad 1891–1953: in *Observer*
(UK) 12 December 1948

23 God's apology for relations.
on friends
Hugh Kingsmill 1889–1949: Michael

Holroyd *The Best of Hugh Kingsmill* (1970)

24 Levin wanted friendship and got friendliness; he wanted steak and they offered spam.
Bernard Malamud 1914–46: *A New Life* (1961)

25 I do not believe that friends are necessarily the people you like best, they are merely the people who got there first.
Peter Ustinov 1921– : *Dear Me* (1977)

Futility

1 Vanity of vanities, saith the Preacher, vanity of vanities; all is vanity.
Bible: Ecclesiastes

2 How weary, stale, flat, and unprofitable
Seem to me all the uses of this world.
William Shakespeare 1564–1616: *Hamlet* (1601)

3 To enlarge or illustrate this power and effect of love is to set a candle in the sun.
Robert Burton 1577–1640: *The Anatomy of Melancholy* (1621–51)

4 To endeavour to work upon the vulgar with fine sense, is like attempting to hew blocks with a razor.
Alexander Pope 1688–1744: *Miscellanies* (1727) "Thoughts on Various Subjects"

5 Who breaks a butterfly upon a wheel?
Alexander Pope 1688–1744: "An Epistle to Dr. Arbuthnot" (1735)

6 "My name is Ozymandias, king of kings:
Look on my works, ye Mighty, and despair!"

Nothing beside remains. Round the decay
Of that colossal wreck, boundless and bare
The lone and level sands stretch far away.
Percy Bysshe Shelley 1792–1822: "Ozymandias" (1819)

7 "Strange friend," I said, "here is no cause to mourn."
"None," said that other, "save the undone years,
The hopelessness. Whatever hope is yours,
Was my life also."
Wilfred Owen 1893–1918: "Strange Meeting" (written 1918)

8 Pathos, piety, courage—they exist, but are identical, and so is filth. Everything exists, nothing has value.
E. M. Forster 1879–1970: *A Passage to India* (1924)

9 Nothing to be done.
Samuel Beckett 1906–89: *Waiting for Godot* (1955)

10 Nothingness haunts being.
Jean-Paul Sartre 1905–80: *Being and Nothingness* (1956)

11 There aren't any good, brave causes left. If the big bang does come, and we all get killed off, it won't be in aid of the old-fashioned, grand design. It'll just be for the Brave New-nothing-very-much-thank-you. About as pointless and inglorious as stepping in front of a bus.
John Osborne 1929–94: *Look Back in Anger* (1956)

12 I'm not going to rearrange the furniture on the deck of the Titanic.
having lost five of the last six primaries as President Ford's campaign manager
Rogers Morton 1914–79: *Washington Post* 16 May 1976

13 It seems that I have spent my entire time trying to make life more rational and that it was all wasted effort.
A. J. Ayer 1910–89: in *Observer* (UK) 17 August 1986

The Future
see also **Foresight**

1 Boast not thyself of to morrow; for thou knowest not what a day may bring forth.
Bible: Proverbs

2 Lord! we know what we are, but know not what we may be.
William Shakespeare 1564–1616: *Hamlet* (1601)

3 For present joys are more to flesh and blood
Than a dull prospect of a distant good.
John Dryden 1631–1700: *The Hind and the Panther* (1687)

4 "We are always doing," says he, "something for Posterity, but I would fain see Posterity do something for us."
Joseph Addison 1672–1719: in *The Spectator* (UK) 20 August 1714

5 The next Augustan age will dawn on the other side of the Atlantic. There will, perhaps, be a Thucydides at Boston, a Xenophon at New York, and, in time, a Virgil at Mexico, and a Newton at Peru. At last, some curious traveller from Lima will visit England and give a description of the ruins of St. Paul's, like the editions of Balbec and Palmyra.
Horace Walpole 1717–97: letter to Horace Mann, 24 November 1774

6 People will not look forward to posterity, who never look backward to their ancestors.
Edmund Burke 1729–97: *Reflections on the Revolution in France* (1790)

7 So many worlds, so much to do, So little done, such things to be.
Alfred, Lord Tennyson 1809–92: *In Memoriam A. H. H.* (1850)

8 He seems to think that posterity is a pack-horse, always ready to be loaded.
Benjamin Disraeli 1804–81: speech, 3 June 1862; attributed

9 You cannot fight against the future. Time is on our side.
W. E. Gladstone 1809–98: speech on the Reform Bill, House of Commons, 27 April 1866

10 You will eat, bye and bye,
In that glorious land above the sky;
Work and pray, live on hay,
You'll get pie in the sky when you die.
Joe Hill 1879–1915: "Preacher and the Slave" (1911 song)

11 Make me a beautiful word for doing things tomorrow; for that surely is a great and blessed invention.
George Bernard Shaw 1856–1950: *Back to Methuselah* (1921)

12 *In the long run* we are all dead.
John Maynard Keynes 1883–1946: *A Tract on Monetary Reform* (1923)

13 I never think of the future. It comes soon enough.
Albert Einstein 1879–1955: in an interview given on the *Belgenland*, December 1930

14 We have trained them [men] to think of the Future as a promised land which favoured heroes attain—not as something which everyone reaches at the rate of sixty minutes an hour, whatever he does, whoever he is.

C. S. Lewis 1898–1963: *The Screwtape Letters* (1942)

15 If you want a picture of the future, imagine a boot stamping on a human face—for ever.
George Orwell 1903–50: *Nineteen Eighty-Four* (1949)

16 They spend their time mostly looking forward to the past.
John Osborne 1929–94: *Look Back in Anger* (1956)

17 The future ain't what it used to be.
Yogi Berra 1925– : attributed

18 More than any other time in history, mankind faces a crossroads. One path leads to despair and utter hopelessness. The other, to total extinction. Let us pray we have the wisdom to choose correctly.
Woody Allen 1935– : *Side Effects* (1980) "My Speech to the Graduates"

19 *announcing that he had ended his association with the cryonics movement, and abandoned his plan to have his head cryonically preserved:*
They have no sense of humor. I was worried I would wake up in fifty years surrounded by people with clipboards.
Timothy Leary 1920–96: in *Daily Telegraph* (UK) 10 May 1996

Games
see **Sports and Games**

Gardens
see also **Flowers**

1 And the Lord God planted a garden eastward in Eden.
Bible: Genesis; cf. **3** below

2 Sowe Carrets in your Gardens, and humbly praise God for them, as for a singular and great blessing.
Richard Gardiner b. *c.* 1533: *Profitable Instructions for the Manuring, Sowing and Planting of Kitchen Gardens* (1599)

3 God Almighty first planted a garden; and, indeed, it is the purest of human pleasures.
Francis Bacon 1561–1626: *Essays* (1625) "Of Gardens" cf. **1** above

4 Annihilating all that's made To a green thought in a green shade.
Andrew Marvell 1621–78: "The Garden" (1681)

5 All gardening is landscape-painting.
Alexander Pope 1688–1744: Joseph Spence *Anecdotes* (1966)

6 But though an old man, I am but a young gardener.
Thomas Jefferson 1743–1826: letter to Charles Willson Peale, 20 August 1811

7 A garden was the primitive prison till man with Promethean felicity and boldness luckily sinned himself out of it.
Charles Lamb 1775–1834: letter to William Wordsworth, 22 January 1830

8 What is a weed? A plant whose virtues have not been discovered.
Ralph Waldo Emerson 1803–82: *Fortune of the Republic* (1878)

9 A garden is a lovesome thing, God wot!
T. E. Brown 1830–97: "My Garden" (1893)

10 The kiss of the sun for pardon, The song of the birds for mirth, One is nearer God's Heart in a garden
Than anywhere else on earth.

Dorothy Frances Gurney 1858–1932: "God's Garden" (1913)

11 All really grim gardeners possess a keen sense of humus.
W. C. Sellar 1898–1951 and **R. J. Yeatman** 1898–1968: *Garden Rubbish* (1930)

12 Let "Dig for Victory" be the motto of every one with a garden and of every able-bodied man and woman capable of digging an allotment in their spare time.
Reginald Dorman-Smith 1899–1977: radio broadcast, 3 October 1939

13 Perennials are the ones that grow like weeds, biennials are the ones that die this year instead of next and hardy annuals are the ones that never come up at all.
Katharine Whitehorn 1928– : *Observations* (1970)

14 I will keep returning to the virtues of sharp and swift drainage, whether a plant prefers to be wet or dry . . . I would have called this book Better Drains, but you would never have bought it or borrowed it for bedtime.
Robin Lane Fox 1946– : *Better Gardening* (1982)

15 I just come and talk to the plants, really—very important to talk to them, they respond I find.
Prince Charles 1948– : television interview, 21 September 1986

16 There can be no other occupation like gardening in which, if you were to creep behind someone at their work, you would find them smiling.
Mirabel Osler: *A Gentle Plea for Chaos* (1989)

The Generation Gap
see also **Old Age, Youth**

1 Tiresome, complaining, a praiser of past times, when he was a boy,
a castigator and censor of the young generation.
Horace 65–8 BC: *Ars Poetica*

2 *Si jeunesse savait; si vieillesse pouvait.*
If youth knew; if age could.
Henri Estienne 1531–98: *Les Prémices* (1594)

3 Age is deformed, youth unkind,
We scorn their bodies, they our mind.
Thomas Bastard 1566–1618: *Chrestoleros* (1598)

4 Crabbed age and youth cannot live together:
Youth is full of pleasance, age is full of care.
William Shakespeare 1564–1616: *The Passionate Pilgrim* (1599)

5 O Man! that from thy fair and shining youth
Age might but take the things Youth needed not!
William Wordsworth 1770–1850: "The Small Celandine" (1807)

6 Youth, which is forgiven everything, forgives itself nothing: age, which forgives itself everything, is forgiven nothing.
George Bernard Shaw 1856–1950: *Man and Superman* (1903)

7 The young have aspirations that never come to pass, the old have reminiscences of what never happened.
Saki 1870–1916: *Reginald* (1904)

8 Where, where but here have Pride and Truth,
That long to give themselves for wage,
To shake their wicked sides at youth
Restraining reckless middle age?
W. B. Yeats 1865–1939: "On hearing that the Students of our New University have joined the Agitation against Immoral Literature" (1910)

9 When I was a boy of 14, my father was so ignorant I could hardly stand to have the old man around. But when I got to be 21, I was astonished at how much the old man had learned in seven years.
Mark Twain 1835–1910: attributed in *Reader's Digest* September 1939, but not traced in his works

10 The young man who has not wept is a savage, and the old man who will not laugh is a fool.
George Santayana 1863–1952: *Dialogues in Limbo* (1925)

11 Every generation revolts against its fathers and makes friends with its grandfathers.
Lewis Mumford 1895– : *The Brown Decades* (1931)

12 Grown-ups never understand anything for themselves, and it is tiresome for children to be always and forever explaining things to them.
Antoine de Saint-Exupéry 1900–44: *Le Petit Prince* (1943)

13 It is the one war in which everyone changes sides.
Cyril Connolly 1903–74: Tom Driberg speech in House of Commons, 30 October 1959

14 We have a saying in the movement that we don't trust anybody over thirty.
Jack Weinberg 1940– : *San Francisco Chronicle* (1965)

Genius

1 Great wits are sure to madness near allied,
And thin partitions do their bounds divide.
John Dryden 1631–1700: *Absalom and Achitophel* (1681)

2 When a true genius appears in the world, you may know him by this sign, that the dunces are all in confederacy against him.
Jonathan Swift 1667–1745: *Thoughts on Various Subjects* (1711)

3 There is more beauty in the works of a great genius who is ignorant of all the rules of art, than in the works of a little genius, who not only knows but scrupulously observes them.
Joseph Addison 1672–1719: in *The Spectator* (UK) 10 September 1714

4 Good God! what a genius I had when I wrote that book.
of A Tale of a Tub
Jonathan Swift 1667–1745: Sir Walter Scott (ed.) *Works of Swift* (1814)

5 The true genius is a mind of large general powers, accidentally determined to some particular direction.
Samuel Johnson 1709–84: *Lives of the English Poets* (1779–81) "Cowley"

6 Genius always finds itself a century too early.
Ralph Waldo Emerson 1803–82: *Journals* (1840)

7 Many a genius has been slow of growth. Oaks that flourish for a thousand years do not spring up into beauty like a reed.
G. H. Lewes 1817–78: *The Spanish Drama* (1846)

8 Since when was genius found respectable?
Elizabeth Barrett Browning 1806–61: *Aurora Leigh* (1857)

9 A person of genius should marry a person of character. Genius does not herd with genius.
Oliver Wendell Holmes, Sr. 1809–94: *The Professor at the Breakfast-Table* (1860)

10 Genius does what it must, and
Talent does what it can.
Owen Meredith 1831–91: "Last
Words of a Sensitive Second-Rate
Poet" (1868)

11 I have nothing to declare except
my genius.
at the New York Custom House
Oscar Wilde 1854–1900: Frank Harris
Oscar Wilde (1918)

12 Genius is one per cent inspiration,
ninety-nine per cent perspiration.
Thomas Alva Edison 1847–1931: said
c. 1903, in *Harper's Monthly
Magazine* September 1932

13 Little minds are interested in the
extraordinary; great minds in the
commonplace.
Elbert Hubbard 1859–1915: *Thousand
and One Epigrams* (1911)

14 A man of genius makes no
mistakes. His errors are volitional
and are the portals of discovery.
James Joyce 1882–1941: *Ulysses*
(1922)

15 Genius is more often found in a
cracked pot than a whole one.
E. B. White 1899–1985: *One Man's
Meat* (1944)

16 Geniuses are the luckiest of
mortals because what they must
do is the same as what they most
want to do.
W. H. Auden 1907–73: Dag
Hammarskjöld *Markings* (1964)

Gifts and Giving
see also **Charity**

1 Enemies' gifts are no gifts and do
no good.
Sophocles *c.* 496–406 BC: *Ajax*

2 Give, and it shall be given unto
you; good measure, pressed down,
and shaken together, and
running over.
Bible: St. Luke

3 It is more blessed to give than to
receive.
Bible: Acts of the Apostles

4 God loveth a cheerful giver.
Bible: II Corinthians

5 Teach us, good Lord, to serve
Thee as Thou deservest:
To give and not to count the cost;
To fight and not to heed the
wounds;
To toil and not to seek for rest;
To labor and not to ask for any
reward
Save that of knowing that we do
Thy will.
St. Ignatius Loyola 1491–1556:
"Prayer for Generosity" (1548)

6 I am not in the giving vein to-
day.
William Shakespeare 1564–1616:
Richard III (1591)

7 When they will not give a doit to
relieve a lame beggar, they will
lay out ten to see a dead Indian.
William Shakespeare 1564–1616: *The
Tempest* (1611)

8 But thousands die, without or
this or that,
Die, and endow a college, or a
cat.
Alexander Pope 1688–1744: *Epistles
to Several Persons* "To Lord
Bathurst" (1733)

9 Presents, I often say, endear
Absents.
Charles Lamb 1775–1834: *Essays of
Elia* (1823) "A Dissertation upon
Roast Pig"

10 Behold, I do not give lectures or a
little charity,
When I give I give myself.
Walt Whitman 1819–92: "Song of
Myself" (written 1855)

11 They gave it me,—for an un-
birthday present.
Lewis Carroll 1832–98: *Through the
Looking-Glass* (1872)

12 When I was one-and-twenty
I heard a wise man say,
"Give crowns and pounds and
    guineas
But not your heart away;
Give pearls away and rubies,
But keep your fancy free."
But I was one-and-twenty,
No use to talk to me.
A. E. Housman 1859–1936: *A
Shropshire Lad* (1896)

13 CHAIRMAN: What is service?
CANDIDATE: The rent we pay for
our room on earth.

*admission ceremony of Toc H (a
society, originally of ex-servicemen
and women, founded after the First
World War to promote Christian
fellowship and social service)*
Tubby Clayton 1885–1972: Tresham
Lever *Clayton of Toc H* (1971)

14 "The more we ask, the more we
have. And, it is fair enough:
asking is not always easy."
"And it is said to be hard to
accept . . . So no wonder we have
so little."
Ivy Compton-Burnett 1884–1969: *The
Mighty and their Fall* (1961)

God
see also **Belief and Unbelief, The
Bible, The Christian Church, Religion**

1 The Lord is my shepherd:
therefore can I lack nothing.
He shall feed me in a green
pasture: and lead me forth beside
the waters of comfort.
Bible: Psalm 23

2 With men this is impossible; but
with God all things are possible.
Bible: St. Matthew

3 He that loveth not knoweth not
God; for God is love.
Bible: I John

4 Jupiter is whatever you see,
whichever way you move.
Lucan AD 39–65: *Pharsalia*

5 Raise the stone, and there thou
shalt find me, cleave the wood
and there am I.
Anonymous: Oxyrhynchus Papyri; B.
P. Grenfell and A. S. Hunt (eds.)
Sayings of Our Lord (1897)

6 Therefore it is necessary to arrive
at a prime mover, put in motion
by no other; and this everyone
understands to be God.
St. Thomas Aquinas c. 1225–74:
Summa Theologicae (c. 1265)

7 The nature of God is a circle of
which the center is everywhere
and the circumference is
nowhere.
Anonymous: said to have been
traced to a lost treatise of
Empedocles; quoted in the *Roman
de la Rose*, and by St. Bonaventura
in *Itinerarius Mentis in Deum*

8 *E'n la sua volontade è nostra pace.*
In His will is our peace.
Dante Alighieri 1265–1321: *Divina
Commedia* "Paradiso"

9 Whatever your heart clings to
and confides in, that is really
your God.
Martin Luther 1483–1546: *Large
Catechism* (1529) "The First
Commandment"

10 Alas, O Lord, to what a state dost
Thou bring those who love Thee!
St. Teresa of Ávila 1512–82: *Interior
Castle*

11 'Twas only fear first in the world
made gods.
Ben Jonson c. 1573–1637: *Sejanus*
(1603)

12 Batter my heart, three-personed
   God; for, you
   As yet but knock, breathe, shine,
   and seek to mend.
   John Donne 1572–1631: *Holy Sonnets*
   (after 1609)

13 I had rather believe all the fables
   in the legend, and the Talmud,
   and the Alcoran, than that this
   universal frame is without a
   mind.
   Francis Bacon 1561–1626: *Essays*
   (1625) "Of Atheism"

14 Though the mills of God grind
   slowly, yet they grind
   exceeding small;
   Though with patience He stands
   waiting, with exactness grinds
   He all.
   Friedrich von Logau 1604–55:
   Sinngedichte (1654) translated by
   Longfellow; Von Logau's first line is
   itself a translation of an anonymous
   verse in Sextus Empiricus *Adversus
   Mathematicos*

15 "God is or he is not." But to
   which side shall we incline? . . .
   Let us weigh the gain and the
   loss in wagering that God is. Let
   us estimate the two chances. If
   you gain, you gain all; if you
   lose, you lose nothing. Wager
   then without hesitation that he is.
   known as Pascal's wager
   Blaise Pascal 1623–62: *Pensées*
   (1670)

16 As you know, God is usually on
   the side of the big squadrons
   against the small.
   Comte de Bussy-Rabutin 1618–93:
   letter to the Comte de Limoges, 18
   October 1677; cf. **Warfare 11**

17 Our God, our help in ages past
   Our hope for years to come,
   Our shelter from the stormy blast,
   And our eternal home.
   Isaac Watts 1674–1748: *The Psalms
   of David Imitated* (1719); "Our God"
   altered to "O God" by John Wesley,
   1738

18 If the triangles were to make a
   God they would give him three
   sides.
   Montesquieu 1689–1755: *Lettres
   Persanes* (1721)

19 If God did not exist, it would be
   necessary to invent him.
   Voltaire 1694–1778: *Épîtres* no. 96
   "A l'Auteur du livre des trois
   imposteurs"

20 God moves in a mysterious way
   His wonders to perform.
   William Cowper 1731–1800: "Light
   Shining out of Darkness" (1779
   hymn)

21 Suppose I had found a *watch*
   upon the ground, and it should
   be enquired how the watch
   happened to be in that place . . .
   the inference, we think, is
   inevitable; that the watch must
   have had a maker, that there
   must have existed, at some time
   and at some place or other, an
   artificer or artificers, who formed
   it for the purpose which we find
   it actually to answer; who
   comprehended its construction,
   and designed its use.
   William Paley 1743–1805: *Natural
   Theology* (1802); cf. **Life Sciences 15**

22 All service ranks the same with
   God—
   With God, whose puppets, best
   and worst,
   Are we: there is no last nor first.
   Robert Browning 1812–89: *Pippa
   Passes* (1841)

23 Up in the mountains of New
   Hampshire, God Almighty has
   hung out a sign to show that
   there He makes men.
   *on the rock formation known as the
   Old Man of the Mountain, in the
   Presidential Range of the White
   Mountains, New Hampshire*
   Daniel Webster 1782–1852:
   attributed

24 Mine eyes have seen the glory of
the coming of the Lord:
He is trampling out the vintage
where the grapes of wrath are
stored;
He hath loosed the fateful
lightning of his terrible swift
sword:
His truth is marching on.
Julia Ward Howe 1819–1910: "Battle
Hymn of the Republic" (1862)

25 Thou shalt have one God only; who
Would be at the expense of two?
Arthur Hugh Clough 1819–61: "The
Latest Decalogue" (1862)

26 I will call no being good, who is
not what I mean when I apply
that epithet to my fellow-
creatures; and if such a being can
sentence me to hell for not so
calling him, to hell I will go.
John Stuart Mill 1806–73:
*Examination of Sir William
Hamilton's Philosophy* (1865)

27 An honest God is the noblest
work of man.
after Pope Essay on Man *(1734) "An
honest man's the noblest work of
God"*
Robert G. Ingersoll 1833–99: *The
Gods* (1876)

28 I am a great & sublime fool. But
then I am God's fool, & all His
works must be contemplated with
respect.
Mark Twain 1835–1910: *Letter to
William Dean Howells* (1877)

29 God is dead: but considering the
state the species Man is in, there
will perhaps be caves, for ages
yet, in which his shadow will be
shown.
Friedrich Nietzsche 1844–1900: *Die
fröhliche Wissenschaft* (1882)

30 God is subtle but he is not
malicious.

Albert Einstein 1879–1955: remark
made at Princeton University, May
1921; R. W. Clark *Einstein* (1973)

31 Better authentic mammon than a
bogus god.
Louis MacNeice 1907–63: *Autumn
Journal* (1939); see **Money 3**

32 It is a mistake to suppose that
God is only, or even chiefly,
concerned with religion.
William Temple 1881–1944: R. V. C.
Bodley *In Search of Serenity* (1955)

33 Operationally, God is beginning to
resemble not a ruler but the last
fading smile of a cosmic Cheshire
cat.
Julian Huxley 1887–1975: *Religion
without Revelation* (1957 ed.)

34 It is the final proof of God's
omnipotence that he need not
exist in order to save us.
Peter De Vries 1910– : *The
Mackerel Plaza* (1958)

35 God has been replaced, as he has
all over the West, with
respectability and air
conditioning.
Imamu Amiri Baraka 1934– :
Midstream (1963)

36 God is really only another artist.
He invented the giraffe, the
elephant, and the cat. He has no
real style. He just goes on trying
other things.
Pablo Picasso 1881–1973: F. Gilot
and C. Lake *Life With Picasso* (1964)

37 God can stand being told by
Professor Ayer and Marghanita
Laski that He doesn't exist.
J. B. Priestley 1894–1984: in *Listener*
(UK) 1 July 1965

38 God seems to have left the
receiver off the hook, and time is
running out.
Arthur Koestler 1905–83: *The Ghost
in the Machine* (1967)

39 God is love, but get it in writing.
Gypsy Rose Lee 1914–70: attributed

40 If only God would give me some clear sign! Like making a large deposit in my name at a Swiss bank.
Woody Allen 1935– : "Selections from the Allen Notebooks" in *New Yorker* 5 November 1973

41 I think it pisses God off if you walk by the color purple in a field somewhere and don't notice it.
Alice Walker 1944– : *The Color Purple* (1982)

42 I am not clear that God manoeuvres physical things . . . After all, a conjuring trick with bones only proves that it is as clever as a conjuring trick with bones.
of the Resurrection
David Jenkins 1925– : "Poles Apart" (BBC radio, 4 October 1984)

43 If I were Her what would really piss me off the worst is that they cannot even get My gender right for Chrissakes.
Roseanne Arnold 1953– : *Roseanne* (1990)

44 Let us do something beautiful for God.
Mother Teresa 1910–97: in *New York Times*, 26 December 1997

Good and Evil
see also **Sin**, **Virtue**

1 He that toucheth pitch shall be defiled therewith.
Bible: Ecclesiasticus

2 It is never right to do wrong or to requite wrong with wrong, or when we suffer evil to defend ourselves by doing evil in return.
Socrates 469–399 BC: Plato *Crito*

3 Every art and every investigation, and likewise every practical pursuit or undertaking, seems to aim at some good: hence it has been well said that the Good is That at which all things aim.
Aristotle 384–322 BC: *Nicomachean Ethics*

4 For the good that I would I do not: but the evil which I would not, that I do.
Bible: Romans

5 Unto the pure all things are pure.
Bible: Titus; cf. **26** below

6 With love for mankind and hatred of sins.
often quoted "Love the sinner but hate the sin"
St. Augustine of Hippo AD 354–430: letter 211; J.-P. Migne (ed.) *Patrologiae Latinae* (1845)

7 If all evil were prevented, much good would be absent from the universe. A lion would cease to live, if there were no slaying of animals; and there would be no patience of martyrs if there were no tyrannical persecution.
St. Thomas Aquinas c. 1225–74: *Summa Theologicae* (c. 1265)

8 *Honi soit qui mal y pense.*
Evil be to him who evil thinks.
Anonymous: motto of the Order of the Garter, originated by Edward III, probably on 23 April of 1348 or 1349

9 For, where God built a church, there the devil would also build a chapel . . . In such sort is the devil always God's ape.
Martin Luther 1483–1546: *Colloquia Mensalia* (1566)

10 I come to bury Caesar, not to praise him.
The evil that men do lives after them,

The good is oft interrèd with their bones.
William Shakespeare 1564–1616: *Julius Caesar* (1599)

11 There is nothing either good or bad, but thinking makes it so.
William Shakespeare 1564–1616: *Hamlet* (1601)

12 By the pricking of my thumbs, Something wicked this way comes.
William Shakespeare 1564–1616: *Macbeth* (1606)

13 For sweetest things turn sourest by their deeds;
Lilies that fester smell far worse than weeds.
William Shakespeare 1564–1616: Sonnet 94

14 Farewell remorse! All good to me is lost;
Evil, be thou my good.
John Milton 1608–74: *Paradise Lost* (1667)

15 BELINDA: Ay, but you know we must return good for evil.
LADY BRUTE: That may be a mistake in the translation.
John Vanbrugh 1664–1726: *The Provoked Wife* (1697)

16 But if he does really think that there is no distinction between virtue and vice, why, Sir, when he leaves our houses, let us count our spoons.
Samuel Johnson 1709–84: James Boswell *Life of Samuel Johnson* (1791) 14 July 1763

17 It is necessary only for the good man to do nothing for evil to triumph.
Edmund Burke 1729–97: attributed (in a number of forms) to Burke, but not found in his writings

18 One impulse from a vernal wood May teach you more of man,
Of moral evil and of good,
Than all the sages can.
William Wordsworth 1770–1850: "The Tables Turned" (1798)

19 He who would do good to another, must do it in minute particulars
General good is the plea of the scoundrel, hypocrite and flatterer.
William Blake 1757–1827: *Jerusalem* (1815)

20 Every sweet hath its sour; every evil its good.
Ralph Waldo Emerson 1803–82: *Essays: First Series, Compensation* (1841)

21 One trembles to think of that mysterious thing in the soul, which seems to acknowledge no human jurisdiction, but in spite of the individual's own innocent self, will still dream horrid dreams, and mutter unmentionable thoughts.
Herman Melville 1819–1902: *Pierre* (1852)

22 It is better to fight for the good, than to rail at the ill.
Alfred, Lord Tennyson 1809–92: *Maud* (1855)

23 Imagine that you are creating a fabric of human destiny with the object of making men happy in the end, giving them peace and rest at last, but that it was essential and inevitable to torture to death only one tiny creature . . . and to found that edifice on its unavenged tears, would you consent to be the architect on those conditions?
Fyodor Dostoevsky 1821–81: *The Brothers Karamazov* (1879–80)

24 A belief in a supernatural source of evil is not necessary; men alone are quite capable of every wickedness.
Joseph Conrad 1857–1924: *Under Western Eyes* (1911)

25 What we call evil is simply ignorance bumping its head in the dark.
Henry Ford 1863–1947: in *Observer* (UK) 16 March 1930

26 To the Puritan all things are impure, as somebody says.
D. H. Lawrence 1885–1930: *Etruscan Places* (1932) "Cerveteri" see **5** above

27 As soon as men decide that all means are permitted to fight an evil, then their good becomes indistinguishable from the evil that they set out to destroy.
Christopher Dawson 1889–1970: *The Judgement of the Nations* (1942)

28 The face of "evil" is always the face of total need.
William S. Burroughs 1914–97: *The Naked Lunch* (1959)

29 It was as though in those last minutes he [Eichmann] was summing up the lessons that this long course in human wickedness had taught us—the lesson of the fearsome, word-and-thought-defying *banality of evil*.
Hannah Arendt 1906–75: *Eichmann in Jerusalem* (1963)

30 Two wrongs don't make a right, but they make a good excuse.
Thomas Szasz 1920– : *The Second Sin* (1973)

Gossip
see also **Reputation, Secrecy**

1 Many have fallen by the edge of the sword: but not so many as have fallen by the tongue.
Bible: Ecclesiasticus

2 *Che ti fa ciò che quivi pispiglia?*
Vien dietro a me, e lascia dir le genti.
What is it to thee what they whisper there? Come after me and let the people talk.
Dante Alighieri 1265–1321: *Divina Commedia* "Purgatorio"

3 Enter Rumour, painted full of tongues.
William Shakespeare 1564–1616: *Henry IV, Part 2* (1597); stage direction

4 Be thou as chaste as ice, as pure as snow, thou shalt not escape calumny.
William Shakespeare 1564–1616: *Hamlet* (1601)

5 How these curiosities would be quite forgot, did not such idle fellows as I am put them down.
John Aubrey 1626–97: *Brief Lives* "Venetia Digby"

6 Love and scandal are the best sweeteners of tea.
Henry Fielding 1707–54: *Love in Several Masques* (1728)

7 While the Town small-talk flows from lip to lip;
Intrigues half-gathered, conversation-scraps,
Kitchen-cabals, and nursery-mishaps.
George Crabbe 1754–1832: *The Borough* (1810)

8 It is a matter of great interest what sovereigns are doing; but as to what Grand Duchesses are doing—Who cares?
Napoleon I 1769–1821: letter, 17 December 1811

9 Every man is surrounded by a neighbourhood of voluntary spies.
Jane Austen 1775–1817: *Northanger Abbey* (1818)

10 Gossip is a sort of smoke that comes from the dirty tobacco-

pipes of those who diffuse it: it proves nothing but the bad taste of the smoker.
George Eliot 1819–80: *Daniel Deronda* (1876)

11 There is only one thing in the world worse than being talked about, and that is not being talked about.
Oscar Wilde 1854–1900: *The Picture of Dorian Gray* (1891)

12 It takes your enemy and your friend, working together, to hurt you to the heart: the one to slander you and the other to get the news to you.
Mark Twain 1835–1910: *Following the Equator* (1897)

13 Like all gossip—it's merely one of those half-alive things that try to crowd out real life.
E. M. Forster 1879–1970: *A Passage to India* (1924)

14 If you haven't got anything good to say about anyone come and sit by me.
maxim embroidered on a cushion
Alice Roosevelt Longworth 1884–1980: Michael Teague *Mrs. L: Conversations with Alice Roosevelt Longworth* (1981)

Government
see also **International Relations, Politics, The Presidency, Society**

1 Let them hate, so long as they fear.
Accius 170–c. 86 BC: from *Atreus*; Seneca *Dialogues*

2 Would that the Roman people had but one neck!
Caligula AD 12–41: Suetonius *Lives of the Caesars* "Gaius Caligula"

3 . . . *Duas tantum res anxius optat, Panem et circenses.*

Only two things does he [the modern citizen] anxiously wish for—bread and circuses.
Juvenal AD c. 60–c. 130: *Satires*

4 Because it is difficult to join them together, it is much safer for a prince to be feared than loved, if he is to fail in one of the two.
Niccolò Machiavelli 1469–1527: *The Prince* (written 1513)

5 Though God hath raised me high, yet this I count the glory of my crown: that I have reigned with your loves.
Elizabeth I 1533–1603. The Golden Speech, 1601

6 I will govern according to the common weal, but not according to the common will.
James I 1566–1625: in December, 1621; J. R. Green *History of the English People* vol. 3 (1879)

7 Dost thou not know, my son, with how little wisdom the world is governed?
Count Oxenstierna 1583–1654: letter to his son, 1648. John Selden, in *Table Talk* (1689) quotes "a certain Pope" (possibly Julius III) saying "Thou little thinkest what *a little foolery governs the whole world!*"

8 During the time men live without a common power to keep them all in awe, they are in that condition which is called war; and such a war as is of every man against every man.
Thomas Hobbes 1588–1679: *Leviathan* (1651)

9 *L'État c'est moi.*
I am the State.
Louis XIV 1638–1715: before the Parlement de Paris, 13 April 1655; probably apocryphal

10 All empire is no more than power in trust.

John Dryden 1631–1700: *Absalom and Achitophel* (1681)

11 Governments need both shepherds and butchers.
Voltaire 1694–1778: "The Piccini Notebooks" (c. 1735–50)

12 Little else is requisite to carry a state to the highest degree of opulence from the lowest barbarism but peace, easy taxes, and a tolerable administration of justice: all the rest being brought about by the natural course of things.
Adam Smith 1723–90: in 1755; *Essays on Philosophical Subjects* (1795)

13 I would not give half a guinea to live under one form of government rather than another. It is of no moment to the happiness of an individual.
Samuel Johnson 1709–84: James Boswell *Life of Samuel Johnson* (1791) 31 March 1772

14 A government of laws, and not of men.
John Adams 1735–1826: *Boston Gazette* (1774) "Novanglus" papers; later incorporated in the Massachusetts Constitution (1780)

15 The happiness of society is the end of government.
John Adams 1735–1826: *Thoughts on Government* (1776)

16 Government, even in its best state, is but a necessary evil . . . Government, like dress, is the badge of lost innocence; the palaces of kings are built upon the ruins of the bowers of paradise.
Thomas Paine 1737–1809: *Common Sense* (1776)

17 My people and I have come to an agreement which satisfies us both. They are to say what they please, and I am to do what I please.

his interpretation of benevolent despotism
Frederick the Great 1712–86: attributed

18 But what is government itself but the greatest of all reflections on human nature? If men were angels, no government would be necessary. If angels were to govern men, neither external nor internal controls on government would be necessary. In framing a government which is to be administered by men over men, the great difficulty lies in this: you must first enable the government to control the governed; and in the next place, oblige it to control itself.
James Madison 1751–1836: *The Federalist*, no. 51 (1788)

19 When, in countries that are called civilized, we see age going to the workhouse and youth to the gallows, something must be wrong in the system of government.
Thomas Paine 1737–1809: *The Rights of Man* pt. 2 (1792)

20 A monarchy is a merchantman which sails well, but will sometimes strike on a rock, and go to the bottom; whilst a republic is a raft which would never sink, but then your feet are always in the water.
Fisher Ames 1758–1808: attributed to Ames, speaking in the House of Representatives, 1795; quoted by R. W. Emerson in *Essays* (1844), but not traced in Ames's speeches

21 Away with the cant of "Measures not men"!—the idle supposition that it is the harness and not the horses that draw the chariot along. If the comparison must be made, if the distinction must be taken, men are everything, measures comparatively nothing.

George Canning 1770–1827: speech on the Army estimates, 8 December 1802; the phrase "measures not men" may be found as early as 1742 (in a letter from Chesterfield to Dr. Chevenix, 6 March)

22 To govern is to choose.
Duc de Lévis 1764–1830: *Maximes et Réflexions* (1812 ed.)

23 America, with the same voice which spoke herself into existence as a nation, proclaimed to mankind the inextinguishable rights of human nature, and the only lawful foundations of government.
John Quincy Adams 1767–1848: *Address* (4 July 1821)

24 The best government is that which governs least.
John L. O'Sullivan 1813–95: *United States Magazine and Democratic Review* (1837)

25 What is understood by republican government in the United States is the slow and quiet action of society upon itself.
Alexis de Tocqueville 1805–59: *Democracy in America* (1835–40)

26 The reluctant obedience of distant provinces generally costs more than it [the territory] is worth.
Lord Macaulay 1800–59: *Essays Contributed to the Edinburgh Review* (1843) "The War of Succession in Spain"

27 No Government can be long secure without a formidable Opposition.
Benjamin Disraeli 1804–81: *Coningsby* (1844)

28 Now, is it to lower the price of corn, or isn't it? It is not much matter which we say, but mind, we must all say *the same.*
on Cabinet government
Lord Melbourne 1779–1848:

attributed; Walter Bagehot *The English Constitution* (1867)

29 This country, with its institutions, belongs to the people who inhabit it. Whenever they shall grow weary of the existing government, they can exercise their constitutional right of amending it, or their revolutionary right to dismember or overthrow it.
Abraham Lincoln 1809–65: first inaugural address, 4 March 1861

30 The Crown is, according to the saying, the "fountain of honour" but the Treasury is the spring of business.
Walter Bagehot 1826–77: *The English Constitution* (1867) "The Cabinet"

31 My faith in the people governing is, on the whole, infinitesimal; my faith in The People governed is, on the whole, illimitable.
Charles Dickens 1812–70: speech at Birmingham and Midland Institute, 27 September 1869

32 The State is not "abolished," *it withers away.*
Friedrich Engels 1820–95: *Anti-Dühring* (1878)

33 The state is like the human body. Not all of its functions are dignified.
Anatole France 1844–1924: *Les Opinions de M. Jerome Coignard* (1893)

34 I work for a Government I despise for ends I think criminal.
John Maynard Keynes 1883–1946: letter to Duncan Grant, 15 December 1917

35 While the State exists, there can be no freedom. When there is freedom there will be no State.
V. I. Lenin 1870–1924: *State and Revolution* (1919)

36 A government which robs Peter to pay Paul can always depend on the support of Paul.
George Bernard Shaw 1856–1950: *Everybody's Political What's What* (1944)

37 BIG BROTHER IS WATCHING YOU.
George Orwell 1903–50: *Nineteen Eighty-Four* (1949)

38 If the Government is big enough to give you everything you want, it is big enough to take away everything you have.
Gerald Ford 1909– : John F. Parker *If Elected* (1960)

39 Today, government is involved in almost every aspect of our lives.
Bernard Baruch 1870–1965: *presenting his papers to Princeton University* (11 May 1964)

40 Government of the busy by the bossy for the bully.
on over-government
Arthur Seldon 1916– : *Capitalism* (1990)

41 We give the impression of being in office but not in power.
Norman Lamont 1942– : speech, House of Commons, 9 June 1993

Gratitude and Ingratitude

1 A joyful and pleasant thing it is to be thankful.
Bible: Psalm 147

2 Blow, blow, thou winter wind, Thou art not so unkind As man's ingratitude.
William Shakespeare 1564–1616: *As You Like It* (1599)

3 How sharper than a serpent's tooth it is To have a thankless child!
William Shakespeare 1564–1616: *King Lear* (1605–6)

4 I once knew a man out of courtesy help a lame dog over a stile, and he for requital bit his fingers.
William Chillingworth 1602–44: *The Religion of Protestants* (1637)

5 A grateful mind By owing owes not, but still pays, at once Indebted and discharged.
John Milton 1608–74: *Paradise Lost* (1667)

6 In most of mankind gratitude is merely a secret hope for greater favors.
Duc de la Rochefoucauld 1613–80: *Maximes* (1678)

7 There are minds so impatient of inferiority, that their gratitude is a species of revenge, and they return benefits, not because recompense is a pleasure, but because obligation is a pain.
Samuel Johnson 1709–84: in *The Rambler* (UK) 15 January 1751

8 My life has crept so long on a broken wing Through cells of madness, haunts of horror and fear, That I come to be grateful at last for a little thing.
Alfred, Lord Tennyson 1809–92: *Maud* (1855)

9 There's plenty of boys that will come hankering and grovelling around you when you've got an apple, and beg the core off of you; but when they've got one, and you beg for the core and remind them how you give them a core one time, they say thank you 'most to death, but there ain't-a-going to be no core.
Mark Twain 1835–1910: *Tom Sawyer Abroad* (1894)

10 That's the way with these directors, they're always biting the hand that lays the golden egg.

Sam Goldwyn 1882–1974: Alva Johnston *The Great Goldwyn* (1937)

11 Never in the field of human conflict was so much owed by so many to so few.
on the skill and courage of British airmen
Winston Churchill 1874–1965: speech, House of Commons, 20 August 1940

Greatness

1 The beauty of Israel is slain upon thy high places: how are the mighty fallen!
Bible: II Samuel

2 Why, man, he doth bestride the narrow world
Like a Colossus; and we petty men
Walk under his huge legs, and peep about
To find ourselves dishonourable graves.
William Shakespeare 1564–1616: *Julius Caesar* (1599)

3 But be not afraid of greatness: some men are born great, some achieve greatness, and some have greatness thrust upon them.
William Shakespeare 1564–1616: *Twelfth Night* (1601)

4 What millions died—that Caesar might be great!
Thomas Campbell 1777–1844: *Pleasures of Hope* (1799)

5 Fleas know not whether they are upon the body of a giant or upon one of ordinary size.
Walter Savage Landor 1775–1864: *Imaginary Conversations* (1824)

6 Is it so bad, then, to be misunderstood? Pythagoras was misunderstood, and Socrates, and Jesus, and Luther, and Copernicus, and Galileo, and Newton, and every pure and wise spirit that ever took flesh. To be great is to be misunderstood.
Ralph Waldo Emerson 1803–82: *Essays* (1841) "Self-Reliance"

7 In me there dwells
No greatness, save it be some far-off touch
Of greatness to know well I am not great.
Alfred, Lord Tennyson 1809–92: *Idylls of the King* "Lancelot and Elaine" (1859)

8 Great men, great nations, have not been boasters and buffoons, but perceivers of the terror of life, and have manned themselves to face it.
Ralph Waldo Emerson 1803–82: *The Conduct of Life, Fate* (1860)

9 In historical events great men—so-called—are but labels serving to give a name to the event, and like labels they have the least possible connection with the event itself.
Leo Tolstoy 1828–1910: *War and Peace* (1868–9)

10 A man is seldom ashamed of feeling that he cannot love a woman so well when he sees a certain greatness in her: nature having intended greatness for men.
George Eliot 1819–80: *Middlemarch* (1871–2)

11 Everything we think of as great has come to us from neurotics. It is they and they alone who found religions and create great works of art. The world will never realize how much it owes to them and what they have suffered in order to bestow their gifts on it.
Marcel Proust 1871–1922: *Guermantes Way* (1921)

12 If I am a great man, then all great men are frauds.
Andrew Bonar Law 1858–1923: Lord

Beaverbrook *Politicians and the War* (1932)

Greed
see also **Money**

1 Greedy for the property of others, extravagant with his own.
Sallust 86–35 BC: *Catiline*

2 *Quid non mortalia pectora cogis, Auri sacra fames!*
To what do you not drive human hearts, cursed craving for gold!
Virgil 70–19 BC: *Aeneid*

3 Whose God is their belly, and whose glory is in their shame.
Bible: Philippians

4 Bell, book, and candle shall not drive me back,
When gold and silver becks me to come on.
William Shakespeare 1564–1616: *King John* (1591–8)

5 What a rare punishment Is avarice to itself!
Ben Jonson c. 1573–1637: *Volpone* (1606)

6 What, if a dear year come or dearth, or some loss? And were it not that they are loath to lay out money on a rope, they would be hanged forthwith, and sometimes die to save charges.
Robert Burton 1577–1640: *The Anatomy of Melancholy* (1621–51)

7 £40,000 a year a moderate income—such a one as a man *might jog on with*.
John George Lambton, Lord Durham 1792–1840: letter from Mr. Creevey to Miss Elizabeth Ord, 13 September 1821

8 Please, sir, I want some more.
Charles Dickens 1812–70: *Oliver Twist* (1838)

9 You shall not crucify mankind upon a cross of gold.
William Jennings Bryan 1860–1925: speech at the Democratic National Convention, Chicago, 1896

10 I'll be sick tonight.
in reply to his mother's warning "You'll be sick tomorrow," when stuffing himself with cakes at tea
Jack Llewelyn-Davies 1894–1959: Andrew Birkin *J. M. Barrie and the Lost Boys* (1979); Barrie used the line in *Little Mary* (1903)

11 If all the rich people in the world divided up their money among themselves there wouldn't be enough to go round.
Christina Stead 1902–83: *House of All Nations* (1938)

12 There is enough in the world for everyone's need, but not enough for everyone's greed.
Frank Buchman 1878–1961: *Remaking the World* (1947)

13 Greed is healthy.
Ivan Boesky 1937– : speech, *University of California Business School in Berkeley* (1986)

14 Greed—for lack of a better word—is good. Greed is right. Greed works.
Stanley Weiser and **Oliver Stone** 1946– : *Wall Street* (1987 film)

Guilt and Innocence

1 Out of the mouth of very babes and sucklings hast thou ordained strength, because of thine enemies.
Bible: Psalm 8

2 He took water, and washed his hands before the multitude, saying, I am innocent of the blood of this just person: see ye to it.
Bible: St. Matthew

3 He that is without sin among
you, let him first cast a stone at
her.
Bible: St. John

4 Suspicion always haunts the
guilty mind;
The thief doth fear each bush an
officer.
William Shakespeare 1564–1616:
Henry VI, Part 3 (1592)

5 Here's the smell of the blood still:
all the perfumes of Arabia will
not sweeten this little hand.
William Shakespeare 1564–1616:
Macbeth (1606)

6 He that first cries out stop thief, is
often he that has stolen the
treasure.
William Congreve 1670–1729: *Love
for Love* (1695)

7 How happy is the blameless
Vestal's lot!
The world forgetting, by the
world forgot.
Alexander Pope 1688–1744: "Eloisa
to Abelard" (1717)

8 It is better that ten guilty persons
escape than one innocent suffer.
William Blackstone 1723–80:
*Commentaries on the Laws of
England* (1765)

9 What hangs people . . . is the
unfortunate circumstance of guilt.
Robert Louis Stevenson 1850–94:
The Wrong Box (with Lloyd
Osbourne, 1889)

10 Of all means to regeneration
Remorse is surely the most
wasteful. It cuts away healthy
tissue with the poisoned. It is a
knife that probes far deeper than
the evil.
E. M. Forster 1879–1970: *Howards
End* (1910)

11 It's better to choose the culprits
than to seek them out.
Marcel Pagnol 1895–1974: *Topaze*
(1930)

12 It is not only our fate but our
business to lose innocence, and
once we have lost that, it is futile
to attempt a picnic in Eden.
Elizabeth Bowen 1899–1973: "Out of
a Book" in *Orion III* (1946)

13 Innocence always calls mutely for
protection, when we would be so
much wiser to guard ourselves
against it: innocence is like a
dumb leper who has lost his bell,
wandering the world meaning no
harm.
Graham Greene 1904–91: *The Quiet
American* (1955)

14 True guilt is guilt at the
obligation one owes to oneself to
be oneself. False guilt is guilt felt
at not being what other people
feel one ought to be or assume
that one is.
R. D. Laing 1927–89: *Self and Others*
(1961)

15 I'd the upbringing a nun would
envy . . . Until I was fifteen I was
more familiar with Africa than
my own body.
Joe Orton 1933–67: *Entertaining Mr.
Sloane* (1964)

16 In former days, everyone found
the assumption of innocence so
easy; today we find fatally easy
the assumption of guilt.
Amanda Cross 1926–　: *Poetic
Justice* (1970)

17 I brought myself down. I gave
them a sword. And they stuck it
in.
Richard Nixon 1913–94: television
interview, 19 May 1977

18 Good women always think it is
their fault when someone else is

being offensive. Bad women never
take the blame for anything.
Anita Brookner 1938– : *Hotel du
Lac* (1984)

Habit
see **Custom and Habit**

Happiness

1 *Nil admirari prope res est una,
Numici,
Solaque quae possit facere et servare
beatum.*
To marvel at nothing is just
about the one and only thing,
Numicius, that can make a man
happy and keep him that way.
Horace 65–8 BC: *Epistles*; cf. **7** below

2 Certainly there is no happiness
within this circle of flesh, nor is it
in the optics of these eyes to
behold felicity; the first day of our
Jubilee is death.
Thomas Browne 1605–82: *Religio
Medici* (1643)

3 But headlong joy is ever on the
wing.
John Milton 1608–74: "The Passion"
(1645)

4 One is never as unhappy as one
thinks, nor as happy as one
hopes.
Duc de la Rochefoucauld 1613–80:
Sentences et Maximes de Morale
(1664)

5 For all the happiness mankind
can gain
Is not in pleasure, but in rest
from pain.
John Dryden 1631–1700: *The Indian
Emperor* (1665)

6 Mirth is like a flash of lightning
that breaks through a gloom of
clouds, and glitters for a moment:
cheerfulness keeps up a kind of
day-light in the mind, and fills it

with a steady and perpetual
serenity.
Joseph Addison 1672–1719: in *The
Spectator* 17 May 1712

7 Not to admire, is all the art I
know,
To make men happy, and to keep
them so.
Alexander Pope 1688–1744:
Imitations of Horace; see **1** above

8 It cannot reasonably be doubted,
but a little miss, dressed in a new
gown for a dancing-school ball,
receives as complete enjoyment as
the greatest orator, who triumphs
in the splendour of his eloquence,
while he governs the passions
and resolutions of a numerous
assembly.
David Hume 1711–76: *Essays: Moral
and Political* (1741–2) "The Sceptic"

9 That all who are happy, are
equally happy, is not true. A
peasant and a philosopher may
be equally *satisfied*, but not
equally *happy*. Happiness consists
in the multiplicity of agreeable
consciousness.
Samuel Johnson 1709–84: James
Boswell *Life of Samuel Johnson*
(1791) February 1766

10 If you will allow me, at my age, a
reflection that is scarcely ever
made at yours, I must say that if
one only knew where one's true
happiness lay one would never
look for it outside the limits
prescribed by the law and by
religion.
Pierre Choderlos de Laclos 1741–
1803: *Les Liaisons dangereuses*
(1782)

11 *Freude, schöner Götterfunken,
Tochter aus Elysium.*
Joy, beautiful radiance of the
gods, daughter of Elysium.
Friedrich von Schiller 1759–1805: "An
die Freude" (1785)

12 Happiness is not an ideal of reason but of imagination.
Immanuel Kant 1724–1804: *Fundamental Principles of the Metaphysics of Ethics* (1785)

13 A large income is the best recipe for happiness I ever heard of. It certainly may secure all the myrtle and turkey part of it.
Jane Austen 1775–1817: *Mansfield Park* (1814)

14 So have I loitered my life away, reading books, looking at pictures, going to plays, hearing, thinking, writing on what pleased me best. I have wanted only one thing to make me happy, but wanting that have wanted everything.
William Hazlitt 1778–1830: *Literary Remains* (1836) "My First Acquaintance with Poets"

15 Happiness is no laughing matter.
Richard Whately 1787–1863: *Apophthegms* (1854)

16 Cheerfulness gives elasticity to the spirit. Spectres fly before it.
Samuel Smiles 1812–1904: *Self-Help* (1859)

17 Ask yourself whether you are happy, and you cease to be so.
John Stuart Mill 1806–73: *Autobiography* (1873)

18 But a lifetime of happiness! No man alive could bear it: it would be hell on earth.
George Bernard Shaw 1856–1950: *Man and Superman* (1903)

19 For if unhappiness develops the forces of the mind, happiness alone is salutary to the body.
Marcel Proust 1871–1922: *Time Regained* (1926)

20 Happiness makes up in height for what it lacks in length.
Robert Frost 1874–1963: title of poem (1942)

21 Happiness is a warm gun.
John Lennon 1940–80: title of song (1968)

22 Happiness is a state of which you are unconscious, of which you are not aware. The moment you are aware that you are happy, you cease to be happy . . . You want to be consciously happy; the moment you are consciously happy, happiness is gone.
Jiddu Krishnamurti 1895–1986: *Penguin Krishnamurti Reader* (1970) "Questions and Answers"

23 Happiness is an imaginary condition, formerly often attributed by the living to the dead, now usually attributed by adults to children, and by children to adults.
Thomas Szasz 1920– : *The Second Sin* (1973)

24 I always say I don't think everyone has the right to happiness or to be loved. Even the Americans have written into their constitution that you have the right to the "pursuit of happiness." You have the right to try but that is all.
Claire Rayner 1931– : G. Kinnock and F. Miller (eds.) *By Faith and Daring* (1993); cf. **Human Rights 3**

Haste and Delay

1 Why tarry the wheels of his chariots?
Bible: Judges

2 He always hurries to the main event and whisks his audience into the middle of things as though they knew already.
Horace 65–8 BC: *Ars Poetica*

3 *Festina lente.*
Make haste slowly.
Augustus 63 BC–AD 14: Suetonius *Lives of the Caesars* "Divus Augustus"

4 I'll put a girdle round about the
earth
In forty minutes.
William Shakespeare 1564–1616: *A
Midsummer Night's Dream* (1595–6)

5 I knew a wise man that had it for
a by-word, when he saw men
hasten to a conclusion, "Stay a
little, that we may make an end
the sooner."
Francis Bacon 1561–1626: *Essays*
(1625) "Of Dispatch"

6 I have protracted my work till
most of those whom I wished to
please have sunk into the grave;
and success and miscarriage are
empty sounds.
Samuel Johnson 1709–84: James
Boswell *Life of Samuel Johnson*
(1791) 1755

7 Though I am always in haste, I
am never in a hurry.
John Wesley 1703–91: letter to Miss
March, 10 December 1777

8 I wish sir, you would practise this
without me. I can't stay dying
here all night.
Richard Brinsley Sheridan 1751–1816:
The Critic (1779)

9 Delay is preferable to error.
Thomas Jefferson 1743–1826: *Letter
to George Washington* (16 May 1792)

10 No admittance till the week after
next!
Lewis Carroll 1832–98: *Through the
Looking-Glass* (1872)

11 He gave her a bright fake smile;
so much of life was a putting-off
of unhappiness for another time.
Nothing was ever lost by delay.
Graham Greene 1904–91: *The Heart
of the Matter* (1948)

12 ESTRAGON: Charming spot.
Inspiring prospects. Let's go.
VLADIMIR: We can't.
ESTRAGON: Why not?

VLADIMIR: We're waiting for
Godot.
Samuel Beckett 1906–89: *Waiting for
Godot* (1955)

13 If anyone believes that our smiles
involve abandonment of the
teaching of Marx, Engels and
Lenin he deceives himself. Those
who wait for that must wait until
a shrimp learns to whistle.
Nikita Khrushchev 1894–1971:
speech in Moscow, 17 September
1955

14 I think we ought to let him hang
there. Let him twist slowly, slowly
in the wind.
*of Patrick Gray, regarding his
nomination as director of the FBI, in
a telephone conversation with John
Dean*
John Ehrlichman 1925– : in
Washington Post 27 July 1973

Hatred
see also **Enemies**

1 Better is a dinner of herbs where
love is, than a stalled ox and
hatred therewith.
Bible: Proverbs

2 I have loved him too much not to
feel any hatred for him.
Jean Racine 1639–99: *Andromaque*
(1667)

3 Dear Bathurst (said he to me one
day) was a man to my very
heart's content: he hated a fool,
and he hated a rogue, and he
hated a whig; he was a very good
hater.
Samuel Johnson 1709–84: Hester
Lynch Piozzi *Anecdotes of . . .
Johnson* (1786)

4 Now hatred is by far the longest
pleasure;
Men love in haste, but they detest
at leisure.

Lord Byron 1788–1824: *Don Juan* (1819–24)

5 The dupe of friendship, and the fool of love; have I not reason to hate and to despise myself? Indeed I do; and chiefly for not having hated and despised the world enough.
William Hazlitt 1778–1830: *The Plain Speaker* (1826) "On the Pleasure of Hating"

6 Gr-r-r—there go, my heart's abhorrence!
Water your damned flower-pots, do!
If hate killed men, Brother Lawrence,
God's blood, would not mine kill you!
Robert Browning 1812–89: "Soliloquy of the Spanish Cloister" (1842)

7 Dante, who loved well because he hated,
Hated wickedness that hinders loving.
Robert Browning 1812–89: "One Word More" (1855)

8 If you hate a person, you hate something in him that is part of yourself. What isn't part of ourselves doesn't disturb us.
Hermann Hesse 1877–1962: *Demian* (1919)

9 One cannot overestimate the power of a good rancorous hatred on the part of the *stupid*. The stupid have so much more industry and energy to expend on hating. They build it up like coral insects.
Sylvia Townsend Warner 1893–1978: diary 26 September 1954

10 I never hated a man enough to give him diamonds back.
Zsa Zsa Gabor 1919– : in *Observer* (UK) 25 August 1957

11 Always give your best, never get discouraged, never be petty; always remember, others may hate you. Those who hate you don't win unless you hate them. And then you destroy yourself.
address to members of his staff on leaving office after his resignation
Richard Nixon 1913–94: on 9 August 1974

12 No one is born hating another person because of the color of his skin, or his background, or his religion. People must learn to hate, and if they can learn to hate, they can be taught to love, for love comes more naturally to the human heart than its opposite.
Nelson Mandela 1918– : *Long Walk to Freedom* (1994)

Health
see **Sickness and Health**

Heaven and Hell

1 But the children of the kingdom shall be cast out into outer darkness: there shall be weeping and gnashing of teeth.
Bible: St. Matthew

2 And I saw a new heaven and a new earth: for the first heaven and the first earth were passed away; and there was no more sea.
Bible: Revelation

3 *PER ME SI VA NELLA CITTÀ DOLENTE.*
PER ME SI VA NELL' ETERNO DOLORE.
PER ME SI VA TRA LA PERDUTA GENTE . . .
LASCIATE OGNI SPERANZA VOI CH'ENTRATE!
Through me is the way to the sorrowful city. Through me is the way to eternal suffering. Through me is the way to join the lost people . . . Abandon all hope, you who enter!
inscription at the entrance to Hell;

the final sentence now often quoted
as "Abandon hope, all ye who enter
here"
Dante Alighieri 1265–1321: *Divina
Commedia* "Inferno"

4 Why, this is hell, nor am I out of
it:
Thinkst thou that I who saw the
face of God,
And tasted the eternal joys of
heaven,
Am not tormented with ten
thousand hells
In being deprived of everlasting
bliss!
Christopher Marlowe 1564–93:
Doctor Faustus (1604)

5 This place is too cold for hell. I'll
devil-porter it no further: I had
thought to have let in some of all
professions, that go the primrose
way to the everlasting bonfire.
William Shakespeare 1564–1616:
Macbeth (1606)

6 And hell itself will pass away,
And leave her dolorous mansions
to the peering day.
John Milton 1608–74: "On the
Morning of Christ's Nativity" (1645)
"The Hymn"

7 So all we know
Of what they do above,
Is that they happy are, and that
they love.
Edmund Waller 1606–87: "Upon the
Death of My Lady Rich" (1645)

8 Were the happiness of the next
world as closely apprehended as
the felicities of this, it were a
martyrdom to live.
Thomas Browne 1605–82:
Hydriotaphia (Urn Burial, 1658)

9 Me miserable! which way shall I
fly
Infinite wrath, and infinite
despair?
Which way I fly is hell; myself
am hell.

John Milton 1608–74: *Paradise Lost*
(1667)

10 Then I saw that there was a way
to Hell, even from the gates of
heaven.
John Bunyan 1628–88: *The Pilgrim's
Progress* (1678)

11 To different minds, the same
world is a hell, and a heaven.
Ralph Waldo Emerson 1803–82:
Journal (20 December 1822)

12 My idea of heaven is, eating *pâté
de foie gras* to the sound of
trumpets.
*the view of Smith's friend Henry
Luttrell*
Sydney Smith 1771–1845: H. Pearson
The Smith of Smiths (1934)

13 I will spend my heaven doing
good on earth.
St. Teresa of Lisieux 1873–97: T. N.
Taylor (ed.) *Soeur Thérèse of Lisieux*
(1912)

14 There is no expeditious road
To pack and label men for God,
And save them by the barrel-load.
Some may perchance, with
strange surprise,
Have blundered into Paradise.
Francis Thompson 1859–1907: "A
Judgement in Heaven" (1913)

15 He has the look of a man who
has been in hell and seen there,
not a hopeless suffering, but
meanness and frippery.
on Dostoevsky
W. Somerset Maugham 1874–1965:
A Writer's Notebook (1949) written
in 1917

16 The true paradises are the
paradises that we have lost.
Marcel Proust 1871–1922: *Time
Regained* (1926)

17 Hell, madam, is to love no more.
Georges Bernanos 1888–1948:

Journal d'un curé de campagne
(1936)

18 Hell is other people.
Jean-Paul Sartre 1905–80: *Huis Clos*
(1944)

19 What is hell?
Hell is oneself,
Hell is alone, the other figures in
it
Merely projections.
T. S. Eliot 1888–1965: *The Cocktail
Party* (1950)

Heroes

1 No man is a hero to his valet.
Mme. Cornuel 1605–94: *Lettres de
Mlle. Aïssé à Madame C* (1787) Letter
13 "De Paris, 1728"; cf. **5** below

2 See, the conquering hero comes!
Sound the trumpets, beat the
drums!
Thomas Morell 1703–84: *Judas
Maccabeus* (1747)

3 In this world I would rather live
two days like a tiger, than two
hundred years like a sheep.
Tipu Sultan c. 1750–99: Alexander
Beatson *A View of the Origin and
Conduct of the War with Tippoo
Sultaun* (1800)

4 So faithful in love, and so
dauntless in war,
There never was knight like the
young Lochinvar.
Sir Walter Scott 1771–1832: *Marmion*
(1808) "Lochinvar"

5 In short, he was a perfect
cavaliero,
And to his very valet seemed a
hero.
Lord Byron 1788–1824: *Beppo* (1818);
cf. **1** above

6 Heroism feels and never reasons
and therefore is always right.
Ralph Waldo Emerson 1803–82:
Essays: First Series, Heroism (1841)

7 Every hero becomes a bore at
last.
Ralph Waldo Emerson 1803–82:
Representative Men (1850)

8 Men reject their prophets and slay
them, but they love their martyrs
and honor those whom they have
slain.
Fyodor Dostoevsky 1821–81: *The
Brothers Karamazov* (1879–80)

9 Heroing is one of the shortest-
lived professions there is.
Will Rogers 1879–1935: newspaper
article, 15 February 1925

10 A fiery horse with the speed of
light, a cloud of dust, and a
hearty, "Hi-yo, Silver!"
Fran Stryker : *The Lone Ranger radio
show* (11 March 1933)

11 Go to Spain and get killed. The
movement needs a Byron.
*on being asked by Stephen Spender
in the 1930s how best a poet could
serve the Communist cause*
Harry Pollitt 1890–1960: Frank
Johnson *Out of Order* (1982);
attributed, perhaps apocryphal

12 ANDREA: Unhappy the land that
has no heroes! . . .
GALILEO: No. Unhappy the land
that needs heroes.
Bertolt Brecht 1898–1956: *The Life of
Galileo* (1939)

13 Faster than a speeding bullet!
More powerful than a locomotive!
Able to leap tall buildings in a
single bound! Look! Up in the sky!
It's a bird! It's a plane! It's
Superman!
George Lother: *Superman* radio
show, first broadcast (12 February
1940)

14 Show me a hero and I will write
you a tragedy.
F. Scott Fitzgerald 1896–1940:

Edmund Wilson (ed.) *The Crack-Up* (1945) "Note-Books E"

15 You don't raise heroes, you raise sons. And if you treat them like sons they'll turn out to be heroes even if it's just in your own eyes.
Walter M. Schirra, Sr. 1894?–1973: *New York Herald Tribune* (3 February 1963)

16 It was involuntary. They sank my boat.
on being asked how he became a war hero
John F. Kennedy 1917–63: Arthur M. Schlesinger, Jr. *A Thousand Days* (1965)

17 Ultimately a hero is a man who would argue with the Gods, and so awakens devils to contest his vision.
Norman Mailer 1923– : *The Presidential Papers* (1976)

History

1 History is philosophy from examples.
Dionysius of Halicarnassus fl. 30–7 BC: *Ars Rhetorica*

2 Whosoever, in writing a modern history, shall follow truth too near the heels, it may happily strike out his teeth.
Walter Ralegh *c.* 1552–1618: *The History of the World* (1614)

3 Happy the people whose annals are blank in history-books!
Montesquieu 1689–1755: attributed to Montesquieu by Thomas Carlyle *History of Frederick the Great*

4 History . . . is, indeed, little more than the register of the crimes, follies, and misfortunes of mankind.
Edward Gibbon 1737–94: *The Decline and Fall of the Roman Empire* (1776–88)

5 What experience and history teach is this—that nations and governments have never learned anything from history, or acted upon any lessons they might have drawn from it.
G. W. F. Hegel 1770–1831: *Lectures on the Philosophy of World History: Introduction* (1830); cf. **8** below

6 History [is] a distillation of rumour.
Thomas Carlyle 1795–1881: *History of the French Revolution* (1837)

7 History is the essence of innumerable biographies.
Thomas Carlyle 1795–1881: *Critical and Miscellaneous Essays* (1838) "On History"

8 Hegel says somewhere that all great events and personalities in world history reappear in one fashion or another. He forgot to add: the first time as tragedy, the second time as farce.
Karl Marx 1818–83: *The Eighteenth Brumaire of Louis Bonaparte* (1852); see **5** above, **18** below

9 History is a gallery of pictures in which there are few originals and many copies.
Alexis de Tocqueville 1805–59: *L'Ancien régime* (1856)

10 That great dust-heap called "history."
Augustine Birrell 1850–1933: *Obiter Dicta* (1884); cf. **Success 27**

11 History is past politics, and politics is present history.
E. A. Freeman 1823–92: *Methods of Historical Study* (1886)

12 It has been said that though God cannot alter the past, historians can; it is perhaps because they can be useful to Him in this respect that He tolerates their existence.

Samuel Butler 1835–1902: *Erewhon Revisited* (1901); see **The Past** 1

13 History is more or less bunk.
Henry Ford 1863–1947: interview with Charles N. Wheeler in *Chicago Tribune* 25 May 1916

14 Human history becomes more and more a race between education and catastrophe.
H. G. Wells 1866–1946: *The Outline of History* (1920)

15 History is not what you thought. *It is what you can remember.*
W. C. Sellar 1898–1951 and **R. J. Yeatman** 1898–1968: *1066 and All That* (1930)

16 History gets thicker as it approaches recent times.
A. J. P. Taylor 1906–90: *English History 1914–45* (1965) bibliography

17 History, like wood, has a grain in it which determines how it splits; and those in authority, besides trying to shape and direct events, sometimes find it more convenient just to let them happen.
Malcolm Muggeridge 1903–90: *The Infernal Grove* (1975)

18 Does history repeat itself, the first time as tragedy, the second time as farce? No, that's too grand, too considered a process. History just burps, and we taste again that raw-onion sandwich it swallowed centuries ago.
Julian Barnes 1946–   : *A History of the World in 10½ Chapters* (1989); see **8** above

The Home and Housework

1 The foxes have holes, and the birds of the air have nests; but the Son of man hath not where to lay his head.
Bible: St. Matthew

2 There is scarcely any less bother in the running of a family than in that of an entire state. And domestic business is no less importunate for being less important.
Montaigne 1533–92: *Essais* (1580)

3 The accent of one's birthplace lingers in the mind and in the heart as it does in one's speech.
Duc de la Rochefoucauld 1613–80: *Maximes* (1678)

4 Show me a man who cares no more for one place than another, and I will show you in that same person one who loves nothing but himself. Beware of those who are homeless by choice.
Robert Southey 1774–1843: *The Doctor* (1812)

5 Mid pleasures and palaces though we may roam,
Be it ever so humble, there's no place like home.
J. H. Payne 1791–1852: *Clari, or, The Maid of Milan* (1823 opera) "Home, Sweet Home"

6 Here lies a poor woman who always was tired,
For she lived in a place where help wasn't hired.
Her last words on earth were, Dear friends I am going
Where washing ain't done nor sweeping nor sewing,
And everything there is exact to my wishes,
For there they don't eat and there's no washing of dishes . . .
Don't mourn for me now, don't mourn for me never,
For I'm going to do nothing for ever and ever.
Anonymous: epitaph in Bushey churchyard, before 1860; destroyed by 1916

7 It is a most miserable thing to feel ashamed of home.
Charles Dickens 1812–70: *Great Expectations* (1861)

8 The ornament of a house is the friends who frequent it.
Ralph Waldo Emerson 1803–82: *Society and Solitude* (1870)

9 What's the good of a home if you are never in it?
George and Weedon Grossmith 1847–1912: *The Diary of a Nobody* (1894)

10 Any old place I can hang my hat is home sweet home to me.
William Jerome 1865–1932: title of song (1901)

11 Home is the girl's prison and the woman's workhouse.
George Bernard Shaw 1856–1950: *Man and Superman* (1903) "Maxims: Women in the Home"

12 Addresses are given to us to conceal our whereabouts.
Saki 1870–1916: *Reginald in Russia* (1910)

13 Hatred of domestic work is a natural and admirable result of civilization.
Rebecca West 1892–1983: in *The Freewoman* (UK) 6 June 1912

14 "Home is the place where, when you have to go there,
They have to take you in."
"I should have called it
Something you somehow haven't to deserve."
Robert Frost 1874–1963: "The Death of the Hired Man" (1914)

15 Many a man who thinks to found a home discovers that he has merely opened a tavern for his friends.
Norman Douglas 1868–1952: *South Wind* (1917)

16 The dust comes secretly day after day,
Lies on my ledge and dulls my shining things.
But O this dust that I shall drive away
Is flowers and Kings,
Is Solomon's temple, poets, Nineveh.
Viola Meynell 1886–1956: "Dusting" (1919)

17 The best
Thing we can do is to make wherever we're lost in
Look as much like home as we can.
Christopher Fry 1907– : *The Lady's not for Burning* (1949)

18 MR. PRITCHARD: I must dust the blinds and then I must raise them.
MRS. OGMORE-PRITCHARD: And before you let the sun in, mind it wipes its shoes.
Dylan Thomas 1914–53: *Under Milk Wood* (1954)

19 By and large, mothers and housewives are the only workers who do not have regular time off. They are the great vacationless class.
Anne Morrow Lindbergh 1906– : *Gift from the Sea* (1955)

20 I think housework is the reason most women go to the office.
Heloise Cruse 1919–77: *Editor & Publisher* (27 April 1963)

21 There was no need to do any housework at all. After the first four years the dirt doesn't get any worse.
Quentin Crisp 1908– : *The Naked Civil Servant* (1968)

22 Conran's Law of Housework—it expands to fill the time available plus half an hour.
Shirley Conran 1932– : *Superwoman 2* (1977)

23 Home is where you come to when you have nothing better to do.
Margaret Thatcher 1925– : in *Vanity Fair* May 1991

Honesty
see also **Deception, Lies and Lying, Truth**

1 Honesty is praised and left to shiver.
Juvenal AD *c.* 60–*c.* 130: *Satires*

2 And those who paint 'em truest praise 'em most.
Joseph Addison 1672–1719: *The Campaign* (1705)

3 "But the Emperor has nothing on at all!" cried a little child.
Hans Christian Andersen 1805–75: *Danish Fairy Legends and Tales* (1846) "The Emperor's New Clothes"

4 Honesty is the best policy; but he who is governed by that maxim is not an honest man.
Richard Whately 1787–1863: *Apophthegms* (1854)

5 The louder he talked of his honor, the faster we counted our spoons.
Ralph Waldo Emerson 1803–82: *The Conduct of Life* (1860)

6 A little sincerity is a dangerous thing, and a great deal of it is absolutely fatal.
Oscar Wilde 1854–1900: *Intentions* (1891)

7 It is always the best policy to speak the truth—unless, of course, you are an exceptionally good liar.
Jerome K. Jerome 1859–1927: in *The Idler* (UK) February 1892

8 Golf . . . is the infallible test. The man who can go into a patch of rough alone, with the knowledge that only God is watching him,

and play his ball where it lies, is the man who will serve you faithfully and well.
P. G. Wodehouse 1881–1975: *The Clicking of Cuthbert* (1922)

9 Always be sincere, even if you don't mean it.
Harry S. Truman 1884–1972: attributed

Hope
see also **Despair, Optimism and Pessimism**

1 Hope deferred maketh the heart sick: but when the desire cometh, it is a tree of life.
Bible: Proverbs

2 I will lift up mine eyes unto the hills: from whence cometh my help.
Bible: Psalm 121

3 *Nil desperandum.*
Never despair.
Horace 65–8 BC: *Odes*

4 Who would have thought my shrivelled heart
Could have recovered greenness?
George Herbert 1593–1633: "The Flower" (1633)

5 I can endure my own despair, But not another's hope.
William Walsh 1663–1708: "Song: Of All the Torments"

6 Hope springs eternal in the human breast:
Man never Is, but always To be blest.
Alexander Pope 1688–1744: *An Essay on Man* Epistle 1 (1733)

7 He that lives upon hope will die fasting.
Benjamin Franklin 1706–90: *Poor Richard's Almanack* (1758)

8 What is hope? nothing but the paint on the face of Existence; the

least touch of truth rubs it off,
and then we see what a hollow-
cheeked harlot we have got hold
of.
Lord Byron 1788–1824: letter to
Thomas Moore, 28 October 1815

9 O, Wind,
If Winter comes, can Spring be
far behind?
Percy Bysshe Shelley 1792–1822:
"Ode to the West Wind" (1819)

10 Providence has given human
wisdom the choice between two
fates: either hope and agitation,
or hopelessness and calm.
Yevgeny Baratynsky 1800–44: "Two
Fates" (1823)

11 Work without hope draws nectar
in a sieve,
And hope without an object
cannot live.
Samuel Taylor Coleridge 1772–1834:
"Work without Hope" (1828)

12 Hopeless hope hopes on and
meets no end,
Wastes without springs and
homes without a friend.
John Clare 1793–1864: "Child
Harold" (written 1841)

13 If hopes were dupes, fears may be
liars.
Arthur Hugh Clough 1819–61: "Say
not the struggle naught availeth"
(1855)

14 He who has never hoped can
never despair.
George Bernard Shaw 1856–1950:
Caesar and Cleopatra (1901)

15 After all, tomorrow is another
day.
Margaret Mitchell 1900–49: *Gone
with the Wind* (1936)

16 Hope raises no dust.
Paul Éluard 1895–1952: "Ailleurs, ici,
partout" (1946)

17 It is the around-the-corner brand
of hope that prompts people to
action, while the distant hope
acts as an opiate.
Eric Hoffer 1902– : *The Ordeal of
Change* (1964)

18 I think it's a fresh, clean page. I
think I go onwards and upwards.
*the day before her divorce was
made absolute*
Sarah, Duchess of York 1959– :
interview on *Sky News* (UK) 29 May
1996

Hospitality
see **Entertaining and Hospitality**

Housework
see **The Home and Housework**

Human Nature
see also **Behavior, Character**

1 A man is a wolf rather than a
man to another man, when he
hasn't yet found out what he's
like.
*often quoted as "A man is a wolf to
another man"*
Plautus c. 250–184 BC: *Asinaria*

2 It is part of human nature to hate
the man you have hurt.
Tacitus AD c. 56–after 117: *Agricola*

3 One touch of nature makes the
whole world kin,
That all with one consent praise
new-born gawds,
Though they are made and
moulded of things past,
And give to dust that is a little
gilt
More laud than gilt o'er-dusted.
William Shakespeare 1564–1616:
Troilus and Cressida (1602)

4 God and the doctor we alike
     adore
   But only when in danger, not
     before;
   The danger o'er, both are alike
     requited,
   God is forgotten, and the Doctor
     slighted.
   John Owen c. 1563–1622: *Epigrams*;
   cf. **Danger** 4

5 O merciful God, grant that the old
   Adam in this Child may be so
   buried, that the new man may be
   raised up in him.
   The Book of Common Prayer 1662:
   Public Baptism of Infants

6 On ev'ry hand it will allow'd be,
   He's just—nae better than he
     shou'd be.
   Robert Burns 1759–96: "A
   Dedication to G[avin] H[amilton]"
   (1786)

7 Subdue your appetites my dears,
   and you've conquered human
   natur.
   Charles Dickens 1812–70: *Nicholas
   Nickleby* (1839)

8 But good God, people don't do
   such things!
   Henrik Ibsen 1828–1906: *Hedda
   Gabler* (1890)

9 Adam was but human—this
   explains it all. He did not want
   the apple for the apple's sake; he
   wanted it only because it was
   forbidden.
   Mark Twain 1835–1910: *Pudd'nhead
   Wilson* (1894)

10 The natural man has only two
    primal passions, to get and beget.
    William Osler 1849–1919: *Science
    and Immortality* (1904)

11 The terrorist and the policeman
    both come from the same basket. .
    Joseph Conrad 1857–1924: *The
    Secret Agent* (1907)

12 That is ever the way. 'Tis all
    jealousy to the bride and good
    wishes to the corpse.
    J. M. Barrie 1860–1937: *Quality
    Street* (1913)

13 There's a man all over for you,
    blaming on his boots the faults of
    his feet.
    Samuel Beckett 1906–89: *Waiting for
    Godot* (1955)

The Human Race

1 And God said, Let us make man
   in our image, after our likeness:
   and let them have dominion over
   the fish of the sea, and over the
   fowl of the air, and over the
   cattle, and over all the earth and
   over every creeping thing that
   creepeth upon the earth.
   Bible: Genesis

2 Man is the measure of all things.
   Protagoras b. c. 485 BC: Plato
   Theaetetus

3 There are many wonderful things,
   and nothing is more wonderful
   than man.
   Sophocles c. 496–406 BC: *Antigone*

4 I am a man, I count nothing
   human foreign to me.
   Terence c. 190–159 BC: *Heauton
   Timorumenos*

5 What a piece of work is a man!
   How noble in reason! how infinite
   in faculty! in form, in moving,
   how express and admirable! in
   action how like an angel! in
   apprehension how like a god! the
   beauty of the world! the paragon
   of animals! And yet, to me, what
   is this quintessence of dust?
   William Shakespeare 1564–1616:
   Hamlet (1601)

6 Thou art the thing itself;
unaccommodated man is no more
but such a poor, bare, forked
animal as thou art.
William Shakespeare 1564–1616:
King Lear (1605–6)

7 Man is a torch borne in the wind;
a dream
But of a shadow, summed with
all his substance.
George Chapman c. 1559–1634:
Bussy D'Ambois (1607–8)

8 How beauteous mankind is! O
brave new world,
That has such people in't.
William Shakespeare 1564–1616: *The
Tempest* (1611)

9 Man is man's A.B.C. There is
none that can
Read God aright, unless he first
spell Man.
Francis Quarles 1592–1644:
Hieroglyphics of the Life of Man
(1638)

10 We carry within us the wonders
we seek without us: there is all
Africa and her prodigies in us.
Thomas Browne 1605–82: *Religio
Medici* (1643)

11 Man is only a reed, the weakest
thing in nature; but he is a
thinking reed.
Blaise Pascal 1623–62: *Pensées*
(1670)

12 What is man in nature? A
nothing in respect of that which
is infinite, an all in respect of
nothing, a middle betwixt nothing
and all.
Blaise Pascal 1623–62: *Pensées*
(1670)

13 Principally I hate and detest that
animal called man; although I
heartily love John, Peter, Thomas,
and so forth.
Jonathan Swift 1667–1745: letter to
Pope, 29 September 1725

14 Know then thyself, presume not
God to scan;
The proper study of mankind is
man.
Alexander Pope 1688–1744: *An
Essay on Man* Epistle 2 (1733)

15 Man is a tool-making animal.
Benjamin Franklin 1706–90: James
Boswell *Life of Samuel Johnson*
(1791) 7 April 1778

16 Out of the crooked timber of
humanity no straight thing can
ever be made.
Immanuel Kant 1724–1804: *Idee zu
einer allgemeinen Geschichte in
weltbürgerlicher Absicht* (1784)

17 Drinking when we are not thirsty
and making love all year round,
madam; that is all there is to
distinguish us from other animals.
**Pierre-Augustin Caron de
Beaumarchais** 1732–99: *Le Mariage
de Figaro* (1785)

18 For Mercy has a human heart
Pity a human face:
And Love, the human form
divine,
And Peace, the human dress.
William Blake 1757–1827: *Songs of
Innocence* (1789) "The Divine Image"

19 Cruelty has a human heart,
And Jealousy a human face;
Terror the human form divine,
And Secrecy the human dress.
William Blake 1757–1827: "A Divine
Image" etched but not included in
Songs of Experience (1794)

20 And much it grieved my heart to
think
What man has made of man.
William Wordsworth 1770–1850:
"Lines Written in Early Spring"
(1798)

21 Providence has not created
mankind entirely independent or
entirely free. It is true that
around every man a fatal circle is

traced, beyond which he cannot pass; but within the wide verge of that circle he is powerful and free.
Alexis de Tocqueville 1805–59: *Democracy in America* (1835–40)

22 Is man an ape or an angel? Now I am on the side of the angels.
Benjamin Disraeli 1804–81: speech at Oxford, 25 November 1864; see **Life Sciences** 5

23 I teach you the superman. Man is something to be surpassed.
Friedrich Nietzsche 1844–1900: *Also Sprach Zarathustra* (1883)

24 I am all at once what Christ is, since he was what I am, and
This Jack, joke, poor potsherd, patch, matchwood, immortal diamond,
Is immortal diamond.
Gerard Manley Hopkins 1844–89: "That Nature is a Heraclitean Fire" (written 1888)

25 Man is the Only Animal that Blushes. Or needs to.
Mark Twain 1835–1910: *Following the Equator* (1897)

26 Ah! what is man? Wherefore does he why? Whence did he whence? Whither is he withering?
Dan Leno 1860–1904: *Dan Leno Hys Booke* (1901)

27 Man, biologically considered, and whatever else he may be into the bargain, is simply the most formidable of all the beasts of prey, and, indeed, the only one that preys systematically on its own species.
William James 1842–1910: in *Atlantic Monthly* December 1904

28 Taking a very gloomy view of the future of the human race, let us suppose that it can only expect to survive for two thousand million years longer, a period about equal to the past age of the earth.

Then, regarded as a being destined to live for three-score years and ten, humanity, although it has been born in a house seventy years old, is itself only three days old.
James Jeans 1877–1946: *Eos* (1928)

29 Many people believe that they are attracted by God, or by Nature, when they are only repelled by man.
William Ralph Inge 1860–1954: *More Lay Thoughts of a Dean* (1931)

30 What is man, when you come to think upon him, but a minutely set, ingenious machine for turning, with infinite artfulness, the red wine of Shiraz into urine?
Isak Dinesen 1885–1962: *Seven Gothic Tales* (1934) "The Dreamers"

31 Man, unlike any other thing organic or inorganic in the universe, grows beyond his work, walks up the stairs of his concepts, emerges ahead of his accomplishments.
John Steinbeck 1902–68: *The Grapes of Wrath* (1939)

32 Man is a useless passion.
Jean-Paul Sartre 1905–80: *L'Être et le néant* (1943)

33 To say, for example, that a man is made up of certain chemical elements is a satisfactory description only for those who intend to use him as a fertilizer.
H. J. Muller 1890–1967: *Science and Criticism* (1943)

34 Man must be invented each day.
Jean-Paul Sartre 1905–80: *Qu'est-ce que la littérature?* (1948)

35 I decline to accept the end of man . . . I believe that man will not merely endure; he will prevail. He is immortal, not because he alone among creatures has an inexhaustible

voice, but because he has a soul,
a spirit capable of compassion
and sacrifice and endurance.
William Faulkner 1897–1962: *speech
accepting the Nobel Prize for
Literature* (10 December 1950)

36 I hate "Humanity" and all such
abstracts: but I love *people*. Lovers
of "Humanity" generally hate
people and children, and keep
parrots or puppy dogs.
Roy Campbell 1901–57: *Light on a
Dark Horse* (1951)

37 We're all of us guinea pigs in the
laboratory of God. Humanity is
just a work in progress.
Tennessee Williams 1911–83: *Camino
Real* (1953)

Human Rights
see also **Equality, Justice**

1 No free man shall be taken or
imprisoned or dispossessed, or
outlawed or exiled, or in any way
destroyed, nor will we go upon
him, nor will we send against him
except by the lawful judgement of
his peers or by the law of the
land.
Magna Carta 1215: clause 39

2 Magna Charta is such a fellow,
that he will have no sovereign.
*on the Lords' Amendment to the
Petition of Right, 17 May 1628*
Edward Coke 1552–1634: J.
Rushworth *Historical Collections*
(1659)

3 We hold these truths to be self-
evident, that all men are created
equal, that they are endowed by
their Creator with certain
unalienable rights, that among
these are life, liberty and the
pursuit of happiness.
**American Declaration of
Independence**: 4 July 1776; from a

draft by Thomas Jefferson (1743–
1826) cf. **Happiness 24**

4 Whatever each man can
separately do, without trespassing
upon others, he has a right to do
for himself; and he has a right to
a fair portion of all which society,
with all its combinations of skill
and force, can do in his favour.
Edmund Burke 1729–97: *Reflections
on the Revolution in France* (1790)

5 *Liberté! Égalité! Fraternité!*
Freedom! Equality! Brotherhood!
*motto of the French Revolution, but
of earlier origin*
Anonymous: the Club des Cordeliers
passed a motion, 30 June 1793,
"that owners should be urged to
paint on the front of their houses, in
large letters, the words: Unity,
indivisibility of the Republic, Liberty,
Equality, Fraternity or death"

6 Any law which violates the
inalienable rights of man is
essentially unjust and tyrannical;
it is not a law at all.
Maximilien Robespierre 1758–94:
Déclaration des droits de l'homme
24 April 1793

7 Natural rights is simple nonsense:
natural and imprescriptible rights,
rhetorical nonsense—nonsense
upon stilts.
Jeremy Bentham 1748–1832:
Anarchical Fallacies (1843)

8 We hold these truths to be self-
evident, that all men and women
are created equal.
Elizabeth Cady Stanton 1815–1902:
*First Woman's Rights Convention,
Seneca Falls, NY* (19–20 July 1848)

9 Its constitution the glittering and
sounding generalities of natural
right which make up the
Declaration of Independence.

Rufus Choate 1799–1859: letter to the Maine Whig State Central Committee, 9 August 1856; cf. **12** below

10 The first duty of a State is to see that every child born therein shall be well housed, clothed, fed and educated, till it attain years of discretion.
John Ruskin 1819–1900: *Time and Tide* (1867)

11 It was we, the people, not we, the white male citizens, nor yet we, the male citizens, but we, the whole people, who formed this Union.
Susan B. Anthony 1820–1906: *speech, New York State* (1873)

12 Glittering generalities! They are blazing ubiquities.
on Rufus Choate
Ralph Waldo Emerson 1803–82: attributed; see **9** above

13 No man can put a chain about the ankle of his fellow man without at last finding the other end fastened about his own neck.
Frederick Douglass *c.* 1818–1895: speech at Civil Rights Mass Meeting, Washington, DC, 22 October 1883

14 The Nineteenth Amendment—I think that's the one that made Women humans by Act of Congress.
Will Rogers 1879–1935: *"Mr. Toastmaster and Democrats"* (30 March 1929)

15 We look forward to a world founded upon four essential human freedoms. The first is freedom of speech and expression—everywhere in the world. The second is freedom of every person to worship God in his own way—everywhere in the world. The third is freedom from want . . . everywhere in the world. The

fourth is freedom from fear . . . anywhere in the world.
Franklin D. Roosevelt 1882–1945: message to Congress, 6 January 1941

16 All human beings are born free and equal in dignity and rights.
Anonymous: *Universal Declaration of Human Rights* (1948) article 1

17 A right is not effectual by itself, but only in relation to the obligation to which it corresponds . . . An obligation which goes unrecognized by anybody loses none of the full force of its existence. A right which goes unrecognized by anybody is not worth very much.
Simone Weil 1909–43: *L'Enracinement* (1949)

18 We have talked long enough in this country about equal rights. We have talked for a hundred years or more. It is time now to write the next chapter, and to write it in the books of law.
Lyndon Baines Johnson 1908–73: speech to Congress, 27 November 1963

19 We are not fighting for integration, nor are we fighting for separation. We are fighting for recognition as human beings. We are fighting for . . . human rights.
Malcolm X 1925–65: *speech, Black Revolution, New York* (1964)

20 The price of championing human rights is a little inconsistency at times.
David Owen 1938– : speech, House of Commons, 30 March 1977

Humility
see **Pride and Humility**

Humor

see also **Wit**

1 A merry heart doeth good like a
medicine.
Bible: Proverbs

2 Delight hath a joy in it either
permanent or present. Laughter
hath only a scornful tickling.
Philip Sidney 1554–86: *The Defence
of Poetry* (1595)

3 A jest's prosperity lies in the ear
Of him that hears it, never in the
tongue
Of him that makes it.
William Shakespeare 1564–1616:
Love's Labour's Lost (1595)

4 Laughter is nothing else but
sudden glory arising from some
sudden conception of some
eminency in ourselves, by
comparison with the infirmity of
others, or with our own formerly.
Thomas Hobbes 1588–1679: *Human
Nature* (1650)

5 I love such mirth as does not
make friends ashamed to look
upon one another next morning.
Izaak Walton 1593–1683: *The
Compleat Angler* (1653)

6 There is nothing more
unbecoming a man of quality
than to laugh; Jesu, 'tis such a
vulgar expression of the passion!
William Congreve 1670–1729: *The
Double Dealer* (1694)

7 Among all kinds of writing, there
is none in which authors are
more apt to miscarry than in
works of humour, as there is
none in which they are more
ambitious to excel.
Joseph Addison 1672–1719: in *The
Spectator* (UK) 10 April 1711

8 I make myself laugh at
everything, for fear of having to
weep at it.

**Pierre-Augustin Caron de
Beaumarchais** 1732–99: *Le Barbier
de Séville* (1775)

9 For what do we live, but to make
sport for our neighbours, and
laugh at them in our turn?
Jane Austen 1775–1817: *Pride and
Prejudice* (1813)

10 Laughter is pleasant, but the
exertion is too much for me.
Thomas Love Peacock 1785–1866:
Nightmare Abbey (1818)

11 'Tis ever thus with simple folk—
an accepted wit has but to say
"Pass the mustard," and they roar
their ribs out!
W. S. Gilbert 1836–1911: *The Yeoman
of the Guard* (1888)

12 We are not amused.
Queen Victoria 1819–1901: attributed;
Caroline Holland *Notebooks of a
Spinster Lady* (1919) 2 January 1900

13 My way of joking is to tell the
truth. It's the funniest joke in the
world.
George Bernard Shaw 1856–1950:
John Bull's Other Island (1907)

14 Everything is funny as long as it
is happening to Somebody Else.
Will Rogers 1879–1935: *The Illiterate
Digest* (1924)

15 Fun is fun but no girl wants to
laugh all of the time.
Anita Loos 1893–1981: *Gentlemen
Prefer Blondes* (1925)

16 What do you mean, funny?
Funny-peculiar or funny ha-ha?
Ian Hay 1876–1952: *The
Housemaster* (1938)

17 Whatever is funny is subversive,
every joke is ultimately a custard
pie . . . A dirty joke is a sort of
mental rebellion.

George Orwell 1903–50: in *Horizon* September 1941 "The Art of Donald McGill"

18 The funniest thing about comedy is that you never know why people laugh. I know *what* makes them laugh but trying to get your hands on the *why* of it is like trying to pick an eel out of a tub of water.
W. C. Fields 1880–1946: R. J. Anobile *A Flask of Fields* (1972)

19 Good taste and humour . . . are a contradiction in terms, like a chaste whore.
Malcolm Muggeridge 1903–90: in *Time* 14 September 1953

20 Laughter would be bereaved if snobbery died.
Peter Ustinov 1921–　: in *Observer* (UK) 13 March 1955

21 Humor is emotional chaos remembered in tranquillity.
James Thurber 1894–1961: in *New York Post* 29 February 1960; see **Poetry 13**

22 Freud's theory was that when a joke opens a window and all those bats and bogeymen fly out, you get a marvellous feeling of relief and elation. The trouble with Freud is that he never had to play the old Glasgow Empire on a Saturday night after Rangers and Celtic had both lost.
Ken Dodd 1931–　: in *Guardian* (UK) 30 April 1991; quoted in many, usually much contracted, forms since the mid-1960s

23 Mark my words, when a society has to resort to the lavatory for its humour, the writing is on the wall.
Alan Bennett 1934–　: *Forty Years On* (1969)

24 People sometimes divide others into those you laugh at and those

you laugh with. The young Auden was someone you could laugh-at-with.
Stephen Spender 1909–95: *W. H. Auden* (1973)

25 The marvellous thing about a joke with a double meaning is that it can only mean one thing.
Ronnie Barker 1929–　: *Sauce* (1977)

26 Nothing is so impenetrable as laughter in a language you don't understand.
William Golding 1911–93: *An Egyptian Journal* (1985)

Hunting, Shooting, and Fishing

1 As no man is born an artist, so no man is born an angler.
Izaak Walton 1593–1683: *The Compleat Angler* (1653)

2 I am, Sir, a Brother of the Angle.
Izaak Walton 1593–1683: *The Compleat Angler* (1653)

3 Most of their discourse was about hunting, in a dialect I understand very little.
Samuel Pepys 1633–1703: diary 22 November 1663

4 The dusky night rides down the sky,
And ushers in the morn;
The hounds all join in glorious cry,
The huntsman winds his horn:
And a-hunting we will go.
Henry Fielding 1707–54: *Don Quixote in England* (1733)

5 My hoarse-sounding horn
Invites thee to the chase, the sport of kings;
Image of war, without its guilt.
William Somerville 1675–1742: *The Chase* (1735); cf. **10** below

6 Fly fishing may be a very
pleasant amusement; but angling
or float fishing I can only
compare to a stick and a string,
with a worm at one end and a
fool at the other.
Samuel Johnson 1709–84: attributed;
Hawker *Instructions to Young
Sportsmen* (1859); also attributed to
Jonathan Swift, in *The Indicator* (UK)
27 October 1819

7 It is very strange, and very
melancholy, that the paucity of
human pleasures should persuade
us ever to call hunting one of
them.
Samuel Johnson 1709–84: Hester
Lynch Piozzi *Anecdotes of . . .
Johnson* (1786)

8 D'ye ken John Peel with his coat
so grey?
D'ye ken John Peel at the break
of the day?
D'ye ken John Peel when he's far
far away
With his hounds and his horn in
the morning?
'Twas the sound of his horn
called me from my bed,
And the cry of his hounds has me
oft-times led;
For Peel's view-hollo would
waken the dead,
Or a fox from his lair in the
morning.
John Woodcock Graves 1795–1886:
"John Peel" (1820)

9 It ar'n't that I loves the fox less,
but that I loves the 'ound more.
R. S. Surtees 1805–64: *Handley
Cross* (1843)

10 'Unting is all that's worth living
for—all time is lost wot is not
spent in 'unting—it is like the
hair we breathe—if we have it
not we die—it's the sport of
kings, the image of war without
its guilt, and only five-and-twenty
per cent of its danger.

R. S. Surtees 1805–64: *Handley
Cross* (1843); cf. 5 above

11 The English country gentleman
galloping after a fox—the
unspeakable in full pursuit of the
uneatable.
Oscar Wilde 1854–1900: *A Woman of
No Importance* (1893)

12 When a man wants to murder a
tiger he calls it sport; when a
tiger wants to murder him, he
calls it ferocity.
George Bernard Shaw 1856–1950:
Man and Superman (1903)

13 The fascination of shooting as a
sport depends almost wholly on
whether you are at the right or
wrong end of a gun.
P. G. Wodehouse 1881–1975:
attributed

14 This fictional account of the day-
by-day life of an English
gamekeeper is still of considerable
interest to outdoor-minded
readers, as it contains many
passages on pheasant raising, the
apprehending of poachers, ways
to control vermin, and other
chores and duties of the
professional gamekeeper.
Unfortunately one is obliged to
wade through many pages of
extraneous material in order to
discover and savour these
sidelights on the management of
a Midlands shooting estate, and
in this reviewer's opinion this
book cannot take the place of J.
R. Miller's *Practical Gamekeeping*.
Anonymous: review of D. H.
Lawrence *Lady Chatterley's Lover*,
attributed to *Field and Stream*, c.
1928

15 I do not see why I should break
my neck because a dog chooses
to run after a nasty smell.
on being asked why he did not hunt
Arthur James Balfour 1848–1930: Ian
Malcolm *Lord Balfour: A Memory*
(1930)

16 A sportsman is a man who, every
now and then, simply has to get
out and kill something. Not that
he's cruel. He wouldn't hurt a fly.
It's not big enough.
Stephen Leacock 1869–1944: *My
Remarkable Uncle* (1942)

17 They do you a decent death on
the hunting-field.
John Mortimer 1923– : *Paradise
Postponed* (1985)

Hypocrisy
see also **Deception**

1 Woe unto them that call evil
good, and good evil.
Bible: Isaiah

2 My tongue swore, but my mind's
unsworn.
on his breaking of an oath
Euripides *c.* 485–*c.* 406 BC:
Hippolytus

3 Beware of false prophets, which
come to you in sheep's clothing,
but inwardly they are ravening
wolves.
Bible: St. Matthew

4 Ye are like unto whited
sepulchres, which indeed appear
beautiful outward, but are within
full of dead men's bones, and of
all uncleanness.
Bible: St. Matthew

5 I want that glib and oily art
To speak and purpose not.
William Shakespeare 1564–1616:
King Lear (1605–6)

6 For neither man nor angel can
discern
Hypocrisy, the only evil that
walks
Invisible, except to God alone.
John Milton 1608–74: *Paradise Lost*
(1667)

7 Hypocrisy is a tribute which vice
pays to virtue.
Duc de la Rochefoucauld 1613–80:
Maximes (1678)

8 Keep up appearances; there lies
the test;
The world will give thee credit for
the rest.
Outward be fair, however foul
within;
Sin if thou wilt, but then in secret
sin.
Charles Churchill 1731–64: *Night*
(1761)

9 Conventionality is not morality.
Self-righteousness is not religion.
To attack the first is not to assail
the last. To pluck the mask from
the face of the Pharisee, is not to
lift an impious hand to the Crown
of Thorns.
Charlotte Brontë 1816–55: *Jane Eyre*
(2nd ed., 1848)

10 As for conforming outwardly, and
living your own life inwardly, I
don't think much of that.
Henry David Thoreau 1817–62: *Letter
to Harrison Blake* (9 August 1850)

11 In the mouths of many men soft
words are like roses that soldiers
put into the muzzles of their
muskets on holidays.
Henry Wadsworth Longfellow 1807–
82: "Table-Talk," *Driftwood* (1857)

12 I sit on a man's back, choking
him and making him carry me,
and yet assure myself and others
that I am very sorry for him and
wish to ease his lot by all possible
means—except by getting off his
back.
Leo Tolstoy 1828–1910: *What Then
Must We Do?* (1886)

13 I hope you have not been leading
a double life, pretending to be
wicked and being really good all
the time. That would be
hypocrisy.

Oscar Wilde 1854–1900: *The Importance of Being Earnest* (1895)

14 Talk about the pews and steeples
And the Cash that goes
therewith!
But the souls of Christian peoples
. . .
Chuck it, Smith!
satirizing F. E. Smith's response to the Welsh Disestablishment Bill (1912)
G. K. Chesterton 1874–1936: "Antichrist" (1915)

15 Hypocrisy is the most difficult and nerve-racking vice that any man can pursue; it needs an unceasing vigilance and a rare detachment of spirit. It cannot, like adultery or gluttony, be practised at spare moments; it is a whole-time job.
W. Somerset Maugham 1874–1965: *Cakes and Ale* (1930)

16 All Reformers, however strict their social conscience, live in houses just as big as they can pay for.
Logan Pearsall Smith 1865–1946: *Afterthoughts* (1931) "Other People"

Hypothesis and Fact
see also **Science**

1 *on "Aristotelian experiments, intended to illustrate a preconceived truth and convince people of its validity":*
A most venomous thing in the making of sciences; for whoever has fixed on his Cause, before he has experimented, can hardly avoid fitting his Experiment to his own Cause . . . rather than the Cause to the truth of the Experiment itself.
Thomas Sprat 1635–1713: *History of the Royal Society* (1667)

2 *Hypotheses non fingo.* I do not feign hypotheses.
Isaac Newton 1642–1727: *Principia Mathematica* (1713 ed.)

3 It may be so, there is no arguing against facts and experiments.
when told of an experiment which appeared to destroy his theory
Isaac Newton 1642–1727: reported by John Conduit, 1726; D. Brewster *Memoirs of Sir Isaac Newton* (1855)

4 It is the nature of an hypothesis, when once a man has conceived it, that it assimilates every thing to itself, as proper nourishment; and, from the first moment of your begetting it, it generally grows the stronger by every thing you see, hear, read, or understand.
Laurence Sterne 1713–68: *Tristram Shandy* (1759–67)

5 Nothing is too wonderful to be true, if it be consistent with the laws of nature, and in such things as these, experiment is the best test of such consistency.
Michael Faraday 1791–1867: diary, 19 March 1849

6 Some circumstantial evidence is very strong, as when you find a trout in the milk.
Henry David Thoreau 1817–62: diary, 11 November 1850

7 Now, what I want is, Facts . . . Facts alone are wanted in life.
Charles Dickens 1812–70: *Hard Times* (1854)

8 False views, if supported by some evidence, do little harm, for everyone takes a salutary pleasure in proving their falseness.
Charles Darwin 1809–82: *The Descent of Man* (1871)

9 How seldom is it that theories stand the wear and tear of practice!
Anthony Trollope 1815–82: *Thackeray* (1879)

10 It is a capital mistake to theorize before you have all the evidence. It biases the judgement.
Arthur Conan Doyle 1859–1930: *A Study in Scarlet* (1888)

11 The great tragedy of Science—the slaying of a beautiful hypothesis by an ugly fact.
T. H. Huxley 1825–95: *Collected Essays* (1893–4) "Biogenesis and Abiogenesis"

12 Roundabout the accredited and orderly fact of every science there ever floats a sort of dust cloud of exceptional observations, of occurences minute and irregular and seldom met with, which it always proves more easy to ignore than to attend to.
William James 1842–1910: attributed

13 The best scale for an experiment is 12 inches to a foot.
John Arbuthnot Fisher 1841–1920: *Memories* (1919)

14 The grand aim of all science [is] to cover the greatest number of empirical facts by logical deduction from the smallest possible number of hypotheses or axioms.
Albert Einstein 1879–1955: Lincoln Barnett *The Universe and Dr. Einstein* (1950 ed.)

15 Aristotle maintained that women have fewer teeth than men; although he was twice married, it never occurred to him to verify this statement by examining his wives' mouths.
Bertrand Russell 1872–1970: *The Impact of Science on Society* (1952)

16 If it looks like a duck, walks like a duck and quacks like a duck, then it just may be a duck.
as a test, during the McCarthy era, of Communist affiliations
Walter Reuther 1907–70: attributed

17 It is a good morning exercise for a research scientist to discard a pet hypothesis every day before breakfast. It keeps him young.
Konrad Lorenz 1903–89: *Das Sogenannte Böse* (1963; translated by Marjorie Latzke as *On Aggression*, 1966)

18 If an elderly but distinguished scientist says that something is possible he is almost certainly right, but if he says that it is impossible he is very probably wrong.
Arthur C. Clarke 1917– : in *New Yorker* 9 August 1969

19 No *good* model ever accounted for *all* the facts since some data was bound to be misleading if not plain wrong.
James Watson 1928– : Francis Crick *Some Mad Pursuit* (1988)

Idealism
see also **Hope**

1 Where there is no vision, the people perish.
Bible: Proverbs

2 Love and a cottage! Eh, Fanny! Ah, give me indifference and a coach and six!
George Colman, the Elder 1732–94 and **David Garrick** 1717–79: *The Clandestine Marriage* (1766); cf. **Love 43**

3 Hitch your wagon to a star.
Ralph Waldo Emerson 1803–82: *Society and Solitude* (1870)

4 We are all in the gutter, but some of us are looking at the stars.
Oscar Wilde 1854–1900: *Lady Windermere's Fan* (1892)

5 I am an idealist. I don't know where I'm going but I'm on the way.
Carl Sandburg 1878–1967: *Incidentals* (1907)

6 A cause may be inconvenient, but
it's magnificent. It's like
champagne or high heels, and
one must be prepared to suffer for
it.
Arnold Bennett 1867–1931: *The Title*
(1918)

7 When they come downstairs from
their Ivory Towers, Idealists are
very apt to walk straight into the
gutter.
Logan Pearsall Smith 1865–1946:
Afterthoughts (1931) "Other People"

8 I submit to you that if a man
hasn't discovered something he
will die for, he isn't fit to live.
Martin Luther King, Jr. 1929–68:
speech in Detroit, 23 June 1963

9 Oh, the vision thing.
*responding to the suggestion that
he turn his attention from short-term
campaign objectives and look to the
longer term*
George Bush 1924– : in *Time* 26
January 1987

Ideas
see also **Hypothesis and Fact, The
Mind, Problems and Solutions,
Thinking**

1 New opinions are always
suspected, and usually opposed,
without any other reason but
because they are not already
common.
John Locke 1632–1704: *An Essay
concerning Human Understanding*
(1690)

2 General notions are generally
wrong.
Lady Mary Wortley Montagu 1689–
1762: letter to her husband Edward
Wortley Montagu, 28 March 1710

3 It was at Rome, on the fifteenth
of October, 1764, as I sat musing
amidst the ruins of the Capitol,
while the barefoot friars were

singing vespers in the Temple of
Jupiter, that the idea of writing
the decline and fall of the city
first started to my mind.
Edward Gibbon 1737–94: *Memoirs of
My Life* (1796)

4 I can't help it, the idea of the
infinite torments me.
Alfred de Musset 1810–57: "L'Espoir
en Dieu" (1838)

5 A stand can be made against
invasion by an army; no stand
can be made against invasion by
an idea.
Victor Hugo 1802–85: *Histoire d'un
Crime* (written 1851–2, published
1877)

6 I share no one's ideas. I have my
own.
Ivan Turgenev 1818–83: *Fathers and
Sons* (1862)

7 Our ideas are only intellectual
instruments which we use to
break into phenomena; we must
change them when they have
served their purpose, as we
change a blunt lancet that we
have used long enough.
Claude Bernard 1813–78: *An
Introduction to the Study of
Experimental Medicine* (1865)

8 For an idea ever to be fashionable
is ominous, since it must
afterwards be always old-
fashioned.
George Santayana 1863–1952: *Winds
of Doctrine* (1913)

9 You see things; and you say
"Why?" But I dream things that
never were; and I say "Why not?"
George Bernard Shaw 1856–1950:
Back to Methuselah (1921)

10 Nothing is more dangerous than
an idea, when you have only one
idea.
Alain 1868–1951: *Propos sur la
religion* (1938)

11 No grand idea was ever born in a conference, but a lot of foolish ideas have died there.
F. Scott Fitzgerald 1896–1940: Edmund Wilson (ed.) *The Crack-Up* (1945) "Note-Books E"

12 Madmen in authority, who hear voices in the air, are distilling their frenzy from some academic scribbler of a few years back.
John Maynard Keynes 1883–1946: *General Theory* (1947 ed.)

13 Resistentialism is concerned with what Things think about men.
Paul Jennings 1918–89: *Even Oddlier* (1952) "Developments in Resistentialism"

14 It is better to entertain an idea than to take it home to live with you for the rest of your life.
Randall Jarrell 1914–65: *Pictures from an Institution* (1954)

15 You can't stop. Composing's not voluntary, you know. There's no choice, you're not free. You're landed with an idea and you have responsibility to that idea.
Harrison Birtwhistle 1934– : in *Observer* (UK) 14 April 1996 "Sayings of the Week"

Idleness
see also **Action and Inaction, Words and Deeds**

1 Go to the ant thou sluggard; consider her ways, and be wise.
Bible: Proverbs

2 Out ye whores, to work, to work, ye whores, go spin.
commonly quoted as "Go spin, you jades, go spin"
William Herbert, Lord Pembroke c. 1501–70: John Aubrey *Brief Lives* (1898 ed.)

3 He that would thrive
Must rise at five;

He that hath thriven
May lie till seven.
John Clarke d. 1658: "Diligentia" (1639)

4 Idleness is only the refuge of weak minds.
Lord Chesterfield 1694–1773: *Letters to his Son* (1774) 20 July 1749

5 If you are idle, be not solitary; if you are solitary, be not idle.
Samuel Johnson 1709–84: letter to Boswell, 27 October 1779

6 A man who has nothing to do with his own time has no conscience in his intrusion on that of others.
Jane Austen 1775–1817: *Sense and Sensibility* (1811)

7 The foul sluggard's comfort: "It will last my time."
Thomas Carlyle 1795–1881: *Critical and Miscellaneous Essays* (1838) "Count Cagliostro. Flight Last"

8 [Brummell] used to say that, whether it was summer or winter, he always liked to have the morning well-aired before he got up.
Beau Brummell 1778–1840: Charles Macfarlane *Reminiscences of a Literary Life* (1917)

9 How dull it is to pause, to make an end,
To rust unburnished, not to shine in use!
As though to breathe were life.
Alfred, Lord Tennyson 1809–92: "Ulysses" (1842)

10 Never do to-day what you can put off till to-morrow.
Punch: in 1849

11 It is impossible to enjoy idling thoroughly unless one has plenty of work to do.
Jerome K. Jerome 1859–1927: *Idle Thoughts of an Idle Fellow* (1886)

12 Oh! how I hate to get up in the morning,
Oh! how I'd love to remain in bed.
Irving Berlin 1888–1989: *Oh! How I Hate to Get Up in the Morning* (1918 song)

Ignorance

1 If one does not know to which port one is sailing, no wind is favourable.
Seneca ("the Younger") c. 4 BC–AD 65: *Epistulae Morales*

2 But those that understood him smiled at one another and shook their heads; but, for mine own part, it was Greek to me.
William Shakespeare 1564–1616: *Julius Caesar* (1599)

3 Lo! the poor Indian, whose untutored mind
Sees God in clouds, or hears him in the wind.
Alexander Pope 1688–1744: *An Essay on Man* Epistle 1 (1733); cf. **Drunkenness 2**

4 Where ignorance is bliss,
'Tis folly to be wise.
Thomas Gray 1716–71: *Ode on a Distant Prospect of Eton College* (1747)

5 Ignorance, madam, pure ignorance.
on being asked why he had defined pastern as the "knee" of a horse
Samuel Johnson 1709–84: James Boswell *Life of Samuel Johnson* (1791) 1755

6 Where people wish to attach, they should always be ignorant. To come with a well-informed mind, is to come with an inability of administering to the vanity of others, which a sensible person would always wish to avoid. A woman especially, if she have the misfortune of knowing any thing, should conceal it as well as she can.
Jane Austen 1775–1817: *Northanger Abbey* (1818)

7 Ignorance is not innocence but sin.
Robert Browning 1812–89: *The Inn Album* (1875)

8 I wish you would read a little poetry sometimes. Your ignorance cramps my conversation.
Anthony Hope 1863–1933: *Dolly Dialogues* (1894)

9 Ignorance is like a delicate exotic fruit; touch it and the bloom is gone. The whole theory of modern education is radically unsound. Fortunately, in England, at any rate, education produces no effect whatsoever.
Oscar Wilde 1854–1900: *The Importance of Being Earnest* (1895)

10 I know nothing—nobody tells me anything.
John Galsworthy 1867–1933: *Man of Property* (1906)

11 You know everybody is ignorant, only on different subjects.
Will Rogers 1879–1935: in *New York Times* 31 August 1924

12 Happy the hare at morning, for she cannot read
The Hunter's waking thoughts.
W. H. Auden 1907–73: *Dog beneath the Skin* (with Christopher Isherwood, 1935)

13 Ignorance is an evil weed, which dictators may cultivate among their dupes, but which no democracy can afford among its citizens.
William Henry Beveridge 1879–1963: *Full Employment in a Free Society* (1944)

14 Nothing in all the world is more dangerous than sincere ignorance and conscientious stupidity.

Martin Luther King, Jr. 1929–68: *Strength to Love* (1963)

15 A bishop wrote gravely to the *Times* inviting all nations to destroy "the formula" of the atomic bomb. There is no simple remedy for ignorance so abysmal.
Peter Medawar 1915–87: *The Hope of Progress* (1972)

16 It was absolutely marvelous working for Pauli. You could ask him anything. There was no worry that he would think a particular question was stupid, since he thought *all* questions were stupid.
Victor Weisskopf 1908– : in *American Journal of Physics* 1977

Imagination

1 For the imagination of man's heart is evil from his youth.
Bible: Genesis

2 The lunatic, the lover, and the poet,
Are of imagination all compact.
William Shakespeare 1564–1616: *A Midsummer Night's Dream* (1595–6)

3 I am giddy, expectation whirls me round.
The imaginary relish is so sweet
That it enchants my sense.
William Shakespeare 1564–1616: *Troilus and Cressida* (1602)

4 That fairy kind of writing which depends only upon the force of imagination.
John Dryden 1631–1700: *King Arthur* (1691)

5 Though our brother is on the rack, as long as we ourselves are at our ease, our senses will never inform us of what he suffers . . . It is by imagination that we can form any conception of what are his sensations.

Adam Smith 1723–90: *Theory of Moral Sentiments* (2nd ed., 1762)

6 Were it not for imagination, Sir, a man would be as happy in the arms of a chambermaid as of a Duchess.
Samuel Johnson 1709–84: James Boswell *Life of Samuel Johnson* (1791) 9 May 1778

7 [Edmund Burke] is not affected by the reality of distress touching his heart, but by the showy resemblance of it striking his imagination. He pities the plumage, but forgets the dying bird.
on Burke's Reflections on the Revolution in France
Thomas Paine 1737–1809: *The Rights of Man* (1791)

8 To see a world in a grain of sand
And a heaven in a wild flower
Hold infinity in the palm of your hand
And eternity in an hour.
William Blake 1757–1827: "Auguries of Innocence" (*c.* 1803)

9 Whither is fled the visionary gleam?
Where is it now, the glory and the dream?
William Wordsworth 1770–1850: "Ode. Intimations of Immortality" (1807)

10 Heard melodies are sweet, but those unheard
Are sweeter; therefore, ye soft pipes, play on;
Not to the sensual ear, but, more endeared,
Pipe to the spirit ditties of no tone.
John Keats 1795–1821: "Ode on a Grecian Urn" (1820)

11 Such writing is a sort of mental masturbation—he is always f—gg—g his *imagination.*—I don't mean that he is indecent but

viciously soliciting his own ideas into a state which is neither poetry nor any thing else but a Bedlam vision produced by raw pork and opium.
of Keats
Lord Byron 1788–1824: letter to John Murray, 9 November 1820

12 The same that oft-times hath
Charmed magic casements,
  opening on the foam
Of perilous seas, in faery lands
  forlorn.
John Keats 1795–1821: "Ode to a Nightingale" (1820)

13 His imagination resembled the wings of an ostrich. It enabled him to run, though not to soar.
Lord Macaulay 1800–59: T. F. Ellis (ed.) *Miscellaneous Writings of Lord Macaulay* (1860) "John Dryden" (1828)

14 He said he should prefer not to know the sources of the Nile, and that there should be some unknown regions preserved as hunting-grounds for the poetic imagination.
George Eliot 1819–80: *Middlemarch* (1871–2)

15 Where there is no imagination there is no horror.
Arthur Conan Doyle 1859–1930: *A Study in Scarlet* (1888)

16 An adventure is only an inconvenience rightly considered. An inconvenience is only an adventure wrongly considered.
G. K. Chesterton 1874–1936: *All Things Considered* (1908) "On Running after one's Hat"

17 Must then a Christ perish in torment in every age to save those that have no imagination?
George Bernard Shaw 1856–1950: *Saint Joan* (1924)

18 Imagination is more important than knowledge.
Albert Einstein 1879–1955: *On Science*

Inaction
see **Action and Inaction**

Inconstancy
see **Constancy and Inconstancy**

Indecision
see also **Certainty and Doubt**

1 Now, the melancholy god protect thee, and the tailor make thy doublet of changeable taffeta, for thy mind is a very opal.
William Shakespeare 1564–1616: *Twelfth Night* (1601)

2 I must have a prodigious quantity of mind; it takes me as much as a week, sometimes, to make it up.
Mark Twain 1835–1910: *The Innocents Abroad* (1869)

3 There is no more miserable human being than one in whom nothing is habitual but indecision.
William James 1842–1910: *The Principles of Psychology* (1890)

4 A very weak-minded fellow I am afraid, and, like the feather pillow, bears the marks of the last person who has sat on him!
of Lord Derby
Earl Haig 1861–1928: letter to Lady Haig, 14 January 1918

5 The Flying Scotsman is no less splendid a sight when it travels north to Edinburgh than when it travels south to London. Mr. Baldwin denouncing sanctions was as dignified as Mr. Baldwin imposing them.
Lord Beaverbrook 1879–1964: in *Daily Express* (UK) 29 May 1937

6 The tragedy of a man who could not make up his mind.
Laurence Olivier 1907–89: introduction to his 1948 screen adaptation of *Hamlet*

7 Often undecided whether to desert a sinking ship for one that might not float, he would make up his mind to sit on the wharf for a day.
of Lord Curzon
Lord Beaverbrook 1879–1964: *Men and Power* (1956)

8 I'll give you a definite maybe.
Sam Goldwyn 1882–1974: attributed

9 A wrong decision isn't forever; it can always be reversed. The losses from a delayed decision *are* forever; they can never be retrieved.
John Kenneth Galbraith 1908– : *A Life in our Times* (1981)

10 The archbishop is usually to be found nailing his colours to the fence.
of Archbishop Runcie
Frank Field 1942– : attributed in *Crockfords 1987/88* (1987); Geoffrey Madan records in his *Notebooks* a similar comment was made about A. J. Balfour, *c.* 1904

Indifference

1 They have mouths, and speak not: eyes have they, and see not. They have ears, and hear not: noses have they, and smell not. They have hands, and handle not: feet have they, and walk not: neither speak they through their throat.
Bible: Psalm 115

2 It is the disease of not listening, the malady of not marking, that I am troubled withal.
William Shakespeare 1564–1616: *Henry IV, Part 2* (1597)

3 All colours will agree in the dark.
Francis Bacon 1561–1626: *Essays* (1625) "Of Unity in Religion"

4 And this the burthen of his song,
For ever used to be,
I care for nobody, not I,
If no one cares for me.
Isaac Bickerstaffe 1733–*c.* 1808: *Love in a Village* (1762) "The Miller of Dee"

5 There is nothing upon the face of the earth so insipid as a medium. Give me love or hate! a friend that will go to jail for me, or an enemy that will run me through the body!
Fanny Burney 1752–1840: *Camilla* (1796)

6 Vacant heart and hand, and eye,—
Easy live and quiet die.
Sir Walter Scott 1771–1832: *The Bride of Lammermoor* (1819)

7 If Jesus Christ were to come to-day, people would not even crucify him. They would ask him to dinner, and hear what he had to say, and make fun of it.
Thomas Carlyle 1795–1881: D. A. Wilson *Carlyle at his Zenith* (1927)

8 The worst sin towards our fellow creatures is not to hate them, but to be indifferent to them: that's the essence of inhumanity.
George Bernard Shaw 1856–1950: *The Devil's Disciple* (1901)

9 Science may have found a cure for most evils; but it has found no remedy for the worst of them all— the apathy of human beings.
Helen Keller 1880–1968: *My Religion* (1927)

10 I wish I could care what you do or where you go but I can't . . . My dear, I don't give a damn.
"Frankly, my dear, I don't give a damn!" in the 1939 screen version by Sidney Howard

Margaret Mitchell 1900–49: *Gone with the Wind* (1936)

11 Catholics and Communists have committed great crimes, but at least they have not stood aside, like an established society, and been indifferent. I would rather have blood on my hands than water like Pilate.
Graham Greene 1904–91: *The Comedians* (1966)

12 When Hitler attacked the Jews I was not a Jew, therefore, I was not concerned. And when Hitler attacked the Catholics, I was not a Catholic, and therefore, I was not concerned. And when Hitler attacked the unions and the industrialists, I was not a member of the unions and I was not concerned. Then, Hitler attacked me and the Protestant church—and there was nobody left to be concerned.
often quoted in the form "In Germany they came first for the Communists, and I didn't speak up because I wasn't a Communist . . . " and so on
Martin Niemöller 1892–1984: in *Congressional Record* 14 October 1968

13 Take sides. Neutrality helps the oppressor, never the victim. Silence encourages the tormentor, never the tormented.
accepting the Nobel Peace Prize
Elie Wiesel 1928– : in *New York Times* 11 December 1986

Ingratitude
see **Gratitude and Ingratitude**

Injustice
see **Justice and Injustice**

Innocence
see **Guilt and Innocence**

Insight
see also **Self-Knowledge**

1 For the Lord seeth not as man seeth: for man looketh on the outward appearance, but the Lord looketh on the heart.
Bible: I Samuel

2 I have striven not to laugh at human actions, not to weep at them, nor to hate them, but to understand them.
Baruch Spinoza 1632–77: *Tractatus Politicus* (1677)

3 He gets at the substance of a book directly; he tears out the heart of it.
on Samuel Johnson
Mary Knowles 1733–1807: James Boswell *The Life of Samuel Johnson* (1791) 15 April 1778

4 If the doors of perception were cleansed everything would appear to man as it is, infinite.
William Blake 1757–1827: *The Marriage of Heaven and Hell* (1790–3)

5 *Tout comprendre rend très indulgent.* To be totally understanding makes one very indulgent.
Mme. de Staël 1766–1817: *Corinne* (1807)

6 Aye on the shores of darkness there is light,
And precipices show untrodden green,
There is a budding morrow in midnight,
There is a triple sight in blindness keen.
John Keats 1795–1821: "To Homer" (written 1818)

7 The only people who remain misunderstood are those who either do not know what they

want or are not worth
understanding.
Ivan Turgenev 1818–83: *Rudin* (1856)

8 If we had a keen vision and
feeling of all ordinary human life,
it would be like hearing the grass
grow and the squirrel's heart
beat, and we should die of that
roar which lies on the other side
of silence.
George Eliot 1819–80: *Middlemarch*
(1871–2)

9 The art of being wise is the art of
knowing what to overlook.
William James 1842–1910: *The
Principles of Psychology* (1890)

10 One sees great things from the
valley; only small things from the
peak.
G. K. Chesterton 1874–1936: *The
Innocence of Father Brown* (1911)

11 It is only with the heart that one
can see rightly; what is essential
is invisible to the eye.
Antoine de Saint-Exupéry 1900–44:
Le Petit Prince (1943)

12 Deprivation is for me what
daffodils were for Wordsworth.
Philip Larkin 1922–85: *Required
Writing* (1983)

Insults

1 The devil damn thee black, thou
cream-faced loon!
Where gott'st thou that goose
look?
William Shakespeare 1564–1616:
Macbeth (1606)

2 How easy it is to call rogue and
villain, and that wittily! But how
hard to make a man appear a
fool, a blockhead, or a knave,
without using any of those
opprobrious terms! To spare the
grossness of the names, and to do
the thing yet more severely, is to

draw a full face, and to make the
nose and cheeks stand out, and
yet not to employ any depth of
shadowing.
John Dryden 1631–1700: *Of Satire*
(1693)

3 An injury is much sooner
forgotten than an insult.
Lord Chesterfield 1694–1773: *Letters
to his Son* (1774) 9 October 1746

4 To-day I pronounced a word
which should never come out of
a lady's lips it was that I called
John a Impudent Bitch.
Marjory Fleming 1803–11: *Journals,
Letters and Verses* (1934)

5 The words she spoke of Mrs.
Harris, lambs could not forgive
. . . nor worms forget.
Charles Dickens 1812–70: *Martin
Chuzzlewit* (1844)

6 He has to learn that petulance is
not sarcasm, and that insolence is
not invective.
of Sir Charles Wood
Benjamin Disraeli 1804–81: speech,
House of Commons, 16 December
1852

7 When you call me that, *smile*!
*"that" referring to "you son-of-a-
bitch"*
Owen Wister 1860–1938: *The
Virginian* (1902)

8 Curse the blasted, jelly-boned
swines, the slimy, the belly-
wriggling invertebrates, the
miserable sodding rotters, the
flaming sods, the snivelling,
dribbling, dithering, palsied, pulse-
less lot that make up England
today. They've got white of egg
in their veins, and their spunk is
that watery it's a marvel they can
breed. They *can* nothing but frog-
spawn—the gibberers! God, how I
hate them!
D. H. Lawrence 1885–1930: letter to
Edward Garnett, 3 July 1912

9 Silence is the most perfect
expression of scorn.
George Bernard Shaw 1856–1950:
Back to Methuselah (1921)

10 JUDGE: You are extremely
offensive, young man.
SMITH: As a matter of fact, we
both are, and the only difference
between us is that I am trying to
be, and you can't help it.
F. E. Smith 1872–1930: 2nd Earl of
Birkenhead *Earl of Birkenhead*
(1933)

11 Okie use' ta mean you was from
Oklahoma. Now it means you're a
dirty son-of-a-bitch. Okie means
you're scum. Don't mean nothing
itself, it's the way they say it.
John Steinbeck 1902–68: *The Grapes
of Wrath* (1939)

12 The *t* is silent, as in *Harlow*.
*to Jean Harlow, who had been
mispronouncing "Margot"*
Margot Asquith 1864–1945: T. S.
Matthews *Great Tom* (1973)

13 BESSIE BRADDOCK: Winston, you're
drunk.
CHURCHILL: Bessie, you're ugly.
But tomorrow I shall be sober.
Winston Churchill 1874–1965: J. L.
Lane (ed.) *Sayings of Churchill*
(1992)

14 Like being savaged by a dead
sheep.
on being criticized by Geoffrey Howe
Denis Healey 1917– : speech in the
House of Commons, 14 June 1978

15 I think I detect sarcasm. I can't
be doing with sarcasm. You know
what they say? Sarcasm is the
greatest weapon of the smallest
mind.
Alan Ayckbourn 1939– : *Woman in
Mind* (1986)

Intelligence and Intellectuals

1 Whoever in discussion adduces
authority uses not intellect but
rather memory.
Leonardo da Vinci 1452–1519:
Edward McCurdy (ed.) *Leonardo da
Vinci's Notebooks* (1906)

2 The height of cleverness is to be
able to conceal it.
Duc de la Rochefoucauld 1613–80:
Maximes (1678)

3 You beat your pate, and fancy
     wit will come:
Knock as you please, there's
     nobody at home.
Alexander Pope 1688–1744:
"Epigram: You beat your pate"
(1732)

4 Sir, I have found you an
argument; but I am not obliged
to find you an understanding.
Samuel Johnson 1709–84: James
Boswell *Life of Samuel Johnson*
(1791) June 1784

5 Our meddling intellect
Mis-shapes the beauteous forms of
     things:—
We murder to dissect.
William Wordsworth 1770–1850:
"The Tables Turned" (1798)

6 "Excellent," I cried. "Elementary,"
said he.
Arthur Conan Doyle 1859–1930: *The
Memoirs of Sherlock Holmes* (1894);
"Elementary, my dear Watson" is
not found in any book by Conan
Doyle, although a review of the film
The Return of Sherlock Holmes in
New York Times 19 October 1929,
states: "In the final scene Dr.
Watson is there with his 'Amazing,
Holmes,' and Holmes comes forth
with his 'Elementary, my dear
Watson, elementary'"

7 He [Hercule Poirot] tapped his
forehead. "These little grey cells.
It is 'up to them.'"

Agatha Christie 1890–1976: *The Mysterious Affair at Styles* (1920)

8 No one in this world, so far as I know—and I have searched the records for years, and employed agents to help me—has ever lost money by underestimating the intelligence of the great masses of the plain people.
H. L. Mencken 1880–1956: in *Chicago Tribune* 19 September 1926

9 *La trahison des clercs.*
The treachery of the intellectuals.
Julien Benda 1867–1956: title of book (1927)

10 "Hullo! friend," I call out, "Won't you lend us a hand?" "I am an intellectual and don't drag wood about," came the answer. "You're lucky," I reply. "I too wanted to become an intellectual, but I didn't succeed."
Albert Schweitzer 1875–1965: *Mitteilungen aus Lambarene* (1928)

11 As a human being, one has been endowed with just enough intelligence to be able to see clearly how utterly inadequate that intelligence is when confronted with what exists.
Albert Einstein 1879–1955: letter to Queen Elisabeth of Belgium, 19 September 1932

12 What is a highbrow? He is a man who has found something more interesting than women.
Edgar Wallace 1875–1932: in *New York Times* 24 January 1932

13 The test of a first-rate intelligence is the ability to hold two opposed ideas in the mind at the same time, and still retain the ability to function.
F. Scott Fitzgerald 1896–1940: in *Esquire* February 1936, "The Crack-Up"

14 Intelligence is quickness to apprehend as distinct from ability, which is capacity to act wisely on the thing apprehended.
Alfred North Whitehead 1861–1947: *Dialogues* (1954) 15 December 1939

15 Eggheads, unite! You have nothing to lose but your yolks!
Adlai Stevenson 1900–65: *remark, presidential campaign* (1952)

16 An intellectual is someone whose mind watches itself.
Albert Camus 1913–60: *Carnets, 1935–42* (1962)

17 It takes little talent to see clearly what lies under one's nose, a good deal of it to know in which direction to point that organ.
W. H. Auden 1907–73: *Dyer's Hand* (1963) "Writing"

18 A spirit of national masochism prevails, encouraged by an effete corps of impudent snobs who characterize themselves as Americans.
Spiro Agnew 1918– : *speech, Republican fundraiser* (19 October 1969)

19 I know I've got a degree. Why does that mean I have to spend my life with intellectuals? I've got a life-saving certificate but I don't spend my evenings diving for a rubber brick with my pyjamas on.
Victoria Wood 1953– : *Mens Sana in Thingummy Doodah* (1990)

International Relations
see also **Countries and Peoples, Diplomacy, Government, Politics**

1 *Il n'y a plus de Pyrénées.* The Pyrenees are no more.
on the accession of his grandson to the throne of Spain, 1700
Louis XIV 1638–1715: attributed to Louis by Voltaire in *Siècle de Louis XIV* (1753); but to the Spanish Ambassador to France in the

Mercure Galant (Paris) November 1700

2 It was easier to conquer it [the East] than to know what to do with it.
Horace Walpole 1717–97: letter to Horace Mann, 27 March 1772

3 Peace, commerce, and honest friendship with all nations— entangling alliances with none.
Thomas Jefferson 1743–1826: inaugural address, 4th of March 1801

4 If you wish to avoid foreign collision, you had better abandon the ocean.
Henry Clay 1777–1852: speech in the House of Representatives, 22 January 1812

5 In matters of commerce the fault of the Dutch
Is offering too little and asking too much.
The French are with equal advantage content,
So we clap on Dutch bottoms just twenty per cent.
George Canning 1770–1827: dispatch, in cipher, to the English ambassador at the Hague, 31 January 1826

6 The Continent will [not] suffer England to be the workshop of the world.
Benjamin Disraeli 1804–81: speech, House of Commons, 15 March 1838

7 Italy is a geographical expression.
discussing the Italian question with Palmerston in 1847
Prince Metternich 1773–1859: *Mémoires, Documents, etc. de Metternich publiés par son fils* (1883)

8 We have no eternal allies and we have no perpetual enemies. Our interests are eternal and perpetual, and those interests it is our duty to follow.

Lord Palmerston 1784–1865: speech, House of Commons, 1 March 1848

9 These wretched colonies will all be independent, too, in a few years, and are a millstone round our necks.
Benjamin Disraeli 1804–81: letter to Lord Malmesbury, 13 August 1852

10 In order that he might rob a neighbour whom he had promised to defend, black men fought on the coast of Coromandel and red men scalped each other by the Great Lakes of North America.
Lord Macaulay 1800–59: *Biographical Essays* (1857) "Frederic the Great"

11 Lord Palmerston, with characteristic levity had once said that only three men in Europe had ever understood [the Schleswig-Holstein question], and of these the Prince Consort was dead, a Danish statesman (unnamed) was in an asylum, and he himself had forgotten it.
Lord Palmerston 1784–1865: R. W. Seton-Watson *Britain in Europe 1789–1914* (1937)

12 Nations touch at their summits.
Walter Bagehot 1826–77: *The English Constitution* (1867)

13 This policy cannot succeed through speeches, and shooting-matches, and songs; it can only be carried out through blood and iron.
Otto von Bismarck 1815–98: speech in the Prussian House of Deputies, 28 January 1886

14 *of British foreign policy:*
A gigantic system of outdoor relief for the aristocracy of Great Britain.
John Bright 1811–89: speech at Birmingham, 29 October 1858

15 In a word, we desire to throw no
   one into the shade [in East Asia],
   but we also demand our own
   place in the sun.
   Prince Bernhard von Bülow 1849–
   1929: speech, Reichstag, 6 December
   1897

16 The day of small nations has long
   passed away. The day of Empires
   has come.
   Joseph Chamberlain 1836–1914:
   speech at Birmingham, 12 May 1904

17 Just for a word "neutrality"—a
   word which in wartime has so
   often been disregarded—just for a
   scrap of paper, Great Britain is
   going to make war on a kindred
   nation who desires nothing better
   than to be friends with her.
   Theobald von Bethmann Hollweg
   1856–1921: summary of a report by
   Sir E. Goschen to Sir Edward Grey;
   *The Diary of Edward Goschen 1900–
   1914* (1980) discusses the
   contentious origins of this statement

18 Armed neutrality is ineffectual
   enough at best.
   Woodrow Wilson 1856–1924: speech
   to Congress, 2 April 1917

19 In the field of world policy I
   would dedicate this Nation to the
   policy of the good neighbor.
   Franklin D. Roosevelt 1882–1945:
   inaugural address, 4 March 1933

20 Since the day of the air, the old
   frontiers are gone. When you
   think of the defence of England
   you no longer think of the chalk
   cliffs of Dover; you think of the
   Rhine. That is where our frontier
   lies.
   Stanley Baldwin 1867–1947: speech,
   House of Commons, 30 July 1934

21 We have learned that we cannot
   live alone, at peace; that our own
   well-being is dependent on the
   well-being of other nations, far
   away. We have learned that we

must live as men, and not as
ostriches, nor as dogs in the
manger. We have learned to be
citizens of the world, members of
the human community.
Franklin D. Roosevelt 1882–1945:
Fourth Inaugural Address (20 January
1945)

22 My [foreign] policy is to be able
   to take a ticket at Victoria Station
   and go anywhere I damn well
   please.
   Ernest Bevin 1881–1951: in *Spectator*
   (UK) 20 April 1951

23 [Winston Churchill] does not talk
   the language of the 20th century
   but that of the 18th. He is still
   fighting Blenheim all over again.
   His only answer to a difficult
   situation is send a gun-boat.
   Aneurin Bevan 1897–1960: speech at
   Labour Party Conference,
   Scarborough, 2 October 1951

24 If you carry this resolution you
   will send Britain's Foreign
   Secretary naked into the
   conference chamber.
   *on a motion proposing unilateral
   nuclear disarmament by the UK*
   Aneurin Bevan 1897–1960: speech at
   Labour Party Conference in Brighton,
   3 October 1957

25 *Ich bin ein Berliner.*
   I am a Berliner.
   *expressing US commitment to the
   support and defense of West Berlin
   (it was later the cause of some
   hilarity, as* ein Berliner *is the
   German name for a doughnut)*
   John F. Kennedy 1917–63: speech in
   West Berlin, 26 June 1963

26 We hope that the world will not
   narrow into a neighborhood
   before it has broadened into a
   brotherhood.
   Lyndon Baines Johnson 1908–73:
   speech at the lighting of the
   Nation's Christmas Tree, 22
   December 1963

27 The great nations have always
acted like gangsters, and the
small nations like prostitutes.
Stanley Kubrick 1928– : in
Guardian (UK) 5 June 1963

28 They're Germans. Don't mention
the war.
John Cleese 1939– and **Connie Booth**:
Fawlty Towers "The Germans" (BBC
TV program, 1975)

29 Whatever it is that the
government does, sensible
Americans would prefer that the
government does it to somebody
else. This is the idea behind
foreign policy.
P. J. O'Rourke 1947– : *Parliament
of Whores* (1991)

30 Europe is in danger of plunging
into a cold peace.
*at the summit meeting of the
Conference on Security and Co-
operation in Europe, December 1994*
Boris Yeltsin 1931– : in *Newsweek*
19 December 1994

Inventions and Discoveries
see also **Science, Technology**

1 Thus were they stained with their
own works: and went a whoring
with their own inventions.
Bible: Psalm 106

2 God hath made man upright; but
they have sought out many
inventions.
Bible: Ecclesiastes

3 *Eureka!* I've got it!
Archimedes *c.* 287–212 BC: Vitruvius
Pollio *De Architectura*

4 It is well to observe the force and
virtue and consequence of
discoveries, and these are to be
seen nowhere more conspicuously
than in those three which were
unknown to the ancients, and of
which the origins, though recent,

are obscure and inglorious;
namely, printing, gunpowder, and
the mariner's needle [the
compass]. For these three have
changed the whole face and state
of things throughout the world.
Francis Bacon 1561–1626: *Novum
Organum* (1620); cf. **Culture 5**

5 As the births of living creatures
at first are ill-shapen, so are all
innovations, which are the births
of time.
Francis Bacon 1561–1626: *Essays*
(1625) "Of Innovations"

6 I don't know what I may seem to
the world, but as to myself, I
seem to have been only like a boy
playing on the sea-shore and
diverting myself in now and then
finding a smoother pebble or a
prettier shell than ordinary,
whilst the great ocean of truth
lay all undiscovered before me.
Isaac Newton 1642–1727: Joseph
Spence *Anecdotes* (ed. J. Osborn,
1966)

7 Thus first necessity invented
stools,
Convenience next suggested
elbow-chairs,
And luxury the accomplished sofa
last.
William Cowper 1731–1800: *The Task*
(1785) "The Sofa"

8 What is the use of a new-born
child?
*when asked what was the use of a
new invention*
Benjamin Franklin 1706–90: J. Parton
Life and Times of Benjamin Franklin
(1864)

9 Then felt I like some watcher of
the skies
When a new planet swims into
his ken;
Or like stout Cortez when with
eagle eyes
He stared at the Pacific—and all
his men

Looked at each other with a wild
    surmise—
Silent, upon a peak in Darien.
John Keats 1795–1821: "On First
Looking into Chapman's Homer"
(1817)

10 Nothing is more contrary to the
organization of the mind, of the
memory, and of the imagination
. . . It's just tormenting the people
with trivia!!!
*on the introduction of the metric
system*
Napoleon I 1769–1821: *Mémoires . . .
écrits à Ste-Hélène* (1823–5)

11 The discovery of a new dish does
more for human happiness than
the discovery of a star.
Anthelme Brillat-Savarin 1755–1826:
Physiologie du Goût (1826)

12 Why sir, there is every possibility
that you will soon be able to tax
it!
*to Gladstone, when asked about the
usefulness of electricity*
Michael Faraday 1791–1867: W. E. H.
Lecky *Democracy and Liberty* (1899
ed.)

13 What one man can invent
another can discover.
Arthur Conan Doyle 1859–1930: *The
Return of Sherlock Holmes* (1905)

14 When man wanted to make a
machine that would walk he
created the wheel, which does not
resemble a leg.
Guillaume Apollinaire 1880–1918: *Les
Mamelles de Tirésias* (1918)

15 Yes, wonderful things.
*when asked what he could see on
first looking into the tomb of
Tutankhamun, 26 November 1922;
his notebook records the words as
"Yes, it is wonderful"*
Howard Carter 1874–1939: H. V. F.
Winstone *Howard Carter and the
discovery of the tomb of
Tutankhamun* (1993)

16 Name the greatest of all the
inventors. Accident.
Mark Twain 1835–1910: *Notebook*
(1935)

17 The unleashed power of the atom
has changed everything save our
modes of thinking and we thus
drift toward unparalleled
catastrophe.
Albert Einstein 1879–1955: telegram
to prominent Americans, 24 May
1946, in *New York Times* 25 May
1946

18 Whatever Nature has in store for
mankind, unpleasant as it may
be, men must accept, for
ignorance is never better than
knowledge.
Enrico Fermi 1901–54: Laura Fermi
Atoms in the Family (1955)

19 Discovery consists of seeing what
everybody has seen and thinking
what nobody has thought.
Albert von Szent-Györgyi 1893–1986:
Irving Good (ed.) *The Scientist
Speculates* (1962)

Jealousy
see **Envy and Jealousy**

Journalism
see **News and Journalism**

Justice and Injustice
see also **The Law and Lawyers**

1 Life for life,
Eye for eye, tooth for tooth.
Bible: Exodus

2 What I say is that "just" or
"right" means nothing but what
is in the interest of the stronger
party.
spoken by Thrasymachus
Plato 429–347 BC: *The Republic*

3 Judge not, that ye be not judged.
Bible: St. Matthew

4 Justice is the constant and perpetual wish to render to every one his due.
Justinian AD 483–565: *Institutes*

5 To no man will we sell, or deny, or delay, right or justice.
Magna Carta 1215: clause 40

6 If the parties will at my hands call for justice, then, all were it my father stood on the one side, and the Devil on the other, his cause being good, the Devil should have right.
Thomas More 1478–1535: William Roper *Life of Sir Thomas More*

7 *Fiat justitia et pereat mundus.* Let justice be done, though the world perish.
Ferdinand I 1503–64: motto; Johannes Manlius *Locorum Communium Collectanea* (1563)

8 The quality of mercy is not strained,
It droppeth as the gentle rain from heaven
Upon the place beneath: it is twice blessed;
It blesseth him that gives and him that takes.
William Shakespeare 1564–1616: *The Merchant of Venice* (1596–8)

9 Use every man after his desert, and who should 'scape whipping?
William Shakespeare 1564–1616: *Hamlet* (1601)

10 You manifestly wrong even the poorest ploughman, if you demand not his free consent.
Charles I 1600–49: The King's Reasons for declining the jurisdiction of the High Court of Justice, 21 January 1649

11 I'm armed with more than complete steel—The justice of my quarrel.
Anonymous: *Lust's Dominion* (1657);

attributed to Marlowe, though of doubtful authorship

12 Here they hang a man first, and try him afterwards.
Molière 1622–73: *Monsieur de Pourceaugnac* (1670)

13 For Justice, though she's painted blind,
Is to the weaker side inclined.
Samuel Butler 1612–80: *Hudibras* pt. 3 (1680)

14 Thwackum was for doing justice, and leaving mercy to heaven.
Henry Fielding 1707–54: *Tom Jones* (1749)

15 A lawyer has no business with the justice or injustice of the cause which he undertakes, unless his client asks his opinion, and then he is bound to give it honestly. The justice or injustice of the cause is to be decided by the judge.
Samuel Johnson 1709–84: James Boswell *Journal of a Tour to the Hebrides* (1785) 15 August 1773

16 Consider what you think justice requires, and decide accordingly. But never give your reasons; for your judgement will probably be right, but your reasons will certainly be wrong.
advice to a newly appointed colonial governor ignorant in the law
William Murray, Lord Mansfield 1705–93: Lord Campbell *The Lives of the Chief Justices of England* (1849)

17 Justice is truth in action.
Benjamin Disraeli 1804–81: speech, House of Commons, 11 February 1851

18 When I hear of an "equity" in a case like this, I am reminded of a blind man in a dark room—looking for a black hat—which isn't there.
Lord Bowen 1835–94: John Alderson Foote *Pie-Powder* (1911)

19 *J'accuse.*
I accuse.
on the Dreyfus affair
Émile Zola 1840–1902: title of an
open letter to the President of the
French Republic in *L'Aurore* 13
January 1898

20 A man who is good enough to
shed his blood for the country is
good enough to be given a
square deal afterwards. More
than that no man is entitled to,
and less than that no man shall
have.
Theodore Roosevelt 1858–1919:
speech at the Lincoln Monument,
Springfield, Illinois, 4 June 1903

21 In England, justice is open to all—
like the Ritz Hotel.
James Mathew 1830–1908: R. E.
Megarry *Miscellany-at-Law* (1955)

22 Injustice is relatively easy to bear;
what stings is justice.
H. L. Mencken 1880–1956:
Prejudices, Third Series (1922)

23 A long line of cases shows that it
is not merely of some
importance, but is of
fundamental importance that
justice should not only be done,
but should manifestly and
undoubtedly be seen to be done.
Gordon Hewart 1870–1943: Rex v.
Sussex Justices, 9 November 1923

24 You may object that it is not a
trial at all; you are quite right,
for it is only a trial if I recognize
it as such.
Franz Kafka 1883–1924: *The Trial*
(1925)

25 Injustice anywhere is a threat to
justice everywhere.
Martin Luther King, Jr. 1929–68:
letter from Birmingham Jail,
Alabama, 16 April 1963

26 If this is justice, I am a banana.
on the libel damages awarded
against Private Eye to Sonia Sutcliffe
Ian Hislop 1960–   : comment, 24
May 1989

Kissing

1 I kissed thee ere I killed thee, no
way but this,
Killing myself to die upon a kiss.
William Shakespeare 1564–1616:
Othello (1602–4)

2 Mr. Grenville squeezed me by the
hand again, kissed the ladies,
and withdrew. He kissed likewise
the maid in the kitchen, and
seemed upon the whole a most
loving, kissing, kind-hearted
gentleman.
William Cowper 1731–1800: letter to
the Revd. John Newton, 29 March
1784

3 O Love, O fire! once he drew
With one long kiss my whole soul
through
My lips, as sunlight drinketh dew.
Alfred, Lord Tennyson 1809–92:
"Fatima" (1832)

4 What of soul was left, I wonder,
when the kissing had to stop?
Robert Browning 1812–89: "A
Toccata of Galuppi's" (1855)

5 I wonder who's kissing her now.
Frank Adams and **Will M. Hough**:
title of song (1909)

6 Where do the noses go? I always
wondered where the noses would
go.
Ernest Hemingway 1899–1961: *For
Whom the Bell Tolls* (1940)

7 When women kiss it always
reminds one of prize-fighters
shaking hands.
H. L. Mencken 1880–1956:
Chrestomathy (1949)

8 My big trouble is that I always
think whoever I'm necking with

is a pretty intelligent person.
J. D. Salinger 1919– : *The Catcher in the Rye* (1951)

9 It's like kissing Hitler.
when asked what it was like to kiss Marilyn Monroe
Tony Curtis 1925– : *A. Hunter Tony Curtis* (1985)

10 I wasn't kissing her, I was just whispering in her mouth.
on being discovered by his wife with a chorus girl
Chico Marx 1891–1961: Groucho Marx and Richard J. Anobile *Marx Brothers Scrapbook* (1973)

Knowledge

1 The fox knows many things—the hedgehog one *big* one.
Archilochus 7th century BC: E. Diehl (ed.) *Anthologia Lyrica Graeca* (3rd ed., 1949–52) cf. **Character 24**

2 He that increaseth knowledge increaseth sorrow.
Bible: Ecclesiastes

3 The price of wisdom is above rubies.
Bible: Job

4 I know nothing except the fact of my ignorance.
Socrates 469–399 BC: Diogenes Laertius *Lives of the Philosophers*

5 Paul, thou art beside thyself; much learning doth make thee mad.
Bible: Acts of the Apostles

6 For now we see through a glass, darkly; but then face to face: now I know in part; but then shall I know even as also I am known.
Bible: I Corinthians

7 Everyman, I will go with thee, and be thy guide,

In thy most need to go by thy side.
spoken by "Knowledge"
Anonymous: *Everyman* (c. 1509–19)

8 *Que sais-je?*
What do I know?
on the position of the skeptic
Montaigne 1533–92: *Essais* (1580)

9 Knowledge itself is power.
Francis Bacon 1561–1626: *Meditationes Sacrae* (1597) "Of Heresies"

10 What song the Syrens sang, or what name Achilles assumed when he hid himself among women, though puzzling questions, are not beyond all conjecture.
Thomas Browne 1605–82: *Hydriotaphia* (Urn Burial, 1658)

11 We have first raised a dust and then complain we cannot see.
George Berkeley 1685–1753: *A Treatise Concerning the Principles of Human Knowledge* (1710)

12 A little learning is a dangerous thing;
Drink deep, or taste not the Pierian spring.
Alexander Pope 1688–1744: *An Essay on Criticism* (1711)

13 There was as great a difference between them as between a man who knew how a watch was made, and a man who could tell the hour by looking on the dial-plate.
Samuel Johnson 1709–84: James Boswell *Life of Samuel Johnson* (1791) Spring 1768

14 And still they gazed, and still the wonder grew,
That one small head could carry all he knew.
Oliver Goldsmith 1730–74: *The Deserted Village* (1770)

15 Knowledge may give weight, but accomplishments give lustre, and many more people see than weigh.
Lord Chesterfield 1694–1773: *Maxims* (1774)

16 Knowledge is of two kinds. We know a subject ourselves, or we know where we can find information upon it.
Samuel Johnson 1709–84: James Boswell *Life of Samuel Johnson* (1791) 18 April 1775

17 Knowledge dwells
In heads replete with thoughts of other men;
Wisdom in minds attentive to their own.
William Cowper 1731–1800: *The Task* (1785) "The Winter Walk at Noon"

18 Does the eagle know what is in the pit?
Or wilt thou go ask the mole:
Can wisdom be put in a silver rod?
Or love in a golden bowl?
William Blake 1757–1827: *The Book of Thel* (1789) "Thel's Motto"

19 Do not all charms fly
At the mere touch of cold philosophy?
There was an awful rainbow once in heaven:
We know her woof, her texture; she is given
In the dull catalogue of common things.
Philosophy will clip an Angel's wings.
John Keats 1795–1821: "Lamia" (1820)

20 Knowledge advances by steps, and not by leaps.
Lord Macaulay 1800–59: T. F. Ellis (ed.) *Miscellaneous Writings of Lord Macaulay* (1860) "History" (1828)

21 Knowledge comes, but wisdom lingers.

22 You will find it a very good practice always to verify your references, sir!
Martin Joseph Routh 1755–1854: John William Burgon *Lives of Twelve Good Men* (1888 ed.)

23 Small sciences are the labours of our manhood: but the round universe is the plaything of the boy.
Walter Bagehot 1826–77: in *National Review* (UK) January 1856 "Edward Gibbon"

24 It is better to know nothing than to know what ain't so.
Josh Billings 1818–85: *Proverb* (1874)

25 No lesson seems to be so deeply inculcated by the experience of life as that you never should trust experts. If you believe the doctors, nothing is wholesome: if you believe the theologians, nothing is innocent: if you believe the soldiers, nothing is safe. They all require to have their strong wine diluted by a very large admixture of insipid common sense.
Lord Salisbury 1830–1903: letter to Lord Lytton, 15 June 1877

26 First come I; my name is Jowett. There's no knowledge but I know it.
I am Master of this college:
What I don't know isn't knowledge.
H. C. Beeching 1859–1919: *The Masque of Balliol*; composed by and current among members of Balliol College in the late 1870s

27 I was gratified to be able to answer promptly, and I did. I said I didn't know.
Mark Twain 1835–1910: *Life on the Mississippi* (1883)

28 If a little knowledge is dangerous,
where is the man who has so
much as to be out of danger?
T. H. Huxley 1825–95: *Collected
Essays* vol. 3 (1895) "On Elementary
Instruction in Physiology" (written
1877)

29 The motto of all the mongoose
family is, "Run and find out."
Rudyard Kipling 1865–1936: *The
Jungle Book* (1897)

30 "Itzig, where are you riding to?"
"Don't ask me, ask the horse."
Sigmund Freud 1856–1939: letter to
Wilhelm Fliess, 7 July 1898

31 I keep six honest serving-men
(They taught me all I knew);
Their names are What and Why
and When
And How and Where and Who.
Rudyard Kipling 1865–1936: *Just So
Stories* (1902) "The Elephant's Child"

32 There is no such thing on earth
as an uninteresting subject; the
only thing that can exist is an
uninterested person.
G. K. Chesterton 1874–1936: *Heretics*
(1905)

33 For lust of knowing what should
not be known,
We take the Golden Road to
Samarkand.
James Elroy Flecker 1884–1915: *The
Golden Journey to Samarkand* (1913)

34 Owl hasn't exactly got Brain, but
he Knows Things.
A. A. Milne 1882–1956: *Winnie-the-
Pooh* (1926)

35 Pedantry is the dotage of
knowledge.
Holbrook Jackson 1874–1948:
Anatomy of Bibliomania (1930)

36 An expert is one who knows
more and more about less and
less.

Nicholas Murray Butler 1862–1947:
commencement address at Columbia
University; attributed

37 An expert is someone who knows
some of the worst mistakes that
can be made in his subject and
who manages to avoid them.
Werner Heisenberg 1901–76: *Der
Teil und das Ganze* (1969)

38 They say that Mitterrand has 100
lovers—one with AIDS, but he
doesn't know which one; Bush
has 100 bodyguards—one a
terrorist, but he doesn't know
which one; Gorbachev has 100
economic advisers—one is smart,
but he doesn't know which one.
Mikhail S. Gorbachev 1931– : *New
York Times* (25 February 1988)

Language
see also **Cursing and Swearing,
Meaning, Words**

1 A word fitly spoken is like apples
of gold in pictures of silver.
Bible: Proverbs

2 Grammer, the ground of al.
William Langland c. 1330–c. 1400:
The Vision of Piers Plowman

3 Syllables govern the world.
John Selden 1584–1654: *Table Talk*
(1689)

4 Good heavens! For more than
forty years I have been speaking
prose without knowing it.
Molière 1622–73: *Le Bourgeois
Gentilhomme* (1671)

5 I have laboured to refine our
language to grammatical purity,
and to clear it from colloquial
barbarisms, licentious idioms, and
irregular combinations.
Samuel Johnson 1709–84: in *The
Rambler* (UK) 14 March 1752

6 The true use of speech is not so
much to express our wants as to
conceal them.

Oliver Goldsmith 1730–74: in *The Bee* (UK) 20 October 1759 "On the Use of Language"

7 Language is the dress of thought.
Samuel Johnson 1709–84: *Lives of the English Poets* (1779–81)

8 In language, the ignorant have prescribed laws to the learned.
Richard Duppa 1770–1831: *Maxims* (1830)

9 Language is fossil poetry.
Ralph Waldo Emerson 1803–82: *Essays. Second Series* (1844) "The Poet"

10 It is hard for a woman to define her feelings in language which is chiefly made by men to express theirs.
Thomas Hardy 1840–1928: *Far from the Madding Crowd* (1874)

11 I will not go down to posterity talking bad grammar.
while correcting proofs of his last Parliamentary speech, 31 March 1881
Benjamin Disraeli 1804–81: Robert Blake *Disraeli* (1966)

12 Her occasional pretty and picturesque use of dialect words—those terrible marks of the beast to the truly genteel.
Thomas Hardy 1840–1928: *The Mayor of Casterbridge* (1886)

13 A definition is the enclosing a wilderness of idea within a wall of words.
Samuel Butler 1835–1902: *Notebooks* (1912)

14 One of our defects as a nation is a tendency to use what have been called "weasel words." When a weasel sucks eggs the meat is sucked out of the egg. If you use a "weasel word" after another, there is nothing left of the other.
Theodore Roosevelt 1858–1919: speech in St. Louis, 31 May 1916

15 The limits of my language mean the limits of my world.
Ludwig Wittgenstein 1889–1951: *Tractatus Logico-Philosophicus* (1922)

16 One picture is worth ten thousand words.
Frederick R. Barnard: in *Printers' Ink* 10 March 1927

17 A phrase is born into the world both good and bad at the same time. The secret lies in a slight, an almost invisible twist. The lever should rest in your hand, getting warm, and you can only turn it once, not twice.
Isaac Babel 1894–c. 1939: *Guy de Maupassant* (1932)

18 The subjunctive mood is in its death throes, and the best thing to do is to put it out of its misery as soon as possible.
W. Somerset Maugham 1874–1965: *A Writer's Notebook* (1949) written in 1941

19 Would you convey my compliments to the purist who reads your proofs and tell him or her that I write in a sort of broken-down patois which is something like the way a Swiss waiter talks, and that when I split an infinitive, God damn it, I split it so it will stay split.
Raymond Chandler 1888–1959: letter to Edward Weeks, 18 January 1947

20 This is the sort of English up with which I will not put.
Winston Churchill 1874–1965: Ernest Gowers *Plain Words* (1948)

21 Where in this small-talking world can I find
A longitude with no platitude?
Christopher Fry 1907– : *The Lady's not for Burning* (1949)

22 Colorless green ideas sleep
furiously.
*illustrating that grammatical
structure is independent of meaning*
Noam Chomsky 1928– : *Syntactic
Structures* (1957)

23 Slang is a language that rolls up
its sleeves, spits on its hands and
goes to work.
Carl Sandburg 1878–1967: in *New
York Times* 13 February 1959

24 Save the gerund and screw the
whale.
Tom Stoppard 1937– : *The Real
Thing* (1988 rev. ed.)

25 Every sentence he manages to
utter scatters its component parts
like pond water from a verb
chasing its own tail.
of George Bush
Clive James 1939– : *The Dreaming
Swimmer* (1992)

Languages
see also **Translation**

1 And Frenssh she spak ful faire
and fetisly,
After the scole of Stratford atte
Bowe,
For Frenssh of Parys was to hire
unknowe.
Geoffrey Chaucer c. 1343–1400: *The
Canterbury Tales* "The General
Prologue"

2 To God I speak Spanish, to
women Italian, to men French,
and to my horse—German.
Charles V 1500–58: attributed; Lord
Chesterfield *Letters to his Son* (1774)

3 It is a thing plainly repugnant to
the Word of God, and the custom
of the Primitive Church, to have
publick Prayer in the Church, or
to minister the Sacraments in a
tongue not understood of the
people.

The Book of Common Prayer 1662:
Articles of Religion (1562)

4 So now they have made our
English tongue a gallimaufry or
hodgepodge of all other speeches.
Edmund Spenser c. 1552–99: *The
Shepherd's Calendar* (1579)

5 Poets that lasting marble seek
Must carve in Latin or in Greek.
Edmund Waller 1606–87: "Of English
Verse" (1645)

6 I am not like a lady at the court
of Versailles, who said: "What a
dreadful pity that the bother at
the tower of Babel should have
got language all mixed up; but
for that, everyone would always
have spoken French."
Voltaire 1694–1778: letter to
Catherine the Great, 26 May 1767

7 I am always sorry when any
language is lost, because
languages are the pedigree of
nations.
Samuel Johnson 1709–84: James
Boswell *Journal of a Tour to the
Hebrides* (1785) 18 September 1773

8 My English text is chaste, and all
licentious passages are left in the
obscurity of a learned language.
*parodied as "decent obscurity" in
the* Anti-Jacobin, *1797–8*
Edward Gibbon 1737–94: *Memoirs of
My Life* (1796)

9 The great breeding people had
gone out and multiplied; colonies
in every clime attest our success;
French is the *patois* of Europe;
English is the language of the
world.
Walter Bagehot 1826–77: in *National
Review* (UK) January 1856 "Edward
Gibbon"

10 I once heard a Californian student
in Heidelberg say, in one of his
calmest moods, that he would

rather decline two drinks than one German adjective.
Mark Twain 1835–1910: *A Tramp Abroad* (1880)

11 Whenever the literary German dives into a sentence, that is the last you are going to see of him till he emerges on the other side of his Atlantic with his verb in his mouth.
Mark Twain 1835–1910: *A Connecticut Yankee in King Arthur's Court* (1889)

12 Written English is now inert and inorganic: not stem and leaf and flower, not even trim and well-joined masonry, but a daub of untempered mortar.
A. E. Housman 1859–1936: in *Cambridge Review* (UK) 1917

13 England and America are two countries divided by a common language.
George Bernard Shaw 1856–1950: attributed in this and other forms, but not found in Shaw's published writings

14 Waiting for the German verb is surely the ultimate thrill.
Flann O'Brien 1911–66: *The Hair of the Dogma* (1977)

15 We are walking lexicons. In a single sentence of idle chatter we preserve Latin, Anglo-Saxon, Norse; we carry a museum inside our heads, each day we commemorate peoples of whom we have never heard.
Penelope Lively 1933– : *Moon Tiger* (1987)

Last Words

1 Crito, we owe a cock to Aesculapius; please pay it and don't forget it.
Socrates 469–399 BC: Plato *Phaedo*

2 *Ave Caesar, morituri te salutant.*
Hail Caesar, those who are about to die salute you.
gladiators saluting the Roman Emperor
Anonymous: Suetonius *Lives of the Caesars* "Claudius"

3 *O sancta simplicitas!*
O holy simplicity!
at the stake, seeing an aged peasant bringing a bundle of twigs to throw on the pile
John Huss *c.* 1372–1415: J. W. Zincgreff and J. L. Weidner *Apophthegmata* (1653)

4 I pray you, master Lieutenant, see me safe up, and my coming down let me shift for my self.
on mounting the scaffold
Thomas More 1478–1535: William Roper *Life of Sir Thomas More*

5 After his head was upon the block, [he] lift it up again, and gently drew his beard aside, and said, *This hath not offended the king.*
Thomas More 1478–1535: Francis Bacon *Apophthegms New and Old* (1625)

6 I am going to seek a great perhaps . . . Bring down the curtain, the farce is played out.
François Rabelais *c.* 1494–*c.* 1553: attributed, though none of his contemporaries authenticated the remarks, which have become part of the "Rabelaisian legend"; Jean Fleury *Rabelais et ses oeuvres* (1877)

7 Be of good comfort Master Ridley, and play the man. We shall this day light such a candle by God's grace in England, as (I trust) shall never be put out.
prior to being burned for heresy, 16 October 1555
Hugh Latimer *c.* 1485–1555: John Foxe *Actes and Monuments* (1570 ed.)

8 All my possessions for a moment of time.
Elizabeth I 1533–1603: attributed, but almost certainly apocryphal

9 For my name and memory, I leave it to men's charitable speeches, and to foreign nations, and the next ages.
Francis Bacon 1561–1626: will, 19 December 1625

10 My design is to make what haste I can to be gone.
Oliver Cromwell 1599–1658: John Morley *Oliver Cromwell* (1900)

11 I am about to take my last voyage, a great leap in the dark.
Thomas Hobbes 1588–1679: John Watkins *Anecdotes of Men of Learning* (1808)

12 Let not poor Nelly starve.
of Nell Gwyn
Charles II 1630–85: Bishop Gilbert Burnet *History of My Own Time* (1724)

13 He had been, he said, an unconscionable time dying; but he hoped that they would excuse it.
Charles II 1630–85: Lord Macaulay *History of England* (1849)

14 This is no time for making new enemies.
on being asked to renounce the Devil on his deathbed
Voltaire 1694–1778: attributed

15 We are all going to Heaven, and Vandyke is of the company.
Thomas Gainsborough 1727–88: attributed; William B. Boulton *Thomas Gainsborough* (1905)

16 Kiss me, Hardy.
Horatio, Lord Nelson 1758–1805: Robert Southey *Life of Nelson* (1813)

17 Oh, my country! how I leave my country!

also variously reported as "How I love my country" "My country! oh, my country!" "I think I could eat one of Bellamy's veal pies"
William Pitt 1759–1806: Earl Stanhope *Life of the Rt. Hon. William Pitt* vol. 3 (1879)

18 Well, I've had a happy life.
William Hazlitt 1778–1830: W. C. Hazlitt *Memoirs of William Hazlitt* (1867)

19 *when his son reminded him that he would soon visit a better land, as he looked out of his window at his Irish estate:*
I doubt it.
Edward Pennefeather Croker d. 1830: attributed; T. Toomey and H. Greensmith *An Antique and Storied Land* (1991)

20 More light!
Johann Wolfgang von Goethe 1749–1832: attributed; actually "Open the second shutter, so that more light can come in"

21 They couldn't hit an elephant at this distance.
immediately prior to being killed by enemy fire at the battle of Spotsylvania in the American Civil War
John Sedgwick d. 1864: Robert E. Denney *The Civil War Years* (1992)

22 Die, my dear Doctor, that's the last thing I shall do!
Lord Palmerston 1784–1865: E. Latham *Famous Sayings and their Authors* (1904)

23 So little done, so much to do.
said on the day of his death
Cecil Rhodes 1853–1902: Lewis Michell *Life of Rhodes* (1910)

24 I am just going outside and may be some time.
Captain Lawrence Oates 1880–1912: Scott's diary entry, 16–17 March 1912; cf. **Epitaphs 23**

25 For God's sake look after our people.
Robert Falcon Scott 1868–1912: last diary entry, 29 March 1912

26 Farewell, my friends. I go to glory.
last words before her scarf caught in a car wheel, breaking her neck
Isadora Duncan 1878–1927: Mary Desti *Isadora Duncan's End* (1929)

27 If this is dying, then I don't think much of it.
Lytton Strachey 1880–1932: Michael Holroyd *Lytton Strachey* vol. 2 (1968)

28 How's the Empire?
to his private secretary on the morning of his death, probably prompted by an article in The Times
George V 1865–1936: letter from Lord Wigram, 31 January 1936

29 Just before she [Stein] died she asked, "What *is* the answer?" No answer came. She laughed and said, "In that case what is the question?" Then she died.
Gertrude Stein 1874–1946: Donald Sutherland *Gertrude Stein, A Biography of her Work* (1951)

30 Now I'll have eine kleine Pause.
Kathleen Ferrier 1912–53: Gerald Moore *Am I Too Loud?* (1962)

31 Why not, why not, why not. Yeah.
Timothy Leary 1920–96: in *Independent* (UK) 1 June 1996; cf. **Death 83, Epitaphs 31**

The Law and Lawyers
see also **Crime and Punishment, Justice and Injustice**

1 Written laws are like spider's webs; they will catch, it is true, the weak and poor, but would be torn in pieces by the rich and powerful.
Anacharsis 6th century BC: Plutarch *Parallel Lives* "Solon"

2 *Salus populi suprema est lex.* The good of the people is the chief law.
Cicero 106–43 BC: *De Legibus*

3 The sabbath was made for man, and not man for the sabbath.
Bible: St. Mark

4 The rusty curb of old father antick, the law.
William Shakespeare 1564–1616: *Henry IV, Part 1* (1597)

5 A parliament can do any thing but make a man a woman, and a woman a man.
Henry Herbert, Lord Pembroke c. 1534–1601: quoted in 4th Earl of Pembroke's speech, 11 April 1648, proving himself Chancellor of Oxford

6 You have a gift, sir, (thank your education),
Will never let you want, while there are men,
And malice, to breed causes.
to a lawyer
Ben Jonson c. 1573–1637: *Volpone* (1605)

7 How long soever it hath continued, if it be against reason, it is of no force in law.
Edward Coke 1552–1634: *The First Part of the Institutes of the Laws of England* (1628)

8 Ignorance of the law excuses no man; not that all men know the law, but because 'tis an excuse every man will plead, and no man can tell how to confute him.
John Selden 1584–1654: *Table Talk* (1689) "Law"

9 Law is a bottomless pit.
John Arbuthnot 1667–1735: *The History of John Bull* (1712)

10 The hungry judges soon the
sentence sign,
And wretches hang that jury-men
may dine.
Alexander Pope 1688–1744: *The
Rape of the Lock* (1714)

11 Laws, like houses, lean on one
another.
Edmund Burke 1729–97: *A Tract on
the Popery Laws*

12 Bad laws are the worst sort of
tyranny.
Edmund Burke 1729–97: *Speech at
Bristol, previous to the Late Election*
(1780)

13 Laws were made to be broken.
Christopher North 1785–1854: in
Blackwood's Magazine (May 1830)

14 "If the law supposes that," said
Mr. Bumble . . . "the law is a ass—
a idiot."
Charles Dickens 1812–70: *Oliver
Twist* (1838)

15 If ever there was a case of clearer
evidence than this of persons
acting together, this case is that
case.
William Arabin 1773–1841: H. B.
Churchill *Arabiniana* (1843)

16 I think that we should be men
first, and subjects afterward. It is
not desirable to cultivate a respect
for the law, so much as for the
right.
Henry David Thoreau 1817–62: *Civil
Disobedience* (1849)

17 The one great principle of the
English law is, to make business
for itself.
Charles Dickens 1812–70: *Bleak
House* (1853)

18 A jury too frequently have at
least one member, more ready to
hang the panel than to hang the
traitor.
Abraham Lincoln 1809–65: letter 12
June 1863

19 I know no method to secure the
repeal of bad or obnoxious laws
so effective as their stringent
execution.
Ulysses S. Grant 1822–85: inaugural
address, 4 March 1869

20 The life of the law has not been
logic; it has been experience.
Oliver Wendell Holmes, Jr. 1841–
1935: *The Common Law* (1881)

21 The Law is the true embodiment
Of everything that's excellent.
It has no kind of fault or flaw,
And I, my Lords, embody the
Law.
W. S. Gilbert 1836–1911: *Iolanthe*
(1882)

22 However harmless a thing is, if
the law forbids it most people will
think it wrong.
W. Somerset Maugham 1874–1965:
A Writer's Notebook (1949) written
in 1896

23 I don't know as I want a lawyer
to tell me what I cannot do. I
hire him to tell me how to do
what I want to do.
J. P. Morgan 1837–1913: Ida M.
Tarbell *The Life of Elbert H. Gary*
(1925)

24 It is obvious that "obscenity" is
not a term capable of exact legal
definition; in the practice of the
Courts, it means "anything that
shocks the magistrate."
Bertrand Russell 1872–1970:
Sceptical Essays (1928) "The
Recrudescence of Puritanism"

25 No poet ever interpreted nature
as freely as a lawyer interprets
the truth.
Jean Giraudoux 1882–1944: *La
Guerre de Troie n'aura pas lieu*
(1935)

26 A verbal contract isn't worth the paper it is written on.
Sam Goldwyn 1882–1974: Alva Johnston *The Great Goldwyn* (1937)

27 The art of cross-examination is not the art of examining crossly. It's the art of leading the witness through a line of propositions he agrees to until he's forced to agree to the *one fatal question*.
Clifford Mortimer d. 1960: John Mortimer *Clinging to the Wreckage* (1982)

28 Loopholes are not always of a fixed dimension. They tend to enlarge as the numbers that pass through wear them away.
Harold Lever 1914– : speech to Finance Bill Committee, 22 May 1968

29 A lawyer with his briefcase can steal more than a hundred men with guns.
Mario Puzo 1920– : *The Godfather* (1969)

30 The South African police would leave no stone unturned to see that nothing disturbed the even terror of their lives.
Tom Sharpe 1928– : *Indecent Exposure* (1973)

31 The Court's opinion will accomplish the seemingly impossible feat of leaving this area of the law more confused than it found it.
William H. Rehnquist 1924– : dissenting opinion in *Roe v. Wade* 1973

32 Not only did we play the race card, we played it from the bottom of the deck.
on the defense's conduct of the O. J. Simpson trial
Robert Shapiro 1942– : interview, 3 October 1995, in *The Times* (UK) 5 October 1995

Leadership

1 They be blind leaders of the blind. And if the blind lead the blind, both shall fall into the ditch.
Bible: St. Matthew; cf. **Conformity 10**

2 Since, then, a prince is necessitated to play the animal well, he chooses among the beasts the fox and the lion, because the lion does not protect himself from traps; the fox does not protect himself from wolves. The prince must be a fox, therefore, to recognize the traps and a lion to frighten the wolves.
Niccolò Machiavelli 1469–1527: *The Prince* (written 1513)

3 I believe my arrival was most welcome, not only to the Commander of the Fleet but almost to every individual in it; and when I came to explain to them the *"Nelson touch,"* it was like an electric shock. Some shed tears, all approved—"It was new—it was singular—it was simple!"
Horatio, Lord Nelson 1758–1805: letter to Lady Hamilton, 1 October 1805

4 I used to say of him that his presence on the field made the difference of forty thousand men.
of Napoleon
Duke of Wellington 1769–1852: Philip Henry Stanhope *Notes of Conversations with the Duke of Wellington* (1888) 2 November 1831

5 Ah well! I am their leader, I really had to follow them!
Alexandre Auguste Ledru-Rollin 1807–74: E. de Mirecourt *Les Contemporains* vol. 14 (1857) "Ledru-Rollin"

6 By the structure of the world we often want, at the sudden occurrence of a grave tempest, to change the helmsman—to replace

the pilot of the calm by the pilot of the storm.
Walter Bagehot 1826–77: *The English Constitution* (1867) "The Cabinet"

7 Just as every conviction begins as a whim so does every emancipator serve his apprenticeship as a crank. A fanatic is a great leader who is just entering the room.
Heywood Broun 1888–1939: in *New York World* 6 February 1928

8 I go the way that Providence dictates with the assurance of a sleepwalker.
Adolf Hitler 1889–1945: speech in Munich, 15 March 1936

9 So long as men worship the Caesars and Napoleons, Caesars and Napoleons will duly arise and make them miserable.
Aldous Huxley 1894–1963: *Ends and Means* (1937)

10 The final test of a leader is that he leaves behind him in other men the conviction and the will to carry on.
Walter Lippmann 1889–1974: in *New York Herald Tribune* 14 April 1945

11 The loyalties which centre upon number one are enormous. If he trips he must be sustained. If he makes mistakes they must be covered. If he sleeps he must not be wantonly disturbed. If he is no good he must be pole-axed. But this last extreme process cannot be carried out every day; and certainly not in the days just after he has been chosen.
Winston Churchill 1874–1965: *The Second World War* vol. 2 (1949)

12 At the age of four with paper hats and wooden swords we're all Generals. Only some of us never grow out of it.
Peter Ustinov 1921– : *Romanoff and Juliet* (1956)

13 I know that the right kind of leader for the Labour Party is a desiccated calculating machine who must not in any way permit himself to be swayed by indignation.
Aneurin Bevan 1897–1960: Michael Foot *Aneurin Bevan* (1973)

14 I don't mind how much my Ministers talk, so long as they do what I say.
Margaret Thatcher 1925– : in *Observer* (UK) 27 January 1980

15 To grasp and hold a vision, that is the very essence of successful leadership—not only on the movie set where I learned it, but everywhere.
Ronald Reagan 1911– : in *The Wilson Quarterly* Winter 1994; attributed

16 The art of leadership is saying no, not yes. It is very easy to say yes.
Tony Blair 1953– : in *Mail on Sunday* (UK) 2 October 1994

17 Leadership is not about being nice. It's about being right and being strong.
Paul Keating 1944– : in *Time* 9 January 1995

Leisure
see also **Work**

1 The wisdom of a learned man cometh by opportunity of leisure: and he that hath little business shall become wise.
Bible: Ecclesiasticus

2 *Id quod est praestantissimum maximeque optabile omnibus sanis et bonis et beatis, cum dignitate otium.*
The thing which is the most outstanding and chiefly to be desired by all healthy and good and well-off persons, is leisure with honor.
Cicero 106–43 BC: *Pro Sestio*

3 If all the year were playing
holidays,
To sport would be as tedious as
to work;
But when they seldom come, they
wished for come.
William Shakespeare 1564–1616:
Henry IV, Part 1 (1597)

4 What is this life if, full of care,
We have no time to stand and
stare.
W. H. Davies 1871–1940: "Leisure"
(1911)

5 A perpetual holiday is a good
working definition of hell.
George Bernard Shaw 1856–1950:
Parents and Children (1914)

6 To be able to fill leisure
intelligently is the last product of
civilization.
Bertrand Russell 1872–1970: *The
Conquest of Happiness* (1930)

7 Cannot avoid contrasting
deliriously rapid flight of time
when on a holiday with very
much slower passage of days, and
even hours, in other and more
familiar surroundings.
E. M. Delafield 1890–1943: *The Diary
of a Provincial Lady* (1930)

8 It was Einstein who made the real
trouble. He announced in 1905
that there was no such thing as
absolute rest. After that there
never was.
Stephen Leacock 1869–1944: *The
Boy I Left Behind Me* (1947)

9 If I am doing nothing, I like to be
doing nothing to some purpose.
That is what leisure means.
Alan Bennett 1934– : *A Question of
Attribution* (1989)

10 *Recreations*: growling, prowling,
scowling and owling.
Nicholas Fairbairn 1933–95: entry in
Who's Who 1990

Letters and Letter-writing

1 Sir, more than kisses, letters
mingle souls.
John Donne 1572–1631: "To Sir Henry
Wotton" (1597–8)

2 I knew one that when he wrote a
letter he would put that which
was most material in the
postscript, as if it had been a
bymatter.
Francis Bacon 1561–1626: *Essays*
(1625) "Of Cunning"

3 All letters, methinks, should be
free and easy as one's discourse,
not studied as an oration, nor
made up of hard words like a
charm.
Dorothy Osborne 1627–95: letter to
William Temple, September 1653

4 I have made this [letter] longer
than usual, only because I have
not had the time to make it
shorter.
Blaise Pascal 1623–62: *Lettres
Provinciales* (1657)

5 A woman seldom writes her mind
but in her postscript.
Richard Steele 1672–1729: in *The
Spectator* (UK) 31 May 1711

6 You bid me burn your letters. But
I must forget you first.
John Adams 1735–1826: letter to
Abigail Adams, 28 April 1776

7 She'll vish there wos more, and
that's the great art o' letter
writin'.
Charles Dickens 1812–70: *Pickwick
Papers* (1837-8)

8 Correspondences are like small-
clothes before the invention of
suspenders; it is impossible to
keep them up.
Sydney Smith 1771–1845: Peter
Virgin *Sydney Smith* (1994)

9 It is wonderful how much news there is when people write every other day; if they wait for a month, there is nothing that seems worth telling.
O. Douglas 1877–1948: *Penny Plain* (1920)

10 A man seldom puts his authentic self into a letter. He writes it to amuse a friend or to get rid of a social or business obligation, which is to say, a nuisance.
H. L. Mencken 1880–1956: *Minority Report* (1956)

11 Don't think that this is a letter. It is only a small eruption of a disease called friendship.
Jean Renoir 1894–1979: letter to Janine Bazin, 12 June 1974

Liberty

1 Let my people go.
Bible: Exodus

2 Not bound to swear allegiance to any master, wherever the wind takes me I travel as a visitor.
Horace 65–8 BC: *Epistles*

3 One Cartwright brought a Slave from Russia, and would scourge him, for which he was questioned: and it was resolved, That England was too pure an Air for Slaves to breathe in.
Anonymous: "In the 11th of Elizabeth" (1568–1569) John Rushworth *Historical Collections* (1680–1722)

4 Why should a man be in love with his fetters, though of gold?
Francis Bacon 1561–1626: *Essay of Death* (1648)

5 Stone walls do not a prison make, Nor iron bars a cage.
Richard Lovelace 1618–58: "To Althea, From Prison" (1649)

6 None can love freedom heartily, but good men; the rest love not freedom, but licence.
John Milton 1608–74: *The Tenure of Kings and Magistrates* (1649)

7 Liberty is, to the lowest rank of every nation, little more than the choice of working or starving.
Samuel Johnson 1709–84: "The Bravery of the English Common Soldier" in *The British Magazine* January 1760

8 Man was born free, and everywhere he is in chains.
Jean-Jacques Rousseau 1712–78: *Du contrat social* (1762)

9 How is it that we hear the loudest yelps for liberty among the drivers of negroes?
Samuel Johnson 1709–84: *Taxation No Tyranny* (1775)

10 I know not what course others may take; but as for me, give me liberty, or give me death!
Patrick Henry 1736–99: speech in Virginia Convention, 23 March 1775

11 The people never give up their liberties but under some delusion.
Edmund Burke 1729–97: speech at County Meeting of Buckinghamshire, 1784; attributed

12 The tree of liberty must be refreshed from time to time with the blood of patriots and tyrants. It is its natural manure.
Thomas Jefferson 1743–1826: letter to W. S. Smith, 13 November 1787

13 The condition upon which God hath given liberty to man is eternal vigilance; which condition if he break, servitude is at once the consequence of his crime, and the punishment of his guilt.
John Philpot Curran 1750–1817: speech on the right of election of the Lord Mayor of Dublin, 10 July 1790

14 O liberty! O liberty! what crimes are committed in thy name!
Mme. Roland 1754–93: A. de Lamartine *Histoire des Girondins* (1847)

15 If men are to wait for liberty till they become wise and good in slavery, they may indeed wait for ever.
Lord Macaulay 1800–59: *Essays Contributed to the Edinburgh Review* (1843) "Milton"

16 Despots themselves do not deny that freedom is excellent: only they desire it for themselves alone, and they maintain that everyone else is altogether unworthy of it.
Alexis de Tocqueville 1805–59: *L'Ancien régime* (1856)

17 The liberty of the individual must be thus far limited: he must not make himself a nuisance to other people.
John Stuart Mill 1806–73: *On Liberty* (1859)

18 The word "freedom" means for me not a point of departure but a genuine point of arrival. The point of departure is defined by the word "order." Freedom cannot exist without the concept of order.
Prince Metternich 1773–1859: *Mein Politisches Testament* (1880)

19 In giving freedom to the slave, we assure freedom to the free— honorable alike in what we give and what we preserve. We shall nobly save, or meanly lose, the last, best hope of earth.
Abraham Lincoln 1809–65: annual message to Congress, 1 December 1862

20 Liberty means responsibility. That is why most men dread it.
George Bernard Shaw 1856–1950: *Man and Superman* (1903) "Maxims: Liberty and Equality"

21 Tyranny is always better organized than freedom.
Charles Péguy 1873–1914: *Basic Verities* (1943) "War and Peace"

22 Freedom is always and exclusively freedom for the one who thinks differently.
Rosa Luxemburg 1871–1919: *Die Russische Revolution* (1918)

23 Liberty is precious—so precious that it must be rationed.
V. I. Lenin 1870–1924: Sidney and Beatrice Webb *Soviet Communism* (1936)

24 It's often better to be in chains than to be free.
Franz Kafka 1883–1924: *The Trial* (1925)

25 It is better to die on your feet than to live on your knees.
Dolores Ibarruri 1895–1989: speech in Paris, 3 September 1936; also attributed to Emiliano Zapata

26 Liberty does not consist merely of denouncing Tyranny, any more than horticulture does of deploring and abusing weeds, or even pulling them out.
Arthur Bryant 1899–1985: in *Illustrated London News* (UK) 24 June 1939

27 I am condemned to be free.
Jean-Paul Sartre 1905–80: *L'Être et le néant* (1943)

28 The enemies of Freedom do not argue; they shout and they shoot.
William Ralph Inge 1860–1954: *End of an Age* (1948)

29 Freedom is the freedom to say that two plus two make four. If that is granted, all else follows.
George Orwell 1903–50: *Nineteen Eighty-Four* (1949)

30 The moment the slave resolves that he will no longer be a slave, his fetters fall. He frees himself and shows the way to others. Freedom and slavery are mental states.
Mahatma Gandhi 1869–1948: *Non-Violence in Peace and War* (1949)

31 Liberty is always unfinished business.
American Civil Liberties Union: title of 36th Annual Report, 1 July 1955–30 June 1956

32 Ask the first man you meet what he means by defending freedom, and he'll tell you privately he means defending the standard of living.
Martin Niemöller 1892–1984: address at Augsburg, January 1958; James Bentley *Martin Niemöller* (1984)

33 Liberty is liberty, not equality or fairness or justice or human happiness or a quiet conscience.
Isaiah Berlin 1909–97: *Two Concepts of Liberty* (1958)

34 Let every nation know, whether it wishes us well or ill, that we shall pay any price, bear any burden, meet any hardship, support any friend, oppose any foe to assure the survival and the success of liberty.
John F. Kennedy 1917–63: inaugural address, 20 January 1961

35 Of course liberty is not license. Liberty in my view is conforming to majority opinion.
Hugh Scanlon 1913– : television interview, 9 August 1977

Libraries
see also **Books, Reading**

1 Come, and take choice of all my library.
And so beguile thy sorrow.

William Shakespeare 1564–1616: *Titus Andronicus* (1590)

2 No place affords a more striking conviction of the vanity of human hopes, than a public library.
Samuel Johnson 1709–84: in *The Rambler* (UK) 23 March 1751

3 A man will turn over half a library to make one book.
Samuel Johnson 1709–84: James Boswell *Life of Samuel Johnson* (1791) 6 April 1775

4 With awe, around these silent walks I tread;
These are the lasting mansions of the dead.
George Crabbe 1754–1832: "The Library" (1808)

5 What a sad want I am in of libraries, of books to gather facts from! Why is there not a Majesty's library in every county town? There is a Majesty's jail and gallows in every one.
Thomas Carlyle 1795–1881: diary 18 May 1832

6 We call ourselves a rich nation, and we are filthy and foolish enough to thumb each other's books out of circulating libraries!
John Ruskin 1819–1900: *Sesame and Lilies* (1865)

7 A man should keep his little brain attic stocked with all the furniture that he is likely to use, and the rest he can put away in the lumber room of his library, where he can get it if he wants it.
Arthur Conan Doyle 1859–1930: *The Adventures of Sherlock Holmes* (1892)

8 A library is thought in cold storage.
Lord Samuel 1870–1963: *A Book of Quotations* (1947)

9 If you file your waste-paper basket for 50 years, you have a public library.
Tony Benn 1925– : in *Daily Telegraph* (UK) 5 March 1994

Lies and Lying
see also **Deception, Truth**

1 The retort courteous . . . the quip modest . . . the reply churlish . . . the reproof valiant . . . the countercheck quarrelsome . . . the lie circumstantial . . . the lie direct.
of the degrees of a lie
William Shakespeare 1564–1616: *As You Like It* (1599)

2 A mixture of a lie doth ever add pleasure.
Francis Bacon 1561–1626: *Essays* (1625) "Of Truth"

3 It is not the lie that passeth through the mind, but the lie that sinketh in, and settleth in it, that doth the hurt.
Francis Bacon 1561–1626: *Essays* (1625) "Of Truth"

4 No mask like open truth to cover lies,
As to go naked is the best disguise.
William Congreve 1670–1729: *The Double Dealer* (1694)

5 He replied that I must needs be mistaken, or that I *said the thing which was not*. (For they have no word in their language to express lying or falsehood.)
Jonathan Swift 1667–1745: *Gulliver's Travels* (1726)

6 Whoever would lie usefully should lie seldom.
Lord Hervey 1696–1743: *Memoirs of the Reign of George II* (ed. J. W. Croker, 1848)

7 Falsehood has a perennial spring.
Edmund Burke 1729–97: *On American Taxation* (1775)

8 He who permits himself to tell a lie once, finds it much easier to do it a second and third time, till at length it becomes habitual; he tells lies without attending to it, and truths without the world's believing him. This falsehood of the tongue leads to that of the heart, and in time depraves all its good dispositions.
Thomas Jefferson 1743–1826: *Letter to Peter Carr* (19 August 1785)

9 I can't tell a lie, Pa; you know I can't tell a lie. I did cut it with my hatchet.
of a cherry tree; the story is most likely an invention of Parson Weems
George Washington 1732–99: M. L. Weems *Life of George Washington* (10th ed., 1810)

10 If you want truth to go round the world you must hire an express train to pull it; but if you want a lie to go round the world, it will fly: it is as light as a feather, and a breath will carry it. It is well said in the old proverb, "a lie will go round the world while truth is pulling its boots on."
C. H. Spurgeon 1834–92: *Gems from Spurgeon* (1859)

11 The lie in the soul is a true lie.
Benjamin Jowett 1817–93: introduction to his translation (1871) of Plato's *Republic*

12 The cruelest lies are often told in silence.
Robert Louis Stevenson 1850–94: *Virginibus Puerisque* (1881)

13 One of the most striking differences between a cat and a

lie is that a cat has only nine lives.
Mark Twain 1835–1910: *Pudd'nhead Wilson* (1894)

14 Matilda told such Dreadful Lies,
It made one Gasp and Stretch one's Eyes.
Hilaire Belloc 1870–1953: *Cautionary Tales* (1907) "Matilda"

15 A little inaccuracy sometimes saves tons of explanation.
Saki 1870–1916: *The Square Egg* (1924)

16 Without lies humanity would perish of despair and boredom.
Anatole France 1844–1924: *La Vie en fleur* (1922)

17 The broad mass of a nation . . . will more easily fall victim to a big lie than to a small one.
Adolf Hitler 1889–1945: *Mein Kampf* (1925)

18 She tells enough white lies to ice a wedding cake.
of Lady Desborough
Margot Asquith 1864–1945: in *Listener* (UK) 11 June 1953

19 One sometimes sees more clearly in the man who lies than in the man who tells the truth. Truth, like the light, blinds. Lying, on the other hand, is a beautiful twilight, which gives to each object its value.
Albert Camus 1913–60: attributed; Lord Trevelyan *Diplomatic Channels* (1973)

20 An abomination unto the Lord, but a very present help in time of trouble.
definition of a lie, an amalgamation of Proverbs 12.22 and Psalms 46.1, often attributed to Adlai Stevenson
Anonymous: Bill Adler *The Stevenson Wit* (1966)

21 In our country the lie has become not just a moral category but a pillar of the State.
Alexander Solzhenitsyn 1918– : 1974 interview, in *The Oak and the Calf* (1975)

Life
see also **Life Sciences, Living and Lifestyles**

1 All that a man hath will he give for his life.
Bible: Job

2 Not to be born is, past all prizing, best.
Sophocles c. 496–406 BC: *Oedipus Coloneus*

3 And life is given to none freehold, but it is leasehold for all.
Lucretius c. 94–55 BC: *De Rerum Natura*

4 "Such," he said, "O King, seems to me the present life of men on earth, in comparison with that time which to us is uncertain, as if when on a winter's night you sit feasting with your ealdormen and thegns,—a single sparrow should fly swiftly into the hall, and coming in at one door, instantly fly out through another."
The Venerable Bede AD 673–735: *Ecclesiastical History of the English People*

5 Life well spent is long.
Leonardo da Vinci 1452–1519: Edward McCurdy (ed.) *Leonardo da Vinci's Notebooks* (1906)

6 The ceaseless labor of your life is to build the house of death.
Montaigne 1533–92: *Essais* (1580)

7 Life is as tedious as a twice-told tale,
Vexing the dull ear of a drowsy man.

William Shakespeare 1564–1616:
King John (1591–8)

8 All the world's a stage,
And all the men and women
merely players:
They have their exits and their
entrances;
And one man in his time plays
many parts,
His acts being seven ages.
William Shakespeare 1564–1616: *As
You Like It* (1599)

9 Life's but a walking shadow, a
poor player,
That struts and frets his hour
upon the stage,
And then is heard no more; it is
a tale
Told by an idiot, full of sound and
fury,
Signifying nothing.
William Shakespeare 1564–1616:
Macbeth (1606)

10 What is life? a frenzy. What is
life? An illusion, a shadow, a
fiction. And the greatest good is
of slight worth, as all life is a
dream, and dreams are dreams.
Pedro Calderón de La Barca 1600–81:
La Vida es Sueño (1636)

11 No arts; no letters; no society; and
which is worst of all, continual
fear and danger of violent death;
and the life of man, solitary, poor,
nasty, brutish, and short.
Thomas Hobbes 1588–1679:
Leviathan (1651)

12 Life is an incurable disease.
Abraham Cowley 1618–67: "To Dr.
Scarborough" (1656)

13 Man that is born of a woman
hath but a short time to live, and
is full of misery.
The Book of Common Prayer 1662:
The Burial of the Dead

14 Man has but three events in his
life: to be born, to live, and to die.

He is not conscious of his birth,
he suffers at his death and he
forgets to live.
Jean de la Bruyère 1645–96: *Les
Caractères ou les moeurs de ce
siècle* (1688) "De l'homme"

15 Dost thou love life? Then do not
squander time; for that's the stuff
life is made of.
Benjamin Franklin 1706–90: *Poor
Richard's Almanack* (1746)

16 Enlarge my life with multitude of
days,
In health, in sickness, thus the
suppliant prays;
Hides from himself his state, and
shuns to know,
That life protracted is protracted
woe.
Samuel Johnson 1709–84: *The Vanity
of Human Wishes* (1749)

17 Man wants but little here below,
Nor wants that little long.
Oliver Goldsmith 1730–74: "Edwin
and Angelina, or the Hermit" (1766);
cf. **Alcohol 11**

18 This world is a comedy to those
that think, a tragedy to those who
feel.
Horace Walpole 1717–97: letter to
Anne, Countess of Upper Ossory, 16
August 1776

19 Life, like a dome of many-
coloured glass,
Stains the white radiance of
Eternity,
Until Death tramples it to
fragments.
Percy Bysshe Shelley 1792–1822:
Adonais (1821)

20 Life is real! Life is earnest!
And the grave is not its goal;
Dust thou art, to dust returnest,
Was not spoken of the soul.
Henry Wadsworth Longfellow 1807–
82: "A Psalm of Life" (1838)

21 I slept, and dreamed that life was
beauty;
I woke, and found that life was
duty.
Ellen Sturgis Hooper 1816–41:
"Beauty and Duty" (1840)

22 Life must be understood
backwards; but . . . it must be
lived forwards.
Sören Kierkegaard 1813–55: *Journals
and Papers* (1843)

23 Youth is a blunder; Manhood a
struggle; Old Age a regret.
Benjamin Disraeli 1804–81:
Coningsby (1844)

24 Our life is frittered away by detail
. . . Simplify, simplify.
Henry David Thoreau 1817–62:
Walden (1854)

25 It is life near the bone where it is
sweetest.
Henry David Thoreau 1817–62:
Walden (1854)

26 The mass of men lead lives of
quiet desperation.
Henry David Thoreau 1817–62:
Walden (1854)

27 Life would be tolerable but for its
amusements.
George Cornewall Lewis 1806–63: in
The Times (UK) 18 September 1872

28 Life is mostly froth and bubble,
Two things stand like stone,
Kindness in another's trouble,
Courage in your own.
Adam Lindsay Gordon 1833–70: *Ye
Wearie Wayfarer* (1866)

29 Cats and monkeys—monkeys and
cats—all human life is there!
Henry James 1843–1916: *The
Madonna of the Future* (1879)

30 *Ah! que la vie est quotidienne.*
Oh, what a day-to-day business
life is.
Jules Laforgue 1860–87: *Complainte
sur certains ennuis* (1885)

31 The life of every man is a diary in
which he means to write one
story, and writes another; and his
humblest hour is when he
compares the volume as it is with
what he vowed to make it.
J. M. Barrie 1860–1937: *The Little
Minister* (1891)

32 Life is like playing a violin solo in
public and learning the
instrument as one goes on.
Samuel Butler 1835–1902: speech at
the Somerville Club, 27 February
1895

33 Life is just one damned thing
after another.
Elbert Hubbard 1859–1915: in
Philistine December 1909; often
attributed to Frank Ward O'Malley;
cf. **38** below

34 And Life is Colour and Warmth
and Light
And a striving evermore for these;
And he is dead, who will not
fight;
And who dies fighting has
increase.
Julian Grenfell 1888–1915: "Into
Battle" (1915)

35 I have measured out my life with
coffee spoons.
T. S. Eliot 1888–1965: "The Love
Song of J. Alfred Prufrock" (1917)

36 Life is not a series of gig lamps
symmetrically arranged; life is a
luminous halo, a semi-
transparent envelope surrounding
us from the beginning of
consciousness to the end.
Virginia Woolf 1882–1941: *The
Common Reader* (1925)

37 Life is a horizontal fall.
Jean Cocteau 1889–1963: *Opium*
(1930)

38 It's not true that life is one damn
thing after another—it's one
damn thing over and over.
Edna St. Vincent Millay 1892–1950:
letter to Arthur Davison Ficke, 24
October 1930; see **33** above

39 Life is just a bowl of cherries.
Lew Brown 1893–1958: title of song
(1931)

40 Birth, and copulation, and death.
That's all the facts when you
come to brass tacks:
Birth, and copulation, and death.
I've been born, and once is
enough.
T. S. Eliot 1888–1965: *Sweeney
Agonistes* (1932)

41 I long ago come to the conclusion
that all life is 6 to 5 against.
Damon Runyon 1884–1946: in
Collier's 8 September 1934, "A Nice
Price"

42 What, knocked a tooth out?
Never mind, dear, laugh it off,
laugh it off; it's all part of life's
rich pageant.
Arthur Marshall 1910–89: *The Games
Mistress* (recorded monologue, 1937)

43 All that matters is love and work.
Sigmund Freud 1856–1939:
attributed

44 The cradle rocks above an abyss,
and common sense tells us that
our existence is but a brief crack
of light between two eternities of
darkness.
Vladimir Nabokov 1899–1977: *Speak,
Memory* (1951)

45 Oh, isn't life a terrible thing,
thank God?
Dylan Thomas 1914–53: *Under Milk
Wood* (1954)

46 As far as we can discern, the sole
purpose of human existence is to
kindle a light in the darkness of
mere being.

Carl Gustav Jung 1875–1961:
Erinnerungen, Träume, Gedanken
(1962)

47 Life, you know, is rather like
opening a tin of sardines. We are
all of us looking for the key. And,
I wonder, how many of you here
tonight have wasted years of
your lives looking behind the
kitchen dressers of this life for
that key.
Alan Bennett 1934– : *Beyond the
Fringe* (1961 revue) "Take a Pew"

48 Life is a gamble at terrible odds—
if it was a bet, you wouldn't take
it.
Tom Stoppard 1937– : *Rosencrantz
and Guildenstern are Dead* (1967)

49 I couldn't have done it otherwise,
gone on I mean. I could not have
gone on through the awful
wretched mess of life without
having left a stain upon the
silence.
Samuel Beckett 1906–89: Deirdre
Bair *Samuel Beckett* (1978)

50 The Answer to the Great
Question Of . . . Life, the Universe
and Everything . . . [is] Forty-two.
Douglas Adams 1952– : *The
Hitchhiker's Guide to the Galaxy*
(1979)

51 Life is a rainbow which also
includes black.
Yevgeny Yevtushenko 1933– : in
Guardian (UK) 11 August 1987

52 At the end of your life you will
never regret not having passed
one more test, winning one more
verdict or not closing one more
deal. You will regret time not
spent with a husband, a child, a
friend or a parent.
Barbara Bush 1925– : *Washington
Post* (2 June 1990)

Life Sciences
see also **Life, Nature, Science, Science and Religion**

1 That which *is* grows, while that which *is not* becomes.
Galen AD 129–199: *On the Natural Faculties*

2 Like following life thro' creatures you dissect,
You lose it in the moment you detect.
Alexander Pope 1688–1744: *Epistles to Several Persons* "To Lord Cobham" (1734)

3 Population, when unchecked, increases in a geometrical ratio. Subsistence only increases in an arithmetical ratio.
Thomas Robert Malthus 1766–1834: *Essay on the Principle of Population* (1798)

4 I have called this principle, by which each slight variation, if useful, is preserved, by the term of Natural Selection.
Charles Darwin 1809–82: *On the Origin of Species* (1859)

5 Was it through his grandfather or his grandmother that he claimed his descent from a monkey?
addressed to T. H. Huxley in the debate on Darwin's theory of evolution
Samuel Wilberforce 1805–73: at a meeting of British Association in Oxford, 30 June 1860; see **Human Race 22, Science and Religion 6**

6 Evolution . . . is—a change from an indefinite, incoherent homogeneity, to a definite coherent heterogeneity.
Herbert Spencer 1820–1903: *First Principles* (1862)

7 [The science of life] is a superb and dazzlingly lighted hall which may be reached only by passing through a long and ghastly kitchen.
Claude Bernard 1813–78: *An Introduction to the Study of Experimental Medicine* (1865)

8 It has, I believe, been often remarked that a hen is only an egg's way of making another egg.
Samuel Butler 1835–1902: *Life and Habit* (1877)

9 The Microbe is so very small
You cannot make him out at all.
But many sanguine people hope
To see him through a microscope.
Hilaire Belloc 1870–1953: "The Microbe" (1897)

10 Men will not be content to manufacture life: they will want to improve on it.
J. D. Bernal 1901–71: *The World, the Flesh and the Devil* (1929)

11 Life exists in the universe only because the carbon atom possesses certain exceptional properties.
James Jeans 1877–1946: *The Mysterious Universe* (1930)

12 Behaviourism is indeed a kind of flat-earth view of the mind . . . it has substituted for the erstwhile anthropomorphic view of the rat, a ratomorphic view of man.
Arthur Koestler 1905–83: *The Ghost in the Machine* (1967)

13 The biologist passes, the frog remains.
sometimes quoted as "Theories pass. The frog remains"
Jean Rostand 1894–1977: *Inquiétudes d'un Biologiste* (1967)

14 Water is life's *mater* and *matrix*, mother and medium. There is no life without water.
Albert von Szent-Györgyi 1893–1986: in *Perspectives in Biology and Medicine* Winter 1971

15 [Natural selection] has no vision, no foresight, no sight at all. If it can be said to play the role of watchmaker in nature, it is the *blind* watchmaker.
Richard Dawkins: *The Blind Watchmaker* (1986); see **God 21**

16 The essence of life is statistical improbability on a colossal scale.
Richard Dawkins: *The Blind Watchmaker* (1986)

17 Almost all aspects of life are engineered at the molecular level, and without understanding molecules we can only have a very sketchy understanding of life itself.
Francis Crick 1916– : *What Mad Pursuit* (1988)

Lifestyles
see **Living and Lifestyles**

Likes and Dislikes
see also **Critics and Criticism, Taste**

1 To business that we love we rise betime,
And go to 't with delight.
William Shakespeare 1564–1616: *Antony and Cleopatra* (1606–7)

2 I do not love thee, Dr. Fell,
The reason why I cannot tell;
But this I know, and know full well,
I do not love thee, Dr. Fell.
written while an undergraduate at Christ Church, Oxford, of which Dr. Fell was Dean
Thomas Brown 1663–1704: translation of an epigram by Martial AD *c.* 40–*c.* 104

3 Ask you what provocation I have had?
The strong antipathy of good to bad.
Alexander Pope 1688–1744: *Imitations of Horace* (1738)

4 All his own geese are swans, as the swans of others are geese.
of Joshua Reynolds
Horace Walpole 1717–97: letter to Anne, Countess of Upper Ossory, 1 December 1786

5 People who like this sort of thing will find this the sort of thing they like.
judgment of a book
Abraham Lincoln 1809–65: G. W. E. Russell *Collections and Recollections* (1898)

6 For I've read in many a novel that, unless they've souls that grovel,
Folks *prefer* in fact a hovel to your dreary marble halls.
C. S. Calverley 1831–84: "In the Gloaming" (1872)

7 I don't care anything about reasons, but I know what I like.
Henry James 1843–1916: *Portrait of a Lady* (1881)

8 Take care to get what you like or you will be forced to like what you get.
George Bernard Shaw 1856–1950: *Man and Superman* (1903) "Maxims: Stray Sayings"

9 Do not do unto others as you would that they should do unto you. Their tastes may not be the same.
George Bernard Shaw 1856–1950: *Man and Superman* (1903) "Maxims for Revolutionists: The Golden Rule"

10 A little of what you fancy does you good.
Fred W. Leigh d. 1924 and **George Arthurs:** title of song (1915)

11 I bet you if I had met him [Trotsky] and had a chat with him, I would have found him a very interesting and human fellow, for I never yet met a man that I didn't like.

Will Rogers 1879–1935: in *Saturday Evening Post* 6 November 1926

12 Tiggers don't like honey.
A. A. Milne 1882–1956: *House at Pooh Corner* (1928)

13 In fact, now that you've got me right down to it, the only thing I didn't like about *The Barretts of Wimpole Street* was the play.
Dorothy Parker 1893–1967: review in *New Yorker* 21 February 1931

14 One would have disliked him [Lord Kitchener] intensely if one had not happened to like him.
Margot Asquith 1864–1945: Henry "Chips" Channon diary 18 September 1939

Living and Lifestyles
see also **Life**

1 Thou shalt love thy neighbor as thyself.
Bible: Leviticus; see also St. Matthew

2 Fear God, and keep his commandments: for this is the whole duty of man.
Bible: Ecclesiastes

3 A man hath no better thing under the sun, than to eat, and to drink, and to be merry.
Bible: Ecclesiastes

4 We live, not as we wish to, but as we can.
Menander 342–c. 292 BC: *The Lady of Andros*

5 Love and do what you will.
St. Augustine of Hippo AD 354–430: *In Epistolam Joannis ad Parthos* (AD 413)

6 *Fay ce que vouldras.*
Do what you like.
François Rabelais c. 1494–c. 1553: *Gargantua* (1534); cf. **16** below

7 Living is my job and my art.
Montaigne 1533–92: *Essais* (1580)

8 Six hours in sleep, in law's grave study six,
Four spend in prayer, the rest on Nature fix.
Edward Coke 1552–1634: translation of a quotation from Justinian *The Pandects*

9 Life is all a VARIORUM,
We regard not how it goes;
Let them cant about DECORUM,
Who have characters to lose.
Robert Burns 1759–96: "The Jolly Beggars" (1799)

10 A man should have the fine point of his soul taken off to become fit for this world.
John Keats 1795–1821: letter to J. H. Reynolds, 22 November 1817

11 Take short views, hope for the best, and trust in God.
Sydney Smith 1771–1845: Lady Holland *Memoir* (1855)

12 Believe me! The secret of reaping the greatest fruitfulness and the greatest enjoyment from life is *to live dangerously!*
Friedrich Nietzsche 1844–1900: *Die fröhliche Wissenschaft* (1882)

13 Living? The servants will do that for us.
Philippe-Auguste Villiers de L'Isle-Adam 1838–89: *Axël* (1890)

14 Do you want to know the great drama of my life? It's that I have put my genius into my life; all I've put into my works is my talent.
Oscar Wilde 1854–1900: André Gide *Oscar Wilde* (1910)

15 Live all you can; it's a mistake not to. It doesn't so much matter what you do in particular, so long as you have your life. If you

haven't had that, what *have* you had?
Henry James 1843–1916: *The Ambassadors* (1903)

16 Do what thou wilt shall be the whole of the Law.
Aleister Crowley 1875–1947: *Book of the Law* (1909); cf. **6** above

17 Never play cards with a man called Doc. Never eat at a place called Mom's. Never sleep with a woman whose troubles are worse than your own.
Nelson Algren 1909– : in *Newsweek* 2 July 1956

18 Man is born to live, not to prepare for life.
Boris Pasternak 1890–1960: *Doctor Zhivago* (1958)

19 Turn on, tune in and drop out.
Timothy Leary 1920–96: lecture, June 1966; *The Politics of Ecstasy* (1968)

20 San Francisco was where the social hemorrhaging was showing up. San Francisco was where the missing children were gathering and calling themselves "hippies."
Joan Didion 1934– : *Slouching Towards Bethlehem* (1968)

Logic and Reason

1 I have no other but a woman's reason:
I think him so, because I think him so.
William Shakespeare 1564–1616: *The Two Gentlemen of Verona* (1592–3)

2 Reasons are not like garments, the worse for wearing.
Robert Devereux, Earl of Essex 1566–1601: letter to Lord Willoughby, 4 January 1599

3 What ever sceptic could inquire for;
For every why he had a wherefore.
Samuel Butler 1612–80: *Hudibras* pt. 1 (1663)

4 I have never yet been able to perceive how anything can be known for truth by consecutive reasoning—and yet it must be.
John Keats 1795–1821: letter to Benjamin Bailey, 22 November 1817

5 I'll not listen to reason . . . Reason always means what someone else has got to say.
Elizabeth Gaskell 1810–65: *Cranford* (1853)

6 "Contrariwise," continued Tweedledee, "if it was so, it might be; and if it were so, it would be: but as it isn't, it ain't. That's logic."
Lewis Carroll 1832–98: *Through the Looking-Glass* (1872)

7 Irrationally held truths may be more harmful than reasoned errors.
T. H. Huxley 1825–95: *Science and Culture and Other Essays* (1881) "The Coming of Age of the Origin of Species"

8 Logical consequences are the scarecrows of fools and the beacons of wise men.
T. H. Huxley 1825–95: *Science and Culture and Other Essays* (1881) "On the Hypothesis that Animals are Automata"

9 [Logic] is neither a science nor an art, but a dodge.
Benjamin Jowett 1817–93: Lionel A. Tollemache *Benjamin Jowett* (1895)

10 "Is there any other point to which you would wish to draw my attention?"
"To the curious incident of the dog in the night-time."
"The dog did nothing in the night-time."
"That was the curious incident," remarked Sherlock Holmes.

Arthur Conan Doyle 1859–1930: *The Memoirs of Sherlock Holmes* (1894)

11 After all, what was a paradox but a statement of the obvious so as to make it sound untrue?
Ronald Knox 1888–1957: *A Spiritual Aeneid* (1918)

12 Logic must take care of itself.
Ludwig Wittgenstein 1889–1951: *Tractatus Logico-Philosophicus* (1922)

13 Only reason can convince us of those three fundamental truths without a recognition of which there can be no effective liberty: that what we believe is not necessarily true; that what we like is not necessarily good; and that all questions are open.
Clive Bell 1881–1964: *Civilization* (1928)

Losing
see **Winning and Losing**

Loss
see **Mourning and Loss**

Love
see also **Courtship, Kissing, Marriage, Relationships, Sex**

1 Many waters cannot quench love, neither can the floods drown it.
Bible: Song of Solomon

2 Let us live, my Lesbia, and let us love, and let us reckon all the murmurs of more censorious old men as worth one farthing. Suns can set and come again: for us, when once our brief light has set, one everlasting night is to be slept.
Catullus c. 84–c. 54 BC: *Carmina*; cf. **Transience 4**

3 *Omnia vincit Amor: et nos cedamus Amori.*
Love conquers all things: let us too give in to Love.
Virgil 70–19 BC: *Eclogues*

4 And now abideth faith, hope, charity, these three; but the greatest of these is charity.
Bible: I Corinthians

5 There is no fear in love; but perfect love casteth out fear.
Bible: I John

6 You who seek an end of love, love will yield to business: be busy, and you will be safe.
Ovid 43 BC–AD c. 17: *Remedia Amoris*

7 Lord, make me an instrument of Your peace!
Where there is hatred let me sow love.
St. Francis of Assisi 1181–1226: "Prayer of St. Francis" attributed

8 The love that moves the sun and the other stars.
Dante Alighieri 1265–1321: *Divina Commedia* "Paradiso"

9 For evere it was, and evere it shal byfalle,
That Love is he that alle thing may bynde,
For may no man fordon the lawe of kynde.
Geoffrey Chaucer c. 1343–1400: *Troilus and Criseyde*

10 God defend me, said Dinadan, for the joy of love is too short, and the sorrow thereof, and what cometh thereof, dureth over long.
Thomas Malory d. 1471: *Le Morte D'Arthur* (1485)

11 If I am pressed to say why I loved him, I feel it can only be explained by replying: "Because it was he; because it was me."
of his friend Étienne de la Boétie
Montaigne 1533–92: *Essais* (1580)

12 What thing is love for (well I
   wot) love is a thing.
   It is a prick, it is a sting,
   It is a pretty, pretty thing.
   George Peele c. 1556–96: *The
   Hunting of Cupid* (c. 1591)

13 Love comforteth like sunshine
   after rain.
   William Shakespeare 1564–1616:
   Venus and Adonis (1593)

14 O! how this spring of love
   resembleth
   The uncertain glory of an April
   day.
   William Shakespeare 1564–1616: *The
   Two Gentlemen of Verona* (1592–3)

15 Where both deliberate, the love is
   slight;
   Who ever loved that loved not at
   first sight?
   Christopher Marlowe 1564–93: *Hero
   and Leander* (1598)

16 The course of true love never did
   run smooth.
   William Shakespeare 1564–1616: *A
   Midsummer Night's Dream* (1595–6)

17 Love looks not with the eyes, but
   with the mind,
   And therefore is winged Cupid
   painted blind.
   William Shakespeare 1564–1616: *A
   Midsummer Night's Dream* (1595–6)

18 Whoever loves, if he do not
   propose
   The right true end of love, he's
   one that goes
   To sea for nothing but to make
   him sick.
   John Donne 1572–1631: "Love's
   Progress" (c. 1600)

19 To be wise, and love,
   Exceeds man's might.
   William Shakespeare 1564–1616:
   Troilus and Cressida (1602)

20 Then, must you speak
   Of one that loved not wisely but
   too well.
   William Shakespeare 1564–1616:
   Othello (1602–4)

21 Love is like linen often changed,
   the sweeter.
   Phineas Fletcher 1582–1650:
   Sicelides (performed 1614)

22 Let me not to the marriage of
   true minds
   Admit impediments. Love is not
   love
   Which alters when it alteration
   finds.
   William Shakespeare 1564–1616:
   Sonnet 116

23 Love made me poet,
   And this I writ;
   My heart did do it,
   And not my wit.
   Elizabeth, Lady Tanfield c. 1565–
   1628: epitaph for her husband, in
   Burford Parish Church, Oxfordshire

24 For God's sake hold your tongue,
   and let me love.
   John Donne 1572–1631: "The
   Canonization"

25 I wonder by my troth, what thou,
   and I
   Did, till we loved, were we not
   weaned till then?
   But sucked on country pleasures,
   childishly?
   Or snorted we in the seven
   sleepers den?
   John Donne 1572–1631: "The Good-
   Morrow"

26 No cord nor cable can so forcibly
   draw, or hold so fast, as love can
   do with a twined thread.
   Robert Burton 1577–1640: *The
   Anatomy of Melancholy* (1621–51)

27 Love is the fart
   Of every heart:
   It pains a man when 'tis kept
   close,

And others doth offend, when 'tis
let loose.
John Suckling 1609–42: "Love's
Offence" (1646)

28 And love's the noblest frailty of
the mind.
John Dryden 1631–1700: *The Indian
Emperor* (1665)

29 It's no longer a burning within
my veins: it's Venus entire
latched onto her prey.
Jean Racine 1639–99: *Phèdre* (1677)

30 Oh, what a dear ravishing thing
is the beginning of an Amour!
Aphra Behn 1640–89: *The Emperor
of the Moon* (1687)

31 The onset and the waning of love
make themselves felt in the
uneasiness experienced at being
alone together.
Jean de la Bruyère 1645–96: *Les
Caractères ou les moeurs de ce
siècle* (1688) "Du Coeur"

32 Say what you will, 'tis better to
be left than never to have been
loved.
William Congreve 1670–1729: *The
Way of the World* (1700)

33 If I were young and handsome as
I was, instead of old and faded as
I am, and you could lay the
empire of the world at my feet,
you should never share the heart
and hand that once belonged to
John, Duke of Marlborough.
*refusing an offer of marriage from
the Duke of Somerset*
Sarah, Duchess of Marlborough 1660–
1744: W. S. Churchill *Marlborough:
His Life and Times* vol. 4 (1938)

34 To say a man is fallen in love,—
or that he is deeply in love,—or
up to the ears in love,—and
sometimes even over head and
ears in it,—carries an idiomatical
kind of implication, that love is a
thing below a man.
Laurence Sterne 1713–68: *Tristram
Shandy* (1759–67)

35 Love is the wisdom of the fool
and the folly of the wise.
Samuel Johnson 1709–84: William
Cooke *Life of Samuel Foote* (1805)

36 Love, in the form in which it
exists in society, is nothing but
the exchange of two fantasies and
the superficial contact of two
bodies.
Nicolas-Sébastien Chamfort 1741–94:
Maximes et Pensées (1796)

37 Love seeketh not itself to please,
Nor for itself hath any care;
But for another gives its ease,
And builds a Heaven in Hell's
despair.
the pebble
William Blake 1757–1827: "The Clod
and the Pebble" (1794)

38 Love seeketh only Self to please,
To bind another to its delight,
Joys in another's loss of ease,
And builds a Hell in Heaven's
despite.
the clod
William Blake 1757–1827: "The Clod
and the Pebble" (1794)

39 O, my Luve's like a red, red rose
That's newly sprung in June;
O my Luve's like the melodie
That's sweetly play'd in tune.
Robert Burns 1759–96: "A Red Red
Rose" (1796); derived from various
folk-songs

40 The cure of a romantic first flame
is a better surety to subsequent
discretion, than all the
exhortations of all the fathers,
and mothers, and guardians, and
maiden aunts in the universe.
Fanny Burney 1752–1840: *Camilla*
(1796)

41 If I love you, what does that
matter to you!
Johann Wolfgang von Goethe 1749–

1832: *Wilhelm Meister's Apprenticeship* (1795-6)

42 No, there's nothing half so sweet
in life
As love's young dream.
Thomas Moore 1779–1852: "Love's
Young Dream" (1807)

43 Love in a hut, with water and a
crust,
Is—Love, forgive us!—cinders,
ashes, dust;
Love in a palace is perhaps at last
More grievous torment than a
hermit's fast.
John Keats 1795–1821: "Lamia"
(1820); cf. **Idealism 2**

44 The magic of first love is our
ignorance that it can ever end.
Benjamin Disraeli 1804–81: *Henrietta
Temple* (1837)

45 In the spring a young man's
fancy lightly turns to thoughts
of love.
Alfred, Lord Tennyson 1809–92:
"Locksley Hall" (1842)

46 What love is, if thou wouldst be
taught,
Thy heart must teach alone—
Two souls with but a single
thought,
Two hearts that beat as one.
Friedrich Halm 1806–71: *Der Sohn
der Wildnis* (1842)

47 My love for Linton is like the
foliage in the woods; time will
change it, I'm well aware, as
winter changes the trees—My
love for Heathcliff resembles the
eternal rocks beneath:—a source
of little visible delight, but
necessary.
Emily Brontë 1818–48: *Wuthering
Heights* (1847)

48 If you could see my legs when I
take my boots off, you'd form
some idea of what unrequited
affection is.

Charles Dickens 1812–70: *Dombey
and Son* (1848)

49 How do I love thee? Let me count
the ways.
Elizabeth Barrett Browning 1806–61:
Sonnets from the Portuguese (1850)
no. 43

50 'Tis better to have loved and lost
Than never to have loved at all.
Alfred, Lord Tennyson 1809–92: *In
Memoriam A. H. H.* (1850)

51 Love's like the measles—all the
worse when it comes late in life.
Douglas Jerrold 1803–57: *The Wit
and Opinions of Douglas Jerrold*
(1859)

52 Love is like any other luxury.
You have no right to it unless
you can afford it.
Anthony Trollope 1815–82: *The Way
We Live Now* (1875)

53 A lover without indiscretion is no
lover at all.
Thomas Hardy 1840–1928: *The Hand
of Ethelberta* (1876)

54 The love that lasts longest is the
love that is never returned.
W. Somerset Maugham 1874–1965:
A Writer's Notebook (1949) written
in 1894

55 I am the Love that dare not
speak its name.
Lord Alfred Douglas 1870–1945:
"Two Loves" (1896)

56 Yet each man kills the thing he
loves,
By each let this be heard,
Some do it with a bitter look,
Some with a flattering word.
The coward does it with a kiss,
The brave man with a sword!
Oscar Wilde 1854–1900: *The Ballad
of Reading Gaol* (1898)

57 To us love says humming that
the heart's stalled motor has

begun working again.
Vladimir Mayakovsky 1893–1930:
"Letter from Paris to Comrade
Kostorov on the Nature of Love"
(1928)

58 Experience shows us that love
does not consist in gazing at each
other but in looking together in
the same direction.
Antoine de Saint-Exupéry 1900–44:
Wind, Sand and Stars (1939)

59 If I can't love Hitler, I can't love
at all.
Rev. A. J. Muste 1885–1967: at a
Quaker meeting 1940; in *New York
Times* 12 February 1967

60 How alike are the groans of love
to those of the dying.
Malcolm Lowry 1909–57: *Under the
Volcano* (1947)

61 You know very well that love is,
above all, the gift of oneself!
Jean Anouilh 1910–87: *Ardèle* (1949)

62 Love is the delusion that one
woman differs from another.
H. L. Mencken 1880–1956:
Chrestomathy (1949)

63 Love. Of course, love. Flames for
a year, ashes for thirty.
Giuseppe di Lampedusa 1896–1957:
The Leopard (1957)

64 Most people experience love,
without noticing that there is
anything remarkable about it.
Boris Pasternak 1890–1960: *Doctor
Zhivago* (1958)

65 All you need is love.
John Lennon 1940–80 and **Paul
McCartney** 1942– : title of song
(1967)

66 Love means not ever having to
say you're sorry.
Erich Segal 1937– : *Love Story*
(1970)

67 Love is just a system for getting
someone to call you darling after
sex.
Julian Barnes 1946– : *Talking It
Over* (1991)

68 Love is one of the answers
humankind invented to stare
death in the face: time ceases to
be a measure, and we can briefly
know paradise.
Octavio Paz 1914– : *The Double
Flame* (1995)

Luck
see **Chance and Luck**

Luxury
see **Wealth and Luxury**

Lying
see **Lies and Lying**

Madness
see also **Fools and Foolishness, The
Mind**

1 Whenever God prepares evil for a
man, He first damages his mind,
with which he deliberates.
Anonymous: scholiastic annotation
to Sophocles's *Antigone*

2 I am never better than when I
am mad. Then methinks I am a
brave fellow; then I do wonders.
But reason abuseth me, and
there's the torment, there's the
hell.
Thomas Kyd 1558–94: *The Spanish
Tragedy* (1592) The Fourth Addition

3 I am but mad north-north-west;
when the wind is southerly, I
know a hawk from a handsaw.
William Shakespeare 1564–1616:
Hamlet (1601)

4 Though this be madness, yet
there is method in't.

William Shakespeare 1564–1616:
Hamlet (1601)

5 O! let me not be mad, not mad,
   sweet heaven;
  Keep me in temper; I would not
   be mad!
William Shakespeare 1564–1616:
King Lear (1605–6)

6 There is a pleasure sure,
  In being mad, which none but
   madmen know!
John Dryden 1631–1700: *The Spanish
Friar* (1681)

7 They called me mad, and I called
  them mad, and damn them, they
  outvoted me.
Nathaniel Lee c. 1653–92: R. Porter
A Social History of Madness (1987)

8 Mad, is he? Then I hope he will
  bite some of my other generals.
  *replying to the Duke of Newcastle,
  who had complained that General
  Wolfe was a madman*
George II 1683–1760: Henry Beckles
Willson *Life and Letters of James
Wolfe* (1909)

9 Babylon in all its desolation is a
  sight not so awful as that of the
  human mind in ruins.
Scrope Davies c. 1783–1852: letter to
Thomas Raikes, May 1835

10 Every one is more or less mad on
  one point.
Rudyard Kipling 1865–1936: *Plain
Tales from the Hills* (1888)

11 I saw the best minds of my
  generation destroyed by madness.
Allen Ginsberg 1926–97: *Howl* (1956)

12 There was only one catch and
  that was Catch-22, which
  specified that a concern for one's
  own safety in the face of dangers
  that were real and immediate was
  the process of a rational mind . . .
  Orr would be crazy to fly more

missions and sane if he didn't, but
if he was sane he had to fly them.
If he flew them he was crazy and
didn't have to; but if he didn't
want to he was sane and had to.
Joseph Heller 1923– : *Catch-22*
(1961)

13 Madness need not be all
  breakdown. It may also be breakthrough.
R. D. Laing 1927–89: *The Politics of
Experience* (1967)

14 If you talk to God, you are
  praying; if God talks to you, you
  have schizophrenia. If the dead
  talk to you, you are a spiritualist;
  if God talks to you, you are a
  schizophrenic.
Thomas Szasz 1920– : *The Second
Sin* (1973)

15 The asylums of this country are
  full of the sound of mind
  disinherited by the out of pocket.
Alan Bennett 1934– : *The Madness
of George III* (performed 1991)

16 The psychopath is the furnace
  that gives no heat.
Derek Raymond 1931–94: *The
Hidden Files* (1992)

Manners
see also **Behavior**

1 Leave off first for manners' sake.
Bible: Ecclesiasticus

2 Evil communications corrupt good
  manners.
Bible: I Corinthians

3 Immodest words admit of no
  defence,
  For want of decency is want of
  sense.
Wentworth Dillon, Lord Roscommon
c. 1633–1685: *Essay on Translated
Verse* (1684)

4 In my mind, there is nothing so illiberal and so ill-bred, as audible laughter.
Lord Chesterfield 1694–1773: *Letters to his Son* (1774) 9 March 1748

5 He is the very pineapple of politeness!
Richard Brinsley Sheridan 1751–1816: *The Rivals* (1775)

6 A man, indeed, is not genteel when he gets drunk; but most vices may be committed very genteelly: a man may debauch his friend's wife genteelly: he may cheat at cards genteelly.
James Boswell 1740–95: *Life of Samuel Johnson* (1791) 6 April 1775

7 The art of pleasing consists in being pleased.
William Hazlitt 1778–1830: *The Round Table* (1817) "On Manner"

8 Ceremony is an invention to take off the uneasy feeling which we derive from knowing ourselves to be less the object of love and esteem with a fellow-creature than some other person is.
Charles Lamb 1775–1834: *Essays of Elia* (1823) "A Bachelor's Complaint of the Behaviour of Married People"

9 Curtsey while you're thinking what to say. It saves time.
Lewis Carroll 1832–98: *Through the Looking-Glass* (1872)

10 Very notable was his distinction between coarseness and vulgarity (coarseness, revealing something; vulgarity, concealing something).
E. M. Forster 1879–1970: *The Longest Journey* (1907)

11 Of Courtesy, it is much less
Than Courage of Heart or Holiness.
Yet in my Walks it seems to me
That the Grace of God is in Courtesy.
Hilaire Belloc 1870–1953: "Courtesy" (1910)

12 Good breeding consists in concealing how much we think of ourselves and how little we think of the other person.
Mark Twain 1835–1910: *Notebooks* (1935)

13 When suave politeness, tempering bigot zeal,
Corrected *I believe* to *One does feel*.
Ronald Knox 1888–1957: "Absolute and Abitofhell" (1913)

14 "Always be civil to the girls, you never know who they may marry" is an aphorism which has saved many an English spinster from being treated like an Indian widow.
Nancy Mitford 1904–73: *Love in a Cold Climate* (1949)

15 To Americans, English manners are far more frightening than none at all.
Randall Jarrell 1914–65: *Pictures from an Institution* (1954)

16 Manners are especially the need of the plain. The pretty can get away with anything.
Evelyn Waugh 1903–66: in *Observer* 15 April 1962

17 The notion that etiquette is bad for children is also detrimental to adults, and not only because their own and other people's children feel free to treat them rudely. If uninhibited childhood is the ideal state of being, surely no one would willingly leave it for a generation charged with responsibility.
Judith Martin 1938– : *Miss Manners Rescues Civilization* (1996)

Marriage
see also **Courtship, Love, Sex**

1 Therefore shall a man leave his father and his mother, and shall

cleave unto his wife: and they
shall be one flesh.
Bible: Genesis

2 What therefore God hath joined
together, let not man put
asunder.
Bible: St. Matthew

3 It is better to marry than to burn.
Bible: I Corinthians

4 Men are April when they woo,
December when they wed: maids
are May when they are maids,
but the sky changes when they
are wives.
William Shakespeare 1564–1616: *As
You Like It* (1599)

5 A young man married is a man
that's marred.
William Shakespeare 1564–1616:
All's Well that Ends Well (1603–4)

6 Wedlock, indeed, hath oft
compared been
To public feasts where meet a
public rout,
Where they that are without
would fain go in
And they that are within would
fain go out.
John Davies 1569–1626: "A
Contention Betwixt a Wife, a Widow,
and a Maid for Precedence" (1608)

7 Wives are young men's
mistresses, companions for middle
age, and old men's nurses.
Francis Bacon 1561–1626: *Essays*
(1625) "Of Marriage and the Single
Life"

8 I would be married, but I'd have
no wife,
I would be married to a single
life.
Richard Crashaw c. 1612–49: "On
Marriage" (1646)

9 Then be not coy, but use your
time;
And while ye may, go marry;

For having lost but once your
prime,
You may for ever tarry.
Robert Herrick 1591–1674: "To the
Virgins, to Make Much of Time"
(1648)

10 Marriage is nothing but a civil
contract.
John Selden 1584–1654: *Table Talk*
(1689) "Marriage"

11 To have and to hold from this day
forward, for better for worse, for
richer for poorer, in sickness and
in health, to love, cherish, and to
obey, till death us do part.
The Book of Common Prayer 1662:
Solemnization of Matrimony
Betrothal

12 A Man may not marry his
Mother.
The Book of Common Prayer 1662: *A
Table of Kindred and Affinity*

13 SHARPER: Thus grief still treads
upon the heels of pleasure:
Married in haste, we may repent
at leisure.
SETTER: Some by experience find
those words mis-placed:
At leisure married, they repent in
haste.
William Congreve 1670–1729: *The
Old Bachelor* (1693)

14 Oh! how many torments lie in the
small circle of a wedding-ring!
Colley Cibber 1671–1757: *The Double
Gallant* (1707)

15 Do you think your mother and I
should have lived comfortably so
long together, if ever we had been
married?
John Gay 1685–1732: *The Beggar's
Opera* (1728)

16 The comfortable estate of
widowhood, is the only hope that
keeps up a wife's spirits.
John Gay 1685–1732: *The Beggar's
Opera* (1728)

17 Where there's marriage without love, there will be love without marriage.
Benjamin Franklin 1706–90: *Poor Richard's Almanack* (1733)

18 Marriage has many pains, but celibacy has no pleasures.
Samuel Johnson 1709–84: *Rasselas* (1759)

19 I . . . chose my wife, as she did her wedding gown, not for a fine glossy surface, but such qualities as would wear well.
Oliver Goldsmith 1730–74: *The Vicar of Wakefield* (1766)

20 O! how short a time does it take to put an end to a woman's liberty!
referring to a wedding
Fanny Burney 1752–1840: diary 20 July 1768

21 The triumph of hope over experience.
of a man who remarried immediately after the death of a wife with whom he had been unhappy
Samuel Johnson 1709–84: James Boswell *Life of Samuel Johnson* (1791) 1770

22 No man is in love when he marries . . . There is something in the formalities of the matrimonial preparations that drive away all the little cupidons.
Fanny Burney 1752–1840: *Camilla* (1796)

23 Still I can't contradict, what so oft has been said,
"Though women are angels, yet wedlock's the devil."
Lord Byron 1788–1824: "To Eliza" (1806)

24 It is a truth universally acknowledged, that a single man in possession of a good fortune, must be in want of a wife.

Jane Austen 1775–1817: *Pride and Prejudice* (1813)

25 Marriage may often be a stormy lake, but celibacy is almost always a muddy horsepond.
Thomas Love Peacock 1785–1866: *Melincourt* (1817)

26 Have you not heard
When a man marries, dies, or turns Hindoo,
His best friends hear no more of him?
Percy Bysshe Shelley 1792–1822: "Letter to Maria Gisborne" (1820)

27 My definition of marriage . . . it resembles a pair of shears, so joined that they cannot be separated; often moving in opposite directions, yet always punishing anyone who comes between them.
Sydney Smith 1771–1845: Lady Holland *Memoir* (1855)

28 Is marriage not an open question, when it is alleged, from the beginning of the work, that such as are in the institution wish to get out, and such as are out wish to get in?
Ralph Waldo Emerson 1803–82: *Representative Men* (1850)

29 It doesn't much signify whom one marries, for one is sure to find next morning that it was someone else.
Samuel Rogers 1763–1855: Alexander Dyce (ed.) *Table Talk of Samuel Rogers* (1860)

30 I have always thought that every woman should marry, and no man.
Benjamin Disraeli 1804–81: *Lothair* (1870)

31 A woman dictates before marriage in order that she may have an appetite for submission afterwards.

George Eliot 1819–80: *Middlemarch* (1871–2)

32 What man thinks of changing himself so as to suit his wife? And yet may expect that women shall put on altogether new characters when they are married, and girls think that they can do so.
Anthony Trollope 1815–82: *Phineas Redux* (1874)

33 A man's mother is his misfortune, but his wife is his fault.
on being urged to marry by his mother
Walter Bagehot 1826–77: in Norman St. John Stevas *Works of Walter Bagehot* (1986) vol. 15 "Walter Bagehot's Conversation"

34 Even quarrels with one's husband are preferable to the ennui of a solitary existence.
Elizabeth Patterson Bonaparte 1785–1879: Eugene L. Didier *The Life and Letters of Madame Bonaparte* (1879)

35 Marriage is like life in this—that it is a field of battle, and not a bed of roses.
Robert Louis Stevenson 1850–94: *Virginibus Puerisque* (1881)

36 To marry is to domesticate the Recording Angel. Once you are married, there is nothing left for you, not even suicide, but to be good.
Robert Louis Stevenson 1850–94: *Virginibus Puerisque* (1881)

37 Nothing perhaps is so efficacious in preventing men from marrying as the tone in which married women speak of the struggles made in that direction by their unmarried friends.
Anthony Trollope 1815–82: *The Way We Live Now*

38 It was very good of God to let Carlyle and Mrs. Carlyle marry one another and so make only two people miserable instead of four.
Samuel Butler 1835–1902: letter to Miss E. M. A. Savage, 21 November 1884

39 In married life three is company and two none.
Oscar Wilde 1854–1900: *The Importance of Being Earnest* (1895)

40 If it were not for the presents, an elopement would be preferable.
George Ade 1866–1944: *Forty Modern Fables* (1901)

41 Marriage is popular because it combines the maximum of temptation with the maximum of opportunity.
George Bernard Shaw 1856–1950: *Man and Superman* (1903) "Maxims: Marriage"

42 When you see what some girls marry, you realize how they must hate to work for a living.
Helen Rowland 1875–1950: *Reflections of a Bachelor Girl* (1909)

43 Hogamus, higamous
Man is polygamous
Higamus, hogamous
Woman monogamous.
William James 1842–1910: in *Oxford Book of Marriage* (1990)

44 Being a husband is a whole-time job. That is why so many husbands fail. They cannot give their entire attention to it.
Arnold Bennett 1867–1931: *The Title* (1918)

45 Chumps always make the best husbands. When you marry, Sally, grab a chump. Tap his forehead first, and if it rings solid, don't hesitate. All the unhappy marriages come from the husbands having brains.
P. G. Wodehouse 1881–1975: *The Adventures of Sally* (1920)

46 A husband is what is left of a lover, after the nerve has been extracted.
Helen Rowland 1875–1950: *A Guide to Men* (1922)

47 Marriage isn't a word . . . it's a *sentence*!
King Vidor 1895–1982: *The Crowd* (1928 film)

48 Marriage always demands the finest arts of insincerity possible between two human beings.
Vicki Baum 1888–1960: *Zwischenfall in Lohwinckel* (1930)

49 By god, D. H. Lawrence was right when he had said there must be a dumb, dark, dull, bitter belly-tension between a man and a woman, and how else could this be achieved save in the long monotony of marriage?
Stella Gibbons 1902–89: *Cold Comfort Farm* (1932)

50 The deep, deep peace of the double-bed after the hurly-burly of the chaise-longue.
on her recent marriage
Mrs. Patrick Campbell 1865–1940: Alexander Woollcott *While Rome Burns* (1934)

51 If you cannot have your dear husband for a comfort and a delight, for a breadwinner and a crosspatch, for a sofa, chair or a hot-water bottle, one can use him as a Cross to be Borne.
Stevie Smith 1902–71: *Novel on Yellow Paper* (1936)

52 Marriage is a bribe to make a housekeeper think she's a householder.
Thornton Wilder 1897–1975: *The Merchant of Yonkers* (1939)

53 Marriage is the waste-paper basket of the emotions.
Sidney Webb 1859–1947: Bertrand Russell *Autobiography* (1967)

54 The value of marriage is not that adults produce children but that children produce adults.
Peter De Vries 1910– : *The Tunnel of Love* (1954)

55 A man in love is incomplete until he has married. Then he's finished.
Zsa Zsa Gabor 1919– : in *Newsweek* 28 March 1960

56 One doesn't have to get anywhere in a marriage. It's not a public conveyance.
Iris Murdoch 1919– : *A Severed Head* (1961)

57 I married beneath me, all women do.
Nancy Astor 1879–1964: in *Dictionary of National Biography 1961–1970* (1981)

58 I think everybody really will concede that on this, of all days, I should begin my speech with the words "My husband and I."
Elizabeth II 1926– : speech at Guildhall, London, on her 25th wedding anniversary, 20 November 1972

59 Marriage is a wonderful invention; but, then again, so is a bicycle repair kit.
Billy Connolly 1942– : Duncan Campbell *Billy Connolly* (1976)

60 Never marry a man who hates his mother, because he'll end up hating you.
Jill Bennett 1931–90: in *Observer* (UK) September 1982

61 There were three of us in this marriage, so it was a bit crowded.
Diana, Princess of Wales 1961–97: interview on *Panorama*, BBC1 TV, 20 November 1995

Mathematics
see also **Quantities and Qualities,
Statistics**

1 Let no one enter who does not
know geometry [mathematics].
*inscription on Plato's door, probably
at the Academy at Athens*
Anonymous: Elias Philosophus *In
Aristotelis Categorias Commentaria*

2 There is no "royal road" to
geometry.
Euclid fl. *c.* 300 BC: addressed to
Ptolemy I; Proclus *Commentary on
the First Book of Euclid's Elementa*

3 If in other sciences we should
arrive at certainty without doubt
and truth without error. it
behoves us to place the
foundations of knowledge in
mathematics.
Roger Bacon *c.* 1220–*c.* 1292: *Opus
Majus*

4 There is divinity in odd numbers,
either in nativity. chance or
death.
William Shakespeare 1564–1616: *The
Merry Wives of Windsor* (1597)

5 Multiplication is vexation,
Division is as bad;
The Rule of Three doth puzzle
me.
And Practice drives me mad.
Anonymous: *Lean's Collectanea* vol.
4 (1904); possibly 16th-century

6 Philosophy is written in that
great book which ever lies before
our eyes—I mean the universe . . .
This book is written in
mathematical language and its
characters are triangles. circles
and other geometrical figures.
without whose help . . . one
wanders in vain through a dark
labyrinth.
*often quoted as "The book of nature
is written . . . "*
Galileo Galilei 1564–1642: *The
Assayer* (1623)

7 They are neither finite quantities,
or quantities infinitely small. nor
yet nothing. May we not call
them the ghosts of departed
quantities?
on Newton's infinitesimals
George Berkeley 1685–1753: *The
Analyst* (1734)

8 The most devilish thing is 8 times
8 and 7 times 7 it is what nature
itselfe cant endure.
Marjory Fleming 1803–11: *Journals,
Letters and Verses* (ed. A. Esdaile,
1934)

9 Mathematics are a species of
Frenchman; if you say something
to them. they translate it into
their own language and presto! it
is something entirely different.
Johann Wolfgang von Goethe 1749–
1832: attributed; R. L. Weber *A
Random Walk in Science* (1973)

10 What would life be like without
arithmetic. but a scene of horrors?
Sydney Smith 1771–1845: letter to
Miss [Lucie Austen]. 22 July 1835

11 I used to love mathematics for its
own sake. and I still do, because
it allows for no hypocrisy and no
vagueness, my two *bêtes noires*.
Stendhal 1783–1842: *La Vie d'Henri
Brulard* (1890)

12 "What's the good of *Mercator's*
North Poles and Equators,
Tropics, Zones and Meridian
lines?"
So the Bellman would cry: and
the crew would reply.
"They are merely conventional
signs!"
Lewis Carroll 1832–98: *The Hunting
of the Snark* (1876)

13 God made the integers, all the
rest is the work of man.
Leopold Kronecker 1823–91:

*Jahrsberichte der Deutschen
Mathematiker Vereinigung*

14 I never could make out what
those damned dots meant.
on decimal points
Lord Randolph Churchill 1849–94: W.
S. Churchill *Lord Randolph Churchill*
(1906)

15 Mathematics, rightly viewed,
possesses not only truth, but
supreme beauty—a beauty cold
and austere, like that of sculpture.
Bertrand Russell 1872–1970:
Philosophical Essays (1910)

16 Mathematics may be defined as
the subject in which we never
know what we are talking about,
nor whether what we are saying
is true.
Bertrand Russell 1872–1970:
Mysticism and Logic (1918)

17 The union of the mathematician
with the poet, fervor with
measure, passion with
correctness, this surely is the
ideal.
William James 1842–1910: *Collected
Essays and Reviews* (1920)

18 Beauty is the first test: there is no
permanent place in the world for
ugly mathematics.
Godfrey Harold Hardy 1877–1947: *A
Mathematician's Apology* (1940)

19 One must divide one's time
between politics and equations.
But our equations are much more
important to me.
Albert Einstein 1879–1955: C. P.
Snow "Einstein" in M. Goldsmith et
al. (eds.) *Einstein* (1980)

20 It is more important to have
beauty in one's equations than to
have them fit experiment.
*he went on to say "The discrepancy
may well be due to minor features
. . . that will get cleared up with
further developments"*

Paul Dirac 1902–84: in *Scientific
American* May 1963

21 Someone told me that each
equation I included in the book
would halve the sales.
Stephen Hawking 1942–   : *A Brief
History of Time* (1988)

Maturity
see also **Experience**

1 More childish valorous than
manly wise.
Christopher Marlowe 1564–93:
Tamburlaine the Great (1590)

2 And so, from hour to hour, we
ripe and ripe,
And then from hour to hour, we
rot and rot:
And thereby hangs a tale.
William Shakespeare 1564–1616: *As
You Like It* (1599)

3 Is not old wine wholesomest, old
pippins toothsomest, old wood
burn brightest, old linen wash
whitest? Old soldiers, sweethearts,
are surest, and old lovers are
soundest.
John Webster c. 1580–c. 1625:
Westward Hoe (1607)

4 Men are but children of a larger
growth;
Our appetites as apt to change as
theirs,
And full as craving too, and full
as vain.
John Dryden 1631–1700: *All for Love*
(1678)

5 At twenty years of age, the will
reigns; at thirty, the wit; and at
forty, the judgment.
Benjamin Franklin 1706–90: *Poor
Richard's Almanack* (1741)

6 The imagination of a boy is
healthy, and the mature
imagination of a man is healthy;
but there is a space of life

between, in which the soul is in a ferment, the character undecided, the way of life uncertain, the ambition thick-sighted: thence proceeds mawkishness.
John Keats 1795–1821: *Endymion* (1818) preface

7 If you can talk with crowds and keep your virtue,
Or walk with Kings—nor lose the common touch,
If neither foes nor loving friends can hurt you,
If all men count with you, but none too much;
If you can fill the unforgiving minute
With sixty seconds' worth of distance run,
Yours is the Earth and everything that's in it,
And—which is more—you'll be a Man, my son!
Rudyard Kipling 1865–1936: "If—" (1910)

8 When you understand what you see, you will no longer be children.
Whittaker Chambers 1901–61: *Witness* (1952)

9 To be adult is to be alone.
Jean Rostand 1894–1977: *Pensées d'un biologiste* (1954)

10 When I was young I hoped that one day I should be able to go into a post office to buy a stamp without feeling nervous and shy: now I realize that I never shall.
Edmund Blunden 1896–1974: Rupert Hart-Davis letter to George Lyttelton, 5 August 1956

11 One's prime is elusive. You little girls, when you grow up, must be on the alert to recognise your prime at whatever time of your life it may occur.
Muriel Spark 1918– : *The Prime of Miss Jean Brodie* (1961)

12 One of the most obvious facts about grown-ups, to a child, is that they have forgotten what it is like to be a child.
Randall Jarrell 1914–65: Christina Stead *The Man Who Loved Children* (1965)

Meaning
see also **Words**

1 I pray thee, understand a plain man in his plain meaning.
William Shakespeare 1564–1616: *The Merchant of Venice* (1596–8)

2 Where more is meant than meets the ear.
John Milton 1608–74: "Il Penseroso" (1645)

3 Egad I think the interpreter is the hardest to be understood of the two!
Richard Brinsley Sheridan 1751–1816: *The Critic* (1779)

4 God and I both knew what it meant once; now God alone knows.
also attributed to Browning, apropos Sordello, in the form "When it was written, God and Robert Browning knew what it meant; now only God knows"
Friedrich Klopstock 1724–1803: C. Lombroso *The Man of Genius* (1891)

5 "Then you should say what you mean," the March Hare went on. "I do," Alice hastily replied; "at least—at least I mean what I say— that's the same thing, you know." "Not the same thing a bit!" said the Hatter. "Why, you might just as well say that "I see what I eat" is the same thing as "I eat what I see!" "
Lewis Carroll 1832–98: *Alice's Adventures in Wonderland* (1865)

6 You see it's like a portmanteau— there are two meanings packed up into one word.

Lewis Carroll 1832–98: *Through the Looking-Glass* (1872)

7 The meaning doesn't matter if it's only idle chatter of a transcendental kind.
W. S. Gilbert 1836–1911: *Patience* (1881)

8 No one means all he says, and yet very few say all they mean, for words are slippery and thought is viscous.
Henry Brooks Adams 1838–1918: *The Education of Henry Adams* (1907)

9 The little girl had the making of a poet in her who, being told to be sure of her meaning before she spoke, said, "How can I know what I think till I see what I say?"
Graham Wallas 1858–1932: *The Art of Thought* (1926)

10 Any general statement is like a cheque drawn on a bank. Its value depends on what is there to meet it.
Ezra Pound 1885–1972: *The ABC of Reading* (1934)

11 It all depends what you mean by . . .
C. E. M. Joad 1891–1953: answering questions on "The Brains Trust" (formerly "Any Questions"), BBC radio (1941–8)

12 If a lady says No, she means Perhaps; if she says Perhaps, she means Yes; if she says Yes, she is no Lady.
If a diplomat says Yes, he means Perhaps; if he says Perhaps, he means No; if he says No, he is no Diplomat.
Lord Dawson of Penn 1864–1945: Francis Watson *Dawson of Penn* (1950)

Means
see **Ways and Means**

Medicine
see also **Sickness and Health**

1 Honor a physician with the honor due unto him for the uses which ye may have of him: for the Lord hath created him.
Bible: Ecclesiasticus

2 Life is short, the art long.
Hippocrates c. 460–357 BC: *Aphorisms*

3 Healing is a matter of time, but it is sometimes also a matter of opportunity.
Hippocrates c. 460–357 BC: *Precepts*

4 Physician, heal thyself.
Bible: St. Luke

5 Confront disease at its onset.
Persius AD 34–62: *Satires*

6 Throw physic to the dogs; I'll none of it.
William Shakespeare 1564–1616: *Macbeth* (1606)

7 The remedy is worse than the disease.
Francis Bacon 1561–1626: *Essays* (1625) "Of Seditions and Troubles"

8 Physicians of all men are most happy; what good success soever they have, the world proclaimeth, and what faults they commit, the earth covereth.
Francis Quarles 1592–1644: *Hieroglyphics of the Life of Man* (1638)

9 We all labour against our own cure, for death is the cure of all diseases.
Thomas Browne 1605–82: *Religio Medici* (1643)

10 GÉRONTE: It seems to me you are locating them wrongly: the heart is on the left and the liver is on the right.
SGANARELLE: Yes, in the old days that was so, but we have changed all that, and we now practice medicine by a completely new method.
Molière 1622–73: *Le médecin malgré lui* (1667)

11 Sciatica: he cured it, by boiling his buttock.
John Aubrey 1626–97: *Brief Lives* "Sir Jonas Moore"

12 Cured yesterday of my disease, I died last night of my physician.
Matthew Prior 1664–1721: "The Remedy Worse than the Disease" (1727)

13 In disease Medical Men guess: if they cannot ascertain a disease, they call it nervous.
John Keats 1795–1821: J. A. Gere and John Sparrow (eds.) *Geoffrey Madan's Notebooks* (1981); attributed

14 No *man*, not even a doctor, ever gives any other definition of what a nurse should be than this— "devoted and obedient." This definition would do just as well for a porter. It might even do for a horse. It would not do for a policeman.
Florence Nightingale 1820–1910: *Notes on Nursing* (1860)

15 It may seem a strange principle to enunciate as the very first requirement in a Hospital that it should do the sick no harm.
Florence Nightingale 1820–1910: *Notes on Hospitals* (1863 ed.) preface

16 Ah, well, then, I suppose that I shall have to die beyond my means.

at the mention of a huge fee for a surgical operation
Oscar Wilde 1854–1900: R. H. Sherard *Life of Oscar Wilde* (1906)

17 If a lot of cures are suggested for a disease, it means that the disease is incurable.
Anton Chekhov 1860–1904: *The Cherry Orchard* (1904)

18 There is at bottom only one genuinely scientific treatment for all diseases, and that is to stimulate the phagocytes.
George Bernard Shaw 1856–1950: *The Doctor's Dilemma* (1911)

19 Every day, in every way, I am getting better and better.
to be said 15 to 20 times, morning and evening
Émile Coué 1857–1926: *De la suggestion et de ses applications* (1915)

20 One finger in the throat and one in the rectum makes a good diagnostician.
William Osler 1849–1919: *Aphorisms from his Bedside Teachings* (1961)

21 We shall have to learn to refrain from doing things merely because we know how to do them.
Theodore Fox 1899–1989: speech to Royal College of Physicians, 18 October 1965

22 I can't stand whispering. Every time a doctor whispers in the hospital, next day there's a funeral.
Neil Simon 1927– : *The Gingerbread Lady* (1970)

23 Formerly, when religion was strong and science weak, men mistook magic for medicine; now, when science is strong and religion weak, men mistake medicine for magic.
Thomas Szasz 1920– : *The Second Sin* (1973)

24 A cousin of mine who was a
casualty surgeon in Manhattan
tells me that he and his
colleagues had a one-word
nickname for bikers: Donors.
Stephen Fry 1957– : *Paperweight*
(1992)

Mediocrity
see **Excellence and Mediocrity**

Meeting and Parting

1 *Atque in perpetuum, frater, ave
atque vale.*
And so, my brother, hail, and
farewell evermore!
Catullus c. 84–c. 54 BC: *Carmina*

2 Fare well my dear child and pray
for me, and I shall for you and all
your friends that we may merrily
meet in heaven.
on the eve of his execution
Thomas More 1478–1535: last letter
to his daughter Margaret Roper, 5
July 1535

3 Good-night, good-night! parting is
such sweet sorrow
That I shall say good-night till it
be morrow.
William Shakespeare 1564–1616:
Romeo and Juliet (1595)

4 Ill met by moonlight, proud
Titania.
William Shakespeare 1564–1616: *A
Midsummer Night's Dream* (1595–6)

5 When shall we three meet again
In thunder, lightning, or in rain?
William Shakespeare 1564–1616:
Macbeth (1606)

6 Since there's no help, come let us
kiss and part,
Nay, I have done: you get no
more of me.
Michael Drayton 1563–1631: *Idea*
(1619) Sonnet 61

7 Gin a body meet a body
Comin thro' the rye,

Gin a body kiss a body
Need a body cry?
Robert Burns 1759–96: "Comin thro'
the rye" (1796)

8 Not many sounds in life, and I
include all urban and all rural
sounds, exceed in interest a knock
at the door.
Charles Lamb 1775–1834: *Essays of
Elia* (1823) "Valentine's Day"

9 The red rose cries, "She is near,
she is near;"
And the white rose weeps, "She is
late;"
The larkspur listens, "I hear, I
hear;"
And the lily whispers, "I wait."
Alfred, Lord Tennyson 1809–92:
Maud (1855)

10 In every parting there is an image
of death.
George Eliot 1819–80: *Scenes of
Clerical Life* (1858)

11 How d'ye do, and how is the old
complaint?
*reputed to be his greeting to all
those he did not know*
Lord Palmerston 1784–1865: A. West
Recollections (1899)

12 Dr. Livingstone, I presume?
Henry Morton Stanley 1841–1904:
How I Found Livingstone (1872)

13 Parting is all we know of heaven,
And all we need of hell.
Emily Dickinson 1830–86: "My life
closed twice before its close"

14 As I was walking up the stair
I met a man who wasn't there.
He wasn't there again today.
I wish, I wish he'd stay away.
Hughes Mearns 1875–1965: lines
written for an amateur play, *The
Psycho-ed* (1910)

15 "Is there anybody there?" said the
Traveller,
Knocking on the moonlit door.

Walter de la Mare 1873–1956: "The Listeners" (1912)

16 Good-bye-ee!—Good-bye-ee!
Wipe the tear, baby dear, from your eye-ee.
Tho' it's hard to part, I know,
I'll be tickled to death to go.
R. P. Weston 1878–1936 and **Bert Lee** 1880–1947: "Good-bye-ee!" (c. 1915 song)

17 She said she always believed in the old addage, "Leave them while you're looking good."
Anita Loos 1893–1981: *Gentlemen Prefer Blondes* (1925)

18 Goodnight, children . . . everywhere.
Derek McCulloch 1897–1967: *Children's Hour* (BBC Radio program; closing words normally spoken by "Uncle Mac" in the 1930s and 1940s)

19 If you can't leave in a taxi you can leave in a huff. If that's too soon, you can leave in a minute and a huff.
Bert Kalmar 1884–1947 et al.: *Duck Soup* (1933 film); spoken by Groucho Marx

20 Why don't you come up sometime, and see me?
usually quoted as "Why don't you come up and see me sometime?"
Mae West 1892–1980: *She Done Him Wrong* (1933 film)

21 Here's looking at you, kid.
Julius J. Epstein 1909– et al.: *Casablanca* (1942 film)

22 We live our lives, for ever taking leave.
Rainer Maria Rilke 1875–1926: *Duineser Elegien* (1948)

Memory

1 Maybe one day it will be cheering to remember even these things.
Virgil 70–19 BC: *Aeneid*

2 Old men forget: yet all shall be forgot,
But he'll remember with advantages
What feats he did that day.
William Shakespeare 1564–1616: *Henry V* (1599)

3 When to the sessions of sweet silent thought
I summon up remembrance of things past.
William Shakespeare 1564–1616: sonnet 30

4 Nobody can remember more than seven of anything.
reason for omitting the eight beatitudes from his catechism
Cardinal Robert Bellarmine 1542–1621: John Bossy *Christianity in the West 1400–1700* (1985)

5 Yesterday I loved, today I suffer, tomorrow I die: but I still think fondly, today and tomorrow, of yesterday.
G. E. Lessing 1729–81: "Lied aus dem Spanischen" (1780)

6 We'll tak a cup o' kindness yet,
For auld lang syne.
Robert Burns 1759–96: "Auld Lang Syne" (1796)

7 You may break, you may shatter the vase, if you will,
But the scent of the roses will hang round it still.
Thomas Moore 1779–1852: "Farewell!—but whenever" (1807)

8 For oft, when on my couch I lie
In vacant or in pensive mood,
They flash upon that inward eye
Which is the bliss of solitude;
And then my heart with pleasure fills,
And dances with the daffodils.
William Wordsworth 1770–1850: "I wandered lonely as a cloud" (1815 ed.)

9 Music, when soft voices die,
Vibrates in the memory—
Odours, when sweet violets
sicken,
Live within the sense they
quicken.
Percy Bysshe Shelley 1792–1822:
"To—: Music, when soft voices die"
(1824)

10 I remember, I remember,
The house where I was born,
The little window where the sun
Came peeping in at morn.
Thomas Hood 1799–1845: "I
Remember" (1826)

11 In looking on the happy autumn-
fields,
And thinking of the days that are
no more.
Alfred, Lord Tennyson 1809–92: *The
Princess* (1847) song (added 1850)

12 And we forget because we must
And not because we will.
Matthew Arnold 1822–88: "Absence"
(1852)

13 Better by far you should forget
and smile
Than that you should remember
and be sad.
Christina Rossetti 1830–94:
"Remember" (1862)

14 I've a grand memory for
forgetting, David.
Robert Louis Stevenson 1850–94:
Kidnapped (1886)

15 I have forgot much, Cynara! gone
with the wind,
Flung roses, roses, riotously, with
the throng,
Dancing, to put thy pale, lost
lilies out of mind.
Ernest Dowson 1867–1900: "Non
Sum Qualis Eram" (1896); also
known as "Cynara" cf. **Constancy 12**

16 Memories are hunting horns
Whose sound dies on the wind.
Guillaume Apollinaire 1880–1918:
"Cors de Chasse" (1912)

17 And suddenly the memory
revealed itself. The taste was that
of the little piece of madeleine
which on Sunday mornings at
Combray . . . my aunt Léonie used
to give me, dipping it first in her
own cup of tea or tisane.
Marcel Proust 1871–1922: *Swann's
Way* (1913, vol. 1 of *Remembrance of
Things Past*)

18 Midnight shakes the memory
As a madman shakes a dead
geranium.
T. S. Eliot 1888–1965: "Rhapsody on
a Windy Night" (1917)

19 Someone said that God gave us
memory so that we might have
roses in December.
J. M. Barrie 1860–1937: Rectorial
Address at St. Andrew's, 3 May 1922

20 In plucking the fruit of memory
one runs the risk of spoiling its
bloom.
Joseph Conrad 1857–1924: *The
Arrow of Gold* (1924 ed.)

21 What beastly incidents our
memories insist on cherishing! . . .
the ugly and disgusting . . . the
beautiful things we have to keep
diaries to remember!
Eugene O'Neill 1888–1953: *Strange
Interlude* (1928)

22 Am in Market Harborough.
Where ought I to be?
telegram sent to his wife in London
G. K. Chesterton 1874–1936:
Autobiography (1936)

23 Our memories are card-indexes
consulted, and then put back in
disorder by authorities whom we
do not control.
Cyril Connolly 1903–74: *The Unquiet
Grave* (1944)

24 Poor people's memory is less
nourished than that of the rich; it
has fewer landmarks in space
because they seldom leave the
place where they live, and fewer
reference points in time ... Of
course, there is the memory of
the heart that they say is the
surest kind, but the heart wears
out with sorrow and labor, it
forgets sooner under the weight
of fatigue.
Albert Camus 1913–60: *The First Man*
(1994)

25 Memories are not shackles,
Franklin, they are garlands.
Alan Bennett 1934– : *Forty Years
On* (1969)

Men

1 Sigh no more, ladies, sigh no
more,
Men were deceivers ever.
William Shakespeare 1564–1616:
Much Ado About Nothing (1598–9)

2 In matters of love men's eyes are
always bigger than their bellies.
They have violent appetites, 'tis
true; but they have soon dined.
John Vanbrugh 1664–1726: *The
Relapse* (1696)

3 Man is to be held only by the
slightest chains, with the idea that
he can break them at pleasure, he
submits to them in sport.
Maria Edgeworth 1768–1849: *Letters
for Literary Ladies* (1795)

4 Men have had every advantage of
us in telling their own story.
Education has been theirs in so
much higher a degree; the pen
has been in their hands.
Jane Austen 1775–1817: *Persuasion*
(1818)

5 Men for the sake of getting a
living forget to live.
Margaret Fuller 1810–50: *Summer on
the Lakes* (1844)

6 A man ... is *so* in the way in the
house!
Elizabeth Gaskell 1810–65: *Cranford*
(1853)

7 Man is Nature's sole mistake!
W. S. Gilbert 1836–1911: *Princess Ida*
(1884)

8 The three most important things
a man has are, briefly, his private
parts, his money, and his
religious opinions.
Samuel Butler 1835–1902: *Further
Extracts from Notebooks* (1934)

9 Every man over forty is a
scoundrel.
George Bernard Shaw 1856–1950:
Man and Superman (1903) "Maxims:
Stray Sayings"

10 If you wish—
... I'll be irreproachably tender;
not a man, but—a cloud in
trousers!
Vladimir Mayakovsky 1893–1930:
"The Cloud in Trousers" (1915)

11 Men build bridges and throw
railroads across deserts, and yet
they contend successfully that the
job of sewing on a button is
beyond them. Accordingly, they
don't have to sew buttons.
Heywood Broun 1888–1939: *Seeing
Things at Night* (1921)

12 Somehow a bachelor never quite
gets over the idea that he is a
thing of beauty and a boy forever.
Helen Rowland 1875–1950: *A Guide
to Men* (1922); see **Beauty 13**

13 It's not the men in my life that
counts—it's the life in my men.
Mae West 1892–1980: *I'm No Angel*
(1933 film)

14 Women want mediocre men, and
men are working hard to be as
mediocre as possible.
Margaret Mead 1901–78: in *Quote
Magazine* 15 June 1958

15 There is, of course, no reason for the existence of the male sex except that sometimes one needs help with moving the piano.
Rebecca West 1892–1983: in *Sunday Telegraph* (UK) 28 June 1970

16 No nice men are good at getting taxis.
Katharine Whitehorn 1928– : in *Observer* (UK) 1977

17 Whatever they may be in public life, whatever their relations with men, in their relations with women, all men are rapists, and that's all they are. They rape us with their eyes, their laws, and their codes.
Marilyn French 1929– : *The Women's Room* (1977)

18 A hard man is good to find.
Mae West 1892–1980: attributed

19 Years ago, manhood was an opportunity for achievement, and now it is a problem to be overcome.
Garrison Keillor 1942– : *The Book of Guys* (1994)

Men and Women
see also **Woman's Role, Women**

1 CAMPASPE: Were women never so fair, men would be false.
APELLES: Were women never so false, men would be fond.
John Lyly c. 1554–1606: *Campaspe* (1584)

2 Just such disparity
As is 'twixt air and angels' purity,
'Twixt women's love, and men's will ever be.
John Donne 1572–1631: "Air and Angels"

3 He for God only, she for God in him.
John Milton 1608–74: *Paradise Lost* (1667)

4 In every age and country, the wiser, or at least the stronger, of the two sexes, has usurped the powers of the state, and confined the other to the cares and pleasures of domestic life.
Edward Gibbon 1737–94: *The Decline and Fall of the Roman Empire* (1776–88)

5 Man's love is of man's life a thing apart,
'Tis woman's whole existence.
Lord Byron 1788–1824: *Don Juan* (1819–24)

6 The man's desire is for the woman; but the woman's desire is rarely other than for the desire of the man.
Samuel Taylor Coleridge 1772–1834: *Table Talk* (1835) 23 July 1827

7 Man is the hunter; woman is his game.
Alfred, Lord Tennyson 1809–92: *The Princess* (1847)

8 'Tis strange what a man may do, and a woman yet think him an angel.
William Makepeace Thackeray 1811–63: *The History of Henry Esmond* (1852)

9 Man dreams of fame while woman wakes to love.
Alfred, Lord Tennyson 1809–92: *Idylls of the King* "Merlin and Vivien" (1859)

10 I expect that Woman will be the last thing civilized by Man.
George Meredith 1828–1909: *The Ordeal of Richard Feverel* (1859)

11 Take my word for it, the silliest woman can manage a clever man; but it takes a very clever woman to manage a fool.
Rudyard Kipling 1865–1936: *Plain Tales from the Hills* (1888)

12 All women become like their mothers. That is their tragedy. No man does. That's his.
Oscar Wilde 1854–1900: *The Importance of Being Earnest* (1895)

13 Of all human struggles there is none so treacherous and remorseless as the struggle between the artist man and the mother woman.
George Bernard Shaw 1856–1950: *Man and Superman* (1903)

14 Women deprived of the company of men pine, men deprived of the company of women become stupid.
Anton Chekhov 1860–1904: *Notebooks* (1921)

15 Every man who is high up loves to think that he has done it all himself; and the wife smiles, and lets it go at that. It's our only joke. Every woman knows that.
J. M. Barrie 1860–1937: *What Every Woman Knows* (performed 1908, published 1918)

16 You are not permitted to kill a woman who has wronged you, but nothing forbids you to reflect that she is growing older every minute. You are avenged 1,440 times a day.
Ambrose Bierce 1842–?1914: *Epigrams* (1909)

17 A woman can forgive a man for the harm he does her, but she can never forgive him for the sacrifices he makes on her account.
W. Somerset Maugham 1874–1965: *The Moon and Sixpence* (1919)

18 Women have served all these centuries as looking-glasses possessing the magic and delicious power of reflecting the figure of a man at twice its natural size.

Virginia Woolf 1882–1941: *A Room of One's Own* (1929)

19 Me Tarzan, you Jane.
summing up his role in Tarzan, the Ape Man *(1932 film)*
Johnny Weissmuller 1904–84: in *Photoplay Magazine* June 1932; the words occur neither in the film nor the original novel, by Edgar Rice Burroughs

20 When women go wrong, men go right after them.
Mae West 1892–1980: *She Done Him Wrong* (1933 film)

21 In the sex-war thoughtlessness is the weapon of the male, vindictiveness of the female.
Cyril Connolly 1903–74: *The Unquiet Grave* (1944)

22 A woman will always have to be better than a man in any job she undertakes.
Eleanor Roosevelt 1884–1962: *My Day* (29 November 1945)

23 It is not in giving life but in risking life that man is raised above the animal; that is why superiority has been accorded in humanity not to the sex that brings forth but to that which kills.
Simone de Beauvoir 1908–86: *The Second Sex* (1949)

24 There is more difference within the sexes than between them.
Ivy Compton-Burnett 1884–1969: *Mother and Son* (1955)

25 I do not think it altogether inappropriate to introduce myself to this audience. I am the man who accompanied Jacqueline Kennedy to Paris, and I have enjoyed it.
John F. Kennedy 1917–63: *remarks at press luncheon, Paris* (1961)

26 Whatever women do they must do twice as well as men to be thought half as good.

Charlotte Whitton 1896–1975: in
Canada Month June 1963

27 Women have very little idea of
how much men hate them.
Germaine Greer 1939– : *The
Female Eunuch* (1971)

28 The best way to hold a man is in
your arms.
Mae West 1892–1980: Joseph
Weintraub *Peel Me a Grape* (1975)

29 Whereas nature turns girls into
women, society has to make boys
into men.
Anthony Stevens: *Archetype* (1982)

30 My mother said it was simple to
keep a man, you must be a maid
in the living room, a cook in the
kitchen and a whore in the
bedroom. I said I'd hire the other
two and take care of the bedroom
bit.
Jerry Hall: in *Observer* (UK) 6
October 1985

31 More and more it appears that,
biologically, men are designed for
short, brutal lives and women for
long miserable ones.
Estelle Ramey: in *Observer* (UK) 7
April 1985

32 A man has every season, while a
woman has only the right to
spring.
Jane Fonda 1937– : in *Daily Mail*
(UK) 13 September 1989

33 A woman without a man is like a
fish without a bicycle.
Gloria Steinem 1934– : attributed

34 In societies where men are truly
confident of their own worth,
women are not merely tolerated
but valued.
Aung San Suu Kyi 1945– : speech
presented on videotape at NGO
Forum on Women, China, early
September 1995

Middle Age

1 *Nel mezzo del cammin di nostra
vita.*
Midway along the path of our life.
Dante Alighieri 1265–1321: *Divina
Commedia* "Inferno"

2 I am resolved to grow fat and
look young till forty, and then
slip out of the world with the first
wrinkle and the reputation of five-
and-twenty.
John Dryden 1631–1700: *The Maiden
Queen* (1668)

3 He who thinks to realize when he
is older the hopes and desires of
youth is always deceiving himself,
for every decade of a man's life
possesses its own kind of
happiness, its own hopes and
prospects.
Johann Wolfgang von Goethe 1749–
1832: *Elective Affinities* (1809)

4 My days are in the yellow leaf;
The flowers and fruits of love are
gone;
The worm, the canker, and the
grief
Are mine alone!
Lord Byron 1788–1824: "On This Day
I Complete my Thirty-Sixth Year"
(1824)

5 I am past thirty, and three parts
iced over.
Matthew Arnold 1822–88: letter to
Arthur Hugh Clough, 12 February
1853

6 Thirty-five is a very attractive
age. London society is full of
women of the very highest birth
who have, of their own free
choice, remained thirty-five for
years.
Oscar Wilde 1854–1900: *The
Importance of Being Earnest* (1895)

7 Mr. Salteena was an elderly man
of 42.

Daisy Ashford 1881–1972: *The Young Visiters* (1919)

8 At eighteen our convictions are hills from which we look; at forty-five they are caves in which we hide.
F. Scott Fitzgerald 1896–1940: "Bernice Bobs her Hair" (1920)

9 The afternoon of human life must also have a significance of its own and cannot be merely a pitiful appendage to life's morning.
Carl Gustav Jung 1875–1961: *The Stages of Life* (1930)

10 Nobody loves a fairy when she's forty.
Arthur W. D. Henley: title of song (1934)

11 One of the pleasures of middle age is to *find out* that one WAS right, and that one was much righter than one knew at say 17 or 23.
Ezra Pound 1885–1972: *ABC of Reading* (1934)

12 Years ago we discovered the exact point, the dead centre of middle age. It occurs when you are too young to take up golf and too old to rush up to the net.
Franklin P. Adams 1881–1960: *Nods and Becks* (1944)

13 After forty a woman has to choose between losing her figure or her face. My advice is to keep your face, and stay sitting down.
Barbara Cartland 1901– : Libby Purves "Luncheon à la Cartland" in *The Times* (UK) 6 October 1993

The Mind
see also **Ideas, Logic and Reason, Madness, Thinking**

1 My mind to me a kingdom is. Such perfect joy therein I find.
Edward Dyer d. 1607: "In praise of a contented mind" (1588); attributed

2 The mind is its own place, and in itself
Can make a heaven of hell, a hell of heaven.
John Milton 1608–74: *Paradise Lost* (1667)

3 The mind is but a barren soil; a soil which is soon exhausted, and will produce no crop, or only one, unless it be continually fertilized and enriched with foreign matter.
Joshua Reynolds 1723–92: *Discourses on Art* 10 December 1774

4 When people will not weed their own minds, they are apt to be overrun with nettles.
Horace Walpole 1717–97: letter to Caroline, Countess of Ailesbury, 10 July 1779

5 To give a sex to mind was not very consistent with the principles of a man [Rousseau] who argued so warmly, and so well, for the immortality of the soul.
often quoted as, "Mind has no sex"
Mary Wollstonecraft 1759–97: *A Vindication of the Rights of Woman* (1792)

6 The only means of strengthening one's intellect is to make up one's mind about nothing—to let the mind be a thoroughfare for all thoughts. Not a select party.
John Keats 1795–1821: letter to George and Georgiana Keats, 24 September 1819

7 Not body enough to cover his mind decently with: his intellect is improperly exposed.
Sydney Smith 1771–1845: Lady Holland *Memoir* (1855)

8 What is Matter?—Never mind. What is Mind?—No matter.
Punch: 1855

9 On earth there is nothing great but man: in man there is nothing great but mind.

William Hamilton 1788–1856:
Lectures on Metaphysics and Logic
(1859); attributed in a Latin form to
Favorinus in Pico di Mirandola (1463–
94) *Disputationes Adversus
Astrologiam Divinatricem*

10 To be conscious is an illness—a
real thorough-going illness.
Fyodor Dostoevsky 1821–81: *Notes
from Underground* (1864)

11 O the mind, mind has mountains;
cliffs of fall
Frightful, sheer, no-man-
fathomed. Hold them cheap
May who ne'er hung there.
Gerard Manley Hopkins 1844–89:
"No worst, there is none" (written
1885)

12 Minds are like parachutes. They
only function when they are
open.
James Dewar 1842–1923: attributed

13 Familiar things happen, and
mankind does not bother about
them. It requires a very unusual
mind to undertake the analysis of
the obvious.
Alfred North Whitehead 1861–1947:
Science and the Modern World
(1925)

14 We are not interested in the fact
that the brain has the consistency
of cold porridge.
Alan Turing 1912–54: A. P. Hodges
Alan Turing: the Enigma (1983)

15 That's the classical mind at work,
runs fine inside but looks dingy
on the surface.
Robert M. Pirsig 1928– : *Zen and
the Art of Motorcycle Maintenance*
(1974)

16 Consciousness . . . is the
phenomenon whereby the
universe's very existence is made
known.
Roger Penrose 1931– : *The
Emperor's New Mind* (1989)

Misfortunes
see also **Adversity**

1 Man is born unto trouble, as the
sparks fly upward.
Bible: Job

2 Misery acquaints a man with
strange bedfellows.
William Shakespeare 1564–1616: *The
Tempest* (1611)

3 All the misfortunes of men derive
from one single thing, which is
their inability to be at ease in a
room.
Blaise Pascal 1623–62: *Pensées*
(1670)

4 In the misfortune of our best
friends, we always find something
which is not displeasing to us.
Duc de la Rochefoucauld 1613–80:
Réflexions ou Maximes Morales
(1665)

5 O Diamond! Diamond! thou little
knowest the mischief done!
*to a dog, who knocked over a
candle which set fire to some papers
and thereby "destroyed the almost
finished labors of some years"*
Isaac Newton 1642–1727: Thomas
Maude *Wensley-Dale . . . a Poem*
(1772); probably apocryphal

6 If Gladstone fell into the Thames,
that would be misfortune; and if
anybody pulled him out, that, I
suppose, would be a calamity.
Benjamin Disraeli 1804–81: Leon
Harris *The Fine Art of Political Wit*
(1965)

7 I had never had a piece of toast
Particularly long and wide,
But fell upon the sanded floor,
And always on the buttered side.
James Payn 1830–98: in *Chambers's
Journal* 2 February 1884

8 I left the room with silent dignity,
but caught my foot in the mat.

George and Weedon Grossmith 1847–
1912: *The Diary of a Nobody* (1894)

9 And always keep a-hold of Nurse
For fear of finding something
worse.
Hilaire Belloc 1870–1953: *Cautionary
Tales* (1907) "Jim"

10 One likes people much better
when they're battered down by a
prodigious siege of misfortune
than when they triumph.
Virginia Woolf 1882–1941: diary 13
August 1921

11 My only solution for the problem
of habitual accidents . . . is to stay
in bed all day. Even then, there is
always the chance that you will
fall out.
Robert Benchley 1889–1945: *Chips
off the old Benchley* (1949)

12 Never cry over spilt milk, because
it may have been poisoned.
to Carlotta Monti
W. C. Fields 1880–1946: Carlotta
Monti with Cy Rice *W. C. Fields and
Me* (1971)

13 The fatal law of gravity: when
you are down everything falls on
you.
Sylvia Townsend Warner 1893–1978:
attributed

14 In the words of one of my more
sympathetic correspondents, it has
turned out to be an "annus
horribilis."
Elizabeth II 1926– : speech at
Guildhall, London, 24 November
1992

Mistakes

1 I would rather be wrong, by God,
with Plato . . . than be correct
with those men.
on Pythagoreans
Cicero 106–43 BC: *Tusculanae
Disputationes*

2 I'm aggrieved when sometimes
even excellent Homer nods.
Horace 65–8 BC: *Ars Poetica*; cf.
Poets 13

3 Leave no rubs nor botches in the
work.
William Shakespeare 1564–1616:
Macbeth (1606)

4 Errors, like straws, upon the
surface flow;
He who would search for pearls
must dive below.
John Dryden 1631–1700: *All for Love*
(1678)

5 Crooked things may be as stiff
and unflexible as straight: and
men may be as positive in error
as in truth.
John Locke 1632–1704: *An Essay
concerning Human Understanding*
(1690)

6 Truth lies within a little and
certain compass, but error is
immense.
Henry St. John, Lord Bolingbroke
1678–1751: *Reflections upon Exile*
(1716)

7 When everyone is wrong,
everyone is right.
Nivelle de la Chaussée 1692–1754:
La Gouvernante (1747)

8 It is worse than a crime, it is a
blunder.
*on hearing of the execution of the
Duc d'Enghien, 1804*
Antoine Boulay de la Meurthe 1761–
1840: C.-A. Sainte-Beuve *Nouveaux
Lundis* (1870)

9 As she frequently remarked when
she made any such mistake, it
would be all the same a hundred
years hence.
Charles Dickens 1812–70: *Nicholas
Nickleby* (1839)

10 "Forward, the Light Brigade!"
Was there a man dismayed?

Not though the soldier knew
Some one had blundered.
Alfred, Lord Tennyson 1809–92: "The
Charge of the Light Brigade" (1854)

11 The man who makes no mistakes
does not usually make anything.
Edward John Phelps 1822–1900:
speech at the Mansion House,
London, 24 January 1889

12 To lose one parent, Mr. Worthing,
may be regarded as a misfortune;
to lose both looks like
carelessness.
Oscar Wilde 1854–1900: *The
Importance of Being Earnest* (1895)

13 The report of my death was an
exaggeration.
*usually quoted as "Reports of my
death have been greatly
exaggerated"*
Mark Twain 1835–1910: in *New York
Journal* 2 June 1897

14 Well, if I called the wrong
number, why did you answer the
phone?
James Thurber 1894–1961: cartoon
caption in *New Yorker* 5 June 1937

15 One Galileo in two thousand
years is enough.
*on being asked to proscribe the
works of Teilhard de Chardin*
Pope Pius XII 1876–1958: attributed;
Stafford Beer *Platform for Change*
(1975)

16 The weak have one weapon: the
errors of those who think they
are strong.
Georges Bidault 1899–1983: in
Observer (UK) 15 July 1962

17 If all else fails, immortality can
always be assured by a
spectacular error.
John Kenneth Galbraith 1908– :
attributed

Moderation
see **Excess and Moderation**

Money
see also **Greed, Poverty, Thrift and
Extravagance, Wealth**

1 Wine maketh merry: but money
answereth all things.
Bible: Ecclesiastes

2 If possible honestly, if not,
somehow, make money.
Horace 65–8 BC: *Epistles*; cf. **Wealth
10**

3 No man can serve two masters
. . . Ye cannot serve God and
mammon.
Bible: St. Matthew; cf. **God 31**

4 The love of money is the root of
all evil.
Bible: I Timothy

5 I can get no remedy against this
consumption of the purse:
borrowing only lingers and
lingers it out, but the disease is
incurable.
William Shakespeare 1564–1616:
Henry IV, Part 2 (1597)

6 Money is like muck, not good
except it be spread.
Francis Bacon 1561–1626: *Essays*
(1625) "Of Seditions and Troubles"

7 But it is pretty to see what money
will do.
Samuel Pepys 1633–1703: diary 21
March 1667

8 Money speaks sense in a
language all nations understand.
Aphra Behn 1640–89: *The Rover* pt.
2 (1681)

9 Money is the sinews of love, as of
war.

George Farquhar 1678–1707: *Love and a Bottle* (1698); see **Warfare 4**

10 Take care of the pence, and the pounds will take care of themselves.
William Lowndes 1652–1724: Lord Chesterfield *Letters to his Son* (1774) 5 February 1750

11 Money, wife, is the true fuller's earth for reputations, there is not a spot or a stain but what it can take out.
John Gay 1685–1732: *The Beggar's Opera* (1728)

12 Money . . . is none of the wheels of trade: it is the oil which renders the motion of the wheels more smooth and easy.
David Hume 1711–76: *Essays: Moral and Political* (1741–2) "Of Money"

13 Whoso has sixpence is sovereign (to the length of sixpence) over all men; commands cooks to feed him, philosophers to teach him, kings to mount guard over him,— to the length of sixpence.
Thomas Carlyle 1795–1881: *Sartor Resartus* (1834)

14 The almighty dollar is the only object of worship.
Anonymous: in *Philadelphia Public Ledger* 2 December 1836

15 Money is coined liberty, and so it is ten times dearer to a man who is deprived of freedom. If money is jingling in his pocket, he is half consoled, even though he cannot spend it.
Fyodor Dostoevsky 1821–81: *House of the Dead* (1862)

16 The force of the guinea you have in your pocket depends wholly on the default of a guinea in your neighbour's pocket. If he did not want it, it would be of no use to you.

John Ruskin 1819–1900: *Unto this Last* (1862)

17 Money is like a sixth sense without which you cannot make a complete use of the other five.
W. Somerset Maugham 1874–1965: *Of Human Bondage* (1915)

18 What is robbing a bank compared with founding a bank?
Bertolt Brecht 1898–1956: *Die Dreigroschenoper* (1928)

19 "My boy," he says, "always try to rub up against money, for if you rub up against money long enough, some of it may rub off on you."
Damon Runyon 1884–1946: in *Cosmopolitan* August 1929, "A Very Honorable Guy"

20 A bank is a place that will lend you money if you can prove that you don't need it.
Bob Hope 1903– : Alan Harrington *Life in the Crystal Palace* (1959)

21 Money, it turned out, was exactly like sex, you thought of nothing else if you didn't have it and thought of other things if you did.
James Baldwin 1924–87: in *Esquire* May 1961 "Black Boy looks at the White Boy"

22 From now the pound abroad is worth 14 per cent or so less in terms of other currencies. It does not mean, of course, that the pound here in Britain, in your pocket or purse or in your bank, has been devalued.
Harold Wilson 1916–95: ministerial broadcast, 19 November 1967

23 Those who have some means think that the most important thing in the world is love. The poor know that it is money.
Gerald Brenan 1894–1987: *Thoughts in a Dry Season* (1978)

24 Pennies don't fall from heaven.
They have to be earned on earth.
Margaret Thatcher 1925– : in
Observer (UK) 18 November 1979

Morality

1 *Cum finis est licitus, etiam media
sunt licita.*
The end justifies the means.
Hermann Busenbaum 1600–68:
Medulla Theologiae Moralis (1650);
literally "When the end is allowed,
the means also are allowed" cf. **13**
below

2 That action is best, which
procures the greatest happiness
for the greatest numbers.
Francis Hutcheson 1694–1746: *An
Inquiry into the Original of our Ideas
of Beauty and Virtue* (1725); see
Society 6

3 We know no spectacle so
ridiculous as the British public in
one of its periodical fits of
morality.
Lord Macaulay 1800–59: *Essays
Contributed to the Edinburgh Review*
(1843) "Moore's *Life of Lord Byron*"

4 And many are afraid of God—
And more of Mrs. Grundy.
Frederick Locker-Lampson 1821–95:
"The Jester's Plea" (1868); see
Behavior 9

5 The highest possible stage in
moral culture is when we
recognize that we ought to
control our thoughts.
Charles Darwin 1809–82: *The
Descent of Man* (1871)

6 Morality is the herd-instinct in
the individual.
Friedrich Nietzsche 1844–1900: *Die
fröhliche Wissenschaft* (1882)

7 Morality is a private and costly
luxury.
Henry Brooks Adams 1838–1918: *The
Education of Henry Adams* (1907)

8 The nation's morals are like its
teeth: the more decayed they are
the more it hurts to touch them.
George Bernard Shaw 1856–1950:
The Shewing-up of Blanco Posnet
(1911)

9 Moral indignation is jealousy with
a halo.
H. G. Wells 1866–1946: *The Wife of
Sir Isaac Harman* (1914)

10 You can't learn too soon that the
most useful thing about a
principle is that it can always be
sacrificed to expediency.
W. Somerset Maugham 1874–1965:
The Circle (1921)

11 Food comes first, then morals.
Bertolt Brecht 1898–1956: *Die
Dreigroschenoper* (1928)

12 The last temptation is the greatest
treason:
To do the right deed for the
wrong reason.
T. S. Eliot 1888–1965: *Murder in the
Cathedral* (1935)

13 The end cannot justify the means,
for the simple and obvious reason
that the means employed
determine the nature of the ends
produced.
Aldous Huxley 1894–1963: *Ends and
Means* (1937); see **1** above

14 It is always easier to fight for
one's principles than to live up to
them.
Alfred Adler 1870–1937: Phyllis
Bottome *Alfred Adler* (1939)

15 Morality's *not* practical. Morality's
a gesture. A complicated gesture
learned from books.
Robert Bolt 1924–95: *A Man for All
Seasons* (1960)

16 If people want a sense of purpose,
they should get it from their
archbishops. They should not

hope to receive it from their
politicians.
to Henry Fairlie, 1963
Harold Macmillan 1894–1986: H.
Fairlie *The Life of Politics* (1968)

17 I probably have a different sense
of morality to most people.
Alan Clark 1928–   : in *Times* (UK) 2
June 1994

Mourning and Loss
see also **Sorrow**

1 And the king was much moved,
and went up to the chamber over
the gate, and wept: and as he
went, thus he said, O my son
Absalom, my son, my son
Absalom! would God I had died
for thee, O Absalom, my son, my
son!
Bible: II Samuel

2 Blessed are they that mourn: for
they shall be comforted.
Bible: St. Matthew

3 Grief fills the room up of my
absent child,
Lies in his bed, walks up and
down with me,
Puts on his pretty looks, repeats
his words,
Remembers me of all his gracious
parts,
Stuffs out his vacant garments
with his form:
Then have I reason to be fond of
grief.
William Shakespeare 1564–1616:
King John (1591–8)

4 All my pretty ones?
Did you say all? O hell-kite! All?
What! all my pretty chickens and
their dam,
At one fell swoop?
William Shakespeare 1564–1616:
Macbeth (1606)

5 O more than moon,
Draw not up seas to drown me in
thy sphere,
Weep me not dead, in thine arms,
but forbear
To teach the sea what it may do
too soon.
John Donne 1572–1631: "A
Valediction: of Weeping"

6 He first deceased; she for a little
tried
To live without him: liked it not,
and died.
Henry Wotton 1568–1639: "Upon the
Death of Sir Albertus Moreton's
Wife" (1651)

7 How often are we to die before
we go quite off this stage? In
every friend we lose a part of
ourselves, and the best part.
Alexander Pope 1688–1744: letter to
Jonathan Swift, 5 December 1732

8 I have something more to do
than feel.
*on the death of his mother, at his
sister Mary's hands*
Charles Lamb 1775–1834: letter to S.
T. Coleridge, 27 September 1796

9 We met . . . Dr. Hall in such very
deep mourning that either his
mother, his wife, or himself must
be dead.
Jane Austen 1775–1817: letter to
Cassandra Austen, 17 May 1799

10 She lived unknown, and few
could know
When Lucy ceased to be;
But she is in her grave, and, oh,
The difference to me!
William Wordsworth 1770–1850:
"She dwelt among the untrodden
ways" (1800)

11 I have had playmates, I have had
companions,
In my days of childhood, in my
joyful school-days,—
All, all are gone, the old familiar
faces.

Charles Lamb 1775–1834: "The Old Familiar Faces"

12 Bombazine would have shown a deeper sense of her loss.
Elizabeth Gaskell 1810–65: *Cranford* (1853)

13 They told me, Heraclitus, they told me you were dead,
They brought me bitter news to hear and bitter tears to shed.
I wept as I remembered how often you and I
Had tired the sun with talking and sent him down the sky.
William Cory 1823–92: "Heraclitus" (1858); translation of Callimachus "Epigram"

14 Dead! and . . . never called me mother.
Mrs. Henry Wood 1814–87: *East Lynne* (dramatized by T. A. Palmer, 1874, the words do not occur in the novel of 1861)

15 I can't think of a more wonderful thanksgiving for the life I have had than that everyone should be jolly at my funeral.
Lord Mountbatten 1900–79: Richard Hough *Mountbatten* (1980)

The Movies and Hollywood
see also **Actors and Acting, The Theater**

1 It is like writing history with lightning. And my only regret is that it is all so terribly true.
on seeing D. W. Griffith's film The Birth of a Nation
Woodrow Wilson 1856–1924: at the White House, 18 February 1915

2 The lunatics have taken charge of the asylum.
on the takeover of United Artists by Charlie Chaplin, Mary Pickford, Douglas Fairbanks, and D. W. Griffith
Richard Rowland c. 1881–1947: Terry

Ramsaye *A Million and One Nights* (1926)

3 A trip through a sewer in a glass-bottomed boat.
of Hollywood
Wilson Mizner 1876–1933: Alva Johnston *The Legendary Mizners* (1953)

4 There is only one thing that can kill the movies, and that is education.
Will Rogers 1879–1935: *Autobiography of Will Rogers* (1949)

5 *on being asked which film he would like to see while convalescing:*
Anything except that damned Mouse.
George V 1865–1936: George Lyttelton letter to Rupert Hart-Davis, 12 November 1959

6 Bring on the empty horses!
said while directing the 1936 film The Charge of the Light Brigade
Michael Curtiz 1888–1962: David Niven *Bring on the Empty Horses* (1975)

7 If we'd had as many soldiers as that, we'd have won the war!
on seeing the number of Confederate troops in Gone with the Wind *at the 1939 premiere*
Margaret Mitchell 1900–49: W. G. Harris *Gable and Lombard* (1976)

8 If my books had been any worse, I should not have been invited to Hollywood, and if they had been any better, I should not have come.
Raymond Chandler 1888–1959: letter to Charles W. Morton, 12 December 1945

9 JOE GILLIS: You used to be in pictures. You used to be big.
NORMA DESMOND: I am big. It's the pictures that got small.
Charles Brackett 1892–1969, **Billy**

Wilder 1906–, and **D.M. Marshman, Jr.**: *Sunset Boulevard* (1950 film)

10 If I made Cinderella, the audience would immediately be looking for a body in the coach.
Alfred Hitchcock 1899–1980: *Newsweek* (11 June 1956)

11 The biggest electric train set any boy ever had!
of the RKO studios
Orson Welles 1915–85: Peter Noble *The Fabulous Orson Welles* (1956)

12 Why should people go out and pay to see bad movies when they can stay at home and see bad television for nothing?
Sam Goldwyn 1882–1974: in *Observer* (UK) 9 September 1956

13 Hollywood money isn't money. It's congealed snow, melts in your hand, and there you are.
Dorothy Parker 1893–1967: Malcolm Cowley *Writers at Work* 1st Series (1958)

14 Photography is truth. The cinema is truth 24 times per second.
Jean-Luc Godard 1930– : *Le Petit Soldat* (1960 film)

15 [Hollywood] is filled with people who make adventure pictures and who have never left this place . . . religious pictures and they haven't been in a church or synagogue for years . . . pictures about love and they have never been in love—ever.
Richard Brooks 1944– : *New York Post* (7 December 1960)

16 [Goldwyn] filled the room with wonderful panic and beat at your mind like a man in front of a slot machine, shaking it for a jackpot.
Ben Hecht 1894–1964: A. Scott Berg *Goldwyn* (1989)

17 A dreary industrial town controlled by hoodlums of enormous wealth, the ethical sense of a pack of jackals and taste so degraded that it befouled everything.
on Hollywood
S. J. Perelman 1904–79: *Paris Review* (1964)

18 No one has a closest friend in Hollywood.
Sheilah Graham 1908?–1988: *The Rest of the Story* (1964)

19 All I need to make a comedy is a park, a policeman and a pretty girl.
Charlie Chaplin 1889–1977: *My Autobiography* (1964)

20 The words "Kiss Kiss Bang Bang" which I saw on an Italian movie poster, are perhaps the briefest statement imaginable of the basic appeal of movies.
Pauline Kael 1919– : *Kiss Kiss Bang Bang* (1968)

21 Pictures are for entertainment, messages should be delivered by Western Union.
Sam Goldwyn 1882–1974: Arthur Marx *Goldwyn* (1976)

22 What we need is a story that starts with an earthquake and works its way up to a climax.
Sam Goldwyn 1882–1974: attributed, perhaps apocryphal

23 I wouldn't say when you've seen one Western you've seen the lot; but when you've seen the lot you get the feeling you've seen one.
Katharine Whitehorn 1928– : *Sunday Best* (1976) "Decoding the West"

24 Words are cheap. The biggest thing you can say is "elephant."
on the universality of silent films
Charlie Chaplin 1889–1977: B. Norman *The Movie Greats* (1981)

25 [The camera] is so refined that it makes it possible for us to shed light on the human soul, to reveal it the more brutally and thereby add to our knowledge new dimensions of the "real."
Ingmar Bergman 1918– : *New York Times* (22 January 1978)

26 Keep it out of focus. I want to win the foreign-picture award.
Billy Wilder 1906– : *Colombo's Hollywood* (1979)

27 *Ce n'est pas une image juste, c'est juste une image.*
This is not a just image, it is just an image.
Jean-Luc Godard 1930– : Colin MacCabe *Godard: Images, Sounds, Politics* (1980)

28 GEORGES FRANJU: Movies should have a beginning, a middle and an end.
JEAN-LUC GODARD: Certainly. But not necessarily in that order.
Jean-Luc Godard 1930– : in *Time* 14 September 1981

29 In Hollywood you don't have happiness, you send out for it.
Rex Reed 1938– : *Chicago Tribune* (16 October 1983)

30 No one "goes Hollywood"—they were that way before they came here. Hollywood just exposed it.
Ronald Reagan 1911– : *People* (9 February 1987)

31 There are no rules in filmmaking. Only sins. And the cardinal sin is dullness.
Frank Capra 1897– : *People* (16 September 1991)

32 From the movies we learn precisely how to hold a champagne flute, kiss a mistress, pull a trigger, turn a phrase . . . [but] the movies spoil us for life; nothing ever lives up to them.

Edmund White 1940– : *Genet* (1993)

33 Giving your book to Hollywood is like turning your daughter into a pimp.
Tom Clancy 1947– : *Guardian Weekly* (25 December 1994)

34 Half the people in Hollywood are dying to be discovered and the other half are afraid they will be.
Lionel Barrymore 1878–1954: *Hollywood, Babble On* (1994)

35 Sex and Art . . . neither ever proved to be as dependable as the filtering of present light through that moving strip of celluloid which projects past images and voices onto a screen.
Gore Vidal 1925– : *Screening History* (1994)

36 [*Gandhi*] looms over the real world like an abandoned space station—eternal, expensive and forsaken.
David Thomson 1941– : *A Biographical Dictionary of Film* (1994)

Murder
see also **Death**

1 Thou shalt not kill.
Bible: Exodus; cf. **10** below

2 Will no one rid me of this turbulent priest?
of Thomas Becket, Archbishop of Canterbury, murdered in Canterbury Cathedral, December 1170
Henry II 1133–89: oral tradition

3 Mordre wol out; that se we day by day.
Geoffrey Chaucer c. 1343–1400: *The Canterbury Tales* "The Nun's Priest's Tale"

4 Murder most foul, as in the best it
is;
But this most foul, strange, and
unnatural.
William Shakespeare 1564–1616:
Hamlet (1601)

5 The coward's weapon, poison.
Phineas Fletcher 1582–1650:
Sicelides (performed 1614)

6 Killing no murder briefly discourst
in three questions.
an apology for tyrannicide
Edward Sexby d. 1658: title of
pamphlet (1657)

7 Assassination is the quickest way.
Molière 1622–73: *Le Sicilien* (1668)

8 Murder considered as one of the
fine arts.
Thomas De Quincey 1785–1859: in
Blackwood's Magazine February
1827; essay title

9 In that case, if we are to abolish
the death penalty, let the
murderers take the first step.
Alphonse Karr 1808–90: in *Les
Guêpes* January 1849

10 Thou shalt not kill; but need'st
not strive
Officiously to keep alive.
Arthur Hugh Clough 1819–61: "The
Latest Decalogue" (1862); cf. 1
above

11 Assassination has never changed
the history of the world.
Benjamin Disraeli 1804–81: speech,
House of Commons, 1 May 1865

12 It was not until several weeks
after he had decided to murder
his wife that Dr. Bickleigh took
any active steps in the matter.
Murder is a serious business.
Francis Iles 1893–1970: *Malice
Aforethought* (1931)

13 Any man has to, needs to, wants
to

Once in a lifetime, do a girl in.
T. S. Eliot 1888–1965: *Sweeney
Agonistes* (1932)

14 Kill a man, and you are an
assassin. Kill millions of men, and
you are a conqueror. Kill
everyone, and you are a god.
Jean Rostand 1894–1977: *Pensées
d'un biologiste* (1939)

15 Roast beef and Yorkshire, or roast
pork and apple sauce, followed up
by suet pudding and driven
home, as it were, by a cup of
mahogany-brown tea, have put
you in just the right mood. Your
pipe is drawing sweetly, the sofa
cushions are soft underneath you,
the fire is well alight, the air is
warm and stagnant. In these
blissful circumstances, what is it
that you want to read about?
   Naturally, about a murder.
George Orwell 1903–50: *Decline of
the English Murder and other essays*
(1965) title essay, written 1946

16 Television has brought back
murder into the home—where it
belongs.
Alfred Hitchcock 1899–1980: in
Observer (UK) 19 December 1965

Music
see also **Musicians, Singing**

1 Is it not strange, that sheeps' guts
should hale souls out of men's
bodies?
William Shakespeare 1564–1616:
Much Ado About Nothing (1598–9)

2 If music be the food of love, play
on;
Give me excess of it, that,
surfeiting,
The appetite may sicken, and so
die.
William Shakespeare 1564–1616:
Twelfth Night (1601)

3 Music helps not the toothache.
George Herbert 1593–1633:
Outlandish Proverbs (1640)

4 Music has charms to soothe a
savage breast.
William Congreve 1670–1729: *The
Mourning Bride* (1697)

5 Of music Dr. Johnson used to say
that it was the only sensual
pleasure without vice.
Samuel Johnson 1709–84: in
European Magazine (1795)

6 A carpenter's hammer, in a warm
summer noon, will fret me into
more than midsummer madness.
But those unconnected, unset
sounds are nothing to the
measured malice of music.
Charles Lamb 1775–1834: *Elia* (1823)

7 Hark, the dominant's persistence
till it must be answered to!
Robert Browning 1812–89: "A
Toccata of Galuppi's" (1855)

8 But I struck one chord of music,
Like the sound of a great Amen.
Adelaide Ann Procter 1825–64: "A
Lost Chord" (1858)

9 Hell is full of musical amateurs:
music is the brandy of the
damned.
George Bernard Shaw 1856–1950:
Man and Superman (1903)

10 There is music in the air.
Edward Elgar 1857–1934: R. J.
Buckley *Sir Edward Elgar* (1905)

11 It is only that which cannot be
expressed otherwise that is worth
expressing in music.
Frederick Delius 1862–1934: in
Sackbut September 1920 "At the
Crossroads"

12 Classic music is th'kind that we
keep thinkin'll turn into a tune.
Frank McKinney ("Kin") Hubbard

1868–1930: *Comments of Abe Martin
and His Neighbors* (1923)

13 Extraordinary how potent cheap
music is.
Noël Coward 1899–1973: *Private
Lives* (1930)

14 Jazz will endure, just as long as
people hear it through their feet
instead of their brains.
John Philip Sousa 1854–1932: Nat
Shapiro (ed.) *An Encyclopedia of
Quotations about Music* (1978)

15 Music begins to atrophy when it
departs too far from the dance . . .
poetry begins to atrophy when it
gets too far from music.
Ezra Pound 1885–1972: *The ABC of
Reading* (1934)

16 The whole trouble with a folk
song is that once you have played
it through there is nothing much
you can do except play it over
again and play it rather louder.
Constant Lambert 1905–51: *Music
Ho!* (1934)

17 The whole problem can be stated
quite simply by asking, "Is there a
meaning to music?" My answer to
that would be, "Yes." And "Can
you state in so many words what
the meaning is?" My answer to
that would be, "No."
Aaron Copland 1900–90: *What to
Listen for in Music* (1939)

18 Jazz music is to be played sweet,
soft, plenty rhythm.
Jelly Roll Morton 1885–1941: *Mister
Jelly Roll* (1950)

19 What a terrible revenge by the
culture of the Negroes on that of
the whites!
of jazz
Ignacy Jan Paderewski 1860–1941:
Nat Shapiro (ed.) *An Encyclopedia of
Quotations about Music* (1978)

20 If she can stand it, I can. Play it!
*usually misquoted as "Play it again,
Sam"*
Julius J. Epstein 1909– et al.:
Casablanca (1942 film); spoken by
Humphrey Bogart

21 Good music is that which
penetrates the ear with facility
and quits the memory with
difficulty.
Thomas Beecham 1879–1961:
speech, *c.* 1950 in *New York Times* 9
March 1961

22 Music is your own experience,
your thoughts, your wisdom. If
you don't live it, it won't come
out of your horn.
Charlie Parker 1920–55: Nat Shapiro
and Nat Hentoff *Hear Me Talkin' to
Ya* (1955)

23 It is like a beautiful woman who
has not grown older, but younger
with time, more slender, more
supple, more graceful.
on the cello
Pablo Casals 1876–1973: in *Time* 29
April 1957

24 I don't know whether I like it,
but it's what I meant.
on his 4th symphony
Ralph Vaughan Williams 1872–1958:
Christopher Headington *Bodley Head
History of Western Music* (1974)

25 Like two skeletons copulating on
a corrugated tin roof.
of the harpsichord
Thomas Beecham 1879–1961: Harold
Atkins and Archie Newman *Beecham
Stories* (1978)

26 If you still have to ask . . . shame
on you.
*when asked what jazz is; sometimes
quoted as, "Man, if you gotta ask
you'll never know"*
Louis Armstrong 1901–71: Max Jones
et al. *Salute to Satchmo* (1970)

27 The tuba is certainly the most
intestinal of instruments—the
very lower bowel of music.
Peter de Vries 1910–93: *The Glory of
the Hummingbird* (1974)

28 Music is spiritual. The music
business is not.
Van Morrison: in *The Times* (UK) 6
July 1990

29 Why waste money on
psychotherapy when you can
listen to the B Minor Mass?
Michael Torke 1961– : in *Observer*
(UK) 23 September 1990 "Sayings of
the Week"

30 Improvisation is too good to leave
to chance.
Paul Simon 1942– : in *Observer*
(UK) 30 December 1990

Musicians
see also **Music**

1 Difficult do you call it, Sir? I wish
it were impossible.
*on the performance of a celebrated
violinist*
Samuel Johnson 1709–84: William
Seward *Supplement to the
Anecdotes of Distinguished Persons*
(1797)

2 I must shut my ears. The man of
sin rubbeth the hair of the horse
to the bowels of the cat.
on hearing a violin being played
John O'Keeffe 1747–1833: *Wild Oats*
(1791)

3 Some cry up Haydn, some
    Mozart,
Just as the whim bites; for my
    part
I care not a farthing candle
For either of them, or for Handel.
Charles Lamb 1775–1834: "Free
Thoughts on Several Eminent
Composers" (1830)

4 Hats off, gentlemen—a genius!
on Chopin
Robert Schumann 1810–56: "An
Opus 2" (1831); H. Pleasants (ed.)
Schumann on Music (1965)

5 Wagner has lovely moments but
awful quarters of an hour.
Gioacchino Rossini 1792–1868: said
to Emile Naumann, April 1867; E.
Naumann *Italienische Tondichter*
(1883)

6 We are the music makers,
We are the dreamers of dreams
. . .
We are the movers and shakers
Of the world for ever, it seems.
Arthur O'Shaughnessy 1844–81:
"Ode" (1874)

7 Everything will pass, and the
world will perish but the Ninth
Symphony [Beethoven's] will
remain.
Michael Bakunin 1814–76: Edmund
Wilson *To The Finland Station* (1940)

8 Please do not shoot the pianist.
He is doing his best.
printed notice in a dancing saloon
Anonymous: Oscar Wilde
Impressions of America "Leadville"
(*c.* 1882–3)

9 I have been told that Wagner's
music is better than it sounds.
Bill Nye 1850–96: Mark Twain
Autobiography (1924)

10 It will be generally admitted that
Beethoven's Fifth Symphony is
the most sublime noise that has
ever penetrated into the ear of
man.
E. M. Forster 1879–1970: *Howards
End* (1910)

11 Ravel refuses the Legion of Honor,
but all his music accepts it.
Erik Satie 1866–1925: Jean Cocteau
Le Discours d'Oxford (1956)

12 As for the slow movement, I
thought it would never end. It
was like being in such a slow
train with so many stops that one
becomes convinced that one has
passed one's station.
*on the performance of a Bruckner
symphony*
Sylvia Townsend Warner 1893–1978:
diary 20 November 1929

13 Bach almost persuades me to be a
Christian.
Roger Fry 1866–1934: Virginia Woolf
Roger Fry (1940)

14 The notes I handle no better than
many pianists. But the pauses
between the notes—ah, that is
where the art resides!
Artur Schnabel 1882–1951: in
Chicago Daily News 11 June 1958

15 Children are given Mozart
because of the small *quantity* of
the notes; grown-ups avoid
Mozart because of the great
quality of the notes.
Artur Schnabel 1882–1951: *My Life
and Music* (1961)

16 Playing "Bop" is like scrabble
with all the vowels missing.
Duke Ellington 1899–1974: in *Look*
10 August 1954

17 There are two golden rules for an
orchestra: start together and
finish together. The public doesn't
give a damn what goes on in
between.
Thomas Beecham 1879–1961: Harold
Atkins and Archie Newman *Beecham
Stories* (1978)

18 Too much counterpoint; what is
worse, Protestant counterpoint.
of Bach
Thomas Beecham 1879–1961: in
Guardian (UK) 8 March 1971

19 Whether the angels play only
Bach in praising God I am not

quite sure; I am sure, however,
that en famille they play Mozart.
Karl Barth 1886–1968: in *New York
Times* 11 December 1968

20 A musician, if he's a messenger,
is like a child who hasn't been
handled too many times by man,
hasn't had too many fingerprints
across his brain.
Jimi Hendrix 1942–70: in *Life
Magazine* (1969)

21 Most people get into bands for
three very simple rock and roll
reasons: to get laid, to get fame,
and to get rich.
Bob Geldof 1954– : in *Melody
Maker* 27 August 1977

22 Ballads and babies. That's what
happened to me.
on reaching the age of fifty
Paul McCartney 1942– : in *Time* 8
June 1992

23 I'm dealing in rock'n'roll. I'm,
like, I'm not a bona fide human
being.
Phil Spector 1940– : attributed

Names

1 God hath also highly exalted him,
and given him a name which is
above every name:
That at the name of Jesus every
knee should bow.
Bible: Philippians

2 What's in a name? that which we
call a rose
By any other name would smell
as sweet.
William Shakespeare 1564–1616:
Romeo and Juliet (1595)

3 JAQUES: I do not like her name.
ORLANDO: There was no thought
of pleasing you when she was
christened.
William Shakespeare 1564–1616: *As
You Like It* (1599)

4 If you call a dog *Hervey*, I shall
love him.
*as the measure of his feeling for
Lord Hervey, who was "a vicious
man, but very kind to me"*
Samuel Johnson 1709–84: James
Boswell *Life of Johnson* (1791) 1737

5 If you should have a boy do not
christen him John . . . 'Tis a bad
name and goes against a man. If
my name had been Edmund I
should have been more fortunate.
John Keats 1795–1821: letter to his
sister-in-law, 13 January 1820

6 A nickname is the heaviest stone
that the devil can throw at a
man.
William Hazlitt 1778–1830: *Sketches
and Essays* (1839) "Nicknames"

7 Fate tried to conceal him by
naming him Smith.
of Samuel Francis Smith
Oliver Wendell Holmes 1809–94:
"The Boys" (1858)

8 With a name like yours, you
might be any shape, almost.
Lewis Carroll 1832–98: *Through the
Looking-Glass* (1872)

9 There may have been
disillusionments in the lives of the
medieval saints, but they would
scarcely have been better pleased
if they could have forseen that
their names would be associated
nowadays chiefly with racehorses
and the cheaper clarets.
Saki 1870–1916: *Reginald* (1904)

10 Dear 338171 (May I call you
338?)
Noël Coward 1899–1973: letter to T.
E. Lawrence, 25 August 1930

11 A self-made man may prefer a self-
made name.
*on Samuel Goldfish changing his
name to Samuel Goldwyn*
Learned Hand 1872–1961: Bosley
Crowther *Lion's Share* (1957)

12 The name of a man is a numbing
blow from which he never
recovers.
Marshall McLuhan 1911–80:
Understanding Media (1964)

13 Every Tom, Dick and Harry is
called Arthur.
*to Arthur Hornblow, who was
planning to name his son Arthur*
Sam Goldwyn 1882–1974: Michael
Freedland *The Goldwyn Touch* (1986)

14 No, I'm breaking it in for a friend.
*when asked if Groucho were his real
name*
Groucho Marx 1895–1977: attributed

15 We do have these extraordinary
names . . . When you see the sign
"African Primates Meeting" you
expect someone to produce
bananas.
*at his retirement service as
Archbishop of Cape Town, 23 June
1996*
Desmond Tutu 1931—: in *Daily
Telegraph* (UK) 24 June 1996

Nature
see also **The Earth, Life Sciences**

1 Nature does nothing without
purpose or uselessly.
Aristotle 384–322 BC: *Politics*

2 In her inventions nothing is
lacking, and nothing is
superfluous.
Leonardo da Vinci 1452–1519:
Edward McCurdy (ed.) *Leonardo da
Vinci's Notebooks* (1906)

3 And this our life, exempt from
public haunt,
Finds tongues in trees, books in
the running brooks,
Sermons in stones, and good in
everything.
William Shakespeare 1564–1616: *As
You Like It* (1599)

4 All things are artificial, for nature
is the art of God.
Thomas Browne 1605–82: *Religio
Medici* (1643)

5 It were happy if we studied
nature more in natural things,
and acted according to nature,
whose rules are few, plain, and
most reasonable.
William Penn 1644–1718: *Some
Fruits of Solitude* (1693)

6 I have learned
To look on nature, not as in the
hour
Of thoughtless youth; but hearing
oftentimes
The still, sad music of humanity.
William Wordsworth 1770–1850:
"Lines composed . . . above Tintern
Abbey" (1798)

7 There is a pleasure in the pathless
woods,
There is a rapture on the lonely
shore,
There is society, where none
intrudes,
By the deep sea, and music in its
roar:
I love not man the less, but
nature more.
Lord Byron 1788–1824: *Childe
Harold's Pilgrimage* (1812–18)

8 The roaring of the wind is my
wife and the stars through the
window pane are my children.
John Keats 1795–1821: letter to
George and Georgiana Keats, 24
October 1818

9 Who trusted God was love indeed
And love Creation's final law—
Though Nature, red in tooth and
claw
With ravine, shrieked against his
creed.
Alfred, Lord Tennyson 1809–92: *In
Memoriam A. H. H.* (1850)

10 It is the marriage of the soul with
Nature that makes the intellect

fruitful, and gives birth to imagination.
Henry David Thoreau 1817–62: *Journal* (21 August 1851)

11 I believe a leaf of grass is no less than the journey-work of the stars,
And the pismire is equally perfect, and a grain of sand, and the egg of the wren,
And the tree toad is a chef-d'oeuvre for the highest,
And the running blackberry would adorn the parlours of heaven.
Walt Whitman 1819–92: "Song of Myself" (written 1855)

12 What a book a devil's chaplain might write on the clumsy, wasteful, blundering, low, and horridly cruel works of nature!
Charles Darwin 1809–82: letter to J. D. Hooker, 13 July 1856

13 Nature is no spendthrift, but takes the shortest way to her ends.
Ralph Waldo Emerson 1803–82: *The Conduct of Life, Fate* (1860)

14 No matter how often you knock at nature's door, she won't answer in words you can understand—for Nature is dumb. She'll vibrate and moan like a violin, but you mustn't expect a song.
Ivan Turgenev 1818–83: *On the Eve* (1860)

15 Nature is not a temple, but a workshop, and man's the workman in it.
Ivan Turgenev 1818–83: *Fathers and Sons* (1862)

16 "I play for Seasons; not Eternities!"
Says Nature.
George Meredith 1828–1909: *Modern Love* (1862)

17 In nature there are neither rewards nor punishments—there are consequences.
Robert G. Ingersoll 1833–99: *Some Reasons Why* (1881)

18 Pile the bodies high at Austerlitz and Waterloo.
Shovel them under and let me work—
I am the grass; I cover all.
Carl Sandburg 1878–1967: "Grass" (1918)

19 For nature, heartless, witless nature,
Will neither care nor know
What stranger's feet may find the meadow
And trespass there and go.
A. E. Housman 1859–1936: *Last Poems* (1922) no. 40

20 Nature, Mr. Allnut, is what we are put into this world to rise above.
James Agee 1909–55: *The African Queen* (1951 film); not in the novel by C. S. Forester

21 BRICK: Well, they say nature hates a vacuum, Big Daddy.
BIG DADDY: That's what they say, but sometimes I think that a vacuum is a hell of a lot better than some of the stuff that nature replaces it with.
Tennessee Williams 1911–83: *Cat on a Hot Tin Roof* (1955)

22 I would feel more optimistic about a bright future for man if he spent less time proving that he can outwit Nature and more time tasting her sweetness and respecting her seniority.
E. B. White 1899–1985: *Essays of E. B. White, "Coon Tree"* (1977)

23 People thought they could explain and conquer nature—yet the outcome is that they

destroyed it and disinherited
themselves from it.
Václav Havel 1936– : Lewis Wolpert
The Unnatural Nature of Science
(1993)

Necessity

1 All places that the eye of heaven
visits
Are to a wise man ports and
happy havens.
Teach thy necessity to reason
thus:
There is no virtue like necessity.
William Shakespeare 1564–1616:
Richard II (1595)

2 Must! Is *must* a word to be
addressed to princes? Little man,
little man! thy father, if he had
been alive, durst not have used
that word.
*to Robert Cecil, on his saying she
must go to bed*
Elizabeth I 1533–1603: J. R. Green *A
Short History of the English People*
(1874)

3 Cruel necessity.
on the execution of Charles I, 1649
Oliver Cromwell 1599–1658: Joseph
Spence *Anecdotes* (1820)

4 Necessity hath no law. Feigned
necessities, imaginary necessities
. . . are the greatest cozenage that
men can put upon the Providence
of God, and make pretences to
break known rules by.
Oliver Cromwell 1599–1658: speech
to Parliament, 12 September 1654

5 Necessity never made a good
bargain.
Benjamin Franklin 1706–90: *Poor
Richard's Almanack* (1735)

6 The superfluous, a very necessary
thing.
Voltaire 1694–1778: *Le Mondain*
(1736)

7 Necessity is the plea for every
infringement of human freedom:
it is the argument of tyrants; it is
the creed of slaves.
William Pitt 1759–1806: speech,
House of Commons, 18 November
1783

News and Journalism

1 Tell it not in Gath, publish it not
in the streets of Askelon.
Bible: II Samuel

2 As cold waters to a thirsty soul,
so is good news from a far
country.
Bible: Proverbs

3 How beautiful upon the
mountains are the feet of him
that bringeth good tidings.
Bible: Isaiah

4 What news on the Rialto?
William Shakespeare 1564–1616: *The
Merchant of Venice* (1596–8)

5 Ill news hath wings, and with the
wind doth go,
Comfort's a cripple and comes
ever slow.
Michael Drayton 1563–1631: *The
Barons' Wars* (1603)

6 The nature of bad news infects
the teller.
William Shakespeare 1564–1616:
Antony and Cleopatra (1606–7)

7 A master passion is the love of
news.
George Crabbe 1754–1832: "The
Newspaper" (1785)

8 The journalists have constructed
for themselves a little wooden
chapel, which they also call the
Temple of Fame, in which they
put up and take down portraits
all day long and make such a
hammering you can't hear
yourself speak.
Georg Christoph Lichtenberg 1742–

99: A. Leitzmann *Georg Christoph Lichtenberg Aphorismen* (1904)

9 In order to enjoy the inestimable benefits that the liberty of the press ensures, it is necessary to submit to the inevitable evils that it creates.
Alexis de Tocqueville 1805–59: *Democracy in America* (1835)

10 The purchaser [of a newspaper] desires an article which he can appreciate at sight; which he can lay down and say, "An excellent article, very excellent; exactly *my own* sentiments."
Walter Bagehot 1826–77: in *National Review* (UK) July 1856 "The Character of Sir Robert Peel"

11 *The Times* has made many ministries.
Walter Bagehot 1826–77: *The English Constitution* (1867) "The Cabinet"

12 All newspaper and journalistic activity is an intellectual brothel from which there is no retreat.
Leo Tolstoy 1828–1910: letter to Prince V. P. Meshchersky, 22 August 1871

13 There are laws to protect the freedom of the press's speech, but none that are worth anything to protect the people from the press.
Mark Twain 1835–1910: "License of the Press" (1873)

14 You furnish the pictures and I'll furnish the war.
message to the artist Frederic Remington in Havana, Cuba, during the Spanish-American War of 1898
William Randolph Hearst 1863–1951: attributed

15 By office boys for office boys.
of the Daily Mail
Lord Salisbury 1830–1903: H. Hamilton Fyfe *Northcliffe, an Intimate Biography* (1930)

16 The men with the muck-rakes are often indispensable to the well-being of society; but only if they know when to stop raking the muck.
Theodore Roosevelt 1858–1919: speech in Washington, 14 April 1906

17 Journalism largely consists in saying "Lord Jones Dead" to people who never knew that Lord Jones was alive.
G. K. Chesterton 1874–1936: *Wisdom of Father Brown* (1914)

18 The power of the press is very great, but not so great as the power to suppress.
Lord Northcliffe 1865–1922: office message, *Daily Mail* (UK) 1918; Reginald Rose and Geoffrey Harmsworth *Northcliffe* (1959)

19 When a dog bites a man, that is not news, because it happens so often. But if a man bites a dog, that is news.
John B. Bogart 1848–1921: F. M. O'Brien *The Story of the* [New York] *Sun* (1918); often attributed to Charles A. Dana

20 Journalists say a thing that they know isn't true, in the hope that if they keep on saying it long enough it *will* be true.
Arnold Bennett 1867–1931: *The Title* (1918)

21 Comment is free, but facts are sacred.
C. P. Scott 1846–1932: in *Manchester Guardian* (UK) 5 May 1921; cf. **32** below

22 Well, all I know is what I read in the papers.
Will Rogers 1879–1935: in *New York Times* 30 September 1923

23 The art of newspaper paragraphing is to stroke a platitude until it purrs like an epigram.

Don Marquis 1878–1937: E. Anthony
O Rare Don Marquis (1962)

24 News is what a chap who doesn't
care much about anything wants
to read. And it's only news until
he's read it. After that it's dead.
Evelyn Waugh 1903–66: *Scoop*
(1938)

25 I ran the paper purely for
propaganda, and with no other
purpose.
of the Daily Express (UK)
Lord Beaverbrook 1879–1964:
evidence to Royal Commission on
the Press, 18 March 1948

26 Small earthquake in Chile. Not
many dead.
*the words with which Cockburn
claimed to have won a competition
at* The Times (UK) *for the dullest
headline*
Claud Cockburn 1904–81: *In Time of
Trouble* (1956)

27 I read the newspapers avidly. It is
my one form of continuous
fiction.
Aneurin Bevan 1897–1960: in *The
Times* (UK) 29 March 1960

28 A good newspaper, I suppose, is a
nation talking to itself.
Arthur Miller 1915– : in *Observer*
(UK) 26 November 1961

29 Freedom of the press in Britain
means freedom to print such of
the proprietor's prejudices as the
advertisers don't object to.
Hannen Swaffer 1879–1962: Tom
Driberg *Swaff* (1974)

30 Success in journalism can be a
form of failure. Freedom comes
from lack of possessions. The
truth-divulging paper must
imitate the tramp and sleep under
a hedge.
Graham Greene 1904–91: in *New
Statesman* (UK) 31 May 1968

31 The press is the enemy.
Richard Nixon 1913–1994: *remark to
aides* (1969)

32 Comment is free but facts are on
expenses.
Tom Stoppard 1937– : *Night and
Day* (1978); see **21** above

33 Rock journalism is people who
can't write interviewing people
who can't talk for people who
can't read.
Frank Zappa 1940–93: Linda Botts
Loose Talk (1980)

34 Whenever I see a newspaper I
think of the poor trees. As trees
they provide beauty, shade and
shelter. But as paper all they
provide is rubbish.
Yehudi Menuhin 1916– : attributed,
1982

35 Blood sport is brought to its
ultimate refinement in the gossip
columns.
Bernard Ingham 1932– : speech, 5
February 1986

36 Journalists belong in the gutter
because that is where the ruling
classes throw their guilty secrets.
Gerald Priestland 1927–91: in
Observer (UK) 22 May 1988

37 Only a fool expects the authorities
to tell him what the news is.
Russell Baker 1925– : *The Good
Times* (1989)

38 Go to where the silence is and
say something.
*accepting an award from Columbia
University for her coverage of the
1991 massacre in East Timor by
Indonesian troops*
Amy Goodman 1957– : in *Columbia
Journalism Review* March/April 1994

39 I don't know. The editor did it
when I was away.
*when asked why he had allowed
Page 3 to develop*

Rupert Murdoch 1931– : in *Guardian* (UK) 25 February 1994

40 When seagulls follow a trawler, it is because they think sardines will be thrown into the sea.
to the media at the end of a press conference, 31 March 1995
Eric Cantona 1966– : in *The Times* 1 April 1995

New Zealand
see **Australia and New Zealand**

Night
see **Day and Night**

Old Age
see also **Middle Age**

1 Then shall ye bring down my grey hairs with sorrow to the grave.
Bible: Genesis

2 The days of our age are threescore years and ten; and though men be so strong that they come to fourscore years: yet is their strength then but labor and sorrow; so soon passeth it away, and we are gone.
Bible: Psalm 90

3 The sixth age shifts
Into the lean and slippered pantaloon,
With spectacles on nose and pouch on side,
His youthful hose well saved a world too wide
For his shrunk shank; and his big manly voice,
Turning again towards childish treble, pipes
And whistles in his sound. Last scene of all,
That ends this strange eventful history,
Is second childishness, and mere oblivion,

Sans teeth, sans eyes, sans taste, sans everything.
William Shakespeare 1564–1616: *As You Like It* (1599)

4 No spring, nor summer beauty hath such grace,
As I have seen in one autumnal face.
John Donne 1572–1631: "The Autumnal" (*c*. 1600)

5 Age will not be defied.
Francis Bacon 1561–1626: *Essays* (1625) "Of Regimen of Health"

6 Every man desires to live long: but no man would be old.
Jonathan Swift 1667–1745: *Thoughts on Various Subjects* (1727 ed.)

7 See how the world its veterans rewards!
A youth of frolics, an old age of cards.
Alexander Pope 1688–1744: *Epistles to Several Persons* "To a Lady" (1735)

8 How happy he who crowns in shades like these,
A youth of labour with an age of ease.
Oliver Goldsmith 1730–74: *The Deserted Village* (1770)

9 Those that desire to write or say anything to me have no time to lose; for time has shaken me by the hand and death is not far behind.
John Wesley 1703–91: letter to Ezekiel Cooper, 1 February 1791

10 The abbreviation of time, and the failure of hope, will always tinge with a browner shade the evening of life.
Edward Gibbon 1737–94: *Memoirs of My Life* (1796)

11 My one fear is that I may live too long. This would be a subject of dread to me.

Thomas Jefferson 1743–1826: *letter to Philip Mazzei* (March 1801)

12 Age does not make us childish, as men tell,
It merely finds us children still at heart.
Johann Wolfgang von Goethe 1749–1832: *Faust* pt. 1 (1808)

13 Grow old along with me!
The best is yet to be.
Robert Browning 1812–89: "Rabbi Ben Ezra" (1864)

14 W'en folks git ole en strucken wid de palsy, dey mus speck ter be laff'd at.
Joel Chandler Harris 1848–1908: *Nights with Uncle Remus* (1883)

15 There's a fascination frantic
In a ruin that's romantic;
Do you think you are sufficiently decayed?
W. S. Gilbert 1836–1911: *The Mikado* (1885)

16 It is better to be seventy years young than forty years old!
Oliver Wendell Holmes 1809–94: reply to invitation from Julia Ward Howe to her seventieth birthday party, 27 May 1889

17 When you are old and grey and full of sleep,
And nodding by the fire, take down this book
And slowly read and dream of the soft look
Your eyes had once, and of their shadows deep.
W. B. Yeats 1865–1939: "When You Are Old" (1893)

18 As a white candle
In a holy place,
So is the beauty
Of an agèd face.
Joseph Campbell 1879–1944: "Old Woman" (1913)

19 I grow old . . . I grow old . . .
I shall wear the bottoms of my trousers rolled.

T. S. Eliot 1888–1965: "The Love Song of J. Alfred Prufrock" (1917)

20 Oh, to be seventy again!
on seeing a pretty girl on his eightieth birthday
Georges Clemenceau 1841–1929: James Agate diary, 19 April 1938; also attributed to Oliver Wendell Holmes, Jr.

21 The older I grow the more I distrust the familiar doctrine that age brings wisdom.
H. L. Mencken 1880–1956: *Prejudices, Third Series* (1922)

22 From the earliest times the old have rubbed it into the young that they are wiser than they, and before the young had discovered what nonsense this was they were old too, and it profited them to carry on the imposture.
W. Somerset Maugham 1874–1965: *Cakes and Ale* (1930)

23 Nothing really wrong with him— only anno domini, but that's the most fatal complaint of all, in the end.
James Hilton 1900–54: *Goodbye, Mr. Chips* (1934)

24 Old age is the most unexpected of all things that happen to a man.
Leon Trotsky 1879–1940: diary 8 May 1935

25 As de old folks always say, Ah'm born but Ah ain't dead. No tellin' what Ah'm liable tuh do yet.
Zora Neale Hurston 1901–60: *Their Eyes Were Watching God* (1937)

26 Growing old is no more than a bad habit which a busy man has no time to form.
André Maurois 1885–1967: *The Art of Living* (1940)

27 You will recognize, my boy, the first sign of old age: it is when you go out into the streets of London and realize for the first time how young the policemen look.
Seymour Hicks 1871–1949: C. R. D. Pulling *They Were Singing* (1952)

28 To me old age is always fifteen years older than I am.
Bernard Baruch 1870–1965: in *Newsweek* 29 August 1955

29 Considering the alternative, it's not too bad at all.
when asked what he felt about the advancing years on his seventy-second birthday
Maurice Chevalier 1888–1972: Michael Freedland *Maurice Chevalier* (1981)

30 What is called the serenity of age is only perhaps a euphemism for the fading power to feel the sudden shock of joy or sorrow.
Arthur Bliss 1891–1975: *As I Remember* (1970)

31 With full-span lives having become the norm, people may need to learn how to be aged as they once had to learn how to be adult.
Ronald Blythe 1922– : *The View in Winter* (1979)

32 If I'd known I was gonna live this long, I'd have taken better care of myself.
on reaching the age of 100
Eubie Blake 1883–1983: in *Observer* (UK) 13 February 1983 "Sayings of the Week"

33 I recently turned sixty. Practically a third of my life is over.
Woody Allen 1935– : in *Observer* (UK) 10 March 1996 "Sayings of the Week"

Openness
see **Secrecy and Openness**

Opinion

1 A plague of opinion! a man may wear it on both sides, like a leather jerkin.
William Shakespeare 1564–1616: *Troilus and Cressida* (1602)

2 Opinion in good men is but knowledge in the making.
John Milton 1608–74: *Areopagitica* (1644)

3 They that approve a private opinion, call it opinion; but they that mislike it, heresy: and yet heresy signifies no more than private opinion.
Thomas Hobbes 1588–1679: *Leviathan* (1651)

4 He that complies against his will,
Is of his own opinion still;
Which he may adhere to, yet disown,
For reasons to himself best known.
Samuel Butler 1612–80: *Hudibras* pt. 3 (1680)

5 Some praise at morning what they blame at night;
But always think the last opinion right.
Alexander Pope 1688–1744: *An Essay on Criticism* (1711)

6 Have not the wisest of men in all ages, not excepting Solomon himself,—have they not had their Hobby-Horses . . . and so long as a man rides his Hobby-Horse peaceably and quietly along the King's highway, and neither compels you or me to get up behind him,—pray, Sir, what have either you or I to do with it?
Laurence Sterne 1713–68: *Tristram Shandy* (1759–67)

7 Every man has a right to utter
what he thinks truth, and every
other man has a right to knock
him down for it. Martyrdom is
the test.
Samuel Johnson 1709–84: James
Boswell *Life of Samuel Johnson*
(1791) 1780

8 A man can brave opinion, a
woman must submit to it.
Mme. de Staël 1766–1817: *Delphine*
(1802)

9 Public opinion is a weak tyrant
compared with our own private
opinion. What a man thinks of
himself, that it is which
determines, or rather, indicates,
his fate.
Henry David Thoreau 1817–62:
Walden (1854)

10 If all mankind minus one were of
one opinion, and only one person
were of the contrary opinion,
mankind would be no more
justified in silencing that one
person, than he, if he had the
power, would be justified in
silencing mankind.
John Stuart Mill 1806–73: *On Liberty*
(1859)

11 There are nine and sixty ways of
constructing tribal lays,
And—every—single—one—of—
them—is—right!
Rudyard Kipling 1865–1936: "In the
Neolithic Age" (1893)

12 It were not best that we should
all think alike; it is difference of
opinion that makes horse-races.
Mark Twain 1835–1910: *Pudd'nhead
Wilson* (1894)

13 The public buys its opinions as it
buys its meat, or takes in its milk,
on the principle that it is cheaper
to do this than to keep a cow. So
it is, but the milk is more likely to
be watered.
Samuel Butler 1835–1902:
Notebooks (1912)

14 Thank God, in these days of
enlightenment and establishment,
everyone has a right to his own
opinions, and chiefly to the
opinion that nobody else has a
right to theirs.
Ronald Knox 1888–1957: *Reunion All
Round* (1914)

15 An intellectual hatred is the
worst,
So let her think opinions are
accursed.
W. B. Yeats 1865–1939: "A Prayer
for My Daughter" (1920)

16 The opinions that are held with
passion are always those for
which no good ground exists;
indeed the passion is the measure
of the holder's lack of rational
conviction.
Bertrand Russell 1872–1970:
Sceptical Essays (1928)

17 Why should you mind being
wrong if someone can show you
that you are?
A. J. Ayer 1910–89: attributed

18 You might very well think that. I
couldn't possibly comment.
*the Chief Whip's habitual response
to questioning*
Michael Dobbs 1948– : *House of
Cards* (televised 1990)

Opportunity

1 Time is that wherein there is
opportunity, and opportunity is
that wherein there is no great
time.
Hippocrates c. 460–357 BC: *Precepts*

2 How oft the sight of means to do
ill deeds
Makes ill deeds done!
William Shakespeare 1564–1616:
King John (1591–8)

3 There is a tide in the affairs of
men,

Which, taken at the flood, leads
  on to fortune;
Omitted, all the voyage of their
  life
Is bound in shallows and in
  miseries.
William Shakespeare 1564–1616:
Julius Caesar (1599); cf. **9** below

4 If any man can shew any just
cause, why they may not lawfully
be joined together, let him now
speak, or else hereafter for ever
hold his peace.
The Book of Common Prayer 1662:
Solemnization of Matrimony

5 But on occasion's forelock
    watchful wait.
John Milton 1608–74: *Paradise
Regained* (1671)

6 We must beat the iron while it is
hot, but we may polish it at
leisure.
John Dryden 1631–1700: *Aeneis*
(1697)

7 Is not a Patron, my Lord, one
who looks with unconcern on a
man struggling for life in the
water, and, when he has reached
ground, encumbers him with
help? The notice which you have
been pleased to take of my
labours, had it been early, had
been kind; but it has been
delayed till I am indifferent, and
cannot enjoy it; till I am solitary,
and cannot impart it; till I am
known, and do not want it.
Samuel Johnson 1709–84: letter to
Lord Chesterfield, 7 February 1755

8 *La carrière ouverte aux talents.*
The career open to the talents.
Napoleon I 1769–1821: Barry E.
O'Meara *Napoleon in Exile* (1822); cf.
10 below

9 There is a tide in the affairs of
women,
Which, taken at the flood, leads—
God knows where.

Lord Byron 1788–1824: *Don Juan*
(1819–24) see **3** above

10 To the very last he [Napoleon]
had a kind of idea; that, namely,
of *La carrière ouverte aux talents,*
The tools to him that can handle
them.
Thomas Carlyle 1795–1881: *Critical
and Miscellaneous Essays* (1838) "Sir
Walter Scott" see **8** above

11 Never the time and the place
And the loved one all together!
Robert Browning 1812–89: "Never
the Time and the Place" (1883)

12 This, if I understand it, is one of
those golden moments of our
history, one of those opportunities
which may come and may go,
but which rarely returns.
W. E. Gladstone 1809–98: speech on
the Second Reading of the Home
Rule Bill, House of Commons, 7 June
1886

13 The time was out of joint, and he
was only too delighted to have
been born to set it right.
of Hurrell Froude
Lytton Strachey 1880–1932: *Eminent
Victorians* (1918) "Cardinal Manning"
see **Circumstance 3**

14 If only I could get down to
Sidcup! I've been waiting for the
weather to break. He's got my
papers, this man I left them with,
it's got it all down there, I could
prove everything.
Harold Pinter 1930– : *The Caretaker*
(1960)

Optimism and Pessimism
see also **Despair, Hope**

1 *Sursum corda.* Lift up your hearts.
The Missal: *The Ordinary of the
Mass*

2 Sin is behovely, but all shall be
well and all shall be well and all
manner of thing shall be well.

Julian of Norwich 1343–after 1416:
Revelations of Divine Love

3 Yet where an equal poise of hope
and fear
Does arbitrate the event, my
nature is
That I incline to hope, rather
than fear,
And gladly banish squint
suspicion.
John Milton 1608–74: *Comus* (1637)

4 When the sun sets, shadows, that
showed at noon
But small, appear most long and
terrible.
Nathaniel Lee *c.* 1653–92: *Oedipus*
(with John Dryden, 1679)

5 In this best of possible worlds . . .
all is for the best.
*usually quoted as "All is for the best
in the best of all possible worlds"*
Voltaire 1694–1778: *Candide* (1759);
cf. **17** below

6 There's a gude time coming.
Sir Walter Scott 1771–1832: *Rob Roy*
(1817)

7 The lark's on the wing;
The snail's on the thorn:
God's in his heaven—
All's right with the world!
Robert Browning 1812–89: *Pippa
Passes* (1841)

8 I have known him come home to
supper with a flood of tears, and
a declaration that nothing was
now left but a jail; and go to bed
making a calculation of the
expense of putting bow-windows
to the house, "in case anything
turned up," which was his
favourite expression.
of Mr. Micawber
Charles Dickens 1812–70: *David
Copperfield* (1850)

9 In front the sun climbs slow, how
slowly,
But westward, look, the land is
bright.

Arthur Hugh Clough 1819–61: "Say
not the struggle naught availeth"
(1855)

10 Nothing to do but work,
Nothing to eat but food,
Nothing to wear but clothes
To keep one from going nude.
Benjamin Franklin King 1857–94:
"The Pessimist"

11 If way to the Better there be, it
exacts a full look at the worst.
Thomas Hardy 1840–1928: "De
Profundis" (1902)

12 My postal-order hasn't come yet.
Frank Richards (Charles Hamilton)
1876–1961: in *Magnet* (1908) "The
Taming of Harry"

13 Are we downhearted?
No! Let 'em all come!
Charles Knight and Kenneth Lyle:
"Here we are! Here we are again!!"
(1914 song)

14 'Twixt the optimist and pessimist
The difference is droll:
The optimist sees the doughnut
But the pessimist sees the hole.
McLandburgh Wilson 1892– :
Optimist and Pessimist (*c.* 1915)

15 Cheer up! the worst is yet to
come!
Philander Chase Johnson 1866–1939:
in *Everybody's Magazine* May 1920

16 Pessimism, when you get used to
it, is just as agreeable as
optimism. Indeed, I think it must
be more agreeable, must have a
more real savour, than optimism—
from the way in which pessimists
abandon themselves to it.
Arnold Bennett 1867–1931: *Things
that have Interested Me* (1921)
"Slump in Pessimism"

17 The optimist proclaims that we
live in the best of all possible
worlds; and the pessimist fears
this is true.

James Branch Cabell 1879–1958: *The
Silver Stallion* (1926); see 5 above

18 I don't consider myself a
pessimist. I think of a pessimist as
someone who is waiting for it to
rain. And I feel soaked to the
skin.
Leonard Cohen 1934–   : in *Observer*
(UK) 2 May 1993

Order and Chaos

1 All things began in order, so shall
they end, and so shall they begin
again; according to the ordainer
of order and mystical
mathematics of the city of
heaven.
Thomas Browne 1605–82: *The
Garden of Cyrus* (1658)

2 But wherefore thou alone?
Wherefore with thee
Came not all hell broke loose?
John Milton 1608–74: *Paradise Lost*
(1667)

3 With ruin upon ruin, rout on
rout,
Confusion worse confounded.
John Milton 1608–74: *Paradise Lost*
(1667)

4 Lo! thy dread empire, Chaos! is
restored;
Light dies before thy uncreating
word;
Thy hand, great Anarch! lets the
curtain fall;
And universal darkness buries all.
Alexander Pope 1688–1744: *The
Dunciad* (1742)

5 Good order is the foundation of
all good things.
Edmund Burke 1729–97: *Reflections
on the Revolution in France* (1790)

6 There are some enterprises in
which a careful disorderliness is
the true method.
Herman Melville 1819–91: *Moby Dick*
(1851)

7 Chaos often breeds life, when
order breeds habit.
Henry Brooks Adams 1838–1918: *The
Education of Henry Adams* (1907)

8 Things fall apart; the centre
cannot hold;
Mere anarchy is loosed upon the
world,
The blood-dimmed tide is loosed,
and everywhere
The ceremony of innocence is
drowned.
W. B. Yeats 1865–1939: "The Second
Coming" (1921)

9 The whole worl's in a state o'
chassis!
Sean O'Casey 1880–1964: *Juno and
the Paycock* (1925)

Originality

1 The saying of the noble and
glorious Aeschylus, who declared
that his tragedies were large cuts
taken from Homer's mighty
dinners.
Aeschylus c. 525–456 BC: Athenaeus
Deipnosophistae

2 Nothing has yet been said that's
not been said before.
Terence c. 190–159 BC: *Eunuchus*

3 It could be said of me that in this
book I have only made up a
bunch of other men's flowers,
providing of my own only the
string that ties them together.
Montaigne 1533–92: *Essais* (1580)

4 They lard their lean books with
the fat of others' works.
Robert Burton 1577–1640: *The
Anatomy of Melancholy* (1621–51)

5 Not wrung from speculations and
subtleties, but from common
sense, and observation; not picked
from the leaves of any author,
but bred among the weeds and
tares of mine own brain.

Thomas Browne 1605–82: *Religio Medici* (1643)

6 The original writer is not he who refrains from imitating others, but he who can be imitated by none.
François-René Chateaubriand 1768–1848: *Le Génie du Christianisme* (1802)

7 Never forget what I believe was observed to you by Coleridge, that every great and original writer, in proportion as he is great and original, must himself create the taste by which he is to be relished.
William Wordsworth 1770–1850: letter to Lady Beaumont, 21 May 1807

8 The truth is that the propensity of man to imitate what is before him is one of the strongest parts of his nature.
Walter Bagehot 1826–77: *Physics and Politics* (1872) "Nation-Making"

9 When 'Omer smote 'is bloomin' lyre,
He'd 'eard men sing by land an' sea;
An' what he thought 'e might require,
'E went an' took—the same as me!
Rudyard Kipling 1865–1936: "When 'Omer smote 'is bloomin' lyre" (1896)

10 What a good thing Adam had. When he said a good thing he knew nobody had said it before.
Mark Twain 1835–1910: *Notebooks* (1935)

11 Immature poets imitate; mature poets steal.
T. S. Eliot 1888–1965: *The Sacred Wood* (1920) "Philip Massinger"

12 If you steal from one author, it's plagiarism; if you steal from many, it's research.

Wilson Mizner 1876–1933: Alva Johnston *The Legendary Mizners* (1953)

13 No plagiarist can excuse the wrong by showing how much of his work he did not pirate.
Learned Hand 1872–1961: *Sheldon v. Metro-Goldwyn Pictures Corp.* 1936

14 When people are free to do as they please, they usually imitate each other. Originality is deliberate and forced, and partakes of the nature of a protest.
Eric Hoffer 1902–83: *Passionate State of Mind* (1955)

15 It is sometimes necessary to repeat what we all know. All mapmakers should place the Mississippi in the same location, and avoid originality.
Saul Bellow 1915– : *Mr. Sammler's Planet* (1969)

16 Let's have some new clichés.
Sam Goldwyn 1882–1974: attributed, perhaps apocryphal

Painting and the Visual Arts

1 I, too, am a painter!
on seeing Raphael's St. Cecilia at Bologna, c. 1525
Correggio c. 1489–1534: L. Pungileoni *Memorie Istoriche de . . . Correggio* (1817)

2 Good painters imitate nature, bad ones spew it up.
Cervantes 1547–1616: *El Licenciado Vidriera* (1613)

3 Remark all these roughnesses, pimples, warts, and everything as you see me; otherwise I will never pay a farthing for it.
to Lely, commonly quoted as "warts and all"
Oliver Cromwell 1599–1658: Horace

Walpole *Anecdotes of Painting in England* vol. 3 (1763)

4 An imitation in lines and colors on any surface of all that is to be found under the sun.
of painting
Nicolas Poussin 1594–1665: letter to M. de Chambray, 1665

5 A mere copier of nature can never produce anything great.
Joshua Reynolds 1723–92: *Discourses on Art* 14 December 1770

6 The sound of water escaping from mill-dams, etc., willows, old rotten planks, slimy posts, and brickwork . . . those scenes made me a painter and I am grateful.
John Constable 1776–1837: letter to John Fisher, 23 October 1821

7 In Claude's landscape all is lovely— all amiable—all is amenity and repose;—the calm sunshine of the heart.
John Constable 1776–1837: lecture, 2 June 1836

8 There are only two styles of portrait painting; the serious and the smirk.
Charles Dickens 1812–70: *Nicholas Nickleby* (1839)

9 *Le dessin est la probité de l'art.*Drawing is the true test of art.
J. A. D. Ingres 1780–1867: *Pensées d'Ingres* (1922)

10 She is older than the rocks among which she sits; like the vampire, she has been dead many times, and learned the secrets of the grave.
of the Mona Lisa
Walter Pater 1839–94: *Studies in the History of the Renaissance* (1873) "Leonardo da Vinci"

11 I have seen, and heard, much of Cockney impudence before now; but never expected to hear a coxcomb ask two hundred guineas for flinging a pot of paint in the public's face.
on Whistler's Nocturne in Black and Gold
John Ruskin 1819–1900: *Fors Clavigera* (1871–84) letter 79, 18 June 1877

12 I own I like definite form in what my eyes are to rest upon: and if landscapes were sold, like the sheets of characters of my boyhood, one penny plain and twopence colored, I should go the length of twopence every day of my life.
Robert Louis Stevenson 1850–94: *Travels with a Donkey* (1879)

13 You should not paint the chair, but only what someone has felt about it.
Edvard Munch 1863–1944: written *c.* 1891 R. Heller *Munch* (1984)

14 Yes madam, Nature is creeping up.
to a lady who had been reminded of his work by an "exquisite haze in the atmosphere"
James McNeill Whistler 1834–1903: D. C. Seitz *Whistler Stories* (1913)

15 Treat nature in terms of the cylinder, the sphere, the cone, all in perspective.
Paul Cézanne 1839–1906: letter to Emile Bernard, 1904; Emile Bernard *Paul Cézanne* (1925)

16 The photographer is like the cod which produces a million eggs in order that one may reach maturity.
George Bernard Shaw 1856–1950: introduction to the catalogue for Alvin Langdon Coburn's exhibition at the Royal Photographic Society, 1906; Bill Jay and Margaret Moore *Bernard Shaw and Photography* (1989)

17 Monet is only an eye, but what an eye!
Paul Cézanne 1839–1906: attributed

18 What I dream of is an art of balance, of purity and serenity devoid of troubling or depressing subject matter . . . a soothing, calming influence on the mind, rather like a good armchair which provides relaxation from physical fatigue.
Henri Matisse 1869–1954: *Notes d'un peintre* (1908)

19 It's with my brush that I make love.
often quoted as "I paint with my prick"
Pierre Auguste Renoir 1841–1919: A. André *Renoir* (1919)

20 Art does not reproduce the visible; rather, it makes visible.
Paul Klee 1879–1940: *Inward Vision* (1958) "Creative Credo" (1920)

21 An active line on a walk, moving freely without a goal. A walk for walk's sake.
Paul Klee 1879–1940: *Pedagogical Sketchbook* (1925)

22 Every time I paint a portrait I lose a friend.
John Singer Sargent 1856–1925: N. Bentley and E. Esar *Treasury of Humorous Quotations* (1951)

23 Do not judge this movement kindly. It is not just another amusing stunt. It is defiant—the desperate act of men too profoundly convinced of the rottenness of our civilization to want to save a shred of its respectability.
Herbert Read 1893–1968: International Surrealist Exhibition Catalogue, New Burlington Galleries, London, 11 June–4 July 1936

24 No, painting is not made to decorate apartments. It's an offensive and defensive weapon against the enemy.
Pablo Picasso 1881–1973: interview with Simone Téry, 24 March 1945, in Alfred H. Barr *Picasso* (1946)

25 I am a painter and I nail my pictures together.
Kurt Schwitters 1887–1948: R. Hausmann *Am Anfang war Dada* (1972)

26 When I was the age of these children I could draw like Raphael: it took me many years to learn how to draw like these children.
to Herbert Read, when visiting an exhibition of childen's drawings
Pablo Picasso 1881–1973: quoted in letter from Read to *The Times* (UK) 27 October 1956

27 Why don't they stick to murder and leave art to us?
on hearing that his statue of Lazarus in New College chapel, Oxford, kept Khrushchev awake at night
Jacob Epstein 1880–1959: attributed

28 Painting is saying "Ta" to God.
Stanley Spencer 1891–1959: letter from Spencer's daughter Shirin to *Observer* (UK) 7 February 1988

29 If Botticelli were alive today he'd be working for *Vogue*.
Peter Ustinov 1921– : in *Observer* (UK) 21 October 1962

30 A product of the untalented, sold by the unprincipled to the utterly bewildered.
on abstract art
Al Capp 1907–79: in *National Observer* (UK) 1 July 1963

31 A photograph is not only an image (as a painting is an image), an interpretation of the real; it is also a trace, something directly stencilled off the real, like a footprint or a death mask.

Susan Sontag 1933– : in *New York Review of Books* 23 June 1977

Parents
see also **The Family, Children**

1 Honour thy father and thy mother.
Bible: Exodus

2 A wise son maketh a glad father: but a foolish son is the heaviness of his mother.
Bible: Proverbs

3 It is a wise father that knows his own child.
William Shakespeare 1564–1616: *The Merchant of Venice* (1596–8)

4 The joys of parents are secret, and so are their griefs and fears.
Francis Bacon 1561–1626: *Essays* (1625) "Of Parents and Children"

5 Diogenes struck the father when the son swore.
Robert Burton 1577–1640: *The Anatomy of Melancholy* (1621–51)

6 A slavish bondage to parents cramps every faculty of the mind.
Mary Wollstonecraft 1759–97: *A Vindication of the Rights of Woman* (1792)

7 Who ran to help me when I fell, And would some pretty story tell, Or kiss the place to make it well? My Mother.
Ann Taylor 1782–1866 and **Jane Taylor** 1783–1824: "My Mother" (1804)

8 The mother's yearning, that completest type of the life in another life which is the essence of real human love, feels the presence of the cherished child even in the debased, degraded man.
George Eliot 1819–80: *Adam Bede* (1859)

9 For the hand that rocks the cradle Is the hand that rules the world.
William Ross Wallace d. 1881: "What rules the world" (1865)

10 There is no slave out of heaven like a loving woman; and, of all loving women, there is no such slave as a mother.
Henry Ward Beecher 1813–87: *Proverbs from Plymouth Pulpit* (1887)

11 If I were damned of body and soul, I know whose prayers would make me whole, Mother o' mine, O mother o' mine.
Rudyard Kipling 1865–1936: *The Light That Failed* (1891)

12 Children begin by loving their parents; after a time they judge them; rarely, if ever, do they forgive them.
Oscar Wilde 1854–1900: *A Woman of No Importance* (1893)

13 Few misfortunes can befall a boy which bring worse consequences than to have a really affectionate mother.
W. Somerset Maugham 1874–1965: *A Writer's Notebook* (1949); written in 1896

14 The natural term of the affection of the human animal for its offspring is six years.
George Bernard Shaw 1856–1950: *Heartbreak House* (1919)

15 The affection you get back from children is sixpence given as change for a sovereign.
Edith Nesbit 1858–1924: J. Briggs *A Woman of Passion* (1987)

16 The fundamental defect of fathers, in our competitive society, is that they want their children to be a credit to them.

Bertrand Russell 1872–1970: *Sceptical Essays* (1928) "Freedom versus Authority in Education"

17 My father was frightened of his mother; I was frightened of my father, and I am damned well going to see to it that my children are frightened of me.
George V 1865–1936: attributed, perhaps apocryphal; Randolph S. Churchill *Lord Derby* (1959)

18 There are no illegitimate children, only illegitimate parents.
MGM paid her a large sum for the line for the 1941 film based on her life, "Blossoms in the Dust"
Edna Gladney: A. Loos *Kiss Hollywood Good-Bye* (1978)

19 Parentage is a very important profession, but no test of fitness for it is ever imposed in the interest of the children.
George Bernard Shaw 1856–1950: *Everybody's Political What's What?* (1944)

20 Here's to the happiest years of our lives
Spent in the arms of other men's wives.
Gentlemen!—Our mothers!
proposing a toast
Edwin Lutyens 1869–1944: Clough Williams-Ellis *Architect Errant* (1971)

21 Parents—especially step-parents—are sometimes a bit of a disappointment to their children. They don't fufil the promise of their early years.
Anthony Powell 1905– : *A Buyer's Market* (1952)

22 It is not that I half knew my mother. I knew half of her: the lower half—her lap, legs, feet, her hands and wrists as she bent forward.
Flann O'Brien 1911–66: *The Hard Life* (1961)

23 There is no good father, that's the rule. Don't lay the blame on men but on the bond of paternity, which is rotten. To beget children, nothing better; to *have* them, what iniquity!
Jean-Paul Sartre 1905–80: *Les Mots* (1964) "Lire"

24 My father would have enjoyed what you have so generously said of me—and my mother would have believed it.
Lyndon B. Johnson 1908–1973: *On receiving an honorary degree from Baylor University* (28 May 1965)

25 A Jewish man with parents alive is a fifteen-year-old boy, and will remain a fifteen-year-old boy until *they die*!
Philip Roth 1933– : *Portnoy's Complaint* (1967)

26 No matter how old a mother is she watches her middle-aged children for signs of improvement.
Florida Scott-Maxwell: *Measure of my Days* (1968)

27 In our society mothers take the place elsewhere occupied by the Fates, the System, Negroes, Communism or Reactionary Imperialist Plots; mothers go on getting blamed until they're eighty, but shouldn't take it personally.
Katharine Whitehorn 1928– : *Observations* (1970)

28 Children always assume the sexual lives of their parents come to a grinding halt at their conception.
Alan Bennett 1934– : *Getting On* (1972)

29 It is only in our advanced and synthetic civilization that mothers no longer sing to the babies they are carrying.
Yehudi Menuhin 1916– : in *Observer* (UK) 4 January 1987

30 Mothers and small towns . . . can be suffocating like an interminable Sunday in an airless house.
Lance Morrow 1939– : *Time* (24 December 1990)

31 I have reached the age when a woman begins to perceive that she is growing into the person she least plans to resemble: her mother.
Anita Brookner 1938– : *Incidents in the Rue Laugier* (1995)

Parting
see **Meeting and Parting**

The Past
see also **History, Memory, The Present**

1 Even a god cannot change the past.
literally "The one thing which even God cannot do is to make undone what has been done"
Agathon b. *c.* 445: Aristotle *Nicomachaean Ethics*; cf. **History 12**

2 *Mais où sont les neiges d'antan?*
But where are the snows of yesteryear?
François Villon b. 1431: *Le Grand Testament* (1461) "Ballade des dames du temps jadis"

3 O! call back yesterday, bid time return.
William Shakespeare 1564–1616: *Richard II* (1595)

4 Antiquities are history defaced, or some remnants of history which have casually escaped the shipwreck of time.
Francis Bacon 1561–1626: *The Advancement of Learning* (1605)

5 There never was a merry world since the fairies left off dancing, and the Parson left conjuring.
John Selden 1584–1654: *Table Talk* (1689)

6 Old mortality, the ruins of forgotten times.
Thomas Browne 1605–82: *Hydriotaphia* (Urn Burial, 1658)

7 Each thing called improvement seems blackened with crimes,
If it tears up one record of blissful old times.
Susanna Blamire 1747–94: "When Home We Return" (*c.* 1790)

8 Think of it, soldiers; from the summit of these pyramids, forty centuries look down upon you.
Napoleon I 1769–1821: speech, 21 July 1798, before the Battle of the Pyramids

9 Thy Naiad airs have brought me home,
To the glory that was Greece
And the grandeur that was Rome.
Edgar Allan Poe 1809–49: "To Helen" (1831)

10 Then none was for a party;
Then all were for the state;
Then the great man helped the poor,
And the poor man loved the great.
Lord Macaulay 1800–59: *Lays of Ancient Rome* (1842) "Horatius"

11 The splendour falls on castle walls
And snowy summits old in story.
Alfred, Lord Tennyson 1809–92: *The Princess* (1847), song (added 1850)

12 The moving finger writes; and, having writ,
Moves on: nor all thy piety nor wit
Shall lure it back to cancel half a line,
Nor all thy tears wash out a word of it.
Edward Fitzgerald 1809–83: *The Rubáiyát of Omar Khayyám* (1859)

13 O God! Put back Thy universe
and give me yesterday.
Henry Arthur Jones 1851–1929 and
Henry Herman 1832–94: *The Silver
King* (1907)

14 What are those blue remembered
hills,
What spires, what farms are
those?
That is the land of lost content,
I see it shining plain,
The happy highways where I
went
And cannot come again.
A. E. Housman 1859–1936: *A
Shropshire Lad* (1896)

15 Those who cannot remember the
past are condemned to repeat it.
George Santayana 1863–1952: *The
Life of Reason* (1905); cf. **23** below

16 They shut the road through the
woods
Seventy years ago.
Weather and rain have undone it
again,
And now you would never know
There was once a road through
the woods.
Rudyard Kipling 1865–1936: "The
Way through the Woods" (1910)

17 Stands the Church clock at ten to
three?
And is there honey still for tea?
Rupert Brooke 1887–1915: "The Old
Vicarage, Grantchester" (1915)

18 The past is the only dead thing
that smells sweet.
Edward Thomas 1878–1917: "Early
one morning in May I set out" (1917)

19 I tell you the past is a bucket of
ashes.
Carl Sandburg 1878–1967: "Prairie"
(1918)

20 Things ain't what they used to
be.
Ted Persons: title of song (1941)

21 In every age "the good old days"
were a myth. No one ever
thought they were good at the
time. For every age has consisted
of crises that seemed intolerable
to the people who lived through
them.
Brooks Atkinson 1894–1984: *Once
Around the Sun* (1951)

22 The past is a foreign country:
they do things differently there.
L. P. Hartley 1895–1972: *The Go-
Between* (1953)

23 Man is a history-making creature
who can neither repeat his past
nor leave it behind.
W. H. Auden 1907–73: *The Dyer's
Hand* (1963) "D. H. Lawrence" see
15 above

24 Hindsight is always twenty-
twenty.
Billy Wilder 1906–   : J. R. Columbo
Wit and Wisdom of the Moviemakers
(1979)

25 The whole peninsula of Florida
was weighted down with regret.
Everyone had left behind a real
life.
*in reference to the large population
of elderly people who retired and
moved to Florida*
Cynthia Ozick 1928–   : *Rosa* (1984)

Patience
see also **Determination, Haste and
Delay**

1 The Lord gave, and the Lord hath
taken away; blessed be the name
of the Lord.
Bible: Job

2 Let patience have her perfect
work.
Bible: James

3 Still have I borne it with a patient
shrug,

For sufferance is the badge of all
our tribe.
William Shakespeare 1564–1616: *The
Merchant of Venice* (1596–8)

4 Beware the fury of a patient man.
John Dryden 1631–1700: *Absalom
and Achitophel* (1681)

5 Our patience will achieve more
than our force.
Edmund Burke 1729–97: *Reflections
on the Revolution in France* (1790)

6 Patience, that blending of moral
courage with physical timidity.
Thomas Hardy 1840–1928: *Tess of
the d'Urbervilles* (1891)

7 We had better wait and see.
*referring to the rumor that the
House of Lords was to be flooded
with new Liberal peers to ensure the
passage of the Finance Bill*
Herbert Asquith 1852–1928: *phrase
used repeatedly in speeches in* 1910;
Roy Jenkins *Asquith* (1964)

8 I am extraordinarily patient,
provided I get my own way in
the end.
Margaret Thatcher 1925–　: in
Observer (UK) 4 April 1989

Patriotism

1 *Dulce et decorum est pro patria
mori.*
Lovely and honorable it is to die
for one's country.
Horace 65–8 BC: *Odes*; cf. **Warfare 32**

2 Not that I loved Caesar less, but
that I loved Rome more.
William Shakespeare 1564–1616:
Julius Caesar (1599)

3 Never was patriot yet, but was a
fool.
John Dryden 1631–1700: *Absalom
and Achitophel* (1681)

4 What pity is it
That we can die but once to serve
our country!

Joseph Addison 1672–1719: *Cato*
(1713)

5 Be England what she will,
With all her faults, she is my
country still.
Charles Churchill 1731–64: *The
Farewell* (1764)

6 Patriotism is the last refuge of a
scoundrel.
Samuel Johnson 1709–84: James
Boswell *Life of Samuel Johnson*
(1791) 7 April 1775

7 I only regret that I have but one
life to lose for my country.
*prior to his execution by the British
for spying*
Nathan Hale 1755–76: Henry Phelps
Johnston *Nathan Hale, 1776* (1914)

8 These are the times that try
men's souls. The summer soldier
and the sunshine patriot will, in
this crisis, shrink from the service
of their country; but he that
stands it *now*, deserves the love
and thanks of men and women.
Thomas Paine 1737–1809: *The Crisis*
(December 1776)

9 Breathes there the man, with soul
so dead,
Who never to himself hath said,
This is my own, my native land!
Sir Walter Scott 1771–1832: *The Lay
of the Last Minstrel* (1805)

10 Our country! In her intercourse
with foreign nations, may she
always be in the right; but our
country, right or wrong.
Stephen Decatur 1779–1820: toast at
Norfolk, Virginia, April 1816; A. S.
Mackenzie *Life of Stephen Decatur*
(1846); cf. **11, 14, 16** below

11 My toast would be, may our
country be always successful, but
whether successful or otherwise,
always right.

John Quincy Adams 1767–1848: letter to John Adams, 1 August 1816; see 10 above

12 A steady patriot of the world alone,
The friend of every country but his own.
on the Jacobin
George Canning 1770–1827: "New Morality" (1821)

13 Our country is the world—our countrymen are all mankind.
William Lloyd Garrison 1805–79: in *The Liberator* (UK) 15 December 1837

14 My country, right or wrong; if right, to be kept right; and if wrong, to be set right!
Carl Schurz 1829–1906: speech, US Senate, 29 February 1872; see 10 above

15 We don't want to fight, yet by jingo! if we do,
We've got the ships, we've got the men, and got the money too.
G. W. Hunt 1829?–1904: "We Don't Want to Fight" (1878 song)

16 "My country, right or wrong," is a thing that no patriot would think of saying except in a desperate case. It is like saying, "My mother, drunk or sober."
G. K. Chesterton 1874–1936: *Defendant* (1901) "Defence of Patriotism" see 10 above

17 If I should die, think only this of me:
That there's some corner of a foreign field
That is for ever England.
Rupert Brooke 1887–1915: "The Soldier" (1914)

18 Standing, as I do, in view of God and eternity, I realize that patriotism is not enough. I must

have no hatred or bitterness towards anyone.
on the eve of her execution for helping Allied soldiers to escape from occupied Belgium
Edith Cavell 1865–1915: in *The Times* (UK) 23 October 1915

19 I vow to thee, my country—all earthly things above—
Entire and whole and perfect, the service of my love.
Cecil Spring-Rice 1859–1918: "I Vow to Thee, My Country" (1918)

20 You'll never have a quiet world till you knock the patriotism out of the human race.
George Bernard Shaw 1856–1950: *O'Flaherty V.C.* (1919)

21 You think you are dying for your country; you die for the industrialists.
Anatole France 1844–1924: in *L'Humanité* 18 July 1922

22 Patriotism is a lively sense of collective responsibility. Nationalism is a silly cock crowing on its own dunghill.
Richard Aldington 1892–1962: *The Colonel's Daughter* (1931)

23 *on H. G. Wells's comment on "an alien and uninspiring court":*
I may be uninspiring, but I'll be damned if I'm an alien!
George V 1865–1936: Sarah Bradford *George VI* (1989); attributed, perhaps apocryphal

24 If I had to choose between betraying my country and betraying my friend, I hope I should have the guts to betray my country.
E. M. Forster 1879–1970: *Two Cheers for Democracy* (1951)

25 And so, my fellow Americans: ask not what your country can do for you—ask what you can do for your country.

John F. Kennedy 1917–63: inaugural address, 20 January 1961

26 I would die for my country but I could never let my country die for me.
Neil Kinnock 1942– : speech at Labour Party Conference, 30 September 1986

27 The cardinal virtue was no longer to love one's country. It was to feel compassion for one's fellow men and women.
writing of his own generation
Noel Annan 1916– : *Our Age* (1990)

Peace
see also **Warfare**

1 The wolf also shall dwell with the lamb, and the leopard shall lie down with the kid; and the calf and the young lion and the fatling together; and a little child shall lead them.
Bible: Isaiah

2 They shall beat their swords into plowshares, and their spears into pruninghooks: nation shall not lift up sword against nation, neither shall they learn war any more.
Bible: Isaiah; cf. **Broadcasting 1**

3 The peace of God, which passeth all understanding, shall keep your hearts and minds through Christ Jesus.
Bible: Philippians; cf. **Christian Church 22**

4 They make a wilderness and call it peace.
Tacitus AD c. 56–after 117: *Agricola*

5 The naked, poor, and manglèd Peace,
Dear nurse of arts, plenties, and joyful births.
William Shakespeare 1564–1616: *Henry V* (1599)

6 . . . Peace hath her victories
No less renowned than war.
John Milton 1608–74: "To the Lord General Cromwell" (written 1652)

7 It's a maxim not to be despised, "Though peace be made, yet it's interest that keeps peace."
Oliver Cromwell 1599–1658: speech to Parliament, 4 September 1654

8 Give peace in our time, O Lord.
The Book of Common Prayer 1662: *Morning Prayer*; cf. **18** below

9 For now I see
Peace to corrupt no less than war to waste.
John Milton 1608–74: *Paradise Lost* (1667)

10 To be prepared for war is one of the most effectual means of preserving peace.
George Washington 1732–99: *first annual address, to both houses of Congress* (8 January 1790)

11 Lord Salisbury and myself have brought you back peace—but a peace I hope with honour.
Benjamin Disraeli 1804–81: speech on returning from the Congress of Berlin, 16 July 1878; cf. **18** below

12 In the arts of peace Man is a bungler.
George Bernard Shaw 1856–1950: *Man and Superman* (1903)

13 War makes rattling good history; but Peace is poor reading.
Thomas Hardy 1840–1928: *The Dynasts* (1904)

14 It is easier to make war than to make peace.
Georges Clemenceau 1841–1929: speech at Verdun, 20 July 1919

15 Peace is indivisible.
Maxim Litvinov 1876–1951: note to the Allies, 25 February 1920

16 I have many times asked myself whether there can be more potent advocates of peace upon earth through the years to come than this massed multitude of silent witnesses to the desolation of war.
George V 1865–1936: message read at Terlincthun Cemetery, Boulogne, 13 May 1922

17 I am not only a pacifist but a militant pacifist. I am willing to fight for peace. Nothing will end war unless the people themselves refuse to go to war.
Albert Einstein 1879–1955: interview with G. S. Viereck, January 1931

18 This is the second time in our history that there has come back from Germany to Downing Street peace with honour. I believe it is peace for our time.
Neville Chamberlain 1869–1940: speech from 10 Downing Street, 30 September 1938; see **8, 11** above

19 One observes, they have gone too long without a war here. Where is morality to come from in such a case, I ask? Peace is nothing but slovenliness, only war creates order.
Bertolt Brecht 1898–1956: *Mother Courage* (1939)

20 The work, my friend, is peace. More than an end of this war—an end to the beginnings of all wars.
Franklin D. Roosevelt 1882–1945: undelivered address for Jefferson Day, 13 April 1945 (the day after Roosevelt died)

21 The grim fact is that we prepare for war like precocious giants and for peace like retarded pygmies.
Lester Pearson 1897–1972: speech in Toronto, 14 March 1955

22 I think that people want peace so much that one of these days governments had better get out of the way and let them have it.
Dwight D. Eisenhower 1890–1969: broadcast discussion, 31 August 1959

23 Give peace a chance.
John Lennon 1940–80 and **Paul McCartney** 1942– : title of song (1969)

24 Enough of blood and tears. Enough.
Yitzhak Rabin 1922–95: at the signing of the Israel-Palestine Declaration, Washington, 13 September 1993

People
see also **Musicians, Poets, Writers**

1 The master of those who know.
of Aristotle
Dante Alighieri 1265–1321: *Divina Commedia* "Inferno"

2 As time requireth, a man of marvellous mirth and pastimes, and sometime of as sad gravity, as who say: a man for all seasons.
of Sir Thomas More
Robert Whittington: *Vulgaria* (1521)

3 The daughter of debate, that eke discord doth sow.
of Mary Queen of Scots
Elizabeth I 1533–1603: George Puttenham (ed.) *The Art of English Poesie* (1589)

4 The wisest fool in Christendom.
of James I of England
Henri IV (Henri of Navarre) 1553–1610: attributed both to Henri IV and Sully

5 Had Cleopatra's nose been shorter, the whole face of the world would have changed.
Blaise Pascal 1623–62: *Pensées* (1670)

6 He had a head to contrive, a
tongue to persuade, and a hand
to execute any mischief.
*of the Parliamentarian John
Hampden*
Edward Hyde, Earl of Clarendon
1609–74: *The History of the
Rebellion* (1703)

7 A merry monarch, scandalous
and poor.
John Wilmot, Lord Rochester 1647–
80: "A Satire on King Charles II"
(1697)

8 Our Garrick's a salad; for in him
we see
Oil, vinegar, sugar, and saltness
agree.
of David Garrick
Oliver Goldsmith 1730–74:
Retaliation (1774)

9 He snatched the lightning shaft
from heaven, and the scepter
from tyrants.
*of Benjamin Franklin, inventor of the
lightning conductor and American
statesman*
A. R. J. Turgot 1727–81: inscription
for a bust

10 If a man were to go by chance at
the same time with Burke under
a shed, to shun a shower, he
would say—"this is an
extraordinary man."
of Edmund Burke
Samuel Johnson 1709–84: James
Boswell *Life of Samuel Johnson*
(1791) 15 May 1784

11 That hyena in petticoats, Mrs.
Wollstonecraft.
of Mary Wollstonecraft
Horace Walpole 1717–97: letter to
Hannah More, 26 January 1795

12 Mad, bad, and dangerous to
know.
of Byron, after their first meeting
Lady Caroline Lamb 1785–1828:
diary, March 1812; Elizabeth Jenkins
Lady Caroline Lamb (1932)

13 An Archangel a little damaged.
of Coleridge
Charles Lamb 1775–1834: letter to
Wordsworth, 26 April 1816

14 He rather hated the ruling few
than loved the suffering many.
of James Mill
Jeremy Bentham 1748–1832: H. N.
Pym (ed.) *Memories of Old Friends,
being Extracts from the Journals and
Letters of Caroline Fox* (1882) 7
August 1840

15 The seagreen Incorruptible.
of Robespierre
Thomas Carlyle 1795–1881: *History
of the French Revolution* (1837)

16 Macaulay is well for a while, but
one wouldn't *live* under Niagara.
Thomas Carlyle 1795–1881: R. M.
Milnes *Notebook* (1838)

17 Out of his surname they have
coined an epithet for a knave,
and out of his Christian name a
synonym for the Devil.
of Niccolò Machiavelli
Lord Macaulay 1800–59: *Essays
Contributed to the Edinburgh Review*
(1843) "Machiavelli"

18 He has occasional flashes of
silence, that make his
conversation perfectly delightful.
of Macaulay
Sydney Smith 1771–1845: Lady
Holland *Memoir* (1855)

19 So you're the little woman who
wrote the book that made this
great war!
*on meeting Harriet Beecher Stowe,
author of* Uncle Tom's Cabin *(1852)*
Abraham Lincoln 1809–65: Carl
Sandburg *Abraham Lincoln: The War
Years* (1936)

20 A sophistical rhetorician,
inebriated with the exuberance of
his own verbosity.
of Gladstone

Benjamin Disraeli 1804–81: in *The Times* (UK) 29 July 1878

21 He was imperfect, unfinished, inartistic; he was worse than provincial—he was parochial.
of H. D. Thoreau
Henry James 1843–1916: *Hawthorne* (1879)

22 There never was a Churchill from John of Marlborough down that had either morals or principles.
W. E. Gladstone 1809–98: in conversation in 1882, recorded by Captain R. V. Briscoe; R. F. Foster *Lord Randolph Churchill* (1981)

23 Fate wrote her a most tremendous tragedy, and she played it in tights.
of Caroline of Brunswick, wife of George IV
Max Beerbohm 1872–1956: *The Yellow Book* (1894)

24 A lath of wood painted to look like iron.
of Lord Salisbury
Otto von Bismarck 1815–98: attributed, but vigorously denied by Sidney Whitman in *Personal Reminiscences of Prince Bismarck* (1902)

25 The first time you meet Winston you see all his faults and the rest of your life you spend in discovering his virtues.
of Churchill
Lady Lytton 1874–1971: letter to Sir Edward Marsh, December 1905

26 Her conception of God was certainly not orthodox. She felt towards Him as she might have felt towards a glorified sanitary engineer; and in some of her speculations she seems hardly to distinguish between the Deity and the Drains.
Lytton Strachey 1880–1932: *Eminent Victorians* (1918) "Florence Nightingale"

27 A good man fallen among Fabians.
of George Bernard Shaw
V. I. Lenin 1870–1924: Arthur Ransome *Six Weeks in Russia in 1919* (1919) "Notes of Conversations with Lenin"

28 He was no striped frieze; he was shot silk.
of Francis Bacon
Lytton Strachey 1880–1932: *Elizabeth and Essex* (1928)

29 He seemed at ease and to have the look of the last gentleman in Europe.
of Oscar Wilde
Ada Leverson 1865–1936: *Letters to the Sphinx* (1930)

30 I thought he was a young man of promise, but it appears he is a young man of promises.
of Winston Churchill
Arthur James Balfour 1848–1930: Winston Churchill *My Early Life* (1930)

31 This extraordinary figure of our time, this syren, this goat-footed bard, this half-human visitor to our age from the hag-ridden magic and enchanted woods of Celtic antiquity.
John Maynard Keynes 1883–1946: *Essays in Biography* (1933) "Mr. Lloyd George"

32 If only Bapu knew the cost of setting him up in poverty!
of Mahatma Gandhi
Sarojini Naidu 1879–1949: A. Campbell-Johnson *Mission with Mountbatten* (1951)

33 He can't see a belt without hitting below it.
of Lloyd George
Margot Asquith 1864–1945: in *Listener* (UK) 11 June 1953

34 A modest man who has a good deal to be modest about.

of Clement Attlee
Winston Churchill 1874–1965: in
*Chicago Sunday Tribune Magazine of
Books* 27 June 1954

35 Few thought he was even a
starter
There were many who thought
themselves smarter
But he ended PM
CH and OM
An earl and a knight of the
garter.
of himself
Clement Attlee 1883–1967: letter to
Tom Attlee, 8 April 1956

36 In a world of voluble hates, he
plotted to make men like, or at
least tolerate one another.
of Stanley Baldwin
G. M. Trevelyan 1876–1962: in
*Dictionary of National Biography
1941–50* (1959)

37 An elderly fallen angel travelling
incognito.
of André Gide
Peter Quennell 1905– : *The Sign of
the Fish* (1960)

38 What, when drunk, one sees in
other women, one sees in Garbo
sober.
of Greta Garbo
Kenneth Tynan 1927–80: *Curtains*
(1961)

39 Too clever by half.
of Iain Macleod
Lord Salisbury 1893–1972: speech,
House of Lords, 7 March 1961

40 She would rather light a candle
than curse the darkness, and her
glow has warmed the world.
*on learning of Eleanor Roosevelt's
death*
Adlai Stevenson 1900–65: in *New
York Times* 8 November 1962

41 [Lloyd George] did not seem to
care which way he travelled

providing he was in the driver's
seat.
Lord Beaverbrook 1879–1964: *The
Decline and Fall of Lloyd George*
(1963)

42 In defeat unbeatable: in victory
unbearable.
of Lord Montgomery
Winston Churchill 1874–1965:
Edward Marsh *Ambrosia and Small
Beer* (1964)

43 The Stag at Bay with the
mentality of a fox at large.
of Harold Macmillan
Bernard Levin 1928– : *The
Pendulum Years* (1970)

44 A high altar on the move.
of Edith Sitwell
Elizabeth Bowen 1899–1973: V.
Glendinning *Edith Sitwell* (1981)

45 So we think of Marilyn who was
every man's love affair with
America, Marilyn Monroe who
was blonde and beautiful and had
a sweet little rinky-dink of a voice
and all the cleanliness of all the
clean American backyards.
Norman Mailer 1923– : *Marilyn*
(1973)

46 It is not necessary that every time
he rises he should give his
famous imitation of a semi-house-
trained polecat.
of Norman Tebbit
Michael Foot 1913– : speech,
House of Commons, 2 March 1978

47 A doormat in a world of boots.
of herself
Jean Rhys *c.* 1890–1979: in *Guardian*
(UK) 6 December 1990

48 Every word she writes is a lie,
including "and" and "the."
of Lillian Hellman
Mary McCarthy 1912–89: in *New
York Times* 16 February 1980

49 The thinking man's crumpet.
of Joan Bakewell
Frank Muir 1920–98: attributed

50 She cannot see an institution without hitting it with her handbag.
of Margaret Thatcher
Julian Critchley 1930– : in *The Times* (UK) 21 June 1982

51 Comrades, this man has a nice smile, but he's got iron teeth.
of Mikhail Gorbachev
Andrei Gromyko 1909–89: speech to Soviet Communist Party Central Committee, 11 March 1985

52 She has the eyes of Caligula, but the mouth of Marilyn Monroe.
of Margaret Thatcher
François Mitterand 1916–96: comment to his new European Minister Roland Dumas; in *Observer* (UK) 25 November 1990

53 A man who so much resembled a Baked Alaska—sweet, warm and gungy on the outside, hard and cold within.
of C. P. Snow
Francis King 1923– : *Yesterday Came Suddenly* (1993)

54 She's a gay man trapped in a woman's body.
of Madonna
Boy George 1961– : *Take It Like a Man* (1995)

Peoples
see **Countries and Peoples**

Perfection
see also **Excellence and Mediocrity**

1 Nothing is an unmixed blessing.
Horace 65–8 BC: *Odes*

2 How many things by season seasoned are

To their right praise and true perfection!
William Shakespeare 1564–1616: *The Merchant of Venice* (1596–8)

3 Perfection is the child of Time.
Joseph Hall 1574–1656: *Works* (1625)

4 Whoever thinks a faultless piece to see,
Thinks what ne'er was, nor is, nor e'er shall be.
Alexander Pope 1688–1744: *An Essay on Criticism* (1711)

5 Pictures of perfection as you know make me sick and wicked.
Jane Austen 1775–1817: letter to Fanny Knight, 23 March 1817

6 Faultily faultless, icily regular, splendidly null,
Dead perfection, no more.
Alfred, Lord Tennyson 1809–92: *Maud* (1855)

7 Faultless to a fault.
Robert Browning 1812–89: *The Ring and the Book* (1868–9)

8 The pursuit of perfection, then, is the pursuit of sweetness and light ... He who works for sweetness and light united, works to make reason and the will of God prevail.
Matthew Arnold 1822–88: *Culture and Anarchy* (1869); see **Virtue 13**

9 Finality is death. Perfection is finality.
Nothing is perfect. There are lumps in it.
James Stephens 1882–1950: *The Crock of Gold* (1912)

Perseverance
see **Determination and Perseverance**

Pessimism
see **Optimisim and Pessimism**

Philosophy
see also **Logic and Reason**

1 The unexamined life is not worth
living.
Socrates 469–399 BC: Plato *Apology*

2 There is nothing so absurd but
some philosopher has said it.
Cicero 106–43 BC: *De Divinatione*

3 No more things should be
presumed to exist than are
absolutely necessary.
William of Occam c. 1285–1349: not
found in this form in his writings,
although he frequently used similar
expressions, e.g. "Plurality should
not be assumed unnecessarily"
Quodlibeta (c. 1324)

4 How charming is divine
philosophy!
Not harsh and crabbèd, as dull
fools suppose,
But musical as is Apollo's lute.
John Milton 1608–74: *Comus* (1637)

5 Some who are far from atheists,
may make themselves merry with
that conceit of thousands of
spirits dancing at once upon a
needle's point.
Ralph Cudworth 1617–88: *The True
Intellectual System of the Universe*
(1678)

6 General propositions are seldom
mentioned in the huts of Indians:
much less are they to be found in
the thoughts of children.
John Locke 1632–1704: *An Essay
concerning Human Understanding*
(1690)

7 The same principles which at first
lead to scepticism, pursued to a
certain point bring men back to
common sense.
George Berkeley 1685–1753: *Three
Dialogues between Hylas and
Philonous* (1734)

8 Superstition sets the whole world
in flames; philosophy quenches
them.
Voltaire 1694–1778: *Dictionnaire
philosophique* (1764) "Superstition"

9 I have tried too in my time to be
a philosopher; but, I don't know
how, cheerfulness was always
breaking in.
Oliver Edwards 1711–91: James
Boswell *Life of Samuel Johnson*
(1791) 17 April 1778

10 I am tempted to say of
metaphysicians what Scaliger
used to say of the Basques: they
are said to understand one
another, but I don't believe a
word of it.
Nicolas-Sébastien Chamfort 1741–94:
Maximes et Pensées (1796)

11 When philosophy paints its grey
on grey, then has a shape of life
grown old. By philosophy's grey
on grey it cannot be rejuvenated
but only understood. The owl of
Minerva spreads its wings only
with the falling of the dusk.
G. W. F. Hegel 1770–1831:
Philosophy of Right (1821)

12 The philosophers have only
interpreted the world in various
ways; the point is to change it.
Karl Marx 1818–83: *Theses on
Feuerbach* (written 1845, published
1888)

13 Metaphysics is the finding of bad
reasons for what we believe upon
instinct; but to find these reasons
is no less an instinct.
F. H. Bradley 1846–1924: *Appearance
and Reality* (1893)

14 What I understand by
"philosopher": a terrible explosive
in the presence of which
everything is in danger.
Friedrich Nietzsche 1844–1900: *Ecce
Homo* (1908) "Die Unzeitgemässen"

15 The Socratic manner is not a game at which two can play.
Max Beerbohm 1872–1956: *Zuleika Dobson* (1911)

16 The safest general characterization of the European philosophical tradition is that it consists of a series of footnotes to Plato.
Alfred North Whitehead 1861–1947: *Process and Reality* (1929)

17 To ask the hard question is simple.
W. H. Auden 1907–73: title of poem (1933)

18 What is your aim in philosophy?— To show the fly the way out of the fly-bottle.
Ludwig Wittgenstein 1889–1951: *Philosophische Untersuchungen* (1953)

19 Students of the heavens are separable into astronomers and astrologers as readily as are the minor domestic ruminants into sheep and goats, but the separation of philosophers into sages and cranks seems to be more sensitive to frames of reference.
W. V. O. Quine 1908– : *Theories and Things* (1981)

Physics
see also **Science**

1 If someone points out to you that your pet theory of the universe is in disagreement with Maxwell's equations—then so much the worse for Maxwell's equations. If it is found to be contradicted by observation—well, these experimentalists do bungle things sometimes. But if your theory is found to be against the second law of thermodynamics I can give you no hope; there is nothing for it but to collapse in deepest humiliation.

Arthur Eddington 1882–1944: *The Nature of the Physical World* (1928)

2 When Rutherford was done with the atom all the solidity was pretty well knocked out of it.
Stephen Leacock 1869–1944: *The Boy I Left Behind Me* (1947)

3 I remembered the line from the Hindu scripture, the *Bhagavad Gita* . . . "I am become death, the destroyer of worlds."
on the explosion of the first atomic bomb near Alamogordo, New Mexico, 16 July 1945
J. Robert Oppenheimer 1904–67: Len Giovannitti and Fred Freed *The Decision to Drop the Bomb* (1965)

4 In some sort of crude sense which no vulgarity, no humor, no overstatement can quite extinguish, the physicists have known sin; and this is a knowledge which they cannot lose.
J. Robert Oppenheimer 1904–67: lecture at Massachusetts Institute of Technology, 25 November 1947

5 If I could remember the names of all these particles I'd be a botanist.
Enrico Fermi 1901–54: R. L. Weber *More Random Walks in Science* (1973)

6 We do not know why they have the masses they do; we do not know why they transform into another the way they do; we do not know anything! The one concept that stands like the Rock of Gibraltar in our sea of confusion is the Pauli [exclusion] principle.
of elementary particles
George Gamow 1904–68: in *Scientific American* July 1959

7 Anybody who is not shocked by this subject has failed to understand it.

of quantum mechanics
Niels Bohr 1885–1962: attributed; in
Nature 23 August 1990

8 All I know about the becquerel is
that, like the Italian lira, you
need an awful lot to amount to
very much.
Arnold Allen: in *Financial Times* (UK)
19 September 1986

Pleasure

1 Everyone is dragged on by their
favorite pleasure.
Virgil 70–19 BC: *Eclogues*

2 Who loves not woman, wine, and
song
Remains a fool his whole life
long.
Martin Luther 1483–1546: attributed;
later inscribed in the Luther room in
the Wartburg, but with no proof of
authorship; cf. **13** below

3 Were it not better done as others
use,
To sport with Amaryllis in the
shade,
Or with the tangles of Neaera's
hair?
John Milton 1608–74: "Lycidas"
(1638)

4 Pleasure is nothing else but the
intermission of pain.
John Selden 1584–1654: *Table Talk*
(1689) "Pleasure"

5 I shouldn't be surprised if the
greatest rule of all weren't to give
pleasure.
Molière 1622–73: *La Critique de
l'école des femmes* (1663)

6 Music and women I cannot but
give way to, whatever my
business is.
Samuel Pepys 1633–1703: diary 9
March 1666

7 "Is there then no more?"
She cries "All this to love and
rapture's due;
Must we not pay a debt to
pleasure too?"
John Wilmot, Lord Rochester 1647–
80: "The Imperfect Enjoyment"
(1680)

8 Pleasure is a *thief* to business.
Daniel Defoe 1660–1731: *The
Complete English Tradesman* (1725)

9 Great lords have their pleasures,
but the people have fun.
Montesquieu 1689–1755: *Pensées et
fragments inédits . . .* vol. 2 (1901)

10 If I had no duties, and no
reference to futurity, I would
spend my life in driving briskly in
a post-chaise with a pretty
woman.
Samuel Johnson 1709–84: James
Boswell *Life of Samuel Johnson*
(1791) 19 September 1777

11 A man enjoys the happiness he
feels, a woman the happiness she
gives.
Pierre Choderlos de Laclos 1741–
1803: *Les Liaisons dangereuses*
(1782)

12 One half of the world cannot
understand the pleasures of the
other.
Jane Austen 1775–1817: *Emma* (1816)

13 Let us have wine and women,
mirth and laughter,
Sermons and soda-water the day
after.
Lord Byron 1788–1824: *Don Juan*
(1819–24) cf. **2** above

14 The greatest pleasure I know, is
to do a good action by stealth,
and to have it found out by
accident.
Charles Lamb 1775–1834: "Table
Talk by the late Elia" in *The
Athenaeum* (UK) 4 January 1834

15 The Puritan hated bear-baiting,
not because it gave pain to the
bear, but because it gave pleasure
to the spectators.
Lord Macaulay 1800–59: *History of
England* vol. 1 (1849)

16 The great pleasure in life is doing
what people say you cannot do.
Walter Bagehot 1826–77: in
Prospective Review (UK) 1853
"Shakespeare"

17 Lying in bed would be an
altogether perfect and supreme
experience if only one had a
coloured pencil long enough to
draw on the ceiling.
G. K. Chesterton 1874–1936:
Tremendous Trifles (1909) "On Lying
in Bed"

18 I admit it is better fun to punt
than to be punted, and that a
desire to have all the fun is nine-
tenths of the law of chivalry.
Dorothy L. Sayers 1893–1957: *Gaudy
Night* (1935)

19 People must not do things for
fun. We are not here for fun.
There is no reference to fun in
any Act of Parliament.
A. P. Herbert 1890–1971: *Uncommon
Law* (1935)

20 All the things I really like to do
are either illegal, immoral, or
fattening.
Alexander Woollcott 1887–1943: R.
E. Drennan *Wit's End* (1973)

21 There's no greater bliss in life
than when the plumber
eventually comes to unblock your
drains. No writer can give that
sort of pleasure.
Victoria Glendinning 1937– : in
Observer (UK) 3 January 1993

22 No pleasure is worth giving up
for the sake of two more years in
a geriatric home in Weston-super-
Mare.

Kingsley Amis 1922–95: in *The
Times* (UK) 21 June 1994; attributed

Poetry
see also **Writing**

1 Skilled or unskilled, we all scribble
poems.
Horace 65–8 BC: *Epistles*

2 "By God," quod he, "for pleynly,
at a word,
Thy drasty rymyng is nat worth a
toord!"
Geoffrey Chaucer c. 1343–1400: *The
Canterbury Tales* "Sir Thopas"

3 I am two fools, I know,
For loving, and for saying so
In whining poetry.
John Donne 1572–1631: "The Triple
Fool"

4 All poets are mad.
Robert Burton 1577–1640: *The
Anatomy of Melancholy* (1621–51)
"Democritus to the Reader"

5 For rhyme the rudder is of verses,
With which like ships they steer
their courses.
Samuel Butler 1612–80: *Hudibras* pt.
1 (1663)

6 Rhyme being no necessary
adjunct or true ornament of poem
or good verse, in longer works
especially, but the invention of a
barbarous age, to set off wretched
matter and lame metre.
John Milton 1608–74: *Paradise Lost*
(1667) "The Verse" (preface, added
1668)

7 All that is not prose is verse; and
all that is not verse is prose.
Molière 1622–73: *Le Bourgeois
Gentilhomme* (1671)

8 Poetry's a mere drug, Sir.
George Farquhar 1678–1707: *Love
and a Bottle* (1698)

9 But when loud surges lash the
   sounding shore,
The hoarse, rough verse should
   like the torrent roar.
When Ajax strives, some rock's
   vast weight to throw,
The line too labours, and the
   words move slow.
Alexander Pope 1688–1744: *An
Essay on Criticism* (1711)

10 BOSWELL: Sir, what is poetry?
JOHNSON: Why Sir, it is much
easier to say what it is not. We
all *know* what light is: but it is
not easy to *tell* what it is.

Samuel Johnson 1709–84: James
Boswell *Life of Samuel Johnson*
(1791) 12 April 1776

11 Some rhyme a neebor's name to
   lash;
Some rhyme (vain thought!) for
   needfu' cash;
Some rhyme to court the countra
   clash,
   An' raise a din;
For me, an aim I never fash;
   I rhyme for fun.
Robert Burns 1759–96: "To J.
S[mith]" (1786)

12 Always waiting and what to do
   or to say in the meantime
I don't know, and who wants
   poets at all in lean years?
Johann Christian Friedrich Hölderlin
1770–1843: "Bread and Wine" (1800-
01)

13 Poetry is the spontaneous
overflow of powerful feelings: it
takes its origin from emotion
recollected in tranquillity.
William Wordsworth 1770–1850:
Lyrical Ballads (2nd ed., 1802); cf.
44 below, **Humor 21, Sorrow 23**

14 A long poem is a test of invention
which I take to be the polar star
of poetry, as fancy is the sails,
and imagination the rudder.

John Keats 1795–1821: letter to
Benjamin Bailey, 8 October 1817

15 That willing suspension of
disbelief for the moment, which
constitutes poetic faith.
Samuel Taylor Coleridge 1772–1834:
Biographia Literaria (1817)

16 Most wretched men
Are cradled into poetry by wrong:
They learn in suffering what they
   teach in song.
Percy Bysshe Shelley 1792–1822:
"Julian and Maddalo" (1818)

17 If poetry comes not as naturally
as the leaves to a tree it had
better not come at all.
John Keats 1795–1821: letter to John
Taylor, 27 February 1818

18 Away! away! for I will fly to thee,
Not charioted by Bacchus and his
   pards,
But on the viewless wings of
   Poesy,
Though the dull brain perplexes
   and retards:
Already with thee! tender is the
   night.
John Keats 1795–1821: "Ode to a
Nightingale" (1820)

19 Poetry is the record of the best
and happiest moments of the
happiest and best minds.
Percy Bysshe Shelley 1792–1822: *A
Defence of Poetry* (written 1821)

20 Poets are the unacknowledged
legislators of the world.
Percy Bysshe Shelley 1792–1822: *A
Defence of Poetry* (written 1821)

21 Prose = words in their best order;—
poetry = the *best* words in the
best order.
Samuel Taylor Coleridge 1772–1834:
Table Talk (1835) 12 July 1827

22 Poetry is certainly something
more than good sense, but it
must be good sense at all events;

just as a palace is more than a house, but it must be a house, at least.
Samuel Taylor Coleridge 1772–1834: *Table Talk* (1835) 9 May 1830

23 Prose is when all the lines except the last go on to the end. Poetry is when some of them fall short of it.
Jeremy Bentham 1748–1832: M. St. J. Packe *The Life of John Stuart Mill* (1954)

24 What is a modern poet's fate? To write his thoughts upon a slate;
The critic spits on what is done, Gives it a wipe—and all is gone.
Thomas Hood 1799–1845: "A Joke" Hallam Tennyson *Alfred Lord Tennyson* (1897)

25 Everything you invent is true: you can be sure of that. Poetry is a subject as precise as geometry.
Gustave Flaubert 1821–80: letter to Louise Colet, 14 August 1853

26 The difference between genuine poetry and the poetry of Dryden, Pope, and all their school, is briefly this: their poetry is conceived and composed in their wits, genuine poetry is conceived and composed in the soul.
Matthew Arnold 1822–88: *Essays in Criticism* Second Series (1888) "Thomas Gray"

27 Mr. Stone's hexameters are verses of no sort, but prose in ribands.
A. E. Housman 1859–1936: in *Classical Review* (UK) 1899

28 I said "a line will take us hours maybe,
Yet if it does not seem a moment's thought
Our stitching and unstitching has been naught."
W. B. Yeats 1865–1939: "Adam's Curse" (1904)

29 Objectivity and again objectivity, and expression: no hindside-before-ness, no straddled adjectives (as "addled mosses dank"), no Tennysonianness of speech; nothing—nothing that you couldn't, in some circumstance, in the stress of some emotion, actually say.
Ezra Pound 1885–1972: letter to Harriet Monroe, January 1915

30 All a poet can do today is warn.
Wilfred Owen 1893–1918: preface (written 1918) in *Poems* (1963)

31 Poetry is not a turning loose of emotion, but an escape from emotion; it is not the expression of personality but an escape from personality.
T. S. Eliot 1888–1965: *The Sacred Wood* (1920) "Tradition and Individual Talent"

32 Poetry is the achievement of the synthesis of hyacinths and biscuits.
Carl Sandburg 1878–1967: in *Atlantic Monthly* March 1923 "Poetry Considered"

33 We make out of the quarrel with others, rhetoric, but of the quarrel with ourselves, poetry.
W. B. Yeats 1865–1939: *Essays* (1924) "Anima Hominis"

34 In our language rhyme is a barrel. A barrel of dynamite. The line is a fuse. The line smoulders to the end and explodes; and the town is blown sky-high in a stanza.
Vladimir Mayakovsky 1893–1930: "Conversation with an Inspector of Taxes about Poetry" (1926)

35 The worst tragedy for a poet is to be admired through being misunderstood.
Jean Cocteau 1889–1963: *Le Rappel à l'ordre* (1926) "Le Coq et l'Arlequin"

36 A poem is never finished; it's always an accident that puts a stop to it—that is to say, gives it to the public.
Paul Valéry 1871–1945: *Littérature* (1930)

37 Experience has taught me, when I am shaving of a morning, to keep watch over my thoughts, because, if a line of poetry strays into my memory, my skin bristles so that the razor ceases to act . . . The seat of this sensation is the pit of the stomach.
A. E. Housman 1859–1936: lecture at Cambridge, 9 May 1933

38 As soon as war is declared it will be impossible to hold the poets back. Rhyme is still the most effective drum.
Jean Giraudoux 1882–1944: *La Guerre de Troie n'aura pas lieu* (1935)

39 Writing a book of poetry is like dropping a rose petal down the Grand Canyon and waiting for the echo.
Don Marquis 1878–1937: E. Anthony *O Rare Don Marquis* (1962)

40 I'd as soon write free verse as play tennis with the net down.
Robert Frost 1874–1963: Edward Lathem *Interviews with Robert Frost* (1966)

41 It is barbarous to write a poem after Auschwitz.
Theodor Adorno 1903–69: I. Buruma *Wages of Guilt* (1994)

42 The notion of expressing sentiments in short lines having similar sounds at their ends seems as remote as mangoes on the moon.
Philip Larkin 1922–85: letter to Barbara Pym, 22 January 1975

43 My favorite poem is the one that starts "Thirty days hath September" because it actually tells you something.
Groucho Marx 1895–1977: Ned Sherrin *Cutting Edge* (1984); attributed

44 Sometimes poetry is emotion recollected in a highly emotional state.
Wendy Cope 1945– : "An Argument with Wordsworth" (1992); see **13** above

Poets

1 The worshipful father and first founder and embellisher of ornate eloquence in our English, I mean Master Geoffrey Chaucer.
William Caxton c. 1421–91: Caxton's edition (c. 1478) of Chaucer's translation of Boethius *De Consolacione Philosophie*

2 Dr. Donne's verses are like the peace of God; they pass all understanding.
James I 1566–1625: remark recorded by Archdeacon Plume (1630–1704)

3 But God, who is able to prevail, wrestled with him, as the Angel did with Jacob, and marked him; marked him for his own.
of John Donne
Izaak Walton 1593–1683: *Life of Donne* (1670 ed.)

4 'Tis sufficient to say, according to the proverb, that here is God's plenty.
of Chaucer
John Dryden 1631–1700: *Fables Ancient and Modern* (1700)

5 Ev'n copious Dryden, wanted, or forgot,
The last and greatest art, the art to blot.
Alexander Pope 1688–1744: *Imitations of Horace* (1737)

6 The living throne, the sapphire-blaze,

Where angels tremble, while they
gaze,
He saw; but blasted with excess of
light,
Closed his eyes in endless night.
of Milton
Thomas Gray 1716–71: *The Progress
of Poesy* (1757)

7 Milton, Madam, was a genius
that could cut a Colossus from a
rock; but could not carve heads
upon cherry-stones.
*to Hannah More, who had expressed
a wonder that the poet who had
written* Paradise Lost *should write
such poor sonnets*
Samuel Johnson 1709–84: James
Boswell *Life of Samuel Johnson*
(1791) 13 June 1784

8 The reason Milton wrote in fetters
when he wrote of Angels and
God, and at liberty when of Devils
and Hell, is because he was a
true Poet, and of the Devil's party
without knowing it.
William Blake 1757–1827: *The
Marriage of Heaven and Hell* (1790–
3)

9 I thought of Chatterton, the
marvellous boy,
The sleepless soul that perished in
its pride.
William Wordsworth 1770–1850:
"Resolution and Independence"
(1807)

10 On Waterloo's ensanguined plain
Full many a gallant man was
slain,
But none, by sabre or by shot,
Fell half so flat as Walter Scott.
*of Scott's poem "The Field of
Waterloo" (1815)*
Anonymous: U. Pope-Hennessy *The
Laird of Abbotsford* (1932)

11 With Donne, whose muse on
dromedary trots,
Wreathe iron pokers into true-
love knots.

Samuel Taylor Coleridge 1772–1834:
"On Donne's Poetry" (1818)

12 A cloud-encircled meteor of the
air,
A hooded eagle among blinking
owls.
of Coleridge
Percy Bysshe Shelley 1792–1822:
"Letter to Maria Gisborne" (1820)

13 We learn from Horace, Homer
sometimes sleeps;
We feel without him: Wordsworth
sometimes wakes.
Lord Byron 1788–1824: *Don Juan*
(1819–24) cf. **Mistakes 2**

14 Out-babying Wordsworth and out-
glittering Keats.
of Tennyson
Edward George Bulwer-Lytton 1803–
73: *The New Timon* (1846)

15 Every man will be a poet if he
can; otherwise a philosopher or
man of science. This proves the
superiority of the poet.
Henry David Thoreau 1817–62:
Journal (1852)

16 He spoke, and loosed our heart in
tears.
He laid us as we lay at birth
On the cool flowery lap of earth.
of Wordsworth
Matthew Arnold 1822–88: "Memorial
Verses, April 1850" (1852)

17 In poetry, no less than in life, he
is "a beautiful and ineffectual
angel, beating in the void his
luminous wings in vain."
Matthew Arnold 1822–88: *Essays in
Criticism* Second Series (1888)
"Shelley" (quoting from his own
essay on Byron in the same work)

18 Chaos, illumined by flashes of
lightning.
on Robert Browning's "style"
Oscar Wilde 1854–1900: Ada
Leverson *Letters to the Sphinx*
(1930)

19 How thankful we ought to be
that Wordsworth was only a poet
and not a musician. Fancy a
symphony by Wordsworth! Fancy
having to sit it out! And fancy
what it would have been if he
had written fugues!
Samuel Butler 1835–1902:
Notebooks (1912)

20 He could not think up to the
height of his own towering style.
of Tennyson
G. K. Chesterton 1874–1936: *The
Victorian Age in Literature* (1912)

21 I see a schoolboy when I think of
him
With face and nose pressed to a
sweet-shop window,
For certainly he sank into his
grave
His senses and his heart
unsatisfied,
And made—being poor, ailing
and ignorant,
Shut out from all the luxury of
the world,
The ill-bred son of a livery stable-
keeper—
Luxuriant song.
of Keats
W. B. Yeats 1865–1939: "Ego
Dominus Tuus" (1917)

22 The high-water mark, so to
speak, of Socialist literature is W.
H. Auden, a sort of gutless
Kipling.
George Orwell 1903–50: *The Road to
Wigan Pier* (1937)

23 *Hugo—hélas!*Hugo—alas!
*when asked who was the greatest
19th-century poet*
André Gide 1869–1951: Claude
Martin *La Maturité d'André Gide*
(1977)

24 To see him fumbling with our
rich and delicate language is to
experience all the horror of seeing
a Sèvres vase in the hands of a
chimpanzee.

of Stephen Spender
Evelyn Waugh 1903–66: in *The
Tablet* (UK) 5 May 1951

25 Self-contempt, well-grounded.
*on the foundation of T. S. Eliot's
work*
F. R. Leavis 1895–1978: in *Times
Literary Supplement* (UK) 21 October
1988

Political Parties

see also **Capitalism and Communism,
Politicians, Politics**

1 Party is little less than an
inquisition, where men are under
such a discipline in carrying on
the common cause, as leaves no
liberty of private opinion.
Lord Halifax 1633–95: *Political,
Moral, and Miscellaneous Thoughts
and Reflections* (1750) "Of Parties"

2 Party-spirit, which at best is but
the madness of many for the gain
of a few.
Alexander Pope 1688–1744: letter to
Edward Blount, 27 August 1714

3 If I could not go to Heaven but
with a party, I would not go
there at all.
Thomas Jefferson 1743–1826: letter
to Francis Hopkinson, 13 March 1789

4 Let me . . . warn you in the most
solemn manner against the
baneful effects of the spirit of
party.
George Washington 1732–99:
President's address retiring from
public life, 17 September 1796

5 What is conservatism? Is it not
adherence to the old and tried,
against the new and untried?
Abraham Lincoln 1809–65: speech,
27 February 1860

6 Party is organized opinion.
Benjamin Disraeli 1804–81: speech at
Oxford, 25 November 1864

7 I always voted at my party's call,
And I never thought of thinking
for myself at all.
W. S. Gilbert 1836–1911: *HMS Pinafore* (1878)

8 Damn your principles! Stick to
your party.
Benjamin Disraeli 1804–81:
attributed to Disraeli and believed to
have been said to Edward George
Bulwer-Lytton; E. Latham *Famous
Sayings and their Authors* (1904)

9 We are Republicans and don't
propose to leave our party and
identify ourselves with the party
whose antecedents are rum,
Romanism, and rebellion.
Samuel Dickinson Burchard 1812–91:
speech at the Fifth Avenue Hotel,
New York, 29 October 1884

10 We are all socialists now.
*during the passage of the 1888
budget, noted for the reduction of
the National Debt*
William Harcourt 1827–1904:
attributed; Hubert Bland "The
Outlook" in G. B. Shaw (ed.) *Fabian
Essays in Socialism* (1889)

11 Then raise the scarlet standard
high!
Within its shade we'll live or die.
Tho' cowards flinch and traitors
sneer,
We'll keep the red flag flying here.
James M. Connell 1852–1929: "The
Red Flag" (1889 song)

12 To the ordinary working man,
the sort you would meet in any
pub on Saturday night, Socialism
does not mean much more than
better wages and shorter hours
and nobody bossing you about.
George Orwell 1903–50: *The Road to
Wigan Pier* (1937)

13 I am reminded of four definitions:
A Radical is a man with both feet
firmly planted—in the air. A

Conservative is a man with two
perfectly good legs who, however,
has never learned to walk
forward. A Reactionary is a
somnambulist walking backwards.
A Liberal is a man who uses his
legs and his hands at the behest—
at the command—of his head.
Franklin D. Roosevelt 1882–1945:
radio address to *New York Herald
Tribune* Forum, 26 October 1939

14 I fear my Socialism is purely
cerebral; I do not like the masses
in the flesh.
Harold Nicolson 1886–1968: letter to
Vita Sackville-West, 7 May 1948

15 The language of priorities is the
religion of Socialism.
Aneurin Bevan 1897–1960: speech at
Labour Party Conference in
Blackpool, England 8 June 1949

16 If they [the Republicans] will stop
telling lies about the Democrats,
we will stop telling the truth
about them.
Adlai Stevenson 1900–65: speech
during 1952 Presidential campaign; J.
B. Martin *Adlai Stevenson and
Illinois* (1976)

17 Under democracy one party
always devotes its energies to
trying to prove that the other
party is unfit to rule—and both
commonly succeed and are right.
H. L. Mencken 1880–1956: *Minority
Report* (1956)

18 I am a free man, an American, a
United States Senator, and a
Democrat, in that order.
Lyndon Baines Johnson 1908–73: in
Texas Quarterly Winter 1958

19 Fascism is not in itself a new
order of society. It is the future
refusing to be born.
Aneurin Bevan 1897–1960: Leon
Harris *The Fine Art of Political Wit*
(1965)

20 There are some of us ... who will
fight and fight and fight again to
save the Party we love.
Hugh Gaitskell 1906–63: speech at
Labour Party Conference, 5 October
1960

21 As usual the Liberals offer a
mixture of sound and original
ideas. Unfortunately none of the
sound ideas is original and none
of the original ideas is sound.
Harold Macmillan 1894–1986: speech
to London Conservatives, 7 March
1961

22 This party is a moral crusade or
it is nothing.
Harold Wilson 1916–95: speech at
the Labour Party Conference, 1
October 1962

23 An independent is a guy who
wants to take the politics out of
politics.
Adlai Stevenson 1900–65: Bill Adler
The Stevenson Wit (1966)

24 This party is a bit like an old
stage-coach. If you drive along at
a rapid rate, everyone aboard is
either so exhilarated or so seasick
that you don't have a lot of
difficulty.
of the Labour Party
Harold Wilson 1916–95: Anthony
Sampson *The Changing Anatomy of
Britain* (1982)

25 Socialism can only arrive by
bicycle.
José Antonio Viera Gallo 1943– :
Ivan Illich *Energy and Equity* (1974)
epigraph

26 The longest suicide note in
history.
*on the Labour Party's election
manifesto* New Hope for Britain
(1983)
Gerald Kaufman 1930– : Denis
Healey *The Time of My Life* (1989)

27 A dead or dying beast lying
across a railway line and
preventing other trains from
getting through.
of the Labour Party in England
Roy Jenkins 1920– : in *Guardian*
(UK) 16 May 1987

28 I have only one firm belief about
the American political system,
and that is this: God is a
Republican and Santa Claus is a
Democrat.
P. J. O'Rourke 1947– : *Parliament
of Whores* (1991)

29 International life is right-wing,
like nature. The social contract is
left-wing, like humanity.
Régis Debray 1940– : *Charles de
Gaulle* (1994)

Politicians
see also **People, Political Parties,
Politics, Speeches**

1 Politicians also have no leisure,
because they are always aiming
at something beyond political life
itself, power and glory, or
happiness.
Aristotle 384–322 BC: *Nicomachean
Ethics*

2 He that goeth about to persuade
a multitude, that they are not so
well governed as they ought to
be, shall never want attentive and
favourable hearers.
Richard Hooker *c.* 1554–1600: *Of the
Laws of Ecclesiastical Polity* (1593)

3 Get thee glass eyes;
And, like a scurvy politician,
   seem
To see the things thou dost not.
William Shakespeare 1564–1616:
King Lear (1605–6)

4 The greatest art of a politician is
to render vice serviceable to the
cause of virtue.

Henry St. John, Lord Bolingbroke
1678–1751: comment (*c.* 1728)
Joseph Spence *Observations,
Anecdotes, and Characters* (1820)

5 If a due participation of office is a
matter of right, how are
vacancies to be obtained? Those
by death are few; by resignation
none.
*usually quoted as, "Few die and
none resign"*
Thomas Jefferson 1743–1826: letter
to E. Shipman and others, 12 July
1801

6 What I want is men who will
support me when I am in the
wrong.
*replying to a politician who said "I
will support you as long as you are
in the right"*
Lord Melbourne 1779–1848: Lord
David Cecil *Lord M* (1954)

7 The greatest gift of any statesman
rests not in knowing what
concessions to make, but
recognizing when to make them.
Prince Metternich 1773–1859:
Concessionen und Nichtconcessionen
(1852)

8 With malice toward none; with
charity for all; with firmness in
the right, as God gives us to see
the right, let us strive on to finish
the work we are in.
Abraham Lincoln 1809–65: Second
Inaugural Address, 4 March 1865

9 A constitutional statesman is in
general a man of common
opinion and uncommon abilities.
Walter Bagehot 1826–77:
Biographical Studies (1881) "The
Character of Sir Robert Peel"

10 All kings is mostly rapscallions.
Mark Twain 1835–1910: *Adventures
of Huckleberry Finn* (1885)

11 An honest politician is one who
when he's bought stays bought.
Simon Cameron 1799–1889:
attributed

12 It could probably be shown by
facts and figures that there is no
distinctly native American
criminal class except Congress.
Mark Twain 1835–1910: *Pudd'nhead
Wilson's New Calendar* (1897)

13 He knows nothing; and he thinks
he knows everything. That points
clearly to a political career.
George Bernard Shaw 1856–1950:
Major Barbara (1907)

14 "Do you pray for the senators, Dr.
Hale?" "No, I look at the senators
and I pray for the country."
Edward Everett Hale 1822–1909: Van
Wyck Brooks *New England Indian
Summer* (1940)

15 He [Labouchère] did not object to
the old man always having a
card up his sleeve, but he did
object to his insinuating that the
Almighty had placed it there.
*on Gladstone's "frequent appeals to
a higher power"*
Henry Labouchère 1831–1912: Earl
Curzon *Modern Parliamentary
Eloquence* (1913)

16 We all know that Prime Ministers
are wedded to the truth, but like
other married couples they
sometimes live apart.
Saki 1870–1916: *The Unbearable
Bassington* (1912)

17 If you want to succeed in politics,
you must keep your conscience
well under control.
David Lloyd George 1863–1945: Lord
Riddell, diary, 23 April 1919

18 Mothers may still want their
favorite sons to grow up to be
President, but, according to a
famous Gallup poll of some years

ago, they do not want them to become politicians in the process.
John F. Kennedy 1917–63: *Profiles in Courage* (1956)

19 Damn it all, you can't have the crown of thorns *and* the thirty pieces of silver.
on his position in the Labour Party in England, c. 1956
Aneurin Bevan 1897–1960: Michael Foot *Aneurin Bevan* (1973)

20 Forever poised between a cliché and an indiscretion.
on the life of a Foreign Secretary
Harold Macmillan 1894–1986: in *Newsweek* 30 April 1956

21 I am not going to spend any time whatsoever in attacking the Foreign Secretary . . . If we complain about the tune, there is no reason to attack the monkey when the organ grinder is present.
during a debate on the Suez crisis
Aneurin Bevan 1897–1960: speech, House of Commons, 16 May 1957

22 A politician is a man who understands government, and it takes a politician to run a government. A statesman is a politician who's been dead 10 or 15 years.
Harry S. Truman 1884–1972: in *New York World Telegram and Sun* 12 April 1958

23 Someone must fill the gap between platitudes and bayonets.
Adlai Stevenson 1900–65: Leon Harris *The Fine Art of Political Wit* (1965)

24 A political leader must keep looking over his shoulder all the time to see if the boys are still there. If they aren't still there, he's no longer a political leader.
Bernard Baruch 1870–1965: in *New York Times* 21 June 1965

25 The ability to foretell what is going to happen tomorrow, next week, next month, and next year. And to have the ability afterwards to explain why it didn't happen.
describing the qualifications desirable in a prospective politician
Winston Churchill 1874–1965: B. Adler *Churchill Wit* (1965)

26 The best time to listen to a politician is when he's on the stump on a street corner in the rain late at night when he's exhausted. Then he doesn't lie.
Theodore H. White 1915–86: *New York Times* (5 January 1969)

27 The first requirement of a statesman is that he be dull.
Dean Acheson 1893–1971: in *Observer* (UK) 21 June 1970

28 In politics, if you want anything said, ask a man. If you want anything done, ask a woman.
Margaret Thatcher 1925– : in 1970; in *People* 15 September 1975

29 He had grown up in a country run by politicians who sent the pilots to man the bombers to kill the babies to make the world safer for children to grow up in.
Ursula K. Le Guin 1929– : *The Lathe of Heaven* (1971)

30 A statesman is a politician who places himself at the service of the nation. A politician is a statesman who places the nation at his service.
Georges Pompidou 1911–74: in *Observer* (UK) 30 December 1973

31 All political lives, unless they are cut off in midstream at a happy juncture, end in failure, because that is the nature of politics and of human affairs.
Enoch Powell 1912– : *Joseph Chamberlain* (1977)

32 In politics you must always keep running with the pack. The moment that you falter and they sense that you are injured, the rest will turn on you like wolves.
R. A. Butler 1902–82: Dennis Walters *Not Always with the Pack* (1989)

33 There are no true friends in politics. We are all sharks circling, and waiting, for traces of blood to appear in the water.
Alan Clark 1928–   : diary 30 November 1990

Politics
see also **Democracy, Elections, Government, International Relations, Political Parties, Politicians, The Presidency**

1 Man is by nature a political animal.
Aristotle 384–322 BC: *Politics*

2 State business is a cruel trade; good nature is a bungler in it.
Lord Halifax 1633–95: *Political, Moral, and Miscellaneous Thoughts and Reflections* (1750) "Wicked Ministers"

3 Most schemes of political improvement are very laughable things.
Samuel Johnson 1709–84: James Boswell *Life of Samuel Johnson* (1791) 26 October 1769

4 Magnanimity in politics is not seldom the truest wisdom; and a great empire and little minds go ill together.
Edmund Burke 1729–97: *On Conciliation with America* (1775)

5 I agree with you that in politics the middle way is none at all.
John Adams 1735–1826: letter to Horatio Gates, 23 March 1776

6 In politics, what begins in fear usually ends in folly.

Samuel Taylor Coleridge 1772–1834: *Table Talk* (1835) 5 October 1830

7 Finality is not the language of politics.
Benjamin Disraeli 1804–81: speech, House of Commons, 28 February 1859

8 Politics is the art of the possible.
Otto von Bismarck 1815–98: in conversation with Meyer von Waldeck, 11 August 1867; cf. **21** below, **Science 26**

9 Politics is perhaps the only profession for which no preparation is thought necessary.
Robert Louis Stevenson 1850–94: *Familiar Studies of Men and Books* (1882) "Yoshida-Torajiro"

10 In politics, there is no use looking beyond the next fortnight.
Joseph Chamberlain 1836–1914: letter from A. J. Balfour to 3rd Marquess of Salisbury, 24 March 1886

11 A statesman . . . must wait until he hears the steps of God sounding through events; then leap up and grasp the hem of his garment.
Otto von Bismarck 1815–98: A. J. P. Taylor *Bismarck* (1955)

12 Politics, as a practice, whatever its professions, has always been the systematic organization of hatreds.
Henry Brooks Adams 1838–1918: *The Education of Henry Adams* (1907)

13 Politics is war without bloodshed while war is politics with bloodshed.
Mao Zedong 1893–1976: lecture, 1938; *Selected Works* (1965)

14 He may be a son of a bitch, but he's our son of a bitch.
on President Somoza of Nicaragua, 1938

Franklin D. Roosevelt 1882–1945:
attributed

15 The trouble with this country is
that there are too many
politicians who believe, with a
conviction based on experience,
that you can fool all of the people
all of the time.
Franklin P. Adams 1881–1960: *Nods
and Becks* (1944); see **Deception 9**

16 All reactionaries are paper tigers.
In appearance, the reactionaries
are terrifying, but in reality they
are not so powerful. From a long-
term point of view, it is not the
reactionaries but the people who
are really powerful.
Mao Zedong 1893–1976: interview
with Anne Louise Strong, August
1946; *Selected Works* (1961)

17 All the contact I have had with
politics has left me feeling as
though I had been drinking out
of spittoons.
Ernest Hemingway 1899–1961: *New
York Times* (17 September 1950)

18 Political language . . . is designed
to make lies sound truthful and
murder respectable, and to give
an appearance of solidity to pure
wind.
George Orwell 1903–50: *Shooting an
Elephant* (1950) "Politics and the
English Language"

19 Men enter local politics solely as a
result of being unhappily married.
C. Northcote Parkinson 1909–93:
Parkinson's Law (1958)

20 Politics are too serious a matter
to be left to the politicians.
*replying to Attlee's remark that "De
Gaulle is a very good soldier and a
very bad politician"*
Charles de Gaulle 1890–1970:
Clement Attlee *A Prime Minister
Remembers* (1961)

21 Politics is not the art of the
possible. It consists in choosing
between the disastrous and the
unpalatable.
John Kenneth Galbraith 1908– :
letter to President Kennedy, 2 March
1962; see **8** above

22 A week is a long time in politics.
*probably first said at the time of the
1964 sterling crisis*
Harold Wilson 1916–95: Nigel Rees
Sayings of the Century (1984)

23 Politics are usually the executive
expression of human immaturity.
Vera Brittain 1893–1970: *Rebel
Passion* (1964)

24 Politics are almost as exciting as
war and quite as dangerous. In
war you can only be killed once,
but in politics—many times.
Winston Churchill 1874–1965:
attributed

25 No. Extreme views, weakly held.
*quoting the response he had given
to the comment "I hear you have
strong political views"*
A. J. P. Taylor 1906–90: letter to Eva
Haraszti Taylor, 16 July 1970; *Letters
To Eva* (1991)

26 That's one of my Goddam
precious American rights, not to
think about politics.
John Updike 1932– : *Rabbit Redux*
(1971)

27 Politics is supposed to be the
second oldest profession. I have
come to realize that it bears a
very close resemblance to the
first.
Ronald Reagan 1911– : at a
conference in Los Angeles, 2 March
1977

28 The silent majority, like a great
soaking-wet shaggy dog banished
from the house during the
Watergate storms, romped back
into the nation's parlor and
shook itself vigorously.

William Safire 1929– : *Safire's New Political Dictionary* (1993)

29 If something makes you cry, you have to do something about it. That's the difference between politics and guilt.
Bill Clinton 1946– : *On the Make* (1994)

Pollution and the Environment
see also **The Earth, Nature**

1 Woe to her that is filthy and polluted, to the oppressing city!
Bible: Zephaniah

2 Woe unto them that join house to house, that lay field to field, till there be no place.
Bible: Isaiah

3 The desert shall rejoice, and blossom as the rose.
Bible: Isaiah

4 It goes so heavily with my disposition that this goodly frame, the earth, seems to me a sterile promontory; this most excellent canopy, the air, look you, this brave o'erhanging firmament, this majestical roof fretted with golden fire, why, it appears no other thing to me but a foul and pestilent congregation of vapours.
William Shakespeare 1564–1616: *Hamlet* (1601)

5 O all ye Green Things upon the Earth, bless ye the Lord: praise him, and magnify him for ever.
The Book of Common Prayer 1662: Benedicite

6 The parks are the lungs of London.
William Pitt, Earl of Chatham 1708–78: speech by William Windham, House of Commons, 30 June 1808

7 And did the Countenance Divine
Shine forth upon our clouded hills?
And was Jerusalem builded here
Among these dark Satanic mills?
William Blake 1757–1827: *Milton* (1804–10) "And did those feet in ancient time"

8 The river Rhine, it is well known,
Doth wash your city of Cologne;
But tell me, Nymphs, what power divine
Shall henceforth wash the river Rhine?
Samuel Taylor Coleridge 1772–1834: "Cologne" (1834)

9 By avarice and selfishness, and a grovelling habit, from which none of us is free, of regarding the soil as property . . . the landscape is deformed.
Henry David Thoreau 1817–62: *Walden* (1854) "The Bean Field"

10 Forget six counties overhung with smoke,
Forget the snorting steam and piston stroke,
Forget the spreading of the hideous town;
Think rather of the pack-horse on the down,
And dream of London, small and white and clean,
The clear Thames bordered by its gardens green.
William Morris 1834–96: *The Earthly Paradise* (1868–70) "Prologue: The Wanderers"

11 And all is seared with trade; bleared, smeared with toil;
And wears man's smudge and shares man's smell.
Gerard Manley Hopkins 1844–89: "God's Grandeur" (written 1877)

12 What would the world be, once bereft
Of wet and wildness? Let them be left,

O let them be left, wildness and wet;
Long live the weeds and the wilderness yet.
Gerard Manley Hopkins 1844–89: "Inversnaid" (written 1881)

13 Wiv a ladder and some glasses,
You could see to 'Ackney Marshes,
If it wasn't for the 'ouses in between.
Edgar Bateman and **George Le Brunn**: "If it wasn't for the 'Ouses in between" (1894 song)

14 Dirt is only matter out of place.
John Chipman Gray 1839–1915: *Restraints on the Alienation of Property* (2nd ed., 1895)

15 Man has been endowed with reason, with the power to create, so that he can add to what he's been given. But up to now he hasn't been a creator, only a destroyer. Forests keep disappearing, rivers dry up, wild life's become extinct, the climate's ruined and the land grows poorer and uglier every day.
Anton Chekhov 1860–1904: *Uncle Vanya* (1897)

16 It will be said of this generation that it found England a land of beauty and left it a land of "beauty spots."
C. E. M. Joad 1891–1953: *The Horrors of the Countryside* (1931)

17 Clear the air! clean the sky! wash the wind!
T. S. Eliot 1888–1965: *Murder in the Cathedral* (1935)

18 Over increasingly large areas of the United States, spring now comes unheralded by the return of the birds, and the early mornings are strangely silent where once they were filled with the beauty of bird song.
Rachel Carson 1907–64: *The Silent Spring* (1962)

19 If I were a Brazilian without land or money or the means to feed my children, I would be burning the rain forest too.
Sting 1951– : in *International Herald Tribune* 14 April 1989

20 The world's ecological balance depends on more than just our ability to restore a balance between civilization's ravenous appetite for resources and the fragile equilibrium of the earth's environment. . . . Each of us must take a greater personal responsibility for this deteriorating global environment.
Al Gore 1948– : *Earth in the Balance* (1992)

Possessions

1 The poor man had nothing, save one little ewe lamb.
Bible: II Samuel

2 How many things I can do without!
on looking at a multitude of wares exposed for sale
Socrates 469–399 BC: Diogenes Laertius *Lives of the Philosophers*

3 Alexander . . . asked him if he lacked anything. "Yes," said he, "that I do: that you stand out of my sun a little."
Diogenes c. 400–c. 325 BC: Plutarch *Parallel Lives* "Alexander"

4 For we brought nothing into this world, and it is certain we can carry nothing out.
Bible: I Timothy

5 There are only two families in the world, as a grandmother of mine used to say: the haves and the have-nots.
Cervantes 1547–1616: *Don Quixote* (1605)

6 Well! some people talk of morality, and some of religion, but give me a little snug property.

Maria Edgeworth 1768–1849: *The Absentee* (1812)

7 Property has its duties as well as its rights.
Thomas Drummond 1797–1840: letter to the Earl of Donoughmore, 22 May 1838

8 Property is theft.
Pierre-Joseph Proudhon 1809–65: *Qu'est-ce que la propriété?* (1840)

9 Things are in the saddle,
And ride mankind.
Ralph Waldo Emerson 1803–82: "Ode" Inscribed to W. H. Channing (1847)

10 Have nothing in your houses that you do not know to be useful, or believe to be beautiful.
William Morris 1834–96: *Hopes and Fears for Art* (1882) "Making the Best of It"

11 Conspicuous consumption of valuable goods is a means of reputability to the gentleman of leisure.
Thorstein Veblen 1857–1929: *Theory of the Leisure Class* (1899)

12 Never be afraid of throwing away what you have, if you *can* throw it away, it is not really yours.
R. H. Tawney 1880–1962: diary 1912, in *Dictionary of National Biography 1961-1970* (1981)

13 People don't resent having nothing nearly as much as too little.
Ivy Compton-Burnett 1884–1969: *A Family and a Fortune* (1939)

14 The goal of all inanimate objects is to resist man and ultimately to defeat him.
Russell Baker 1925– : *The New York Times* (18 June 1968)

15 Inanimate objects are classified scientifically into three major

categories—those that don't work, those that break down, and those that get lost.
Russell Baker 1925– : *The New York Times* (18 June 1968)

16 Man must choose whether to be rich in things or in the freedom to use them.
Ivan Illich 1926– : *Deschooling Society* (1971)

17 If men are to respect each other for what they are, they must cease to respect each other for what they own.
A. J. P. Taylor 1906–90: *Politicians, Socialism and Historians* (1980)

Poverty
see also **Money, Wealth**

1 What mean ye that ye beat my people to pieces, and grind the faces of the poor?
Bible: Isaiah

2 The poor always ye have with you.
Bible: St. John

3 The misfortunes of poverty carry with them nothing harder to bear than that it makes men ridiculous.
Juvenal AD *c.* 60–*c.* 130: *Satires*

4 I want there to be no peasant in my kingdom so poor that he is unable to have a chicken in his pot every Sunday.
Henri IV (Henri of Navarre) 1553–1610: Hardouin de Péréfixe *Histoire de Henry le Grand* (1681); cf.
Progress 12

5 Come away; poverty's catching.
Aphra Behn 1640–89: *The Rover* pt. 2 (1681)

6 Give me not poverty lest I steal.
Daniel Defoe 1660–1731: in *Review* 15 September 1711; later

incorporated into *Moll Flanders* (1721)

7 Let not ambition mock their
useful toil,
Their homely joys, and destiny
obscure;
Nor grandeur hear with a
disdainful smile,
The short and simple annals of
the poor.
Thomas Gray 1716–71: *Elegy Written in a Country Churchyard* (1751)

8 Laws grind the poor, and rich
men rule the law.
Oliver Goldsmith 1730–74: *The Traveller* (1764)

9 Resolve not to be poor: whatever
you have, spend less. Poverty is a
great enemy to human happiness;
it certainly destroys liberty, and it
makes some virtues impracticable,
and others extremely difficult.
Samuel Johnson 1709–84: letter to
Boswell, 7 December 1782

10 The murmuring poor, who will
not fast in peace.
George Crabbe 1754–1832: "The
Newspaper" (1785)

11 The poor are Europe's blacks.
Nicolas-Sébastien Chamfort 1741–94:
Maximes et Pensées (1796)

12 Single women have a dreadful
propensity for being poor—which
is one very strong argument in
favour of matrimony.
Jane Austen 1775–1817: letter to
Fanny Knight, 13 March 1817

13 It's a wery remarkable
circumstance . . . that poverty and
oysters always seem to go
together.
Charles Dickens 1812–70: *Pickwick Papers* (1837)

14 Oh! God! that bread should be so
dear,
And flesh and blood so cheap!

Thomas Hood 1799–1845: "The Song
of the Shirt" (1843)

15 Economy was always "elegant,"
and money-spending always
"vulgar" and ostentatious— a
sort of sour-grapeism, which
made us very peaceful and
satisfied.
Elizabeth Gaskell 1810–65: *Cranford*
(1853)

16 They [the poor] have to labor in
the face of the majestic equality of
the law, which forbids the rich as
well as the poor to sleep under
bridges, to beg in the streets, and
to steal bread.
Anatole France 1844–1924: *Le Lys
rouge* (1894)

17 Like dear St. Francis of Assisi I
am wedded to Poverty: but in my
case the marriage is not a
success.
Oscar Wilde 1854–1900: letter June
1899

18 The greatest of evils and the
worst of crimes is poverty.
George Bernard Shaw 1856–1950:
Major Barbara (1907)

19 The poor cannot always reach
those whom they want to love,
and they can hardly ever escape
from those whom they no longer
love.
E. M. Forster 1879–1970: *Howards
End* (1910)

20 She was poor but she was honest
Victim of a rich man's game.
First he loved her, then he left
her,
And she lost her maiden name
. . .
It's the same the whole world
over,
It's the poor wot gets the blame,
It's the rich wot gets the gravy.
Ain't it all a bleedin' shame?
Anonymous: "She was Poor but she

was Honest" sung by British soldiers in World War I

21 She was not so much a person as an implication of dreary poverty, like an open door in a mean house that lets out the smell of cooking cabbage and the screams of children.
Rebecca West 1892–1983: *The Return of the Soldier* (1918)

22 There's nothing surer,
The rich get rich and the poor get children.
Gus Kahn 1886–1941 and **Raymond B. Egan** 1890–1952: "Ain't We Got Fun" (1921 song)

23 Brother can you spare a dime?
E. Y. Harburg 1898–1981: title of song (1932)

24 We shall have to walk and live a Woolworth life hereafter.
anticipating the aftermath of World War II
Harold Nicolson 1886–1968: diary 4 June 1941

25 Anyone who has ever struggled with poverty knows how extremely expensive it is to be poor.
James Baldwin 1924–87: *Nobody Knows My Name* (1961) "Fifth Avenue, Uptown: a letter from Harlem"

26 We were poor when I was young, but the difference then was the government didn't come around telling you you were poor.
Ronald Reagan 1911– : *Time* (7 July 1986)

27 When I give food to the poor they call me a saint. When I ask why the poor have no food they call me a communist.
Helder Camara 1909– : attributed

28 I never saw a beggar yet who would recognize guilt if it bit him on his unwashed ass.

Tony Parsons 1953– : *Dispatches from the Front Line of Popular Culture* (1994)

Power

1 It is much safer to be in a subordinate position than in authority.
Thomas à Kempis c. 1380–1471: *The Imitation of Christ*

2 Man, proud man,
Drest in a little brief authority.
William Shakespeare 1564–1616: *Measure for Measure* (1604)

3 All rising to great place is by a winding stair.
Francis Bacon 1561–1626: *Essays* (1625) "Of Great Place"

4 Power is so apt to be insolent and Liberty to be saucy, that they are very seldom upon good terms.
Lord Halifax 1633–95: *Political, Moral, and Miscellaneous Thoughts and Reflections* (1750) "Of Prerogative, Power and Liberty"

5 Nature has left this tincture in the blood,
That all men would be tyrants if they could.
Daniel Defoe 1660–1731: *The History of the Kentish Petition* (1712–13)

6 A fly, Sir, may sting a stately horse and make him wince; but one is but an insect, and the other is a horse still.
Samuel Johnson 1709–84: James Boswell *Life of Samuel Johnson* (1791) 1754

7 Those who have been once intoxicated with power, and have derived any kind of emolument from it, even though but for one year, can never willingly abandon it.
Edmund Burke 1729–97: *Letter to a Member of the National Assembly* (1791)

8 I shall be an autocrat: that's my trade. And the good Lord will forgive me: that's his.
Catherine the Great 1729–96: attributed; cf. **Forgiveness 13**

9 The strongest poison ever known
Came from Caesar's laurel crown.
William Blake 1757–1827: "Auguries of Innocence" (c. 1803)

10 The good old rule
Sufficeth them, the simple plan,
That they should take who have the power,
And they should keep who can.
William Wordsworth 1770–1850: "Rob Roy's Grave" (1807)

11 The fundamental article of my political creed is that despotism, or unlimited sovereignty, or absolute power, is the same in a majority of a popular assembly, an aristocratic council, an oligarchical junto, and a single emperor.
John Adams 1735–1826: letter to Thomas Jefferson, 13 November 1815

12 You shall have joy, or you shall have power, said God; you shall not have both.
Ralph Waldo Emerson 1803–82: *Journal* (October 1842)

13 I claim not to have controlled events, but confess plainly that events have controlled me.
Abraham Lincoln 1809–65: letter to A. G. Hodges, 4 April 1864

14 "The question is," said Humpty Dumpty, "which is to be master— that's all."
Lewis Carroll 1832–98: *Through the Looking-Glass* (1872); cf. **19** below

15 Power tends to corrupt and absolute power corrupts absolutely.
Lord Acton 1834–1902: letter to Bishop Mandell Creighton, 3 April 1887

16 Whatever happens we have got
The Maxim Gun, and they have not.
Hilaire Belloc 1870–1953: *The Modern Traveller* (1898)

17 Every Communist must grasp the truth, "Political power grows out of the barrel of a gun."
Mao Zedong 1893–1976: speech, 6 November 1938

18 The finest plans are always ruined by the littleness of those who ought to carry them out, for the Emperors can actually do nothing.
Bertolt Brecht 1898 1956: *Mother Courage* (1939)

19 "But," said Alice, "the question is whether you can make a word mean different things." "Not so," said Humpty-Dumpty, "the question is which is to be the master. That's all." We are the masters at the moment, and not only at the moment, but for a very long time to come.
often quoted as "We are the masters now"
Hartley Shawcross 1902– : speech, House of Commons, 2 April 1946; see **14** above

20 Who controls the past controls the future: who controls the present controls the past.
George Orwell 1903–50: *Nineteen Eighty-Four* (1949)

21 A friend in power is a friend lost.
Henry Brooks Adams 1838–1918: *The Education of Henry Adams* (1907)

22 You only have power over people as long as you don't take *everything* away from them. But when you've robbed a man of *everything* he's no longer in your power — he's free again.
Alexander Solzhenitsyn 1918– : *The First Circle* (1968)

23 Power is the great aphrodisiac.
Henry Kissinger 1923– : in *New York Times* 19 January 1971

24 Power? It's like a Dead Sea fruit. When you achieve it, there is nothing there.
Harold Macmillan 1894–1986: Anthony Sampson *The New Anatomy of Britain* (1971)

25 Seven months ago I could give a single command and 541,000 people would immediately obey it. Today I can't get a plumber to come to my house.
H. Norman Schwarzkopf III 1934– : *Newsweek* (11 November 1991)

Practicality

1 This man hath the right sow by the ear.
of Thomas Cranmer, June 1529
Henry VIII 1491–1547: *Acts and Monuments of John Foxe* ["Fox's Book of Martyrs"], 1570

2 A dead woman bites not.
pressing for the execution of Mary Queen of Scots in 1587
Patrick, Lord Gray d. 1612: oral tradition; William Camden *Annals of the Reign of Queen Elizabeth* (1615)

3 My lord, we make use of you, not for your bad legs, but for your good head.
to William Cecil, who suffered from gout
Elizabeth I 1533–1603: F. Chamberlin *Sayings of Queen Elizabeth* (1923)

4 Common sense is the best distributed commodity in the world, for every man is convinced that he is well supplied with it.
René Descartes 1596–1650: *Le Discours de la méthode* (1637)

5 And he gave it for his opinion, that whoever could make two ears of corn or two blades of grass to grow upon a spot of ground where only one grew before, would deserve better of mankind, and do more essential service to his country than the whole race of politicians put together.
Jonathan Swift 1667–1745: *Gulliver's Travels* (1726) "A Voyage to Brobdingnag"

6 'Tis use alone that sanctifies expense,
And splendour borrows all her rays from sense.
Alexander Pope 1688–1744: *Epistles to Several Persons* "To Lord Burlington" (1731)

7 Whenever our neighbour's house is on fire, it cannot be amiss for the engines to play a little on our own.
Edmund Burke 1729–97: *Reflections on the Revolution in France* (1790)

8 *La mort, sans phrases.*Death, without rhetoric.
voting in the French Convention for the death of Louis XVI, 16 January 1793
Emmanuel Joseph Sieyès 1748–1836: attributed, but afterwards repudiated by Sieyès *Le Moniteur* 20 January 1793 records his vote as "La mort"

9 How horrible it is to have so many people killed!—And what a blessing that one cares for none of them!
after the battle of Albuera, 16 May 1811
Jane Austen 1775–1817: letter to Cassandra Austen, 31 May 1811

10 Put your trust in God, my boys, and keep your powder dry.
Valentine Blacker 1728–1823: "Oliver's Advice" often attributed to Oliver Cromwell himself

11 It's grand, and you canna expect to be baith grand and comfortable.
J. M. Barrie 1860–1937: *The Little Minister* (1891)

12 So I really think that American gentlemen are the best after all, because kissing your hand may make you feel very very good but a diamond and safire bracelet lasts forever.
Anita Loos 1893–1981: *Gentlemen Prefer Blondes* (1925)

13 Be nice to people on your way up because you'll meet 'em on your way down.
Wilson Mizner 1876–1933: Alva Johnston *The Legendary Mizners* (1953)

14 Praise the Lord and pass the ammunition.
moving along a line of sailors passing ammunition by hand to the deck
Howell Forgy 1908–83: at Pearl Harbor, 7 December 1941; later the title of a song by Frank Loesser, 1942

15 Common sense is is nothing more than a deposit of prejudices laid down in the mind before you reach eighteen.
Albert Einstein 1879–1955: Lincoln Barnett *The Universe and Dr. Einstein* (1950 ed.)

16 Life is too short to stuff a mushroom.
Shirley Conran 1932–   : *Superwoman* (1975)

Praise and Flattery

1 But when I tell him he hates flatterers,
He says he does, being then most flattered.
William Shakespeare 1564–1616: *Julius Caesar* (1599)

2 Give 'em words;
Pour oil into their ears, and send them hence.
Ben Jonson c. 1573–1637: *Volpone* (1606)

3 It has been well said that "the arch-flatterer with whom all the petty flatterers have intelligence is a man's self."
Francis Bacon 1561–1626: *Essays* (1625) "Of Love"

4 Nothing so soon the drooping spirits can raise
As praises from the men, whom all men praise.
Abraham Cowley 1618–67: "Ode upon a Copy of Verses of My Lord Broghill's" (1663)

5 Of whom to be dispraised were no small praise.
John Milton 1608–74: *Paradise Regained* (1671)

6 He who discommendeth others obliquely commendeth himself.
Thomas Browne 1605–82: *Christian Morals* (1716)

7 Damn with faint praise, assent with civil leer,
And without sneering, teach the rest to sneer.
of Addison
Alexander Pope 1688–1744: "An Epistle to Dr. Arbuthnot" (1735)

8 Madam, before you flatter a man so grossly to his face, you should consider whether or not your flattery is worth his having.
to Hannah More
Samuel Johnson 1709–84: Fanny Burney's diary, August 1778

9 And even the ranks of Tuscany Could scarce forbear to cheer.
Lord Macaulay 1800–59: *Lays of Ancient Rome* (1842) "Horatius"

10 The advantage of doing one's praising for oneself is that one can lay it on so thick and exactly in the right places.
Samuel Butler 1835–1902: *The Way of All Flesh* (1903)

11 I suppose flattery hurts no one,
that is, if he doesn't inhale.
Adlai Stevenson 1900–65: television
broadcast, 30 March 1952

12 If you are flattering a woman, it
pays to be a little more subtle.
You don't have to bother with
men, they believe any compliment
automatically.
Alan Ayckbourn 1939– : *Round and
Round the Garden* (1975)

Prayer

1 O gods, grant me this in return
for my piety.
Catullus *c.* 84–*c.* 54 BC: *Carmina*

2 Ask, and it shall be given you;
seek, and ye shall find; knock,
and it shall be opened unto you.
Bible: St. Matthew

3 God be in my head,
And in my understanding.
Anonymous: *Sarum Missal* (11th
century)

4 My words fly up, my thoughts
remain below:
Words without thoughts never to
heaven go.
William Shakespeare 1564–1616:
Hamlet (1601)

5 I throw myself down in my
Chamber, and I call in, and invite
God, and his Angels thither, and
when they are there, I neglect
God and his Angels, for the noise
of a fly, for the rattling of a
coach, for the whining of a door.
John Donne 1572–1631: *LXXX
Sermons* (1640) 12 December 1626
"At the Funeral of Sir William
Cokayne"

6 O Lord! thou knowest how busy I
must be this day: if I forget thee,
do not thou forget me.
*prayer before the Battle of Edgehill,
1642*
Jacob Astley 1579–1652: Sir Philip
Warwick *Memoires* (1701)

7 At my devotion I love to use the
civility of my knee, my hat, and
hand.
Thomas Browne 1605–82: *Religio
Medici* (1643)

8 Be still and cool in thy own mind
and spirit from thy own thoughts,
and then thou wilt feel the
principle of God to turn thy mind
to the Lord God.
George Fox 1624–91: diary 1658

9 No praying, it spoils business.
Thomas Otway 1652–85: *Venice
Preserved* (1682)

10 O God, if there be a God, save my
soul, if I have a soul!
*prayer of a common soldier before
the battle of Blenheim, 1704*
Anonymous: in *Notes and Queries* 9
October 1937

11 Work as if you were to live a
hundred years, Pray as if you
were to die tomorrow.
Benjamin Franklin 1706–90: *Poor
Richard's Almanack* (1757)

12 One single grateful thought raised
to heaven is the most perfect
prayer.
G. E. Lessing 1729–81: *Minna von
Barnhelm* (1767)

13 Did not God
Sometimes withhold in mercy
what we ask,
We should be ruined at our own
request.
Hannah More 1745–1833: *Moses in
the Bulrushes* (1782)

14 He prayeth well, who loveth well
Both man and bird and beast.
He prayeth best, who loveth best
All things both great and small.
Samuel Taylor Coleridge 1772–1834:
"The Rime of the Ancient Mariner"
(1798)

15 And lips say, "God be pitiful,"
Who ne'er said, "God be praised."
Elizabeth Barrett Browning 1806–61:
"The Cry of the Human" (1844)

16 I am just going to pray for you at
St. Paul's, but with no very lively
hope of success.
Sydney Smith 1771–1845: H. Pearson
The Smith of Smiths (1934)

17 More things are wrought by
    prayer
Than this world dreams of.
Alfred, Lord Tennyson 1809–92:
Idylls of the King "The Passing of
Arthur" (1869)

18 Whatever a man prays for, he
prays for a miracle. Every prayer
reduces itself to this: Great God,
grant that twice two be not four.
Ivan Turgenev 1818–83: *Poems in
Prose* (1881) "Prayer"

19 To lift up the hands in prayer
gives God glory, but a man with
a dungfork in his hand, a woman
with a slop-pail, give him glory
too. He is so great that all things
give him glory if you mean they
should.
Gerard Manley Hopkins 1844–89:
"The Principle or Foundation" (1882)

20 You can't pray a lie.
Mark Twain 1835–1910: *Adventures
of Huckleberry Finn* (1885)

21 Bernard always had a few prayers
in the hall and some whiskey
afterwards as he was rarther
pious but Mr. Salteena was not
very addicted to prayers so he
marched up to bed.
Daisy Ashford 1881–1972: *The Young
Visiters* (1919)

22 Often when I pray I wonder if I
am not posting letters to a nonexistent address.
C. S. Lewis 1898–1963: letter to
Arthur Greeves, 24 December 1930;

W. Hooper (ed.) *They Stand
Together* (1979)

23 The wish for prayer is a prayer in
itself.
Georges Bernanos 1888–1948:
Journal d'un curé de campagne
(1936)

24 School prayer . . . bears about as
much resemblance to real
spiritual experience as that freeze-
dried astronaut food bears to a
nice standing rib roast.
Anna Quindlen 1953– : *New York
Times* (7 December 1994)

Pregnancy and Birth

1 In sorrow thou shalt bring forth
children.
Bible: Genesis

2 The queen of Scots is this day
leichter of a fair son, and I am
but a barren stock.
Elizabeth I 1533–1603: Sir James
Melville *Memoirs of His Own Life*
(1827 ed.)

3 Men should be bewailed at their
birth, and not at their death.
Montesquieu 1689–1755: *Lettres
Persanes* (1721)

4 I wish either my father or my
mother, or indeed both of them,
as they were in duty both equally
bound to it, had minded what
they were about when they begot
me.
Laurence Sterne 1713–68: *Tristram
Shandy* (1759–67)

5 Our birth is but a sleep and a
    forgetting . . .
Not in entire forgetfulness,
And not in utter nakedness,
But trailing clouds of glory do we
    come.
William Wordsworth 1770–1850:
"Ode. Intimations of Immortality"
(1807)

6 I s'pect I growed. Don't think
nobody never made me.
said by Topsy
Harriet Beecher Stowe 1811–96:
Uncle Tom's Cabin (1852)

7 What you say of the pride of
giving life to an immortal soul is
very fine, dear, but I own I can
not enter into that; I think much
more of our being like a cow or a
dog at such moments; when our
poor nature becomes so very
animal and unecstatic.
Queen Victoria 1819–1901: letter to
the Princess Royal, 15 June 1858

8 In the dark womb where I began
My mother's life made me a man.
Through all the months of
    human birth
Her beauty fed my common
    earth.
I cannot see, nor breathe, nor
    stir,
But through the death of some of
    her.
John Masefield 1878–1967: "C. L.
M." (1910)

9 We want better reasons for
having children than not
knowing how to prevent them.
Dora Russell 1894–1986: *Hypatia*
(1925)

10 Good work, Mary. We all knew
you had it in you.
*telegram to Mrs. Sherwood on the
arrival of her baby*
Dorothy Parker 1893–1967:
Alexander Woollcott *While Rome
Burns* (1934)

11 Death and taxes and childbirth!
There's never any convenient
time for any of them.
Margaret Mitchell 1900–49: *Gone
with the Wind* (1936)

12 A fast word about oral
contraception. I asked a girl to go
to bed with me and she said "no."

Woody Allen 1935– : at a nightclub
in Washington, April 1965

13 If men could get pregnant,
abortion would be a sacrament.
Florynce Kennedy 1916– : in *Ms.*
March 1973

14 The right of privacy . . . is broad
enough to encompass a woman's
decision whether or not to
terminate her pregnancy.
Harry Andrew Blackmun 1908– :
Roe v. Wade (1973)

15 Protestant women may take the
pill. Roman Catholic women must
keep taking The Tablet.
Irene Thomas: in *Guardian* (UK) 28
December 1990

Prejudice and Tolerance
see also **Race and Racism**

1 *Sine ira et studio.*
With neither anger nor partiality.
Tacitus AD *c.* 56–after 117: *Annals*

2 Hear the other side.
St. Augustine of Hippo AD 354–430:
*De Duabus Animabus contra
Manicheos*

3 Mr. Doctor, that loose gown
becomes you so well I wonder
your notions should be so
narrow.
*to the Puritan Dr. Humphreys, as he
was about to kiss her hand on her
visit to Oxford in 1566*
Elizabeth I 1533–1603: F. Chamberlin
Sayings of Queen Elizabeth (1923)

4 Sir Roger told them, with the air
of a man who would not give his
judgement rashly, that much
might be said on both sides.
Joseph Addison 1672–1719: in *The
Spectator* (UK) 20 July 1711

5 There is, however, a limit at
which forbearance ceases to be a
virtue.

Edmund Burke 1729–97:
*Observations on a late Publication
on the Present State of the Nation*
(2nd ed., 1769)

6 Drive out prejudices through the
door, and they will return
through the window.
Frederick the Great 1712–86: letter to
Voltaire, 19 March 1771

7 Without the aid of prejudice and
custom, I should not be able to
find my way across the room.
William Hazlitt 1778–1830: "On
Prejudice" (1830)

8 It is never too late to give up our
prejudices.
Henry David Thoreau 1817–62:
Walden (1854)

9 Tolerance is only another name
for indifference.
W. Somerset Maugham 1874–1965:
A Writer's Notebook (1949) written
in 1896

10 Bigotry may be roughly defined as
the anger of men who have no
opinions.
G. K. Chesterton 1874–1936: *Heretics*
(1905)

11 *definition of a compromise:*
An agreement between two men
to do what both agree is wrong.
Lord Edward Cecil 1867–1918: letter,
3 September 1911

12 Make hatred hated!
to public school teachers
Anatole France 1844–1924: speech in
Tours, August 1919; Carter Jefferson
*Anatole France: The Politics of
Scepticism* (1965)

13 I decline utterly to be impartial as
between the fire brigade and the
fire.
*replying to complaints of his bias in
editing the* British Gazette *during the
General Strike*

Winston Churchill 1874–1965:
speech, House of Commons, 7 July
1926

14 Bigotry tries to keep truth safe in
its hand
With a grip that kills it.
Rabindranath Tagore 1861–1941:
Fireflies (1928)

15 Intolerance of groups is often,
strangely enough, exhibited more
strongly against small differences
than against fundamental ones.
Sigmund Freud 1856–1939: *Moses
and Monotheism* (1938)

16 You might as well fall flat on
your face as lean over too far
backward.
James Thurber 1894–1961: "The Bear
Who Let It Alone" in *New Yorker* 29
April 1939

17 Four legs good, two legs bad.
George Orwell 1903–50: *Animal Farm*
(1945)

18 We should therefore claim, in the
name of tolerance, the right not
to tolerate the intolerant.
Karl Popper 1902–94: *The Open
Society and Its Enemies* (1945)

19 When people feel deeply,
impartiality is bias.
Lord Reith 1889–1971: *Into the Wind*
(1945)

20 PLEASE ACCEPT MY RESIGNATION. I
DON'T WANT TO BELONG TO ANY
CLUB THAT WILL ACCEPT ME AS A
MEMBER.
Groucho Marx 1895–1977: *Groucho
and Me* (1959)

Preparation and Readiness

1 The voice of him that crieth in
the wilderness, Prepare ye the
way of the Lord.
Bible: Isaiah

2 Watch therefore: for ye know not what hour your Lord doth come.
Bible: St. Matthew

3 Not a mouse
Shall disturb this hallowed house:
I am sent with broom before,
To sweep the dust behind the door.
William Shakespeare 1564–1616: *A Midsummer Night's Dream* (1595–6)

4 No time like the present.
Mrs. Manley 1663–1724: *The Lost Lover* (1696)

5 "Anne, sister Anne, do you see nothing coming?" And her sister Anne replied, "I see nothing but the sun showing up the dust, and the grass looking green."
Charles Perrault 1628–1703: "Blue Beard" (1697)

6 Barkis is willin'.
Charles Dickens 1812–70: *David Copperfield* (1850)

7 I think the necessity of being *ready* increases. Look to it.
Abraham Lincoln 1809–65: the whole of a letter to Governor Andrew Curtin of Pennsylvania, 8 April 1861

8 The scouts' motto is founded on my initials, it is: BE PREPARED, which means, you are always to be in a state of readiness in mind and body to do your duty.
Robert Baden-Powell 1857–1941: *Scouting for Boys* (1908)

9 Go ahead, make my day.
Joseph C. Stinson 1947– : *Sudden Impact* (1983 film); spoken by Clint Eastwood

The Present
see also **The Past**

1 *Carpe diem, quam minimum credula postero.*

Seize the day, put no trust in the future.
Horace 65–8 BC: *Odes*

2 Take therefore no thought for the morrow: for the morrow shall take thought for the things of itself. Sufficient unto the day is the evil thereof.
Bible: St. Matthew

3 Can ye not discern the signs of the times?
Bible: St. Matthew

4 What is love? 'tis not hereafter;
Present mirth hath present laughter;
What's to come is still unsure:
William Shakespeare 1564–1616: *Twelfth Night* (1601)

5 Praise they that will times past, I joy to see
My self now live: this age best pleaseth me.
Robert Herrick 1591–1674: "The Present Time Best Pleaseth" (1648)

6 The present is the funeral of the past,
And man the living sepulchre of life.
John Clare 1793–1864: "The present is the funeral of the past" (written 1845)

7 In any weather, at any hour of the day or night, I have been anxious to improve the nick of time, and notch it on my stick too; to stand on the meeting of two eternities, the past and the future, which is precisely the present moment; to toe that line.
Henry David Thoreau 1817–62: *Walden* (1854) "Economy"

8 Ah, fill the cup:—what boots it to repeat
How time is slipping underneath our feet:
Unborn TO-MORROW, and dead YESTERDAY,

Why fret about them if TO-DAY be sweet!
Edward Fitzgerald 1809–83: *The Rubáiyát of Omar Khayyám* (1859)

9 The rule is, jam to-morrow and jam yesterday—but never jam today.
Lewis Carroll 1832–98: *Through the Looking-Glass* (1872); cf. **Foresight 10**

10 The only living life is in the past and future . . . the present is an interlude . . . strange interlude in which we call on past and future to bear witness we are living.
Eugene O'Neill 1888–1953: *Strange Interlude* (1928)

11 Like a monkey scratching for the wrong fleas, every age assiduously seeks out in itself those vices which it does not in fact have, while ignoring the large, red, beady-eyed crawlers who scuttle around unimpeded.
Katharine Whitehorn 1928– : *Observations* (1970)

12 Below my window . . . the blossom is out in full now . . . I *see* it is the whitest, frothiest, blossomiest blossom that there ever could be, and I can see it. Things are both more trivial than they ever were, and more important than they ever were, and the difference between the trivial and the important doesn't seem to matter. But the nowness of everything is absolutely wondrous.
on his heightened awareness of things, in the face of his imminent death
Dennis Potter 1935–94: television interview with Melvyn Bragg, March 1994

The Presidency

see also **America**, **Politicians**

1 My country has in its wisdom contrived for me the most insignificant office that ever the invention of man contrived or his imagination conceived.
of the vice-presidency
John Adams 1735–1826: letter to Abigail Adams, 19 December 1793

2 A citizen, first in war, first in peace, and first in the hearts of his countrymen.
Henry Lee 1756–1818: *Funeral Oration on the death of General Washington* (1800)

3 As President, I have no eyes but constitutional eyes; I cannot see you.
Abraham Lincoln 1809–65: reply to the South Carolina Commissioners; attributed

4 We have exchanged the Washingtonian dignity for the Jeffersonian simplicity, which was, in truth, only another name for the Jacksonian vulgarity.
Henry Codman Potter 1835–1908: *Bishop Potter's Address* (1890) 30 April 1889

5 Log-cabin to White House.
William Roscoe Thayer 1859–1923: title of biography (1910) of James Garfield (1831–81)

6 He [Calvin Coolidge] slept more than any other President, whether by day or by night. Nero fiddled, but Coolidge only snored.
H. L. Mencken 1880–1956: in *American Mercury* April 1933

7 How do they know?
reaction to the death of President Calvin Coolidge in 1933
Dorothy Parker 1893–1967: Malcolm Cowley *Writers at Work* 1st Series (1958)

8 When I was a boy I was told that anybody could become President. I'm beginning to believe it.
Clarence Darrow 1857–1938: Irving Stone *Clarence Darrow for the Defense* (1941)

9 In America any boy may become President and I suppose it's just one of the risks he takes!
Adlai Stevenson 1900–65: speech in Indianapolis, 26 September 1952

10 Probably the greatest concentration of talent and genius in this house except for perhaps those times when Thomas Jefferson ate alone.
of a White House dinner for Nobel Prizewinners
John F. Kennedy 1917–63: in *New York Times* 30 April 1962

11 No easy problems ever come to the President of the United States. If they are easy to solve, somebody else has solved them.
Dwight D. Eisenhower 1890–1969: *Parade Magazine* (8 April 1962)

12 No, *no. Jimmy Stewart* for governor—Reagan for his best friend.
on hearing that Ronald Reagan was seeking nomination as Governor of California, 1966
Jack Warner 1892–1978: Max Wilk *The Wit and Wisdom of Hollywood* (1972)

13 The vice-presidency isn't worth a pitcher of warm piss.
John Nance Garner 1868–1967: O. C. Fisher *Cactus Jack* (1978)

14 He'll sit right here and he'll say do this, do that! And nothing will happen. Poor Ike—it won't be a bit like the Army.
Harry S. Truman 1884–1972: *Harry S. Truman* (1973)

15 The answer to the runaway Presidency is not the messenger-boy Presidency. The American democracy must discover a middle way between making the President a tsar and making him a puppet.
Arthur M. Schlesinger, Jr. 1917– : *The Imperial Presidency* (1973); preface

16 There can be no whitewash at the White House.
on Watergate
Richard Nixon 1913–94: television speech, 30 April 1973

17 Anybody that wants the presidency so much that he'll spend two years organizing and campaigning for it is not to be trusted with the office.
David Broder 1929– : in *Washington Post* 18 July 1973

18 I am a Ford, not a Lincoln.
Gerald Ford 1909– : on taking the vice-presidential oath, 6 December 1973

19 The US presidency is a Tudor monarchy plus telephones.
Anthony Burgess 1917–93: George Plimpton (ed.) *Writers at Work* 4th Series (1977)

20 When the President does it, that means that it is not illegal.
Richard Nixon 1913–94: David Frost *I Gave Them a Sword* (1978)

21 Richard Nixon impeached himself. He gave us Gerald Ford as his revenge.
Bella Abzug 1920– : in *Rolling Stone*; Linda Botts *Loose Talk* (1980)

22 A triumph of the embalmer's art.
of Ronald Reagan
Gore Vidal 1925– : in *Observer* (UK) 26 April 1981

23 Ronald Reagan . . . is attempting a great breakthrough in political technology—he has been perfecting the Teflon-coated

Presidency. He sees to it that nothing sticks to him.
Patricia Schroeder 1940– : speech in the US House of Representatives, 2 August 1983

24 Poor George, he can't help it—he was born with a silver foot in his mouth.
of George Bush
Ann Richards 1933– : keynote speech at the Democratic convention, in *Independent* (UK) 20 July 1988

25 Somewhere out in this audience may even be someone who will one day follow in my footsteps, and preside over the White House as the President's spouse. I wish him well!
Barbara Bush 1925– : remarks at Wellesley College Commencement, 1 June 1990

26 I will seek the presidency with nothing to fall back on but the judgment of the people and with nowhere to go but the White House or home.
announcing his decision, as a presidential candidate, to relinquish his Senate seat and position as majority leader
Robert ("Bob") Dole 1923– : on Capitol Hill, 15 May 1996

Pride and Humility
see also **Self-Esteem and Self-Assertion**

1 Pride goeth before destruction, and an haughty spirit before a fall.
Bible: Proverbs

2 Blessed are the meek: for they shall inherit the earth.
Bible: St. Matthew; cf. **11** below, **Wealth 26**

3 *Qualis artifex pereo!*
What an artist dies with me!

Nero AD 37–68: Suetonius *Lives of the Caesars* "Nero"

4 It is an hard matter for a man to go down into the valley of Humiliation . . . and to catch no slip by the way.
John Bunyan 1628–88: *The Pilgrim's Progress* (1678)

5 He that is down needs fear no fall,
He that is low no pride.
He that is humble ever shall
Have God to be his guide.
John Bunyan 1628–88: *The Pilgrim's Progress* (1684) "Shepherd Boy's Song"

6 God's revenge against vanity.
to David Garrick, who had asked him what he thought of a heavy shower of rain falling on the day of the Shakespeare Jubilee, organized by and chiefly starring Garrick himself
Samuel Foote 1720–77: W. Cooke *Memoirs of Samuel Foote* (1805)

7 We are so very 'umble.
Charles Dickens 1812–70: *David Copperfield* (1850)

8 I can trace my ancestry back to a protoplasmal primordial atomic globule. Consequently, my family pride is something in-conceivable. I can't help it. I was born sneering.
W. S. Gilbert 1836–1911: *The Mikado* (1885)

9 The tumult and the shouting dies—
The captains and the kings depart—
Still stands Thine ancient Sacrifice,
An humble and a contrite heart.
Lord God of Hosts, be with us yet,
Lest we forget—lest we forget!
Rudyard Kipling 1865–1936: "Recessional" (1897); cf. **Food 14**

10 The clever men at Oxford
Know all that there is to be knowed.

But they none of them know one
half as much
As intelligent Mr. Toad!
Kenneth Grahame 1859–1932: *Wind
in the Willows* (1908)

11 We have the highest authority for
believing that the meek shall
inherit the earth; though I have
never found any particular
corroboration of this aphorism in
the records of Somerset House.
F. E. Smith 1872–1930: *Contemporary
Personalities* (1924); see **2** above

12 I have often wished I had time to
cultivate modesty . . . But I am
too busy thinking about myself.
Edith Sitwell 1887–1964: in *Observer*
(UK) 30 April 1950

13 No one can make you feel inferior
without your consent.
Eleanor Roosevelt 1884–1962: in
Catholic Digest August 1960

14 In 1969 I published a small book
on Humility. It was a pioneering
work which has not, to my
knowledge, been superseded.
Lord Longford 1905–   : in *Tablet* 22
January 1994

Problems and Solutions
see also **Ways and Means**

1 Probable impossibilities are to be
preferred to improbable
possibilities.
Aristotle 384–322 BC: *Poetics*

2 One hears only those questions
for which one is able to find
answers.
Friedrich Nietzsche 1844–1900: *The
Gay Science* (1882)

3 How often have I said to you that
when you have eliminated the
impossible, whatever remains,
however improbable, must be the
truth?

Arthur Conan Doyle 1859–1930: *The
Sign of Four* (1890)

4 The fascination of what's difficult
Has dried the sap out of my
veins, and rent
Spontaneous joy and natural
content
Out of my heart.
W. B. Yeats 1865–1939: "The
Fascination of What's Difficult"
(1910)

5 Another nice mess you've gotten
me into.
Stan Laurel 1890–1965: *Another Fine
Mess* (1930 film) and many other
Laurel and Hardy films; spoken by
Oliver Hardy

6 It isn't that they can't see the
solution. It is that they can't see
the problem.
G. K. Chesterton 1874–1936: *Scandal
of Father Brown* (1935)

7 We haven't got the money, so
we've got to think!
Ernest Rutherford 1871–1937: in
Bulletin of the Institute of Physics
(1962); cf. **10** below

8 What we're saying today is that
you're either part of the solution
or you're part of the problem.
Eldridge Cleaver 1935–   : speech in
San Francisco, 1968; R. Scheer
*Eldridge Cleaver, Post Prison
Writings and Speeches* (1969)

9 Houston, we've had a problem.
*on Apollo 13 space mission, 14 April
1970*
James Lovell 1928–   : in *The Times*
(UK) 15 April 1970

10 Rutherford was a disaster. He
started the "something for
nothing" tradition . . . the notion
that research can always be done
on the cheap . . . The war taught
us differently. If you want quick
and effective results you must put
the money in.

Edward Bullard 1907–80: P. Grosvenor and J. McMillan *The British Genius* (1973); see **7** above

11 In my experience, the worst thing you can do to an important problem is discuss it. You know, I really do think this whole business of non-communication is one of the more poignant fallacies of our zestfully overexplanatory age.
Simon Gray 1936– : *Otherwise Engaged* (1975)

12 If a problem is too difficult to solve, one cannot claim that it is solved by pointing at all the efforts made to solve it.
Hannes Alfven 1908–95: quoted by Lord Flowers in 1976; A. Sampson *The Changing Anatomy of Britain* (1982)

Progress
see also **Change**

1 The thing that hath been, it is that which shall be; and that which is done is that which shall be done: and there is no new thing under the sun.
Bible: Ecclesiastes

2 Forgetting those things which are behind, and reaching forth unto those things which are before, I press toward the mark.
Bible: Philippians

3 We are like dwarfs on the shoulders of giants, so that we can see more than they, and things at a greater distance, not by virtue of any sharpness of sight on our part, or any physical distinction, but because we are carried high and raised up by their giant size.
Bernard of Chartres d. c. 1130: John of Salisbury *The Metalogicon* (1159)

4 If I have seen further it is by standing on the shoulders of giants.
Isaac Newton 1642–1727: letter to Robert Hooke, 5 February 1676

5 Not to go back, is somewhat to advance,
And men must walk at least before they dance.
Alexander Pope 1688–1744: *Imitations of Horace*

6 Nothing in progression can rest on its original plan. We may as well think of rocking a grown man in the cradle of an infant.
Edmund Burke 1729–97: *Letter to the Sheriffs of Bristol* (1777)

7 The European talks of progress because by an ingenious application of some scientific acquirements he has established a society which has mistaken comfort for civilization.
Benjamin Disraeli 1804–81: *Tancred* (1847)

8 From time to time, in the towns, I open a newspaper. Things seem to be going at a dizzy rate. We are dancing not on a volcano, but on the rotten seat of a latrine.
Gustave Flaubert 1821–80: letter to Louis Bouilhet, 14 November 1850

9 Belief in progress is a doctrine of idlers and Belgians. It is the individual relying upon his neighbors to do his work.
Charles Baudelaire 1821–67: *Journaux intimes* (1887) "Mon coeur mis à nu"

10 The reasonable man adapts himself to the world: the unreasonable one persists in trying to adapt the world to himself. Therefore all progress depends on the unreasonable man.
George Bernard Shaw 1856–1950: *Man and Superman* (1903)

11 One step forward two steps back.
V. I. Lenin 1870–1924: title of book
(1904)

12 The slogan of progress is
changing from the full dinner pail
to the full garage.
*sometimes paraphrased as, "a car in
every garage and a chicken in every
pot"*
Herbert Hoover 1874–1964: speech
in New York, 22 October 1928; cf.
Poverty 4

13 Want is one only of five giants on
the road of reconstruction . . . the
others are Disease, Ignorance,
Squalor and Idleness.
William Henry Beveridge 1879–1963:
Social Insurance and Allied Services
(1942)

14 "Change" is scientific, "progress"
is ethical; change is indubitable,
whereas progress is a matter of
controversy.
Bertrand Russell: *Unpopular Essays*
(1950) "Philosophy and Politics"

15 Man aspires to the stars. But if he
can get his sewage and refuse
distributed and utilised in orderly
fashion he will be doing very
well.
Roy Bridger: in *The Times* (UK) 13
July 1959

16 Is it progress if a cannibal uses
knife and fork?
Stanislaw Lec 1909–66: *Unkempt
Thoughts* (1962)

Publishing
see also **Books**

1 I, according to my copy, have
done set it in imprint, to the
intent that noble men may see
and learn the noble acts of
chivalry, the gentle and virtuous
deeds that some knights used in
those days.
William Caxton *c.* 1421–91: Thomas

Malory *Le Morte D'Arthur* (1485)
prologue

2 You shall see them on a beautiful
quarto page where a neat rivulet
of text shall meander through a
meadow of margin.
Richard Brinsley Sheridan 1751–1816:
The School for Scandal (1777)

3 Never literary attempt was more
unfortunate than my Treatise of
Human Nature. It fell *dead-born
from the press.*
David Hume 1711–76: *My Own Life*
(1777)

4 The poem will please if it is lively—
if it is stupid it will fail—but I will
have none of your damned
cutting and slashing.
Lord Byron 1788–1824: letter to his
publisher John Murray, 6 April 1819

5 Publish and be damned.
*replying to Harriette Wilson's
blackmail threat, c. 1825*
Duke of Wellington 1769–1852:
attributed

6 For you know, dear—I may,
without vanity, hint—
Though an angel should write,
still 'tis *devils* must print.
Thomas Moore 1779–1852: *The
Fudges in England* (1835)

7 Now Barabbas was a publisher.
*alteration in a Bible of the verse
"Now Barabbas was a robber"*
Thomas Campbell 1777–1844:
attributed, in Samuel Smiles *A
Publisher and his Friends* (1891);
also attributed, wrongly, to Byron;
cf. **12** below

8 University printing presses exist,
and are subsidised by the
Government for the purpose of
producing books which no one
can read; and they are true to
their high calling.
Francis M. Cornford 1874–1943:

Microcosmographia Academica
(1908)

9 For several days after my first
book was published I carried it
about in my pocket, and took
surreptitious peeps at it to make
sure that the ink had not faded.
J. M. Barrie 1860–1937: speech at
the Critics' Circle in London, 26 May
1922

10 Whence came the intrusive
comma on p. 4? It did not fall
from the sky.
A. E. Housman 1859–1936: letter to
the Richards Press, 3 July 1930

11 Being published by the Oxford
University Press is rather like
being married to a duchess: the
honour is almost greater than the
pleasure.
G. M. Young 1882–1959: Rupert Hart-
Davis letter to George Lyttelton, 29
April 1956

12 I always thought Barabbas was a
much misunderstood man . . .
a publisher's view
Peter Grose: letter 25 May 1983; see
7 above

13 If I had been someone not very
clever, I would have done an
easier job like publishing. That's
the easiest job I can think of.
A. J. Ayer 1910–89: attributed

Punctuality

1 You come most carefully upon
your hour.
William Shakespeare 1564–1616:
Hamlet (1601)

2 I was nearly kept waiting.
Louis XIV 1638–1715: attribution
queried, among others, by E.
Fournier in *L'Esprit dans l'Histoire*
(1857)

3 Recollect that painting and
punctuality mix like oil and
vinegar, and that genius and
regularity are utter enemies, and
must be to the end of time.
Thomas Gainsborough 1727–88:
letter to the Hon. Edward Stratford,
1 May 1772

4 Punctuality is the politeness of
kings.
Louis XVIII 1755–1824: *Souvenirs de
J. Lafitte* (1844); attributed

5 But think how early I go.
*when criticized for continually
arriving late for work in the City in
1919*
Lord Castlerosse 1891–1943: Leonard
Mosley *Castlerosse* (1956); remark
also claimed by Howard Dietz at
MGM

6 We've been waiting 700 years,
you can have the seven minutes.
*on arriving at Dublin Castle for the
handover by British forces on 16
January 1922, and being told that he
was seven minutes late*
Michael Collins 1880–1922: Tim Pat
Coogan *Michael Collins* (1990);
attributed, perhaps apocryphal

7 I have noticed that the people
who are late are often so much
jollier than the people who have
to wait for them.
E. V. Lucas 1868–1938: *365 Days
and One More* (1926)

8 We must leave exactly on time
. . . From now on everything must
function to perfection.
to a station-master
Benito Mussolini 1883–1945: Giorgio
Pini *Mussolini* (1939)

9 My Aunt Minnie would always be
punctual and never hold up
production, but who would pay
to see my Aunt Minnie?
on Marilyn Monroe's unpunctuality
Billy Wilder 1906– : P. F. Boller
and R. L. Davis *Hollywood
Anecdotes* (1988)

10 Punctuality is the virtue of the
bored.
Evelyn Waugh 1903–66: diary 26
March 1962

11 Cathedral time is five minutes
later than standard time.
Anonymous: order of service leaflet,
Christ Church Cathedral, Oxford,
1990s

Punishment
see **Crime and Punishment**

Quantities and Qualities

1 Thick as autumnal leaves that
strew the brooks
In Vallombrosa,
High overarched imbower.
John Milton 1608–74: *Paradise Lost*
(1667)

2 So, naturalists observe, a flea
Hath smaller fleas that on him
prey;
And these have smaller fleas to
bite 'em,
And so proceed *ad infinitum*.
Jonathan Swift 1667–1745: "On
Poetry" (1733)

3 I think no virtue goes with size.
Ralph Waldo Emerson 1803–82:
"The Titmouse" (1867)

4 I'll sing you twelve O.
Green grow the rushes O.
What is your twelve O?
Twelve for the twelve apostles,
Eleven for the eleven who went to
heaven,
Ten for the ten commandments,
Nine for the nine bright shiners,
Eight for the eight bold rangers,
Seven for the seven stars in the
sky,
Six for the six proud walkers,
Five for the symbol at your door,
Four for the Gospel makers,
Three for the rivals,
Two, two, the lily-white boys,

Clothed all in green O,
One is one and all alone
And ever more shall be so.
Anonymous: "The Dilly Song"
existing in various versions from the
nineteenth century

5 It is our national joy to mistake
for the first-rate, the fecund rate.
Dorothy Parker 1893–1967: review of
Sinclair Lewis *Dodsworth*; in *New
Yorker* 16 March 1929

Quotations

1 Confound those who have said
our remarks before us.
Aelius Donatus 4th century: St.
Jerome *Commentary on Ecclesiastes*

2 Classical quotation is the *parole* of
literary men all over the world.
Samuel Johnson 1709–84: James
Boswell *Life of Samuel Johnson*
(1791) 8 May 1781

3 He liked those literary cooks
Who skim the cream of others'
books;
And ruin half an author's graces
By plucking bon-mots from their
places.
Hannah More 1745–1833: *Florio*
(1786)

4 A proverb is one man's wit and
all men's wisdom.
Lord John Russell 1792–1878: R. J.
Mackintosh *Sir James Mackintosh*
(1835)

5 I hate quotation. Tell me what
you know.
Ralph Waldo Emerson 1803–82:
diary May 1849

6 Next to the originator of a good
sentence is the first quoter of it.
Ralph Waldo Emerson 1803–82:
Letters and Social Aims (1876)

7 He wrapped himself in quotations—
as a beggar would enfold himself
in the purple of emperors.

Rudyard Kipling 1865–1936: *Many Inventions* (1893)

8 OSCAR WILDE: How I wish I had said that.
WHISTLER: You will, Oscar, you will.
James McNeill Whistler 1834–1903: R. Ellman *Oscar Wilde* (1987)

9 You must not treat my immortal works as quarries to be used at will by the various hacks whom you may employ to compile anthologies.
A. E. Housman 1859–1936: letter to his publisher Grant Richards, 29 June 1907

10 An anthology is like all the plums and orange peel picked out of a cake.
Walter Raleigh 1861–1922: letter to Mrs. Robert Bridges, 15 January 1915

11 But I have long thought that if you knew a column of advertisements by heart, you could achieve unexpected felicities with them. You can get a happy quotation anywhere if you have the eye.
Oliver Wendell Holmes, Jr. 1841–1935: letter to Harold Laski, 31 May 1923

12 It is a good thing for an uneducated man to read books of quotations.
Winston Churchill 1874–1965: *My Early Life* (1930)

13 Misquotation is, in fact, the pride and privilege of the learned. A widely-read man never quotes accurately, for the rather obvious reason that he has read too widely.
Hesketh Pearson 1887–1964: *Common Misquotations* (1934)

14 The surest way to make a monkey of a man is to quote him.
Robert Benchley 1889–1945: *My Ten Years in a Quandary* (1936)

15 To-day I am a lamppost against which no anthologist lifts his leg.
James Agate 1877–1947: diary 21 August 1941

16 The nice thing about quotes is that they give us a nodding acquaintance with the originator which is often socially impressive.
Kenneth Williams 1926–88: *Acid Drops* (1980)

17 Windbags can be right. Aphorists can be wrong. It is a tough world.
James Fenton 1949– : in *Times* (UK) 21 February 1985

Race and Racism
see also **Equality, Prejudice and Tolerance**

1 You call me misbeliever, cut-throat dog,
And spit upon my Jewish gabardine,
And all for use of that which is mine own.
William Shakespeare 1564–1616: *The Merchant of Venice* (1596–8)

2 My mother bore me in the southern wild,
And I am black, but O! my soul is white;
White as an angel is the English child:
But I am black as if bereaved of light.
William Blake 1757–1827: "The Little Black Boy" (1789)

3 When I recovered a little I found some black people about me . . . I asked them if we were not to be eaten by those white men with horrible looks, red faces, and loose hair.
Olaudah Equiano c. 1745–c. 1797: *Narrative of the Life of Olaudah Equiano* (1789)

4 Am I not a man and a brother.
legend on Wedgwood cameo,
depicting a kneeling Negro slave in
chains
Josiah Wedgwood 1730–95: E.
Darwin *The Botanic Garden* pt. 1
(1791)

5 You have seen how a man was
made a slave; you shall see how
a slave was made a man.
Frederick Douglass *c.* 1818–1895:
Narrative of the Life of Frederick
Douglass (1845)

6 The only good Indian is a dead
Indian.
at Fort Cobb, January 1869
Philip Henry Sheridan 1831–88:
attributed

7 Because a man has a black face
and a different religion from our
own, there is no reason why he
should be treated as a brute.
Edward VII 1841–1910: letter to Lord
Granville, 30 November 1875

8 The so-called white races are
really pinko-grey.
E. M. Forster 1879–1970: *A Passage*
to India (1924)

9 If my theory of relativity is
proven correct, Germany will
claim me as a German and
France will declare that I am a
citizen of the world. Should my
theory prove untrue, France will
say that I am a German and
Germany will declare that I am a
Jew.
Albert Einstein 1879–1955: address
at the Sorbonne, Paris, possibly
early December 1929; in *New York*
Times 16 February 1930

10 I herewith commission you to
carry out all preparations with
regard to . . . a *total solution* of the
Jewish question in those
territories of Europe which are
under German influence.
instructions to Heydrich, 31 July 1941

Hermann Goering 1893–1946: W. L.
Shirer *The Rise and Fall of the Third*
Reich (1962)

11 You gotta say this for the white
race—its self-confidence knows no
bounds. Who else could go to a
small island in the South Pacific
where there's no poverty, no
crime, no unemployment, no war
and no worry—and call it a
"primitive society"?
Dick Gregory 1932– : *From the Back*
of the Bus (1962)

12 I want to be the white man's
brother, not his brother-in-law.
Martin Luther King, Jr. 1929–68: in
New York Journal-American 10
September 1962

13 Segregation now, segregation
tomorrow and segregation
forever!
George Wallace 1919– : inaugural
speech as Governor of Alabama, 14
January 1963

14 There are no "white" or "colored"
signs on the foxholes or
graveyards of battle.
John F. Kennedy 1917–63: message
to Congress on proposed Civil Rights
Bill, 19 June 1963

15 Being a star has made it possible
for me to get insulted in places
where the average Negro could
never *hope* to go and get insulted.
Sammy Davis Jnr. 1925–90: *Yes I*
Can (1965)

16 It comes as a great shock around
the age of 5, 6 or 7 to discover
that the flag to which you have
pledged allegiance, along with
everybody else, has not pledged
allegiance to you. It comes as a
great shock to see Gary Cooper
killing off the Indians and,
although you are rooting for Gary
Cooper, that the Indians are you.
speaking for the proposition that
"The American Dream is at the

expense of the American Negro"
James Baldwin 1924–87: Cambridge
Union, England, 17 February 1965

17 As I look ahead, I am filled with
foreboding. Like the Roman, I
seem to see "the River Tiber
foaming with much blood."
*on the probable consequences of
immigration*
Enoch Powell 1912–   : speech at the
Annual Meeting of the West
Midlands Area Conservative Political
Centre, Birmingham, 20 April 1968;
see **Warfare** 5

18 Black is beautiful when it is a
slum kid studying to enter
college, when it is a man learning
new skills for a new job, or a
slum mother battling to give her
kids a chance for a better life. But
white is beautiful, too, when it
helps change society to make our
system work for black people also.
White is ugly when it oppresses
blacks—and so is black ugly
when black people exploit other
blacks. No race has a monopoly
on vice or virtue, and the worth
of an individual is not related to
the color of his skin.
Whitney Moore Young, Jr. 1921–71:
*Beyond Racism: Building an Open
Society* (1969)

19 When I look out at this
convention, I see the face of
America, red, yellow, brown,
black, and white. We are all
precious in God's sight—the real
rainbow coalition.
Jesse Jackson 1941–   : speech at
Democratic National Convention,
Atlanta, 19 July 1988

Rank and Title
see also **Class**

1 New nobility is but the act of
power, but ancient nobility is the
act of time.

Francis Bacon 1561–1626: *Essays*
(1625) "Of Nobility"

2 'Tis from high life high characters
are drawn;
A saint in crape is twice a saint
in lawn.
Alexander Pope 1688–1744: "To Lord
Cobham" (1734)

3 Nobility is a graceful ornament to
the civil order. It is the
Corinthian capital of polished
society.
Edmund Burke 1729–97: *Reflections
on the Revolution in France* (1790)

4 The rank is but the guinea's
stamp,
The man's the gowd for a' that!
Robert Burns 1759–96: "For a' that
and a' that" (1790)

5 All that class of equivocal
generation, which in some
countries is called *aristocracy*, and
in others *nobility*, is done away,
and the peer is exalted into MAN.
of France
Thomas Paine 1737–1809: *The
Rights of Man* (1791)

6 I am an ancestor.
*taunted on his lack of ancestry when
made Duke of Abrantes, 1807*
Marshal Junot 1771–1813: attributed

7 I agree with you that there is a
natural aristocracy among men.
The grounds of this are virtue
and talents.
Thomas Jefferson 1743–1826: letter
to John Adams, 28 October 1813

8 Kind hearts are more than
coronets,
And simple faith than Norman
blood.
Alfred, Lord Tennyson 1809–92:
"Lady Clara Vere de Vere" (1842)

9 Whenever he met a great man he
grovelled before him, and my-

lorded him as only a free-born
Briton can do.
William Makepeace Thackeray 1811–
63: *Vanity Fair* (1847–8)

10 The order of nobility is of great
use, too, not only in what it
creates, but in what it prevents. It
prevents the rule of wealth—the
religion of gold. This is the
obvious and natural idol of the
Anglo-Saxon.
Walter Bagehot 1826–77: *The
English Constitution* (1867)

11 Tyndall, I must remain plain
Michael Faraday to the last; and
let me now tell you, that if I
accepted the honour which the
Royal Society desires to confer
upon me, I would not answer for
the integrity of my intellect for a
single year.
*on being offered the Presidency of
the Royal Society*
Michael Faraday 1791–1867: J.
Tyndall *Faraday as a Discoverer*
(1868)

12 Titles distinguish the mediocre,
embarrass the superior, and are
disgraced by the inferior.
George Bernard Shaw 1856–1950:
Man and Superman (1903)

13 A medal glitters, but it also casts
a shadow.
*a reference to the envy caused by
the award of honors*
Winston Churchill 1874–1965: in 1941;
Kenneth Rose *King George V* (1983)

14 An aristocracy in a republic is
like a chicken whose head has
been cut off: it may run about in
a lively way, but in fact it is dead.
Nancy Mitford 1904–73: *Noblesse
Oblige* (1956)

15 There is no stronger craving in
the world than that of the rich
for titles, except perhaps that of
the titled for riches.

Hesketh Pearson 1887–1964: *The
Pilgrim Daughters* (1961)

Readiness
see **Preparation and Readiness**

Reading
see also **Books**

1 POLONIUS: What do you read, my
lord?
HAMLET: Words, words, words.
William Shakespeare 1564–1616:
Hamlet (1601)

2 Who reads
Incessantly, and to his reading
brings not
A spirit and judgement equal or
superior
(And what he brings, what needs
he elsewhere seek?)
Uncertain and unsettled still
remains,
Deep-versed in books and shallow
in himself.
John Milton 1608–74: *Paradise
Regained* (1671)

3 Choose an author as you choose
a friend.
Wentworth Dillon, Lord Roscommon
c. 1633–85: *Essay on Translated
Verse* (1684)

4 He had read much, if one
considers his long life; but his
contemplation was much more
than his reading. He was wont to
say that if he had read as much
as other men, he should have
known no more than other men.
John Aubrey 1626–97: *Brief Lives*
"Thomas Hobbes"

5 Reading is to the mind what
exercise is to the body.
Richard Steele 1672–1729: in *The
Tatler* (UK) 18 March 1710

6 The bookful blockhead, ignorantly
read,
With loads of learned lumber in
his head.
Alexander Pope 1688–1744: *An
Essay on Criticism* (1711)

7 A man ought to read just as
inclination leads him; for what he
reads as a task will do him little
good.
Samuel Johnson 1709–84: James
Boswell *Life of Samuel Johnson*
(1791) 14 July 1763

8 Digressions, incontestably, are the
sunshine;—they are the life, the
soul of reading:—take them out
of this book for instance,—you
might as well take the book along
with them.
Laurence Sterne 1713–68: *Tristram
Shandy* (1759–67)

9 Much have I travelled in the
realms of gold,
And many goodly states and
kingdoms seen.
John Keats 1795–1821: "On First
Looking into Chapman's Homer"
(1817)

10 'Tis the good reader that makes
the good book; . . . in every book
he finds passages which seem
confidences or asides hidden from
all else and unmistakably meant
for his ear.
Ralph Waldo Emerson 1802–82:
Society and Solitude, Success (1870)

11 People say that life is the thing,
but I prefer reading.
Logan Pearsall Smith 1865–1946:
Afterthoughts (1931) "Myself"

12 [*The Compleat Angler*] is
acknowledged to be one of the
world's books. Only the trouble is
that the world doesn't read its
books, it borrows a detective story
instead.
Stephen Leacock 1869–1944: *The
Boy I Left Behind Me* (1947)

13 The primary object of a student of
literature is to be delighted. His
duty is to enjoy himself: his efforts
should be directed to developing
his faculty of appreciation.
Lord David Cecil 1902–86: *Reading
as one of the Fine Arts* (1949)

14 Curiously enough, one cannot
read a book: one can only reread
it. A good reader, a major reader,
an active and creative reader is a
rereader.
Vladimir Nabokov 1899–1977:
Lectures on Literature (1980) "Good
Readers and Good Writers"

15 Any writer worth his salt knows
that only a small proportion of
literature does more than partly
compensate people for the
damage they have suffered in
learning to read.
Rebecca West 1892–1983: Peter
Vansittart *Path from a White Horse*
(1985)

16 Only a handful of students now
enter Yale with an authentic
passion for reading. You cannot
teach someone to love great
poetry if they come to you
without such love. How can you
teach solitude? Real reading is a
lonely activity and does not teach
anyone to become a better citizen.
Perhaps the ages of reading—
Aristocratic, Democratic, Chaotic—
now reach terminus, and the
reborn Theocratic era will be
almost wholly an oral and visual
culture.
Harold Bloom 1932– : *The Western
Canon* (1994)

Reality
see also **Appearance, Hypothesis and
Fact**

1 Every thing, saith Epictetus, hath
two handles, the one to be held
by, the other not.

Robert Burton 1577–1640: *The Anatomy of Melancholy* (1621–51)

2 I refute it *thus*.
kicking a large stone by way of refuting Bishop Berkeley's theory of the non-existence of matter
Samuel Johnson 1709–84: James Boswell *Life of Samuel Johnson* (1791) 6 August 1763

3 All theory, dear friend, is grey, but the golden tree of actual life springs ever green.
Johann Wolfgang von Goethe 1749–1832: *Faust* pt. 1 (1808) "Studierzimmer"

4 What is rational is actual and what is actual is rational.
G. W. F. Hegel 1770–1831: *Grundlinien der Philosophie des Rechts* (1821)

5 All that we see or seem
Is but a dream within a dream.
Edgar Allan Poe 1809–49: "A Dream within a Dream" (1849)

6 Do you think that the things people make fools of themselves about are any less real and true than the things they behave sensibly about? They are more true: they are the only things that are true.
George Bernard Shaw 1856–1950: *Candida* (1898)

7 BLANCHE: I don't want realism.
MITCH: Naw, I guess not.
BLANCHE: I'll tell you what I want. Magic!
Tennessee Williams: *A Streetcar Named Desire* (1947)

8 Reality goes bounding past the satirist like a cheetah laughing as it lopes ahead of the greyhound.
Claud Cockburn 1904–81: *Crossing the Line* (1958)

9 Perhaps the rare and simple pleasure of being seen for what one is compensates for the misery of being it.
Margaret Drabble 1939– : *A Summer Bird-Cage* (1963)

10 The camera makes everyone a tourist in other people's reality, and eventually in one's own.
Susan Sontag 1933– : in *New York Review of Books* 18 April 1974

Reason
see **Logic and Reason**

Rebellion
see **Revolution and Rebellion**

Relationships
see also **Friendship, Hatred, Love**

1 Am I my brother's keeper?
Bible: Genesis

2 Difficult or easy, pleasant or bitter, you are the same you: I cannot live with you—or without you.
Martial AD *c.* 40–*c.* 104: *Epigrammata*

3 He who has a thousand friends has not a friend to spare,
And he who has one enemy will meet him everywhere.
Ali ibn-Abi-Talib *c.* 602–661: *A Hundred Sayings*

4 Friendship is constant in all other things
Save in the office and affairs of love.
William Shakespeare 1564–1616: *Much Ado About Nothing* (1598–9)

5 In necessary things, unity; in doubtful things, liberty; in all things, charity.
Richard Baxter 1615–91: motto

6 Friendship is a disinterested commerce between equals; love,

an abject intercourse between
tyrants and slaves.
Oliver Goldsmith 1730–74: *The Good-
Natured Man* (1768)

7 Ships that pass in the night, and
    speak each other in passing;
Only a signal shown and a
    distant voice in the darkness;
So on the ocean of life we pass
    and speak one another,
Only a look and a voice; then
    darkness again and a silence.
Henry Wadsworth Longfellow 1807–
82: *Tales of a Wayside Inn* pt. 3
(1874)

8 I hold this to be the highest task
    for a bond between two people:
    that each protects the solitude of
    the other.
Rainer Maria Rilke 1875–1926: letter
to Paula Modersohn-Becker, 12
February 1902

9 Love, friendship, respect do not
    unite people as much as common
    hatred for something.
Anton Chekhov 1860–1904:
Notebooks (1921)

10 Accident counts for much in
    companionship as in marriage.
Henry Brooks Adams 1838–1918: *The
Education of Henry Adams* (1907)

11 Personal relations are the
    important thing for ever and ever,
    and not this outer life of
    telegrams and anger.
E. M. Forster 1879–1970: *Howards
End* (1910)

12 I may be wrong, but I have never
    found deserting friends conciliates
    enemies.
Margot Asquith 1864–1945: *Lay
Sermons* (1927)

13 She experienced all the cosiness
    and irritation which can come
    from living with thoroughly nice

people with whom one has
nothing in common.
Barbara Pym 1913–80: *Less than
Angels* (1955)

14 Almost all of our relationships
    begin and most of them continue
    as forms of mutual exploitation, a
    mental or physical barter, to be
    terminated when one or both
    parties run out of goods.
W. H. Auden 1907–73: *The Dyer's
Hand* (1963)

15 There are those who never stretch
    out the hand for fear it will be
    bitten. But those who never
    stretch out the hand will never
    feel it clasped in friendship.
Michael Heseltine 1933– : *Where
There's a Will* (1987)

16 There is no improper relationship.
    denying allegations of a sexual affair
Bill Clinton 1946– : in *New York
Times* 22 January 1998

Religion
see also **The Bible, The Christian
Church, Clergy, God, Prayer, Science
and Religion**

1 Is that which is holy loved by the
    gods because it is holy, or is it
    holy because it is loved by the
    gods?
Plato 429–347 BC: *Euthyphro*

2 *Tantum religio potuit suadere
    malorum.*
So much wrong could religion
    induce.
Lucretius c. 94–55 BC: *De Rerum
Natura*

3 Render therefore unto Caesar the
    things which are Caesar's; and
    unto God the things that are
    God's.
Bible: St. Matthew

4 I count religion but a childish
toy,
And hold there is no sin but
ignorance.
Christopher Marlowe 1564–93: *The
Jew of Malta* (*c.* 1592)

5 Had I but served my God with
half the zeal
I served my king, he would not in
mine age
Have left me naked to mine
enemies.
William Shakespeare 1564–1616:
Henry VIII (1613)

6 A verse may find him, who a
sermon flies,
And turn delight into a sacrifice.
George Herbert 1593–1633: "The
Church Porch" (1633)

7 One religion is as true as another.
Robert Burton 1577–1640: *The
Anatomy of Melancholy* (1621–51)

8 For it is with the mysteries of our
religion, as with wholesome pills
for the sick, which swallowed
whole, have the virtue to cure;
but chewed, are for the most part
cast up again without effect.
Thomas Hobbes 1588–1679:
Leviathan (1651)

9 Men have lost their reason in
nothing so much as their religion,
wherein stones and clouts make
martyrs.
Thomas Browne 1605–82:
Hydriotaphia (Urn Burial, 1658)

10 A good honest and painful
sermon.
Samuel Pepys 1633–1703: diary 17
March 1661

11 They are for religion when in rags
and contempt; but I am for him
when he walks in his golden
slippers, in the sunshine and with
applause.
John Bunyan 1628–88: *The Pilgrim's
Progress* (1678)

12 "People differ in their discourse
and profession about these
matters, but men of sense are
really but of one religion." . . .
"Pray, my lord, what religion is
that which men of sense agree
in?" "Madam," says the earl
immediately, "men of sense never
tell it."
1st Earl of Shaftesbury 1621–83:
Bishop Gilbert Burnet *History of My
Own Time* vol. 1 (1724)

13 We have just enough religion to
make us hate, but not enough to
make us love one another.
Jonathan Swift 1667–1745: *Thoughts
on Various Subjects* (1711)

14 I went to America to convert the
Indians; but oh, who shall
convert me?
John Wesley 1703–91: diary 24
January 1738

15 Putting moral virtues at the
highest, and religion at the
lowest, religion must still be
allowed to be a collateral security,
at least, to virtue; and every
prudent man will sooner trust to
two securities than to one.
Lord Chesterfield 1694–1773: *Letters
to his Son* (1774) 8 January 1750

16 It is our first duty to serve society,
and, after we have done that, we
may attend wholly to the
salvation of our own souls. A
youthful passion for abstracted
devotion should not be
encouraged.
Samuel Johnson 1709–84: James
Boswell *Life of Samuel Johnson*
(1791) February 1766

17 As to religion, I hold it to be the
indispensable duty of government
to protect all conscientious
professors thereof, and I know of
no other business which
government hath to do therewith.
Thomas Paine 1737–1809: *Common
Sense* (1776)

18 Orthodoxy is my doxy;
heterodoxy is another man's
doxy.
William Warburton 1698–1779: to
Lord Sandwich; Joseph Priestley
Memoirs (1807)

19 My country is the world, and my
religion is to do good.
Thomas Paine 1737–1809: *The
Rights of Man* pt. 2 (1792)

20 Old religious factions are
volcanoes burnt out.
Edmund Burke 1729–97: speech on
the petition of the Unitarians, 11
May 1792

21 Any system of religion that has
any thing in it that shocks the
mind of a child cannot be a true
system.
Thomas Paine 1737–1809: *The Age
of Reason* pt. 1 (1794)

22 In vain with lavish kindness
The gifts of God are strown;
The heathen in his blindness
Bows down to wood and stone.
Reginald Heber 1783–1826: "From
Greenland's icy mountains" (1821
hymn); cf. **Armed Forces 23**

23 I am always most religious upon
a sunshiny day.
Lord Byron 1788–1824: "Detached
Thoughts" 15 October 1821

24 Religion's in the heart, not in the
knees.
Douglas Jerrold 1803–57: *The Devil's
Ducat* (1830)

25 Religion . . . is the opium of the
people.
Karl Marx 1818–83: *A Contribution
to the Critique of Hegel's Philosophy
of Right* (1843–4)

26 Things have come to a pretty
pass when religion is allowed to
invade the sphere of private life.
on hearing an evangelical sermon
Lord Melbourne 1779–1848: G. W. E.

Russell *Collections and Recollections*
(1898)

27 'Tis not the dying for a faith
that's so hard, Master Harry—
every man of every nation has
done that—'tis the living up to it
that is difficult.
William Makepeace Thackeray 1811–
63: *The History of Henry Esmond*
(1852)

28 The true meaning of religion is
thus not simply morality, but
morality touched by emotion.
Matthew Arnold 1822–88: *Literature
and Dogma* (1873)

29 So long as man remains free he
strives for nothing so incessantly
and so painfully as to find
someone to worship.
Fyodor Dostoevsky 1821–81: *The
Brothers Karamazov* (1879–80)

30 There is only one religion, though
there are a hundred versions of it.
George Bernard Shaw 1856–1950:
Plays Pleasant and Unpleasant
(1898)

31 So many gods, so many creeds,
So many paths that wind and
wind,
While just the art of being kind
Is all the sad world needs.
Ella Wheeler Wilcox 1855–1919: "The
World's Need"

32 These damned mystics with a
private line to God ought to be
compelled to disconnect. I cannot
see that they have done anything
save prevent necessary change.
Harold Laski 1893–1950: letter to
Oliver Wendell Holmes, 29 January
1919

33 To become a popular religion, it
is only necessary for a
superstition to enslave a
philosophy.
William Ralph Inge 1860–1954: *Idea
of Progress* (1920)

34 There's no reason to bring religion into it. I think we ought to have as great a regard for religion as we can, so as to keep it out of as many things as possible.
Sean O'Casey 1880–1964: *The Plough and the Stars* (1926)

35 Religion is the frozen thought of men out of which they build temples.
Jiddu Krishnamurti 1895–1986: in *Observer* (UK) 22 April 1928

36 Religion may in most of its forms be defined as the belief that the gods are on the side of the Government.
Bertrand Russell 1872–1970: attributed

37 Religions are kept alive by heresies, which are really sudden explosions of faith. Dead religions do not produce them.
Gerald Brenan 1894–1987: *Thoughts in a Dry Season* (1978)

38 Religion to me has always been the wound, not the bandage.
Dennis Potter 1935–94: television interview with Melvyn Bragg, March 1994

Repentance
see **Forgiveness and Repentance**

Reputation
see also **Fame**

1 A good name is rather to be chosen than great riches.
Bible: Proverbs

2 Caesar's wife must be above suspicion.
Julius Caesar 100–44 BC: oral tradition, based on Plutarch *Parallel Lives* "Julius Caesar"

3 Woe unto you, when all men shall speak well of you!
Bible: St. Luke

4 *Non è il mondan romore altro che un fiato*
di vento, ch'or vien quinci ed or qien quindi,
e muta nome perchè muta lato.
The reputation which the world bestows
is like the wind, that shifts now here now there,
its name changed with the quarter whence it blows.
Dante Alighieri 1265–1321: *Divina Commedia* "Purgatorio"

5 The purest treasure mortal times afford
Is spotless reputation; that away,
Men are but gilded loam or painted clay.
William Shakespeare 1564–1616: *Richard II* (1595)

6 What is honour? A word. What is that word, honour? Air. A trim reckoning! Who hath it? He that died o' Wednesday. Doth he feel it? No. Doth he hear it? No. It is insensible then? Yea, to the dead. But will it not live with the living? No. Why? Detraction will not suffer it. Therefore I'll none of it: honour is a mere scutcheon: and so ends my catechism.
William Shakespeare 1564–1616: *Henry IV, Part 1* (1597)

7 Who steals my purse steals trash;
'tis something, nothing;
'Twas mine, 'tis his, and has been slave to thousands;
But he that filches from me my good name
Robs me of that which not enriches him,
And makes me poor indeed.
William Shakespeare 1564–1616: *Othello* (1602–4)

8 O! I have lost my reputation. I have lost the immortal part of

myself, and what remains is
bestial.
William Shakespeare 1564–1616:
Othello (1602–4)

9 Men's evil manners live in brass;
their virtues
We write in water.
William Shakespeare 1564–1616:
Henry VIII (1613)

10 They come together like the
Coroner's Inquest, to sit upon the
murdered reputations of the week.
William Congreve 1670–1729: *The
Way of the World* (1700)

11 At ev'ry word a reputation dies.
Alexander Pope 1688–1744: *The
Rape of the Lock* (1714)

12 He left the name, at which the
world grew pale,
To point a moral, or adorn a tale.
of Charles XII of Sweden
Samuel Johnson 1709–84: *The Vanity
of Human Wishes* (1749)

13 Oh, fond attempt to give a
deathless lot
To names ignoble, born to be
forgot!
William Cowper 1731–1800: "On
Observing Some Names of Little
Note Recorded in the Biographia
Britannica" (1782)

14 We owe respect to the living; to
the dead we owe only truth.
Voltaire 1694–1778: "Première Lettre
sur Oedipe" in *Oeuvres* (1785)

15 "If I should die," said I to myself,
"I have left no immortal work
behind me—nothing to make my
friends proud of my memory—but
I have loved the principle of
beauty in all things, and if I had
had time I would have made
myself remembered."
John Keats 1795–1821: letter to
Fanny Brawne, *c.* February 1820

16 The devil's most devilish when
respectable.

Elizabeth Barrett Browning 1806–61:
Aurora Leigh (1857)

17 What is merit? The opinion one
man entertains of another.
Lord Palmerston 1784–1865: Thomas
Carlyle *Shooting Niagara: and After?*
(1867)

18 Honor is like a match, you can
only use it once.
Marcel Pagnol 1895–1974: *Marius*
(1946)

19 I'm the girl who lost her
reputation and never missed it.
Mae West 1892–1980: P. F. Boller
and R. L. Davis *Hollywood
Anecdotes* (1988)

20 You can't shame or humiliate
modern celebrities. What used to
be called shame and humiliation
is now called publicity.
P. J. O'Rourke 1947–   : *Give War a
Chance* (1992)

Revenge

1 Vengeance is mine; I will repay,
saith the Lord.
Bible: Romans

2 Indeed, revenge is always the
pleasure of a paltry, feeble, tiny
mind.
Juvenal AD *c.* 60–*c.* 130: *Satires*

3 Men should be either treated
generously or destroyed, because
they take revenge for slight
injuries—for heavy ones they
cannot.
Niccolò Machiavelli 1469–1527: *The
Prince* (written 1513)

4 Caesar's spirit, ranging for
revenge,
With Ate by his side, come hot
from hell,
Shall in these confines, with a
monarch's voice
Cry, "Havoc!" and let slip the
dogs of war;

William Shakespeare 1564–1616:
Julius Caesar (1599)

5 Revenge is a kind of wild justice,
which the more man's nature
runs to, the more ought law to
weed it out.
Francis Bacon 1561–1626: *Essays*
(1625) "Of Revenge"

6 A man that studieth revenge
keeps his own wounds green.
Francis Bacon 1561–1626: *Essays*
(1625) "Of Revenge"

7 Heaven has no rage, like love to
hatred turned,
Nor Hell a fury, like a woman
scorned.
William Congreve 1670–1729: *The
Mourning Bride* (1697)

8 Sweet is revenge—especially to
women.
Lord Byron 1788–1824: *Don Juan*
(1819–24)

9 We hand folks over to God's
mercy, and show none ourselves.
George Eliot 1819–80: *Adam Bede*
(1859)

10 *Sic semper tyrannis!* The South is
avenged.
*having shot President Lincoln, 14
April 1865*
John Wilkes Booth 1838–65: "*Sic
semper tyrannis* [Thus always to
tyrants]"—motto of the State of
Virginia; in *New York Times* 15 April
1865 (the second part of the
statement possibly apocryphal)

11 It may be that vengeance is
sweet, and that the gods forbade
vengeance to men because they
reserved for themselves so
delicious and intoxicating a drink.
But no one should drain the cup
to the bottom. The dregs are often
filthy-tasting.
Winston Churchill 1874–1965: *The
River War* (1899)

12 Beware of the man who does not
return your blow: he neither
forgives you nor allows you to
forgive yourself.
George Bernard Shaw 1856–1950:
Man and Superman (1903)

13 I like to write when I feel spiteful;
it's like having a good sneeze.
D. H. Lawrence 1885–1930: letter to
Lady Cynthia Asquith, *c.* 25
November 1913

14 The Germans, if this Government
is returned, are going to pay
every penny; they are going to be
squeezed as a lemon is squeezed—
until the pips squeak.
Eric Geddes 1875–1937: speech at
Cambridge, 10 December 1918

15 If you start throwing hedgehogs
under me, I shall throw a couple
of porcupines under you.
Nikita Khrushchev 1894–1971: in
New York Times 7 November 1963

Revolution and Rebellion

1 A desperate disease requires a
dangerous remedy.
Guy Fawkes 1570–1606: remark, 6
November 1605

2 The surest way to prevent
seditions (if the times do bear it)
is to take away the matter of
them.
Francis Bacon 1561–1626: *Essays*
(1625) "Of Seditions and Troubles"

3 Rebellion to tyrants is obedience
to God.
John Bradshaw 1602–59:
suppositious epitaph; Henry S.
Randall *Life of Thomas Jefferson*
(1865)

4 When the people contend for
their liberty, they seldom get
anything by their victory but new
masters.
Lord Halifax 1633–95: *Political,
Moral, and Miscellaneous Thoughts*

and Reflections (1750) "Of Prerogative, Power and Liberty"

5 He wished . . . that all the great men in the world and all the nobility could be hanged, and strangled with the guts of priests.
quoting "an ignorant, uneducated man" often quoted as "I should like . . . the last of the kings to be strangled with the guts of the last priest"
Jean Meslier *c.* 1664–1733: *Testament* (1864)

6 *Après nous le déluge.*
After us the deluge.
Madame de Pompadour 1721–64: Madame du Hausset *Mémoires* (1824)

7 Stand your ground. Don't fire unless fired upon, but if they mean to have a war let it begin here.
John Parker 1729–75: *to his Minutemen at Lexington, Massachusetts* (19 April 1775)

8 A little rebellion now and then is a good thing.
Thomas Jefferson 1743–1826: letter to James Madison, 30 January 1787

9 LOUIS XVI: It is a big revolt.
LA ROCHEFOUCAULD-LIANCOURT: No, Sir, a big revolution.
on a report reaching Versailles of the Fall of the Bastille, 1789
Duc de la Rochefoucauld-Liancourt 1747–1827: F. Dreyfus *La Rochefoucauld-Liancourt* (1903)

10 Kings will be tyrants from policy when subjects are rebels from principle.
Edmund Burke 1729–97: *Reflections on the Revolution in France* (1790)

11 There was reason to fear that the Revolution, like Saturn, might devour in turn each one of her children.

Pierre Vergniaud 1753–93: Alphonse de Lamartine *Histoire des Girondins* (1847)

12 Bliss was it in that dawn to be alive,
But to be young was very heaven!
William Wordsworth 1770–1850: "The French Revolution, as it Appeared to Enthusiasts" (1809)

13 A share in two revolutions is living to some purpose.
Thomas Paine 1737–1809: Eric Foner *Tom Paine and Revolutionary America* (1976)

14 Those who have served the cause of the revolution have ploughed the sea.
Simón Bolívar 1783–1830: attributed

15 Maximilien Robespierre was nothing but the hand of Jean Jacques Rousseau, the bloody hand that drew from the womb of time the body whose soul Rousseau had created.
Heinrich Heine 1797–1856: *Zur Geschichte der Religion und Philosophie in Deutschland* (1834)

16 Revolutions are not made; they come. A revolution is as natural a growth as an oak. It comes out of the past. Its foundations are laid far back.
Wendell Phillips 1811–84: speech 8 January 1852

17 The social order destroyed by a revolution is almost always better than that which immediately preceded it, and experience shows that the most dangerous moment for a bad government is generally that in which it sets about reform.
Alexis de Tocqueville 1805–59: *L'Ancien régime* (1856)

18 Better to abolish serfdom from above than to wait till it begins to abolish itself from below.

Czar Alexander II 1818–81: speech in Moscow, 30 March 1856

19 I know, and all the world knows, that revolutions never go backward.
William Seward 1801–72: speech at Rochester, 25 October 1858

20 Anarchism is a game at which the police can beat you.
George Bernard Shaw 1856–1950: *Misalliance* (1914)

21 I will die like a true-blue rebel. Don't waste any time in mourning—organize.
prior to his death by firing squad
Joe Hill 1879–1915: farewell telegram to Bill Haywood, 18 November 1915

22 Ten days that shook the world.
of the Russian revolution
John Reed 1887–1920: title of book (1919)

23 "There won't be any revolution in America," said Isadore. Nikitin agreed. "The people are all too clean. They spend all their time changing their shirts and washing themselves. You can't feel fierce and revolutionary in a bathroom."
Eric Linklater 1899–1974: *Juan in America* (1931)

24 Not believing in force is the same thing as not believing in gravitation.
Leon Trotsky 1879–1940: G. Maximov *The Guillotine at Work* (1940)

25 All modern revolutions have ended in a reinforcement of the State.
Albert Camus 1913–60: *L'Homme révolté* (1951)

26 What is a rebel? A man who says no.

Albert Camus 1913–60: *L'Homme révolté* (1951)

27 History will absolve me.
Fidel Castro 1926– : title of pamphlet (1953)

28 Those who make peaceful revolution impossible will make violent revolution inevitable.
John F. Kennedy 1917–63: speech at the White House, 13 March 1962

29 The most radical revolutionary will become a conservative on the day after the revolution.
Hannah Arendt 1906–75: in *New Yorker* 12 September 1970

30 Revolutions are celebrated when they are no longer dangerous.
Pierre Boulez 1925– : in *Guardian* 13 January 1989

31 It is the tradition of the rebel who resists and says no to the intolerable absurdities of life, and by doing so makes an affirmative statement.
of Dwight Macdonald
Michael Wreszin: *A Rebel in Defence of Tradition: the Life and Politics of Dwight Macdonald* (1994)

Rivers

1 Because of you your land never pleads for showers, nor does its parched grass pray to Jupiter the Rain-giver.
of the River Nile
Tibullus *c.* 50–19 BC: *Elegies*

2 And look, how Thames, enriched with many a flood . . .
Glides on, with pomp of waters, unwithstood,
Unto the ocean.
Samuel Daniel 1563–1619: *The Civil Wars* (1595)

3 Sweet Thames, run softly, till I end my song.

Edmund Spenser c. 1552–99:
Prothalamion (1596)

4 Sabrina fair,
  Listen where thou art sitting
  Under the glassy, cool,
     translucent wave,
  In twisted braids of lilies knitting
  The loose train of thy amber-
     dropping hair.
  *Sabrina, the nymph of the River
  Severn*
  John Milton 1608–74: *Comus* (1637)

5 And he spoke to the river Tiber,
  As it rolls by the towers of Rome.
  Oh, Tiber! father Tiber
  To whom the Romans pray,
  A Roman's life, a Roman's arms,
  Take thou in charge this day!
  Lord Macaulay 1800–59: *Lays of
  Ancient Rome* (1842) "Horatius"

6 Way down upon the Swanee
     River,
  Far, far, away,
  There's where my heart is
     turning ever;
  There's where the old folks stay.
  Stephen Collins Foster 1826–64:
  "The Old Folks at Home" (1851
  song)

7 I come from haunts of coot and
     hern,
  I make a sudden sally
  And sparkle out among the fern,
  To bicker down a valley.
  Alfred, Lord Tennyson 1809–92:
  "The Brook" (1855)

8 Then I saw the Congo, creeping
     through the black,
  Cutting through the forest with a
     golden track.
  Vachel Lindsay 1879–1931: "The
  Congo" (1914)

9 The Thames is liquid history.
  *to an American who had compared
  the Thames disparagingly with the
  Mississippi*
  John Burns 1858–1943: in *Daily Mail*
  (UK) 25 January 1943

Royalty

1 Whoso pulleth out this sword of
  this stone and anvil is rightwise
  King born of all England.
  Thomas Malory d. 1471: *Le Morte
  D'Arthur* (1470)

2 The anger of the sovereign is
  death.
  Duke of Norfolk 1473?–1554: William
  Roper *Life of Sir Thomas More*

3 I know I have the body of a weak
  and feeble woman, but I have the
  heart and stomach of a king, and
  of a king of England too.
  Elizabeth I 1533–1603: speech to the
  troops at Tilbury on the approach of
  the Armada, 1588

4 Not all the water in the rough
     rude sea
  Can wash the balm from an
     anointed king.
  William Shakespeare 1564–1616:
  Richard II (1595)

5 Uneasy lies the head that wears a
     crown.
  William Shakespeare 1564–1616:
  Henry IV, Part 2 (1597)

6 I think the king is but a man, as
  I am: the violet smells to him as
  it doth to me.
  William Shakespeare 1564–1616:
  Henry V (1599)

7 There's such divinity doth hedge
     a king,
  That treason can but peep to
     what it would.
  William Shakespeare 1564–1616:
  Hamlet (1601)

8 The king is truly *parens patriae*,
  the polite father of his people.
  James I 1566–1625: speech to
  Parliament, 21 March 1610

9 He is the fountain of honour.
  Francis Bacon 1561–1626: *An Essay*

of a King (1642); attribution doubtful;
cf. **Government** 30

10 A subject and a sovereign are
clean different things.
Charles I 1600–49: speech on the
scaffold, 30 January 1649

11 But methought it lessened my
esteem of a king, that he should
not be able to command the rain.
Samuel Pepys 1633–1703: diary 19
July 1662

12 I see it is impossible for the King
to have things done as cheap as
other men.
Samuel Pepys 1633–1703: diary 21
July 1662

13 Titles are shadows, crowns are
empty things,
The good of subjects is the end of
kings.
Daniel Defoe 1660–1731: *The True-
Born Englishman* (1701)

14 The Right Divine of Kings to
govern wrong.
Alexander Pope 1688–1744: *The
Dunciad* (1742)

15 God save our gracious king!
Long live our noble king!
God save the king!
Anonymous: "God save the King,"
attributed to various authors,
including Henry Carey *c.* 1687–1743
see Percy Scholes *God save the King*
(1942)

16 The influence of the Crown has
increased, is increasing, and
ought to be diminished.
John Dunning 1731–83: resolution
passed in the House of Commons, 6
April 1780

17 Monarchy is only the string that
ties the robber's bundle.
Percy Bysshe Shelley 1792–1822: *A
Philosophical View of Reform*
(written 1819–20)

18 The king neither administers nor
governs, he reigns.
Louis Adolphe Thiers 1797–1877: in
Le National, 4 February 1830

19 I will be good.
*on being shown a chart of the line
of succession, 11 March 1830*
Queen Victoria 1819–1901: Theodore
Martin *The Prince Consort* (1875)

20 The Emperor is everything,
Vienna is nothing.
Prince Metternich 1773–1859: letter
to Count Bombelles, 5 June 1848

21 George the First was always
reckoned
Vile, but viler George the Second;
And what mortal ever heard
Any good of George the Third?
When from earth the Fourth
descended
God be praised the Georges ended!
Walter Savage Landor 1775–1864:
epigram in *The Atlas*, 28 April 1855

22 Above all things our royalty is to
be reverenced, and if you begin to
poke about it you cannot
reverence it . . . Its mystery is its
life. We must not let in daylight
upon magic.
Walter Bagehot 1826–77: *The
English Constitution* (1867)

23 It has been said, not truly, but
with a possible approximation to
truth, that in 1802 every
hereditary monarch was insane.
Walter Bagehot 1826–77: *The
English Constitution* (1867)

24 The Sovereign has, under a
constitutional monarchy such as
ours, three rights—the right to be
consulted, the right to encourage,
the right to warn.
Walter Bagehot 1826–77: *The
English Constitution* (1867)

25 Everyone likes flattery; and when
you come to Royalty you should
lay it on with a trowel.

Benjamin Disraeli 1804–81: to
Matthew Arnold; G. W. E. Russell
Collections and Recollections (1898)

26 We could not go anywhere
without sending word ahead so
that life might be put on parade
for us.
Infanta Eulalia of Spain 1864–1958:
Court Life from Within (1915)

27 After I am dead, the boy will ruin
himself in twelve months.
*on his son, the future King Edward
VIII*
George V 1865–1936: Keith
Middlemas and John Barnes *Baldwin*
(1969)

28 At long last I am able to say a
few words of my own . . . you
must believe me when I tell you
that I have found it impossible to
carry the heavy burden of
responsibility and to discharge my
duties as King as I would wish to
do without the help and support
of the woman I love.
Edward VIII 1894–1972: radio
broadcast following his abdication,
11 December 1936

29 The whole world is in revolt.
Soon there will be only five Kings
left—the King of England, the
King of Spades, the King of Clubs,
the King of Hearts and the King
of Diamonds.
King Farouk 1920–65: addressed to
the author at a conference in Cairo,
1948; Lord Boyd-Orr *As I Recall*
(1966)

30 For seventeen years he did
nothing at all but kill animals
and stick in stamps.
of King George V
Harold Nicolson 1886–1968: diary 17
August 1949

31 The family firm.
description of the British monarchy
George VI 1895–1952: attributed

32 Royalty is the gold filling in a
mouthful of decay.
John Osborne 1929–94: "They call it
cricket" in T. Maschler (ed.)
Declaration (1957)

33 I don't enjoy my public
obligations. I was not made to
cut ribbons and kiss babies.
Princess Michael of Kent 1945– : in
Life November 1986

34 I'd like to be a queen in people's
hearts but I don't see myself
being Queen of this country.
Diana, Princess of Wales 1961–97:
interview on *Panorama*, BBC1 TV, 20
November 1995

Russia

1 God of frostbite, God of famine,
beggars, cripples by the yard,
farms with no crops to examine—
that's him, that's your Russian
God.
Prince Peter Vyazemsky 1792–1878:
"The Russian God" (1828)

2 This empire, vast as it is, is only
a prison to which the emperor
holds the key.
of Russia
**Astolphe Louis Léonard, Marquis de
Custine** 1790–1857: *La Russie en
1839*; at Peterhof, 23 July 1839

3 [Are not] you too, Russia,
speeding along like a spirited
troika that nothing can overtake?
. . . Everything on earth is flying
past, and looking askance, other
nations and states draw aside and
make way.
Nikolai Gogol 1809–52: *Dead Souls*
(1842)

4 Russia has two generals in whom
she can confide—Generals Janvier
[January] and Février [February].
Nicholas I 1796–1855: attributed;
Punch 10 March 1855

5 Through reason Russia can't be known,
No common yardstick can avail you:
She has a nature all her own —
Have faith in her, all else will fail you.
F. I. Tyutchev 1803–73: "Through reason Russia can't be known" (1866)

6 Every country has its own constitution; ours is absolutism moderated by assassination.
Anonymous: Ernst Friedrich Herbert, Count Münster, quoting "an intelligent Russian," in *Political Sketches of the State of Europe, 1814–1867* (1868)

7 The Lord God has given us vast forests, immense fields, wide horizons; surely we ought to be giants, living in such a country as this.
Anton Chekhov 1860–1904: *The Cherry Orchard* (1904)

8 They are strangely primitive in the completeness with which they surrender themselves to emotion . . . like Aeolian harps upon which a hundred winds play a hundred melodies, and so it seems as though the instrument were of unimaginable complexity.
on the Russians
W. Somerset Maugham 1874–1965: *A Writers Notebook* (1949) written in 1917

9 I cannot forecast to you the action of Russia. It is a riddle wrapped in a mystery inside an enigma.
Winston Churchill 1874–1965: radio broadcast, 1 October 1939

10 [Russian Communism is] the illegitimate child of Karl Marx and Catherine the Great.
Clement Attlee 1883–1967: speech at Aarhus University, 11 April 1956

11 Miles of cornfields, and ballet in the evening.
Alan Hackney: *Private Life* (1958); later filmed as *I'm All Right Jack*, 1959

12 Russia can be an empire or a democracy, but it cannot be both.
Zbigniew Brzezinski 1928– : in *Foreign Affairs* March/April 1994

13 Today is the last day of an era past.
at a Berlin ceremony to end the Soviet military presence in Germany
Boris Yeltsin 1931– : in *Guardian* (UK) 1 September 1994

Satisfaction and Discontent

1 My soul, do not seek immortal life, but exhaust the realm of the possible.
Pindar 518–438 BC: *Pythian Odes*

2 So long as the great majority of men are not deprived of either property or honor, they are satisfied.
Niccolò Machiavelli 1469–1527: *The Prince* (written 1513)

3 Some have too much, yet still do crave;
I little have, and seek no more.
They are but poor, though much they have,
And I am rich with little store.
They poor, I rich; they beg, I give;

They lack, I leave; they pine, I live.
Edward Dyer d. 1607: "In praise of a contented mind" (1588)

4 Who doth ambition shun
And loves to live i' the sun,
Seeking the food he eats,
And pleased with what he gets.
William Shakespeare 1564–1616: *As You Like It* (1599)

5 'Tis just like a summer birdcage
in a garden; the birds that are
without despair to get in, and the
birds that are within despair, and
are in a consumption, for fear
they shall never get out.
John Webster c. 1580–c. 1625: *The
White Devil* (1612)

6 The heart is a small thing, but
desireth great matters. It is not
sufficient for a kite's dinner, yet
the whole world is not sufficient
for it.
Francis Quarles 1592–1644: *Emblems*
(1635)

7 About six or seven o'clock, I walk
out Into a common that lies hard
by the house, where a great
many young wenches keep sheep
and cows and sit in the shade
singing of ballads . . . I talk to
them, and find they want nothing
to make them the happiest people
in the world, but the knowledge
that they are so.
Dorothy Osborne 1627–95: letter to
William Temple, 2 June 1653

8 We loathe our manna, and we
long for quails.
John Dryden 1631–1700: *The Medal*
(1682)

9 Happy the man, and happy he
alone,
He, who can call to-day his own:
He who, secure within, can say,
To-morrow do thy worst, for I
have lived to-day.
John Dryden 1631–1700: translation
of Horace *Odes*

10 The stoical scheme of supplying
our wants, by lopping off our
desires, is like cutting off our feet
when we want shoes.
Jonathan Swift 1667–1745: *Thoughts
on Various Subjects* (1711)

11 An elegant sufficiency, content,
Retirement, rural quiet, friendship,
books.
James Thomson 1700–48: *The
Seasons* (1746) "Spring"

12 I am content, I do not care,
Wag as it will the world for me.
John Byrom 1692–1763: "Careless
Content" (1773)

13 Plain living and high thinking are
no more:
The homely beauty of the good
old cause
Is gone.
William Wordsworth 1770–1850: "O
friend! I know not which way I must
look" (1807)

14 That all was wrong because not
all was right.
George Crabbe 1754–1832: "The
Convert" (1812)

15 It is a flaw
In happiness, to see beyond our
bourn—
It forces us in summer skies to
mourn:
It spoils the singing of the
nightingale.
John Keats 1795–1821: "To J. H.
Reynolds, Esq." (written 1818)

16 In pale contented sort of
discontent.
John Keats 1795–1821: "Lamia"
(1820)

17 Ah! *Vanitas Vanitatum!* Which of
us is happy in this world? Which
of us has his desire? or, having it,
is satisfied?—Come, children, let
us shut up the box and the
puppets, for our play is played
out.
William Makepeace Thackeray 1811–
63: *Vanity Fair* (1847–8); cf. **Futility 1**

18 Oh, the little more, and how
much it is!
And the little less, and what
worlds away!
Robert Browning 1812–89: "By the
Fireside" (1855)

19 It is an uneasy lot at best, to be what we call highly taught and yet not to enjoy: to be present at this great spectacle of life and never to be liberated from a small hungry shivering self.
George Eliot 1819–80: *Middlemarch* (1871–2)

20 A book of verses underneath the bough,
A jug of wine, a loaf of bread—and Thou
Beside me singing in the wilderness—
Oh, wilderness were paradise enow!
Edward Fitzgerald 1809–83: *The Rubáiyát of Omar Khayyám* (1879 ed.)

21 I'm afraid you've got a bad egg, Mr. Jones.
Oh no, my Lord, I assure you! Parts of it are excellent!
Punch: cartoon caption, 1895, showing a curate breakfasting with his bishop

22 As long as I have a want, I have a reason for living. Satisfaction is death.
George Bernard Shaw 1856–1950: *Overruled* (1916)

23 Content is disillusioning to behold: what is there to be content about?
Virginia Woolf 1882–1941: diary 5 May 1920

24 He spoke with a certain what-is-it in his voice, and I could see that, if not actually disgruntled, he was far from being gruntled.
P. G. Wodehouse 1881–1975: *The Code of the Woosters* (1938)

25 When you don't have any money, the problem is food. When you have money, it's sex. When you have both it's health.

J. P. Donleavy 1926– : *The Ginger Man* (1955)

26 Let us be frank about it: most of our people have never had it so good.
Harold Macmillan 1894–1986: speech at Bedford, 20 July 1957; "You Never Had It So Good" was the Democratic Party slogan during the 1952 US election campaign

27 You ask if they were happy. This is not a characteristic of a European. To be contented—that's for the cows.
Coco Chanel 1883–1971: A. Madsen *Coco Chanel* (1990)

Science
see also **Arts and Sciences, Hypothesis and Fact, Inventions and Discoveries, Life Sciences, Physics, Science and Religion, Technology**

1 Lucky is he who has been able to understand the causes of things.
of Lucretius
Virgil 70–19 BC: *Georgics*

2 That all things are changed, and that nothing really perishes, and that the sum of matter remains exactly the same, is sufficiently certain.
Francis Bacon 1561–1626: *Cogitationes de Natura Rerum*

3 Books must follow sciences, and not sciences books.
Francis Bacon 1561–1626: *Resuscitatio* (1657)

4 He had been eight years upon a project for extracting sun-beams out of cucumbers, which were to be put into vials hermetically sealed, and let out to warm the air in raw inclement summers.
Jonathan Swift 1667–1745: *Gulliver's Travels* (1726)

5 The changing of bodies into light, and light into bodies, is very conformable to the course of Nature, which seems delighted with transmutations.
Isaac Newton 1642–1727: *Opticks* (1730 ed.)

6 Nature, and Nature's laws lay hid in night.
God said, *Let Newton be!* and all was light.
Alexander Pope 1688–1744: "Epitaph: Intended for Sir Isaac Newton" (1730)

7 Where observation is concerned, chance favors only the prepared mind.
Louis Pasteur 1822–95: address given on the inauguration of the Faculty of Science, University of Lille, 7 December 1854

8 There are no such things as applied sciences, only applications of science.
Louis Pasteur 1822–95: address, Lyons, 11 September 1872

9 In research the horizon recedes as we advance, and is no nearer at sixty than it was at twenty. As the power of endurance weakens with age, the urgency of the pursuit grows more intense . . . And research is always incomplete.
Mark Pattison 1813–84: *Isaac Casaubon* (1875)

10 Scientific truth should be presented in different forms, and should be regarded as equally scientific whether it appears in the robust form and the vivid colouring of a physical illustration, or in the tenuity and paleness of a symbolic expression.
James Clerk Maxwell 1831–79: attributed; in *Physics Teacher* December 1969

11 When you can measure what you are speaking about, and express it in numbers, you know something about it; but when you cannot measure it, when you cannot express it in numbers, your knowledge is of a meagre and unsatisfactory kind: it may be the beginning of knowledge, but you have scarcely, in your thoughts, advanced to the stage of *science*, whatever the matter may be.
often quoted as "If you cannot measure it, then it is not science"
Lord Kelvin 1824–1907: *Popular Lectures and Addresses* vol. 1 (1889) "Electrical Units of Measurement," delivered 3 May 1883

12 There is something fascinating about science. One gets such wholesale returns of conjecture out of such a trifling investment of fact.
Mark Twain 1835–1910: *Life on the Mississippi* (1883)

13 Science is nothing but trained and organized common sense, differing from the latter only as a veteran may differ from a raw recruit: and its methods differ from those of common sense only as far as the guardsman's cut and thrust differ from the manner in which a savage wields his club.
T. H. Huxley 1825–95: *Collected Essays* (1893–4) "The Method of Zadig"

14 Science is built up of facts, as a house is built of stones; but an accumulation of facts is no more a science than a heap of stones is a house.
Henri Poincaré 1854–1912: *Science and Hypothesis* (1905)

15 The outcome of any serious research can only be to make two questions grow where one question grew before.
Thorstein Veblen 1857–1929: *University of California Chronicle* (1908) "Evolution of the Scientific Point of View"

16 In science the credit goes to the man who convinces the world, not to the man to whom the idea first occurs.
Francis Darwin 1848–1925: in *Eugenics Review* April 1914 "Francis Galton"

17 There is no more reason to believe that man descended from some inferior animal than there is to believe that a stately mansion has descended from a small cottage.
William Jennings Bryan 1860–1925: in the Scopes "monkey" trial (28 July 1925)

18 I ask you to look both ways. For the road to a knowledge of the stars leads through the atom; and important knowledge of the atom has been reached through the stars.
Arthur Eddington 1882–1944: *Stars and Atoms* (1928)

19 It is much easier to make measurements than to know exactly what you are measuring.
J. W. N. Sullivan 1886–1937: comment, 1928; R. L. Weber *More Random Walks in Science* (1982)

20 Science means simply the aggregate of all the recipes that are always successful. The rest is literature.
Paul Valéry 1871–1945: *Moralités* (1932)

21 The whole of science is nothing more than a refinement of everyday thinking.
Albert Einstein 1879–1955: *Physics and Reality* (1936)

22 All science is either physics or stamp collecting.
Ernest Rutherford 1871–1937: J. B. Birks *Rutherford at Manchester* (1962)

23 The aim of science is not to open the door to infinite wisdom, but to set a limit to infinite error.
Bertolt Brecht 1898–1956: *Life of Galileo* (1939)

24 The importance of a scientific work can be measured by the number of previous publications it makes it superfluous to read.
David Hilbert 1862–1943: attributed; Lewis Wolpert *The Unnatural Nature of Science* (1993)

25 A new scientific truth does not triumph by convincing its opponents and making them see the light, but rather because its opponents eventually die, and a new generation grows up that is familiar with it.
Max Planck 1858–1947: *A Scientific Autobiography* (1949)

26 If politics is the art of the possible, research is surely the art of the soluble. Both are immensely practical-minded affairs.
Peter Medawar 1915–87: in *New Statesman* (UK) 19 June 1964; cf. **Politics 8**

27 The essence of science: ask an impertinent question, and you are on the way to a pertinent answer.
Jacob Bronowski 1908–74: *The Ascent of Man* (1973)

28 Basic research is what I am doing when I don't know what I am doing.
Wernher von Braun 1912–77: R. L. Weber *A Random Walk in Science* (1973)

29 Modern science was largely conceived of as an answer to the servant problem.
Fran Lebowitz 1946– : *Metropolitan Life* (1978)

30 In effect, we have redefined the task of science to be the discovery

of laws that will enable us to predict events up to the limits set by the uncertainty principle.
Stephen Hawking 1942– : *A Brief History of Time* (1988)

31 To mistrust science and deny the validity of the scientific method is to resign your job as a human. You'd better go look for work as a plant or wild animal.
P. J. O'Rourke 1947– : *Parliament of Whores* (1991)

32 Not explaining science seems to me perverse. When you're in love, you want to tell the world.
Carl Sagan 1934–96: *Washington Post* (9 January 1994)

Science and Religion

1 It is God who is the ultimate reason of things, and the knowledge of God is no less the beginning of science than his essence and will are the beginning of beings.
Gottfried Wilhelm Leibniz 1646–1716: *Letter on a General Principle Useful in Explaining the Laws of Nature* (1687)

2 An Aristotle was but the rubbish of an Adam, and Athens but the rudiments of Paradise.
Robert South 1634–1716: *Twelve Sermons . . .* (1692)

3 If ignorance of nature gave birth to the Gods, knowledge of nature is destined to destroy them.
Paul Henri, Baron d'Holbach 1723–89: *Système de la Nature* (1770)

4 We are perpetually moralists, but we are geometricians only by chance. Our intercourse with intellectual nature is necessary; our speculations upon matter are voluntary and at leisure.
Samuel Johnson 1709–84: *Lives of the English Poets* (1779–81) "Milton"

5 The atoms of Democritus
And Newton's particles of light
Are sands upon the Red sea shore
Where Israel's tents do shine so bright.
William Blake 1757–1827: *MS Note-Book*

6 I asserted—and I repeat—that a man has no reason to be ashamed of having an ape for his grandfather. If there were an ancestor whom I should feel shame in recalling it would rather be a *man*—a man of restless and versatile intellect—who, not content with an equivocal success in his own sphere of activity, plunges into scientific questions with which he has no real acquaintance, only to obscure them by an aimless rhetoric, and distract the attention of his hearers from the real point at issue by eloquent digressions and skilled appeals to religious prejudice.
replying to Bishop Samuel Wilberforce in the debate on Darwin's theory of evolution
T. H. Huxley 1825–95: at a meeting of the British Association in Oxford, 30 June 1860; see **Life Sciences 5**

7 Terms like grace, new birth, justification . . . terms, in short, which with St. Paul are literary terms, theologians have employed as if they were scientific terms.
Matthew Arnold 1822–88: *Literature and Dogma* (1873)

8 Science without religion is lame, religion without science is blind.
Albert Einstein 1879–1955: *Science, Philosophy and Religion: a Symposium* (1941)

9 We have grasped the mystery of the atom and rejected the Sermon on the Mount.
Omar N. Bradley 1893–1981: speech on Armistice Day, 1948

10 There is no evil in the atom; only in men's souls.
Adlai Stevenson 1900–65: speech at Hartford, Connecticut, 18 September 1952

11 The scientist who yields anything to theology, however slight, is yielding to ignorance and false pretences, and as certainly as if he granted that a horse-hair put into a bottle of water will turn into a snake.
H. L. Mencken 1880–1956: *Minority Report* (1956)

12 The means by which we live have outdistanced the ends for which we live. Our scientific power has outrun our spiritual power. We have guided missiles and misguided men.
Martin Luther King, Jr. 1929–68: *Strength to Love* (1963)

13 Science offers the best answers to the meaning of life. Science offers you the privilege before you die of understanding why you were ever born in the first place.
Richard Dawkins 1941– : in *Break the Science Barrier with Richard Dawkins* (UK Channel 4) 1 September 1996

The Sea

1 One deep calleth another, because of the noise of the water-pipes: all thy waves and storms are gone over me.
Bible: Psalm 42

2 They that go down to the sea in ships: and occupy their business in great waters;
These men see the works of the Lord: and his wonders in the deep.
Bible: Psalm 107

3 And there was no more sea.
Bible: Revelation

4 Full fathom five thy father lies;
Of his bones are coral made:
Those are pearls that were his eyes:
Nothing of him that doth fade,
But doth suffer a sea-change
Into something rich and strange.
William Shakespeare 1564–1616: *The Tempest* (1611)

5 Now would I give a thousand furlongs of sea for an acre of barren ground.
William Shakespeare 1564–1616: *The Tempest* (1611)

6 The dominion of the sea, as it is an ancient and undoubted right of the crown of England, so it is the best security of the land . . . The wooden walls are the best walls of this kingdom.
Thomas Coventry 1578–1640: speech to the Judges, 17 June 1635

7 What is a ship but a prison?
Robert Burton 1577–1640: *The Anatomy of Melancholy* (1621–51)

8 Water, water, everywhere,
And all the boards did shrink;
Water, water, everywhere,
Nor any drop to drink.
Samuel Taylor Coleridge 1772–1834: "The Rime of the Ancient Mariner" (1798)

9 It [the Channel] is a mere ditch, and will be crossed as soon as someone has the courage to attempt it.
Napoleon I 1769–1821: letter to Consul Cambacérès, 16 November 1803

10 Roll on, thou deep and dark blue Ocean—roll!
Ten thousand fleets sweep over thee in vain;
Man marks the earth with ruin—his control
Stops with the shore.
Lord Byron 1788–1824: *Childe Harold's Pilgrimage* (1812–18)

11 A wet sheet and a flowing sea,
   A wind that follows fast
   And fills the white and rustling
      sail
   And bends the gallant mast.
   Allan Cunningham 1784–1842: "A
   Wet Sheet and a Flowing Sea"
   (1825)

12 Rocked in the cradle of the deep.
   Emma Hart Willard 1787–1870: title
   of song (1840), inspired by a
   prospect of the Bristol Channel

13 Break, break, break,
   On thy cold grey stones, O Sea!
   And I would that my tongue
      could utter
   The thoughts that arise in me.
   Alfred, Lord Tennyson 1809–92:
   "Break, Break, Break" (1842)

14 Now the great winds shorewards
      blow;
   Now the salt tides seawards flow;
   Now the wild white horses play.
   Champ and chafe and toss in the
      spray.
   Matthew Arnold 1822–88: "The
   Forsaken Merman" (1842)

15 I love to sail forbidden seas, and
   land on barbarous coasts.
   Herman Melville 1819–91: *Moby Dick*
   (1851)

16 Let the most absent-minded of
   men be plunged in his deepest
   reveries—stand that man upon
   his legs, set his feet a-going, and
   he will infallibly lead you to
   water, if water there be in all that
   region . . . Meditation and water
   are wedded forever.
   Herman Melville 1819–91: *Moby Dick*
   (1851)

17 If blood be the price of admiralty,
   Lord God, we ha' paid in full!
   Rudyard Kipling 1865–1936: "The
   Song of the Dead" (1896)

18 I must go down to the sea again,
   to the lonely sea and the sky,

And all I ask is a tall ship and a
   star to steer her by,
And the wheel's kick and the
   wind's song and the white sail's
   shaking,
And a grey mist on the sea's face
   and a grey dawn breaking.
John Masefield 1878–1967: "Sea
Fever"; "I must down to the seas" in
the original of 1902, possibly a
misprint

19 "A man who is not afraid of the
   sea will soon be drownded," he
   said "for he will be going out on
   a day he shouldn't. But we do be
   afraid of the sea, and we do only
   be drownded now and again."
   John Millington Synge 1871–1909:
   The Aran Islands (1907)

20 The dragon-green, the luminous,
      the dark, the serpent-haunted
      sea.
   James Elroy Flecker 1884–1915: "The
   Gates of Damascus" (1913)

21 The snotgreen sea. The
   scrotumtightening sea.
   James Joyce 1882–1941: *Ulysses*
   (1922)

22 The sea hates a coward!
   Eugene O'Neill 1888–1953: *Mourning
   becomes Electra* (1931)

23 The sea lies all about us. The
   commerce of all lands must cross
   it. The very winds that move over
   the lands have been cradled on
   its broad expanse and seek ever
   to return to it. The continents
   themselves dissolve and pass to
   the sea, in grain after grain of
   eroded land. So the rains that
   rose from it return again in
   rivers. In its mysterious past it
   encompasses all the dim origin of
   life and receives in the end, after,
   it may be, many transmutations,
   the dead husks of that same life.
   For all at last returns to the sea—
   to Oceanus, the ocean river, like

the ever-flowing stream of time,
the beginning and the end.
Rachel Carson 1907–64: *The Sea Around Us* (1951)

The Seasons
see also **Festivals and Celebrations, Weather**

1 Sumer is icumen in,
Lhude sing cuccu!
Groweth sed, and bloweth med,
And springth the wude nu.
Anonymous: "Cuckoo Song" (*c.* 1250), sung annually at Reading Abbey (UK) gateway and first recorded by John Fornset, a monk of Reading Abbey; cf. **24** below

2 In a somer seson, whan softe was the sonne.
William Langland *c.* 1330–*c.* 1400: *The Vision of Piers Plowman*

3 Whan that Aprill with his shoures soote
The droghte of March hath perced to the roote.
Geoffrey Chaucer *c.* 1343–1400: *The Canterbury Tales* "The General Prologue"

4 When icicles hang by the wall,
And Dick the shepherd, blows his nail,
And Tom bears logs into the hall,
And milk comes frozen home in pail,
When blood is nipped and ways be foul,
Then nightly sings the staring owl,
Tu-who;
Tu-whit, tu-who—a merry note,
While greasy Joan doth keel the pot.
William Shakespeare 1564–1616: *Love's Labour's Lost* (1595)

5 That time of year thou mayst in me behold
When yellow leaves, or none, or few, do hang

Upon those boughs which shake against the cold,
Bare ruined choirs, where late the sweet birds sang.
William Shakespeare 1564–1616: Sonnet 73

6 It was no summer progress. A cold coming they had of it, at this time of the year; just, the worst time of the year, to take a journey, and specially a long journey, in. The ways deep, the weather sharp, the days short, the sun farthest off *in solstitio brumali*, the very dead of Winter.
Lancelot Andrewes 1555–1626: *Of the Nativity* (1622)

7 In those vernal seasons of the year, when the air is calm and pleasant, it were an injury and sullenness against nature not to go out, and see her riches, and partake in her rejoicing with heaven and earth.
John Milton 1608–74: *Of Education* (1644)

8 I sing of brooks, of blossoms, birds, and bowers:
Of April, May, of June, and July-flowers.
I sing of May-poles, Hock-carts, wassails, wakes,
Of bride-grooms, brides, and of their bridal-cakes.
Robert Herrick 1591–1674: "The Argument of his Book" from *Hesperides* (1648)

9 The way to ensure summer in England is to have it framed and glazed in a comfortable room.
Horace Walpole 1717–97: letter to Revd. William Cole, 28 May 1774

10 Snowy, Flowy, Blowy,
Showery, Flowery, Bowery,
Hoppy, Croppy, Droppy,
Breezy, Sneezy, Freezy.
George Ellis 1753–1815: "The Twelve Months"

11 Season of mists and mellow
   fruitfulness,
   Close bosom-friend of the
   maturing sun;
   Conspiring with him how to load
   and bless
   With fruit the vines that round
   the thatch-eaves run.
   John Keats 1795–1821: "To Autumn"
   (1820)

12 The English winter—ending in
   July,
   To recommence in August.
   Lord Byron 1788–1824: *Don Juan*
   (1819–24)

13 Summer has set in with its usual
   severity.
   Samuel Taylor Coleridge 1772–1834:
   letter from Charles Lamb to Vincent
   Novello, 9 May 1826

14 A tedious season they await
   Who hear November at the gate.
   Alexander Pushkin 1799–1837:
   Eugene Onegin (1833)

15 No warmth, no cheerfulness, no
   healthful ease,
   No comfortable feel in any
   member—
   No shade, no shine, no butterflies,
   no bees,
   No fruits, no flowers, no leaves,
   no birds,—
   November!
   Thomas Hood 1799–1845: "No!"
   (1844)

16 Oh, to be in England
   Now that April's there,
   And whoever wakes in England
   Sees, some morning, unaware,
   That the lowest boughs and the
   brushwood sheaf
   Round the elm-tree bole are in
   tiny leaf,
   While the chaffinch sings on the
   orchard bough
   In England—now!
   Robert Browning 1812–89: "Home-
   Thoughts, from Abroad" (1845)

17 The word May is a perfumed
   word. It is an illuminated initial.
   It means youth, love, song, and
   all that is beautiful in life.
   Henry Wadsworth Longfellow 1807–
   82: *journal entry* (1 May 1861)

18 Coldly, sadly descends
   The autumn evening. The Field
   Strewn with its dank yellow drifts
   Of withered leaves, and the elms,
   Fade into dimness apace,
   Silent;—hardly a shout
   From a few boys late at their
   play!
   Matthew Arnold 1822–88: "Rugby
   Chapel, November 1857" (1867)

19 November is the most
   disagreeable month in the whole
   year.
   Louisa May Alcott 1832–88: *Little
   Women* (1868)

20 May is a pious fraud of the
   almanac.
   James Russell Lowell 1819–91:
   "Under the Willows" (1869)

21 In the bleak mid-winter
   Frosty wind made moan,
   Earth stood hard as iron,
   Water like a stone.
   Christina Rossetti 1830–94: "Mid-
   Winter" (1875)

22 In winter I get up at night
   And dress by yellow candle-light.
   In summer, quite the other way,—
   I have to go to bed by day.
   Robert Louis Stevenson 1850–94:
   "Bed in Summer" (1885)

23 Loveliest of trees, the cherry now
   Is hung with bloom along the
   bough,
   And stands about the woodland
   ride
   Wearing white for Eastertide.
   A. E. Housman 1859–1936: *A
   Shropshire Lad* (1896)

24 Winter is icummen in,
   Lhude sing Goddamm,

Raineth drop and staineth slop,
And how the wind doth ramm!
Sing: Goddamm.
Ezra Pound 1885–1972: "Ancient
Music" (1917); see **1** above

25 April is the cruellest month,
breeding
Lilacs out of the dead land,
mixing
Memory and desire, stirring
Dull roots with spring rain.
Winter kept us warm, covering
Earth in forgetful snow, feeding
A little life with dried tubers.
T. S. Eliot 1888–1965: *The Waste
Land* (1922)

26 I want to go south, where there
is no autumn, where the cold
doesn't crouch over one like a
snow-leopard waiting to pounce.
The heart of the North is dead,
and the fingers of cold are corpse
fingers.
D. H. Lawrence 1885–1930: letter to
J. Middleton Murry, 3 October 1924

27 All things on earth point home in
old October: sailors to sea,
travelers to walls and fences,
hunters to field and hollow and
the long voice of the hounds, the
lover to the love he has forsaken.
Thomas Wolfe 1900–38: *Of Time and
the River* (1935)

28 It is about five o'clock in an
evening that the first hour of
spring strikes—autumn arrives in
the early morning, but spring at
the close of a winter day.
Elizabeth Bowen 1899–1973: *The
Death of the Heart* (1938)

29 June is bustin' out all over.
Oscar Hammerstein II 1895–1960:
title of song (1945)

30 August creates as she slumbers,
replete and satisfied.
Joseph Wood Krutch 1893–1970:
Twelve Seasons (1949)

31 The most serious charge which
can be brought against New
England is not Puritanism but
February.
Joseph Wood Krutch 1893–1970: *The
Twelve Seasons* (1949)

32 One swallow does not make a
summer, but one skein of geese,
cleaving the murk of a March
thaw, is the spring.
Aldo Leopold 1886–1948: *A Sand
County Almanack* (1949)

33 What of October, that ambiguous
month, the month of tension, the
unendurable month?
Doris Lessing 1919– : *Martha Quest*
(1952)

34 For man, autumn is a time of
harvest, of gathering together.
For nature, it is a time of sowing,
of scattering abroad.
Edwin Way Teale 1899–1980:
Autumn Across America (1956)

35 August is a wicked month.
Edna O'Brien 1936– : title of novel
(1965)

Secrecy and Openness

1 DUKE: And what's her history?
VIOLA: A blank, my lord. She
never told her love,
But let concealment, like a worm
i' the bud,
Feed on her damask cheek.
William Shakespeare 1564–1616:
Twelfth Night (1601)

2 I would not open windows into
men's souls.
Elizabeth I 1533–1603: oral tradition,
the words very possibly originating
in a letter drafted by Bacon; J. B.
Black *Reign of Elizabeth 1558–1603*
(1936)

3 For secrets are edged tools,
And must be kept from children
and from fools.

John Dryden 1631–1700: *Sir Martin Mar-All* (1667)

4 Love ceases to be a pleasure, when it ceases to be a secret.
Aphra Behn 1640–89: *The Lover's Watch* (1686)

5 I know that's a secret, for it's whispered every where.
William Congreve 1670–1729: *Love for Love* (1695)

6 Three may keep a secret, if two of them are dead.
Benjamin Franklin 1706–1790: *Poor Richard's Almanack* (1735)

7 Secrets with girls, like loaded guns with boys,
Are never valued till they make a noise.
George Crabbe 1754–1832: *Tales of the Hall* (1819) "The Maid's Story"

8 Stolen sweets are always sweeter,
Stolen kisses much completer,
Stolen looks are nice in chapels,
Stolen, stolen, be your apples.
Leigh Hunt 1784–1859: "Song of Fairies Robbing an Orchard" (1830)

9 We never knows wot's hidden in each other's hearts; and if we had glass winders there, we'd need keep the shutters up, some on us, I do assure you!
Charles Dickens 1812–70: *Martin Chuzzlewit* (1844)

10 We seek him here, we seek him there,
Those Frenchies seek him everywhere.
Is he in heaven?—Is he in hell?
That demmed, elusive Pimpernel?
Baroness Orczy 1865–1947: *The Scarlet Pimpernel* (1905)

11 After the first silence the small man said to the other: "Where does a wise man hide a pebble?" And the tall man answered in a low voice: "On the beach." The small man nodded, and after a short silence said: "Where does a wise man hide a leaf?" And the other answered: "In the forest."
G. K. Chesterton 1874–1936: *The Innocence of Father Brown* (1911)

12 I shall be but a short time tonight. I have seldom spoken with greater regret, for my lips are not yet unsealed. Were these troubles over I would make a case, and I guarantee that not a man would go into the lobby against us.
on the Abyssinian crisis; usually quoted "My lips are sealed"
Stanley Baldwin 1867–1947: speech, House of Commons, 10 December 1935

13 Once the toothpaste is out of the tube, it is awfully hard to get it back in.
on the Watergate affair
H. R. Haldeman 1929– : to John Dean, 8 April 1973

14 That's another of those irregular verbs, isn't it? I give confidential briefings; you leak; he has been charged under Section 2a of the Official Secrets Act.
Jonathan Lynn 1943– and **Antony Jay** 1930– : *Yes Prime Minister* (1987) vol. 2 "Man Overboard"

15 In the culture I grew up in you did your work and you did not put your arm around it to stop other people from looking—you took the earliest possible opportunity to make knowledge available.
on modern medical research
James Black 1924– : in *Daily Telegraph* (UK) 11 December 1995

16 *contrasting political advisers with elected politicians:*
I sometimes call them the people who live in the dark. Everything they do is in hiding . . .

Everything we do is in the light.
They live in the dark.
Clare Short 1946– : in *New
Statesman* (UK) 9 August 1996

The Self

1 If I am not for myself who is for
me; and being for my own self
what am I? If not now when?
Hillel "The Elder" *c.* 60 BC–AD *c.* 9:
Pirqe Aboth

2 I am made all things to all men.
Bible: I Corinthians

3 A man should keep for himself a
little back shop, all his own, quite
unadulterated, in which he
establishes his true freedom and
chief place of seclusion and
solitude.
Montaigne 1533–92: *Essais* (1580)

4 This above all: to thine own self
be true,
And it must follow, as the night
the day,
Thou canst not then be false to
any man.
William Shakespeare 1564–1616:
Hamlet (1601)

5 Who is it that can tell me who I
am?
William Shakespeare 1564–1616:
King Lear (1605–6)

6 But I do nothing upon my self,
and yet I am mine own
Executioner.
John Donne 1572–1631: *Devotions
upon Emergent Occasions* (1624)

7 It is the nature of extreme self-
lovers, as they will set a house on
fire, and it were but to roast their
eggs.
Francis Bacon 1561–1626: *Essays*
(1625) "Of Wisdom for a Man's Self"

8 The self is hateful.
Blaise Pascal 1623–62: *Pensées*
(1670)

9 It is not contrary to reason to
prefer the destruction of the
whole world to the scratching of
my finger.
David Hume 1711–76: *A Treatise
upon Human Nature* (1739)

10 Nothing can bring you peace but
yourself. Nothing can bring you
peace but the triumph of
principles.
Ralph Waldo Emerson 1803–82:
Essays: First Series (1841)

11 I am—yet what I am, none cares
or knows;
My friends forsake me like a
memory lost:
I am the self-consumer of my
woes.
John Clare 1793–1864: "I Am" (1848)

12 What other dungeon is so dark as
one's own heart! What jailer so
inexorable as one's self.
Nathaniel Hawthorne 1804–64: *The
House of the Seven Gables* (1851)

13 Do I contradict myself?
Very well then I contradict
myself,
(I am large, I contain multitudes.)
Walt Whitman 1819–92: "Song of
Myself" (written 1855)

14 I sound my barbaric yawp over
the roofs of the world.
Walt Whitman 1819–92: "Song of
Myself" (written 1855)

15 I am a writer who came of a
sheltered life. A sheltered life can
be a daring life as well. For all
serious daring starts from within.
Eudora Welty 1909– : *One Writer's
Beginnings* (1984)

16 It matters not how strait the gate,
How charged with punishments
the scroll,
I am the master of my fate:
I am the captain of my soul.
W. E. Henley 1849–1903: "Invictus.
In Memoriam R.T.H.B." (1888)

17 The men who really believe in themselves are all in lunatic asylums.
G. K. Chesterton 1874–1936: *Orthodoxy* (1908)

18 Rose is a rose is a rose, is a rose.
Gertrude Stein 1874–1946: *Sacred Emily* (1913)

19 I am I plus my surroundings, and if I do not preserve the latter I do not preserve myself.
José Ortega y Gasset 1883–1955: *Meditaciones del Quijote* (1914)

20 I will not serve that in which I no longer believe whether it call itself my home, my fatherland or my church: and I will try to express myself in some mode of life or art as freely as I can and as wholly as I can, using for my defence the only arms I allow myself to use, silence, exile, and cunning.
James Joyce 1882–1941: *A Portrait of the Artist as a Young Man* (1916)

21 Each had his past shut in him like the leaves of a book known to him by heart; and his friends could only read the title.
Virginia Woolf 1882–1941: *Jacob's Room* (1922)

22 Through the Thou a person becomes I.
Martin Buber 1878–1965: *Ich und Du* (1923)

23 We are all serving a life-sentence in the dungeon of self.
Cyril Connolly 1903–74: *The Unquiet Grave* (1944)

24 The whole human way of life has been destroyed and ruined. All that's left is the bare, shivering human soul, stripped to the last shred, the naked force of the human psyche for which nothing has changed because it was always cold and shivering and reaching out to its nearest neighbor, as cold and lonely as itself.
Boris Pasternak 1890–1960: *Doctor Zhivago* (1958)

25 The image of myself which I try to create in my own mind in order that I may love myself is very different from the image which I try to create in the minds of others in order that they may love me.
W. H. Auden 1907–73: *Dyer's Hand* (1963) "Hic et Ille"

26 My one regret in life is that I am not someone else.
Woody Allen 1935– : Eric Lax *Woody Allen and his Comedy* (1975)

27 Human beings have an inalienable right to invent themselves; when that right is pre-empted it is called brain-washing.
Germaine Greer 1939– : in *The Times* (UK) 1 February 1986

28 "You" your joys and your sorrows, your memories and ambitions, your sense of personal identity and free will, are in fact no more than the behaviour of a vast assembly of nerve cells and their associated molecules.
Francis Crick 1916– : *The Astonishing Hypothesis: The Scientific Search for the Soul* (1994)

29 There is perhaps no better a demonstration of the folly of human conceits than this distant image of our tiny world.
Carl Sagan 1934–96: *Time* (9 January 1995)

Self-Esteem and Self-Assertion
see also **Pride and Humility**

1 Seest thou a man wise in his own conceit? There is more hope of a fool than of him.
Bible: Proverbs

2 Lord I am not worthy that thou
shouldest come under my roof.
Bible: St. Matthew

3 It was prettily devised of Aesop,
"The fly sat upon the axletree of
the chariot-wheel and said, what
a dust do I raise."
Francis Bacon 1561–1626: *Essays*
(1625) "Of Vain-Glory"

4 Oft-times nothing profits more
Than self esteem, grounded on
    just and right
Well managed.
John Milton 1608–74: *Paradise Lost*
(1667)

5 Where he falls short, 'tis Nature's
    fault alone;
Where he succeeds, the merit's all
    his own.
of the actor, Thomas Sheridan
Charles Churchill 1731–64: *The
Rosciad* (1761)

6 The axis of the earth sticks out
visibly through the center of each
and every town or city.
Oliver Wendell Holmes 1809–94: *The
Autocrat of the Breakfast-Table*
(1858)

7 He was like a cock who thought
the sun had risen to hear him
crow.
George Eliot 1819–80: *Adam Bede*
(1859)

8 To be commonly above others,
still more to think yourself above
others, is to be below them every
now and then, and sometimes
much below.
Walter Bagehot 1826–77: in *National
Review* (UK) July 1859 "John Milton"

9 As for conceit, what man will do
any good who is not conceited?
Nobody holds a good opinion of a
man who has a low opinion of
himself.
Anthony Trollope 1815–82: *Orley
Farm* (1862)

10 *on the suggestion that his attacks on
John Bright were too harsh as
Bright was a self-made man:*
I know he is and he adores his
maker.
Benjamin Disraeli 1804–81: Leon
Harris *The Fine Art of Political Wit*
(1965)

11 You must stir it and stump it,
And blow your own trumpet,
Or trust me, you haven't a
    chance.
W. S. Gilbert 1836–1911: *Ruddigore*
(1887)

12 It is easy—terribly easy— to
shake a man's faith in himself. To
take advantage of that to break a
man's spirit is devil's work.
George Bernard Shaw 1856–1950:
Candida (1898)

13 The affair between Margot
Asquith and Margot Asquith will
live as one of the prettiest love
stories in all literature.
Dorothy Parker 1893–1967: review of
Margot Asquith's *Lay Sermons* in
New Yorker 22 October 1927

14 He fell in love with himself at first
sight and it is a passion to which
he has always remained faithful.
Anthony Powell 1905– : *The
Acceptance World* (1955)

15 I had felt for a long time, that if I
was ever told to get up so a white
person could sit, that I would
refuse to do so.
Rosa Parks 1913– : *recalling her
refusal to give up her seat on a
Montgomery, Alabama, bus* (1
December 1955)

16 I'm the greatest.
Muhammad Ali (Cassius Clay) 1942– :
catch-phrase used from 1962, in
Louisville Times 16 November 1962

17 I know of no case where a man
added to his dignity by standing
on it.

Winston Churchill 1874–1965:
attributed

18 That's it baby, when you got it,
flaunt it.
Mel Brooks 1926– : *The Producers*
(1968 film)

19 Pavarotti is not vain, but
conscious of being unique.
Peter Ustinov 1921– : in
Independent (UK) on Sunday 12
September 1993

Self-Interest
see also **Self-Sacrifice**

1 *Cui bono?*
To whose profit?
Cicero 106–43 BC: *Pro Roscio
Amerino*; quoting L. Cassius
Longinus Ravilla

2 Men are nearly always willing to
believe what they wish.
Julius Caesar 100–44 BC: *De Bello
Gallico*

3 To rise by other's fall
I deem a losing gain;
All states with others' ruins built
To ruin run amain.
Robert Southwell *c.* 1561–95:
"Content and Rich" (1595)

4 Thus God and nature linked the
gen'ral frame,
And bade self-love and social be
the same.
Alexander Pope 1688–1744: *An
Essay on Man* Epistle 3 (1733)

5 And this is law, I will maintain,
Unto my dying day, Sir,
That whatsoever King shall reign,
I will be the Vicar of Bray, sir!
Anonymous: "The Vicar of Bray"
(1734 song)

6 *Il faut cultiver notre jardin.* We
must cultivate our garden.
Voltaire 1694–1778: *Candide* (1759)

7 It is not from the benevolence of
the butcher, the brewer, or the
baker, that we expect our dinner,
but from their regard to their
own interest. We address
ourselves not to their humanity
but their self love.
Adam Smith 1723–90: *Wealth of
Nations* (1776)

8 All sensible people are selfish, and
nature is tugging at every
contract to make the terms of it
fair.
Ralph Waldo Emerson 1803–82: *The
Conduct of Life* (1860)

9 It's "Damn you, Jack — I'm all
right!" with you chaps.
David Bone 1874–1959:
Brassbounder (1910)

10 We are all special cases. We all
want to appeal against
something! Everyone insists on his
innocence, at all costs, even if it
means accusing the rest of the
human race and heaven.
Albert Camus 1913–60: *La Chute*
(1956)

11 He would, wouldn't he?
*on being told that Lord Astor
claimed that her allegations,
concerning himself and his house
parties at Cliveden, were untrue*
Mandy Rice-Davies 1944– : at the
trial of Stephen Ward, 29 June 1963

12 Fourteen heart attacks and he
had to die in my week. In MY
week.
*when ex-President Eisenhower's
death prevented her photograph
appearing on the cover of* Newsweek
Janis Joplin 1943–70: in *New Musical
Express* 12 April 1969

13 We are now in the Me Decade—
seeing the upward roll of . . . the
third great religious wave in
American history . . . and this one
has the mightiest, holiest roll of
all, the beat that goes . . . *Me* . . .

Me . . . Me . . . Me.
Tom Wolfe 1931– : *Mauve Gloves
and Madmen* (1976)

Self-Knowledge

1 I do not know whether I was
then a man dreaming I was a
butterfly, or whether I am now a
butterfly dreaming I am a man.
Zhuangzi c. 369–286 BC: *Chuang Tzu*
(1889)

2 Why beholdest thou the mote
that is in thy brother's eye, but
considerest not the beam that is
in thine own eye?
Bible: St. Matthew

3 Alas! 'tis true I have gone here
and there,
And made myself a motley to the
view,
Gored mine own thoughts, sold
cheap what is most dear,
Made old offences of affections
new.
William Shakespeare 1564–1616:
Sonnet 110

4 He knows the universe and does
not know himself.
Jean de la Fontaine 1621–95: *Fables*
(1678–9) "Démocrite et les
Abdéritains"

5 Satire is a sort of glass, wherein
beholders do generally discover
everybody's face but their own.
Jonathan Swift 1667–1745: *The
Battle of the Books* (1704)

6 All our knowledge is, ourselves to
know.
Alexander Pope 1688–1744: *An
Essay on Man* Epistle 4 (1734)

7 At thirty a man suspects himself
a fool;
Knows it at forty, and reforms his
plan;
At fifty chides his infamous delay,
Pushes his prudent purpose to
resolve;

In all the magnanimity of
thought
Resolves; and re-resolves; then
dies the same.
Edward Young 1683–1765: *Night
Thoughts* (1742–5)

8 O wad some Pow'r the giftie gie
us
To see oursels as others see us!
It wad frae mony a blunder free
us,
And foolish notion.
Robert Burns 1759–96: "To a Louse"
(1786)

9 The Vision of Christ that thou
dost see
Is my vision's greatest enemy
Thine has a great hook nose like
thine
Mine has a snub nose like to
mine.
William Blake 1757–1827: *The
Everlasting Gospel* (c. 1818)

10 How little do we know that
which we are!
How less what we may be!
Lord Byron 1788–1824: *Don Juan*
(1819–24)

11 I do not know myself, and God
forbid that I should.
Johann Wolfgang von Goethe 1749–
1832: J. P. Eckermann *Gespräche mit
Goethe* (1836–48) 10 April 1829

12 Resolve to be thyself: and know,
that he
Who finds himself, loses his
misery.
Matthew Arnold 1822–88: "Self-
Dependence" (1852)

13 I went to the woods because I
wished to live deliberately, to
front only the essential facts of
life, and see if I could not learn
what it had to teach, and not,
when I came to die, discover that
I had not lived.
Henry David Thoreau 1817–62:
Walden (1854)

14 No, when the fight begins within
himself,
A man's worth something.
Robert Browning 1812–89: "Bishop
Blougram's Apology" (1855)

15 The tragedy of a man who has
found himself out.
J. M. Barrie 1860–1937: *What Every
Woman Knows* (performed 1908,
published 1918)

16 The excursion is the same when
you go looking for your sorrow as
when you go looking for your
joy.
Eudora Welty 1909– : *The Wide Net*
(1943)

17 Between the ages of twenty and
forty we are engaged in the
process of discovering who we
are, which involves learning the
difference between accidental
limitations which it is our duty to
outgrow and the necessary
limitations of our nature beyond
which we cannot trespass with
impunity.
W. H. Auden 1907–73: *Dyer's Hand*
(1963) "Reading"

18 There are few things more painful
than to recognise one's own
faults in others.
John Wells 1936– : in *Observer*
(UK) 23 May 1982

19 [Alfred Hitchcock] thought of
himself as looking like Cary
Grant. That's tough, to think of
yourself one way and look
another.
Tippi Hedren 1935– : interview in
California, 1982; P. F. Boller and R.
L. Davis *Hollywood Anecdotes* (1988)

Self-Sacrifice
see also **Self-Interest**

1 Greater love hath no man than
this, that a man lay down his life
for his friends.
Bible: St. John

2 Does the silk-worm expend her
yellow labours
For thee? for thee does she undo
herself?
Thomas Middleton *c.* 1580–1627:
The Revenger's Tragedy (1607)

3 I am no longer my own, but
yours. Put me to what you will,
rank me with whom you will; put
me to doing, put me to suffering;
let me be employed for you or
laid aside for you, exalted for you
or brought low for you; let me be
full, let me be empty; let me have
all things, let me have nothing.
Methodist Service Book 1975: The
Covenant Prayer (based on the
words of Richard Alleine in the First
Covenant Service, 1782)

4 Deny yourself! You must deny
yourself!
That is the song that never ends.
Johann Wolfgang von Goethe 1749–
1832: *Faust* pt. 1 (1808)
"Studierzimmer"

5 Am I prepared to lay down my
life for the British female?
Really, who knows? . . .
Ah, for a child in the street I
could strike; for the full-blown
lady—
Somehow, Eustace, alas! I have
not felt the vocation.
Arthur Hugh Clough 1819–61:
Amours de Voyage (1858)

6 It is a far, far better thing that I
do, than I have ever done; it is a
far, far better rest that I go to,
than I have ever known.
*Sydney Carton's thoughts on the
steps of the guillotine, taking the*

place of Charles Darnay whom he
has smuggled out of prison
Charles Dickens 1812–70: *A Tale of
Two Cities* (1859)

7 From the standpoint of pure
reason, there are no good
grounds to support the claim that
one should sacrifice one's own
happiness to that of others.
W. Somerset Maugham 1874–1965:
A Writer's Notebook (1949) written
in 1896

8 Self-sacrifice enables us to
sacrifice other people without
blushing.
George Bernard Shaw 1856–1950:
Man and Superman (1903) "Maxims:
Self-Sacrifice"

9 I gave my life for freedom — This
I know:
For those who bade me fight had
told me so.
William Norman Ewer 1885–1976:
"Five Souls" (1917)

10 A woman will always sacrifice
herself if you give her the
opportunity. It is her favourite
form of self-indulgence.
W. Somerset Maugham 1874–1965:
The Circle (1921)

11 I do not think you have ever
realised the shock, which the
attitude you took up caused your
family and the whole nation. It
seemed inconceivable to those
who had made such sacrifices
during the war that you, as their
King, refused a lesser sacrifice.
Queen Mary 1867–1953: letter to the
Duke of Windsor, July 1938

12 I have nothing to offer but blood,
toil, tears and sweat.
Winston Churchill 1874–1965:
speech, House of Commons, 13 May
1940

13 She's the sort of woman who
lives for others—you can always

tell the others by their hunted
expression.
C. S. Lewis 1898–1963: *The
Screwtape Letters* (1942)

The Senses
see also **The Body**

1 I have heard of thee by the
hearing of the ear: but now mine
eye seeth thee.
Bible: Job

2 By convention there is color, by
convention sweetness, by
convention bitterness, but in
reality there are atoms and space.
Democritus c. 460–c. 370 BC:
fragment 125

3 Warble, child; make passionate
my sense of hearing.
William Shakespeare 1564–1616:
Love's Labour's Lost (1595)

4 Nor will the sweetest delight of
gardens afford much comfort in
sleep; wherein the dullness of that
sense shakes hands with
delectable odours; and though in
the bed of Cleopatra, can hardly
with any delight raise up the
ghost of a rose.
Thomas Browne 1605–82: *The
Garden of Cyrus* (1658)

5 When I consider how my light is
spent,
E're half my days, in this dark
world and wide,
And that one talent which is
death to hide
Lodged with me useless.
on his blindness
John Milton 1608–74: "When I
consider how my light is spent"
(1673)

6 Whatever withdraws us from the
power of our senses; whatever
makes the past, the distant, or
the future predominate over the
present, advances us in the
dignity of thinking beings.

Samuel Johnson 1709–84: *A Journey to the Western Islands of Scotland* (1775)

7 O for a life of sensations rather than of thoughts!
John Keats 1795–1821: letter to Benjamin Bailey, 22 November 1817

8 Any nose
May ravage with impunity a rose.
Robert Browning 1812–89: *Sordello* (1840)

9 You see, but you do not observe.
Arthur Conan Doyle 1859–1930: *The Adventures of Sherlock Holmes* (1892)

10 Friday I tasted life. It was a vast morsel. A Circus passed the house— still I feel the red in my mind though the drums are out. The Lawn is full of south and the odors tangle, and I hear to-day for the first time the river in the tree.
Emily Dickinson 1830–86: letter to Mrs. J. G. Holland, May 1866

11 Does it matter?—losing your sight? . . .
There's such splendid work for the blind;
And people will always be kind,
As you sit on the terrace remembering
And turning your face to the light.
Siegfried Sassoon 1886–1967: "Does it Matter?" (1918)

12 The three great elemental sounds in nature are the sound of rain, the sound of wind in a primeval wood, and the sound of outer ocean on a beach.
Henry Beston 1888–1968: *The Outermost House*, "The Headlong Wave" (1928)

13 Fortissimo at last!
on seeing Niagara Falls

Gustav Mahler 1860–1911: K. Blaukopf *Gustav Mahler* (1973)

14 The important thing is not the camera but the eye.
Alfred Eisenstaedt 1898–1995: *New York Times* (26 September 1994)

Sex
see also **Love, Marriage**

1 Someone asked Sophocles, "How is your sex-life now? Are you still able to have a woman?" He replied, "Hush, man; most gladly indeed am I rid of it all, as though I had escaped from a mad and savage master."
Sophocles c. 496–406 BC: Plato *Republic*

2 Give me chastity and continency— but not yet!
St. Augustine of Hippo AD 354–430: *Confessions* (AD 397–8)

3 And after wyn on Venus moste I thynke,
For al so siker as cold engendreth hayl,
A likerous mouth moste han a likerous tayl.
Geoffrey Chaucer c. 1343–1400: *The Canterbury Tales* "The Wife of Bath's Prologue"

4 Licence my roving hands, and let them go,
Behind, before, above, between, below.
O my America, my new found land,
My kingdom, safeliest when with one man manned.
John Donne 1572–1631: "To His Mistress Going to Bed" (c. 1595)

5 Is it not strange that desire should so many years outlive performance?
William Shakespeare 1564–1616: *Henry IV, Part 2* (1597)

6 Your daughter and the Moor are
now making the beast with two
backs.
William Shakespeare 1564–1616:
Othello (1602–4)

7 Die: die for adultery! No:
The wren goes to't, and the small
gilded fly
Does lecher in my sight.
Let copulation thrive.
William Shakespeare 1564–1616:
King Lear (1605–6)

8 The expense of spirit in a waste of
shame
Is lust in action.
William Shakespeare 1564–1616:
Sonnet 129

9 This trivial and vulgar way of
coition; it is the foolishest act a
wise man commits in all his life,
nor is there any thing that will
more deject his cooled
imagination, when he shall
consider what an odd and
unworthy piece of folly he hath
committed.
Thomas Browne 1605–82: *Religio
Medici* (1643)

10 He in a few minutes ravished this
fair creature, or at least would
have ravished her, if she had not,
by a timely compliance, prevented
him.
Henry Fielding 1707–54: *Jonathan
Wild* (1743)

11 The Duke returned from the wars
today and did pleasure me in his
top-boots.
Sarah, Duchess of Marlborough 1660–
1744: oral tradition, attributed in
various forms; see I. Butler *Rule of
Three* (1967)

12 Eighth and lastly. They are so
grateful!!
Benjamin Franklin 1706–90: *Reasons
for Preferring an Elderly Mistress*
(1745)

13 What is commonly called love,
namely the desire of satisfying a
voracious appetite with a certain
quantity of delicate white human
flesh.
Henry Fielding 1707–54: *Tom Jones*
(1749)

14 I'll come no more behind your
scenes, David; for the silk
stockings and white bosoms of
your actresses excite my amorous
propensities.
Samuel Johnson 1709–84: James
Boswell *Life of Samuel Johnson*
(1791) 1750

15 It is amusing that a virtue is
made of the vice of chastity; and
it's a pretty odd sort of chastity at
that, which leads men straight
into the sin of Onan, and girls to
the waning of their color.
Voltaire 1694–1778: letter to M.
Mariott, 28 March 1766

16 The pleasure is momentary, the
position ridiculous, and the
expense damnable.
Lord Chesterfield 1694–1773:
attributed

17 It is true from early habit, one
must make love mechanically as
one swims. I was once very fond
of both, but now as I never swim
unless I tumble into the water, I
don't make love till almost
obliged.
Lord Byron 1788–1824: letter 10
September 1812

18 Not tonight, Josephine.
Napoleon I 1769–1821: attributed,
but probably apocryphal; R. H.
Horne *The History of Napoleon*
(1841) describes the circumstances in
which the affront may have occurred

19 A little still she strove, and much
repented,
And whispering "I will ne'er
consent"—consented.

Lord Byron 1788–1824: *Don Juan* (1819–24)

20 I want you to assist me in forcing her on board the lugger; once there, I'll frighten her into marriage.
since quoted as "Once aboard the lugger and the maid is mine"
John Benn Johnstone 1803–91: *The Gipsy Farmer* (performed 1845)

21 Bed. No woman is worth more than a fiver unless you're in love with her. Then she's worth all she costs you.
W. Somerset Maugham 1874–1965: *A Writer's Notebook* (1949) written in 1903

22 'Tisn't beauty, so to speak, nor good talk necessarily. It's just It. Some women'll stay in a man's memory if they once walked down a street.
Rudyard Kipling 1865–1936: *Traffics and Discoveries* (1904)

23 When I hear his steps outside my door I lie down on my bed, close my eyes, open my legs, and think of England.
Lady Hillingdon 1857–1940: diary 1912 (original untraced, perhaps apocryphal); J. Gathorne-Hardy *The Rise and Fall of the British Nanny* (1972)

24 You're neither unnatural, nor abominable, nor mad; you're as much a part of what people call nature as anyone else; only you're unexplained as yet— you've not got your niche in creation.
on lesbianism
Radclyffe Hall 1883–1943: *The Well of Loneliness* (1928)

25 Chastity—the most unnatural of all the sexual perversions.
Aldous Huxley 1894–1963: *Eyeless in Gaza* (1936)

26 Pornography is the attempt to insult sex, to do dirt on it.
D. H. Lawrence 1885–1930: *Phoenix* (1936) "Pornography and Obscenity"

27 Give a man a free hand and he'll try to put it all over you.
Mae West 1892–1980: *Klondike Annie* (1936 film)

28 But did thee feel the earth move?
Ernest Hemingway 1899–1961: *For Whom the Bell Tolls* (1940)

29 It doesn't matter what you do in the bedroom as long as you don't do it in the street and frighten the horses.
Mrs. Patrick Campbell 1865–1940: Daphne Fielding *The Duchess of Jermyn Street* (1964)

30 Continental people have sex life; the English have hot-water bottles.
George Mikes 1912– : *How to be an Alien* (1946)

31 Modest? My word, no . . . He was an all-the-lights-on man.
Henry Reed 1914–86: *A Very Great Man Indeed* (1953 radio play)

32 Lolita, light of my life, fire of my loins. My sin, my soul.
Vladimir Nabokov 1899–1977: *Lolita* (1955)

33 Many years ago I chased a woman for almost two years, only to discover that her tastes were exactly like mine: we both were crazy about girls.
Groucho Marx 1895–1977: letter 28 March 1955

34 I think Lawrence tried to portray this [sex] relation as in a real sense an act of holy communion. For him flesh was sacramental of the spirit.
as defense witness in the case against Penguin Books for publishing Lady Chatterley's Lover

Bishop John Robinson 1919–83: in
The Times (UK) 28 October 1960

35 He said it was artificial
respiration, but now I find I am
to have his child.
Anthony Burgess 1917–93: *Inside
Mr. Enderby* (1963)

36 I have heard some say . . .
[homosexual] practices are
allowed in France and in other
NATO countries. We are not
French, and we are not other
nationals. We are British, thank
God!
*on the 2nd reading of the Sexual
Offences Bill*
Bernard Law Montgomery 1887–1976:
speech, House of Lords, 24 May
1965

37 The orgasm has replaced the
Cross as the focus of longing and
the image of fulfilment.
Malcolm Muggeridge 1903–90:
Tread Softly (1966)

38 When I look back on the paint of
sex, the love like a wild fox so
ready to bite, the antagonism
that sits like a twin beside love,
and contrast it with affection, so
deeply unrepeatable, of two
people who have lived a life
together (and of whom one must
die), it's the affection I find richer.
It's that I would have again. Not
all those doubtful rainbow colors.
(But then she's old, one must
say.)
Enid Bagnold 1889–1981:
Autobiography (1969)

39 My dear fellow, buggers can't be
choosers.
*on being told he should not marry
anyone as plain as his fiancée*
Maurice Bowra 1898–1971: Hugh
Lloyd-Jones *Maurice Bowra: a
Celebration* (1974); possibly
apocryphal

40 Is sex dirty? Only if it's done
right.

Woody Allen 1935– : *Everything
You Always Wanted to Know about
Sex* (1972 film)

41 Traditionally, sex has been a very
private, secretive activity. Herein
perhaps lies its powerful force for
uniting people in a strong bond.
As we make sex less secretive, we
may rob it of its power to hold
men and women together.
Thomas Szasz 1920– : *The Second
Sin* (1973)

42 Is that a gun in your pocket, or
are you just glad to see me?
*usually quoted as "Is that a pistol in
your pocket . . . "*
Mae West 1892–1980: Joseph
Weintraub *Peel Me a Grape* (1975)

43 On bisexuality: It immediately
doubles your chances for a date
on Saturday night.
Woody Allen 1935– : in *New York
Times* 1 December 1975

44 Seduction is often difficult to
distinguish from rape. In
seduction, the rapist bothers to
buy a bottle of wine.
Andrea Dworkin 1946– : speech to
women at *Harper & Row*, 1976; in
Letters from a War Zone (1988)

45 If homosexuality were the normal
way, God would have made
Adam and Bruce.
Anita Bryant 1940– : in *New York
Times* 5 June 1977

46 Don't knock masturbation. It's
sex with someone I love.
Woody Allen 1935– : *Annie Hall*
(1977 film, with Marshall Brickman)

47 That [sex] was the most fun I
ever had without laughing.
Woody Allen 1935– : *Annie Hall*
(1977 film, with Marshall Brickman)

48 *at the age of ninety-seven, Blake
was asked at what age the sex drive
goes:*

You'll have to ask somebody older than me.
Eubie Blake 1883–1983: in *Ned Sherrin in his Anecdotage* (1993)

49 I am that twentieth-century failure, a happy undersexed celibate.
Denise Coffey: Ned Sherrin *Cutting Edge* (1984)

50 I know it [sex] does make people happy, but to me it is just like having a cup of tea.
having been acquitted of running a brothel in South London
Cynthia Payne 1934– : in *Observer* (UK) 8 February 1987

51 Personally I know nothing about sex because I've always been married.
Zsa Zsa Gabor 1919– : in *Observer* (UK) 16 August 1987

Shakespeare
see also **Actors and Acting, The Theater**

1 He was not of an age, but for all time!
Ben Jonson c. 1573–1637: "To the Memory of My Beloved, the Author, Mr. William Shakespeare" (1623)

2 Thou hadst small Latin, and less Greek.
Ben Jonson c. 1573–1637: "To the Memory of My Beloved, the Author, Mr. William Shakespeare" (1623)

3 His mind and hand went together: And what he thought, he uttered with that easiness, that we have scarce received from him a blot.
John Heming 1556–1630 and **Henry Condell** d. 1627: First Folio Shakespeare (1623) preface

4 The players have often mentioned it as an honour to Shakespeare that in his writing, whatsoever he penned, he never blotted out a line. My answer hath been "Would he had blotted a thousand" . . . But he redeemed his vices with his virtues. There was ever more in him to be praised than to be pardoned.
Ben Jonson c. 1573–1637: *Timber, or Discoveries made upon Men and Matter* (1641) "De Shakespeare Nostrati"

5 [Shakespeare] is the very Janus of poets; he wears almost everywhere two faces; and you have scarce begun to admire the one, ere you despise the other.
John Dryden 1631–1700: *Essay on the Dramatic Poetry of the Last Age* (1672)

6 Shakespeare has united the powers of exciting laughter and sorrow not only in one mind but in one composition . . . That this is a practice contrary to the rules of criticism will be readily allowed; but there is always an appeal open from criticism to nature.
Samuel Johnson 1709–84: *Plays of William Shakespeare* . . . (1765) preface

7 Was there ever such stuff as great part of Shakespeare? Only one must not say so! But what think you?—what?—Is there not sad stuff? what?—what?
George III 1738–1820: to Fanny Burney; Fanny Burney, diary, 19 December 1785

8 Scorn not the Sonnet; Critic, you have frowned,
Mindless of its just honours; with this key
Shakespeare unlocked his heart.
William Wordsworth 1770–1850: "Scorn not the Sonnet" (1827)

9 Others abide our question. Thou art free.
We ask and ask: Thou smilest and art still,

Out-topping knowledge.
Matthew Arnold 1822–88:
"Shakespeare" (1849)

10 With the single exception of
Homer, there is no eminent
writer, not even Sir Walter Scott,
whom I can despise so entirely as
I despise Shakespeare when I
measure my mind against his.
George Bernard Shaw 1856–1950: in
Saturday Review 26 September 1896

11 Shakespeare is so tiring. You
never get a chance to sit down
unless you're a king.
Josephine Hull 1886–1957: in *Time*
16 November 1953

12 Shakespeare—the nearest thing in
incarnation to the eye of God.
Laurence Olivier 1907–89: in
Kenneth Harris Talking To (1971) "Sir
Laurence Olivier"

Sickness and Health
see also **Medicine**

1 Life's not just being alive, but
being well.
Martial AD *c.* 40–*c.* 104: *Epigrammata*

2 *Orandum est ut sit mens sana in
corpore sano.*
You should pray to have a sound
mind in a sound body.
Juvenal AD *c.* 60–*c.* 130: *Satires*

3 Diseases desperate grown,
By desperate appliances are
relieved,
Or not at all.
William Shakespeare 1564–1616:
Hamlet (1601)

4 Look to your health; and if you
have it, praise God, and value it
next to a good conscience; for
health is the second blessing that
we mortals are capable of; a
blessing that money cannot buy.
Izaak Walton 1593–1683: *The
Compleat Angler* (1653)

5 Here am I, dying of a hundred
good symptoms.
Alexander Pope 1688–1744: to
George, Lord Lyttelton, 15 May 1744;
Joseph Spence *Anecdotes* (ed. J.
Osborn, 1966)

6 How few of his friends' houses
would a man choose to be at
when he is sick.
Samuel Johnson 1709–84: James
Boswell *Life of Samuel Johnson*
(1791) 1783

7 The sovereign invigorator of the
body is exercise, and of all the
exercises, walking is best.
Thomas Jefferson 1743–1826: *letter
to Thomas Mann Randolph, Jr.* (27
August 1786)

8 Give me health and a day and I
will make the pomp of emperors
seem ridiculous.
Ralph Waldo Emerson 1803–82:
Nature (1836, 1849)

9 It is a most extraordinary thing,
but I never read a patent
medicine advertisement without
being impelled to the conclusion
that I am suffering from the
particular disease therein dealt
with in its most virulent form.
Jerome K. Jerome 1859–1927: *Three
Men in a Boat* (1889)

10 I enjoy convalescence. It is the
part that makes illness worth
while.
George Bernard Shaw 1856–1950:
Back to Methuselah (1921)

11 Human nature seldom walks up
to the word "cancer."
Rudyard Kipling 1865–1936: *Debits
and Credits* (1926)

12 The biggest disease today is not
leprosy or tuberculosis, but rather
the feeling of being unwanted,
uncared for and deserted by
everybody.

Mother Teresa 1910–97: in *The Observer* (UK) 3 October 1971

13 Illness is the night-side of life, a more onerous citizenship. Everyone who is born holds dual citizenship, in the kingdom of the well and in the kingdom of the sick.
Susan Sontag 1933– : in *New York Review of Books* 26 January 1978

14 An illness in stages, a very long flight of steps that led assuredly to death, but whose every step represented a unique apprenticeship. It was a disease that gave death time to live and its victims time to die, time to discover time, and in the end to discover life.
on AIDS
Hervé Guibert 1955–91: *To the Friend who did not Save my Life* (1991)

15 I now begin the journey that will lead me into the sunset of my life.
statement to the American people revealing that he had Alzheimer's disease, 1994
Ronald Reagan 1911– : in *Daily Telegraph* (UK) 5 January 1995

Silence

1 Silence is a woman's finest ornament.
Auctoritates Aristotelis: a compilation of medieval propositions

2 Shallow brooks murmur most, deep silent slide away.
Philip Sidney 1554–86: *Arcadia* (1581)

3 Silence is only commendable In a neat's tongue dried and a maid not vendible.
William Shakespeare 1564–1616: *The Merchant of Venice* (1596–8)

4 Silence is the virtue of fools.
Francis Bacon 1561–1626: *De Dignitate et Augmentis Scientiarum* (1623)

5 No voice; but oh! the silence sank Like music on my heart.
Samuel Taylor Coleridge 1772–1834: "The Rime of the Ancient Mariner" (1798)

6 And then there crept A little noiseless noise among the leaves, Born of the very sigh that silence heaves.
John Keats 1795–1821: "I stood tip-toe upon a little hill" (1817)

7 Thou still unravished bride of quietness, Thou foster-child of silence and slow time.
John Keats 1795–1821: "Ode on a Grecian Urn" (1820)

8 Under all speech that is good for anything there lies a silence that is better. Silence is deep as Eternity; speech is shallow as Time.
Thomas Carlyle 1795–1881: *Critical and Miscellaneous Essays* (1838) "Sir Walter Scott"

9 Speech is often barren; but silence also does not necessarily brood over a full nest. Your still fowl, blinking at you without remark, may all the while be sitting on one addled egg; and when it takes to cackling will have nothing to announce but that addled delusion.
George Eliot 1819–80: *Felix Holt* (1866)

10 Elected Silence, sing to me And beat upon my whorlèd ear.
Gerard Manley Hopkins 1844–89: "The Habit of Perfection" (written 1866)

11 It is good practice to leave a few things unsaid.
Elbert Hubbard 1856–1915: *The Roycroft Dictionary and Book of Epigrams* (1923)

12 Drawing on my fine command of
language, I said nothing.
Robert Benchley 1889–1945: *Chips
off the Old Benchley* (1949)

Similarity and Difference

1 The road up and the road down
are one and the same.
Heraclitus c. 540–c. 480 BC: H. Diels
and W. Kranz *Die Fragmente der
Vorsokratiker* (7th ed., 1954)
fragment 60

2 Comparisons are odorous.
William Shakespeare 1564–1616:
Much Ado About Nothing (1598–9)

3 These hands are not more like.
William Shakespeare 1564–1616:
Hamlet (1601)

4 Here's metal more attractive.
William Shakespeare 1564–1616:
Hamlet (1601)

5 Feel by turns the bitter change
Of fierce extremes, extremes by
change more fierce.
John Milton 1608–74: *Paradise Lost*
(1667)

6 Dark with excessive bright.
John Milton 1608–74: *Paradise Lost*
(1667)

7 When Greeks joined Greeks, then
was the tug of war!
Nathaniel Lee c. 1653–92: *The Rival
Queens* (1677)

8 No caparisons, Miss, if you please!—
Caparisons don't become a young
woman.
Richard Brinsley Sheridan 1751–1816:
The Rivals (1775)

9 Near all the birds
Will sing at dawn,—and yet we
do not take
The chaffering swallow for the
holy lark.
Elizabeth Barrett Browning 1806–61:
Aurora Leigh (1857)

10 One of the most common defects
of half-instructed minds is to
think much of that in which they
differ from others, and little of
that in which they agree with
others.
on the evils of sectarianism
Walter Bagehot 1826–77: in
Economist (UK) 11 June 1870

11 If we cannot end now our
differences, at least we can help
make the world safe for diversity.
John F. Kennedy 1917–63: address at
American University, Washington, DC,
10 June 1963

Sin
see also **Good and Evil**

1 Be sure your sin will find you out.
Bible: Numbers

2 There is no peace, saith the Lord,
unto the wicked.
Bible: Isaiah

3 If thine eye offend thee, pluck it
out, and cast it from thee: it is
better for thee to enter into life
with one eye, rather than having
two eyes to be cast into hell fire.
Bible: St. Matthew

4 The blasphemy against the Holy
Ghost shall not be forgiven unto
men.
Bible: St. Matthew

5 The wages of sin is death.
Bible: Romans

6 No one ever suddenly became
depraved.
Juvenal AD c. 60–c. 130: *Satires*

7 We make ourselves a ladder out
of our vices if we trample the
vices themselves underfoot.
St. Augustine of Hippo AD 354–430:
Sermon no. 176 ("On the Ascension
of the Lord")

8 I have sinned exceedingly in thought, word, and deed, through my fault, through my fault, through my most grievous fault.
The Missal: *The Ordinary of the Mass*

9 O wombe! O bely! O stynkyng cod Fulfilled of dong and of corrupcioun!
Geoffrey Chaucer c. 1343–1400: *The Canterbury Tales* "The Pardoner's Tale"

10 And see ye not yon braid, braid road,
That lies across the lily leven?
That is the Path of Wickedness,
Though some call it the Road to Heaven.
Anonymous: "Thomas the Rhymer" (traditional ballad)

11 Commit
The oldest sins the newest kind of ways.
William Shakespeare 1564–1616: *Henry IV, Part 2* (1597)

12 Nothing emboldens sin so much as mercy.
William Shakespeare 1564–1616: *Timon of Athens* (c. 1607)

13 But he that hides a dark soul, and foul thoughts
Benighted walks under the midday sun;
Himself is his own dungeon.
John Milton 1608–74: *Comus* (1637)

14 I should renounce the devil and all his works, the pomps and vanity of this wicked world, and all the sinful lusts of the flesh.
The Book of Common Prayer 1662: *Catechism*

15 We have erred, and strayed from thy ways like lost sheep. We have followed too much the devices and desires of our own hearts.
The Book of Common Prayer 1662: *Morning Prayer* General Confession

16 Had laws not been, we never had been blamed;
For not to know we sin is innocence.
William D'Avenant 1606–68: "The Philosopher's Disquisition directed to the Dying Christian" (1672)

17 It is public scandal that constitutes offense, and to sin in secret is not to sin at all.
Molière 1622–73: *Le Tartuffe* (1669)

18 Vice came in always at the door of necessity, not at the door of inclination.
Daniel Defoe 1660–1731: *Moll Flanders* (1721)

19 Vice is a monster of so frightful mien,
As, to be hated, needs but to be seen;
Yet seen too oft, familiar with her face,
We first endure, then pity, then embrace.
Alexander Pope 1688–1744: *An Essay on Man* Epistle 2 (1733)

20 I waive the quantum o' the sin;
The hazard of concealing;
But och! it hardens a' within,
And petrifies the feeling!
Robert Burns 1759–96: "Epistle to a Young Friend" (1786)

21 Vice is detestable; I banish all its appearances from my coteries; and I would banish its reality, too, were I sure I should then have any thing but empty chairs in my drawing-room.
Fanny Burney 1752–1840: *Camilla* (1796)

22 All men that are ruined are ruined on the side of their natural propensities.
Edmund Burke 1729–97: *Two Letters on the Proposals for Peace with the Regicide Directory* (9th ed., 1796)

23 That Calvinistic sense of innate depravity and original sin from whose visitations, in some shape or other, no deeply thinking mind is always and wholly free.
Herman Melville 1819–91: *Hawthorne and His Mosses* (1850)

24 She [the Catholic Church] holds that it were better for sun and moon to drop from heaven, for the earth to fail, and for all the many millions who are upon it to die of starvation in extremest agony, as far as temporal affliction goes, than that one soul, I will not say, should be lost, but should commit one single venial sin, should tell one wilful untruth ... or steal one poor farthing without excuse.
John Henry Newman 1801–90: *Lectures on Anglican Difficulties* (1852)

25 For the sin ye do by two and two ye must pay for one by one!
Rudyard Kipling 1865–1936: "Tomlinson" (1892)

26 We are punished by our sins, not for them.
Elbert Hubbard 1856–1915: *The Note Book* (1927)

27 When I'm good, I'm very, very good, but when I'm bad, I'm better.
Mae West 1892–1980: *I'm No Angel* (1933 film)

28 *when asked by Mrs. Coolidge what a sermon had been about:*
"Sins," he said. "Well, what did he say about sin?" "He was against it."
Calvin Coolidge 1872–1933: John H. McKee *Coolidge: Wit and Wisdom* (1933); perhaps apocryphal

29 There is a charm about the forbidden that makes it unspeakably desirable.
Mark Twain 1835–1910: *Notebook* (1935)

30 All sins are attempts to fill voids.
Simone Weil 1909–43: *La Pesanteur et la grâce* (1948)

31 Shoot all the bluejays you want, if you can hit 'em, but remember it's a sin to kill a mockingbird.
Harper Lee 1926– : *To Kill a Mockingbird* (1960)

32 There are different kinds of wrong. The people sinned against are not always the best.
Ivy Compton-Burnett 1884–1969: *The Mighty and their Fall* (1961)

33 All sin tends to be addictive, and the terminal point of addiction is what is called damnation.
W. H. Auden 1907–73: *A Certain World* (1970) "Hell"

34 Sins become more subtle as you grow older. You commit sins of despair rather than lust.
Piers Paul Read 1941– : in *Daily Telegraph* (UK) 3 October 1990

Singing
see also **Music**

1 So was hir joly whistle wel ywet.
Geoffrey Chaucer c. 1343–1400: *The Canterbury Tales* "The Reeve's Tale"

2 The exercise of singing is delightful to Nature, and good to preserve the health of man. It doth strengthen all parts of the breast, and doth open the pipes.
William Byrd 1543–1623: *Psalms, Sonnets and Songs* (1588)

3 I can suck melancholy out of a song as a weasel sucks eggs.
William Shakespeare 1564–1616: *As You Like It* (1599)

4 If a man were permitted to make all the ballads, he need not care who should make the laws of a nation.
Andrew Fletcher of Saltoun 1655–1716: "An Account of a Conversation concerning a Right Regulation of Government for the Good of Mankind. In a Letter to the Marquis of Montrose" (1704)

5 Today if something is not worth saying, people sing it.
Pierre-Augustin Caron de Beaumarchais 1732–99: *Le Barbier de Séville* (1775)

6 An exotic and irrational entertainment, which has been always combated, and always has prevailed.
of Italian opera
Samuel Johnson 1709–84: *Lives of the English Poets* (1779–81) "Hughes"

7 Sentimentally I am disposed to harmony. But organically I am incapable of a tune.
Charles Lamb 1775–1834: *Essays of Elia* (1823) "A Chapter on Ears"

8 Nothing can be more disgusting than an oratorio. How absurd to see 500 people fiddling like madmen about Israelites in the Red Sea!
Sydney Smith 1771–1845: Hesketh Pearson *The Smith of Smiths* (1934)

9 Every tone [of the songs of the slaves] was a testimony against slavery, and a prayer to God for deliverance from chains.
Frederick Douglass c. 1818–1895: *Narrative of the Life of Frederick Douglass* (1845)

10 A wandering minstrel I—
A thing of shreds and patches.
Of ballads, songs and snatches,
And dreamy lullaby!
W. S. Gilbert 1836–1911: *The Mikado* (1885)

11 I only know two tunes. One of them is "Yankee Doodle" and the other isn't.
Ulysses S. Grant 1822–85: Nat Shapiro (ed.) *An Encyclopedia of Quotations about Music* (1978)

12 You think that's noise—you ain't heard nuttin' yet!
first said in a café, competing with the din from a neighboring building site, in 1906; subsequently an aside in the 1927 film The Jazz Singer
Al Jolson 1886–1950: Martin Abramson *The Real Story of Al Jolson* (1950); also the title of a Jolson song, 1919, in the form "You Ain't Heard Nothing Yet"

13 Everyone suddenly burst out singing;
And I was filled with such delight
As prisoned birds must find in freedom.
Siegfried Sassoon 1886–1967: "Everyone Sang" (1919)

14 An unalterable and unquestioned law of the musical world required that the German text of French operas sung by Swedish artists should be translated into Italian for the clearer understanding of English-speaking audiences.
Edith Wharton 1862–1937: *The Age of Innocence* (1920)

15 People are wrong when they say that the opera isn't what it used to be. It is what it used to be— that's what's wrong with it.
Noël Coward 1899–1973: *Design for Living* (1933)

16 Opera is when a guy gets stabbed in the back and, instead of bleeding, he sings.
Ed Gardner 1901–63: in *Duffy's Tavern* (radio program, 1940s)

17 No opera plot can be sensible, for in sensible situations people do not sing. An opera plot must be,

in both senses of the word, a melodrama.
W. H. Auden 1907–73: in *Times Literary Supplement* (UK) 2 November 1967

18 Words make you think a thought. Music makes you feel a feeling. A song makes you feel a thought.
E. Y. Harburg 1898–1981: lecture given at the New York YMCA in 1970

19 He was an average guy who could carry a tune.
Crosby's own suggestion for his epitaph
Bing Crosby 1903–77: in *Newsweek* 24 October 1977

20 It's the building. That acoustic would make a fart sound like a sevenfold Amen.
on King's College Chapel
David Willcocks 1919– : *Ned Sherrin in his Anecdotage* (1993)

Situation
see **Circumstance and Situation**

The Skies
see also **The Universe**

1 And God made two great lights; the greater light to rule the day, and the lesser light to rule the night: he made the stars also.
Bible: Genesis

2 And ther he saugh, with ful avysement
The erratik sterres, herkenyng armonye
With sownes ful of hevenyssh melodie.
Geoffrey Chaucer c. 1343–1400: *Troilus and Criseyde*

3 Look, how the floor of heaven Is thick inlaid with patines of bright gold:
There's not the smallest orb which thou behold'st

But in this motion like an angel sings
Still quiring to the young-eyed cherubins.
William Shakespeare 1564–1616: *The Merchant of Venice* (1596–8)

4 Queen and huntress, chaste and fair,
Now the sun is laid to sleep,
Seated in thy silver chair,
State in wonted manner keep:
Hesperus entreats thy light,
Goddess, excellently bright.
Ben Jonson c. 1573–1637: *Cynthia's Revels* (1600)

5 The moon's an arrant thief,
And her pale fire she snatches from the sun.
William Shakespeare 1564–1616: *Timon of Athens* (c. 1607)

6 Busy old fool, unruly sun,
Why dost thou thus,
Through windows, and through curtains call on us?
Must to thy motions lovers' seasons run?
John Donne 1572–1631: "The Sun Rising"

7 But it does move.
after his recantation, that the earth moves around the sun, in 1632
Galileo Galilei 1564–1642: attributed; Baretti *Italian Library* (1757) possibly has the earliest appearance of the phrase

8 The evening star,
Love's harbinger.
John Milton 1608–74: *Paradise Lost* (1667)

9 The hornèd Moon, with one bright star
Within the nether tip.
Samuel Taylor Coleridge 1772–1834: "The Rime of the Ancient Mariner" (1798)

10 Twinkle, twinkle, little star,
How I wonder what you are!

Up above the world so high,
Like a diamond in the sky!
Ann Taylor 1782–1866 and **Jane
Taylor** 1783–1824: "The Star" (1806)

11 I am the daughter of Earth and
    Water,
And the nursling of the Sky;
I pass through the pores of the
    ocean and shores;
I change, but I cannot die.
Percy Bysshe Shelley 1792–1822:
"The Cloud" (1819)

12 And like a dying lady, lean and
    pale,
Who totters forth, wrapped in a
    gauzy veil.
Percy Bysshe Shelley 1792–1822:
"The Waning Moon" (1824)

13 Look at the stars! look, look up at
    the skies!
O look at all the fire-folk sitting in
    the air!
The bright boroughs, the circle-
    citadels there!
Gerard Manley Hopkins 1844–89:
"The Starlight Night" (written 1877)

14 The night has a thousand eyes,
And the day but one;
Yet the light of the bright world
    dies,
With the dying sun.
F. W. Bourdillon 1852–1921: "Light"
(1878)

15 Slowly, silently, now the moon
Walks the night in her silver
    shoon.
Walter de la Mare 1873–1956:
"Silver" (1913)

16 The heaventree of stars hung
with humid nightblue fruit.
James Joyce 1882–1941: *Ulysses*
(1922)

17 The moon is nothing
But a circumambulating
    aphrodisiac
Divinely subsidized to provoke the
    world

Into a rising birth-rate.
Christopher Fry 1907– : *The Lady's
not for Burning* (1949)

18 Houston, Tranquillity Base here.
The Eagle has landed.
on landing on the moon
"Buzz" Aldrin 1930– : in *The Times*
(UK) 21 July 1969

Sleep
see also **Dreams**

1 The sleep of a laboring man is
sweet.
Bible: Ecclesiastes

2 Care-charmer Sleep, son of the
    sable Night,
Brother to Death, in silent
    darkness born.
Samuel Daniel 1563–1619: *Delia*
(1592) Sonnet 54

3 Not to be a-bed after midnight is
to be up betimes.
William Shakespeare 1564–1616:
Twelfth Night (1601)

4 Golden slumbers kiss your eyes,
Smiles awake you when you rise:
Sleep, pretty wantons, do not cry,
And I will sing a lullaby.
Thomas Dekker 1570–1641: *Patient
Grissil* (1603)

5 Blessings on him who invented
sleep, the mantle that covers all
human thoughts, the food that
satisfies hunger, the drink that
slakes thirst, the fire that warms
cold, the cold that moderates
heat, and, lastly, the common
currency that buys all things, the
balance and weight that equalizes
the shepherd and the king, the
simpleton and the sage.
Cervantes 1547–1616: *Don Quixote*
(1605)

6 Methought I heard a voice cry,
    "Sleep no more!

Macbeth does murder sleep," the
    innocent sleep,
Sleep that knits up the ravelled
    sleave of care,
The death of each day's life, sore
    labour's bath,
Balm of hurt minds, great
    nature's second course.
William Shakespeare 1564–1616:
Macbeth (1606)

7 What hath night to do with
    sleep?
John Milton 1608–74: *Comus* (1637)

8 We term sleep a death, and yet it
    is waking that kills me, and
    destroys those spirits which are
    the house of life.
Thomas Browne 1605–82: *Religio
Medici* (1643)

9 And so to bed.
Samuel Pepys 1633–1703: diary 20
April 1660

10 'Tis the voice of the sluggard; I
    heard him complain,
    "You have waked me too soon, I
    must slumber again."
As the door on its hinges, so he
    on his bed,
Turns his sides and his shoulders
    and his heavy head.
Isaac Watts 1674–1748: "The
Sluggard" (1715)

11 Tired Nature's sweet restorer,
    balmy sleep!
Edward Young 1683–1765: *Night
Thoughts* (1742–5)

12 Turn the key deftly in the oilèd
    wards,
And seal the hushèd casket of my
    soul.
John Keats 1795–1821: "Sonnet to
Sleep" (written 1819)

13 Must we to bed indeed? Well
    then,
Let us arise and go like men,
And face with an undaunted
    tread
The long black passage up to bed.

Robert Louis Stevenson 1850–94:
"North-West Passage. Good-Night"
(1885)

14 The cool kindliness of sheets, that
    soon
Smooth away trouble; and the
    rough male kiss
Of blankets.
Rupert Brooke 1887–1915: "The
Great Lover" (1914)

15 Early to rise and early to bed
makes a male healthy and
    wealthy and dead.
James Thurber 1894–1961: "The
Shrike and the Chipmunks" in *New
Yorker* 18 February 1939

16 I love sleep because it is both
pleasant and safe to use.
Fran Lebowitz 1946– : *Metropolitan
Life* (1978)

Smoking

1 Whether it divine tobacco were,
Or panachaea, or polygony,
She found, and brought it to her
    patient dear.
Edmund Spenser c. 1552–99: *The
Faerie Queen* (1596)

2 A custom loathsome to the eye,
hateful to the nose, harmful to
the brain, dangerous to the lungs,
and in the black, stinking fume
thereof, nearest resembling the
horrible Stygian smoke of the pit
that is bottomless.
James I 1566–1625: *A Counterblast
to Tobacco* (1604)

3 The lungs of the tobacconist are
rotted, the liver spotted, the brain
smoked like the backside of the
pig-woman's booth here, and the
whole body within, black as her
pan you saw e'en now without.
Ben Jonson c. 1573–1637:
Bartholomew Fair (1614)

4 He who lives without tobacco is
not worthy to live.

Molière 1622–73: *Don Juan* (performed 1665)

5 The pipe with solemn interposing puff,
Makes half a sentence at a time enough;
The dozing sages drop the drowsy strain,
Then pause, and puff—and speak, and pause again.
William Cowper 1731–1800: "Conversation" (1782)

6 This very night I am going to leave off tobacco! Surely there must be some other world in which this unconquerable purpose shall be realized.
Charles Lamb 1775–1834: letter to Thomas Manning, 26 December 1815

7 I toiled after it, sir, as some men toil after virtue.
on being asked "how he had acquired his power of smoking at such a rate"
Charles Lamb 1775–1834: Thomas Noon Talfourd *Memoirs of Charles Lamb* (1892)

8 The sweet post-prandial cigar.
Robert Buchanan 1841–1901: "De Berny" (1874)

9 Lastly (and this is, perhaps, the golden rule), no woman should marry a teetotaller, or a man who does not smoke.
Robert Louis Stevenson 1850–94: *Virginibus Puerisque* (1881)

10 The roots of tobacco plants must go clear through to hell.
Thomas Alva Edison 1847–1931: *American Heritage* (12 July 1885)

11 A cigarette is the perfect type of a perfect pleasure. It is exquisite, and it leaves one unsatisfied. What more can one want?

Oscar Wilde 1854–1900: *The Picture of Dorian Gray* (1891)

12 The wretcheder one is, the more one smokes; and the more one smokes, the wretcheder one gets— a vicious circle!
George du Maurier 1834–96: *Peter Ibbetson* (1892)

13 What this country needs is a really good 5-cent cigar.
Thomas R. Marshall 1854–1925: in *New York Tribune* 4 January 1920

14 I smoked my first cigarette and kissed my first woman on the same day. I have never had time for tobacco since.
Arturo Toscanini 1867–1957: in *Observer* (UK) 30 June 1946

15 But the cigarette, well, I love stroking this lovely tube of delight.
Dennis Potter 1935–94: television interview with Melvyn Bragg, March 1994

Society
see also **Government, Human Race**

1 No man is an Island, entire of it self; every man is a piece of the Continent, a part of the main; if a clod be washed away by the sea, Europe is the less, as well as if a promontory were.
John Donne 1572–1631: *Devotions upon Emergent Occasions* (1624)

2 The only way by which any one divests himself of his natural liberty and puts on the bonds of civil society is by agreeing with other men to join and unite into a community.
John Locke 1632–1704: *Second Treatise of Civil Government* (1690)

3 Society is indeed a contract . . . it becomes a partnership not only between those who are living, but

between those who are living,
those who are dead, and those
who are to be born.
Edmund Burke 1729–97: *Reflections
on the Revolution in France* (1790)

4 The general will rules in society
as the private will governs each
separate individual.
Maximilien Robespierre 1758–94:
Lettres à ses commettans (2nd
series) 5 January 1793

5 Only in the state does man have
a rational existence . . . Man owes
his entire existence to the state,
and has his being within it alone.
Whatever worth and spiritual
reality he possesses are his solely
by virtue of the state.
G. W. F. Hegel 1770–1831: *Lectures
on the Philosophy of World History:
Introduction* (1830)

6 The greatest happiness of the
greatest number is the foundation
of morals and legislation.
Jeremy Bentham 1748–1832: *The
Commonplace Book*; Bentham
claimed that either Joseph Priestley
(1733–1804) or Cesare Beccaria
(1738–94) passed on the "sacred
truth"; see **Morality 2**

7 Wherever a man goes, men will
pursue him and paw him with
their dirty institutions, and, if
they can, constrain him to belong
to their desperate oddfellow
society.
Henry David Thoreau 1817–62:
Walden (1854) "The Village"

8 When society requires to be
rebuilt, there is no use in
attempting to rebuild it on the old
plan.
John Stuart Mill 1806–73:
Dissertations and Discussions vol. 1
(1859) "Essay on Coleridge"

9 From each according to his
abilities, to each according to his
needs.

Karl Marx 1818–83: *Critique of the
Gotha Programme* (written 1875, but
of earlier origin)

10 The Social Contract is nothing
more or less than a vast
conspiracy of human beings to lie
to and humbug themselves and
one another for the general Good.
Lies are the mortar that bind the
savage individual man into the
social masonry.
H. G. Wells 1866–1946: *Love and Mr.
Lewisham* (1900)

11 Society is based on the
assumption that everyone is alike
and no one is alive.
Hugh Kingsmill 1889–1949: Michael
Holroyd *Hugh Kingsmill* (1964)

12 If a free society cannot help the
many who are poor, it cannot
save the few who are rich.
John F. Kennedy 1917–63: inaugural
address, 20 January 1961

13 In your time we have the
opportunity to move not only
toward the rich society and the
powerful society, but upward to
the Great Society.
Lyndon Baines Johnson 1908–73:
speech at University of Michigan, 22
May 1964

14 We started off trying to set up a
small anarchist community, but
people wouldn't obey the rules.
Alan Bennett 1934– : *Getting On*
(1972)

15 There is no such thing as Society.
There are individual men and
women, and there are families.
Margaret Thatcher 1925– : in
Woman's Own 31 October 1987

Solitude

1 It is not good that the man
should be alone; I will make him
an help meet for him.
Bible: Genesis; cf. **18**, **19** below

2 He who is unable to live in society, or who has no need because he is sufficient for himself, must be either a beast or a god.
Aristotle 384–322 BC: *Politics*

3 Never less idle than when wholly idle, nor less alone than when wholly alone.
Cicero 106–43 BC: *De Officiis*

4 My wife, who, poor wretch, is troubled with her lonely life.
Samuel Pepys 1633–1703: diary 19 December 1662

5 In solitude
What happiness? who can enjoy alone,
Or all enjoying, what contentment find?
John Milton 1608–74: *Paradise Lost* (1667)

6 I am monarch of all I survey,
My right there is none to dispute;
From the centre all round to the sea
I am lord of the foul and the brute.
William Cowper 1731–1800: "Verses Supposed to be Written by Alexander Selkirk" (1782); Selkirk (1621–1721) was the prototype of "Robinson Crusoe"

7 'Tis the last rose of summer
Left blooming alone;
All her lovely companions
Are faded and gone.
Thomas Moore 1779–1852: "'Tis the last rose of summer" (1807)

8 To fly from, need not be to hate, mankind.
Lord Byron 1788–1824: *Childe Harold's Pilgrimage* (1812–18)

9 Anythin' for a quiet life, as the man said wen he took the sitivation at the lighthouse.
Charles Dickens 1812–70: *Pickwick Papers* (1837)

10 I long for scenes where man hath never trod
A place where woman never smiled or wept
There to abide with my Creator God.
John Clare 1793–1864: "I Am" (1848)

11 It is a fine thing to be out on the hills alone. A man can hardly be a beast or a fool alone on a great mountain.
Francis Kilvert 1840–79: diary 29 May 1871

12 Down to Gehenna or up to the Throne,
He travels the fastest who travels alone.
Rudyard Kipling 1865–1936: "L'Envoi" (*The Story of the Gadsbys*, 1890)

13 I will arise and go now, and go to Innisfree,
And a small cabin build there, of clay and wattles made;
Nine bean rows will I have there, a hive for the honey bee,
And live alone in the bee-loud glade.
W. B. Yeats 1865–1939: "The Lake Isle of Innisfree" (1893)

14 My heart is a lonely hunter that hunts on a lonely hill.
Fiona McLeod 1855–1905: "The Lonely Hunter" (1896); reworked by Carson McCullers as "The heart is a lonely hunter" for the title of a novel, 1940

15 We live, as we dream—alone.
Joseph Conrad 1857–1924: *Heart of Darkness* (1902)

16 Man goes into the noisy crowd to drown his own clamour of silence.
Rabindranath Tagore 1861–1941: "Stray Birds" (1916)

17 I want to be alone.
Greta Garbo 1905–90: *Grand Hotel*

(1932 film), the phrase already being associated with Garbo

18 God created man and, finding him not sufficiently alone, gave him a companion to make him feel his solitude more keenly.
Paul Valéry 1871–1945: *Tel Quel 1* (1941); see **1** above

19 [Barrymore] would quote from Genesis the text which says, "It is not good for man to be alone," and then add, "But O my God, what a relief."
John Barrymore 1882–1942: Alma Power-Waters *John Barrymore* (1941); see **1** above

20 We're all of us sentenced to solitary confinement inside our own skins, for life!
Tennessee Williams 1911–83: *Orpheus Descending* (1958)

21 The loneliness of the long-distance runner.
Alan Sillitoe 1928– : title of novel (1959)

22 What Chekhov saw in our failure to communicate was something positive and precious: the private silence in which we live, and which enables us to endure our own solitude.
V. S. Pritchett 1900– : *Myth Makers* (1979)

23 Thirty years is a very long time to live alone and life doesn't get any nicer.
on widowhood, at the age of 92
Frances Partridge 1900– : G. Kinnock and F. Miller *By Faith and Daring* (1993)

Solutions
see **Problems and Solutions**

Sorrow
see also **Mourning and Loss, Suffering**

1 By the waters of Babylon we sat down and wept: when we remembered thee, O Sion.
Bible: Psalm 137

2 *Sunt lacrimae rerum et mentem mortalia tangunt.*
There are tears shed for things even here and mortality touches the heart.
Virgil 70–19 BC: *Aeneid*

3 . . . *Nessun maggior dolore, Che ricordarsi del tempo felice Nella miseria.*
There is no greater pain than to remember a happy time when one is in misery.
Dante Alighieri 1265–1321: *Divina Commedia* "Inferno"

4 Silence augmenteth grief, writing increaseth rage,
Staled are my thoughts, which loved and lost, the wonder of our age.
Edward Dyer d. 1607: "Elegy on the Death of Sir Philip Sidney" (1593); previously attributed to Fulke Greville, 1554–1628

5 If you have tears, prepare to shed them now.
William Shakespeare 1564–1616: *Julius Caesar* (1599)

6 When sorrows come, they come not single spies,
But in battalions.
William Shakespeare 1564–1616: *Hamlet* (1601)

7 Indeed the tears live in an onion that should water this sorrow.
William Shakespeare 1564–1616: *Antony and Cleopatra* (1606–7)

8 We think caged birds sing, when indeed they cry.

John Webster *c.* 1580–*c.* 1625: *The White Devil* (1612)

9 All my joys to this are folly,
Naught so sweet as Melancholy.
Robert Burton 1577–1640: *The Anatomy of Melancholy* (1621–51)

10 Nothing is here for tears.
John Milton 1608–74: *Samson Agonistes* (1671)

11 Grief is a species of idleness.
Samuel Johnson 1709–84: letter to Mrs. Thrale, 17 March 1773

12 Go—you may call it madness, folly;
You shall not chase my gloom away.
There's such a charm in melancholy,
I would not, if I could, be gay.
Samuel Rogers 1763–1855: "To —, 1814"

13 For a tear is an intellectual thing;
And a sigh is the sword of an Angel King.
William Blake 1757–1827: *Jerusalem* (1815)

14 There's not a joy the world can give like that it takes away.
Lord Byron 1788–1824: "Stanzas for Music" (1816)

15 But when the melancholy fit shall fall
Sudden from heaven like a weeping cloud,
That fosters the droop-headed flowers all,
And hides the green hill in an April shroud;
Then glut thy sorrow on a morning rose,
Or on the rainbow of the salt sand-wave.
John Keats 1795–1821: "Ode on Melancholy" (1820)

16 I tell you, hopeless grief is passionless.

Elizabeth Barrett Browning 1806–61: "Grief" (1844)

17 Tears, idle tears, I know not what they mean,
Tears from the depth of some divine despair.
Alfred, Lord Tennyson 1809–92: *The Princess* (1847), song (added 1850)

18 Áh! ás the heart grows older
It will come to such sights colder
By and by, nor spare a sigh
Though worlds of wanwood leafmeal lie;
And yet you *will* weep and know why.
Gerard Manley Hopkins 1844–89: "Spring and Fall: to a young child" (written 1880)

19 MEDVEDENKO: Why do you wear black all the time?
MASHA: I'm in mourning for my life. I'm unhappy.
Anton Chekhov 1860–1904: *The Seagull* (1896)

20 Laugh and the world laughs with you;
Weep, and you weep alone;
For the sad old earth must borrow its mirth,
But has trouble enough of its own.
Ella Wheeler Wilcox 1855–1919: "Solitude"

21 All the old statues of Victory have wings: but Grief has no wings. She is the unwelcome lodger that squats on the hearth-stone between us and the fire and will not move or be dislodged.
Arthur Quiller-Couch 1863–1944: Armistice Day anniversary sermon, Cambridge, November 1923

22 Men who are unhappy, like men who sleep badly, are always proud of the fact.
Bertrand Russell 1872–1970: *The Conquest of Happiness* (1930)

23 Sorrow is tranquillity remembered in emotion.
Dorothy Parker 1893–1967: *Here Lies* (1939) "Sentiment" see **Poetry 13**

24 He felt the loyalty we all feel to unhappiness—the sense that that is where we really belong.
Graham Greene 1904–91: *The Heart of the Matter* (1948)

25 Noble deeds and hot baths are the best cures for depression.
Dodie Smith 1896–1990: *I Capture the Castle* (1949)

26 How small and selfish is sorrow. But it bangs one about until one is senseless.
shortly after the death of George VI
Queen Elizabeth, the Queen Mother 1900– : letter to Edith Sitwell, 1952; Victoria Glendinning *Edith Sitwell* (1983)

27 No one ever told me that grief felt so like fear.
C. S. Lewis 1898–1963: *A Grief Observed* (1961)

28 All I have I would have given gladly not to be standing here today.
following the assassination of J. F. Kennedy
Lyndon Baines Johnson 1908–73: first speech to Congress as President, 27 November 1963

29 Total grief is like a minefield. No knowing when one will touch the tripwire.
Sylvia Townsend Warner 1893–1978: diary 11 December 1969

Speech
see also **Conversation**

1 The words of his mouth were softer than butter, having war in his heart: his words were smoother than oil, and yet they be very swords.
Bible: Psalm 55

2 Then said they unto him, Say now Shibboleth: and he said Sibboleth: for he could not frame to pronounce it right. Then they took him, and slew him.
Bible: Judges

3 The reason why we have two ears and only one mouth is that we may listen the more and talk the less.
to a youth who was talking nonsense
Zeno 333–261 BC: Diogenes Laertius *Lives of the Philosophers*

4 The tongue can no man tame; it is an unruly evil.
Bible: James

5 Somwhat he lipsed, for his wantownesse,
To make his Englissh sweete upon his tonge.
Geoffrey Chaucer c. 1343–1400: *The Canterbury Tales* "The General Prologue"

6 It has been well said, that heart speaks to heart, whereas language only speaks to the ears.
St. Francis de Sales 1567–1622: letter to the Archbishop of Bourges, 5 October 1604, which John Henry Newman paraphrased for his motto as "*cor ad cor loquitur* [heart speaks to heart]"

7 Her voice was ever soft,
Gentle and low, an excellent thing in woman.
William Shakespeare 1564–1616: *King Lear* (1605–6)

8 I do not much dislike the matter, but
The manner of his speech.
William Shakespeare 1564–1616: *Antony and Cleopatra* (1606–7)

9 Continual eloquence is tedious.
Blaise Pascal 1623–62: *Pensées* (1670)

10 Most men make little other use of
their speech than to give evidence
against their own understanding.
Lord Halifax 1633–95: *Political,
Moral, and Miscellaneous Thoughts
and Reflections* (1750) "Of Folly and
Fools"

11 Here comes the orator! with his
flood of words, and his drop of
reason.
Benjamin Franklin 1706–90: *Poor
Richard's Almanack* (October 1735)

12 Faith, that's as well said, as if I
had said it myself.
Jonathan Swift 1667–1745: *Polite
Conversation* (1738)

13 No, Sir, because I have time to
think before I speak, and don't
ask impertinent questions.
*when asked if he found his
stammering very inconvenient*
Erasmus Darwin 1731–1802:
"Reminiscences of My Father's
Everyday Life," an appendix by
Francis Darwin to his edition of
Charles Darwin *Autobiography* (1877)

14 When you have nothing to say,
say nothing.
Charles Caleb Colton c. 1780–1832:
Lacon (1820)

15 A tart temper never mellows with
age, and a sharp tongue is the
only edged tool that grows keener
with constant use.
Washington Irving 1783–1859: *The
Sketch Book* (1820)

16 And, when you stick on
        conversation's burrs,
Don't strew your pathway with
        those dreadful *urs.*
Oliver Wendell Holmes 1809–94: "A
Rhymed Lesson" (1848)

17 Human speech is like a cracked
kettle on which we tap crude
rhythms for bears to dance to,
while we long to make music that
will melt the stars.

Gustave Flaubert 1821–80: *Madame
Bovary* (1857)

18 Speech is the small change of
silence.
George Meredith 1828–1909: *The
Ordeal of Richard Feverel* (1859)

19 Take care of the sense, and the
sounds will take care of
themselves.
Lewis Carroll 1832–98: *Alice's
Adventures in Wonderland* (1865)

20 Half the sorrows of women would
be averted if they could repress
the speech they know to be
useless; nay, the speech they
have resolved not to make.
George Eliot 1819–80: *Felix Holt*
(1866)

21 To Trinity Church, Dorchester.
The rector in his sermon delivers
himself of mean images in a very
sublime voice, and the effect is
that of a glowing landscape in
which clothes are hung up to dry.
Thomas Hardy 1840–1928:
Notebooks 1 February 1874

22 I don't want to talk grammar, I
want to talk like a lady.
George Bernard Shaw 1856–1950:
Pygmalion (1916)

23 What can be said at all can be
said clearly; and whereof one
cannot speak thereof one must be
silent.
Ludwig Wittgenstein 1889–1951:
Tractatus Logico-Philosophicus
(1922)

24 If you don't say anything, you
won't be called on to repeat it.
Calvin Coolidge 1872–1933: (1933)

25 Speech is civilization itself. The
word, even the most
contradictory word, preserves
contact—it is silence which
isolates.

Thomas Mann 1875–1955: *The Magic Mountain* (1924)

26 Nagging is the repetition of unpalatable truths.
Edith Summerskill 1901–80: speech to the Married Women's Association, House of Commons, 14 July 1960

27 If, sir, I possessed, as you suggest, the power of conveying unlimited sexual attraction through the potency of my voice, I would not be reduced to accepting a miserable pittance from the BBC for interviewing a faded female in a damp basement.
reply to Mae West's manager who asked "Can't you sound a bit more sexy when you interview her?"
Gilbert Harding 1907–60: S. Grenfell *Gilbert Harding by his Friends* (1961)

28 Sentence structure is innate but whining is acquired.
Woody Allen 1935– : "Remembering Needleman" (1976)

Speeches

1 Grasp the subject, the words will follow.
Cato the Elder 234–149 BC: Caius Julius Victor *Ars Rhetorica*

2 Friends, Romans, countrymen, lend me your ears.
William Shakespeare 1564–1616: *Julius Caesar* (1599)

3 I am no orator, as Brutus is;
But, as you know me all, a plain, blunt man,
That love my friend.
William Shakespeare 1564–1616: *Julius Caesar* (1599)

4 But all was false and hollow; though his tongue
Dropped manna, and could make the worse appear
The better reason.
John Milton 1608–74: *Paradise Lost* (1667)

5 The keenness of his sabre was blunted by the difficulty with which he drew it from the scabbard; I mean, the hesitation and ungracefulness of his delivery took off from the force of his arguments.
of Henry Fox, 1755
Horace Walpole 1717–97: *Memoirs of the Reign of King George II* (1846)

6 And adepts in the speaking trade
Keep a cough by them ready made.
Charles Churchill 1731–64: *The Ghost* (1763)

7 Not merely a chip of the old "block," but the old block itself.
on the younger Pitt's maiden speech, February 1781
Edmund Burke 1729–97: N. W. Wraxall *Historical Memoirs of My Own Time* (1904 ed.)

8 The Right Honourable gentleman is indebted to his memory for his jests, and to his imagination for his facts.
Richard Brinsley Sheridan 1751–1816: speech in reply to Mr. Dundas; T. Moore *Life of Sheridan* (1825)

9 The brilliant chief, irregularly great,
Frank, haughty, rash,—the Rupert of Debate!
on Edward Stanley, Lord Derby
Edward George Bulwer-Lytton 1803–73: *The New Timon* (1846); a similar term had been used by Disraeli in 1844

10 Preach not because you have to say something, but because you have something to say.
Richard Whately 1787–1863: *Apophthegms* (1854)

11 I absorb the vapour and return it as a flood.
on public speaking

W. E. Gladstone 1809–98: Lord Riddell *Some Things That Matter* (1927 ed.)

12 He is one of those orators of whom it was well said, "Before they get up, they do not know what they are going to say; when they are speaking, they do not know what they are saying; and when they have sat down, they do not know what they have said."
of Lord Charles Beresford
Winston Churchill 1874–1965: speech, House of Commons, 20 December 1912

13 M. Clemenceau . . . is one of the greatest living orators, but he knows that the finest eloquence is that which gets things done and the worst is that which delays them.
David Lloyd George 1863–1945: speech at Paris Peace Conference, 18 January 1919

14 Seventy minutes had passed before Mr. Lloyd George arrived at his proper theme. He spoke for a hundred and seventeen minutes, in which period he was detected only once in the use of an argument.
Arnold Bennett 1867–1931: *Things that have Interested Me* (1921)

15 If I am to speak for ten minutes, I need a week for preparation; if fifteen minutes, three days; if half an hour, two days; if an hour, I am ready now.
Woodrow Wilson 1856–1924: Josephus Daniels *The Wilson Era* (1946)

16 Public speaking is like the winds of the desert: it blows constantly without doing any good.
when asked, at the inception of the UN in 1945, why he (as Saudi Arabian minister) was the only

delegate not to have delivered a speech
Faisal: Y. Karsh *Karsh: A 50-Year Retrospective* (1983)

17 Attlee is a charming and intelligent man, but as a public speaker he is, compared to Winston [Churchill], like a village fiddler after Paganini.
Harold Nicolson 1886–1968: diary 10 November 1947

18 If I talk over people's heads, Ike must talk under their feet.
Adlai Stevenson 1900–65: during the Presidential campaign of 1952; Bill Adler *The Stevenson Wit* (1966)

19 He mobilized the English language and sent it into battle to steady his fellow countrymen and hearten those Europeans upon whom the long dark night of tyranny had descended.
of Winston Churchill
Ed Murrow 1908–65: broadcast, 30 November 1954

20 It was the nation and the race dwelling all round the globe that had the lion's heart. I had the luck to be called upon to give the roar. I also hope that I sometimes suggested to the lion the right place to use his claws.
Winston Churchill 1874–1965: speech at Westminster Hall, 30 November 1954

21 I take the view, and always have, that if you cannot say what you are going to say in twenty minutes you ought to go away and write a book about it.
Lord Brabazon 1884–1964: speech, House of Lords, 21 June 1955

22 Listening to a speech by Chamberlain is like paying a visit to Woolworth's: everything in its place and nothing above sixpence.

Aneurin Bevan 1897–1960: Michael
Foot *Aneurin Bevan* (1962)

23 I do not object to people looking
at their watches when I am
speaking. But I strongly object
when they start shaking them to
make certain they are still going.
Lord Birkett 1883–1962: in *Observer*
(UK) 30 October 1960

24 Do you remember that in
classical times when Cicero had
finished speaking, the people said,
"How well he spoke," but when
Demosthenes had finished
speaking, they said, "Let us
march."
introducing John F. Kennedy in 1960
Adlai Stevenson 1900–65: Bert
Cochran *Adlai Stevenson*

25 A speech from Ernest Bevin on a
major occasion had all the
horrific fascination of a public
execution. If the mind was left
immune, eyes and ears and
emotions were riveted.
Michael Foot 1913– : *Aneurin Bevan*
(1962)

26 Humming, Hawing and
Hesitation are the three Graces of
contemporary Parliamentary
oratory.
Julian Critchley 1930– :
Westminster Blues (1985)

Sports and Games
see also **Football; Hunting, Shooting,
and Fishing; Winning and Losing**

1 There is plenty of time to win this
game, and to thrash the
Spaniards too.
*receiving news of the Armada while
playing bowls on Plymouth Hoe*
Francis Drake c. 1540–96: attributed,
in *Dictionary of National Biography*
(1917–)

2 When we have matched our
rackets to these balls,

We will in France, by God's
grace, play a set
Shall strike his father's crown
into the hazard.
William Shakespeare 1564–1616:
Henry V (1599)

3 Chaos umpire sits,
And by decision more embroils
the fray.
John Milton 1608–74: *Paradise Lost*
(1667)

4 I am sorry I have not learned to
play at cards. It is very useful in
life: it generates kindness and
consolidates society.
Samuel Johnson 1709–84: James
Boswell *Journal of a Tour to the
Hebrides* (1785) 21 November 1773

5 What a sad old age you are
preparing for yourself.
*to a young diplomat who boasted of
his ignorance of whist*
Charles-Maurice de Talleyrand 1754–
1838: J. Amédée Pichot *Souvenirs
Intimes sur M. de Talleyrand* (1870)

6 The only athletic sport I ever
mastered was backgammon.
Douglas Jerrold 1803–57: Walter
Jerrold *Douglas Jerrold* (1914)

7 Jolly boating weather,
And a hay harvest breeze,
Blade on the feather,
Shade off the trees
Swing, swing together
With your body between your
knees.
William Cory 1823–92: "Eton Boating
Song" in *Eton Scrap Book* (1865)

8 The harmless art of knucklebones
has seen the fall of the Roman
empire and the rise of the United
States.
Robert Louis Stevenson 1850–94:
Across the Plains (1892) "The
Lantern-Bearers"

9 And it's not for the sake of a
ribboned coat,

Or the selfish hope of a season's
fame,
But his Captain's hand on his
shoulder smote—
"Play up! play up! and play the
game!"
Henry Newbolt 1862–1938: "Vitaï
Lampada" (1897)

10 To play billiards well is a sign of
an ill-spent youth.
Charles Roupell: attributed; D.
Duncan *Life of Herbert Spencer*
(1908)

11 Take me out to the ball game,
Take me out with the crowd.
Buy me some peanuts and cracker-
jack—
I don't care if I never get back.
Jack Norworth 1879–1959: *Take Me
Out to the Ball Game* (1908)

12 Golf is a good walk spoiled.
Mark Twain 1835–1910: Alex Ayres
*Greatly Exaggerated: the Wit and
Wisdom of Mark Twain* (1988);
attributed

13 Honey, I just forgot to duck.
*to his wife, on losing the World
Heavyweight title, 23 September
1926*
Jack Dempsey 1895–1983: J. and B.
P. Dempsey *Dempsey* (1977); after a
failed attempt on his life in 1981,
Ronald Reagan quipped to his wife,
"Honey, I forgot to duck"

14 We was robbed!
*after Jack Sharkey beat Max
Schmeling (of whom Jacobs was
manager) in the heavyweight title
fight, 21 June 1932*
Joe Jacobs 1896–1940: Peter Heller *In
This Corner* (1975)

15 I called off his players' names as
they came marching up the steps
behind him . . . All nice guys.
They'll finish last. Nice guys.
Finish last.
*casual remark at a practice in the
presence of a number of journalists,
July 1946*
Leo Durocher 1906–91: *Nice Guys
Finish Last* (1975)

16 The theory and practice of
gamesmanship or The art of
winning games without actually
cheating.
Stephen Potter 1900–69: title of
book (1947)

17 *when asked by the coroner if he had
intended to "get Doyle in trouble":*
Mister, it's my *business* to get him
in trouble.
*following the death of Jimmy Doyle
from his injuries after fighting
Robinson, 24 June 1947*
Sugar Ray Robinson 1920–89: Sugar
Ray Robinson with Dave Anderson
Sugar Ray (1970)

18 All the time he's boxing he's
thinking. All the time he was
thinking, I was hitting him.
Jack Dempsey 1895–1983: *New
Yorker* (13 May 1950)

19 Serious sport has nothing to do
with fair play. It is bound up with
hatred, jealousy, boastfulness, and
disregard of all the rules.
George Orwell 1903–50: *Shooting an
Elephant* (1950) "I Write as I Please"

20 One of the chief duties of the fan
is to engage in arguments with
the man behind him. This
department of the game has been
allowed to run down fearfully.
Robert Benchley 1889–1945: *The
Baseball Reader* (1951)

21 Don't look back. Something may
be gaining on you.
a baseball pitcher's advice
Satchel Paige 1906–82: in *Collier's*
13 June 1953

22 What I know most surely about
morality and the duty of man I
owe to sport.

*often quoted as, " . . . I owe to
football"*
Albert Camus 1913–60: Herbert R.
Lottman *Albert Camus* (1979)

23 The ball climbed on a diagonal
line into the vast volume of air
over center field . . . in the books
while it was still in the sky.
John Updike 1932– : *Sports
Illustrated* (2 October 1960)

24 Ideally, the umpire should
combine the integrity of a
Supreme Court justice, the
physical agility of an acrobat, the
endurance of Job and the
imperturbability of Buddha.
Anonymous: *Time* (1961)

25 Float like a butterfly, sting like a
bee.
summary of his boxing strategy
Muhammad Ali (Cassius Clay)
1942– : G. Sullivan *Cassius Clay
Story* (1964); probably originated by
Drew "Bundini" Brown

26 You don't save a pitcher for
tomorrow. Tomorrow it may rain.
Leo Durocher 1905–91: *New York
Times* (16 May 1965)

27 In America, it is sport that is the
opiate of the masses.
Russell Baker 1925– : *New York
Times* (3 October 1967)

28 I used to think the only use for it
was to give small boys something
else to kick besides me.
of sport
Katharine Whitehorn 1928– :
Observations (1970)

29 Blind people came to the game
just to listen to his fast ball.
of Tom Seaver
Reggie Jackson 1946– : *Sports
Illustrated* (4 January 1973)

30 All you have to do is keep the
five players who hate your guts

away from the five who are
undecided.
on baseball
Casey Stengel 1891–1975: John
Samuel (ed.) *The Guardian Book of
Sports Quotes* (1985)

31 Think! How the hell are you gonna
think and hit at the same time?
Yogi Berra 1925– : *Nice Guys Finish
Seventh* (1976)

32 Football isn't a contact sport, it's
a collision sport. Dancing is a
contact sport.
Vince Lombardi 1913–1970: *Sports in
America* (1976)

33 A yammer of radio announcers
. . . a grouse of ballplayers . . . a
conceit of managers . . . a dawdle
of magnates . . . a braille of
umpires and a bibulation of
sportswriters.
Walter W. ("Red") Smith 1905–82:
Sporting News (4 December 1976)

34 Trying to sneak a pitch past Rod
Carew is like trying to sneak the
sunrise past a rooster.
Amos Otis 1947– : *Time* (18 July
1977)

35 Fame vaporizes, money goes with
the wind, and all that's left is
character.
O. J. Simpson 1947– : *Juice: O. J.
Simpson's Life* (1977)

36 The trouble with referees is that
they just don't care which side
wins.
Tom Canterbury: in *Guardian* (UK)
24 December 1980 "Sports Quotes
of the Year"

37 You cannot be serious!
John McEnroe 1959– : said to
tennis umpire at Wimbledon, early
1980s

38 Corned-beef sandwiches were
good enough for him, but for the
catfish he'd bought at least a
pound of filet steak.

Jonathan Rabin 1942– : *Old Glory* (1982)

39 If people don't want to come out to the ball park, nobody's going to stop 'em.
Yogi Berra 1925– : attributed

40 New Yorkers love it when you spill your guts out there. Spill your guts at Wimbledon and they make you stop and clean it up.
Jimmy Connors 1952– : at Flushing Meadow; in *Guardian* (UK) 24 December 1984 "Sports Quotes of the Year"

41 Where do they get the money to come out here every day and bet? . . . It's the money they save on neckties and razor blades.
Alfred Vanderbilt 1912– : *Red* (1986)

42 Design has taken the place of what sailing used to be.
Dennis Conner 1943– : *Time* (9 February 1987)

43 The thing about sport, any sport, is that swearing is very much part of it.
Jimmy Greaves 1940– : in *Observer* (UK) 1 January 1989

44 Playing snooker gives you firm hands and helps to build up character. It is the ideal recreation for dedicated nuns.
attending a snooker championship at Tyburn convent as emissary of the Pope
Luigi Barbarito 1922– : in *Daily Telegraph* 15 November 1989

45 He wasn't a pitcher, he was Zeus, the mound was his Olympus, and the curve ball, that was his thunderbolt, streaking through space until it reached the plate, where it suddenly fell to earth.
on John Weiss as a 21-year-old semi-pro reliever

Charles Hirshberg 1917– : *Life* (May 1990)

46 Some kids want to join the circus . . . Others want to be big-league baseball players . . . When I came to the Yankees, I got to do both.
Graig Nettles 1944– : *Newsweek* (6 August 1990)

47 Baseball, it is said, is only a game. True. And the Grand Canyon is only a hole in Arizona. Not all holes, or games, are created equal.
George F. Will 1941– : *Men At Work: The Craft of Baseball* (1990)

48 Greek philosophers considered sport a religious and civic—in a word, moral—undertaking. Sport, they said, is morally serious because mankind's noblest aim is the loving contemplation of worthy things, such as beauty and courage.
George F. Will 1941– : *Men At Work: The Craft of Baseball* (1990)

49 It is an old baseball joke that big-inning baseball is affirmed in the Bible, in Genesis. "In the big inning, God created . . ."
George F. Will 1941– : *Men At Work: The Craft of Baseball* (1990)

50 Going to college offered me the chance to play football for four more years.
Ronald Reagan 1911– : *An American Life* (1990)

51 Boxing's just show business with blood.
Frank Bruno 1961– : in *Guardian* (UK) 20 November 1991; also attributed to David Belasco in 1915

52 Baseball is very big with my people. It figures. It's the only way we can get to shake a bat at a white man without starting a riot.

Dick Gregory 1932– : D. H. Nathan
(ed.) *Baseball Quotations* (1991)

53 The game begins in the spring,
when everything else begins
again, and it blossoms in the
summer, filling the afternoons
and evenings, and then as soon
as the chill rains come, it stops
and leaves you to face the fall
alone.
A. Bartlett Giamatti 1938–89: *Bart*
(1991)

54 He could throw a lamb chop past
a wolf.
on Lefty Grove
Westbrook Pegler 1894–1969:
Baseball's Greatest Quotations
(1991)

55 Who's the horse to beat? I've got
to beat them all.
Mike Smith: *New York Times* (8 May
1994)

56 Baseball gives every American
boy a chance to excel. Not just to
be as good as someone else, but
to be better. This is the nature of
man and the name of the game.
Ted Williams 1918– : *Baseball*
(1994)

57 Playing baseball for a living was
like having a license to steal.
Pete Rose 1941– : *Baseball* (1994)

58 Here is a game in which there is
no clock, the defense holds the
ball, though it has rigid rules,
every park is different, the
greatest heroes fail seven times
out of ten, a game that's born in
the spring dies in the fall. This is
life.
on baseball
Kenneth L. Burns 1953– :
Washington Post (4 July 1994)

59 That's a home run in an elevator
shaft.
*in reference to Phil Rizzuto's high
pop-up*

Leo Durocher 1905–91: *Washington
Post* (1 August 1994)

60 [I]nfield practice is more mystic
ritual than preparation,
encouraging the big-leaguer, no
less than the duffer in the stands,
to believe in spite of all evidence
to the contrary, that playing ball
is a snap.
Roger Angell 1920– : *Baseball*
(1994)

61 Football combines the two worst
features of modern American life:
it's violence punctuated by
committee meetings.
George F. Will 1941– : *Baseball
(PBS series)* (1994)

62 [The] baseball strike has pitted
greedy owners against grasping
players, killed one World Series,
stymied the President, polarized
Congress, disgusted the country
and threatened to shut down the
national pastime as we know it.
Kitty Kelley 1942– : *New York
Times* (25 February 1995)

Statistics
see also **Mathematics, Quantities and
Qualities**

1 We are just statistics, born to
consume resources.
Horace 65–8 BC: *Epistles*

2 A witty statesman said, you
might prove anything by figures.
Thomas Carlyle 1795–1881: *Chartism*
(1839)

3 Every moment dies a man,
Every moment one is born.
Alfred, Lord Tennyson 1809–92:
"The Vision of Sin" (1842); cf. **4**
below

4 Every moment dies a man,
Every moment 1¹⁄₁₆ is born.
Charles Babbage 1792–1871: parody
of Tennyson's "Vision of Sin" in an

unpublished letter to the poet; in
New Scientist 4 December 1958: see
3 above

5 There are three kinds of lies: lies,
damned lies and statistics.
Benjamin Disraeli 1804–81:
attributed; Mark Twain
Autobiography (1924)

6 He uses statistics as a drunken
man uses lampposts—for support
rather than for illumination.
Andrew Lang 1844–1912: attributed

7 [The War Office kept three sets of
figures:] one to mislead the
public, another to mislead the
Cabinet, and the third to mislead
itself.
Herbert Asquith 1852–1928: Alistair
Horne *Price of Glory* (1962)

8 The so-called science of poll-
taking is not a science at all but
a mere necromancy. People are
unpredictable by nature, and
although you can take a nation's
pulse, you can't be sure that the
nation hasn't just run up a flight
of stairs.
E. B. White 1899–1985: in *New
Yorker* 13 November 1948

9 From the fact that there are
400,000 species of beetles on this
planet, but only 8,000 species of
mammals, he [Haldane]
concluded that the Creator, if He
exists, has a special preference for
beetles.
J. B. S. Haldane 1892–1964: report of
lecture, 7 April 1951

10 One of the thieves was saved.
(*Pause*) It's a reasonable
percentage.
Samuel Beckett 1906–89: *Waiting for
Godot* (1955)

Storytelling
see **Fiction and Storytelling**

Strength and Weakness

1 I am poured out like water, and
all my bones are out of joint: my
heart also in the midst of my
body is even like melting wax.
Bible: Psalm 22

2 A threefold cord is not quickly
broken.
Bible: Ecclesiastes

3 If God be for us, who can be
against us?
Bible: Romans

4 The gods are on the side of the
stronger.
Tacitus AD *c.* 56–after 117: *Histories*

5 One hair of a woman can draw
more than a hundred pair of
oxen.
James Howell *c.* 1593–1666: *Familiar
Letters* (1645–55)

6 The concessions of the weak are
the concessions of fear.
Edmund Burke 1729–97: *On
Conciliation with America* (1775)

7 Under a spreading chestnut tree
The village smithy stands;
The smith, a mighty man is he,
With large and sinewy hands;
And the muscles of his brawny
arms
Are strong as iron bands.
Henry Wadsworth Longfellow 1807–
82: "The Village Blacksmith" (1839)

8 The thing is, you see, that the
strongest man in the world is the
man who stands most alone.
Henrik Ibsen 1828–1906: *An Enemy
of the People* (1882)

9 The weak are strong because they
are reckless. The strong are weak
because they have scruples.
Otto von Bismarck 1815–98: quoted
by Henry Kissinger to James
Callaghan, 1975; James Callaghan
Time and Change (1987)

10 I am as strong as a bull moose
and you can use me to the limit.
*"Bull Moose" subsequently became
the popular name of the Progressive
Party*
Theodore Roosevelt 1858–1919: letter
to Mark Hanna, 27 June 1900

11 This is the law of the Yukon, that
only the Strong shall thrive;
That surely the Weak shall perish,
and only the Fit survive.
Robert W. Service 1874–1958: "The
Law of the Yukon" (1907)

12 Strength through joy.
Robert Ley 1890–1945: German
Labour Front slogan from 1933

13 Our cock won't fight.
*of Edward VIII, said to Winston
Churchill during the abdication crisis
of 1936*
Lord Beaverbrook 1879–1964:
Frances Donaldson *Edward VIII*
(1974)

14 If you can't stand the heat, get
out of the kitchen.
Harry Vaughan: in *Time* 28 April
1952; associated with Harry S.
Truman, but attributed by him to
Vaughan, his "military jester"

15 The most potent weapon in the
hands of the oppressor is the
mind of the oppressed.
Steve Biko 1946–77: statement as
witness, 3 May 1976

16 Toughness doesn't have to come
in a pinstripe suit.
Dianne Feinstein 1933– : in *Time* 4
June 1984

Style
see also **Language**

1 I strive to be brief, and I become
obscure.
Horace 65–8 BC: *Ars Poetica*

2 Works of serious purpose and
grand promises often have a
purple patch or two stitched on,
to shine far and wide.
Horace 65–8 BC: *Ars Poetica*

3 I have revered always not crude
verbosity, but holy simplicity.
St. Jerome c. AD 342–420: letter "Ad
Pammachium"

4 More matter with less art.
William Shakespeare 1564–1616:
Hamlet (1601)

5 He does it with a better grace,
but I do it more natural.
William Shakespeare 1564–1616:
Twelfth Night (1601)

6 When we see a natural style, we
are quite surprised and delighted,
for we expected to see an author
and we find a man.
Blaise Pascal 1623–62: *Pensées*
(1670)

7 Style is the dress of thought; a
modest dress,
Neat, but not gaudy, will true
critics please.
Samuel Wesley 1662–1735: "An
Epistle to a Friend concerning
Poetry" (1700)

8 True wit is Nature to advantage
dressed,
What oft was thought, but ne'er
so well expressed.
Alexander Pope 1688–1744: *An
Essay on Criticism* (1711)

9 Proper words in proper places,
make the true definition of a
style.
Jonathan Swift 1667–1745: *Letter to
a Young Gentleman lately entered
into Holy Orders* 9 January 1720

10 These things [subject matter] are
external to the man; style is the
man.

Comte de Buffon 1707–88: *Discours sur le style*; address given to the Académie Française, 25 August 1753

11 Dr. Johnson's sayings would not appear so extraordinary, were it not for his bow-wow way.
Henry Herbert, Lord Pembroke 1734–94: James Boswell *Life of Samuel Johnson* (1791) 27 March 1775

12 The moving accident is not my trade;
To freeze the blood I have no ready arts:
'Tis my delight, alone in summer shade,
To pipe a simple song for thinking hearts.
William Wordsworth 1770–1850: "Hart-Leap Well" (1800)

13 Style is life! It is the very life-blood of thought!
Gustave Flaubert 1821–80: letter to Louise Colet, 7 September 1853

14 The web, then, or the pattern; a web at once sensuous and logical, an elegant and pregnant texture: that is style, that is the foundation of the art of literature.
Robert Louis Stevenson 1850–94: *The Art of Writing* (1905) "On some technical Elements of Style in Literature" (written 1885)

15 People think that I can teach them style. What stuff it all is! Have something to say, and say it as clearly as you can. That is the only secret of style.
Matthew Arnold 1822–88: G. W. E. Russell *Collections and Recollections* (1898)

16 Detection is, or ought to be, an exact science, and should be treated in the same cold and unemotional manner. You have attempted to tinge it with romanticism, which produces much the same effect as if you worked a love-story or an elopement into the fifth proposition of Euclid.
Arthur Conan Doyle 1859–1930: *The Sign of Four* (1890)

17 I don't wish to sign my name, though I am afraid everybody will know who the writer is: one's style is one's signature always.
sending a letter for publication
Oscar Wilde 1854–1900: letter to the *Daily Telegraph* (UK), 2 February 1891

18 As to the Adjective: when in doubt, strike it out.
Mark Twain 1835–1910: *Pudd'nhead Wilson* (1894)

19 No flowers, by request.
summarizing the principle of conciseness for contributors to the Dictionary of National Biography
Alfred Ainger 1837–1904: speech to contributors, 8 July 1897

20 No iron can stab the heart with such force as a full stop put just at the right place.
Isaac Babel 1894–c. 1939: *Guy de Maupassant* (1932)

21 "Feather-footed through the plashy fen passes the questing vole" . . . "Yes," said the Managing Editor. "That must be good style."
Evelyn Waugh 1903–66: *Scoop* (1938)

22 The Mandarin style . . . is beloved by literary pundits, by those who would make the written word as unlike as possible to the spoken one.
Cyril Connolly 1903–74: *Enemies of Promise* (1938)

23 It's not what I do, but the way I do it. It's not what I say, but the way I say it.
Mae West 1892–1980: G. Eells and S. Musgrove *Mae West* (1989)

Success and Failure
see also **Winning and Losing**

1 The race is not to the swift, nor
the battle to the strong.
Bible: Ecclesiastes

2 *Veni, vidi, vici.*
I came, I saw, I conquered.
Julius Caesar 100–44 BC: inscription
displayed in Caesar's Pontic triumph,
according to Suetonius *Lives of the
Caesars* "Divus Julius"; or, according
to Plutarch *Parallel Lives* "Julius
Caesar," written in a letter by
Caesar, announcing the victory of
Zela that concluded the Pontic
campaign

3 These success encourages: they
can because they think they can.
Virgil 70–19 BC: *Aeneid*

4 For what shall it profit a man, if
he shall gain the whole world,
and lose his own soul?
Bible: St. Mark

5 Of all I had, only honor and life
have been spared.
*usually quoted "All is lost save
honour"*
Francis I of France 1494–1547: letter
to his mother following his defeat at
Pavia, 1525

6 MACBETH: If we should fail,—
LADY MACBETH: We fail!
But screw your courage to the
sticking-place,
And we'll not fail.
William Shakespeare 1564–1616:
Macbeth (1606)

7 'Tis not in mortals to command
success,
But we'll do more, Sempronius;
we'll deserve it.
Joseph Addison 1672–1719: *Cato*
(1713)

8 I shall be like that tree, I shall die
at the top.

Jonathan Swift 1667–1745: Sir Walter
Scott (ed.) *Works of Swift* (1814)

9 The conduct of a losing party
never appears right: at least it
never can possess the only
infallible criterion of wisdom to
vulgar judgements—success.
Edmund Burke 1729–97: *Letter to a
Member of the National Assembly*
(1791)

10 As he rose like a rocket, he fell
like the stick.
*on Edmund Burke losing the
parliamentary debate on the French
Revolution to Charles James Fox*
Thomas Paine 1737–1809: *Letter to
the Addressers on the late
Proclamation* (1792)

11 The sublime and the ridiculous
are often so nearly related, that it
is difficult to class them
separately. One step above the
sublime, makes the ridiculous;
and one step above the ridiculous,
makes the sublime again.
Thomas Paine 1737–1809: *The Age
of Reason* pt. 2 (1795); cf. **12** below

12 There is only one step from the
sublime to the ridiculous.
*to De Pradt, Polish ambassador,
after the retreat from Moscow in
1812*
Napoleon I 1769–1821: D. G. De
Pradt *Histoire de l'Ambassade dans
le grand-duché de Varsovie en 1812*
(1815); cf. **11** above

13 Half the failures in life arise from
pulling in one's horse as he is
leaping.
Julius Hare 1795–1855 and **Augustus
Hare** 1792–1834: *Guesses at Truth*
(1827)

14 'Tis better to have fought and
lost,
Than never to have fought at all.
Arthur Hugh Clough 1819–61:
"Peschiera" (1854)

15 If one advances confidently in the direction of his dreams, and endeavors to live the life which he has imagined, he will meet with a success unexpected in common hours.
Henry David Thoreau 1817–62: *Walden* (1854)

16 It was roses, roses, all the way.
Robert Browning 1812–89: "The Patriot" (1855)

17 Success is counted sweetest
By those who ne'er succeed.
To comprehend a nectar
Requires sorest need.
Emily Dickinson 1830–86: "Success is counted sweetest" (1859)

18 To burn always with this hard, gemlike flame, to maintain this ecstasy, is success in life.
Walter Pater 1839–94: *Studies in the History of the Renaissance* (1873)

19 I have climbed to the top of the greasy pole.
on becoming Prime Minister
Benjamin Disraeli 1804–81: W. Monypenny and G. Buckle *Life of Benjamin Disraeli* vol. 4 (1916)

20 Success is a science; if you have the conditions, you get the result.
Oscar Wilde 1854–1900: letter March–April 1883

21 All you need in this life is ignorance and confidence; then success is sure.
Mark Twain 1835–1910: letter to Mrs. Foote, 2 December 1887

22 I never climbed any ladder: I have achieved eminence by sheer gravitation.
George Bernard Shaw 1856–1950: *The Irrational Knot* (1905)

23 The moral flabbiness born of the exclusive worship of the bitch-goddess *success*.
William James 1842–1910: letter to H. G. Wells, 11 September 1906

24 Success, like charity, covers a multitude of sins.
Alfred Thayer Mahan 1840–1914: *Naval Strategy* (1911)

25 The world continues to offer glittering prizes to those who have stout hearts and sharp swords.
F. E. Smith 1872–1930: Rectorial Address, Glasgow University, 7 November 1923

26 Anybody seen in a bus over the age of 30 has been a failure in life.
Loelia, Duchess of Westminster 1902–93: in *The Times* (UK) 4 November 1993 (obituary); habitual remark

27 You [the Mensheviks] are pitiful isolated individuals; you are bankrupts; your role is played out. Go where you belong from now on — into the dustbin of history!
Leon Trotsky 1879–1940: *History of the Russian Revolution* (1933); cf. **History 10**

28 How to win friends and influence people.
Dale Carnegie 1888–1955: title of book (1936)

29 The common idea that success spoils people by making them vain, egotistic and self-complacent is erroneous; on the contrary it makes them, for the most part, humble, tolerant and kind. Failure makes people bitter and cruel.
W. Somerset Maugham 1874–1965: *Summing Up* (1938)

30 Success is relative:
It is what we can make of the mess we have made of things.
T. S. Eliot 1888–1965: *The Family Reunion* (1939)

31 Victory has a hundred fathers, but no-one wants to recognize defeat as his own.

Count Galeazzo Ciano 1903–44:
diary, 9 September 1942

32 If *A* is a success in life, then *A*
equals *x* plus *y* plus *z*. Work is *x*;
y is play; and *z* is keeping your
mouth shut.
Albert Einstein 1879–1955: in
Observer (UK) 15 January 1950

33 The world is made of people who
never quite get into the first team
and who just miss the prizes at
the flower show.
Jacob Bronowski 1908–74: *Face of
Violence* (1954)

34 The theory seems to be that as
long as a man is a failure he is
one of God's children, but that as
soon as he succeeds he is taken
over by the Devil.
H. L. Mencken 1880–1956: *Minority
Report* (1956)

35 Sweet smell of success.
Ernest Lehman 1920– : title of
book and film (1957)

36 Flops are a part of life's menu,
and I've never been a girl to miss
out on any of the courses.
Rosalind Russell 1911–76: *New York
Herald Tribune* (11 April 1957)

37 Success took me to her bosom
like a maternal boa constrictor.
Noël Coward 1899–1973: Sheridan
Morley *A Talent to Amuse* (1969)

38 For a writer, success is always
temporary, success is only a
delayed failure. And it is
incomplete.
Graham Greene 1904–91: *A Sort of
Life* (1971)

39 Whenever a friend succeeds, a
little something in me dies.
Gore Vidal 1925– : in *Sunday
Times Magazine* (UK) 16 September
1973

40 Is it possible to succeed without
any act of betrayal?
Jean Renoir 1894–1979: *My Life and
My Films* (1974)

41 Go on failing. Go on. Only next
time, try to fail better.
*to an actor who had lamented, "I'm
failing"*
Samuel Beckett 1906–89: Tony
Richardson *Long Distance Runner*
(1993)

42 Nick played great and I played
poor. There were no two ways
about it.
*on losing the golf Masters
tournament to Nick Faldo*
Greg Norman 1955– : in *Observer*
(UK) 21 April 1996

Suffering
see also **Mourning and Loss, Sorrow,
Sympathy and Consolation**

1 They that sow in tears: shall reap
in joy.
He that now goeth on his way
weeping, and beareth forth good
seed: shall doubtless come again
with joy, and bring his sheaves
with him.
Bible: Psalm 126

2 Out of the deep have I called unto
thee, O Lord: Lord, hear my voice.
Bible: Psalm 130

3 Nothing happens to anybody
which he is not fitted by nature
to bear.
Marcus Aurelius AD 121–80:
Meditations

4 *Tu proverai sì come sa di sale
Lo pane altrui, e com'è duro calle
Lo scendere e'l salir per l'altrui
    scale.*
You shall find out how salt is the
taste of another man's bread, and
how hard is the way up and
down another man's stairs.

Dante Alighieri 1265–1321: *Divina Commedia* "Paradiso"

5 If you bear the cross gladly, it will bear you.
Thomas à Kempis c. 1380–1471: *The Imitation of Christ*

6 He jests at scars, that never felt a wound.
William Shakespeare 1564–1616: *Romeo and Juliet* (1595)

7 The worst is not,
So long as we can say, "This is the worst."
William Shakespeare 1564–1616: *King Lear* (1605–6)

8 Our torments also may in length of time
Become our elements.
John Milton 1608–74: *Paradise Lost* (1667)

9 No pain, no palm; no thorns, no throne; no gall, no glory; no cross, no crown.
William Penn 1644–1718: *No Cross, No Crown* (1669 pamphlet)

10 To each his suff'rings, all are men,
Condemned alike to groan;
The tender for another's pain,
Th' unfeeling for his own.
Thomas Gray 1716–71: *Ode on a Distant Prospect of Eton College* (1747)

11 Fade far away, dissolve, and quite forget
What thou among the leaves hast never known,
The weariness, the fever, and the fret
Here, where men sit and hear each other groan;
Where palsy shakes a few, sad, last grey hairs,
Where youth grows pale, and spectre-thin, and dies;
Where but to think is to be full of sorrow

And leaden-eyed despairs.
John Keats 1795–1821: "Ode to a Nightingale" (1820)

12 Suffering is permanent, obscure and dark,
And shares the nature of infinity.
William Wordsworth 1770–1850: *The Borderers* (1842)

13 I love the majesty of human suffering.
Alfred de Vigny 1797–1863: *La Maison du Berger* (1844)

14 Sorrow and silence are strong, and patient endurance is godlike.
Henry Wadsworth Longfellow 1807–82: *Evangeline* (1847)

15 For frequent tears have run
The colours from my life.
Elizabeth Barrett Browning 1806–61: *Sonnets from the Portuguese* (1850)

16 After great pain, a formal feeling comes—
The Nerves sit ceremonious, like Tombs—
The stiff Heart questions was it He, that bore,
And Yesterday, or Centuries before?
Emily Dickinson 1830–86: "After great pain, a formal feeling comes" (1862)

17 Thank you, madam, the agony is abated.
aged four, having had hot coffee spilt over his legs
Lord Macaulay 1800–59: G. O. Trevelyan *Life and Letters of Lord Macaulay* (1876)

18 The toad beneath the harrow knows
Exactly where each tooth-point goes;
The butterfly upon the road
Preaches contentment to that toad.

Rudyard Kipling 1865–1936: "Pagett, MP" (1886)

19 What does not kill me makes me stronger.
Friedrich Nietzsche 1844–1900: *Twilight of the Idols* (1889)

20 Nothing begins, and nothing ends,
That is not paid with moan;
For we are born in other's pain,
And perish in our own.
Francis Thompson 1859–1907: "Daisy" (1913)

21 Tragedy ought really to be a great kick at misery.
D. H. Lawrence 1885–1930: letter to A. W. McLeod, 6 October 1912

22 It is not true that suffering ennobles the character; happiness does that sometimes, but suffering, for the most part, makes men petty and vindictive.
W. Somerset Maugham 1874–1965: *The Moon and Sixpence* (1919)

23 Too long a sacrifice
Can make a stone of the heart.
O when may it suffice?
W. B. Yeats 1865–1939: "Easter, 1916" (1921)

24 The point is that nobody likes having salt rubbed into their wounds, even if it is the salt of the earth.
Rebecca West 1892–1983: *The Salt of the Earth* (1935)

25 We can't all be happy, we can't all be rich, we can't all be lucky . . . Some must cry so that others may be able to laugh the more heartily.
Jean Rhys c. 1890–1979: *Good Morning, Midnight* (1939)

26 Tragedy is clean, it is restful, it is flawless.
Jean Anouilh 1910–87: *Antigone* (1944)

27 Willy Loman never made a lot of money. His name was never in the paper. He's not the finest character that ever lived. But he's a human being, and a terrible thing is happening to him. So attention must be paid.
Arthur Miller 1915– : *Death of a Salesman* (1949)

28 How can you expect a man who's warm to understand one who's cold?
Alexander Solzhenitsyn 1918– : *One Day in the Life of Ivan Denisovich* (1962)

Suicide

1 For who would bear the whips and scorns of time,
The oppressor's wrong, the proud man's contumely,
The pangs of disprized love, the law's delay,
The insolence of office, and the spurns
That patient merit of the unworthy takes,
When he himself might his quietus make
With a bare bodkin?
William Shakespeare 1564–1616: *Hamlet* (1601)

2 O! that this too too solid flesh would melt,
Thaw, and resolve itself into a dew;
Or that the Everlasting had not fixed
His canon 'gainst self-slaughter!
William Shakespeare 1564–1616: *Hamlet* (1601)

3 What Cato did, and Addison approved,
Cannot be wrong.
lines found on his desk after he, too, had taken his own life
Eustace Budgell 1686–1737: Colley Cibber *Lives of the Poets* (1753)

4 In chains and darkness, wherefore
   should I stay,
   And mourn in prison, while I
   keep the key?
   Lady Mary Wortley Montagu 1689–
   1762: "Verses on Self-Murder"
   (1749)

5 All this buttoning and
   unbuttoning.
   Anonymous: 18th-century suicide
   note

6 Nor at all can tell
   Whether I mean this day to end
   myself,
   Or lend an ear to Plato where he
   says,
   That men like soldiers may not
   quit the post
   Allotted by the Gods.
   Alfred, Lord Tennyson 1809–92:
   "Lucretius" (1868)

7 The thought of suicide is a great
   source of comfort: with it a calm
   passage is to be made across
   many a bad night.
   Friedrich Nietzsche 1844–1900:
   Jenseits von Gut und Böse (1886)

8 A suicide kills two people,
   Maggie, that's what it's for!
   Arthur Miller 1915– : *After the Fall*
   (1964)

9 Suicide . . . is about life, being in
   fact the sincerest form of criticism
   life gets.
   Wilfrid Sheed 1930– : *The Good
   Word* (1978)

10 Suicide is no more than a trick
   played on the calendar.
   Tom Stoppard 1937– : *The Dog It
   Was That Died* (1983)

The Supernatural

1 Then a spirit passed before my
   face; the hair of my flesh stood
   up.
   Bible: Job

2 May the gods avert this omen.
   Cicero 106–43 BC: *Third Philippic*

3 For we wrestle not against flesh
   and blood, but against
   principalities, against powers,
   against the rulers of the darkness
   of this world, against spiritual
   wickedness in high places.
   Bible: Ephesians

4 GLENDOWER: I can call spirits from
   the vasty deep.
   HOTSPUR: Why, so can I, or so can
   any man;
   But will they come when you do
   call for them?
   William Shakespeare 1564–1616:
   Henry IV, Part 1 (1597)

5 There are more things in heaven
   and earth, Horatio,
   Than are dreamt of in your
   philosophy.
   William Shakespeare 1564–1616:
   Hamlet (1601); cf. **Universe 7**

6 Double, double toil and trouble;
   Fire burn and cauldron bubble.
   William Shakespeare 1564–1616:
   Macbeth (1606)

7 Is this a dagger which I see
   before me,
   The handle toward my hand?
   Come, let me clutch thee:
   I have thee not, and yet I see
   thee still.
   Art thou not, fatal vision, sensible
   To feeling as to sight? or art thou
   but
   A dagger of the mind, a false
   creation,
   Proceeding from the heat-
   oppressed brain?
   William Shakespeare 1564–1616:
   Macbeth (1606)

8 There is a superstition in avoiding
   superstition.
   Francis Bacon 1561–1626: *Essays*
   (1625) "Of Superstition"

9 Go, and catch a falling star,
   Get with child a mandrake root,

Tell me, where all past years are,
Or who cleft the Devil's foot.
John Donne 1572–1631: "Song: Go
and catch a falling star"

10 Anno 1670, not far from
Cirencester, was an apparition;
being demanded whether a good
spirit or a bad? returned no
answer, but disappeared with a
curious perfume and most
melodious twang. Mr. W. Lilly
believes it was a fairy.
John Aubrey 1626–97: *Miscellanies*
(1696) "Apparitions"

11 All argument is against it; but all
belief is for it.
of the existence of ghosts
Samuel Johnson 1709–84: James
Boswell *Life of Samuel Johnson*
(1791) 31 March 1778

12 Superstition is the religion of
feeble minds.
Edmund Burke 1729–97: *Reflections
on the Revolution in France* (1790)

13 Superstition is the poetry of life.
Johann Wolfgang von Goethe 1749–
1832: *Maximen und Reflexionen*
(1819) "Literatur und Sprache"

14 Out flew the web and floated wide;
The mirror cracked from side to
side;
"The curse is come upon me,"
cried
The Lady of Shalott.
Alfred, Lord Tennyson 1809–92: "The
Lady of Shalott" (1832, revised 1842)

15 Up the airy mountain,
Down the rushy glen,
We daren't go a-hunting,
For fear of little men.
William Allingham 1824–89: "The
Fairies" (1850)

16 There are fairies at the bottom of
our garden!
Rose Fyleman 1877–1957: "The
Fairies" (1918)

17 From ghoulies and ghosties and
long-leggety beasties
And things that go bump in the
night,
Good Lord, deliver us!
Anonymous: "The Cornish or West
Country Litany"; Francis T.
Nettleinghame *Polperro Proverbs
and Others* (1926)

18 I always knew the living talked
rot, but it's nothing to the rot the
dead talk.
on spiritualism
Margot Asquith 1864–1945: Chips
Channon, diary, 20 December 1937

Surprise

1 O wonderful, wonderful, and most
wonderful wonderful! and yet
again wonderful, and after that,
out of all whooping!
William Shakespeare 1564–1616: *As
You Like It* (1599)

2 Surprises are foolish things. The
pleasure is not enhanced, and the
inconvenience is often
considerable.
Jane Austen 1775–1817: *Emma* (1816)

3 I'm Gormed—and I can't say no
fairer than that!
Charles Dickens 1812–70: *David
Copperfield* (1850)

4 "Curiouser and curiouser!" cried
Alice.
Lewis Carroll 1832–98: *Alice's
Adventures in Wonderland* (1865)

5 When Gregor Samsa awoke one
morning from uneasy dreams he
found himself transformed in his
bed into a gigantic insect.
Franz Kafka 1883–1924: *The
Metamorphosis* (1915)

6 I turned to Aunt Agatha, whose
demeanour was now rather like
that of one who, picking daisies
on the railway, has just caught
the down express in the small of
the back.

P. G. Wodehouse 1881–1975: *The Inimitable Jeeves* (1923)

7 It was quite the most incredible event that has ever happened to me in my life. It was almost as incredible as if you fired a 15-inch shell at a piece of tissue paper and it came back and hit you.
on the back-scattering effect of metal foil on alpha-particles
Ernest Rutherford 1871–1937: E. N. da C. Andrade *Rutherford and the Nature of the Atom* (1964)

8 Nobody expects the Spanish Inquisition! Our chief weapon is surprise—surprise and fear . . . fear and surprise . . . our two weapons are fear and surprise—and ruthless efficiency . . . our *three* weapons are fear and surprise and ruthless efficiency and an almost fanatical devotion to the Pope . . . our *four* . . . no . . . *Amongst* our weapons—amongst our weaponry—are such elements as fear, surprise . . . I'll come in again.
Graham Chapman 1941–89 et al.: *Monty Python's Flying Circus* (BBC TV program, 1970)

Swearing
see **Cursing and Swearing**

Sympathy and Consolation

1 Heaven and Earth are not ruthful; To them the Ten Thousand Things are but as straw dogs.
Ten Thousand Things = *all life forms*; straw dogs = *sacrificial tokens*
Lao-tsu c. 604–c. 531 BC: *Tao-Tê-Ching*

2 If you want me to weep, you must first feel grief yourself.
Horace 65–8 BC: *Ars Poetica*

3 O divine Master, grant that I may not so much seek

To be consoled as to console; To be understood as to understand.
St. Francis of Assisi 1181–1226: "Prayer of St. Francis"; attributed

4 She wolde wepe, if that she saugh a mous
Kaught in a trappe, if it were deed or bledde.
Geoffrey Chaucer c. 1343–1400: *The Canterbury Tales* "The General Prologue"

5 For pitee renneth soone in gentil herte.
Geoffrey Chaucer c. 1343–1400: *The Canterbury Tales* "The Knight's Tale"

6 But yet the pity of it, Iago! O! Iago, the pity of it, Iago!
William Shakespeare 1564–1616: *Othello* (1602–4)

7 Yet I do fear thy nature; It is too full o' the milk of human kindness
To catch the nearest way.
William Shakespeare 1564–1616: *Macbeth* (1606)

8 We are all strong enough to bear the misfortunes of others.
Duc de la Rochefoucauld 1613–80: *Maximes* (1678)

9 A feeling heart is a blessing that no one, who has it, would be without; and it is a moral security of innocence; since the heart that is able to partake of the distress of another, cannot wilfully give it.
Samuel Richardson 1689–1761: *History of Sir Charles Grandison* (1754)

10 If a madman were to come into this room with a stick in his hand, no doubt we should pity the state of his mind; but our primary consideration would be to take care of ourselves. We

should knock him down first, and pity him afterwards.
Samuel Johnson 1709–84: House of Commons, 3 April 1776

11 Our sympathy is cold to the relation of distant misery.
Edward Gibbon 1737–94: *The Decline and Fall of the Roman Empire* (1776–88)

12 Then cherish pity, lest you drive an angel from your door.
William Blake 1757–1827: "Holy Thursday" (1789)

13 Hatred is a tonic, it makes one live, it inspires vengeance; but pity kills, it makes our weakness weaker.
Honoré de Balzac 1799–1850: *La Peau de Chagrin* (1831)

14 Pity is the feeling which arrests the mind in the presence of whatsoever is grave and constant in human sufferings and unites it with the human sufferer. Terror is the feeling which arrests the mind in the presence of whatsoever is grave and constant in human sufferings and unites it with the secret cause.
James Joyce 1882–1941: *A Portrait of the Artist as a Young Man* (1916)

15 I can sympathize with people's pains, but not with their pleasures. There is something curiously boring about somebody else's happiness.
Aldous Huxley 1894–1963: *Limbo* (1920)

16 Only the hopeless are starkly sincere and . . . only the unhappy can either give or take sympathy.
Jean Rhys c. 1890–1979: *The Left Bank* (1927)

17 Any victim demands allegiance.
Graham Greene 1904–91: *The Heart of the Matter* (1948)

18 The fact that I have no remedy for the sorrows of the world is no reason for my accepting yours. It simply supports the strong probability that yours is a fake.
H. L. Mencken 1880–1956: *Minority Report* (1956)

Taste

1 *Elegantiae arbiter.*
The arbiter of taste.
of Petronius
Tacitus AD c. 56–after 117: *Annals*

2 The play, I remember, pleased not the million; 'twas caviare to the general.
William Shakespeare 1564–1616: *Hamlet* (1601)

3 Between good sense and good taste there is the same difference as between cause and effect.
Jean de la Bruyère 1645–96: *Les Caractères ou les moeurs de ce siècle* (1688) "Des Jugements"

4 Our tastes greatly alter. The lad does not care for the child's rattle, and the old man does not care for the young man's whore.
Samuel Johnson 1709–84: James Boswell *Life of Samuel Johnson* (1791) Spring 1766

5 Could we teach taste or genius by rules, they would be no longer taste and genius.
Joshua Reynolds 1723–92: *Discourses on Art* 14 December 1770

6 Rules and models destroy genius and art.
William Hazlitt 1778–1830: *Sketches and Essays* (1839) "On Taste"

7 She had
A heart—how shall I say?—too soon made glad,
Too easily impressed; she liked whate'er
She looked on, and her looks went everywhere.

Robert Browning 1812–89: "My Last
Duchess" (1842)

8 A difference of taste in jokes is a
great strain on the affections.
George Eliot 1819–80: *Daniel
Deronda* (1876)

9 Taste is the feminine of genius.
Edward Fitzgerald 1809–83: letter to
J. R. Lowell, October 1877

10 Nowhere probably is there more
true feeling, and nowhere worse
taste, than in a churchyard.
Benjamin Jowett 1817–93: Evelyn
Abbott and Lewis Campbell (eds.)
Letters of Benjamin Jowett (1899)

11 The requirement of conspicuous
wastefulness is not commonly
present, consciously, in our
canons of taste, but it is none the
less present as a constraining
norm, selectively shaping and
sustaining our sense of what is
beautiful, and guiding our
discrimination with respect to
what may legitimately be
approved as beautiful and what
may not.
Thorstein Veblen 1857–1929: *Theory
of the Leisure Class* (1899)

12 *of the wallpaper in the room where
he was dying:*
One of us must go.
Oscar Wilde 1854–1900: attributed,
probably apocryphal

13 Good taste is better than bad
taste, but bad taste is better than
no taste, and men without
individuality have no taste—at
any rate no taste that they can
impose on their publics.
Arnold Bennett 1867–1931: in
Evening Standard (UK) 21 August
1930

14 The kind of people who always go
on about whether a thing is in
good taste invariably have very
bad taste.

Joe Orton 1933–67: in *Transatlantic
Review* Spring 1967

15 Never criticize Americans. They
have the best taste that money
can buy.
Miles Kington 1941– : *Welcome to
Kington* (1989)

Taxes

1 Money has no smell.
*quashing an objection to a tax on
public lavatories*
Vespasian AD 9–79: traditional
summary; Suetonius *Lives of the
Caesars* "Vespasian"

2 Neither will it be, that a people
overlaid with taxes should ever
become valiant and martial.
Francis Bacon 1561–1626: *Essays*
(1625) "Of the True Greatness of
Kingdoms"

3 *Excise.* A hateful tax levied upon
commodities.
Samuel Johnson 1709–84: *A
Dictionary of the English Language*
(1755)

4 Taxation without representation
is tyranny.
James Otis 1725–83: watchword (*c.*
1761) of the American Revolution; in
Dictionary of American Biography

5 To tax and to please, no more
than to love and to be wise, is
not given to men.
Edmund Burke 1729–97: *On
American Taxation* (1775)

6 There is no art which one
government sooner learns of
another than that of draining
money from the pockets of the
people.
Adam Smith 1723–90: *Wealth of
Nations* (1776)

7 The art of government is to make
two-thirds of a nation pay all it
possibly can pay for the benefit of
the other third.

Voltaire 1694–1778: attributed; Walter Bagehot *The English Constitution* (1867)

8 All taxes must, at last, fall upon agriculture.
Edward Gibbon 1737–1794: quoting Artaxerxes, in *The Decline and Fall of the Roman Empire* (1776–88)

9 In this world nothing can be said to be certain, except death and taxes.
Benjamin Franklin 1706–90: letter to Jean Baptiste Le Roy, 13 November 1789

10 Of all debts, men are least willing to pay taxes. What a satire is this on government!
Ralph Waldo Emerson 1803–82: *Essays: First Series* (1844)

11 The Chancellor of the Exchequer is a man whose duties make him more or less of a taxing machine. He is intrusted with a certain amount of misery which it is his duty to distribute as fairly as he can.
Robert Lowe 1811–92: speech, House of Commons, 11 April 1870

12 What is the difference between a taxidermist and a tax collector? The taxidermist takes only your skin.
Mark Twain 1835–1910: *Mark Twain's Notebook* (30 December 1902)

13 Death is the most convenient time to tax rich people.
David Lloyd George 1863–1945: in *Lord Riddell's Intimate Diary of the Peace Conference and After, 1918–23* (1933)

14 Income Tax has made more Liars out of the American people than Golf.
Will Rogers 1879–1935: *The Illiterate Digest* (1924) "Helping the Girls with their Income Taxes"

15 Taxes, after all, are the dues that we pay for the privileges of membership in an organized society.
Franklin D. Roosevelt 1882–1945: *Campaign address* (21 October 1936)

16 Only the little people pay taxes.
Leona Helmsley *c.* 1920– : addressed to her housekeeper in 1983, and reported at her trial for tax evasion; in *New York Times* 12 July 1989

17 Read my lips: no new taxes.
George Bush 1924– : campaign pledge on taxation, in *New York Times* 19 August 1988

Teaching
see **Education and Teaching**

Technology
see also **Inventions and Discoveries, Science**

1 Give me but one firm spot on which to stand, and I will move the earth.
on the action of a lever
Archimedes *c.* 287–212 BC: Pappus *Synagoge*

2 I sell here, Sir, what all the world desires to have—POWER.
of his engineering works
Matthew Boulton 1728–1809: James Boswell *Life of Samuel Johnson* (1791) 22 March 1776

3 Man is a tool-using animal . . . Without tools he is nothing, with tools he is all.
Thomas Carlyle 1795–1881: *Sartor Resartus* (1834)

4 This extraordinary metal [iron], the soul of every manufacture, and the mainspring perhaps of civilised society.

Samuel Smiles 1812–1904: *Men of Invention and Industry* (1884)

5 One machine can do the work of fifty ordinary men. No machine can do the work of one extraordinary man.
Elbert Hubbard 1859–1915: *Thousand and One Epigrams* (1911)

6 Your worship is your furnaces,
Which, like old idols, lost obscenes,
Have molten bowels; your vision is
Machines for making more machines.
Gordon Bottomley 1874–1948: "To Ironfounders and Others" (1912)

7 Machines are worshipped because they are beautiful, and valued because they confer power; they are hated because they are hideous, and loathed because they impose slavery.
Bertrand Russell 1872–1970: *Sceptical Essays* (1928) "Machines and Emotions"

8 Science finds, industry applies, man conforms.
Anonymous: subtitle of guidebook to 1933 Chicago World's Fair

9 This is not the age of pamphleteers. It is the age of the engineers. The spark-gap is mightier than the pen.
Lancelot Hogben 1895–1975: *Science for the Citizen* (1938)

10 The biggest obstacle to professional writing is the necessity for changing a typewriter ribbon.
Robert Benchley 1889–1945: *Chips off the old Benchley* (1949) "Learn to Write"

11 One servant is worth a thousand gadgets.
Joseph Alois Schumpeter 1883–1950:

John Kenneth Galbraith *A Life in our Times* (1981)

12 Mechanics, not microbes, are the menace to civilization.
Norman Douglas 1868–1952: introduction to *The Norman Douglas Limerick Book* (1967)

13 Technology . . . the knack of so arranging the world that we need not experience it.
Max Frisch 1911– : *Homo Faber* (1957)

14 The Britain that is going to be forged in the white heat of this revolution will be no place for restrictive practices or for outdated methods on either side of industry.
usually quoted as "the white heat of the technological revolution"
Harold Wilson 1916–95: speech at the Labour Party Conference, 1 October 1963

15 Man is still the most extraordinary computer of all.
John F. Kennedy 1917–63: (21 May 1963)

16 The medium is the message.
Marshall McLuhan 1911–80: *Understanding Media* (1964)

17 Any sufficiently advanced technology is indistinguishable from magic.
Arthur C. Clarke 1917– : *The Lost Worlds of 2001* (1972)

18 The danger always exists that our technology will serve as a buffer between us and nature, a block between us and the deeper dimensions of our own experience.
Rollo May 1909–94: *The Courage to Create* (1975)

19 To err is human but to really foul things up requires a computer.
Anonymous: *Farmers' Almanac for 1978* "Capsules of Wisdom"

20 A modern computer hovers between the obsolescent and the nonexistent.
Sydney Brenner 1927– : attributed in *Science* 5 January 1990

21 Computers are anti-Faraday machines. He said he couldn't understand anything until he could count it, while computers count everything and understand nothing.
Ralph Cornes: in *Guardian* (UK) 28 March 1991

22 Thanks to modern technology . . . history now comes equipped with a fast-forward button.
Gore Vidal 1925– : *Screening History* (1992)

23 The thing with high-tech is that you always end up using scissors.
David Hockney 1937– : in *Observer* (UK) 10 July 1994

Temptation

1 Get thee behind me, Satan.
Bible: St. Matthew

2 And lead us not into temptation, but deliver us from evil.
Bible: St. Matthew

3 Watch and pray, that ye enter not into temptation: the spirit indeed is willing but the flesh is weak.
Bible: St. Matthew

4 Is this her fault or mine?
The tempter or the tempted, who sins most?
William Shakespeare 1564–1616: *Measure for Measure* (1604)

5 From all the deceits of the world, the flesh, and the devil,
Good Lord, deliver us.
The Book of Common Prayer 1662: *The Litany*

6 What's done we partly may compute,
But know not what's resisted.
Robert Burns 1759–96: "Address to the Unco Guid" (1787)

7 It may almost be a question whether such wisdom as many of us have in our mature years has not come from the dying out of the power of temptation, rather than as the results of thought and resolution.
Anthony Trollope 1815–82: *The Small House at Allington* (1864)

8 Why comes temptation but for man to meet
And master and make crouch beneath his foot,
And so be pedestalled in triumph?
Robert Browning 1812–89: *The Ring and the Book* (1868–9)

9 I can resist everything except temptation.
Oscar Wilde 1854–1900: *Lady Windermere's Fan* (1892)

10 There are several good protections against temptations, but the surest is cowardice.
Mark Twain 1835–1910: *Following the Equator* (1897)

11 Temptations came to him, in middle age, tentatively and without insistence, like a neglected butcher-boy who asks for a Christmas box in February for no more hopeful reason than that he didn't get one in December.
Saki 1870–1916: *The Chronicles of Clovis* (1911)

12 A blonde to make a bishop kick a hole in a stained glass window.
Raymond Chandler 1888–1959: *Farewell, My Lovely* (1940)

13 He that but looketh on a plate of
ham and eggs to lust after it,
hath already committed breakfast
with it in his heart.
C. S. Lewis 1898–1963: letter 10
March 1954

14 This extraordinary pride in being
exempt from temptation that you
have not yet risen to the level of!
Eunuchs boasting of their
chastity!
C. S. Lewis 1898–1963: "Unreal
Estates" in Kingsley Amis and Robert
Conquest (eds.) *Spectrum IV* (1965)

15 I've looked on a lot of women
with lust. I've committed adultery
in my heart many times. This is
something that God recognizes I
will do — and I have done it —
and God forgives me for it.
Jimmy Carter 1924– : in *Playboy*
November 1976

The Theater
see also **Actors and Acting,
Shakespeare**

1 Tragedy is thus a representation
of an action that is worth serious
attention, complete in itself and of
some amplitude . . . by means of
pity and fear bringing about the
purgation of such emotions.
Aristotle 384–322 BC: *Poetics*

2 For what's a play without a
woman in it?
Thomas Kyd 1558–94: *The Spanish
Tragedy* (1592)

3 Can this cockpit hold
The vasty fields of France? or may
we cram
Within this wooden O the very
casques
That did affright the air at
Agincourt?
William Shakespeare 1564–1616:
Henry V (1599)

4 The play's the thing
Wherein I'll catch the conscience
of the king.
William Shakespeare 1564–1616:
Hamlet (1601)

5 Then to the well-trod stage anon,
If Jonson's learnèd sock be on,
Or sweetest Shakespeare fancy's
child,
Warble his native wood-notes
wild.
John Milton 1608–74: "L'Allegro"
(1645)

6 Ay, now the plot thickens very
much upon us.
**George Villiers, 2nd Duke of
Buckingham** 1628–87: *The Rehearsal*
(1672)

7 Damn them! They will not let my
play run, but they steal my
thunder!
*on hearing his new thunder effects
used at a performance of* Macbeth,
*following the withdrawal of one of
his own plays after only a short run*
John Dennis 1657–1734: William S.
Walsh *A Handy-Book of Literary
Curiosities* (1893)

8 There still remains, to mortify a
wit,
The many-headed monster of the
pit.
Alexander Pope 1688–1744:
Imitations of Horace

9 "Do you come to the play
without knowing what it is?" "O
yes, Sir, yes, very frequently; I
have no time to read play-bills;
one merely comes to meet one's
friends, and show that one's
alive."
Fanny Burney 1752–1840: *Evelina*
(1778)

10 It is better to have written a
damned play, than no play at all—
it snatches a man from obscurity.
Frederic Reynolds 1764–1841: *The
Dramatist* (1789)

11 The composition of a tragedy requires *testicles*.
on being asked why no woman had ever written "a tolerable tragedy"
Voltaire 1694–1778: letter from Byron to John Murray, 2 April 1817

12 The play-bill, which is said to have announced the tragedy of Hamlet, the character of the Prince of Denmark being left out.
commonly alluded to as "Hamlet without the Prince"
Sir Walter Scott 1771–1832: *The Talisman* (1825)

13 NINA: Your play's hard to act, there are no living people in it.
TREPLEV: Living people! We should show life neither as it is nor as it ought to be, but as we see it in our dreams.
Anton Chekhov 1860–1904: *The Seagull* (1896)

14 The theater, when all is said and done, is not life in miniature, but life enormously magnified, life hideously exaggerated.
H. L. Mencken 1880–1956: *Prejudices: First Series* (1919)

15 *Étonne-moi.* Astonish me.
to Jean Cocteau
Sergei Diaghilev 1872–1929: Wallace Fowlie (ed.) *Journals of Jean Cocteau* (1956)

16 The drama is make-believe. It does not deal with truth but with effect.
W. Somerset Maugham 1874–1965: *The Summing Up* (1938)

17 There's no business like show business.
Irving Berlin 1888–1989: title of song (1946)

18 We never closed.
of the Windmill Theatre, London, during World War II

Vivian van Damm *c.* 1889–1960: *Tonight and Every Night* (1952)

19 The theater is the primary evidence of a nation's culture.
James Thurber 1894–1961: *New York Times* (27 July 1952)

20 Some mystery should be left in the revelation of character in a play, just as a great deal of mystery is always left in the revelation of character in life, even in one's own character to himself.
Tennessee Williams 1911–83: stage directions, *Cat on a Hot Tin Roof* (1955)

21 Shaw is like a train. One just speaks the words and sits in one's place. But Shakespeare is like bathing in the sea—one swims where one wants.
Vivien Leigh 1913–67: letter from Harold Nicolson to Vita Sackville-West, 1 February 1956

22 It's a sound you can't get in the movies or television . . . the sound of a wonderful, deep silence that means you've hit them where they live.
Shelley Winters 1922– : *Theater Arts* (June 1956)

23 Don't clap too hard—it's a very old building.
John Osborne 1929–94: *The Entertainer* (1957)

24 There is nothing that one can say about acting, writing, producing or directing that cannot be revoked in the next breath. Nothing is immutable. The logic of one year is a folly of the next.
Moss Hart 1904–61: *Act One* (1959)

25 The unencumbered stage encourages the truth operative in everyone. The less seen, the more heard. The eye is the enemy of the ear in real drama.

Thornton Wilder 1897–1975: *New York Times* (6 November 1961)

26 Satire is what closes Saturday night.
George S. Kaufman 1889–1961: Scott Meredith *George S. Kaufman and his Friends* (1974)

27 Surely no other American institution is so bound around and tightened up by rules, strictures, adages, and superstitions as the Broadway theater.
James Thurber 1894–1961: *Collecting Himself* (1989)

28 The weasel under the cocktail cabinet.
on being asked what his plays were about
Harold Pinter 1930– : J. Russell Taylor *Anger and After* (1962)

29 I go to the theatre to be entertained, I want to be taken out of myself, I don't want to see lust and rape and incest and sodomy and so on, I can get all that at home.
Alan Bennett 1934– : Alan Bennett et al. *Beyond the Fringe* (1963) "Man of Principles"

30 I can do you blood and love without the rhetoric, and I can do you blood and rhetoric without the love, and I can do you all three concurrent or consecutive, but I can't do you love and rhetoric without the blood. Blood is compulsory—they're all blood, you see.
Tom Stoppard 1937– : *Rosencrantz and Guildenstern are Dead* (1967)

31 I've never much enjoyed going to plays . . . The unreality of painted people standing on a platform saying things they've said to each other for months is more than I can overlook.
John Updike 1932– : George

Plimpton (ed.) *Writers at Work* 4th Series (1977)

32 The most magical moment in the theater is a silence so complete that you can't even hear people breathe. It means that you've got them.
Hume Cronyn 1911– : *Time* (2 April 1990)

33 It's a play that after you've been there for a short while, you wonder how long this is going to take.
Garrison Keillor 1942– : *New Yorker* (2 January 1995)

Thinking
see also **Ideas, The Mind**

1 His thinking does not produce smoke after the flame, but light after smoke.
Horace 65–8 BC: *Ars Poetica*

2 Whatsoever things are true, whatsoever things are honest, whatsoever things are just, whatsoever things are pure, whatsoever things are lovely, whatsoever things are of good report; if there be any virtue and if there be any praise, think on these things.
Bible: Philippians

3 To change your mind and to follow him who sets you right is to be nonetheless the free agent that you were before.
Marcus Aurelius AD 121–80: *Meditations*

4 Yond' Cassius has a lean and hungry look;
He thinks too much: such men are dangerous.
William Shakespeare 1564–1616: *Julius Caesar* (1599)

5 *Cogito, ergo sum.*
I think, therefore I am.

René Descartes 1596–1650: *Le Discours de la méthode* (1637)

6 A man, doubtful of his dinner, or trembling at a creditor, is not much disposed to abstracted meditation, or remote enquiries.
Samuel Johnson 1709–84: *Lives of the English Poets* (1779–81) "Collins"

7 Two things fill the mind with ever new and increasing wonder and awe, the more often and the more seriously reflection concentrates upon them: the starry heaven above me and the moral law within me.
Immanuel Kant 1724–1804: *Critique of Practical Reason* (1788)

8 I never could find any man who could think for two minutes together.
Sydney Smith 1771–1845: *Sketches of Moral Philosophy* (1849)

9 Thinking is, or ought to be, a coolness and a calmness; and our poor hearts throb, and our poor brains beat too much for that.
Herman Melville 1819–91: *Moby Dick* (1851)

10 There is one disadvantage which the man of philosophical habits of mind suffers, as compared with the man of action. While he is taking an enlarged and rational view of the matter before him, he lets his chance slip through his fingers.
Oliver Wendell Holmes, Sr. 1809–94: *The Professor at the Breakfast-Table* (1860)

11 Stung by the splendour of a sudden thought.
Robert Browning 1812–89: "A Death in the Desert" (1864)

12 How often misused words generate misleading thoughts.
Herbert Spencer 1820–1903: *Principles of Ethics* (1879)

13 It is quite a three-pipe problem, and I beg that you won't speak to me for fifty minutes.
Arthur Conan Doyle 1859–1930: *The Adventures of Sherlock Holmes* (1892)

14 Sometimes I sits and thinks, and then again I just sits.
Punch: 1906

15 How can I tell what I think till I see what I say?
E. M. Forster 1879–1970: *Aspects of the Novel* (1927)

16 Pooh began to feel a little more comfortable, because when you are a Bear of Very Little Brain, and you Think of Things, you find sometimes that a Thing which seemed very Thingish inside you is quite different when it gets out into the open and has other people looking at it.
A. A. Milne 1882–1956: *The House at Pooh Corner* (1928)

17 A man of action forced into a state of thought is unhappy until he can get out of it.
John Galsworthy 1867–1933: *Maid in Waiting* (1931)

18 Heretics are the only bitter remedy against the entropy of human thought.
Yevgeny Zamyatin 1884–1937: "Literature, Revolution and Entropy" quoted in *The Dragon and other Stories* (1967) introduction

19 *Doublethink* means the power of holding two contradictory beliefs in one's mind simultaneously, and accepting both of them.
George Orwell 1903–50: *Nineteen Eighty-Four* (1949)

20 He can't think without his hat.
Samuel Beckett 1906–89: *Waiting for Godot* (1955)

21 It is a far, far better thing to have a firm anchor in nonsense than to put out on the troubled seas of thought.
John Kenneth Galbraith 1908– : *The Affluent Society* (1958)

22 What was once thought can never be unthought.
Friedrich Dürrenmatt 1921– : *The Physicists* (1962)

23 The real question is not whether machines think but whether men do.
B. F. Skinner 1904–90: *Contingencies of Reinforcement* (1969)

Thoroughness
see also **Determination and Perseverance**

1 Whatsoever thy hand findeth to do, do it with thy might.
Bible: Ecclesiastes

2 There must be a beginning of any great matter, but the continuing unto the end until it be thoroughly finished yields the true glory.
Francis Drake c. 1540–96: dispatch to Sir Francis Walsingham, 17 May 1587

3 The shortest way to do many things is to do only one thing at once.
Samuel Smiles 1812–1904: *Self-Help* (1859)

Thrift and Extravagance
see also **Debt and Borrowing, Poverty, Wealth**

1 Plenty has made me poor.
Ovid 43 BC–AD c. 17: *Metamorphoses*

2 Thrift, thrift, Horatio! the funeral baked meats
Did coldly furnish forth the marriage tables.

William Shakespeare 1564–1616: *Hamlet* (1601)

3 In squandering wealth was his peculiar art:
Nothing went unrewarded, but desert.
Beggared by fools, whom still he found too late:
He had his jest, and they had his estate.
John Dryden 1631–1700: *Absalom and Achitophel* (1681)

4 Up and down the City Road,
In and out the Eagle,
That's the way the money goes—
Pop goes the weasel!
W. R. Mandale: "Pop Goes the Weasel" (1853 song); also attributed to Charles Twiggs

5 Economy is going without something you do want in case you should, some day, want something you probably won't want.
Anthony Hope 1863–1933: *The Dolly Dialogues* (1894)

6 From the foregoing survey of conspicuous leisure and consumption, it appears that the utility of both alike for the purposes of reputability lies in the element of waste that is common to both. In the one case it is a waste of time and effort, in the other it is a waste of goods.
Thorstein Veblen 1857–1929: *Theory of the Leisure Class* (1899)

7 All decent people live beyond their incomes nowadays, and those who aren't respectable live beyond other peoples'.
Saki 1870–1916: *Chronicles of Clovis* (1911)

8 We could have saved sixpence. We have saved fivepence. (*Pause*) But at what cost?
Samuel Beckett 1906–89: *All That Fall* (1957)

Time
see also **Transience**

1 To every thing there is a season,
and a time to every purpose
under the heaven:
A time to be born, and a time to
die; a time to plant, and a time to
pluck up that which is planted;
A time to kill, and a time to heal;
a time to break down, and a time
to build up;
A time to weep, and a time to
laugh; a time to mourn, and a
time to dance.
Bible: Ecclesiastes

2 *Sed fugit interea, fugit inreparabile*
tempus.
But meanwhile it is flying,
irretrievable time is flying.
usually quoted as "tempus fugit
[time flies]"
Virgil 70–19 BC: *Georgics*

3 *Tempus edax rerum.*
Time the devourer of everything.
Ovid 43 BC–AD *c.* 17: *Metamorphoses*

4 Time is a violent torrent; no
sooner is a thing brought to sight
than it is swept by and another
takes its place.
Marcus Aurelius AD 121–80:
Meditations

5 Every instant of time is a pinprick
of eternity.
Marcus Aurelius AD 121–80:
Meditations

6 I am Time grown old to destroy
the world,
Embarked on the course of world
annihilation.
Bhagavad Gita 250 BC–AD 250: ch. 11

7 Time is . . . Time was . . . Time is
past.
Robert Greene *c.* 1560–92: *Friar*
Bacon and Friar Bungay (1594)

8 Now hast thou but one bare hour
to live,
And then thou must be damned
perpetually.
Stand still, you ever-moving
spheres of heaven,
That time may cease, and
midnight never come.
Christopher Marlowe 1564–93:
Doctor Faustus (1604)

9 I wasted time, and now doth time
waste me.
William Shakespeare 1564–1616:
Richard II (1595)

10 Time hath, my lord, a wallet at
his back,
Wherein he puts alms for
oblivion.
William Shakespeare 1564–1616:
Troilus and Cressida (1602)

11 To-morrow, and to-morrow, and
to-morrow,
Creeps in this petty pace from day
to day,
To the last syllable of recorded
time;
And all our yesterdays have
lighted fools
The way to dusty death.
William Shakespeare 1564–1616:
Macbeth (1606)

12 Even such is Time, which takes in
trust
Our youth, our joys, and all we
have,
And pays us but with age and
dust.
Walter Ralegh *c.* 1552–1618: written
the night before his death, and
found in his Bible in the Gate-house
at Westminster

13 Who can speak of eternity
without a solecism, or think
thereof without an ecstasy? Time
we may comprehend, 'tis but five
days elder than ourselves.
Thomas Browne 1605–82: *Religio*
Medici (1643)

14 There was never any thing by the
wit of man so well devised, or so
sure established, which in
continuance of time hath not
been corrupted.
The Book of Common Prayer 1662:
The Preface Concerning the Service
of the Church

15 But at my back I always hear
Time's wingèd chariot hurrying
near:
And yonder all before us lie
Deserts of vast eternity.
Andrew Marvell 1621–78: "To His
Coy Mistress" (1681)

16 Time, like an ever-rolling stream,
Bears all its sons away.
Isaac Watts 1674–1748: "O God, our
help in ages past" (1719 hymn)

17 I recommend to you to take care
of minutes: for hours will take
care of themselves.
Lord Chesterfield 1694–1773: *Letters
to his Son* (1774) 6 November 1747

18 Remember that time is money.
Benjamin Franklin 1706–90: *Advice
to a Young Tradesman* (1748)

19 Time makes more converts than
reason.
Thomas Paine 1737–1809: *Common
Sense* (1776)

20 O aching time! O moments big as
years!
John Keats 1795–1821: "Hyperion: A
Fragment" (1820)

21 Time is the great physician.
Benjamin Disraeli 1804–81: *Henrietta
Temple* (1837)

22 Men talk of killing time, while
time quietly kills them.
Dion Boucicault 1820–90: *London
Assurance* (1841)

23 As if you could kill time without
injuring eternity.

Henry David Thoreau 1817–62:
Walden (1854) "Economy"

24 Time is but the stream I go a-
fishing in.
Henry David Thoreau 1817–62:
Walden (1854)

25 He said, "What's time? Leave
Now for dogs and apes!
Man has Forever."
Robert Browning 1812–89: "A
Grammarian's Funeral" (1855)

26 Lost, yesterday, somewhere
between Sunrise and Sunset, two
golden hours, each set with sixty
diamond minutes. No reward is
offered, for they are gone forever.
Horace Mann 1796–1859: "Lost, Two
Golden Hours"

27 The woods decay, the woods
decay and fall,
The vapours weep their burthen
to the ground,
Man comes and tills the field and
lies beneath,
And after many a summer dies
the swan.
Alfred, Lord Tennyson 1809–92:
"Tithonus" (1860, revised 1864)

28 Time goes, you say? Ah no!
Alas, Time stays, *we* go.
Henry Austin Dobson 1840–1921:
"The Paradox of Time" (1877)

29 The years like great black oxen
tread the world,
And God the herdsman goads
them on behind,
And I am broken by their passing
feet.
W. B. Yeats 1865–1939: *The
Countess Cathleen* (1895)

30 The Principle of Unripe Time is
that people should not do at the
present moment what they think
right at that moment, because
the moment at which they think
it right has not yet arrived . . .
Time, by the way, is like the

medlar; it has a trick of going
rotten before it is ripe.
Francis M. Cornford 1874–1943:
Microcosmographia Academica
(1908)

31 Time, you old gipsy man,
Will you not stay,
Put up your caravan
Just for one day?
Ralph Hodgson 1871–1962: "Time,
You Old Gipsy Man" (1917)

32 Ah! the clock is always slow;
It is later than you think.
Robert W. Service 1874–1958: "It Is
Later Than You Think" (1921)

33 Half our life is spent trying to find
something to do with the time we
have rushed through life trying to
save.
Will Rogers 1879–1935: letter in *New
York Times* 29 April 1930

34 Three o'clock is always too late
or too early for anything you
want to do.
Jean-Paul Sartre 1905–80: *La Nausée*
(1938)

35 Time has too much credit . . . It is
not a great healer. It is an
indifferent and perfunctory one.
Sometimes it does not heal at all.
And sometimes when it seems to,
no healing has been necessary.
Ivy Compton-Burnett 1884–1969:
Darkness and Day (1951)

36 VLADIMIR: That passed the time.
ESTRAGON: It would have passed
in any case.
VLADIMIR: Yes, but not so rapidly.
Samuel Beckett 1906–89: *Waiting for
Godot* (1955)

37 The distinction between past,
present and future is only an
illusion, however persistent.
Albert Einstein 1879–1955: letter to
Michelangelo Besso, 21 March 1955

Title
see **Rank and Title**

Tolerance
see **Prejudice and Tolerance**

The Town
see **The Country and the Town**

Towns and Cities
see also **London**

1 He could boast that he inherited
it brick and left it marble.
referring to the city of Rome
Augustus 63 BC–AD 14: Suetonius
Lives of the Caesars "Divus
Augustus"

2 Once did she hold the gorgeous
East in fee,
And was the safeguard of the
West.
William Wordsworth 1770–1850: "On
the Extinction of the Venetian
Republic" (1807)

3 Sun-girt city, thou hast been
Ocean's child, and then his queen;
Now is come a darker day,
And thou soon must be his prey.
of Venice
Percy Bysshe Shelley 1792–1822:
"Lines written amongst the
Euganean Hills" (1818)

4 While stands the Coliseum, Rome
shall stand;
When falls the Coliseum, Rome
shall fall;
And when Rome falls—the
World.
Lord Byron 1788–1824: *Childe
Harold's Pilgrimage* (1812–18)

5 Let there be light! said Liberty,
And like sunrise from the sea,
Athens arose!
Percy Bysshe Shelley 1792–1822:
Hellas (1822)

6 Moscow: those syllables can start
A tumult in the Russian heart.
Alexander Pushkin 1799–1837:
Eugene Onegin (1833)

7 It is from the midst of this putrid
sewer that the greatest river of
human industry springs up and
carries fertility to the whole
world. From this foul drain pure
gold flows forth.
of Manchester, England
Alexis de Tocqueville 1805–59:
*Voyage en Angleterre et en Irlande
de 1835* 2 July 1835

8 Match me such marvel, save in
Eastern clime,—
A rose-red city—half as old as
Time!
John William Burgon 1813–88: *Petra*
(1845)

9 Oxford is on the whole more
attractive than Cambridge to the
ordinary visitor; and the traveller
is therefore recommended to visit
Cambridge first, or to omit it
altogether if he cannot visit both.
Karl Baedeker 1801–59: *Great Britain*
(1887) Route 30 "From London to
Oxford"

10 Petersburg, the most abstract and
premeditated city on earth.
Fyodor Dostoevsky 1821–81: *Notes
from Underground* (1864)

11 Beautiful city! so venerable, so
lovely, so unravaged by the fierce
intellectual life of our century, so
serene! . . . whispering from her
towers the last enchantments of
the Middle Age . . . Home of lost
causes, and forsaken beliefs, and
unpopular names, and impossible
loyalties!
of Oxford
Matthew Arnold 1822–88: *Essays in
Criticism* First Series (1865)

12 Towery city and branchy between
towers;
Cuckoo-echoing, bell-swarmèd,
lark-charmèd, rook-racked,
river-rounded.
Gerard Manley Hopkins 1844–89:
"Duns Scotus's Oxford" (written
1879)

13 A Boston man is the east wind
made flesh.
Thomas Gold Appleton 1812–84:
attributed

14 And this is good old Boston,
The home of the bean and the
cod,
Where the Lowells talk to the
Cabots
And the Cabots talk only to God.
John Collins Bossidy 1860–1928:
verse spoken at Holy Cross College
alumni dinner in Boston,
Massachusetts, 1910

15 STREETS FLOODED. PLEASE ADVISE.
*telegraph message on arriving in
Venice*
Robert Benchley 1889–1945: R. E.
Drennan (ed.) *Wits End* (1973)

16 Last week, I went to Philadelphia,
but it was closed.
W. C. Fields 1880–1946: Richard J.
Anobile *Godfrey Daniels* (1975)

17 A big hard-boiled city with no
more personality than a paper
cup.
of Los Angeles
Raymond Chandler 1888–1959: *The
Little Sister* (1949)

18 Hollywood is a place where
people from Iowa mistake each
other for stars.
Fred Allen 1894–1956: Maurice
Zolotow *No People like Show People*
(1951)

19 This is Red Hook, not Sicily . . .
This is the gullet of New York
swallowing the tonnage of the
world.

Arthur Miller 1915– : *A View from the Bridge* (1955)

20 Paris is a movable feast.
Ernest Hemingway 1899–1961: *A Movable Feast* (1964) epigraph

21 Venice is like eating an entire box of chocolate liqueurs in one go.
Truman Capote 1924–84: in *Observer* (UK) 26 November 1961

22 Washington is a city of southern efficiency and northern charm.
John F. Kennedy 1917–63: Arthur M. Schlesinger, Jr. *A Thousand Days* (1965)

23 Chicago is the great American city. New York is one of the capitals of the world and Los Angeles is a constellation of plastic, San Francisco is a lady, Boston has become Urban Renewal, Philadelphia and Baltimore and Washington wink like dull diamonds in the smog of Eastern Megalopolis, and New Orleans is unremarkable past the French Quarter. Detroit is a one-trade town, Pittsburgh has lost its golden triangle, St. Louis has become the golden arch of the corporation, and nights in Kansas City close early. The oil depletion allowance makes Houston and Dallas naught but checkerboards for this sort of game. But Chicago is a great American city. Perhaps it is the last of the great American cities.
Norman Mailer 1923– : *Miami and the Siege of Chicago* (1968)

24 New York makes one think of the collapse of civilization, about Sodom and Gomorrah, the end of the world. The end wouldn't come as a surprise here. Many people already bank on it.
Saul Bellow 1915– : *Mr. Sammler's Planet* (1970)

25 By God what a site! By man what a mess!
of Sydney

Clough Williams-Ellis 1883–1978: *Architect Errant* (1971)

Transience
see also **Opportunity, Time**

1 Like that of leaves is a generation of men.
Homer: *The Iliad*

2 For a thousand years in thy sight are but as yesterday: seeing that is past as a watch in the night.
Bible: Psalm 90

3 All flesh is as grass, and all the glory of man as the flower of grass. The grass withereth, and the flower thereof falleth away.
Bible: I Peter

4 My sweetest Lesbia let us live and love,
And though the sager sort our deeds reprove,
Let us not weigh them: Heav'n's great lamps do dive
Into their west, and straight again revive,
But soon as once set is our little light,
Then must we sleep one ever-during night.
Thomas Campion 1567–1620: *A Book of Airs* (1601); translation of Catullus *Carmina*; see **Love 2**

5 Gather ye rosebuds while ye may,
Old Time is still a-flying:
And this same flower that smiles to-day,
To-morrow will be dying.
Robert Herrick 1591–1674: "To the Virgins, to Make Much of Time" (1648)

6 But transient is the smile of fate:
A little rule, a little sway,
A sunbeam in a winter's day,
Is all the proud and mighty have
Between the cradle and the grave.
John Dyer 1700–58: *Grongar Hill* (1726)

7 Ah! Posthumus, the years, the
    years
Glide swiftly on, nor can our
    tears
Or piety the wrinkled age
    forefend,
Or for one hour retard th'
    inevitable end.
Christopher Smart 1722–71:
translation of Horace *Odes*

8 The rainbow comes and goes,
And lovely is the rose.
William Wordsworth 1770–1850:
"Ode. Intimations of Immortality"
(1807)

9 Though nothing can bring back
    the hour
Of splendour in the grass, of glory
    in the flower;
We will grieve not, rather find
Strength in what remains behind
    . . .
In the faith that looks through
    death,
In years that bring the
    philosophic mind.
William Wordsworth 1770–1850:
"Ode. Intimations of Immortality"
(1807)

10 Oh! ever thus, from childhood's
    hour,
I've seen my fondest hopes decay;
I never loved a tree or flower,
But 'twas the first to fade away.
I never nursed a dear gazelle,
To glad me with its soft black eye,
But when it came to know me
    well,
And love me, it was sure to die!
Thomas Moore 1779–1852: *Lalla
Rookh* (1817) "The Fire-Worshippers";
cf. **Disillusion 10, Value 14**

11 He who binds to himself a joy
Doth the winged life destroy
But he who kisses the joy as it
    flies
Lives in Eternity's sunrise.
William Blake 1757–1827: *MS Note-
Book*

12 They are not long, the days of
    wine and roses:
Out of a misty dream
Our path emerges for a while,
    then closes
Within a dream.
Ernest Dowson 1867–1900: "Vitae
Summa Brevis" (1896)

13 A rainbow and a cuckoo's song
May never come together again;
May never come
This side the tomb.
W. H. Davies 1871–1940: "A Great
Time" (1914)

14 Look thy last on all things lovely,
Every hour.
Walter de la Mare 1873–1956: "Fare
Well" (1918)

15 He will be just like the scent on a
pocket handkerchief.
*on being asked what place Arthur
Balfour would have in history*
David Lloyd George 1863–1945:
Thomas Jones diary 9 June 1922

16 Treaties, you see, are like girls
and roses: they last while they
last.
Charles de Gaulle 1890–1970: speech
at Elysée Palace, 2 July 1963

Translation

1 Such is our pride, our folly, or
    our fate,
That few, but such as cannot
    write, translate.
John Denham 1615–69: "To Richard
Fanshaw" (1648)

2 He is translation's thief that
    addeth more,
As much as he that taketh from
    the store
Of the first author.
Andrew Marvell 1621–78: "To His
Worthy Friend Dr. Witty" (1651)

3 Some hold translations not unlike
to be
The wrong side of a Turkey
tapestry.
James Howell c. 1593–1666: *Familiar
Letters* (1645–55)

4 It is a pretty poem, Mr. Pope, but
you must not call it Homer.
*when pressed by Pope to comment
on "My Homer," i.e. his translation
of Homer's* Iliad
Richard Bentley 1662–1742: John
Hawkins (ed.) *The Works of Samuel
Johnson* (1787)

5 The vanity of translation; it were
as wise to cast a violet into a
crucible that you might discover
the formal principle of its colour
and odour, as seek to transfuse
from one language to another the
creations of a poet. The plant
must spring again from its seed,
or it will bear no flower.
Percy Bysshe Shelley 1792–1822: *A
Defence of Poetry* (written 1821)

6 Never forget, gentlemen, never
forget that this is *not* the Bible.
This, gentlemen, is only a
translation of the Bible.
*to a meeting of his diocesan clergy,
as he held up a copy of the
"Authorized Version"*
Richard Whately 1787–1863: H. Solly
These Eighty Years (1893)

7 A translation is no translation
unless it will give you the music
of a poem along with the words
of it.
John Millington Synge 1871–1909:
The Aran Islands (1907)

8 The original Greek is of great use
in elucidating Browning's
translation of the *Agamemnon*.
Robert Yelverton Tyrrell 1844–1914:
Ulick O'Connor *Oliver St. John
Gogarty* (1964); cf. **11** below

9 Translations (like wives) are
seldom strictly faithful if they are
in the least attractive.
Roy Campbell 1901–57: in *Poetry
Review* June–July 1949

10 It has never occurred to Anderson
that one foreign language can be
translated into another. He
assumes that every strange
tongue exists only by virtue of its
not being English.
Tom Stoppard 1937– : *Where Are
They Now?* (1973)

11 The original is unfaithful to the
translation.
on Henley's translation of Beckford's
Vathek
Jorge Luis Borges 1899–1986: *Sobre
el "Vathek" de William Beckford*; in
Obras Completas (1974); cf. **8** above

Transportation

1 The driving is like the driving of
Jehu, the son of Nimshi; for he
driveth furiously.
Bible: II Kings

2 There was a rocky valley between
Buxton and Bakewell . . . You
enterprised a railroad . . . you
blasted its rocks away . . . And
now, every fool in Buxton can be
at Bakewell in half-an-hour, and
every fool in Bakewell at Buxton.
John Ruskin 1819–1900: *Praeterita*
vol. 3 (1889)

3 Quinquireme of Nineveh from
distant Ophir
Rowing home to haven in sunny
Palestine,
With a cargo of ivory,
And apes and peacocks,
Sandalwood, cedarwood, and
sweet white wine.
John Masefield 1878–1967:
"Cargoes" (1903)

4 Dirty British coaster with a salt-
caked smoke stack,
Butting through the Channel in
the mad March days,
With a cargo of Tyne coal,

Road-rails, pig lead,
Firewood, ironware, and cheap
tin trays.
John Masefield 1878–1967:
"Cargoes" (1903)

5 There is *nothing*—absolutely
nothing—half so much worth
doing as simply messing about in
boats.
Kenneth Grahame 1859–1932: *The
Wind in the Willows* (1908)

6 The poetry of motion! The *real*
way to travel! The *only* way to
travel! Here today—in next week
tomorrow! Villages skipped, towns
and cities jumped—always
somebody else's horizon! O bliss!
O poop-poop! O my! O my!
on the car
Kenneth Grahame 1859–1932: *The
Wind in the Willows* (1908)

7 What good is speed if the brain
has oozed out on the way?
Karl Kraus 1874–1936: in *Die Fackel*
September 1909 "The Discovery of
the North Pole"

8 Railway termini. They are our
gates to the glorious and the
unknown. Through them we pass
out into adventure and sunshine,
to them, alas! we return.
E. M. Forster 1879–1970: *Howards
End* (1910)

9 Sir, Saturday morning, although
recurring at regular and well-
foreseen intervals, always seems
to take this railway by surprise.
W. S. Gilbert 1836–1911: letter to the
station-master at Baker Street, on
the Metropolitan line; John Julius
Norwich *Christmas Crackers* (1980)

10 Walk! Not bloody likely. I am
going in a taxi.
George Bernard Shaw 1856–1950:
Pygmalion (1916)

11 To George F. Babbitt, as to most
prosperous citizens of Zenith, his

motor car was poetry and
tragedy, love and heroism. The
office was his pirate ship but the
car his perilous excursion ashore.
Sinclair Lewis 1885–1951: *Babbitt*
(1922)

12 [There are] only two classes of
pedestrians in these days of
reckless motor traffic—the quick,
and the dead.
Lord Dewar 1864–1930: George
Robey *Looking Back on Life* (1933)

13 Home James, and don't spare the
horses.
Fred Hillebrand 1893– : title of
song (1934)

14 It looks like a poached egg—we
can't make that.
*on seeing the Morris Minor
prototype in 1945*
Lord Nuffield 1877–1963: attributed

15 I think that cars today are almost
the exact equivalent of the great
Gothic cathedrals: I mean the
supreme creation of an era,
conceived with passion by
unknown artists, and consumed
in image if not in usage by a
whole population which
appropriates them as a purely
magical object.
Roland Barthes 1915–80:
Mythologies (1957) "La nouvelle
Citroën"

16 The automobile changed our
dress, manners, social customs,
vacation habits, the shape of our
cities, consumer purchasing
patterns, common tastes and
positions in intercourse.
John Keats 1920– : *The Insolent
Chariots* (1958)

17 There is no class of person more
moved by hatred than the
motorist and the policeman is a
convenient receptacle for his
feeling.
C. W. Hewitt: speech to the Lawyers'

Club of the London School of
Economics, 22 October 1959

18 The car has become an article of
dress without which we feel
uncertain, unclad and incomplete
in the urban compound.
Marshall McLuhan 1911–80:
Understanding Media (1964)

19 We have now to plan no longer
for soft little animals pottering
about on their own two legs, but
for hard steel canisters hurtling
about with these same little
animals inside them.
Hugh Casson 1910–   : Clough
Williams-Ellis *Around the World in
90 Years* (1978)

20 There are only two emotions in a
plane: boredom and terror.
Orson Welles 1915–85: interview to
celebrate his 70th birthday, in *The
Times* (UK) 6 May 1985

Travel and Exploration
see also **Countries and Peoples**

1 And the Lord said unto Satan,
Whence comest thou? Then Satan
answered the Lord, and said,
From going to and fro in the
earth, and from walking up and
down in it.
Bible: Job

2 They change their clime, not their
frame of mind, who rush across
the sea.
Horace 65–8 BC: *Epistles*

3 Now the boundary of Britain is
revealed, and everything
unknown is held to be glorious.
*reporting the speech of a British
leader, Calgacus*
Tacitus AD *c.* 56–after 117: *Agricola*

4 Ay, now am I in Arden; the more
fool I. When I was at home I was
in a better place; but travellers
must be content.

William Shakespeare 1564–1616: *As
You Like It* (1599)

5 They are ill discoverers that think
there is no land, when they can
see nothing but sea.
Francis Bacon 1561–1626: *The
Advancement of Learning* (1605)

6 He disdains all things above his
reach, and preferreth all countries
before his own.
Thomas Overbury 1581–1613:
Miscellaneous Works (1632) "An
Affected Traveller"

7 Travel, in the younger sort, is a
part of education; in the elder, a
part of experience. He that
travelleth into a country before
he hath some entrance into the
language, goeth to school, and
not to travel.
Francis Bacon 1561–1626: *Essays*
(1625) "Of Travel"

8 See one promontory (said
Socrates of old), one mountain,
one sea, one river, and see all.
Robert Burton 1577–1640: *The
Anatomy of Melancholy* (1621–51)

9 So geographers, in Afric-maps,
With savage-pictures fill their
    gaps;
And o'er unhabitable downs
Place elephants for want of
    towns.
Jonathan Swift 1667–1745: "On
Poetry" (1733)

10 I always love to begin a journey
on Sundays, because I shall have
the prayers of the church, to
preserve all that travel by land, or
by water.
Jonathan Swift 1667–1745: *Polite
Conversation* (1738)

11 So it is in travelling; a man must
carry knowledge with him, if he
would bring home knowledge.
Samuel Johnson 1709–84: James

Boswell *Life of Samuel Johnson*
(1791) 17 April 1778

12 Worth seeing, yes; but not worth
going to see.
on the Giant's Causeway
Samuel Johnson 1709–84: James
Boswell *Life of Samuel Johnson*
(1791) 12 October 1779

13 Travelling is the ruin of all
happiness! There's no looking at a
building here after seeing Italy.
Fanny Burney 1752–1840: *Cecilia*
(1782)

14 O the flummery of a birth place!
Cant! Cant! Cant! It is enough to
give a spirit the guts-ache.
on visiting Burns's birthplace
John Keats 1795–1821: letter to John
Hamilton Reynolds, 11 July 1818

15 I am become a name;
For always roaming with a
hungry heart
Alfred, Lord Tennyson 1809–92:
"Ulysses" (1842)

16 Go West, young man, go West!
John L. B. Soule 1815–91: in *Terre
Haute* [Indiana] *Express* (1851)

17 It is not worthwhile to go around
the world to count the cats in
Zanzibar.
Henry David Thoreau 1817–62:
Walden (1854) "Conclusion"

18 It was a melancholy day for
human nature when that stupid
Lord Anson, after beating about
for three years, found himself
again at Greenwich. The
circumnavigation of our globe
was accomplished, but the
illimitable was annihilated and a
fatal blow [dealt] to all
imagination.
Benjamin Disraeli 1804–81: written
1860, in *Reminiscences* (ed. H. and
M. Swartz, 1975)

19 "Abroad," that large home of
ruined reputations.
George Eliot 1819–80: *Felix Holt*
(1866)

20 Of all noxious animals, too, the
most noxious is a tourist. And of
all tourists the most vulgar, ill-
bred, offensive and loathsome is
the British tourist.
Francis Kilvert 1840–79: diary 5 April
1870

21 The best thing about traveling is
going home.
Charles Dudley Warner 1829–1900:
The Whims of Travel (12 September
1875)

22 For my part, I travel not to go
anywhere, but to go. I travel for
travel's sake. The great affair is to
move.
Robert Louis Stevenson 1850–94:
Travels with a Donkey (1879)

23 To travel hopefully is a better
thing than to arrive, and the true
success is to labor.
Robert Louis Stevenson 1850–94:
Virginibus Puerisque (1881)

24 When you set out for Ithaka
ask that your way be long.
Constantine Cavafy 1863–1933:
"Ithaka" (1911)

25 In these days of rapid and
convenient travel . . . to come
from Leighton Buzzard does not
necessarily denote any great
strength of character. It might
only mean mere restlessness.
Saki 1870–1916: *The Chronicles of
Clovis* (1911)

26 Great God! this is an awful place.
of the South Pole
Robert Falcon Scott 1868–1912: diary
17 January 1912

27 A man travels the world in
search of what he needs and
returns home to find it.

George Moore 1852–1933: *The Brook
Kerith* (1916)

28 How 'ya gonna keep 'em down
on the farm (after they've seen
Paree)?
Sam M. Lewis 1885–1959 and **Joe
Young** 1889–1939: title of song
(1919)

29 I like my "abroad" to be Catholic
and sensual.
Henry ("Chips") Channon 1897–1958:
diary 18 January 1924

30 In America there are two classes
of travel—first class, and with
children.
Robert Benchley 1889–1945: *Pluck
and Luck* (1925)

31 As the traveler who has once
been from home is wiser than he
who has never left his own
doorstep, so a knowledge of one
other culture should sharpen our
ability to scrutinize more steadily,
to appreciate more lovingly, our
own.
Margaret Mead 1901–78: *Coming of
Age in Samoa* (1928)

32 São Paulo is like Reading, only
much farther away.
Peter Fleming 1907–71: *Brazilian
Adventure* (1933)

33 Frogs . . . are slightly better than
Huns or Wops, but abroad is
unutterably bloody and foreigners
are fiends.
Nancy Mitford 1904–73: *The Pursuit
of Love* (1945)

34 That life-quickening atmosphere
of a big railway station where
everything is something trembling
on the brink of something else.
Vladimir Nabokov 1899–1977: *Spring
in Fialta and other stories* (1956)
"Spring in Fialta"

35 Thanks to the interstate highway
system, it is now possible to
travel from coast to coast without
seeing anything.
Charles Kuralt 1934–97: *On the
Road* (1980)

36 In the middle ages people were
tourists because of their religion,
whereas now they are tourists
because tourism is their religion.
Robert Runcie 1921– : speech in
London, 6 December 1988

37 The Devil himself had probably re-
designed Hell in the light of
information he had gained from
observing airport layouts.
Anthony Price 1928– : *The Memory
Trap* (1989)

Treachery
see **Trust and Treachery**

Trees

1 Something sweet is the whisper of
the pine, O goatherd, that makes
her music by yonder springs.
Theocritus *c.* 300–260 BC: *Idylls*

2 Generations pass while some trees
stand, and old families last not
three oaks.
Thomas Browne 1605–82:
Hydriotaphia (Urn Burial, 1658)

3 He that plants trees loves others
beside himself.
Thomas Fuller 1654–1734:
Gnomologia (1732)

4 The poplars are felled, farewell to
the shade
And the whispering sound of the
cool colonnade.
William Cowper 1731–1800: "The
Poplar-Field" (written 1784)

5 O leave this barren spot to me!
Spare, woodman, spare the
beechen tree.
Thomas Campbell 1777–1844: "The
Beech-Tree's Petition" (1800)

6 Woodman, spare that tree!
Touch not a single bough!
In youth it sheltered me,
And I'll protect it now.
George Pope Morris 1802–64:
"Woodman, Spare That Tree" (1830)

7 Willows whiten, aspens quiver,
Little breezes dusk and shiver.
Alfred, Lord Tennyson 1809–92:
"The Lady of Shalott" (1832, revised
1842)

8 Laburnums, dropping-wells of fire.
Alfred, Lord Tennyson 1809–92: *In
Memoriam A. H. H.* (1850)

9 And since to look at things in
bloom
Fifty springs are little room,
About the woodlands I will go
To see the cherry hung with
snow.
A. E. Housman 1859–1936: *A
Shropshire Lad* (1896)

10 Of all the trees that grow so fair,
Old England to adorn,
Greater are none beneath the
Sun,
Than Oak, and Ash, and Thorn.
Rudyard Kipling 1865–1936: *Puck of
Pook's Hill* (1906) "A Tree Song"

11 For pines are gossip pines the
wide world through
And full of runic tales to sigh or
sing.
James Elroy Flecker 1884–1915:
Golden Journey to Samarkand (1913)
"Brumana"

12 I like trees because they seem
more resigned to the way they
have to live than other things do.
Willa Cather 1873–1947: *O Pioneers!*
(1913)

Trust and Treachery

1 O put not your trust in princes,
nor in any child of man: for there
is no help in them.
Bible: Psalm 146

2 *Equo ne credite, Teucri.
Quidquid id est, timeo Danaos et
dona ferentes.*
Do not trust the horse, Trojans.
Whatever it is, I fear the Greeks
even when they bring gifts.
Virgil 70–19 BC: *Aeneid*

3 *Et tu, Brute?*
You too, Brutus?
Julius Caesar 100–44 BC: traditional
rendering of Suetonius *Lives of the
Caesars* "Divus Julius"

4 This night, before the cock crow,
thou shalt deny me thrice.
Bible: St. Matthew

5 *Quis custodiet ipsos custodes?*
Who is to guard the guards
themselves?
Juvenal AD *c.* 60–*c.* 130: *Satires*

6 The smylere with the knyf under
the cloke.
Geoffrey Chaucer *c.* 1343–1400: *The
Canterbury Tales* "The Knight's Tale"

7 I know what it is to be a subject,
what to be a Sovereign, what to
have good neighbours, and
sometimes meet evil-willers.
*the traditional version concludes:
"and in trust I have found treason"*
Elizabeth I 1533–1603: speech to a
Parliamentary deputation at
Richmond, 12 November 1586; John
Neale *Elizabeth I and her
Parliaments 1584–1601* (1957), from
a report "which the Queen herself
heavily amended in her own hand"

8 Treason doth never prosper,
what's the reason?
For if it prosper, none dare call it
treason.
John Harington 1561–1612: *Epigrams*
(1618)

9 Suspicions amongst thoughts are
like bats amongst birds, they ever
fly by twilight.
Francis Bacon 1561–1626: *Essays*
(1625) "Of Suspicion"

10 There is nothing makes a man
suspect much, more than to
know little.
Francis Bacon 1561–1626: *Essays*
(1625) "Of Suspicion"

11 Caesar had his Brutus—Charles
the First, his Cromwell—and
George the Third—("Treason,"
cried the Speaker) . . . *may profit
by their example.* If *this* be treason,
make the most of it.
Patrick Henry 1736–99: speech in the
Virginia assembly, May 1765

12 The first vows sworn by two
creatures of flesh and blood were
made at the foot of a rock that
was crumbling to dust; they
called as witness to their
constancy a heaven which never
stays the same for one moment;
everything within them and
around them was changing, and
they thought their hearts were
exempt from vicissitudes.
Children!
Denis Diderot 1713–84: *Oeuvres
romanesques* (1981)

13 There is no infidelity when there
has been no love.
Honoré de Balzac 1799–1850: letter
to Mme. Hanska, August 1833; in
The Penguin Book of Infidelities
(1994)

14 *to the Emperor of Russia, who had
spoken bitterly of those who had
betrayed the cause of Europe:*
That, Sire, is a question of dates.
*often quoted as, "treason is a
matter of dates"*
Charles-Maurice de Talleyrand 1754–
1838: Duff Cooper *Talleyrand* (1932)

15 Just for a handful of silver he left
us,
Just for a riband to stick in his
coat.
*of Wordsworth's apparent betrayal
of his radical principles by accepting
the position of poet laureate*

Robert Browning 1812–89: "The Lost
Leader" (1845)

16 And trust me not at all or all in
all.
Alfred, Lord Tennyson 1809–92:
Idylls of the King "Merlin and
Vivien" (1859)

17 A promise made is a debt unpaid,
and the trail has its own stern
code.
Robert W. Service 1874–1958: "The
Cremation of Sam McGee" (1907)

18 To trust people is a luxury in
which only the wealthy can
indulge; the poor cannot afford it.
E. M. Forster 1879–1970: *Howards
End* (1910)

19 The thing on the blind side of the
heart,
On the wrong side of the door,
The green plant groweth,
menacing
Almighty lovers in the Spring;
There is always a forgotten thing,
And love is not secure.
G. K. Chesterton 1874–1936: *The
Ballad of the White Horse* (1911)

20 Anyone can rat, but it takes a
certain amount of ingenuity to re-
rat.
*on rejoining the Conservatives
twenty years after leaving them for
the Liberals, c. 1924*
Winston Churchill 1874–1965: Kay
Halle *Irrepressible Churchill* (1966)

21 The night of the long knives.
Adolf Hitler 1889–1945: phrase given
to the massacre of Ernst Roehm and
his associates by Hitler on 29–30
June 1934, taken from an early Nazi
marching song; subsequently
associated with Harold Macmillan's
Cabinet dismissals of 13 July 1962

22 He trusted neither of them as far
as he could spit, and he was a
poor spitter, lacking both distance
and control.

P. G. Wodehouse 1881–1975: *Money in the Bank* (1946)

23 We have to distrust each other. It's our only defense against betrayal.
Tennessee Williams 1911–83: *Camino Real* (1953)

24 Greater love hath no man than this, that he lay down his friends for his life.
on Harold Macmillan sacking seven of his Cabinet on 13 July 1962
Jeremy Thorpe 1929– : D. E. Butler and Anthony King *The General Election of 1964* (1965); see **Self-Sacrifice 1**

25 To betray, you must first belong.
Kim Philby 1912–88: in *Sunday Times* (UK) 17 December 1967

26 Judas was paid! I am sacrificing my whole political life.
response to a heckler's call of "Judas," having advised Conservatives to vote Labour at the coming general election
Enoch Powell 1912– : speech at Bull Ring, Birmingham, 23 February 1974

27 He who wields the knife never wears the crown.
Michael Heseltine 1933– : in *New Society* 14 February 1986

Truth
see also **Honesty, Lies and Lying**

1 Great is Truth, and mighty above all things.
Bible: I Esdras

2 But, my dearest Agathon, it is truth which you cannot contradict; you can without any difficulty contradict Socrates.
Socrates 469–399 BC: Plato *Symposium*

3 Plato is dear to me, but dearer still is truth.
Aristotle 384–322 BC: attributed

4 And ye shall know the truth, and the truth shall make you free.
Bible: St. John

5 Truth will come to light; murder cannot be hid long.
William Shakespeare 1564–1616: *The Merchant of Venice* (1596–8)

6 What is truth? said jesting Pilate; and would not stay for an answer.
Francis Bacon 1561–1626: *Essays* (1625) "Of Truth"

7 Who says that fictions only and false hair
Become a verse? Is there in truth no beauty?
Is all good structure in a winding stair?
George Herbert 1593–1633: "Jordan (1)" (1633)

8 Many from . . . an inconsiderate zeal unto truth, have too rashly charged the troops of error, and remain as trophies unto the enemies of truth.
Thomas Browne 1605–82: *Religio Medici* (1643)

9 Though all the winds of doctrine were let loose to play upon the earth, so Truth be in the field, we do injuriously by licensing and prohibiting to misdoubt her strength. Let her and Falsehood grapple; who ever knew Truth put to the worse, in a free and open encounter?
John Milton 1608–74: *Areopagitica* (1644)

10 True and False are attributes of speech, not of things. And where speech is not, there is neither Truth nor Falsehood.
Thomas Hobbes 1588–1679: *Leviathan* (1651)

11 It is one thing to show a man that he is in error, and another to put him in possession of truth.
John Locke 1632–1704: *An Essay concerning Human Understanding* (1690)

12 I design plain truth for plain people.
John Wesley 1703–91: *Sermons on Several Occasions* (1746)

13 They make truth serve as a stalking-horse to error.
Henry St. John, Lord Bolingbroke 1678–1751: *Letters on the Study and Use of History* (1752)

14 It is commonly said, and more particularly by Lord Shaftesbury, that ridicule is the best test of truth.
Lord Chesterfield 1694–1773: *Letters to his Son* (1774) 6 February 1752

15 In lapidary inscriptions a man is not upon oath.
Samuel Johnson 1709–84: James Boswell *Life of Samuel Johnson* (1791) 1775

16 If God were to hold out enclosed in His right hand all Truth, and in His left hand just the active search for Truth, though with the condition that I should always err therein, and He should say to me: Choose! I should humbly take His left hand and say: Father! Give me this one; absolute Truth belongs to Thee alone.
G. E. Lessing 1729–81: *Eine Duplik* (1778)

17 A truth that's told with bad intent
Beats all the lies you can invent.
William Blake 1757–1827: "Auguries of Innocence" (*c.* 1803)

18 I am certain of nothing but the holiness of the heart's affections and the truth of imagination— what the imagination seizes as

beauty must be truth—whether it existed before or not.
John Keats 1795–1821: letter to Benjamin Bailey, 22 November 1817; cf. **Beauty 14**

19 'Tis strange—but true; for truth is always strange;
Stranger than fiction.
Lord Byron 1788–1824: *Don Juan* (1819–24)

20 Truth, like a torch, the more it's shook it shines.
William Hamilton 1788–1856: *Discussions on Philosophy* (1852)

21 Rather than love, than money, than fame, give me truth.
Henry David Thoreau 1817–62: *Walden* (1854)

22 Truth is generally the best vindication against slander.
Abraham Lincoln 1809–65: *Letter to Secretary Stanton* (14 July 1864)

23 What I tell you three times is true.
Lewis Carroll 1832–98: *The Hunting of the Snark* (1876)

24 It is the customary fate of new truths to begin as heresies and to end as superstitions.
T. H. Huxley 1825–95: *Science and Culture and Other Essays* (1881) "The Coming of Age of the Origin of Species"

25 The truth is rarely pure, and never simple.
Oscar Wilde 1854–1900: *The Importance of Being Earnest* (1895)

26 Truth is the most valuable thing we have. Let us economize it.
Mark Twain 1835–1910: *Following the Equator* (1897); cf. **36** below

27 He who does not bellow the truth when he knows the truth makes himself the accomplice of liars and forgers.

Charles Péguy 1873–1914: *Basic Verities* (1943) "Lettre du Provincial" 21 December 1899

28 A platitude is simply a truth repeated until people get tired of hearing it.
Stanley Baldwin 1867–1947: speech, House of Commons, 29 May 1924

29 Truth is a pathless land, and you cannot approach it by any path whatsoever, by any religion, by any sect.
Jiddu Krishnamurti 1895–1986: speech in Holland, 3 August 1929

30 The truth is often a terrible weapon of aggression. It is possible to lie, and even to murder, for the truth.
Alfred Adler 1870–1937: *The Problems of Neurosis* (1929)

31 The truth which makes men free is for the most part the truth which men prefer not to hear.
Herbert Agar 1897–1980: *A Time for Greatness* (1942)

32 There are no whole truths; all truths are half-truths. It is trying to treat them as whole truths that plays the devil.
Alfred North Whitehead 1861–1947: *Dialogues* (1954)

33 Truth exists; only lies are invented.
Georges Braque 1882–1963: *Le Jour et la nuit: Cahiers 1917–52*

34 One of the favourite maxims of my father was the distinction between the two sorts of truths, profound truths recognized by the fact that the opposite is also a profound truth, in contrast to trivialities where opposites are obviously absurd.
Niels Bohr 1885–1962: S. Rozental *Niels Bohr* (1967)

35 Truth is not merely what we are thinking, but also why, to whom and under what circumstances we say it.
Václav Havel 1936– : *Temptation* (1985)

36 It contains a misleading impression, not a lie. It was being economical with the truth.
the phrase "economy of truth" was earlier used by Edmund Burke (1729–97)
Robert Armstrong 1927– : referring to a letter during the "Spycatcher" trial, Supreme Court, New South Wales, in *Daily Telegraph* (UK) 19 November 1986; cf. **26** above

37 In exceptional circumstances it is necessary to say something that is untrue in the House of Commons.
William Waldegrave 1946– : in *Guardian* (UK) 9 March 1994

Unbelief
see **Belief and Unbelief**

The Universe
see also **The Earth, The Skies**

1 Had I been present at the Creation, I would have given some useful hints for the better ordering of the universe.
on studying the Ptolemaic system
Alfonso "the Wise" of Castile 1221–84: attributed

2 The eternal silence of these infinite spaces [the heavens] terrifies me.
Blaise Pascal 1623–62: *Pensées* (1670)

3 *on hearing that Margaret Fuller "accepted the universe":*
"Gad! she'd better!"
Thomas Carlyle 1795–1881: William James *Varieties of Religious Experience* (1902)

4 Not a sound. The universe sleeps,
resting a huge ear on its paw
with mites of stars.
Vladimir Mayakovsky 1893–1930:
"The Cloud in Trousers" (1915)

5 The world is disgracefully
managed, one hardly knows to
whom to complain.
Ronald Firbank 1886–1926: *Vainglory*
(1915)

6 The world is everything that is
the case.
Ludwig Wittgenstein 1889–1951:
Tractatus Logico-Philosophicus
(1922)

7 Now, my own suspicion is that
the universe is not only queerer
than we suppose, but queerer
than we *can* suppose . . . I suspect
that there are more things in
heaven and earth than are
dreamed of, or can be dreamed of,
in any philosophy.
J. B. S. Haldane 1892–1964: *Possible
Worlds and Other Essays* (1927)
"Possible Worlds" see **The
Supernatural 5**

8 From the intrinsic evidence of his
creation, the Great Architect of
the Universe now begins to
appear as a pure mathematician.
James Jeans 1877–1946: *The
Mysterious Universe* (1930)

9 This, now, is the judgement of
our scientific age—the third
reaction of man upon the
universe! This universe is not
hostile, nor yet is it friendly. It is
simply indifferent.
John H. Holmes 1879–1964: *The
Sensible Man's View of Religion*
(1932)

10 For one of those gnostics, the
visible universe was an illusion
or, more precisely, a sophism.
Mirrors and fatherhood are
abominable because they multiply
it and extend it.

Jorge Luis Borges 1899–1986: *Tlön,
Uqbar, Orbis Tertius* (1941)

11 *on Felix Bloch's stating that space
was the field of linear operations:*
Nonsense. Space is blue and birds
fly through it.
Werner Heisenberg 1901–76: Felix
Bloch "Heisenberg and the early
days of quantum mechanics," in
Physics Today December 1976

12 Space isn't remote at all. It's only
an hour's drive away if your car
could go straight upwards.
Fred Hoyle: in *Observer* (UK) 9
September 1979

13 If we find the answer to that
[why it is that we and the
universe exist], it would be the
ultimate triumph of human
reason—for then we would know
the mind of God.
Stephen Hawking 1942– : *A Brief
History of Time* (1988)

14 Space is almost infinite. As a
matter of fact, we think it is
infinite.
Dan Quayle 1947– : in *Daily
Telegraph* (UK) 8 March 1989

15 It is often said that there is no
such thing as a free lunch. The
Universe, however, is a free
lunch.
Alan Guth 1947– : in *Harpers*
November 1994

Universities
see also **Education and Teaching**

1 A Clerk there was of Oxenford
also,
That unto logyk hadde longe ygo.
As leene was his hors as is a
rake,
And he was nat right fat, I
undertake,
But looked holwe, and therto
sobrely.
Geoffrey Chaucer c. 1343–1400: *The

Canterbury Tales "The General
Prologue"

2 Universities incline wits to
sophistry and affectation.
Francis Bacon 1561–1626: *Valerius
Terminus of the Interpretation of
Nature*

3 Aye, 'tis well enough for a
servant to be bred at an
University. But the education is a
little too pedantic for a
gentleman.
William Congreve 1670–1729: *Love
for Love* (1695)

4 The discipline of colleges and
universities is in general
contrived, not for the benefit of
the students, but for the interest,
or more properly speaking, for the
ease of the masters.
Adam Smith 1723–90: *Wealth of
Nations* (1776)

5 To the University of Oxford I
acknowledge no obligation; and
she will as cheerfully renounce
me for a son, as I am willing to
disclaim her for a mother. I spent
fourteen months at Magdalen
College: they proved the fourteen
months the most idle and
unprofitable of my whole life.
Edward Gibbon 1737–94: *Memoirs of
My Life* (1796)

6 The most prominent requisite to a
lecturer, though perhaps not
really the most important, is a
good delivery; for though to all
true philosophers science and
nature will have charms
innumerable in every dress, yet I
am sorry to say that the
generality of mankind cannot
accompany us one short hour
unless the path is strewed with
flowers.
Michael Faraday 1791–1867: *Advice
to a Lecturer* (1960); from his letters
and notebook written at age 21

7 You will hear more good things
on the outside of a stagecoach
from London to Oxford than if
you were to pass a twelvemonth
with the undergraduates, or
heads of colleges, of that famous
university.
William Hazlitt 1778–1830: *Table
Talk* (1821)

8 The true University of these days
is a collection of books.
Thomas Carlyle 1795–1881: *On
Heroes, Hero-Worship, and the
Heroic* (1841)

9 A classic lecture, rich in
sentiment,
With scraps of thundrous epic
lilted out
By violet-hooded Doctors, elegies
And quoted odes, and jewels five-
words-long,
That on the stretched forefinger of
all Time
Sparkle for ever.
Alfred, Lord Tennyson 1809–92: *The
Princess* (1847)

10 A whaleship was my Yale College
and my Harvard.
Herman Melville 1819–91: *Moby Dick*
(1851)

11 Nor can I do better, in conclusion,
than impress upon you the study
of Greek literature, which not
only elevates above the vulgar
herd, but leads not infrequently to
positions of considerable
emolument.
Thomas Gaisford 1779–1855:
Christmas Day Sermon in the
Cathedral, Oxford; W. Tuckwell
Reminiscences of Oxford (2nd ed.,
1907)

12 A University should be a place of
light, of liberty, and of learning.
Benjamin Disraeli 1804–81: speech,
House of Commons, 11 March 1873

13 Undergraduates owe their
happiness chiefly to the

consciousness that they are no longer at school. The nonsense which was knocked out of them at school is all put gently back at Oxford or Cambridge.
Max Beerbohm 1872–1956: *More* (1899)

14 Very nice sort of place, Oxford, I should think, for people that like that sort of place. They teach you to be a gentleman there. In the Polytechnic they teach you to be an engineer or such like.
George Bernard Shaw 1856–1950: *Man and Superman* (1903)

15 Gentlemen: I have not had your advantages. What poor education I have received has been gained in the University of Life.
Horatio Bottomley 1860–1933: speech at the Oxford Union, 2 December 1920

16 Our American professors like their literature clear and cold and pure and very dead.
Sinclair Lewis 1885–1951: Nobel Prize Address, 12 December 1930

17 I am told that today rather more than 60 per cent of the men who go to the universities go on a Government grant. This is a new class that has entered upon the scene . . . They are scum.
W. Somerset Maugham 1874–1965: in *Sunday Times* (UK) 25 December 1955

18 I don't think one "comes down" from Jimmy's university. According to him, it's not even red brick, but white tile.
John Osborne 1929–94: *Look Back in Anger* (1956)

19 The delusion that there are thousands of young people about who are capable of benefiting from university training, but have somehow failed to find their way there, is . . . a necessary

component of the expansionist case . . . More will mean worse.
Kingsley Amis 1922–95: in *Encounter* (UK) July 1960

20 College is a refuge from hasty judgment.
Robert Frost 1874–1963: *Quote* (9 July 1961)

21 It might be said now that I have the best of both worlds. A Harvard education and a Yale degree.
John F. Kennedy 1917–63: *New York Times* (12 June 1962)

22 Princeton is a wonderful little spot. A quaint and ceremonious village of puny demigods on stilts.
Albert Einstein 1879–1955: *Philadelphia* (August 1975)

23 City of perspiring dreams.
of Cambridge, England
Frederic Raphael 1931– : *The Glittering Prizes* (1976)

24 This is a noble day on which to remember one of the great dropouts of Columbia, Alexander Hamilton.
Henry F. Graff 1921– : *New York Times* (11 April 1987)

25 Why am I the first Kinnock in a thousand generations to be able to get to a university?
later plagiarized by the American politician Joe Biden
Neil Kinnock 1942– : speech in party political broadcast, 21 May 1987

26 Princeton sent me a rejection letter so elegantly worded that I still think of myself as an alumnus.
Newton L. ("Newt") Gingrich 1943– : *Newsweek* (9 January 1995)

Value

1 Thirty spokes share the wheel's
   hub;
   It is the centre hole that makes it
   useful.
   Shape clay into a vessel;
   It is the space within that makes
   it useful.
   Cut doors and windows for a
   room;
   It is the holes which make it
   useful.
   Therefore profit comes from what
   is there;
   Usefulness from what is not there.
   Lao-tsu c. 604–c. 531 BC: *Tao-Tê-Ching*

2 A living dog is better than a dead
   lion.
   Bible: Ecclesiastes

3 Neither cast ye your pearls before
   swine.
   Bible: St. Matthew

4 Men do not weigh the stalk for
   that it was,
   When once they find her flower,
   her glory, pass.
   Samuel Daniel 1563–1619: *Delia*
   (1592) sonnet 32

5 O monstrous! but one half-
   pennyworth of bread to this
   intolerable deal of sack!
   William Shakespeare 1564–1616:
   Henry IV, Part 1 (1597)

6 Of one whose hand,
   Like the base Indian, threw a
   pearl away
   Richer than all his tribe.
   William Shakespeare 1564–1616:
   Othello (1602–4)

7 When the well's dry, we know
   the worth of water.
   Benjamin Franklin 1706–90: *Poor
   Richard's Almanack* (1746)

8 Then on the shore
   Of the wide world I stand alone
   and think
   Till love and fame to nothingness
   do sink.
   John Keats 1795–1821: "When I have
   fears that I may cease to be"
   (written 1818)

9 It is not that pearls fetch a high
   price *because* men have dived for
   them; but on the contrary, men
   dive for them because they fetch
   a high price.
   Richard Whately 1787–1863:
   *Introductory Lectures on Political
   Economy* (1832)

10 An acre in Middlesex is better
    than a principality in Utopia.
    Lord Macaulay 1800–59: *Essays
    Contributed to the Edinburgh Review*
    (1843) "Lord Bacon"

11 Every man is wanted, and no
    man is wanted much.
    Ralph Waldo Emerson 1803–82:
    Essays. Second Series (1844)
    "Nominalist and Realist"

12 You can calculate the worth of a
    man by the number of his
    enemies, and the importance of a
    work of art by the harm that is
    spoken of it.
    Gustave Flaubert 1821–80: letter to
    Louise Colet, 14 June 1853

13 Nothink for nothink 'ere, and
    precious little for sixpence.
    Punch: in 1869

14 I never loved a dear Gazelle—
    *Nor anything that cost me much:
    High prices profit those who sell,
    But why should I be fond of such?*
    Lewis Carroll 1832–98:
    Phantasmagoria (1869) "Theme with
    Variations" see **Transience** 10

15 It has long been an axiom of
    mine that the little things are
    infinitely the most important.

Arthur Conan Doyle 1859–1930:
Adventures of Sherlock Holmes
(1892)

16 Oh I see said the Earl but my
own idear is that these things are
as piffle before the wind.
Daisy Ashford 1881–1972: *The Young
Visiters* (1919)

17 There is less in this than meets
the eye.
*on a revival of Maeterlinck's play
"Aglavaine and Selysette"*
Tallulah Bankhead 1903–68:
Alexander Woollcott *Shouts and
Murmurs* (1922)

Violence

1 Force, unaided by judgement,
collapses through its own weight.
Horace 65–8 BC: *Odes*

2 Resist not evil: but whosoever
shall smite thee on thy right
cheek, turn to him the other also.
Bible: St. Matthew; cf. **6** below

3 All they that take the sword shall
perish with the sword.
Bible: St. Matthew

4 Who overcomes
By force, hath overcome but half
his foe.
John Milton 1608–74: *Paradise Lost*
(1667)

5 The use of force alone is but
temporary. It may subdue for a
moment; but it does not remove
the necessity of subduing again;
and a nation is not governed,
which is perpetually to be
conquered.
Edmund Burke 1729–97: *On
Conciliation with America* (1775)

6 Wisdom has taught us to be calm
and meek,
To take one blow, and turn the
other cheek;
It is not written what a man shall
do

If the rude caitiff smite the other
too!
Oliver Wendell Holmes 1809–94:
"Non-Resistance" (1861); see **2**
above

7 If you strike a child take care that
you strike it in anger, even at the
risk of maiming it for life. A blow
in cold blood neither can nor
should be forgiven.
George Bernard Shaw 1856–1950:
Man and Superman (1903) "Maxims:
How to Beat Children"

8 Non-violence is the first article of
my faith. It is also the last article
of my creed.
Mahatma Gandhi 1869–1948: speech
at Shahi Bag, 18 March 1922, on a
charge of sedition

9 A man may build himself a
throne of bayonets, but he cannot
sit on it.
*quoted by Boris Yeltsin at the time
of the failed military coup in Russia,
August 1991*
William Ralph Inge 1860–1954:
Philosophy of Plotinus (1923)

10 Where force is necessary, there it
must be applied boldly, decisively
and completely. But one must
know the limitations of force; one
must know when to blend force
with a maneuver, a blow with an
agreement.
Leon Trotsky 1879–1940: *What Next?*
(1932)

11 In violence, we forget who we
are.
Mary McCarthy 1912–89: *On the
Contrary* (1961) "Characters in
Fiction"

12 A riot is at bottom the language
of the unheard.
Martin Luther King, Jr. 1929–68:
Where Do We Go From Here? (1967)

13 I say violence is necessary. It is as
American as cherry pie.

H. Rap Brown 1943– : speech at Washington, 27 July 1967

14 The only thing that's been a worse flop than the organization of non-violence has been the organization of violence.
Joan Baez 1941– : *Daybreak* (1970)

15 Not hard enough.
when asked how hard she had slapped a policeman
Zsa Zsa Gabor 1919– : in *Independent* (UK) 21 September 1989

Virtue
see also **Good and Evil, Sin**

1 He preferred to be rather than to seem good.
of Cato
Sallust 86–35 BC: *Catiline*

2 Strait is the gate, and narrow is the way, which leadeth unto life, and few there be that find it.
Bible: St. Matthew

3 Be sober, be vigilant; because your adversary the devil, as a roaring lion, walketh about, seeking whom he may devour.
Bible: I Peter

4 *Puro e disposto a salire alle stelle.*
Pure and ready to mount to the stars.
Dante Alighieri 1265–1321: *Divina Commedia* "Purgatorio"

5 Would that we had spent one whole day well in this world!
Thomas à Kempis c. 1380–1471: *The Imitation of Christ*

6 We may not look at our pleasure to go to heaven in feather-beds; it is not the way.
Thomas More 1478–1535: William Roper *Life of Sir Thomas More*

7 How far that little candle throws his beams!
So shines a good deed in a naughty world.
William Shakespeare 1564–1616: *The Merchant of Venice* (1596–8)

8 Dost thou think, because thou art virtuous, there shall be no more cakes and ale?
William Shakespeare 1564–1616: *Twelfth Night* (1601)

9 Virtue is like a rich stone, best plain set.
Francis Bacon 1561–1626: *Essays* (1625) "Of Beauty"

10 I cannot praise a fugitive and cloistered virtue, unexercised and unbreathed, that never sallies out and sees her adversary, but slinks out of the race, where that immortal garland is to be run for, not without dust and heat.
John Milton 1608–74: *Areopagitica* (1644)

11 Only the actions of the just Smell sweet, and blossom in their dust.
James Shirley 1596–1666: *The Contention of Ajax and Ulysses* (1659)

12 I am not the less human for being devout.
Molière 1622–73: *Le Tartuffe* (1669)

13 Instead of dirt and poison we have rather chosen to fill our hives with honey and wax; thus furnishing mankind with the two noblest of things, which are sweetness and light.
Jonathan Swift 1667–1745: *The Battle of the Books* (1704) **Perfection 8**

14 When men grow virtuous in their old age, they only make a sacrifice to God of the devil's leavings.
Alexander Pope 1688–1744:

Miscellanies (1727) "Thoughts on
Various Subjects"

15 Virtue she finds too painful an
endeavour,
Content to dwell in decencies for
ever.
Alexander Pope 1688–1744: *Epistles
to Several Persons* "To a Lady"
(1735)

16 Let humble Allen, with an
awkward shame,
Do good by stealth, and blush to
find it fame.
Alexander Pope 1688–1744:
Imitations of Horace (1738)

17 The virtue which requires to be
ever guarded is scarce worth the
sentinel.
Oliver Goldsmith 1730–74: *The Vicar
of Wakefield* (1766)

18 When we are planning for
posterity, we ought to remember
that virtue is not hereditary.
Thomas Paine 1737–1809: *Common
Sense* (1776)

19 Tell me, ye divines, which is the
most virtuous man, he who
begets twenty bastards, or he who
sacrifices an hundred thousand
lives?
Horace Walpole 1717–97: letter to Sir
Horace Mann, 7 July 1778

20 Our intentions make blackguards
of us all; our weakness in
carrying them out we call
probity.
Pierre Choderlos de Laclos 1741–
1803: *Les Liaisons Dangereuses*
(1782) letter 66

21 Minute attention to propriety
stops the growth of virtue.
Mary Wollstonecraft 1759–97: letter
to Everina Wollstonecraft, 4 March
1787

22 Virtue knows to a farthing what
it has lost by not having been
vice.

Horace Walpole 1717–97: L.
Kronenberger *The Extraordinary Mr.
Wilkes* (1974)

23 Feelings too
Of unremembered pleasure: such,
perhaps,
As may have had no trivial
influence
On that best portion of a good
man's life,
His little, nameless,
unremembered, acts
Of kindness and of love.
William Wordsworth 1770–1850:
"Lines composed a few miles above
Tintern Abbey" (1798)

24 How pleasant it is, at the end of
the day,
No follies to have to repent;
But reflect on the past, and be
able to say,
That my time has been properly
spent.
Ann Taylor 1782–1866 and **Jane
Taylor** 1783–1824: "The Way to be
Happy" (1806)

25 The greatest offence against
virtue is to speak ill of it.
William Hazlitt 1778–1830: *Sketches
and Essays* (1839) "On Cant and
Hypocrisy"

26 My strength is as the strength of
ten,
Because my heart is pure.
Alfred, Lord Tennyson 1809–92: "Sir
Galahad" (1842)

27 More people are flattered into
virtue than bullied out of vice.
R. S. Surtees 1805–64: *The Analysis
of the Hunting Field* (1846)

28 As for Doing-good, that is one of
the professions which are full.
Henry David Thoreau 1817–62:
Walden (1854)

29 Be good, sweet maid, and let who
will be clever.

Charles Kingsley 1819–75: "A Farewell" (1858)

30 Good, but not religious-good.
Thomas Hardy 1840–1928: *Under the Greenwood Tree* (1872)

31 It is better to be beautiful than to be good. But . . . it is better to be good than to be ugly.
Oscar Wilde 1854–1900: *The Picture of Dorian Gray* (1891)

32 Few things are harder to put up with than the annoyance of a good example.
Mark Twain 1835–1910: *Pudd'nhead Wilson* (1894)

33 If some great Power would agree to make me always think what is true and do what is right, on condition of being turned into a sort of clock and wound up every morning before I got out of bed, I should instantly close with the offer.
T. H. Huxley 1825–95: "On Descartes' *Discourse on Method*" (written 1870)

34 No people do so much harm as those who go about doing good.
Mandell Creighton 1843–1901: *The Life and Letters of Mandell Creighton* by his wife (1904)

35 What is virtue but the Trade Unionism of the married?
George Bernard Shaw 1856–1950: *Man and Superman* (1903)

36 I expect to pass through this world but once; any good thing therefore that I can do, or any kindness that I can show to any fellow-creature, let me do it now; let me not defer or neglect it, for I shall not pass this way again.
Stephen Grellet 1773–1855: attributed; see John o' London *Treasure Trove* (1925) for some of the many other claimants to authorship

37 "Goodness, what beautiful diamonds!"
"Goodness had nothing to do with it."
Mae West 1892–1980: *Night After Night* (1932 film)

38 I'm as pure as the driven slush.
Tallulah Bankhead 1903–68: in *Saturday Evening Post* 12 April 1947

39 Terrible is the temptation to be good.
Bertolt Brecht 1898–1956: *The Caucasian Chalk Circle* (1948)

40 What after all
Is a halo? It's only one more thing to keep clean.
Christopher Fry 1907– : *The Lady's not for Burning* (1949)

41 I used to be Snow White . . . but I drifted.
Mae West 1892–1980: Joseph Weintraub *Peel Me a Grape* (1975)

Visual Arts
see **Painting and the Visual Arts**

Warfare
see also **The Armed Forces**, **Peace**, **Wars**

1 He saith among the trumpets, Ha, ha; and he smelleth the battle afar off, the thunder of the captains, and the shouting.
Bible: Job

2 We make war that we may live in peace.
Aristotle 384–322 BC: *Nicomachean Ethics*

3 Laws are silent in time of war.
Cicero 106–43 BC: *Pro Milone*

4 The sinews of war, unlimited money.
Cicero 106–43 BC: *Fifth Philippic*; cf. **Money 9**

5 I see wars, horrible wars, and the Tiber foaming with much blood.
Virgil 70–19 BC: *Aeneid*; cf. **Race 17**

6 Wars begin when you will, but they do not end when you please.
Niccolò Machiavelli 1469–1527: *History of Florence* (1521–4)

7 Once more unto the breach, dear friends, once more;
Or close the wall up with our English dead!
In peace there's nothing so becomes a man
As modest stillness and humility:
But when the blast of war blows in our ears,
Then imitate the action of the tiger;
Stiffen the sinews, summon up the blood,
Disguise fair nature with hard-favoured rage.
William Shakespeare 1564–1616: *Henry V* (1599)

8 For what can war, but endless war still breed?
John Milton 1608–74: "On the Lord General Fairfax at the Siege of Colchester" (written 1648)

9 Force, and fraud, are in war the two cardinal virtues.
Thomas Hobbes 1588–1679: *Leviathan* (1651)

10 One to destroy, is murder by the law;
And gibbets keep the lifted hand in awe;
To murder thousands, takes a specious name,
"War's glorious art," and gives immortal fame.
Edward Young 1683–1765: *The Love of Fame* (1725–8)

11 God is on the side not of the heavy battalions, but of the best shots.
Voltaire 1694–1778: "The Piccini Notebooks" (c. 1735–50) cf. **God 16**

12 Among the calamities of war may be jointly numbered the diminution of the love of truth, by the falsehoods which interest dictates and credulity encourages.
Samuel Johnson 1709–84: in *The Idler* 11 November 1758; possibly the source of "When war is declared, Truth is the first casualty," epigraph to Arthur Ponsonby's *Falsehood in Wartime* (1928); attributed also to Hiram Johnson, speaking in the US Senate, 1918, but not recorded in his speech

13 There never was a good war, or a bad peace.
Benjamin Franklin 1706–90: letter to Josiah Quincy, 11 September 1783

14 War is the national industry of Prussia.
Comte de Mirabeau 1749–91: attributed to Mirabeau by Albert Sorel (1842–1906), based on Mirabeau's introduction to *De la monarchie prussienne sous Frédéric le Grand* (1788)

15 In war, three-quarters turns on personal character and relations; the balance of manpower and materials counts only for the remaining quarter.
Napoleon I 1769–1821: "Observations sur les affaires d'Espagne, Saint-Cloud, 27 août 1808"

16 Next to a battle lost, the greatest misery is a battle gained.
Duke of Wellington 1769–1852: in *Diary of Frances, Lady Shelley 1787–1817* (ed. R. Edgcumbe)

17 Everything is very simple in war, but the simplest thing is difficult. These difficulties accumulate and produce a friction which no man

can imagine exactly who has not
seen war.
Karl von Clausewitz 1780–1831: *On
War* (1832–4)

18 War is nothing but a
continuation of politics with the
admixture of other means.
*commonly rendered as "War is the
continuation of politics by other
means"*
Karl von Clausewitz 1780–1831: *On
War* (1832–4)

19 He knew that the essence of war
is violence, and that moderation
in war is imbecility.
Lord Macaulay 1800–59: *Essays
Contributed to the Edinburgh Review*
(1843) "John Hampden"

20 All the business of war, and
indeed all the business of life, is
to endeavour to find out what
you don't know by what you do;
that's what I called "guessing
what was at the other side of the
hill."
Duke of Wellington 1769–1852: in
The Croker Papers (1885)

21 It is well that war is so terrible.
We should grow too fond of it.
Robert E. Lee 1807–70: after the
battle of Fredericksburg, December
1862; attributed

22 There is many a boy here to-day
who looks on war as all glory,
but, boys, it is all hell.
William Tecumseh Sherman 1820–91:
speech at Columbus, Ohio, 11
August 1880

23 Everlasting peace is a dream, and
not even a pleasant one; and war
is a necessary part of God's
arrangement of the world . . .
Without war the world would
deteriorate into materialism.
Helmuth von Moltke 1800–91: letter
to Dr. J. K. Bluntschli, 11 December
1880

24 *of possible German involvement in
the Balkans:*
Not worth the healthy bones of a
single Pomeranian grenadier.
Otto von Bismarck 1815–98: George
O. Kent *Bismarck and his Times*
(1978); cf. **49** below

25 BATTLE, *n.* A method of untying
with the teeth a political knot
that would not yield to the
tongue.
Ambrose Bierce 1842–*c.* 1914: *The
Cynic's Word Book* (1906)

26 Yes; quaint and curious war is!
You shoot a fellow down
You'd treat if met where any bar
is,
Or help to half-a-crown.
Thomas Hardy 1840–1928: "The Man
he Killed" (1909)

27 War is hell, and all that, but it
has a good deal to recommend it.
It wipes out all the small
nuisances of peace-time.
Ian Hay 1876–1952: *The First
Hundred Thousand* (1915)

28 I have a rendezvous with Death
At some disputed barricade.
Alan Seeger 1888–1916: "I Have a
Rendezvous with Death" (1916)

29 Once lead this people into war
and they will forget there ever
was such a thing as tolerance.
Woodrow Wilson 1856–1924: John
Dos Passos *Mr. Wilson's War* (1917)

30 My subject is War, and the pity
of War.
The Poetry is in the pity.
Wilfred Owen 1893–1918: preface
(written 1918) in *Poems* (1963)

31 I am beginning to rub my eyes at
the prospect of peace . . . One will
at last fully recognize that the
dead are not only dead for the
duration of the war.
Cynthia Asquith 1887–1960: diary 7
October 1918

32 If you could hear, at every jolt,
the blood
Come gargling from the froth-
corrupted lungs,
Obscene as cancer, bitter as the
cud
Of vile, incurable sores on
innocent tongues,—
My friend, you would not tell
with such high zest
To children ardent for some
desperate glory,
The old Lie: Dulce et decorum est
Pro patria mori.
Wilfred Owen 1893–1918: "Dulce et
Decorum Est" see **Patriotism** 1

33 Waste of Blood, and waste of
Tears,
Waste of youth's most precious
years,
Waste of ways the saints have
trod,
Waste of Glory, waste of God,
War!
G. A. Studdert Kennedy 1883–1929:
"Waste" (1919)

34 When we, the Workers, all
demand: "What are WE fighting
for?" . . .
Then, then we'll end that stupid
crime, that devil's madness—
War.
Robert W. Service 1874–1958:
"Michael" (1921)

35 War hath no fury like a non-
combatant.
C. E. Montague 1867–1928:
Disenchantment (1922)

36 You can't say civilization don't
advance, however, for in every
war they kill you in a new way.
Will Rogers 1879–1935: in *New York
Times* 23 December 1929

37 War is too serious a matter to
entrust to military men.
Georges Clemenceau 1841–1929:
attributed to Clemenceau, e.g. in
Hampden Jackson *Clemenceau and*

the Third Republic (1946); but also
to Briand and Talleyrand

38 The bomber will always get
through. The only defence is in
offence, which means that you
have to kill more women and
children more quickly than the
enemy if you want to save
yourselves.
Stanley Baldwin 1867–1947: speech,
House of Commons, 10 November
1932

39 The sword is the axis of the
world and its power is absolute.
Charles de Gaulle 1890–1970: *Vers
l'armée de métier* (1934)

40 We can manage without butter
but not, for example, without
guns. If we are attacked we can
only defend ourselves with guns
not with butter.
Joseph Goebbels 1897–1945: speech
in Berlin, 17 January 1936

41 We have no butter . . . but I ask
you—would you rather have
butter or guns? . . . preparedness
makes us powerful. Butter merely
makes us fat.
Hermann Goering 1893–1946: speech
at Hamburg, 1936; W. Frischauer
Goering (1951)

42 I have seen war. I have seen war
on land and sea. I have seen
blood running from the wounded.
I have seen men coughing out
their gassed lungs. I have seen
the dead in the mud. I have seen
cities destroyed. I have seen 200
limping, exhausted men come out
of line—the survivors of a
regiment of 1,000 that went
forward 48 hours before. I have
seen children starving. I have
seen the agony of mothers and
wives. I hate war.
Franklin D. Roosevelt 1882–1945:
speech at Chautauqua, NY, 14
August 1936

43 There are not fifty ways of fighting, there's only one, and that's to win. Neither revolution nor war consists in doing what one pleases.
André Malraux 1901–76: *L'Espoir* (1937)

44 In war, whichever side may call itself the victor, there are no winners, but all are losers.
Neville Chamberlain 1869–1940: speech at Kettering, 3 July 1938

45 War always finds a way.
Bertolt Brecht 1898–1956: *Mother Courage* (1939)

46 Probably the battle of Waterloo *was* won on the playing-fields of Eton, but the opening battles of all subsequent wars have been lost there.
George Orwell 1903–50: *The Lion and the Unicorn* (1941) "England Your England" see **Wars 12**

47 What difference does it make to the dead, the orphans and the homeless, whether the mad destruction is wrought under the name of totalitarianism or the holy name of liberty or democracy?
Mahatma Gandhi 1869–1948: *Non-Violence in Peace and War* (1942)

48 Older men declare war. But it is youth who must fight and die.
Herbert Hoover 1874–1964: speech at the Republican National Convention, Chicago, 27 June 1944

49 I would not regard the whole of the remaining cities of Germany as worth the bones of one British Grenadier.
supporting the continued strategic bombing of German cities
Arthur Harris 1892–1984: letter to Norman Bottomley, deputy Chief of Air Staff, 29 March 1945; Max Hastings *Bomber Command* (1979); cf. **24** above

50 I suppose if I had lost the war, I would have been tried as a war criminal. Fortunately, we were on the winning side.
of World War II
Curtis E. LeMay 1906–90: *The New Yorker* (10 March 1945)

51 I have never met anyone who wasn't against war. Even Hitler and Mussolini were, according to themselves.
David Low 1891–1963: in *New York Times Magazine* 10 February 1946

52 The quickest way of ending a war is to lose it.
George Orwell 1903–50: in *Polemic* (UK) May 1946

53 The world has achieved brilliance without conscience. Ours is a world of nuclear giants and ethical infants.
Omar N. Bradley 1893–1981: *Address on Armistice Day* (1948)

54 In war: resolution. In defeat: defiance. In victory: magnanimity. In peace: goodwill.
Winston Churchill 1874–1965: *The Second World War* vol. 1 (1948)

55 In war there is no second prize for the runner-up.
Omar N. Bradley 1893–1981: in *Military Review* February 1950

56 The time not to become a father is eighteen years before a world war.
E. B. White 1899–1985: *The Second Tree from the Corner* (1953)

57 Every gun that is made, every warship launched, every rocket fired signifies, in the final sense, a theft from those who hunger and are not fed, those who are cold and are not clothed. This world in arms is not spending money alone. It is spending the sweat of its laborers, the genius of its

scientists, the hopes of its children.
Dwight D. Eisenhower 1890–1969: speech in Washington, 16 April 1953

58 A bigger bang for a buck.
Anonymous: Charles E. Wilson's defense policy, in *Newsweek* 22 March 1954

59 Mankind must put an end to war or war will put an end to mankind.
John F. Kennedy 1917–63: speech to United Nations General Assembly, 25 September 1961

60 Dead battles, like dead generals, hold the military mind in their dead grip and Germans, no less than other peoples, prepare for the last war.
Barbara W. Tuchman 1912–89: *August 1914* (1962)

61 Rule 1, on page 1 of the book of war, is: "Do not march on Moscow" . . . [Rule 2] is: "Do not go fighting with your land armies in China."
Bernard Law Montgomery 1887–1976: speech, House of Lords, 30 May 1962

62 History is littered with the wars which everybody knew would never happen.
Enoch Powell 1912– : speech to the Conservative Party Conference, 19 October 1967

63 War is the most exciting and dramatic thing in life. In fighting to the death you feel terribly relaxed when you manage to come through.
Moshe Dayan 1915–81: in *Observer* (UK) 13 February 1972

64 War is capitalism with the gloves off and many who go to war know it but they go to war because they don't want to be a hero.

Tom Stoppard 1937– : *Travesties* (1975)

65 I love the smell of napalm in the morning. It smells like victory.
John Milius and **Francis Ford Coppola** 1939– : *Apocalypse Now* (1979 film)

66 You're not here to die for your country. You're here to make those so-and-so's die for theirs.
John H. ("Iron Mike") Michaelis 1912– : *Time* (11 November 1985)

67 When you're in the battlefield, survival is all there is. Death is the only great emotion.
Sam Fuller: in *Guardian* (UK) 26 February 1991

68 I'll tell you what war is about. You've got to kill people, and when you've killed enough they stop fighting.
Curtis E. LeMay 1906–90: *New Yorker* (19 June 1995)

Wars
see also **World War I, World War II**

1 Men said openly that Christ and His saints slept.
of twelfth-century England during the civil war between Stephen and Matilda
Anonymous: *Anglo-Saxon Chronicle* for 1137

2 The singeing of the King of Spain's Beard.
on the expedition to Cadiz, 1587
Francis Drake *c.* 1540–96: Francis Bacon *Considerations touching a War with Spain* (1629)

3 The dimensions of this mercy are above my thoughts. It is, for aught I know, a crowning mercy.
on the battle of Worcester, 1651
Oliver Cromwell 1599–1658: letter to William Lenthall, Speaker of the

Parliament of England, 4 September
1651

4 They now *ring* the bells, but they
will soon *wring* their hands.
*on the declaration of war with
Spain, 1739*
Robert Walpole 1676–1745: W. Coxe
Memoirs of Sir Robert Walpole
(1798)

5 What a glorious morning is this.
*on hearing gunfire at Lexington, 19
April 1775; traditionally quoted
"What a glorious morning for
America"*
Samuel Adams 1722–1803: J. K.
Hosmer *Samuel Adams* (1886)

6 Men, you are all marksmen—
don't one of you fire until you see
the white of their eyes.
at Bunker Hill, 1775
Israel Putnam 1718–90: R.
Frothingham *History of the Siege of
Boston* (1873); also attributed to
William Prescott, 1726–95

7 We beat them to-day or Molly
Stark's a widow.
John Stark 1728–1822: before the
battle of Bennington, 16 August
1777; in *Cyclopaedia of American
Biography*

8 It is the object only of war that
makes it honorable. And if there
was ever a just war since the
world began, it is this in which
America is now engaged.
Thomas Paine 1737–1809: *The
American Crisis, no. 5* (21 March
1778)

9 *Guerra a cuchillo.*
War to the knife.
*at the siege of Saragossa, 4 August
1808, replying to the suggestion that
he should surrender*
José de Palafox 1780–1847: as
reported; he actually said: "*Guerra y
cuchillo* [War and the knife]"; José
Gòmez de Arteche y Moro *Guerra de
la Independencia* (1875)

10 Up Guards and at them!
Duke of Wellington 1769–1852: in
The Battle of Waterloo by a Near
Observer [J. Booth] (1815); later
denied by Wellington

11 Hard pounding this, gentlemen;
let's see who will pound longest.
at the battle of Waterloo
Duke of Wellington 1769–1852: Sir
Walter Scott *Paul's Letters* (1816)

12 The battle of Waterloo was won
on the playing fields of Eton.
Duke of Wellington 1769–1852: oral
tradition, but not found in this form
of words; C. F. R. Montalembert *De
l'avenir politique de l'Angleterre*
(1856); cf. **Warfare 46**

13 Half a league, half a league,
Half a league onward,
All in the valley of Death
Rode the six hundred . . .
Cannon to right of them,
Cannon to left of them,
Cannon in front of them
Volleyed and thundered.
Alfred, Lord Tennyson 1809–92: "The
Charge of the Light Brigade" (1854)

14 The angel of death has been
abroad throughout the land; you
may almost hear the beating of
his wings.
*on the effects of the war in the
Crimea*
John Bright 1811–89: speech, House
of Commons, 23 February 1855

15 *J'y suis, j'y reste.*
Here I am, and here I stay.
*at the taking of the Malakoff fortress
during the Crimean War, 8
September 1855*
Comte de Macmahon 1808–93: G.
Hanotaux *Histoire de la France
Contemporaine* (1903–8)

16 There is Jackson with his
Virginians, standing like a stone
wall. Let us determine to die here,
and we will conquer.
referring to General T. J.

("Stonewall") Jackson at the battle
of Bull Run, 21 July, 1861 (in which
Bee himself was killed)
Barnard Elliott Bee 1823–61: B.
Perley Poore *Perley's Reminiscences*
(1886)

17 All quiet along the Potomac to-
night,
No sound save the rush of the
river,
While soft falls the dew on the
face of the dead—
The picket's off duty forever.
Ethel Lynn Beers 1827–79: "The
Picket Guard" (1861); the first line is
also attributed to George B.
McClellan (1826–85)

18 Give them the cold steel, boys!
Lewis Addison Armistead 1817–63:
attributed during the American Civil
War, 1863

19 Hold the fort, for I am coming.
*suggested by a flag message from
General W. T. Sherman near Atlanta,
October 1864*
Philip Paul Bliss 1838–76: *Gospel
Hymns and Sacred Songs* (1875)

20 Don't cheer, men; those poor
devils are dying.
John Woodward ("Jack") Philip 1840–
1900: at the battle of Santiago, 4
July 1898; in *Dictionary of American
Biography* vol. 14 (1934)

21 The Cavaliers (Wrong but
Wromantic) and the Roundheads
(Right but Repulsive).
*of the two sides in the English Civil
War*
W. C. Sellar 1898–1951 and **R. J.
Yeatman** 1898–1968: *1066 and All
That* (1930)

22 Wars may be fought with
weapons, but they are won by
men. It is the spirit of the men
who follow and of the man who
leads that gains the victory.
George S. Patton 1885–1945: *Cavalry
Journal* (September 1933)

23 Red China is not the powerful
nation seeking to dominate the
world. Frankly, in the opinion of
the Joint Chiefs of Staff, this
strategy would involve us in the
wrong war, at the wrong place,
at the wrong time, and with the
wrong enemy.
Omar N. Bradley 1893–1981: *US
Cong. Senate Comm. on Armed
Services* (1951)

24 We are not about to send
American boys 9 or 10,000 miles
away from home to do what
Asian boys ought to be doing for
themselves.
Lyndon Baines Johnson 1908–73:
speech at Akron University, 21
October 1964

25 They've got to draw in their
horns and stop their aggression,
or we're going to bomb them
back into the Stone Age.
on the North Vietnamese
Curtis E. LeMay 1906–90: *Mission
with LeMay* (1965)

26 It became necessary to destroy
the town to save it.
*statement by unidentified US Army
Major, referring to Ben Tre in
Vietnam*
Anonymous: Associated Press
Report, *New York Times* 8 February
1968

27 Just rejoice at that news and
congratulate our forces and the
Marines . . . Rejoice!
*on the recapture of South Georgia;
usually quoted as "Rejoice, rejoice"*
Margaret Thatcher 1925– : to
newsmen outside Downing Street,
25 April 1982

28 I counted them all out and I
counted them all back.
*on the number of British airplanes
(which he was not permitted to
disclose) joining the raid on Port
Stanley in the Falkland Islands*

Brian Hanrahan 1949– : BBC broadcast report, 1 May 1982

29 GOTCHA!
Anonymous: headline on the sinking of the *General Belgrano*, in *Sun* 4 May 1982

30 The Falklands thing was a fight between two bald men over a comb.
Jorge Luis Borges 1899–1986: in *Time* 14 February 1983

31 A line has been drawn in the sand.
George Bush 1924– : (8 August 1990)

32 The mother of battles.
popular interpretation of his description of the approaching Gulf War
Saddam Hussein 1937– : speech in Baghdad, 6 January 1991; *The Times*, 7 January 1991, reported that Saddam had no intention of relinquishing Kuwait and was ready for the "mother of all wars"

Ways and Means

1 It is in life as it is in ways, the shortest way is commonly the foulest, and surely the fairer way is not much about.
Francis Bacon 1561–1626: *The Advancement of Learning* (1605)

2 *Dans ce pays-ci il est bon de tuer de temps en temps un amiral pour encourager les autres.*
In this country [England] it is thought well to kill an admiral from time to time to encourage the others.
referring to the execution of Admiral John Byng, 1757
Voltaire 1694–1778: *Candide* (1759)

3 A servant's too often a negligent elf;
—If it's business of consequence,
DO IT YOURSELF!

R. H. Barham 1788–1845: "The Ingoldsby Penance!—Moral" (1842)

4 They sought it with thimbles, they sought it with care;
They pursued it with forks and hope;
They threatened its life with a railway-share;
They charmed it with smiles and soap.
Lewis Carroll 1832–98: *The Hunting of the Snark* (1876)

5 The color of the cat doesn't matter as long as it catches the mice.
quoting a Chinese proverb
Deng Xiaoping 1904–97: in *Financial Times* (UK) 18 December 1986

Weakness
see **Strength and Weakness**

Wealth and Luxury
see also **Money**

1 A land flowing with milk and honey.
Bible: Exodus

2 Lay not up for yourselves treasures upon earth, where moth and rust doth corrupt, and where thieves break through and steal:
But lay up for yourselves treasures in heaven.
Bible: St. Matthew

3 It is easier for a camel to go through the eye of a needle, than for a rich man to enter into the kingdom of God.
Bible: St. Matthew

4 I glory
More in the cunning purchase of my wealth
Than in the glad possession.
Ben Jonson c. 1573–1637: *Volpone* (1606)

5 Riches are for spending.
Francis Bacon 1561–1626: *Essays* (1625) "Of Expense"

6 Let none admire
That riches grow in hell; that soil may best
Deserve the precious bane.
John Milton 1608–74: *Paradise Lost* (1667)

7 Do you not daily see fine clothes, rich furniture, jewels and plate are more inviting than beauty unadorned?
Aphra Behn 1640–89: *The Rover* pt. 2 (1681)

8 It was very prettily said, that we may learn the little value of fortune by the persons on whom heaven is pleased to bestow it.
Richard Steele 1672–1729: in *The Tatler* (UK) 27 July 1710

9 We are all Adam's children but silk makes the difference.
Thomas Fuller 1654–1734: *Gnomologia* (1732)

10 Get place and wealth, if possible, with grace;
If not, by any means get wealth and place.
Alexander Pope 1688–1744: *Imitations of Horace* (1738); cf. **Money 2**

11 The chief enjoyment of riches consists in the parade of riches.
Adam Smith 1723–90: *Wealth of Nations* (1776)

12 We are not here to sell a parcel of boilers and vats, but the potentiality of growing rich, beyond the dreams of avarice.
at the sale of Thrale's brewery
Samuel Johnson 1709–84: James Boswell *Life of Samuel Johnson* (1791) 6 April 1781

13 The love of wealth is therefore to be traced, as either a principal or

accessory motive, at the bottom of all that the Americans do; this gives to all their passions a sort of family likeness.
Alexis de Tocqueville 1805–59: *Democracy in America* (1835)

14 "Two nations; between whom there is no intercourse and no sympathy; who are as ignorant of each other's habits, thoughts, and feelings, as if they were dwellers in different zones, or inhabitants of different planets . . . " "You speak of—" said Egremont, hesitatingly, "THE RICH AND THE POOR."
Benjamin Disraeli 1804–81: *Sybil* (1845)

15 Give us the luxuries of life, and we will dispense with its necessities.
John Lothrop Motley 1814–77: Oliver Wendell Holmes *Autocrat of the Breakfast-Table* (1857–8)

16 The man who dies . . . rich dies disgraced.
Andrew Carnegie 1835–1919: in *North American Review* June 1889 "Wealth"

17 In every well-governed state, wealth is a sacred thing; in democracies it is the only sacred thing.
Anatole France 1844–1924: *L'Île des pingouins* (1908)

18 To be clever enough to get all that money, one must be stupid enough to want it.
G. K. Chesterton 1874–1936: *Wisdom of Father Brown* (1914)

19 Her voice is full of money.
F. Scott Fitzgerald 1896–1940: *The Great Gatsby* (1925)

20 Let me tell you about the very rich. They are different from you and me.
F. Scott Fitzgerald 1896–1940: *All the*

Sad Young Men (1926) "Rich Boy"
to which Ernest Hemingway replied,
"Yes, they have more money," in
Esquire August 1936 "The Snows of
Kilimanjaro"

21 To suppose, as we all suppose,
that we could be rich and not
behave as the rich behave, is like
supposing that we could drink all
day and keep absolutely sober.
Logan Pearsall Smith 1865–1946:
Afterthoughts (1931) "In the World"

22 The necessities were going by
default to save the luxuries until I
hardly knew which were
necessities and which luxuries.
Frank Lloyd Wright 1867–1959:
Autobiography (1945)

23 The greater the wealth, the
thicker will be the dirt.
John Kenneth Galbraith 1908– :
The Affluent Society (1958)

24 I want to spend, and spend, and
spend.
*said to reporters on arriving to
collect her husband's football pools
winnings of £152,000*
Vivian Nicholson 1936– : in *Daily
Herald* (UK) 28 September 1961

25 I've been rich and I've been poor:
rich is better.
Sophie Tucker c. 1884–1966:
attributed

26 The meek shall inherit the earth,
but not the mineral rights.
John Paul Getty 1892–1976: Robert
Lenzner *The Great Getty*; attributed;
see **Pride 2**

27 Having money is rather like being
a blonde. It is more fun but not
vital.
Mary Quant 1934– : in *Observer*
(UK) 2 November 1986

28 If you really want to make a
million . . . the quickest way is to
start your own religion.

Anonymous: previously attributed to
L. Ron Hubbard 1911–86 in B.
Corydon and L. Ron Hubbard, Jr. *L.
Ron Hubbard* (1987), but attribution
subsequently rejected by L. Ron
Hubbard, Jr., who also dissociated
himself from the book

Weather

1 "After sharpest shoures," quath
Pees "most shene is the sonne;
Is no weder warmer than after
watry cloudes."
Pees = *Peace*
William Langland c. 1330–c. 1400:
The Vision of Piers Plowman

2 For I have seyn of a ful misty
morwe
Folowen ful ofte a myrie someris
day.
Geoffrey Chaucer c. 1343–1400:
Troilus and Criseyde

3 So foul and fair a day I have not
seen.
William Shakespeare 1564–1616:
Macbeth (1606)

4 When two Englishmen meet, their
first talk is of the weather.
Samuel Johnson 1709–84: in *The
Idler* (UK) 24 June 1758

5 The best sun we have is made of
Newcastle coal.
Horace Walpole 1717–97: letter to
George Montagu, 15 June 1768

6 The frost performs its secret
ministry,
Unhelped by any wind.
Samuel Taylor Coleridge 1772–1834:
"Frost at Midnight" (1798)

7 It is impossible to live in a
country which is continually
under hatches . . . Rain! Rain!
Rain!
John Keats 1795–1821: letter to J. H.
Reynolds from Devon, England 10
April 1818

8 O wild West Wind, thou breath of
Autumn's being,
Thou, from whose unseen
presence the leaves dead
Are driven, like ghosts from an
enchanter fleeing,
Yellow, and black, and pale, and
hectic red,
Pestilence-stricken multitudes.
Percy Bysshe Shelley 1792–1822:
"Ode to the West Wind" (1819)

9 This is a London particular . . . A
fog, miss.
Charles Dickens 1812–70: *Bleak
House* (1853)

10 Welcome, wild North-easter!
Shame it is to see
Odes to every zephyr;
Ne'er a verse to thee.
Charles Kingsley 1819–75: "Ode to
the North-East Wind" (1858)

11 There is a sumptuous variety
about the New England weather
that compels the stranger's
admiration—and regret. The
weather is always doing
something there; always attending
strictly to business; always getting
up new designs and trying them
on the people to see how they will
go.
Mark Twain 1835–1910: speech to
New England Society, 22 December
1876

12 When men were all asleep the
snow came flying,
In large white flakes falling on
the city brown,
Stealthily and perpetually settling
and loosely lying,
Hushing the latest traffic of the
drowsy town.
Robert Bridges 1844–1930: "London
Snow" (1890)

13 The rain, it raineth on the just
And also on the unjust fella:
But chiefly on the just, because
The unjust steals the just's
umbrella.

Lord Bowen 1835–94: Walter Sichel
Sands of Time (1923); see **Equality 1**

14 On Wenlock Edge the wood's in
trouble;
His forest fleece the Wrekin
heaves;
The gale, it plies the saplings
double,
And thick on Severn snow the
leaves.
A. E. Housman 1859–1936: *A
Shropshire Lad* (1896)

15 The fog comes
on little cat feet.
It sits looking
over harbor and city
on silent haunches
and then moves on.
Carl Sandburg 1878–1967: "Fog"
(1916)

16 The yellow fog that rubs its back
upon the window-panes.
T. S. Eliot 1888–1965: "The Love
Song of J. Alfred Prufrock" (1917)

17 This is the weather the cuckoo
likes,
And so do I;
When showers betumble the
chestnut spikes,
And nestlings fly.
Thomas Hardy 1840–1928:
"Weathers" (1922)

18 Thank heaven, the sun has gone
in, and I don't have to go out
and enjoy it.
Logan Pearsall Smith 1865–1946:
Afterthoughts (1931)

19 It ain't a fit night out for man or
beast.
W. C. Fields 1880–1946: adopted by
Fields but claimed by him not to be
original; letter, 8 February 1944

20 The first fall of snow is not only
an event, but it is a magical
event. You go to bed in one kind
of world and wake up to find
yourself in another quite different,

and if this is not enchantment,
then where is it to be found?
J. B. Priestley 1894–1984: *Apes and
Angels* (1928) "First Snow"

21 A woman rang to say she heard
there was a hurricane on the
way. Well don't worry, there
isn't.
*weather forecast on the night before
serious gales in southern England*
Michael Fish: BBC TV, 15 October
1987

22 Wet spring had merged
imperceptibly into bleak autumn.
For months the sky had remained
a depthless grey. Sometimes it
rained, but mostly it was just dull
. . . It was like living inside
Tupperware.
Bill Bryson 1951– : *The Lost
Continent* (1989)

23 It was the wrong kind of snow.
explaining disruption on British Rail
Terry Worrall: in *The Independent*
(UK) 16 February 1991

Winning and Losing
see also **Success and Failure**

1 One more such victory and we
are lost.
*on defeating the Romans at
Asculum, 279 BC*
Pyrrhus 319–272 BC: Plutarch *Parallel
Lives* "Pyrrhus"

2 The only safe course for the
defeated is to expect no safety.
Virgil 70–19 BC: *Aeneid*

3 The happy state of winning the
palm without the dust of racing.
Horace 65–8 BC: *Epistles*

4 Know ye not that they which run
in a race run all, but one
receiveth the prize.
Bible: I Corinthians

5 *Vae victis.*
Down with the defeated!

cry (already proverbial) of the Gallic
King, Brennus, on capturing Rome
(390 BC)
Livy 59 BC–AD 17: *Ab Urbe Condita*

6 Eclipse first, the rest nowhere.
*comment on a horse-race at Epsom,
3 May 1769; Eclipse was the most
famous racehorse of the 18th
century, one of the ancestors in the
direct male line of all thoroughbred
racehorses throughout the world*
Dennis O'Kelly c. 1720–87: in *Annals
of Sporting* (1822); *Dictionary of
National Biography* gives the
occasion as the Queen's Plate at
Winchester, 1769

7 When in doubt, win the trick.
Edmond Hoyle 1672–1769: *Hoyle's
Games Improved* (ed. Charles Jones,
1790) "Twenty-four Short Rules for
Learners" (though attributed to
Hoyle, this may well have been an
editorial addition by Jones, since it
is not found in earlier editions)

8 "The game," said he, "is never
lost till won."
George Crabbe 1754–1832: *Tales of
the Hall* (1819) "Gretna Green"

9 The politicians of New York . . .
see nothing wrong in the rule,
that to the victor belong the
spoils of the enemy.
William Learned Marcy 1786–1857:
speech to the Senate, 25 January
1832

10 For everything you have missed,
you have gained something else;
and for everything you gain, you
lose something.
Ralph Waldo Emerson 1803–82:
Essays: First Series, Compensation
(1841)

11 We are not interested in the
possibilities of defeat; they do not
exist.
*on the Boer War during "Black
Week," December 1899*

Queen Victoria 1819–1901: Lady Gwendolen Cecil *Life of Robert, Marquis of Salisbury* (1931)

12 Anybody can Win, unless there happens to be a Second Entry.
George Ade 1866–1944: *Fables in Slang* (1900)

13 The important thing in life is not the victory but the contest; the essential thing is not to have won but to have fought well.
Baron Pierre de Coubertin 1863–1937: speech on the Olympic Games, London, 24 July 1908

14 What's lost upon the roundabouts we pulls up on the swings!
Patrick Reginald Chalmers 1872–1942: "Roundabouts and Swings" (1912)

15 What is our aim? . . . Victory, victory at all costs, victory in spite of all terror; victory, however long and hard the road may be; for without victory, there is no survival.
Winston Churchill 1874–1965: speech, House of Commons, 13 May 1940

16 The war situation has developed not necessarily to Japan's advantage.
announcing Japan's surrender, in a broadcast to his people after atom bombs had destroyed Hiroshima and Nagasaki
Emperor Hirohito 1901–89: on 15 August 1945

17 Sure, winning isn't everything. It's the only thing.
Henry ("Red") Sanders: in *Sports Illustrated* 26 December 1955; often attributed to Vince Lombardi

18 Of course I want to win it . . . I'm not here to have a good time, nor to keep warm and dry.
while leading the field, in wet weather, during the PGA golf championship
Nick Faldo 1957– : in *Guardian* (UK) 25 May 1996

Wit
see also **Humor**

1 I am not only witty in myself, but the cause that wit is in other men.
William Shakespeare 1564–1616: *Henry IV, Part 2* (1597)

2 Brevity is the soul of wit.
William Shakespeare 1564–1616: *Hamlet* (1601); cf. **10** below

3 A thing well said will be wit in all languages.
John Dryden 1631–1700: *An Essay of Dramatic Poesy* (1668)

4 And wit's the noblest frailty of the mind.
Thomas Shadwell c. 1642–92: *A True Widow* (1679)

5 Wit will shine
Through the harsh cadence of a rugged line.
John Dryden 1631–1700: "To the Memory of Mr. Oldham" (1684)

6 A wit with dunces, and a dunce with wits.
Alexander Pope 1688–1744: *The Dunciad* (1742)

7 There's no possibility of being witty without a little ill-nature; the malice of a good thing is the barb that makes it stick.
Richard Brinsley Sheridan 1751–1816: *The School for Scandal* (1777)

8 His wit invites you by his looks to come,
But when you knock it never is at home.
William Cowper 1731–1800: "Conversation" (1782)

9 Wit is the epitaph of an emotion.
Friedrich Nietzsche 1844–1900:
Menschliches, Allzumenschliches
(1867–80)

10 Impropriety is the soul of wit.
W. Somerset Maugham 1874–1965:
The Moon and Sixpence (1919); see
2 above

11 There's a hell of a distance
between wise-cracking and wit.
Wit has truth in it; wise-cracking
is simply callisthenics with words.
Dorothy Parker 1893–1967: in *Paris
Review* Summer 1956

12 Epigram: a wisecrack that played
Carnegie Hall.
Oscar Levant 1906–72: in *Coronet*
September 1958

Woman's Role
see also **Men and Women**

1 The First Blast of the Trumpet
Against the Monstrous Regiment
of Women.
regiment = *rule or government over
a country; directed against the rule
of Mary Tudor in England and Mary
of Lorraine in Scotland (as regent for
her daughter Mary Queen of Scots)*
John Knox *c.* 1505–72: title of
pamphlet (1558)

2 I am obnoxious to each carping
tongue,
Who says my hand a needle
better fits,
A poet's pen, all scorn, I should
thus wrong.
Anne Bradstreet *c.* 1612–72: "The
Prologue" (1650)

3 Why then should women be
denied the benefits of instruction?
If knowledge and understanding
had been useless additions to the
sex, God almighty would never
have given them capacities.
Daniel Defoe 1660–1731: *An Essay

Upon Projects (1697) "Of Academies:
An Academy for Women"

4 Be to her virtues very kind;
Be to her faults a little blind;
Let all her ways be unconfined;
And clap your padlock—on her
mind.
Matthew Prior 1664–1721: "An
English Padlock" (1705)

5 If all men are born free, how is it
that all women are born slaves?
Mary Astell 1668–1731: *Some
Reflections upon Marriage* (1706 ed.)

6 A woman's preaching is like a
dog's walking on his hinder legs.
It is not done well; but you are
surprised to find it done at all.
Samuel Johnson 1709–84: James
Boswell *Life of Samuel Johnson*
(1791) 31 July 1763

7 In the new code of laws which I
suppose it will be necessary for
you to make I desire you would
remember the ladies, and be more
generous and favorable to them
than your ancestors. Do not put
such unlimited power into the
hands of the husbands.
Remember all men would be
tyrants if they could.
Abigail Adams 1744–1818: letter to
John Adams, 31 March 1776

8 How much it is to be regretted,
that the British ladies should ever
sit down contented to polish,
when they are able to reform; to
entertain, when they might
instruct; and to dazzle for an
hour, when they are candidates
for eternity!
Hannah More 1745–1833: *Essays on
Various Subjects . . . for Young
Ladies* (1777) "On Dissipation"

9 A man is in general better pleased
when he has a good dinner upon
his table, than when his wife
talks Greek.
Samuel Johnson 1709–84: John

Hawkins (ed.) *The Works of Samuel Johnson* (1787) "Apophthegms, Sentiments, Opinions, etc."

10 Can anything be more absurd than keeping women in a state of ignorance, and yet so vehemently to insist on their resisting temptation?
Vicesimus Knox 1752–1821: Mary Wollstonecraft *A Vindication of the Rights of Woman* (1792)

11 I do not wish them [women] to have power over men; but over themselves.
Mary Wollstonecraft 1759–97: *A Vindication of the Rights of Woman* (1792)

12 Religion is an all-important matter in a public school for girls. Whatever people say, it is the mother's safeguard, and the husband's. What we ask of education is not that girls should think, but that they should believe.
Napoleon I 1769–1821: "Note sur L'Établissement D'Écouen" 15 May 1807

13 With fingers weary and worn,
With eyelids heavy and red,
A woman sat, in unwomanly rags,
Plying her needle and thread—
Stitch! stitch! stitch!
In poverty, hunger, and dirt.
And still with a voice of dolorous pitch
She sang the "Song of the Shirt."
Thomas Hood 1799–1845: "The Song of the Shirt" (1843)

14 Woman stock is rising in the market. I shall not live to see women vote, but I'll come and rap at the ballot box.
Lydia Maria Child 1802–80: letter to Sarah Shaw, 3 August 1856

15 I should like to know what is the proper function of women, if it is

not to make reasons for husbands to stay at home, and still stronger reasons for bachelors to go out.
George Eliot 1819–80: *The Mill on the Floss* (1860)

16 I want to be something so much worthier than the doll in the doll's house.
Charles Dickens 1812–70: *Our Mutual Friend* (1865)

17 The Queen is most anxious to enlist every one who can speak or write to join in checking this mad, wicked folly of "Woman's Rights," with all its attendant horrors, on which her poor feeble sex is bent, forgetting every sense of womanly feeling and propriety.
Queen Victoria 1819–1901: letter to Theodore Martin, 29 May 1870

18 The one point on which all women are in furious secret rebellion against the existing law is the saddling of the right to a child with the obligation to become the servant of a man.
George Bernard Shaw 1856–1950: *Getting Married* (1911)

19 We are here to claim our right as women, not only to be free, but to fight for freedom. That it is our right as well as our duty.
Christabel Pankhurst 1880–1958: in *Votes for Women* 31 March 1911

20 I myself have never been able to find out precisely what feminism is: I only know that people call me a feminist whenever I express sentiments that differentiate me from a doormat or a prostitute.
Rebecca West 1892–1983: in *The Clarion* 14 November 1913

21 I . . . understand why the saints were rarely married women. I am convinced it has nothing inherently to do, as I once supposed, with chastity or children. It has to do primarily

with distractions . . . Woman's
normal occupations in general
run counter to creative life, or
contemplative life or saintly life.
Anne Morrow Lindbergh 1906– :
Gift from the Sea (1955)

22 The only position for women in
SNCC is prone.
Stokely Carmichael 1941– :
response to a question about the
position of women at a Student
Nonviolent Coordinating Committee
conference, November 1964

23 Woman is the nigger of the
world.
Yoko Ono 1933– : remark made in
a 1968 interview for *Nova* magazine
and adopted by John Lennon as the
title of a song (1972)

24 But if God had wanted us to
think just with our wombs, why
did He give us a brain?
Clare Booth Luce 1903–87: in *Life* 16
October 1970

25 Because of their age-long training
in human relations—for that is
what feminine intuition really is—
women have a special
contribution to make to any
group enterprise, and I feel it is
up to them to contribute the
kinds of awareness that relatively
few men . . . have incorporated
through their education.
Margaret Mead 1901–78: *Blackberry
Winter* (1972)

26 Always suspect any job men
willingly vacate for women.
Jill Tweedie 1936–93: *It's Only Me*
(1980)

27 We are becoming the men we
wanted to marry.
Gloria Steinem 1934– : in *Ms* July/
August 1982

28 I didn't fight to get women out
from behind the vacuum cleaner
to get them onto the board of
Hoover.
Germaine Greer 1939– : in
Guardian (UK) 27 October 1986

29 Feminism is the most
revolutionary idea there has ever
been. Equality for women
demands a change in the human
psyche more profound then
anything Marx dreamed of. It
means valuing parenthood as
much as we value banking.
Polly Toynbee 1946– : in *Guardian*
(UK) 19 January 1987

30 I suppose I could have stayed
home, baked cookies and had
teas. . . . The work that I have
done as a professional, a public
advocate, has been aimed . . . to
assure that women can make the
choices . . . whether it's full-time
career, full-time motherhood or
some combination.
Hillary Rodham Clinton 1947– :
Quoted in Time (14 September 1992)

Women
see also **Men and Women**

1 This is now bone of my bones,
and flesh of my flesh: she shall be
called Woman, because she was
taken out of Man.
Bible: Genesis

2 Who can find a virtuous woman?
for her price is far above rubies.
Bible: Proverbs

3 The greatest glory of a woman is
to be least talked about by men.
Pericles c. 495–429 BC: Thucydides
History of the Peloponnesian War

4 *Varium et mutabile semper
Femina.*
Fickle and changeable always is
woman.
Virgil 70–19 BC: *Aeneid*

5 And what is bettre than
wisedoom? Womman. And

what is bettre than a good womman? Nothyng.
Geoffrey Chaucer c. 1343–1400: *The Canterbury Tales* "The Tale of Melibee"

6 Frailty, thy name is woman!
William Shakespeare 1564–1616: *Hamlet* (1601)

7 The weaker sex, to piety more prone.
William Alexander, Earl of Stirling c. 1567–1640: "Doomsday" 5th Hour (1637)

8 She floats, she hesitates; in a word, she's a woman.
Jean Racine 1639–99: *Athalie* (1691)

9 When once a woman has given you her heart, you can never get rid of the rest of her body.
John Vanbrugh 1664–1726: *The Relapse* (1696)

10 She knows her man, and when you rant and swear,
Can draw you to her *with a single hair*.
John Dryden 1631–1700: translation of Persius *Satires*

11 I have never had any great esteem for the generality of the fair sex, and my only consolation for being of that gender has been the assurance it gave me of never being married to anyone amongst them.
Lady Mary Wortley Montagu 1689–1762: letter to Mrs. Calthorpe, 7 December 1723

12 Woman's at best a contradiction still.
Alexander Pope 1688–1744: *Epistles to Several Persons* "To a Lady" (1735)

13 Women, then, are only children of a larger growth.
Lord Chesterfield 1694–1773: *Letters to his Son* (1774) 5 September 1748

14 Here's to the maiden of bashful fifteen
Here's to the widow of fifty
Here's to the flaunting, extravagant quean;
And here's to the housewife that's thrifty.
Richard Brinsley Sheridan 1751–1816: *The School for Scandal* (1777)

15 Auld nature swears, the lovely dears
Her noblest work she classes, O;
Her prentice han' she tried on man,
An' then she made the lasses, O.
Robert Burns 1759–96: "Green Grow the Rashes, O" (1787)

16 O Woman! in our hours of ease,
Uncertain, coy, and hard to please,
And variable as the shade
By the light quivering aspen made;
When pain and anguish wring the brow,
A ministering angel thou!
Sir Walter Scott 1771–1832: *Marmion* (1808)

17 All the privilege I claim for my own sex . . . is that of loving longest, when existence or when hope is gone.
Jane Austen 1775–1817: *Persuasion* (1818)

18 I have met with women whom I really think would like to be married to a poem and to be given away by a novel.
John Keats 1795–1821: letter to Fanny Brawne, 8 July 1819

19 In her first passion woman loves her lover,
In all the others all she loves is love.
Lord Byron 1788–1824: *Don Juan* (1819–24)

20 Eternal Woman draws us upward.

Johann Wolfgang von Goethe 1749–1832: *Faust* pt. 2 (1832) "Hochgebirg"

21 If I were asked . . . to what the singular prosperity and growing strength of that people [the Americans] ought mainly to be attributed, I should reply: To the superiority of their women.
Alexis de Tocqueville 1805–59: *Democracy in America* (1835)

22 The woman is so hard
Upon the woman.
Alfred, Lord Tennyson 1809–92: *The Princess* (1847)

23 Only the male intellect, clouded by sexual impulse, could call the undersized, narrow-shouldered, broad-hipped, and short-legged sex the fair sex.
Arthur Schopenhauer 1788–1860: "On Women" (1851)

24 The happiest women, like the happiest nations, have no history.
George Eliot 1819–80: *The Mill on the Floss* (1860)

25 Women—one half the human race at least—care fifty times more for a marriage than a ministry.
Walter Bagehot 1826–77: *The English Constitution* (1867) "The Monarchy"

26 Woman was God's second blunder.
Friedrich Nietzsche 1844–1900: *Der Antichrist* (1888)

27 One should never trust a woman who tells one her real age. A woman who would tell one that, would tell one anything.
Oscar Wilde 1854–1900: *A Woman of No Importance* (1893)

28 When you get to a man in the case,
They're like as a row of pins—

For the Colonel's Lady an' Judy O'Grady
Are sisters under their skins!
Rudyard Kipling 1865–1936: "The Ladies" (1896)

29 Women have, commonly, a very positive moral sense; that which they will, is right; that which they reject, is wrong; and their will, in most cases, ends by settling the moral.
Henry Brooks Adams 1838–1918: *The Education of Henry Adams* (1907)

30 The prime truth of woman, the universal mother . . . that if a thing is worth doing, it is worth doing badly.
G. K. Chesterton 1874–1936: *What's Wrong with the World* (1910) "Folly and Female Education"

31 The female of the species is more deadly than the male.
Rudyard Kipling 1865–1936: "The Female of the Species" (1919)

32 The perpetual hunger to be beautiful and that thirst to be loved which is the real curse of Eve.
Jean Rhys c. 1890–1979: *The Left Bank* (1927) "Illusion"

33 Certain women should be struck regularly, like gongs.
Noël Coward 1899–1973: *Private Lives* (1930)

34 The great and almost only comfort about being a woman is that one can always pretend to be more stupid than one is and no one is surprised.
Freya Stark 1893–1993: *The Valleys of the Assassins* (1934)

35 The great question that has never been answered and which I have not yet been able to answer, despite my thirty years of research into the feminine soul, is "What does a woman want?"

Sigmund Freud 1856–1939: to Marie Bonaparte; Ernest Jones *Sigmund Freud: Life and Work* (1955)

36 One is not born a woman: one becomes one.
Simone de Beauvoir 1908–86: *Le deuxième sexe* (1949)

37 There is nothin' like a dame.
Oscar Hammerstein II 1895–1960: title of song (1949)

38 Slamming their doors, stamping their high heels, banging their irons and saucepans—the eternal flaming racket of the female.
John Osborne 1929–94: *Look Back in Anger* (1956)

39 Women never have young minds. They are born three thousand years old.
Shelagh Delaney 1939– : *A Taste of Honey* (1959)

40 A liberated woman is one who has sex before marriage and a job after.
Gloria Steinem 1934– : *Newsweek* (28 March 1960)

41 From birth to 18 a girl needs good parents. From 18 to 35, she needs good looks. From 35 to 55, good personality. From 55 on, she needs good cash.
Sophie Tucker 1884–1966: Michael Freedland *Sophie* (1978)

42 Being an old maid is like death by drowning, a really delightful sensation after you cease to struggle.
Edna Ferber 1887–1968: R. E. Drennan *Wit's End* (1973)

43 Sisterhood is powerful.
Robin Morgan 1941– : title of book (1970)

44 Being a woman is of special interest only to aspiring male transsexuals. To actual women, it is merely a good excuse not to play football.
Fran Lebowitz 1946– : *Metropolitan Life* (1978)

45 You can now see the Female Eunuch the world over . . . spreading herself wherever blue jeans and Coca-Cola may go. Wherever you see nail varnish, lipstick, brassieres, and high heels, the Eunuch has set up her camp.
Germaine Greer 1939– : *The Female Eunuch* (20th anniversary ed., 1991)

Wordplay
see also **Wit**

1 A man who could make so vile a pun would not scruple to pick a pocket.
John Dennis 1657–1734: editorial note in *The Gentleman's Magazine* (1781)

2 Apt Alliteration's artful aid.
Charles Churchill 1731–64: *The Prophecy of Famine* (1763)

3 A quibble is to Shakespeare, what luminous vapours are to the traveller; he follows it at all adventures, it is sure to lead him out of his way and sure to engulf him in the mire.
Samuel Johnson 1709–84: *Plays of William Shakespeare . . .* (1765)

4 If I reprehend any thing in this world, it is the use of my oracular tongue, and a nice derangement of epitaphs!
Richard Brinsley Sheridan 1751–1816: *The Rivals* (1775)

5 What is an Epigram? a dwarfish whole,
Its body brevity, and wit its soul.
Samuel Taylor Coleridge 1772–1834: "Epigram" (1809)

6 Those who cannot miss an
opportunity of saying a good
thing . . . are not to be trusted
with the management of any
great question.
William Hazlitt 1778–1830:
Characteristics (1823)

7 [A pun] is a pistol let off at the
ear; not a feather to tickle the
intellect.
Charles Lamb 1775–1834: *Last
Essays of Elia* (1833) "Popular
Fallacies"

8 I summed up all systems in a
phrase, and all existence in an
epigram.
Oscar Wilde 1854–1900: letter, from
Reading Prison, to Lord Alfred
Douglas, January–March 1897

9 Up with your damned nonsense
will I put twice, or perhaps once,
but sometimes always, by God,
never.
Hans Richter 1843–1916: attributed

10 You merely loop the loop on a
commonplace and come down
between the lines.
*when asked how to make an
epigram by a young man in the
flying corps*
W. Somerset Maugham 1874–1965:
A Writer's Notebook (1949) written
in 1933

11 The conclusion of your syllogism,
I said lightly, is fallacious, being
based upon licensed premises.
Flann O'Brien 1911–66: *At Swim-Two-
Birds* (1939)

12 Many of us can still remember
the social nuisance of the
inveterate punster. This man
followed conversation as a shark
follows a ship.
Stephen Leacock 1869–1944: *The
Boy I Left Behind Me* (1947)

Words

see also **Language, Meaning, Names,
Words and Deeds**

1 And once sent out a word takes
wing beyond recall.
Horace 65–8 BC: *Epistles*

2 Throughout the world, if it were
sought,
Fair words enough a man shall
find.
They be good cheap; they cost
right naught;
Their substance is but only wind.
Thomas Wyatt *c.* 1503–42:
"Throughout the world, if it were
sought" (1557)

3 But words are words; I never yet
did hear
That the bruisèd heart was
piercèd through the ear.
William Shakespeare 1564–1616:
Othello (1602–4)

4 Words are the tokens current and
accepted for conceits, as moneys
are for values.
Francis Bacon 1561–1626: *The
Advancement of Learning* (1605)

5 Words are wise men's counters,
they do but reckon by them: but
they are the money of fools, that
value them by the authority of an
Aristotle, a Cicero, or a Thomas,
or any other doctor whatsoever, if
but a man.
Thomas Hobbes 1588–1679:
Leviathan (1651)

6 Words are like leaves; and where
they most abound,
Much fruit of sense beneath is
rarely found.
Alexander Pope 1688–1744: *An
Essay on Criticism* (1711)

7 I am not yet so lost in
lexicography as to forget that
words are the daughters of earth,
and that things are the sons of

heaven. Language is only the instrument of science, and words are but the signs of ideas: I wish, however, that the instrument might be less apt to decay, and that signs might be permanent, like the things which they denote.
Samuel Johnson 1709–84: *A Dictionary of the English Language* (1755)

8 A word to the wise is enough, and many words won't fill a bushel.
Benjamin Franklin 1706–90: *Poor Richard's Almanack, Preface: Courteous Reader* (1758)

9 It's exactly where a thought is lacking
That, just in time, a word shows up instead.
Johann Wolfgang von Goethe 1749–1832: *Faust* (1808)

10 "Do you spell it with a "V" or a "W"?" inquired the judge. "That depends upon the taste and fancy of the speller, my Lord," replied Sam [Weller].
Charles Dickens 1812–70: *Pickwick Papers* (1837)

11 "When *I* use a word," Humpty Dumpty said in a rather scornful tone, "it means just what I choose it to mean—neither more nor less."
Lewis Carroll 1832–98: *Through the Looking-Glass* (1872)

12 Some word that teems with hidden meaning—like Basingstoke.
W. S. Gilbert 1836–1911: *Ruddigore* (1887)

13 Summer afternoon—summer afternoon . . . the two most beautiful words in the English language.
Henry James 1843–1916: Edith Wharton *A Backward Glance* (1934)

14 I fear those big words, Stephen said, which make us so unhappy.
James Joyce 1882–1941: *Ulysses* (1922)

15 Words are, of course, the most powerful drug used by mankind.
Rudyard Kipling 1865–1936: speech, 14 February 1923

16 My spelling is Wobbly. It's good spelling but it Wobbles, and the letters get in the wrong places.
A. A. Milne 1882–1956: *Winnie-the-Pooh* (1926)

17 The Greeks had a word for it.
Zoë Akins 1886–1958: title of play (1930)

18 I gotta use words when I talk to you.
T. S. Eliot 1888–1965: *Sweeney Agonistes* (1932)

19 Words are chameleons, which reflect the color of their environment.
Learned Hand 1872–1961: in *Commissioner v. National Carbide Corp.* (1948)

20 There is no use indicting words, they are no shoddier than what they peddle.
Samuel Beckett 1906–89: *Malone Dies* (1958)

21 Man does not live by words alone, despite the fact that he sometimes has to eat them.
Adlai Stevenson 1900–65: *The Wit and Wisdom of Adlai Stevenson* (1965)

22 MIKE: There's no word in the Irish language for what you were doing.
WILSON: In Lapland they have no word for snow.
Joe Orton 1933–67: *The Ruffian on the Stair* (rev. ed. 1967)

23 In my youth there were words
you couldn't say in front of a girl;
now you can't say "girl."
Tom Lehrer 1928– : interview in
The Oldie 1996; in *Sunday Telegraph*
(UK) 10 March 1996

Words and Deeds

1 But be ye doers of the word, and
not hearers only.
Bible: James

2 Woord is but wynd; leff woord
and tak the dede.
John Lydgate c. 1370–c. 1451:
Secrets of Old Philosophers

3 If to do were as easy as to know
what were good to do, chapels
had been churches, and poor
men's cottages princes' palaces. It
is a good divine that follows his
own instructions; I can easier
teach twenty what were good to
be done, than be one of the
twenty to follow mine own
teaching.
William Shakespeare 1564–1616: *The
Merchant of Venice* (1596–8)

4 Do not, as some ungracious
pastors do,
Show me the steep and thorny
way to heaven,
Whiles, like a puffed and reckless
libertine,
Himself the primrose path of
dalliance treads,
And recks not his own rede.
William Shakespeare 1564–1616:
Hamlet (1601)

5 Oh that thou hadst like others
been all words,
And no performance.
Philip Massinger 1583–1640: *The
Parliament of Love* (1624)

6 Here lies a great and mighty king
Whose promise none relies on;
He never said a foolish thing,
Nor ever did a wise one.
on Charles II

John Wilmot, Lord Rochester 1647–
80: "The King's Epitaph"
(alternatively "Here lies our
sovereign lord the King") in C. E.
Doble et al. *Thomas Hearne:
Remarks and Collections* (1885–1921)
17 November 1706; cf. **7** below

7 This is very true: for my words
are my own, and my actions are
my ministers'.
reply to Lord Rochester's epitaph
Charles II 1630–85: in *Thomas
Hearne: Remarks and Collections*
(1885–1921) 17 November 1706; cf. **6**
above

8 Because half a dozen grasshoppers
under a fern make the field ring
with their importunate chink,
whilst thousands of great cattle,
reposed beneath the shadow of
the British oak, chew the cud and
are silent, pray do not imagine
that those who make the noise
are the only inhabitants of the
field.
Edmund Burke 1729–97: *Reflections
on the Revolution in France* (1790)

9 I prefer the talents of action—of
war—of the senate—or even of
science—to all the speculations of
those mere dreamers of another
existence.
Lord Byron 1788–1824: letter to
Annabella Milbanke, 29 November
1813

10 The end of man is an action and
not a thought, though it were the
noblest.
Thomas Carlyle 1795–1881: *Sartor
Resartus* (1834)

11 Considering how foolishly people
act and how pleasantly they
prattle, perhaps it would be better
for the world if they talked more
and did less.
W. Somerset Maugham 1874–1965: *A
Writer's Notebook* (1949) written in
1892

12 People who could not tell a lathe
from a lawn mower and have
never carried the responsibilities
of management never tire of
telling British management off for
its alleged inefficiency.
Keith Joseph 1918–94: in *The Times*
(UK) 9 August 1974

Work
see also **Employment, Idleness,
Leisure**

1 In the sweat of thy face shalt
thou eat bread.
Bible: Genesis

2 For it is commonly said:
completed labors are pleasant.
Cicero 106–43 BC: *De Finibus*

3 Come unto me, all ye that labor
and are heavy laden, and I will
give you rest . . .
For my yoke is easy, and my
burden is light.
Bible: St. Matthew

4 If any would not work, neither
should he eat.
Bible: II Thessalonians

5 O, how full of briers is this
working-day world!
William Shakespeare 1564–1616: *As
You Like It* (1599)

6 The labour we delight in physics
pain.
William Shakespeare 1564–1616:
Macbeth (1606)

7 We spend our midday sweat, our
midnight oil;
We tire the night in thought, the
day in toil.
Francis Quarles 1592–1644: *Emblems*
(1635)

8 Why should he, with wealth and
honour blest,
Refuse his age the needful hours
of rest?

Punish a body which he could
not please;
Bankrupt of life, yet prodigal of
ease?
John Dryden 1631–1700: *Absalom
and Achitophel* (1681)

9 How doth the little busy bee
Improve each shining hour,
And gather honey all the day
From every opening flower!
Isaac Watts 1674–1748: "Against
Idleness and Mischief" (1715)

10 When men are employed, they
are best contented; for on the
days they worked they were goodnatured and cheerful, and, with
the consciousness of having done
a good day's work, they spent the
evening jollily; but on our idle
days they were mutinous and
quarrelsome.
Benjamin Franklin 1706–90:
Autobiography (1868)

11 If you have great talents, industry
will improve them: if you have
but moderate abilities, industry
will supply their deficiency.
Joshua Reynolds 1723–92:
Discourses on Art 11 December 1769

12 The world is too much with us;
late and soon,
Getting and spending, we lay
waste our powers.
William Wordsworth 1770–1850:
"The world is too much with us"
(1807)

13 Whether we consider the manual
industry of the poor, or the
intellectual exertions of the
superior classes, we shall find that
diligent occupation, if not
criminally perverted from its
purposes, is at once the
instrument of virtue and the
secret of happiness. Man cannot
be safely trusted with a life of
leisure.
Hannah More 1745–1833: *Christian
Morals* (1813)

14 Who first invented work—and
tied the free
And holy-day rejoicing spirit
down
To the ever-haunting importunity
Of business?
Charles Lamb 1775–1834: letter to
Bernard Barton, 11 September 1822

15 My life is one demd horrid grind!
Charles Dickens 1812–70: *Nicholas
Nickleby* (1839)

16 Blessèd are the horny hands of
toil!
James Russell Lowell 1819–91: "A
Glance Behind the Curtain" (1844)

17 For men must work, and women
must weep,
And there's little to earn, and
many to keep,
Though the harbour bar be
moaning.
Charles Kingsley 1819–75: "The
Three Fishers" (1858)

18 Labour without joy is base.
Labour without sorrow is base.
Sorrow without labour is base.
Joy without labour is base.
John Ruskin 1819–1900: *Time and
Tide* (1867)

19 Generations have trod, have trod,
have trod;
And all is seared with trade;
bleared, smeared with toil.
Gerard Manley Hopkins 1844–89:
"God's Grandeur" (written 1877)

20 I like work: it fascinates me. I can
sit and look at it for hours. I love
to keep it by me: the idea of
getting rid of it nearly breaks my
heart.
Jerome K. Jerome 1859–1927: *Three
Men in a Boat* (1889)

21 Work is the curse of the drinking
classes.
Oscar Wilde 1854–1900: H. Pearson
Life of Oscar Wilde (1946)

22 Far and away the best prize that
life offers is the chance to work
hard at work worth doing.
Theodore Roosevelt 1858–1919:
Labor Day speech (1903)

23 Perfect freedom is reserved for the
man who lives by his own work
and in that work does what he
wants to do.
R. G. Collingwood 1889–1943:
Speculum Mentis (1924)

24 That state is a state of slavery in
which a man does what he likes
to do in his spare time and in his
working time that which is
required of him.
Eric Gill 1882–1940: *Art nonsense
and Other Essays* (1929)

25 The test of a vocation is the love
of the drudgery it involves.
Logan Pearsall Smith 1865–1946:
Afterthoughts (1931) "Art and
Letters"

26 There is no substitute for hard
work.
Thomas Alva Edison 1847–1931: *Life*
(1932)

27 *Arbeit macht frei.* Work liberates.
Anonymous: words inscribed on the
gates of Dachau concentration camp,
1933, and subsequently on those of
Auschwitz

28 Work expands so as to fill the
time available for its completion.
C. Northcote Parkinson 1909–93:
Parkinson's Law (1958)

29 Without work, all life goes rotten,
but when work is soulless, life
stifles and dies.
Albert Camus 1913–60: attributed; E.
F. Schumacher *Good Work* (1979)

30 If work was a good thing the rich
would have it all and not let you
do it.
Elmore Leonard 1925– : *Split
Images* (1961)

31 Work was like a stick. It had two ends. When you worked for the knowing you gave them quality; when you worked for a fool you simply gave him eye-wash.
Alexander Solzhenitsyn 1918– : *One Day in the Life of Ivan Denisovich* (1962)

32 It's true hard work never killed anybody, but I figure why take the chance?
Ronald Reagan 1911– : interview, *Guardian* (UK) 31 March 1987

33 I have long been of the opinion that if work were such a splendid thing the rich would have kept more of it for themselves.
Bruce Grocott 1940– : in *Observer* (UK) 22 May 1988

World War I
see also **The Armed Forces, Warfare, Wars, World War II**

1 If there is ever another war in Europe, it will come out of some damned silly thing in the Balkans.
Otto von Bismarck 1815–98: quoted in speech, House of Commons, 16 August 1945

2 The lamps are going out all over Europe; we shall not see them lit again in our lifetime.
on the eve of World War I
Edward Grey 1862–1933: *25 Years* (1925)

3 Do your duty bravely. Fear God. Honour the King.
Lord Kitchener 1850–1916: message to soldiers of the British Expeditionary Force, August 1914

4 *Gott strafe England!*
God punish England!
Alfred Funke b. 1869: *Schwert und Myrte* (1914)

5 Belgium put the kibosh on the Kaiser.
Alf Ellerton: title of song (1914)

6 Now, God be thanked Who has matched us with His hour,
And caught our youth, and wakened us from sleeping,
With hand made sure, clear eye, and sharpened power,
To turn, as swimmers into cleanness leaping.
Rupert Brooke 1887–1915: "Peace" (1914)

7 Oh! we don't want to lose you but we think you ought to go
For your King and your Country both need you so.
Paul Alfred Rubens 1875–1917: "Your King and Country Want You" (1914 song)

8 My center is giving way, my right is retreating, situation excellent, I am attacking.
Ferdinand Foch 1851–1929: message sent during the first Battle of the Marne, September 1914; R. Recouly *Foch* (1919)

9 In Flanders fields the poppies blow
Between the crosses, row on row.
John McCrae 1872–1918: "In Flanders Fields" (1915)

10 There's something wrong with our bloody ships today, Chatfield.
David Beatty 1871–1936: at the Battle of Jutland, 1916; Winston Churchill *The World Crisis 1916–1918* (1927)

11 *Ils ne passeront pas.*
They shall not pass.
Anonymous: slogan used by the French army at the defense of Verdun in 1916; variously attributed to Marshal Pétain and to General Robert Nivelle, and taken up by the Republicans in the Spanish Civil War in the form "*No pasarán!*"; cf. **Defiance 9**

12 *Lafayette, nous voilà!*
Lafayette, we are here.
Charles E. Stanton 1859–1933: at the
tomb of Lafayette in Paris, 4 July
1917

13 Over there, over there,
Send the word, send the word
    over there
That the Yanks are coming, the
    Yanks are coming . . .
We'll be over, we're coming over
And we won't come back till it's
    over, over there.
George M. Cohan 1878–1942: "Over
There" (1917 song)

14 My home policy: I wage war; my
foreign policy: I wage war. All the
time I wage war.
Georges Clemenceau 1841–1929:
speech to French Chamber of
Deputies, 8 March 1918

15 At eleven o'clock this morning
came to an end the cruellest and
most terrible war that has ever
scourged mankind. I hope we
may say that thus, this fateful
morning, came to an end all
wars.
David Lloyd George 1863–1945:
speech, House of Commons, 11
November 1918

16 This is not a peace treaty, it is an
armistice for twenty years.
Ferdinand Foch 1851–1929: at the
signing of the Treaty of Versailles,
1919; Paul Reynaud *Mémoires* (1963)

17 All quiet on the western front.
Erich Maria Remarque 1898–1970:
English title of *Im Westen nichts
Neues* (1929 novel)

18 You are all a lost generation.
*of the young who served in the First
World War; phrase borrowed (in
translation) from a French garage
mechanic, whom Stein heard
address it disparagingly to an
incompetent apprentice*
Gertrude Stein 1874–1946: Ernest

Hemingway subsequently took it as
his epigraph to *The Sun Also Rises*
(1926)

19 Oh what a lovely war.
Joan Littlewood 1914– and **Charles
Chilton** 1914– : title of stage show
(1963)

20 The First World War had begun—
imposed on the statesmen of
Europe by railway timetables.
A. J. P. Taylor 1906–90: *The First
World War* (1963)

World War II
see also **The Armed Forces, Warfare,
Wars, World War I**

1 How horrible, fantastic, incredible
it is that we should be digging
trenches and trying on gas-masks
here because of a quarrel in a far
away country between people of
whom we know nothing.
*on Germany's annexation of the
Sudetenland*
Neville Chamberlain 1869–1940:
radio broadcast, 27 September 1938

2 We're gonna hang out the
washing on the Siegfried Line.
Jimmy Kennedy and **Michael Carr**:
title of song (1939)

3 We shall not flag or fail. We shall
go on to the end. We shall fight
in France, we shall fight on the
seas and oceans, we shall fight
with growing confidence and
growing strength in the air, we
shall defend our island, whatever
the cost may be. We shall fight
on the beaches, we shall fight on
the landing grounds, we shall
fight in the fields and in the
streets, we shall fight in the hills;
we shall never surrender.
Winston Churchill 1874–1965:
speech, House of Commons, 4 June
1940

4 This little steamer, like all her brave and battered sisters, is immortal. She'll go sailing proudly down the years in the epic of Dunkirk. And our great-grand-children, when they learn how we began this war by snatching glory out of defeat, and then swept on to victory, may also learn how the little holiday steamers made an excursion to hell and came back glorious.
J. B. Priestley 1894–1984: radio broadcast, 5 June 1940

5 France has lost a battle. But France has not lost the war!
Charles de Gaulle 1890–1970: proclamation, 18 June 1940

6 Let us therefore brace ourselves to our duty, and so bear ourselves that, if the British Commonwealth and its Empire last for a thousand years, men will still say, "This was their finest hour."
Winston Churchill 1874–1965: speech, House of Commons, 18 June 1940

7 I'm glad we've been bombed. It makes me feel I can look the East End in the face.
Queen Elizabeth, the Queen Mother 1900– : to a London policeman, 13 September 1940

8 We have the men—the skill—the wealth—and above all, the will . . . We must be the great arsenal of democracy.
Franklin D. Roosevelt 1882–1945: "Fireside Chat" radio broadcast, 29 December 1940

9 Yesterday, December 7, 1941—a date which will live in infamy—the United States of America was suddenly and deliberately attacked by naval and air forces of the Empire of Japan.
Franklin D. Roosevelt 1882–1945: address to Congress, 8 December 1941

10 Sighted sub, sank same.
on sinking a Japanese submarine in the Atlantic region (the first US naval success in the war)
Donald Mason 1913– : radio message, 28 January 1942

11 I came through and I shall return.
on reaching Australia, having broken through Japanese lines en route from Corregidor
Douglas MacArthur 1880–1964: statement in Adelaide, 20 March 1942

12 Don't let's be beastly to the Germans
When our Victory is ultimately won.
Noël Coward 1899–1973: "Don't Let's Be Beastly to the Germans" (1943 song)

13 I think we might be going a bridge too far.
expressing reservations about the Arnhem "Market Garden" operation
Frederick ("Boy") Browning 1896–1965: to Field Marshal Montgomery, 10 September 1944

14 The Third Fleet's sunken and damaged ships have been salvaged and are retiring at high speed toward the enemy.
on hearing claims that the Japanese had virtually annihilated the US fleet
W. F. ("Bull") Halsey 1882–1959: report, 14 October 1944

15 Nuts!
Anthony McAuliffe 1898–1975: replying to the German demand for surrender at Bastogne, Belgium, 22 December 1944

16 Götterdämmerung without the gods.
of the use of atomic bombs against the Japanese
Dwight Macdonald 1906–82: in *Politics* September 1945 "The Bomb"

17 It may almost be said, "Before
Alamein we never had a victory.
After Alamein we never had a
defeat."
Winston Churchill 1874–1965:
Second World War (1951)

Worry

1 O polished perturbation! golden
care!
That keep'st the ports of slumber
open wide
To many a watchful night!
William Shakespeare 1564–1616:
Henry IV, Part 2 (1597)

2 What though care killed a cat,
thou hast mettle enough in thee
to kill care.
William Shakespeare 1564–1616:
Much Ado About Nothing (1598–9)

3 In trouble to be troubled
Is to have your trouble doubled.
Daniel Defoe 1660–1731: *The Farther
Adventures of Robinson Crusoe*
(1719)

4 Nothing puzzles me more than
time and space; and yet nothing
troubles me less, as I never think
about them.
Charles Lamb 1775–1834: letter to
Thomas Manning, 2 January 1810

5 What's the use of worrying?
It never was worth while,
So, pack up your troubles in your
old kit-bag,
And smile, smile, smile.
George Asaf 1880–1951: "Pack up
your Troubles" (1915 song)

6 Neurosis is the way of avoiding
non-being by avoiding being.
Paul Tillich 1886–1965: *The Courage
To Be* (1952)

7 I'm not [biting my fingernails].
I'm biting my knuckles. I finished
the fingernails months ago.
while directing Cleopatra *(1963)*

Joseph L. Mankiewicz 1909– : Dick
Sheppard *Elizabeth* (1975)

8 We are, perhaps uniquely among
the earth's creatures, the
worrying animal. We worry away
our lives, fearing the future,
discontent with the present,
unable to take in the idea of
dying, unable to sit still.
Lewis Thomas 1913– : *The Medusa
and the Snail* (1979)

9 A neurosis is a secret you don't
know you're keeping.
Kenneth Tynan 1927–80: Kathleen
Tynan *Life of Kenneth Tynan* (1987)

Writers
see also **Poets, Shakespeare, Writing**

1 Will you have all in all for prose
and verse? Take the miracle of
our age, Sir Philip Sidney.
Richard Carew 1555–1620: William
Camden *Remains concerning Britain*
(1614) "The Excellency of the English
Tongue"

2 That great Cham of literature,
Samuel Johnson.
Tobias Smollett 1721–71: letter to
John Wilkes, 16 March 1759

3 Why, Sir, if you were to read
Richardson for the story, your
impatience would be so much
fretted that you would hang
yourself.
Samuel Johnson 1709–84: James
Boswell *Life of Samuel Johnson*
(1791) 6 April 1772

4 What should I do with your
strong, manly, spirited sketches,
full of variety and glow?—How
could I possibly join them on to
the little bit (two inches wide) of
ivory on which I work with so
fine a brush, as produces little
effect after much labour?
Jane Austen 1775–1817: letter to J.
Edward Austen, 16 December 1816

5 The Big Bow-Wow strain I can do
myself like any now going; but
the exquisite touch, which
renders ordinary commonplace
things and characters interesting,
from the truth of the description
and the sentiment, is denied to
me.
of Jane Austen
Sir Walter Scott 1771–1832: diary 14
March 1826

6 Swift was *anima Rabelaisii habitans
in sicco*—the soul of Rabelais
dwelling in a dry place.
Samuel Taylor Coleridge 1772–1834:
Table Talk (1835) 15 June 1830

7 Johnson hewed passages through
the Alps, while Gibbon levelled
walks through parks and gardens.
George Colman, the Younger 1762–
1836: *Random Records* (1830)

8 Thou large-brained woman and
large-hearted man.
Elizabeth Barrett Browning 1806–61:
"To George Sand—A Desire" (1844)

9 A rake among scholars, and a
scholar among rakes.
of Richard Steele
Lord Macaulay 1800–59: *Essays
Contributed to the Edinburgh Review*
(1850) "The Life and Writings of
Addison"

10 He describes London like a special
correspondent for posterity.
Walter Bagehot 1826–77: *National
Review* (UK) 7 October 1858 "Charles
Dickens"

11 He never leaves off . . . and he
always has two packages of
manuscript in his desk, besides
the one he's working on, and the
one that's being published.
*on her husband Anthony Trollope,
1815–82*
Rose Trollope 1820–1917: Julian
Hawthorne *Shapes that Pass:
Memories of Old Days* (1928)

12 Meredith's a prose Browning, and
so is Browning.
Oscar Wilde 1854–1900: *Intentions*
(1891) "The Critic as Artist"

13 A louse in the locks of literature.
of Churton Collins
Alfred, Lord Tennyson 1809–92:
Evan Charteris *Life and Letters of Sir
Edmund Gosse* (1931)

14 Hardy went down to botanize in
the swamp, while Meredith
climbed towards the sun.
Meredith became, at his best, a
sort of daintily dressed Walt
Whitman: Hardy became a sort of
village atheist brooding and
blaspheming over the village idiot.
G. K. Chesterton 1874–1936: *The
Victorian Age in Literature* (1912)

15 It is leviathan retrieving pebbles.
It is a magnificent but painful
hippopotamus resolved at any
cost, even at the cost of its
dignity, upon picking up a pea
which has got into a corner of its
den.
of Henry James
H. G. Wells 1866–1946: *Boon* (1915)

16 E. M. Forster never gets any
further than warming the teapot.
He's a rare fine hand at that. Feel
this teapot. Is it not beautifully
warm? Yes, but there ain't going
to be no tea.
Katherine Mansfield 1888–1923:
diary, May 1917

17 The humour of Dostoievsky is the
humour of a bar-loafer who ties a
kettle to a dog's tail.
W. Somerset Maugham 1874–1965:
A Writer's Notebook (1949) written
in 1917

18 The cheerful clatter of Sir James
Barrie's cans as he went round
with the milk of human kindness.
Philip Guedalla 1889–1944: *Supers
and Supermen* (1920) "Some Critics"

19 The work of Henry James has always seemed divisible by a simple dynastic arrangement into three reigns: James I, James II, and the Old Pretender.
Philip Guedalla 1889–1944: *Supers and Supermen* (1920)

20 The scratching of pimples on the body of the bootboy at Claridges.
of James Joyce's Ulysses
Virginia Woolf 1882–1941: letter to Lytton Strachey, 24 April 1922

21 A dogged attempt to cover the universe with mud, an inverted Victorianism, an attempt to make crossness and dirt succeed where sweetness and light failed.
of James Joyce's Ulysses
E. M. Forster 1879–1970: *Aspects of the Novel* (1927)

22 Poor Henry, he's spending eternity wandering round and round a stately park and the fence is just too high for him to peep over and they're having tea just too far away for him to hear what the countess is saying.
of Henry James
W. Somerset Maugham 1874–1965: *Cakes and Ale* (1930)

23 It was like watching someone organize her own immortality. Every phrase and gesture was studied. Now and again, when she said something a little out of the ordinary, she wrote it down herself in a notebook.
of Virginia Woolf
Harold Laski 1893–1950: letter to Oliver Wendell Holmes, 30 November 1930

24 Shaw's plays are the price we pay for Shaw's prefaces.
James Agate 1877–1947: diary 10 March 1933

25 She is so odd a blend of Little Nell and Lady Macbeth. It is not so much the familiar phenomenon of a hand of steel in a velvet glove as a lacy sleeve with a bottle of vitriol concealed in its folds.
of Dorothy Parker
Alexander Woollcott 1887–1943: *While Rome Burns* (1934)

26 When a young man came up to him in Zurich and said, "May I kiss the hand that wrote *Ulysses?*" Joyce replied, somewhat like King Lear, "No, it did lots of other things too."
James Joyce 1882–1941: Richard Ellmann *James Joyce* (1959)

27 Coleridge was a drug addict. Poe was an alcoholic. Marlowe was stabbed by a man whom he was treacherously trying to stab. Pope took money to keep a woman's name out of a satire; then wrote a piece so that she could still be recognized anyhow. Chatterton killed himself. Byron was accused of incest. *Do you still want to be a writer—and if so, why?*
Bennett Cerf 1898–1971: *Shake Well Before Using* (1948)

28 English literature's performing flea.
of P. G. Wodehouse
Sean O'Casey 1880–1964: P. G. Wodehouse *Performing Flea* (1953)

29 I enjoyed talking to her, but thought *nothing* of her writing. I considered her "a beautiful little knitter."
of Virginia Woolf
Edith Sitwell 1887–1964: letter to Geoffrey Singleton, 11 July 1955

30 The mama of dada.
of Gertrude Stein
Clifton Fadiman 1904– : *Party of One* (1955)

31 He could not blow his nose without moralising on the state of the handkerchief industry.
of George Orwell

Cyril Connolly 1903–74: in *Sunday Times* (UK) 29 September 1968

32 We were put to Dickens as children but it never quite took. That unremitting humanity soon had me cheesed off.
Alan Bennett 1934– : *The Old Country* (1978)

Writing
see also **Books, Fiction and Story-telling, Originality, Poetry, Style, Words, Writers**

1 It is a foolish thing to make a long prologue, and to be short in the story itself.
Bible: II Maccabees

2 You will have written exceptionally well if, by skilful arrangement of your words, you have made an ordinary one seem original.
Horace 65–8 BC: *Ars Poetica*

3 *Tenet insanabile multos
Scribendi cacoethes et aegro in corde
senescit.*
Many suffer from the incurable disease of writing, and it becomes chronic in their sick minds.
Juvenal AD c. 60–c. 130: *Satires*

4 Go, litel bok, go, litel myn tragedye,
Ther God thi makere yet, er that he dye,
So sende mygth to make in som comedye!
Geoffrey Chaucer c. 1343–1400: *Troilus and Criseyde*

5 In the mind, as in the body, there is the necessity of getting rid of waste, and a man of active literary habits will write for the fire as well as for the press.
Jerome Cardan 1501–76: William Osler *Aequanimites* (1904); epigraph

6 And, as imagination bodies forth
The forms of things unknown, the poet's pen
Turns them to shapes, and gives to airy nothing
A local habitation and a name.
William Shakespeare 1564–1616: *A Midsummer Night's Dream* (1595–6)

7 If all the earth were paper white
And all the sea were ink
'Twere not enough for me to write
As my poor heart doth think.
John Lyly c. 1554–1606: "If all the earth were paper white"

8 So all my best is dressing old words new,
Spending again what is already spent.
William Shakespeare 1564–1616: sonnet 76

9 The last thing one knows in constructing a work is what to put first.
Blaise Pascal 1623–62: *Pensées* (1670)

10 Of every four words I write, I strike out three.
Nicolas Boileau 1636–1711: *Satire (2). A M. Molière* (1665)

11 What in me is dark
Illumine, what is low raise and support;
That to the height of this great argument
I may assert eternal providence,
And justify the ways of God to men.
John Milton 1608–74: *Paradise Lost* (1667); cf. **Alcohol 16**

12 Learn to write well, or not to write at all.
John Sheffield, 1st Duke of Buckingham and Normanby 1648–1721: "An Essay upon Satire" (1689)

13 Eye Nature's walks, shoot Folly as it flies,

And catch the Manners living as
they rise.
Laugh where we must, be candid
where we can;
But vindicate the ways of God to
man.
Alexander Pope 1688–1744: *An
Essay on Man* Epistle 1 (1733)

14 A man may write at any time, if
he will set himself doggedly to it.
Samuel Johnson 1709–84: James
Boswell *Life of Samuel Johnson*
(1791) March 1750

15 Writing, when properly managed
(as you may be sure I think mine
is) is but a different name for
conversation.
Laurence Sterne 1713–68: *Tristram
Shandy* (1759–67)

16 Any fool may write a most
valuable book by chance, if he
will only tell us what he heard
and saw with veracity.
Thomas Gray 1716–71: letter to
Horace Walpole, 25 February 1768

17 You write with ease, to show
your breeding,
But easy writing's vile hard
reading.
Richard Brinsley Sheridan 1751–1816:
"Clio's Protest" (written 1771,
published 1819)

18 Read over your compositions, and
where ever you meet with a
passage which you think is
particularly fine, strike it out.
Samuel Johnson 1709–84: quoting a
college tutor; James Boswell *Life of
Samuel Johnson* (1791) 30 April 1773

19 No man but a blockhead ever
wrote, except for money.
Samuel Johnson 1709–84: James
Boswell *Life of Samuel Johnson*
(1791) 5 April 1776

20 Another damned, thick, square
book! Always scribble, scribble,
scribble! Eh! Mr. Gibbon?
William Henry, Duke of Gloucester
1743–1805: Henry Best *Personal and
Literary Memorials* (1829); also
attributed to the Duke of
Cumberland and King George III; D.
M. Low *Edward Gibbon* (1937)

21 Let other pens dwell on guilt and
misery. I quit such odious
subjects as soon as I can.
Jane Austen 1775–1817: *Mansfield
Park* (1814)

22 Until you understand a writer's
ignorance, presume yourself
ignorant of his understanding.
Samuel Taylor Coleridge 1772–1834:
Biographia Literaria (1817)

23 I am convinced more and more
day by day that fine writing is
next to fine doing the top thing
in the world.
John Keats 1795–1821: letter to J. H.
Reynolds, 24 August 1819

24 The true antithesis to knowledge,
in this case, is not *pleasure*, but
power. All that is literature seeks
to communicate power; all that is
not literature, to communicate
knowledge.
Thomas De Quincey 1785–1859:
*Letters to a Young Man whose
Education has been Neglected*, in
the *London Magazine* January–July
1823; De Quincey adds that he is
indebted for this distinction to
"many years' conversation with Mr.
Wordsworth"

25 When my sonnet was rejected, I
exclaimed, "Damn the age; I will
write for Antiquity!"
Charles Lamb 1775–1834: letter to B.
W. Proctor 22 January 1829

26 Beneath the rule of men entirely
great
The pen is mightier than the
sword.
Edward George Bulwer-Lytton 1803–
73: *Richelieu* (1839)

27 When once the itch of literature comes over a man, nothing can cure it but the scratching of a pen.
Samuel Lover 1797–1868: *Handy Andy* (1842)

28 A losing trade, I assure you, sir: literature is a drug.
George Borrow 1803–81: *Lavengro* (1851)

29 Writers, like teeth, are divided into incisors and grinders.
Walter Bagehot 1826–77: *Estimates of some Englishmen and Scotchmen* (1858) "The First Edinburgh Reviewers"

30 They shut me up in prose—
As when a little girl
They put me in the closet—
Because they liked me "still."
Emily Dickinson 1830–86: "They shut me up in prose" (c. 1862)

31 Three hours a day will produce as much as a man ought to write.
Anthony Trollope 1815–82: *Autobiography* (1883)

32 The business of the poet and novelist is to show the sorriness underlying the grandest things, and the grandeur underlying the sorriest things.
Thomas Hardy 1840–1928: notebook entry for 19 April 1885

33 A writer must be as objective as a chemist: he must abandon the subjective line; he must know that dung-heaps play a very reasonable part in a landscape, and that evil passions are as inherent in life as good ones.
Anton Chekhov 1860–1904: letter to M. V. Kiselev, 14 January 1887

34 One man is as good as another until he has written a book.
Benjamin Jowett 1817–93: Evelyn Abbott and Lewis Campbell (eds.) *Life and Letters of Benjamin Jowett* (1897)

35 Only connect! . . . Only connect the prose and the passion, and both will be exalted, and human love will be seen at its height.
E. M. Forster 1879–1970: *Howards End* (1910)

36 The tip's a good one, as for literature
It gives no man a sinecure.
And no one knows, at sight, a masterpiece.
And give up verse, my boy,
There's nothing in it.
Ezra Pound 1885–1972: *Hugh Selwyn Mauberley* (1920) "Mr. Nixon"

37 True literature can exist only where it is created not by diligent and trustworthy officials, but by madmen, heretics, dreamers, rebels and skeptics. But when a writer must be sensible . . . there can be no bronze literature, there can only be a newspaper literature, which is read today, and used for wrapping soap tomorrow.
Yevgeny Zamyatin 1884–1937: "I am Afraid" (1921)

38 A woman must have money and a room of her own if she is to write fiction.
Virginia Woolf 1882–1941: *A Room of One's Own* (1929)

39 I am a camera with its shutter open, quite passive, recording, not thinking.
Christopher Isherwood 1904–86: *Goodbye to Berlin* (1939) "Berlin Diary" Autumn 1930

40 Remarks are not literature.
Gertrude Stein 1874–1946: *Autobiography of Alice B. Toklas* (1933)

41 Literature is news that STAYS news.

Ezra Pound 1885–1972: *The ABC of Reading* (1934)

42 Literature is the art of writing something that will be read twice; journalism what will be read once.
Cyril Connolly 1903–74: *Enemies of Promise* (1938)

43 There is no need for the writer to eat a whole sheep to be able to tell you what mutton tastes like. It is enough if he eats a cutlet. But he should do that.
W. Somerset Maugham 1874–1965: *A Writer's Notebook* (1949) written in 1941

44 A writer's ambition should be . . . to trade a hundred contemporary readers for ten readers in ten years' time and for one reader in a hundred years.
Arthur Koestler 1905–83: in *New York Times Book Review* 1 April 1951

45 Writing is not a profession but a vocation of unhappiness.
Georges Simenon 1903–89: interview in *Paris Review* Summer 1955

46 The writer's only responsibility is to his art. He will be completely ruthless if he is a good one. . . . If a writer has to rob his mother, he will not hesitate; the *Ode on a Grecian Urn* is worth any number of old ladies.
William Faulkner 1897–1962: in *Paris Review* Spring 1956

47 The most essential gift for a good writer is a built-in, shock-proof shit detector. This is the writer's radar and all great writers have had it.
Ernest Hemingway 1899–1961: in *Paris Review* Spring 1958

48 A writer must refuse, therefore, to allow himself to be transformed into an institution.
Jean-Paul Sartre 1905–80: refusing the Nobel Prize at Stockholm, 22 October 1964

49 Good prose is like a window-pane.
George Orwell 1903–50: *Collected Essays* (1968) vol. 1 "Why I Write"

50 If you can't annoy somebody with what you write, I think there's little point in writing.
Kingsley Amis 1922–95: in *Radio Times* 1 May 1971

51 The writer must be universal in sympathy and an outcast by nature: only then can he see clearly.
Julian Barnes 1946– : *Flaubert's Parrot* (1984)

52 Writing fiction has developed in me an abiding respect for the unknown in a human lifetime and a sense of where to look for the threads, how to follow, how to connect, find in the thick of the tangle what clear line persists. The strands are all there: to the memory nothing is ever really lost.
Eudora Welty 1909– : *One Writer's Beginnings* (1984)

53 The shelf life of the modern hardback writer is somewhere between the milk and the yoghurt.
Calvin Trillin: in *Sunday Times* (UK) 9 June 1991; attributed

Youth
see also **Children, Generation Gap**

1 Whom the gods love dies young.
Menander 342–c. 292 BC: *Dis Exapaton*

2 In delay there lies no plenty;
Then come kiss me, sweet and twenty,
Youth's a stuff will not endure.
William Shakespeare 1564–1616: *Twelfth Night* (1601)

3 My salad days,
When I was green in judgment.
William Shakespeare 1564–1616:
Antony and Cleopatra (1606–7)

4 Young men are fitter to invent
than to judge, fitter for execution
than for counsel, and fitter for
new projects than for settled
business.
Francis Bacon 1561–1626: *Essays*
(1625) "Of Youth and Age"

5 To find a young fellow that is
neither a wit in his own eye, nor
a fool in the eye of the world, is a
very hard task.
William Congreve 1670–1729: *Love
for Love* (1695)

6 The atrocious crime of being a
young man . . . I shall neither
attempt to palliate nor deny.
William Pitt, Earl of Chatham 1708–
78: speech, House of Commons, 2
March 1741

7 In gallant trim the gilded vessel
goes;
Youth on the prow, and Pleasure
at the helm.
Thomas Gray 1716–71: "The Bard"
(1757)

8 Heaven lies about us in our
infancy!
Shades of the prison-house begin
to close
Upon the growing boy.
William Wordsworth 1770–1850:
"Ode. Intimations of Immortality"
(1807)

9 Live as long as you may, the first
twenty years are the longest half
of your life.
Robert Southey 1774–1843: *The
Doctor* (1812)

10 The Youth of a Nation are the
trustees of Posterity.
Benjamin Disraeli 1804–81: *Sybil*
(1845)

11 In our youth is our strength; in
our inexperience, our wisdom.
Herman Melville 1819–91: *White-
Jacket* (1850)

12 I remember my youth and the
feeling that will never come back
any more—the feeling that I
could last for ever, outlast the
sea, the earth, and all men; the
deceitful feeling that lures us on
to joys, to perils, to love, to vain
effort—to death; the triumphant
conviction of strength, the heat of
life in the handful of dust, the
glow in the heart that with every
year grows dim, grows cold,
grows small, and expires—and
expires, too soon, too soon—
before life itself.
Joseph Conrad 1857–1924: *Youth*
(1902)

13 I'm not young enough to know
everything.
J. M. Barrie 1860–1937: *The
Admirable Crichton* (performed 1902,
published 1914)

14 Youth would be an ideal state if it
came a little later in life.
Herbert Henry Asquith 1852–1928: in
Observer (UK) 15 April 1923

15 It is better to waste one's youth
than to do nothing with it at all.
Georges Courteline 1858–1929: *La
Philosophie de Georges Courteline*
(1948)

16 What music is more enchanting
than the voices of young people,
when you can't hear what they
say?
Logan Pearsall Smith 1865–1946:
Afterthoughts (1931) "Age and
Death"

17 Being young is not having any
money; being young is not
minding not having any money.
Katharine Whitehorn 1928– :
Observations (1970)

18 Youth is something very new:
twenty years ago no one
mentioned it.
Coco Chanel 1883–1971: Marcel
Haedrich *Coco Chanel, Her Life, Her
Secrets* (1971)

19 Remember that as a teenager you
are at the last stage in your life
when you will be happy to hear
that the phone is for you.
Fran Lebowitz 1946– : *Social
Studies* (1981)

20 Youth is vivid rather than happy,
but memory always remembers
the happy things.
Bernard Lovell 1913– : in *The
Times* (UK) 20 August 1993

21 Being young is greatly
overestimated . . . Any failure
seems so total. Later on you
realize you can have another go.
Mary Quant 1934–: interview in
Observer (UK) 5 May 1996

Author Index

Abzug, Bella: PRESIDENCY 21

Accius: GOVERNMENT 1

Ace, Goodman: BROADCASTING 3

Acheson, Dean: ADMINISTRATION 26, BRITAIN 8, POLITICIANS 27

Acton, Lord: POWER 15

Adams, Abigail: CHARACTER 10; FASHION 4; WOMAN'S ROLE 7

Adams, Douglas: ADVICE 15; LIFE 50

Adams, Frank: KISSING 5

Adams, Franklin P.: MIDDLE AGE 12; POLITICS 15

Adams, Henry Brooks: ACHIEVEMENT 26; EDUCATION 27; EXPERIENCE 15; FRIENDSHIP 19; MEANING 8; MORALITY 7; ORDER 7; POLITICS 12; POWER 21; RELATIONSHIPS 10; WOMEN 29

Adams, John: AMERICA 3; CULTURE 3; GOVERNMENT 14, 15; LETTERS 6; POLITICS 5; POWER 11; PRESIDENCY 1

Adams, John Quincy: GOVERNMENT 23; PATRIOTISM 11

Adams, Samuel: WARS 5

Adamson, Harold: CRISES 11

Addison, Joseph: ARGUMENT 4; BUSINESS 4; CHRISTMAS 4; DEFIANCE 7; FUTURE 4; GENIUS 3; HAPPINESS 6; HONESTY 2; HUMOR 7; PATRIOTISM 4; PREJUDICE 4; SUCCESS 7

Ade, George: DRUNKENNESS 8; MARRIAGE 40; WINNING 12

Adenauer, Konrad: CHARACTER 25

Adler, Alfred: MORALITY 14; TRUTH 30

Adorno, Theodor: POETRY 41

Aeschylus: ORIGINALITY 1

Agar, Herbert: TRUTH 31

Agate, James: AMERICA 28; CERTAINTY 17; DIARIES 8; EMPLOYMENT 21; QUOTATIONS 15; WRITERS 24

Agathon: PAST 1

Agee, James: NATURE 19

Agesilaus: CIRCUMSTANCE 1

Agnew, Spiro: INTELLIGENCE 18

Ainger, Alfred: STYLE 19

Akins, Zoë: WORDS 17

Alain: IDEAS 10

Alcott, Louisa May: SEASONS 19

Alcuin: DEMOCRACY 1

Aldington, Richard: PATRIOTISM 22

Aldrich, Henry: ALCOHOL 3

Aldrin, "Buzz": SKIES 18

Alexander II: REVOLUTION 18

Alexander, Cecil Frances: CLASS 9

Alexander, William, Earl of Stirling: WOMEN 7

Alfonso "the Wise" of Castile: UNIVERSE 1

Alfven, Hannes: PROBLEMS 12

Algren, Nelson: LIVING 17

Ali, Muhammad (Cassius Clay): SELF-ESTEEM 16; SPORTS 25

Alighieri, Dante: ACHIEVEMENT 5; CONSCIENCE 2; GOD 8; GOSSIP 2; HEAVEN 3; LOVE 8; MIDDLE AGE 1; PEOPLE 1; REPUTATION 4; SORROW 3; SUFFERING 4; VIRTUE 4

Allen, Arnold: PHYSICS 8

Allen, Fred: ADMINISTRATION 19; AMERICA 29; TOWNS 18

Allen, Woody: BODY 23; COOPERATION 14; DEATH 80; FUTURE 18; GOD 40; OLD AGE 33; PREGNANCY 12; SELF 26; SEX 40, 43, 46, 47; SPEECH 28

Allingham, William: SUPERNATURAL 15

Ambrose, St.: BEHAVIOR 2

American Civil Liberties Union: LIBERTY 31

American Declaration of Independence: HUMAN RIGHTS 3

Amery, Leo: DETERMINATION 18

Ames, Fisher: GOVERNMENT 20

Amies, Hardy: DRESS 20

Amis, Kingsley: BODY 20; DRUNKENNESS 11; PLEASURE 22; UNIVERSITIES 19; WRITING 50

Anacharsis: LAW 1

Andersen, Hans Christian: HONESTY 3

Anderson, Maxwell: FAME 17

Andrewes, Lancelot: SEASONS 6

Angell, Roger: SPORTS 60

Annan, Noel: PATRIOTISM 27

Anonymous: ACTORS 5; ALCOHOL 20; ANIMALS 16; APPEARANCE 19; ARMED FORCES 10, 11, 31; BROADCASTING 4; BUSINESS 3; CAUTION 1; CHILDREN 28; CHOICE 13; CHRISTIAN CHURCH 15; CRISES 18; CURSING 10; DANCE 8; DETERMINATION 4; EPITAPHS 4, 12, 31; EXCESS 1; EXPERIENCE 20; FAME 7; FOOLS 5; GOD 5, 7; GOOD AND EVIL 8; HOME 6; HUMAN RIGHTS 5, 16; HUNTING 14; JUSTICE 11; KNOWLEDGE 7; LAST WORDS 2;

RACE 18, 19;
IMAGINATION 8;
INSIGHT 4; KNOWLEDGE
18; LOVE 37, 38;
POETS 8; POLLUTION 7;
POWER 9; RACE 2;
SCIENCE AND RELIGION
5; SELF-KNOWLEDGE 9;
SORROW 13; SYMPATHY
12; TRANSIENCE 11;
TRUTH 17

Blamire, Susanna: PAST
7

Bliss, Arthur: OLD AGE
30

Bliss, Philip Paul: WARS
19

Bloom, Harold: READING
16

Blunden, Edmund:
MATURITY 10

Blythe, Ronald:
EMPLOYMENT 25; OLD
AGE 31

Boaz, David: DRUGS 9

Boesky, Ivan: GREED 13

Bogart, John B.: NEWS
19

Bohr, Niels: BELIEF 23;
PHYSICS 7; TRUTH 34

Boileau, Nicolas: FOOLS 7;
WRITING 10

Bolívar, Simón:
REVOLUTION 14

Bolingbroke, Lord (Henry
St. John): CHANCE 3;
MISTAKES 6;
POLITICIANS 4; TRUTH
13

Bolt, Robert: MORALITY
15

Bonaparte, Elizabeth
Patterson: MARRIAGE
34

Bone, David: SELF-
INTEREST 9

Bonhoeffer, Dietrich:
CHARACTER 23

Book of Common Prayer,
The: ACTION 8;
CAPITALISM 1; DAY 6;
DEATH 31, 32;
FORGIVENESS 5; HUMAN
NATURE 5; LANGUAGES
3; LIFE 13; MARRIAGE
11, 12; OPPORTUNITY 4;

PEACE 8; POLLUTION 5;
SIN 14, 15;
TEMPTATION 5; TIME
14

Booth, Connie:
INTERNATIONAL
RELATIONS 28

Booth, John Wilkes:
REVENGE 10

Boren, James H.:
ADMINISTRATION 25

Borges, Jorge Luis:
CHANCE 13;
TRANSLATION 11;
UNIVERSE 10; WARS 30

Borgia, Cesare: AMBITION
2

Borrow, George: WRITING
28

Bosquet, Pierre: ARMED
FORCES 18

Bossidy, John Collins:
TOWNS 14

Boswell, James:
CONVERSATION 2;
DIARIES 1; MANNERS 6

Bottomley, Gordon:
TECHNOLOGY 6

Bottomley, Horatio:
CRIME 30; UNIVERSITIES
15

Boucicault, Dion: TIME
22

Boulez, Pierre:
REVOLUTION 30

Boulton, Harold Edwin:
ENGLAND 18

Boulton, Matthew:
TECHNOLOGY 2

Bourdillon, F. W.: SKIES
14

Bowen, Elizabeth:
ABSENCE 7; ARTS 28;
CHILDREN 24; ENVY 10;
EXPERIENCE 19; FATE
13; GUILT 12; PEOPLE
44; SEASONS 28

Bowen, Lord: JUSTICE 18;
WEATHER 13

Bowra, Maurice: CLERGY
18; ENTERTAINING 14;
SEX 39

Brabazon, Lord: SPEECHES
21

Brackett, Charles:
BUSINESS 16; MOVIES 9

Bradford, John:
CIRCUMSTANCE 2

Bradley, F. H.:
PHILOSOPHY 13

Bradley, Omar N.:
ARMED FORCES 39;
SCIENCE AND RELIGION
9; WARFARE 53, 55;
WARS 23

Bradshaw, John:
REVOLUTION 3

Bradstreet, Anne:
WOMAN'S ROLE 2

Bramah, Ernest:
CONVERSATION 17

Branson, Richard:
EMPLOYMENT 27

Braque, Georges: ARTS
AND SCIENCES 8; TRUTH
33

Braun, Wernher von:
SCIENCE 28

Brecht, Bertolt: DRESS 15;
HEROES 12; MONEY 18;
MORALITY 11; PEACE
19; POWER 18; SCIENCE
23; VIRTUE 39;
WARFARE 45

Brenan, Gerald: MONEY
23; RELIGION 37

Brenner, Sydney:
TECHNOLOGY 20

Brereton, Jane: FOOLS 12

Breton, Nicholas:
ENEMIES 5

Bridger, Roy: PROGRESS
15

Bridges, Robert:
WEATHER 12

Bright, John:
INTERNATIONAL
RELATIONS 14; WARS
14

Brillat-Savarin,
Anthelme: COOKING
10, 11; INVENTIONS 11

British Board of Film
Censors: CENSORSHIP
10

Brittain, Vera: POLITICS
23

Broder, David:
PRESIDENCY 17

Brodrick, St. John:
CONVERSATION 14

Bronowski, Jacob:

Carlyle, Jane: CHARACTER
13
Carlyle, Thomas:
ADVERSITY 4;
BIOGRAPHY 3, 4;
CULTURE 5; FRANCE 6;
HISTORY 6, 7; IDLENESS
7; INDIFFERENCE 7;
LIBRARIES 5; MONEY 13;
OPPORTUNITY 10;
PEOPLE 15, 16; SILENCE
8; STATISTICS 2;
TECHNOLOGY 3;
UNIVERSE 3;
UNIVERSITIES 8; WORDS
AND DEEDS 10
Carmichael, J. W.:
EDUCATION 43
Carmichael, Stokely:
WOMAN'S ROLE 22
Carnegie, Andrew:
WEALTH 16
Carnegie, Dale: SUCCESS
28
Carr, Michael: WORLD
WAR II 2
Carroll, Lewis:
ACHIEVEMENT 22;
APPEARANCE 12;
BEGINNING 12;
BEHAVIOR 13; BELIEF
19; BOOKS 13;
CONVERSATION 12;
DANCE 6;
DETERMINATION 17;
GIFTS 11; HASTE 10;
LOGIC 6; MANNERS 9;
MATHEMATICS 12;
MEANING 5, 6; NAMES
8; POWER 14; PRESENT
9; SPEECH 19; SURPRISE
4; TRUTH 23; VALUE
14; WAYS 4; WORDS
11
Carson, Edward: ARMED
FORCES 35
Carson, Rachel:
POLLUTION 18; SEA
23
Carter, Henry: AUSTRALIA
2
Carter, Howard:
INVENTIONS 15
Carter, Jimmy:
ARGUMENT 20;
TEMPTATION 15

Cartier, Jacques: CANADA
1
Cartland, Barbara:
MIDDLE AGE 13
Cartwright, John:
DEMOCRACY 6
Cary, Lucius, Lord
Falkland: CHANGE 7
Casals, Pablo: MUSIC
23
Casimir, Comte de
Montrond: CAUTION 4;
ENVY 8
Casson, Hugh:
TRANSPORTATION 19
Castlerosse, Lord:
PUNCTUALITY 5
Castro, Fidel: CAPITALISM
20; REVOLUTION 27
Cather, Willa: TREES
12
Catherine the Great:
POWER 8
Cato the Elder: ENEMIES 2;
SPEECHES 1
Catullus: LOVE 2;
MEETING 1; PRAYER 1
Cavafy, Constantine:
CULTURE 9; TRAVEL 24
Cavell, Edith: PATRIOTISM
18
Caxton, William: POETS 1;
PUBLISHING 1
Ceauçescu, Nicolae:
ENEMIES 16
Cecil, Lord David:
READING 13
Cecil, Lord Edward:
PREJUDICE 11
Cecil, Lord Hugh:
CHRISTIAN CHURCH 28
Centlivre, Susannah:
BRIBERY 5
Cerf, Bennett: WRITERS
27
Cervantes: PAINTING 2;
POSSESSIONS 5; SLEEP
5
Cézanne, Paul: PAINTING
15, 17
Chalmers, Patrick
Reginald: WINNING 14
Chamberlain, Joseph:
INTERNATIONAL
RELATIONS 16; POLITICS
10

Chamberlain, Neville:
PEACE 18; WARFARE
44; WORLD WAR II 1
Chambers, Whittaker:
MATURITY 8
Chamfort, Nicolas-
Sébastien: CHARACTER
12; LOVE 36;
PHILOSOPHY 10;
POVERTY 11
Chandler, Raymond:
CRIME 32; FICTION 16;
LANGUAGE 19; MOVIES
8; TEMPTATION 12;
TOWNS 17
Chanel, Coco: EMOTIONS
22; SATISFACTION 27;
YOUTH 18
Channon, Henry
("Chips"): BIOGRAPHY
14; DIARIES 5;
DIPLOMACY 10; TRAVEL
29
Chaplin, Charlie: MOVIES
19, 24
Chapman, George:
EDUCATION 9; ENGLAND
4; HUMAN RACE 7
Chapman, Graham:
DEATH 78; SURPRISE 8
Charles I: APOLOGY 1;
JUSTICE 10; ROYALTY
10
Charles II: ARMED FORCES
4; BEHAVIOR 4;
CHARACTER 6; LAST
WORDS 12, 13; WORDS
AND DEEDS 7
Charles V: LANGUAGES 2
Charles, Prince:
ARCHITECTURE 18;
GARDENS 15
Charles-Joseph, Prince de
Ligne: DIPLOMACY 4
Chase, Salmon Portland:
AMERICA 16
Chateaubriand, François-
René: ORIGINALITY 6
Chaucer, Geoffrey:
ACTION 2; APPEARANCE
2; BEAUTY 3; BEHAVIOR
3; BIRDS 1; BRIBERY 3;
CHARACTER 2;
EDUCATION 4, 5;
FLOWERS 1; LANGUAGES
1; LOVE 9; MURDER 3;

POETRY 2; SEASONS 3; SEX 3; SIN 9; SINGING 1; SKIES 2; SPEECH 5; SYMPATHY 4, 5; TRUST 6; UNIVERSITIES 1; WEATHER 2; WOMEN 5; WRITING 4

Chekhov, Anton: BEAUTY 21; FRIENDSHIP 18; MEDICINE 17; MEN AND WOMEN 14; POLLUTION 15; RELATIONSHIPS 9; RUSSIA 7; SORROW 19; THEATER 13; WRITING 33

Cherry-Garrard, Apsley: EPITAPHS 23

Chesterfield, Lord: ADVICE 5, 6; BEHAVIOR 4; BRITAIN 2; CHANCE 5; CONVERSATION 3; EDUCATION 14; EXPERIENCE 4; IDLENESS 4; INSULTS 3; KNOWLEDGE 15; MANNERS 4; RELIGION 15; SEX 16; TIME 17; TRUTH 14; WOMEN 13

Chesterton, G. K.: ALCOHOL 18; ANIMALS 13; ARTS AND SCIENCES 4; CHANGE 24; CHRISTIAN CHURCH 23; CRIME 26; CUSTOM 12; ENGLAND 21; FICTION 11; FOOD 18; HYPOCRISY 14; IMAGINATION 16; INSIGHT 10; KNOWLEDGE 32; MEMORY 22; NEWS 17; PATRIOTISM 16; PLEASURE 17; POETS 20; PREJUDICE 10; PROBLEMS 6; SECRECY 11; SELF 17; TRUST 19; WEALTH 18; WOMEN 30; WRITERS 14

Chevalier, Maurice: OLD AGE 29

Child, Lydia Maria: WOMAN'S ROLE 14

Chillingworth, William: GRATITUDE 4

Chilton, Charles: WORLD WAR I 19

Choate, Rufus: HUMAN RIGHTS 9

Chomsky, Noam: LANGUAGE 22

Christie, Agatha: EXPERIENCE 21; INTELLIGENCE 7

Church, Francis Pharcellus: CHRISTMAS 8

Churchill, Charles: DECEPTION 7; EXCELLENCE 3; HYPOCRISY 8; PATRIOTISM 5; SELF-ESTEEM 5; SPEECHES 6; WORDPLAY 2

Churchill, Lord Randolph: MATHEMATICS 14

Churchill, Winston: ACHIEVEMENT 30; ALCOHOL 31; ANIMALS 18; ARMED FORCES 36; BEGINNING 13; BRITAIN 6; CAPITALISM 14; CHARACTER 27; CHILDREN 26; CRISES 9, 10; CULTURE 14; DEMOCRACY 20; DIPLOMACY 13, 14; EDUCATION 32; EXAMINATIONS 6; FOOD 23; GRATITUDE 11; INSULTS 13; LANGUAGE 20; LEADERSHIP 11; PEOPLE 34, 42; POLITICIANS 25; POLITICS 24; PREJUDICE 13; QUOTATIONS 12; RANK 13; REVENGE 11; RUSSIA 9; SELF-ESTEEM 17; SELF-SACRIFICE 12; SPEECHES 12, 20; TRUST 20; WARFARE 54; WINNING 15; WORLD WAR II 3, 6, 17

Ciano, Count Galeazzo: SUCCESS 31

Cibber, Colley: MARRIAGE 14

Cicero: BEHAVIOR 1; COUNTRIES 1; LAW 2; LEISURE 2; MISTAKES 1; PHILOSOPHY 2; SELF-INTEREST 1; SOLITUDE 3;

SUPERNATURAL 2; WARFARE 3, 4; WORK 2

Cioran, E. M.: ACTION 19

Clancy, Tom: MOVIES 33

Clare, John: COUNTRIES 11; DEATH 51; HOPE 12; PRESENT 6; SELF 11; SOLITUDE 10

Clarendon, Earl of (Edward Hyde): PEOPLE 6

Clark, Alan: ADMINISTRATION 29; CHARACTER 32; MORALITY 17; POLITICIANS 33

Clarke, Arthur C.: EARTH 9; HYPOTHESIS 18; TECHNOLOGY 17

Clarke, John: IDLENESS 3

Claudius Caecus, Appius: FATE 2

Clausewitz, Karl von: WARFARE 17, 18

Clay, Cassius (Muhammad Ali): SELF-ESTEEM 16; SPORTS 24

Clay, Henry: AMBITION 16; AMERICA 9; DIPLOMACY 3; INTERNATIONAL RELATIONS 4

Clayton, Tubby: GIFTS 13

Cleaver, Eldridge: PROBLEMS 8

Cleese, John: DEATH 78; INTERNATIONAL RELATIONS 28

Clemenceau, Georges: DIPLOMACY 9; OLD AGE 20; PEACE 14; WARFARE 37; WORLD WAR I 14

Clement XIII, Pope: CHANGE 12

Cleveland, Grover: ARMED FORCES 21

Clinton, Bill: ACHIEVEMENT 38; DRUGS 10; POLITICS 29; RELATIONSHIPS 16

Clinton, Hillary Rodham: WOMAN'S ROLE 30

Clive, Lord: EXCESS 8; FATE 8

Clough, Arthur Hugh:
ACHIEVEMENT 20;
BELIEF 17; CRIME 20;
ENVY 9; EXPERIENCE 11;
GOD 25; HOPE 13;
MURDER 10; OPTIMISM
9; SELF-SACRIFICE 5;
SUCCESS 14

Cockburn, Claud: NEWS
26; REALITY 8

Cocteau, Jean: BEHAVIOR
20; CHOICE 10; LIFE 37;
POETRY 35

Coffey, Denise: SEX 49

Cohan, George M.:
AMERICA 21; FAME 16;
WORLD WAR I 13

Cohen, John: CURSING 8

Cohen, Leonard:
OPTIMISM 18

Coke, Desmond:
COOPERATION 9

Coke, Edward: BUSINESS
2; HUMAN RIGHTS 2;
LAW 8

Coleridge, Samuel Taylor:
ACTORS 3; CHRISTIAN
CHURCH 14; DAY 9;
EXPERIENCE 6, 8; HOPE
11; MEN AND WOMEN
6; POETRY 15, 21, 22;
POETS 11; POLITICS 6;
POLLUTION 8; PRAYER
14; SEA 8; SEASONS 13;
SILENCE 5; SKIES 9;
WEATHER 6;
WORDPLAY 5; WRITERS
6; WRITING 22

Colette: EMOTIONS 15

Collingwood, Admiral:
ACHIEVEMENT 15

Collingwood, R. G.:
WORK 23

Collins, Michael:
PUNCTUALITY 6

Colman, George, the
Elder: IDEALISM 2

Colman, George, the
Younger: AMBITION 11;
WRITERS 7

Colombo, John Robert:
CANADA 5

Colton, Charles Caleb:
COUNTRY AND TOWN
10; EXAMINATIONS 1;
SPEECH 14

Commager, Henry Steele:
FORESIGHT 11

Compton-Burnett, Ivy:
CRUELTY 10; GIFTS 14;
MEN AND WOMEN 24;
POSSESSIONS 13; SIN 32;
TIME 35

Conant, James B.:
EDUCATION 42

Condell, Henry:
SHAKESPEARE 3

Congreve, William:
APPEARANCE 5; BEAUTY
8; BEHAVIOR 5;
COURTSHIP 4; GUILT 6;
HUMOR 6; LIES 4; LOVE
32; MARRIAGE 13;
MUSIC 4; REPUTATION
10; REVENGE 7;
SECRECY 5;
UNIVERSITIES 3; YOUTH
5

Connell, James M.:
POLITICAL PARTIES 11

Conner, Dennis: SPORTS
42

Connolly, Billy:
MARRIAGE 59

Connolly, Cyril: ARTS 29;
BODY 18; CLASS 21;
COUNTRY AND TOWN
19; CRITICS 29, 31;
CULTURE 18;
GENERATION GAP 13;
MEMORY 23; MEN AND
WOMEN 21; SELF 23;
STYLE 22; WRITERS 31;
WRITING 42

Connolly, James:
CAPITALISM 7

Connors, Jimmy: SPORTS
40

Conrad, Joseph: ACTION
14; AMBITION 18;
APOLOGY 5; ENEMIES
12; FEAR 8; GOOD AND
EVIL 24; HUMAN
NATURE 11; MEMORY
20; SOLITUDE 15;
YOUTH 12

Conran, Shirley: HOME
22; PRACTICALITY 16

Constable, John: BEAUTY
15; PAINTING 6, 7

Constant, Benjamin:
ARTS 4

Constantine the Great:
CHRISTIAN CHURCH 4

Conybeare, Eliza:
CERTAINTY 13

Cook, A. J.: EMPLOYMENT
17

Cook, Eliza: CRIME 19

Coolidge, Calvin:
AMERICA 24; DEBT 13;
SIN 28; SPEECH 24

Coomaraswamy, Ananda:
ARTS 25

Cooper, Diana: FRANCE
10

Cooper, Duff:
APPEARANCE 15

Cope, Wendy: POETRY 44

Copland, Aaron: MUSIC
17

Coppola, Francis Ford:
WARFARE 65

Corneille, Pierre: ACTION
6; DANGER 5; DUTY 2

Cornes, Ralph:
TECHNOLOGY 21

Cornfeld, Bernard:
AMBITION 21

Cornford, Francis M.:
ADMINISTRATION 7;
CUSTOM 13; DECEPTION
12; PUBLISHING 8; TIME
30

Cornuel, Mme.: HEROES 1

Coronation Service: BIBLE
4

Correggio: PAINTING 1

Cory, William: MOURNING
13; SPORTS 7

Cosby, Bill: FAMILY 21

Coubertin, Baron Pierre
de: WINNING 13

Coué, Émile: MEDICINE 19

Countess Morphy:
COOKING 29

Courteline, Georges:
YOUTH 15

Coventry, Thomas: SEA
6

Coward, Noël: ACTORS 8,
17; EPITAPHS 29;
MUSIC 13; NAMES 10;
SINGING 15; SUCCESS
37; WOMEN 33;
WORLD WAR II 12

Cowley, Abraham:
CHANGE 8; COUNTRY

18; SOCIETY 13;
SORROW 28; WARS 24
Johnson, Philander
Chase: OPTIMISM 15
Johnson, Philip:
ARCHITECTURE 15
Johnson, Samuel:
ACHIEVEMENT 9, 13;
ADVERTISING 1;
ALCOHOL 6; ARGUMENT
7; ARMED FORCES 8;
BEHAVIOR 7; BELIEF 11;
BIOGRAPHY 1; BOOKS 6;
CATS 3; CHANGE 10;
CHARACTER 8;
CONVERSATION 4, 5;
COOKING 5; COURAGE
11; CRITICS 6, 7;
DEATH 39, 40; DESPAIR
3; DRUNKENNESS 3;
EDUCATION 15, 16;
EMPLOYMENT 6;
EQUALITY 4; EXCESS 7;
FAME 11; FAMILIARITY
4; FOOD 5, 7;
FRIENDSHIP 8, 10;
GENIUS 5; GOOD AND
EVIL 16; GOVERNMENT
13; GRATITUDE 7;
HAPPINESS 9; HASTE 6;
HATRED 3; HUNTING 6,
7; IDLENESS 5;
IGNORANCE 5;
IMAGINATION 6;
INTELLIGENCE 4; JUSTICE
15; KNOWLEDGE 13, 16;
LANGUAGE 5, 7;
LANGUAGES 7; LIBERTY
7, 9; LIBRARIES 2, 3;
LIFE 16; LOVE 35;
MARRIAGE 18, 21;
MUSIC 5; MUSICIANS 1;
NAMES 4; OPINION 7;
OPPORTUNITY 1;
PATRIOTISM 6; PEOPLE
10; PLEASURE 10;
POETRY 3; POETS 7;
POLITICS 3; POVERTY 9;
POWER 6; PRAISE 8;
QUOTATIONS 2;
READING 7; REALITY 2;
RELIGION 16;
REPUTATION 12;
SCIENCE AND RELIGION
4; SENSES 6; SEX 14;
SHAKESPEARE 6;

SICKNESS 6; SINGING 6;
SORROW 11; SPORTS 4;
SUPERNATURAL 11;
SYMPATHY 10; TASTE 4;
TAXES 3; THINKING 6;
TRAVEL 11, 12; TRUTH
15; WARFARE 12;
WEALTH 12; WEATHER
4; WOMAN'S ROLE 6, 9;
WORDPLAY 3; WORDS 7;
WRITERS 3; WRITING
14, 18, 19
Johnstone, John Benn:
SEX 20
Johst, Hanns: CULTURE
16
Jolson, Al: SINGING 12
Jones, Henry Arthur:
PAST 13
Jones, John Paul:
DETERMINATION 12
Jones, Paul M.:
EXPERIENCE 18
Jonson, Ben: DRESS 2;
EDUCATION 8; EPITAPHS
8; GOD 11; GREED 5;
LAW 6; PRAISE 2;
SHAKESPEARE 1, 2, 4;
SKIES 4; SMOKING 3;
WEALTH 4
Joplin, Janis: SELF-
INTEREST 12
Joseph, Keith: WORDS
AND DEEDS 12
Jowett, Benjamin: FAITH
10; LIES 11; LOGIC 9;
TASTE 10; WRITING
34
Joyce, James: ARTS 22;
GENIUS 14; SEA 21;
SELF 20; SKIES 16;
SYMPATHY 14; WORDS
14; WRITERS 26
Judd, Naomi: EXPERIENCE
25
Julius Caesar: AMBITION
1; CRISES 1;
REPUTATION 2; SELF-
INTEREST 2; SUCCESS 2;
TRUST 3
Julian of Norwich:
OPTIMISM 2
Jung, Carl Gustav: BELIEF
30; CHILDREN 23, 33;
DRUGS 6; EMOTIONS 20;
LIFE 46; MIDDLE AGE 9

"Junius": ELECTIONS 1
Junot, Marshal: RANK 6
Justinian: JUSTICE 4
Juvenal: BRIBERY 2;
CHILDREN 4; CRIME 4;
DETERMINATION 3;
GOVERNMENT 3;
HONESTY 1; POVERTY 3;
REVENGE 2; SICKNESS 2;
SIN 6; TRUST 5;
WRITING 3

Kael, Pauline: MOVIES 20
Kafka, Franz: JUSTICE 24;
LIBERTY 24; SURPRISE 5
Kahn, Gus: POVERTY 22
Kalmar, Bert: MEETING
19
Kant, Immanuel: CAUSES
7; HAPPINESS 12;
HUMAN RACE 16;
THINKING 7
Karr, Alphonse: CHANGE
19; MURDER 9
Kaufman, George S.:
THEATER 26
Kaufman, Gerald:
POLITICAL PARTIES 26
Kaunda, Kenneth:
COUNTRIES 28
Keating, Paul: AUSTRALIA
17; LEADERSHIP 17
Keats, John: ABSENCE 4;
ALCOHOL 8;
APPEARANCE 9; BEAUTY
13, 14; BIRDS 7;
CERTAINTY 5; CHANGE
14; CONSTANCY 9;
CREATIVITY 3; DAY 11;
DEATH 42; DESPAIR 6;
DREAMS 4; EMOTIONS 9;
EPITAPHS 17;
EXPERIENCE 7;
FESTIVALS 2; FLOWERS
7; FOOD 11;
IMAGINATION 10, 12;
INSIGHT 6; INVENTIONS
9; KNOWLEDGE 19;
LIVING 10; LOGIC 4;
LOVE 43; MATURITY 6;
MEDICINE 13; MIND 6;
NAMES 5; NATURE 8;
POETRY 14, 17, 18;
READING 9;
REPUTATION 15;
SATISFACTION 15, 16;

12; DUTY 14;
GENERATION GAP 7;
HOME 12; LIES 15;
NAMES 9; POLITICIANS
16; TEMPTATION 11;
THRIFT 7; TRAVEL 25

Sales, St. Francis de:
SPEECH 6

Salinger, J. D.: KISSING 8

Salisbury, Lord: ARMED
FORCES 27; CHARITY
10; DIPLOMACY 7;
EUROPE 6; KNOWLEDGE
25; NEWS 15; PEOPLE
39

Sallust: BRIBERY 1; GREED
1; VIRTUE 1

Samuel, Lord: LIBRARIES
8

Sandburg, Carl: IDEALISM
5; LANGUAGE 23;
NATURE 17; PAST 19;
POETRY 32; WEATHER
15

Sanders, Henry ("Red"):
WINNING 17

Sandwich, Lord:
ADMINISTRATION 3

Santayana, George:
CUSTOM 11; EXCESS 14;
FAMILY 11; FASHION 6;
GENERATION GAP 10;
IDEAS 8; PAST 15

Sarah, Duchess of
Marlborough: LOVE 33;
SEX 11

Sarah, Duchess of York:
HOPE 18

Sargent, John Singer:
PAINTING 22

Sarony, Leslie: DEATH 73

Sarraute, Nathalie:
BROADCASTING 6

Sartre, Jean-Paul: BELIEF
31; CRIME 33; DESPAIR
14; DISILLUSION 23;
FUTILITY 10; HEAVEN
18; HUMAN RACE 32,
34; LIBERTY 27;
PARENTS 23; TIME 34;
WRITING 48

Sassoon, Siegfried:
ARMED FORCES 29;
SENSES 11; SINGING 13

Satie, Erik: MUSICIANS 11

Sayers, Dorothy L.:

ADVERTISING 7;
PLEASURE 18

Scanlon, Hugh: LIBERTY
35

Scargill, Arthur: CLASS
31

Schelling, Friedrich von:
ARCHITECTURE 4

Schiller, Friedrich von:
FOOLS 17; HAPPINESS
11

Schirra, Walter M., Sr.:
HEROES 15

Schlesinger, Arthur M.,
Jr.: PRESIDENCY 15

Schnabel, Artur:
MUSICIANS 14, 15

Schopenhauer, Arthur:
WOMEN 23

Schroeder, Patricia:
PRESIDENCY 23

Schulberg, Budd:
ACHIEVEMENT 33

Schumacher, E. F.:
ECONOMICS 10, 11

Schumann, Robert:
MUSICIANS 4

Schumpeter, Joseph Alois:
ECONOMICS 5;
TECHNOLOGY 11

Schurz, Carl: PATRIOTISM
14

Schwarzkopf, H. Norman
III: ARMED FORCES 47,
48, 50; POWER 25

Schweitzer, Albert:
INTELLIGENCE 10

Schwitters, Kurt:
PAINTING 25

Scott, C. P.:
BROADCASTING 2; NEWS
21

Scott, Robert Falcon:
COURAGE 19; DANGER
8; LAST WORDS 25;
TRAVEL 26

Scott, Sir Walter: CHANCE
6; DECEPTION 8;
EMOTIONS 10; ENEMIES
9; FOOLS 18;
FORGIVENESS 11;
HEROES 4; INDIFFERENCE
6; OPTIMISM 6;
PATRIOTISM 9; THEATER
12; WOMEN 16;
WRITERS 5

Scott-Maxwell, Florida:
PARENTS 26

Searle, Ronald:
CHRISTMAS 10

Sedgwick, John: LAST
WORDS 21

Seeger, Alan: WARFARE
28

Seeger, Pete: EXPERIENCE
22

Segal, Erich: LOVE 66

Selden, John: BIBLE 3;
FAMILIARITY 3;
LANGUAGE 3; LAW 8;
MARRIAGE 10; PAST 5;
PLEASURE 4

Seldon, Arthur:
GOVERNMENT 40

Sellar, W. C.: DEBT 12;
EXAMINATIONS 5;
GARDENS 11; HISTORY
15; WARS 21

Seneca ("the Younger"):
COOKING 1; DEATH 10;
EDUCATION 3;
IGNORANCE 1

Service, Robert W.:
STRENGTH 11; TIME 32;
TRUST 17; WARFARE
34

Seward, William:
REVOLUTION 19

Sexby, Edward: MURDER
6

Shadwell, Thomas: WIT
4

Shaffer, Peter:
CONFORMITY 13;
CULTURE 25

Shaftesbury, 1st Earl of:
RELIGION 12

Shakespeare, William:
ACHIEVEMENT 7;
ACTION 5; ACTORS 1;
ADVERSITY 2; AMBITION
4, 7; APPEARANCE 3;
ARGUMENT 3; ARMED
FORCES 2; BEAUTY 6;
BEGINNING 5, 6; BIBLE
1; BODY 3; BRIBERY 4;
CAUSES 4; CHANGE 4;
CHARACTER 3; CHARITY
4; CHILDREN 8; CHOICE
2; CIRCUMSTANCE 3, 4;
CLASS 3, 4; CONSCIENCE
3, 4; CONSTANCY 2;

•Shelley, Mary:
CONFORMITY 4; DESPAIR
5

Shelley, Percy Bysshe:
BIRDS 6; DEATH 43, 44;
DREAMS 5; FLOWERS 8;
FUTILITY 6; HOPE 9;
LIFE 19; MARRIAGE 26;
MEMORY 9; POETRY 16,
19, 20; POETS 12;
ROYALTY 17; SKIES 11,
12; TOWNS 3, 5;
TRANSLATION 5;
WEATHER 8

Sheridan, Philip Henry:
RACE 6

Sheridan, Richard
Brinsley: APPEARANCE
6; COURAGE 9; CRISES 5;
CRITICS 9;
DETERMINATION 10;
FASHION 3; HASTE 8;
MANNERS 5; MEANING
3; PUBLISHING 2;
SIMILARITY 8; SPEECHES
8; WIT 7; WOMEN 14;
WORDPLAY 4; WRITING
17

Sherman, William
Tecumseh: ELECTIONS 5;
WARFARE 22

Shirley, James: DEATH 27;
VIRTUE 11

Short, Clare: SECRECY 16

Sibelius, Jean: CRITICS
28

Sidney, Philip: AMBITION
3; CHARITY 3;
CONSTANCY 1; FICTION
2; FRANCE 2; HUMOR 2;
SILENCE 2

Sieyès, Emmanuel Joseph:
ACHIEVEMENT 16;
PRACTICALITY 8

Sillitoe, Alan: SOLITUDE
21

Simenon, Georges:
WRITING 45

Simon, Neil: BODY 22;
MEDICINE 22

Simon, Paul: MUSIC 30

Simonides: ARTS 1;
EPITAPHS 1

Simpson, Alan: BODY 19

Simpson, O. J.: SPORTS
35

Sims, George R.:
CHRISTMAS 7

Sisson, C. H.:
ADMINISTRATION 21

Sitwell, Edith: PRIDE 12;
WRITERS 29

Sitwell, Osbert: CLASS 17

Skinner, B. F.: EDUCATION
38; THINKING 23

Smart, Christopher: CATS
2; CHARITY 6;
TRANSIENCE 7

Smiles, Samuel: COOKING
19; HAPPINESS 16;
TECHNOLOGY 4;
THOROUGHNESS 3

Smith, Adam: BUSINESS
7, 8; GOVERNMENT 12;
IMAGINATION 5; SELF-
INTEREST 7; TAXES 6;
UNIVERSITIES 4;
WEALTH 11

Smith, Dodie: FAMILY 14;
SORROW 25

Smith, Edgar: CLASS 15

Smith, F. E.: CAPITALISM
12; INSULTS 10; PRIDE
11; SUCCESS 25

Smith, Logan Pearsall:
AMBITION 19; BODY 17;
BOOKS 19; CONSCIENCE
8; DREAMS 9; FASHION
7; HYPOCRISY 16;
IDEALISM 7; READING
11; WEALTH 21;
WEATHER '18; WORK
25; YOUTH 16

Smith, Mike: SPORTS
55

Smith, Stevie: DEATH 77;
MARRIAGE 51

Smith, Sydney:
ARCHITECTURE 5; BOOKS
10; CIRCUMSTANCE 7;
CLERGY 11, 14, 15;
COOKING 16; COUNTRIES
8; COUNTRY AND TOWN
12; CRITICS 16; DEATH
47; DEMOCRACY 10;
FOOD 12; HEAVEN 12;
LETTERS 8; LIVING 11;
MARRIAGE 27;
MATHEMATICS 10;
MIND 7; PEOPLE 18;
PRAYER 16; SINGING 8;
THINKING 8

Smith, Walter W.
("Red"): SPORTS 33

Smollett, Tobias:
WRITERS 2

Socrates: CONSCIENCE 1;
GOOD AND EVIL 2;
KNOWLEDGE 4; LAST
WORDS 1; PHILOSOPHY
1; POSSESSIONS 2;
TRUTH 2

Solzhenitsyn, Alexander:
CAPITALISM 24, 26;
CENSORSHIP 16; CRIME
34; LIES 21; POWER 22;
SUFFERING 28; WORK
31

Somerville, William:
HUNTING 5

Somoza, Anastasio:
ELECTIONS 11

Sontag, Susan: CRITICS
35; PAINTING 31;
REALITY 10; SICKNESS
13

Sophocles: GIFTS 1;
HUMAN RACE 3; LIFE 2;
SEX 1

Soule, John L. B.: TRAVEL
16

Sousa, John Philip:
MUSIC 14

South, Robert: SCIENCE
AND RELIGION 2

Southey, Robert: ARTS 5;
COUNTRIES 7; DEATH
41; HOME 4; YOUTH 9

Southwell, Robert:
CHANGE 3; SELF-
INTEREST 3

Spark, Muriel: MATURITY
11

Sparrow, John: DOGS 12;
ELECTIONS 6; EPITAPHS
30

Spector, Phil: MUSICIANS
23

Spencer, Herbert: CRIME
17; EQUALITY 6; FOOLS
21; FRANCE 8; LIFE
SCIENCES 6; THINKING
12

Spencer, Stanley:
PAINTING 28

Spender, Stephen:
HUMOR 24

Spenser, Edmund: